More praise for

GOD'S CRUCIBLE

"Vivid and illuminating."   —Anna Mundow, *Boston Globe*

"In *God's Crucible*, answers to many urgent questions, currently in the public discourse, can be deduced."   —Eric Ormsby, *New York Times*

"Lewis is a consummate storyteller and *God's Crucible* will help make this increasingly important period of history more popularly accessible."
                —Jason Webster, *New Statesman*

"A thrilling and colorful narrative."   —Tom Holland, *Literary Review*

"A stirring . . . account of the rise of Islam . . . deals with the broad sweep of history with commendable enthusiasm."
                —Simon Barton, *Times Higher Education Supplement*

"This superb portrayal by NYU history professor Lewis of the fraught half-millennium during which Islam and Christianity uneasily coexisted on the continent just beginning to be known as Europe displays the formidable scholarship and magisterial ability to synthesize vast quantities of material that won him Pulitzer Prizes for both volumes of W. E. B. Du Bois. In characteristically elegant prose, Lewis shows Islam arising in the power vacuum left by the death throes of the empires of newly Christianized Rome and Persian Iran. . . . Lewis clear-sightedly lays out the strengths and weaknesses of both worlds."   —*Publishers Weekly*, starred review

"*God's Crucible* traces in astonishing detail the development of relations between Muslims and the adherents of other faiths, especially Christians in the Byzantine Empire and in the emerging polities of medieval Europe. The attentive reader comes to understand that jihad is not a permanent and unchanging feature of Islam, but a dynamic product of a complex relationship—a relationship in which the West has been an active participant, and not just the victim of Muslim violence."

—Jonathan Berkey, author of *The Formation of Islam*

"David Lewis's range is really remarkable, and this surely is a major contribution to a still understudied and much misunderstood period of history." —Paul Kennedy, author of *The Rise and Fall of the Great Powers*

"This is a wonderfully interesting contribution to understanding the modern world in the light of genuine, rather than dogmatic, history. The role of the Arab culture and of Muslim leaders and intellectuals in the making of Europe a thousand years ago remains profoundly relevant to a world so undermined by uninformed reasoning today."

—Amartya Sen, author of *Identity and Violence*

"A first-rate scholar with a rare gift for synthesizing vast swaths of material. . . . He makes a persuasive case."

—Lisa Montanarelli, *San Francisco Chronicle*

"This marvelous book offers a magisterial—and splendidly readable—guide to the history of the cultures of the Mediterranean world, as Rome declined and Islam exploded out of Arabia, showing how Europe and Christianity were shaped through the conflict with the Muslims of El-Andalus. In exploring for us the intricate relations between Christianity and Islam, David Levering Lewis confirms Dionysus of Halicarnassus's claim that history is philosophy taken from examples."

—Anthony Appiah, author of *Cosmopolitanism*

"This thoughtful overview sheds welcome light on an increasingly relevant period of history. . . . A work of clear-eyed scholarship—and occasionally challenging vocabulary." —*Kirkus Reviews*

"Lewis' unfailingly ornate . . . prose . . . draw[s] one into considering . . . a fruitful and frequently overlooked period of cultural interaction."

—Brendan Driscoll, *Booklist*

GOD'S CRUCIBLE

GOD'S CRUCIBLE

ISLAM AND THE
MAKING OF EUROPE,
570 TO 1215

David Levering Lewis

Liveright Publishing Corporation
A division of W. W. Norton & Company
Independent Publishers Since 1923
New York London

Excerpt from *The Song of Roland*, translated, with an introduction and notes by Glyn
Burgess. Penguin Classics, 1990. Copyright © Glyn Burgess, 1990. Reproduced by
permission of Penguin Books Ltd. Excerpt of "Battle of Alfuente," from *Medieval
Iberia: Readings from Christian, Muslim, and Jewish Sources*. Olivia R. Constable, ed.
University of Pennsylvania Press, 1997. Reprinted by permission of the
University of Pennsylvania Press.

For information about permission to reproduce selections from this book,
write to Permissions, W. W. Norton & Company, Inc.,
500 Fifth Avenue, New York, NY 10110

For information about special discounts for bulk purchases, please contact
W. W. Norton Special Sales at specialsales@wwnorton.com or 800-233-4830

Manufacturing by LSC Communications Harrisonburg
Book design by Dana Sloan
Production manager: Anna Oler

ISBN 978-1-63149-430-7 pbk.

Liveright Publishing Corporation
500 Fifth Avenue, New York, N.Y. 10110
www.wwnorton.com

W. W. Norton & Company Ltd.
15 Carlisle Street, London W1D 3BS

1 2 3 4 5 6 7 8 9 0

To Marissa

Contents

LIST OF ILLUSTRATIONS · ix

LIST OF MAPS · xi

CHRONOLOGY · xiii

NOTES ON USAGE · xix

PREFACE · xxi

1. The Superpowers · 3

2. "The Arabs Are Coming!" · 29

3. *"Jihad!"* · 57

4. The Co-opted Caliphate and the Stumbling *Jihad* · 85

5. The Year 711 · 105

6. Picking Up the Pieces after Rome · 137

7. The Myth of Poitiers · 160

8. The Fall and Rise of the Umayyads · 184

9. Saving the Popes · 209

10. An Empire of Force and Faith · 224

11. Carolingian *Jihads*: Roncesvalles and Saxony · 251

12. The Great Mosque · 268

13. The First Europe, Briefly · 282

14. Equipoise—Delicate and Doomed · 304

15. Disequilibrium, Pelayo's Revenge · 333

16. Knowledge Transmitted, Rationalism Repudiated:
    Ibn Rushd and Musa ibn Maymun · 367

ACKNOWLEDGMENTS · 381

NOTES · 385

GLOSSARY · 423

GENEALOGIES · 433

BIBLIOGRAPHY · 439

CREDITS · 449

INDEX · 451

List of Illustrations

Emperor Justinian I, Bishop Maximianus, and attendants. Detail of mosaic (ca. 547 CE) from the north wall of the apse, Basilica of San Vitale, Ravenna, Italy. · 3

Ka'aba. Holiest place in Islam and direction faced by Muslims during prayer. The destination of the *hajj*. · 29

Al-Aqsa Mosque. Arabic for "the farthest mosque," derived from Muhammad's night journey from Mecca to Jerusalem, where he ascended to heaven. Shrine was begun by Caliph 'Abd al-Malik and completed by Caliph al-Walid (709–15 CE). Al-Aqsa forms part of the Noble Sanctuary, known to Jews and Christians as the Temple Mount. · 57

The Great Mosque at Kairouan, Tunisia. Begun in 670 CE by Uqba ibn Nafi, conqueror of the Maghreb; demolished and rebuilt in 703 and significantly enlarged under the Aghlabids in 836 and 863. · 85

Visigothic Tower. Panorama at Medina-Sidonia, not far from the Visigothic debacle at the hands of Tariq ibn Ziyad, 711 CE. · 105

Baptism of Clovis, December 25, 496 CE, in Reims Cathedral. Clovis, consolidator of the Merovingian dynasty, was the first Christian king of the Franks. He formally converted to Catholicism after defeating the Alamanni at Tolbiac in 496. · 137

Charles Martel, King of the Franks, at the Battle of Poitiers, 732 CE. · 160

Mosque at Karbala. Shrine of *imam* Husayn, martyred by the Umayyads in 680 CE. · 184

Late-Roman or early-Byzantine "iron crown" of Lombardy (also known as the crown of Theodelinda). Fifth-century Chapel of Theodelinda in the Duomo, Monza, Italy. · 209

Castel Sant'Angelo. Emperor Hadrian's mausoleum, erected in Rome between 135 and 139 CE. It served as a papal fortress, residence, and prison in the fourteenth century. · 224

Roland's monument. Twentieth-century Basque stone marker of the putative spot at Roncesvalles where Roland fell in 778 CE. · 251

Forest of columns, interior of Cordoba's Great Mosque. Begun by Amir 'Abd al-Rahman I in 775 CE. The last of several augmentations executed under Caliph Hisham II (r. 976–1012 CE). · 268

Charlemagne presenting the forest of Kinsheim. Nonliterate monogram of Charlemagne, 779 CE. · 282

The splendid shrine in Aachen Cathedral to which Charlemagne's remains were removed at the beginning of the thirteenth century. A marble Roman sarcophagus had served as the emperor's original interment vessel. · 304

Statue of El Cid, Burgos Cathedral. · 333

Detail of *The School of Athens*, fresco painted by Raphael in 1509–10 for the Stanza della Segnatura in the Apostolic Palace, Vatican City. Averroës (Ibn Rushd), turbaned, observes Pythagoras from the far left. · 367

List of Maps

Middle Eastern Empires, Late Sixth Century CE · xxvi

Terminal Conflict between Eastern Roman Empire
and Sassanian Iran · 64

The Conquest of Spain and Portugal · 121

The *Ta'ifa* Kingdoms of Iberia · 322

Christian Spain and Muslim Enclave · 362

Chronology

53 BCE: Marcus Licinius Crassus attacks the Parthians

260 CE: Shapur defeats and captures Publius Licinius Valerian

325: Council of Nicaea

378: Tervingi and Greuthingi, barbarians, destroy Roman legions; Emperor Valens commits suicide

380: Theodosius declares Christianity official faith of Roman Empire

409–410: Barbarians cross Pyrenees into Iberian peninsula

410: Sack of Rome

451: Battle of Châlons: Roman coalition of Franks and Visigoths withstands Attila's Huns

476: Downfall of Western Roman Empire

482–511: Clovis I founds, rules (Catholic) Merovingian Frankish kingdom

507: Clovis defeats Gothic ruler Alaric II at Vouillé

527–565: Reign of Justinian I, "last Roman emperor"

531–579: Khosrow I rules as king of Sassanian Empire

570: Birth of Muhammad

589: Third Toledo Council; Visigoth monarchy embraces Catholicism

591: Peace between Maurice of Eastern Roman Empire and Khosrow II

603: Iran (Khosrow II) declares war on Eastern Roman Empire

610: Angel Gabriel visits Muhammad

614: Shahrbaraz occupies Jerusalem and removes True Cross from Church of the Resurrection

622: *Hijra:* Muhammad goes to Yathrib, initiating struggle with Mecca; Heraclius defeats Iranians in Cappadocia, first in series of Graeco-Roman victories

624: Battle of Badr

625: Battle of Uhud

627: Battle of the Trench; Battle of Nineveh: Heraclius defeats Sassanian army

628: Treaty of Hudaybiyya

629: Jews of Khaybar oasis put to the sword; Muhammad sends invasion force into Jordan

630: Muhammad enters Mecca; peace treaty ratified between Iranians and Graeco-Romans

632: Muhammad dies, sparking struggle for succession

634: Abu Bakr, the first caliph, dies, after having started to assemble the Qur'an

636: Caliph 'Umar's armies commence conquest with the Battle of Jabiya-Yarmuk against Graeco-Romans

641: 'Amr ibn al-As occupies Alexandria

642: Zoroastrian Iran collapses with battles of al-Qadisiyya (636–37) and Nihawand (642)

644: 'Umar, second *rashidun* caliph, stabbed to death by Iranian slave; 'Uthman becomes third caliph

650–656: Definitive Qur'an produced under 'Uthman ibn Affan

656: Ali becomes caliph; first Muslim civil war (*fitna*); so-called *coup d'état* by Grimoald

661: Ali dies; *Dar al-Islam* divides into warring clans; Mu'awiya becomes first Umayyad caliph

680: Mu'awiya's son Yazid becomes first caliph through heredity rather than deliberation; death of Muhammad's grandson Husayn at Karbala

682: Berbers defeat and kill Uqba ibn Nafi, roll Arabs back to Qayarawan (Kairouan)

684: Battle of Marj Rahit

686–741: Rule of Charles Martel

690: Arabs fight Graeco-Romans, taking Carthage and removing Roman superpower from Africa

711: Conquest of Iberia: Tariq ibn Ziyad crosses Strait of Gibraltar; Battle of Guadalete

712: Musa ibn Nusayr arrives in southern Spain, June–July

716: Battle of Amblève: Martel secures his power base

717–718: Covadonga: Pelayo and followers skirmish with Arab unit; siege of Constantinople

721: Battle of Toulouse: Frankish Duke Odo defeats Umayyad army; Arabs take Carcassonne and Nîmes

731: Duke Odo of Aquitaine's defeat; Arabs and Berbers invade southwestern Gaul

732: Battle of Poitiers (Moussais-la-Bataille)

739–740: Uqba ibn al-Hajjaj al-Saluli invades Charles Martel's Francia

741: Battle of the Nobles

749: Abu Muslim's forces capture Kufa; Aistulf becomes Lombard king

750: Overthrow of Umayyad Caliphate

750–1258: Abbasid Caliphate: al-Mansur moves capital from Damascus to Baghdad

751: Battle of Talas in T'ang China; Arabs discover China's papermaking secrets; end of Merovingian dynasty

754: Pippin the Short crowned king by Pope Stephen II, starting Carolingian dynasty; invades Lombard stronghold at Pavia

756–788: ʿAbd al-Rahman I, *amir* of *al-Andalus*

759: Arabs lose Narbonne

763: Battle of Carmona: ʿAbd al-Rahman I attacks Yemeni forces

768: Death of Pippin I, succeeded by his sons Charlemagne and Carloman

771: Death of Carloman: Charlemagne becomes sole ruler

772/775–780: Charlemagne's campaigns against Saxons

773/74: Charlemagne's conquest of the Lombard kingdom; first expedition to Rome; Charlemagne names himself king of the Franks and the Lombards

778: Roncevalles (Roncevaux): Charlemagne's campaign to *al-Andalus*

782: Saxon revolt under Widukind; massacre at Verden; ʿAbd al-Rahman I takes Zaragoza

785: Construction of *La Mezquita* started under ʿAbd al-Rahman I; baptism of Widukind at Attigny

786: Harun al-Rashid, greatest of Abbasid caliphs, begins his reign

788: Charlemagne, with Pope Adrian's blessing, takes Tassilo's lands; ʿAbd al-Rahman I dies

792–793: Revolt of Pippin the Hunchback against his father, Charlemagne

793: Muslims, under Hisham I, invade Asturias, Navarra, Septimania, and Languedoc

795: Avar kingdom destroyed; Charlemagne's Spanish March

800: Christmas Day coronation of Charlemagne as emperor by Pope Leo III

805: Al-Rabad conspiracy in Cordoba

814: Death of Charlemagne, succeeded by his son Louis the Pious

843: Treaty of Verdun

844: Battle of Clavijo

846: Arabs pillage Rome: St. Peter's and St. Paul's looted

850s: Death of Christian fanatics dubbed "Mozarabic martyrs"

909: Fatimids establish Shiʾite Tunisian caliphate

912–961: ʿAbd al-Rahman III reigns; assumes title of caliph in 929

928: *Amir* ʿAbd al-Rahman III conquers Bobastro

929: ʿAbd al-Rahman III constructs *Madinat al-Zahra*

976–1002: "Reign" of al-Mansur

1009: Cordovan revolt against Amirids; destruction of *Madinat al-Zahra* and death of Hisham II

1027: Ibn Hazm publishes *The Ring of the Dove*

1031: Formal dissolution of Cordoba's Umayyad Caliphate; emergence of *taʾifas*

1040s: Ferdinand invades Muslim region of Galicia

1064: Norman, French, and Italian troops attack Barbastro in northern Spain

1085: Muslim surrender of Toledo to Alfonso VI ("the Brave") of Castile

1086: Almoravids arrive; Yusuf ibn Tashufin defeats Alfonso VI in Battle of Zallaqa

1095: Pope Urban II summons First Crusade

1128: Portugal emerges from Castilian dominance

1143: Latin translation of Qur'an by Robert of Ketton
1147: Almohads arrive (Ibn Tumart)
1148: Moses Maimonides and family flee Cordoba for Almeria
1171: Averroës is *gadi* in Cordoba
1190: Maimonides's *Guide for the Perplexed*
1198–1216: Papacy of Innocent III
1212: Battle of Las Navas de Tolosa (battle in Iberia between Muslims and Christians)
1215: Fourth Lateran Council and sumptuary decree against Jews; Albigensian Crusade

Notes on Usage

T IME UNFOLDS in this book within two eras: Before the Common Era (BCE) and in the Common Era (CE) in which we still live. The presumptuous "Before Christ" (BC) and "*anno Domini*" (AD) cede to an ecumenism cognizant of historical interdependence and parity. I recognize, however, that the convenience of this notation along with the pluralistic rationale animating it will not satisfy many Muslim readers, for the compelling reason that "real time" begins in Islam with the *hijra* (*anno Hegirae*)—the departure of the Prophet Muhammad from Mecca to Medina in 622 CE. Ideally, therefore, significant Common Era dates such as the defeat of the Iranian empire at al-Qadisiyya in 636 and the conquest of Visigothic Spain in 711 might have been rendered contiguously as AH 14 and AH 92, respectively. Only in rare instances has this been done, however. Similarly, two or three instances excepted, the reader will find no corresponding dates from the Hebrew calendar whose foundational year (*anno mundi*) is computed 3760 AM years before the Common Era.

The time is fast approaching when Arabic names and terms, unfamiliar and difficult though they are to people formed by Western culture, should be reproduced in historical works intended for a wide readership avid for information and understanding precisely as they are written in Standard Arabic with their diacritical notations. Because we are still some years away from such literacy, however, an author's challenge is to

make the unfamiliar and difficult congenial without travesty or trivializa-
tion. For the most part, diacritical marks have been omitted in the
transliteration from Arabic. Exceptions obtain in cases where recent academic literature in English discloses a degree of uniformity in preserving
certain prominent personalities, important place names, and significant
terms and concepts more or less close to the original Arabic. Readers
acquainted with Spanish history may find it occasionally necessary to
think twice before recognizing ʿAbd al-Rahman or al-Mansur as the
more familiar Abderaman or Almanzor.

The reader will encounter Latin and an abundance of terms from
European languages other than English, doubtless some of which might
better have served their purpose translated, notwithstanding a loss in
aural resonance. Most foreign words here are essential. They are integral
to this book's narrative and, aided where needed by a comprehensive
glossary, well worth the reader's patience.

Preface

WITHOUT my realizing it at the time, the idea for this book germinated a quarter-century ago in Khartoum. An ambitious three-month research junket from Southern California in the summer of 1982 carried me from Paris to Istanbul by way of the Republic of Djibouti, Ethiopia, Sudan, and Egypt. My time in the Sudanese capital, just shy of a month, was spent reading old British army intelligence files on the activities of the Muslim fundamentalists who had stopped the East African advance of the British Empire for the better part of a decade after 1885. To Victorian England's astonishment and continental Europe's unconcealed relish, the ragged dervishes of the "Messenger of Allah" (*al-Mahdi*) and "the Successor" (*al-Khalifah*) held the world's mightiest empire at bay. The history of the Sudan's *Mahdiyya* regime comprised a large part of *The Race to Fashoda: European Colonialism and African Resistance in the Scramble for Africa* (1989), the book written partly from my rewarding Khartoum sojourn of 1982.

Four years later, the secular Republic of the Sudan vanished after Sunni extremists, led by ideological descendants of the Mahdists, came to power. There had been definite indications of what was in store for the republic not long after my return home. On September 8, 1983, in violation of the country's ten-year-old constitution, an embattled government courted the support of Islamic fundamentalists by attempting to impose *Sharia* upon a national population geographically and ethnically divided between Muslims in the North and animists and Christians in the South. As years passed, the cautionary experience of having observed the power and appeal of Islamic fundamentalism in Khartoum (even if only from my lateral vision) began to register with a growing insistence— all the more so as it came to seem reasonably certain that the supreme modernizing empire of the twentieth century, the United States, was sleepwalking on a collision course with Islam similar to Great Britain's at the end of the nineteenth century.

The logic of that costly confrontation seemed transparent to me as the serial assaults on the symbols and instruments of American power unfolded in the Middle East and East Africa during the 1990s. For a historian, thinking about the present means thinking about the past in the present. To know something of Islam's remarkable seven-hundred-year presence in Europe is to contemplate a slice of history that might seem too remote in time to speak to the concerns of our postmodern present— even though much of the Muslim world stands in relationship to Europe and the United States today as much of a ramshackle Christian world once stood in relationship to a highly advanced Islamic one. Yet it is in this long, fraught saga of cultural roles reversed and political hegemonies upended that we can discern many of the causes for the troubled history being made in the twenty-first century.

At the beginning of the eighth century, the Arabs brought one of history's greatest revolutions in power, religion, culture, and wealth to Dark Ages Europe. The Arabs were to stay there until the end of the fifteenth century, and for much of that time—until roughly the beginning of the twelfth century—Islam in *al-Andalus* (Muslim Spain) was generally religiously tolerant and, above all, economically robust. The Arab advance beyond the Pyrenees petered out by the end of their first European century, but not, as in the lore and history of the West, because of Christian military success. The *jihad* east of the Pyrenees eventually failed because of a revolution within the world of Islam (*Dar al-Islam*). *God's Crucible: Islam and the Making of Europe, 570 to 1215*, animates the history ensuing from this epic forfeiture of what the Arabs called the "Great Land" (*al-Ard al-*

Kabirah), one of the most significant losses in world history and certainly
the most consequential since the fall of the Western Roman Empire. So
much of what has occurred since, occurred because of it.

The Battle of Poitiers, which intercepted Islam as it rounded the
Pyrenees in 732, and the martyrdom almost a half-century afterward
of Roland and his peers at Roncevaux (Roncesvalles), were consolidating and celebrated events in the emerging identity of the people
called "Europenses" for the first time by an obscure eighth-century
Spanish priest. *God's Crucible* engages a perspective rarely addressed by
the scholarship about Europe's long age of Islamo-Christian cohabi-
tation. In that perspective, the Battle of Poitiers and the *Song of Roland*
are pivotal moments in the creation of an economically retarded,
balkanized, and fratricidal Europe that, by defining itself in opposition to Islam, made virtues out of hereditary aristocracy, persecutory
religious intolerance, cultural particularism, and perpetual war. The
massacre at Roncevaux gave the "West" an iconic hero who embodied
caste supremacy and unrestrained martial valor: Roland, an eighth-
century prototype of the American cowboy. Poitiers and Roncevaux
nurtured an ideology of Holy War and, in time, of national arrogance
to counter the advance of Islam.

Most of history is indisputably written by the winners, yet "winning"
at Poitiers actually meant that the economic, scientific, and cultural levels that Europeans attained in the thirteenth century could almost certainly have been achieved more than three centuries earlier had they
been included in the Muslim world empire. With few exceptions,
Edward Gibbon's well-known pronouncement has influenced the value
judgments rendered by historians as to the desirable outcome from the
competition between these two world orders. A shiver passed through
the great eighteenth-century historian as he famously wrote of what
might have followed an Arab victory at Poitiers: "Perhaps the interpretation of the Koran would now be taught in the schools of Oxford, and her
pulpits might demonstrate to a circumcised people the sanctity and truth
of the revelation of Mahomet."[1]

Historical value judgments aside, what cultural, scientific, and tech-

nical achievements there were east of the mountain barrier in the awakening Europe were indispensably stimulated and facilitated by the learning flowing in a gathering volume out of *al-Andalus*. For some seventy-five
years, even after the fall of Muslim Toledo in 1085, an "Indian summer"
of interfaith collaboration of Christian, Muslim, and Jew prevailed—
what contemporaries called the *convivencia*—notwithstanding the redou-
bling of Muslim and Catholic fanaticism. The conveyor belt at Toledo
transmitted most of what Paris, Cologne, Padua, and Rome knew of
Aristotle and Plato, Euclid and Galen, the "Hindu numbers," and Arab
astronomy. This narrative of symbiosis ended after the second decade of
the thirteenth century. The lauded *convivencia* was chased into oblivion by
Muslim and Christian holy warriors respectively shouting, "God is great!"
("*Allahu akbar*") and "St. James the Moorslayer!" ("*Santiago Matamoros!*"). By
then, the exceptional civilization presided over by the Umayyad *amirs* and
caliphs of Cordoba for 275 years was but a memory cherished by Spain's
Moriscos and reviled by its Christians. The main outlines of this story
trace the rise, for centuries thereafter, of a reciprocally reassuring ignorance and of an addiction to war as the substitute for the complexities of
coexistence.

   God's Crucible is, as I've said, the product of hindsight, the delayed
inspiration of an African research sojourn. It so happens that I jotted
down the book's earliest field notes on September 11 in Rabat, Morocco,
the first day of my topographical research junket.[2] The year was 2001. I
thought then, on that staggering day, as I still do, that large historical outcomes are far more often contingent than inevitable, and that if so, then
it behooves all of us in a time of heightened global interaction to resist
the eschatologies of the cultural and political simplifiers.

   Although the arc of my professional interests have been eclectic, I
would insist that there is a certain logic to its design. From Martin
Luther King, Jr., and Alfred Dreyfus, to the progenitors of the Harlem
Renaissance, and the leaders who temporarily retarded the imperial
scramble for Africa, to the spectacular W. E. B. Du Bois, the central concern was the critical yet sympathetic exploration of lives exemplifying—
uniquely or in some combination—courage or integrity, intellect or

calculation in the face of injustice, religious exclusion, and organized plunder. *God's Crucible,* as the story of the rise and decline of a civilization in Europe (if not quite a European civilization), abundantly incorporates such concerns.

David Levering Lewis
New York City and Milan, New York, 2007

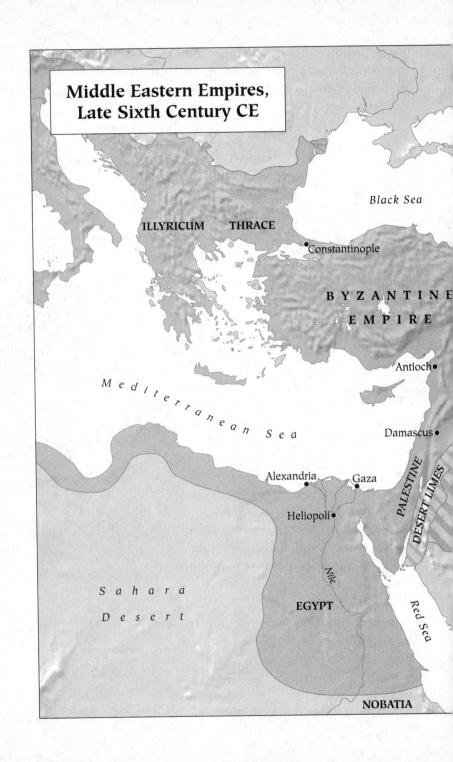

Middle Eastern Empires, Late Sixth Century CE

Black Sea

ILLYRICUM   THRACE

• Constantinople

B Y Z A N T I N E
E M P I R E

Antioch •

M e d i t e r r a n e a n   S e a

Damascus •

Alexandria
•   Gaza
•

PALESTINE

DESERT LIMES

Heliopoli •

Nile

S a h a r a
D e s e r t

EGYPT

Red Sea

NOBATIA

KHAZARS

BULGARS

ALANS

KHAZARS

IBERIA

LAZICA

DARRAN

Caspian Sea

Armenia

Edessa

MEDIA

TABARISTAN

GURGAN

KHURASAN

Tigris

SASSANIAN

EMPIRE

Ctesiphon

IRAQ

MESOPOTAMIA

Alhira

KHUZISTAN

GHASS-
ANIDS

Euphrates

FARS

LAKHMIDS

KIRMAN

KINDA

Persian Gulf

BAHRAYNI

N

Yathrib
(Medina)

W   E

S

0   200 miles

0   200 kilometers

Byzantine Empire

Sassanian Empire

Ghassanids (allies of Byzantium)

Lakhmids (allies of the Sassanians)

autonomous "desert *limes*" frontier zone

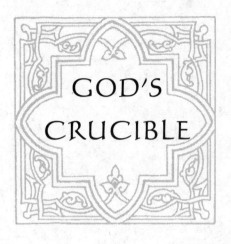

GOD'S
CRUCIBLE

The Superpowers

I SLAM rose when Rome fell. Why and how that happened is the necessary beginning of *God's Crucible*: why, in the early years of the seventh century of the Common Era, the road opened wide to Islam for world conquest; how, in a time frame that passed in the blinking of an eye, the Arabs accomplished the greatest revolution in power, religion, culture, and wealth in history—all of which made Europe Europe. Historians have a plethora of autopsy reports to explain the decline and fall of the Roman Empire. But none trumps the explanatory power of death by imperial misadventure with Iran.[1] Graeco-Latin Rome and Persian Iran were mirror-image empires in their military expansion, lawgiving, cultural attainment, road building, and architectural exuberance—expanding universes whose violence at points of contact resembled the explosive interface of matter and antimatter. Theirs was the systole–diastole of a seven-century competition in arms, institutions, and cultures in which almost all of Asia Minor's peoples were obliged to participate.

The notable exceptions were the Arabs living in the blazing-hot Hijaz along the Arabian peninsula's Red Sea littoral and the vast and empty plateau of the Najd to the east. These Semite tribes remained for the most part below the geopolitical radar of the two superpowers dominating the Fertile Crescent. The tribes of Arabia's inner peninsula, whose caravans out of oasis towns plied north as far as Jordan and south as far as Yemen, largely escaped being sucked into the tremendous imperial vortices of the region until the end of the sixth century. They were remote spectators who played what was a marginal role at best in the Fertile Crescent, that arc rising from the lands of the eastern Mediterranean shore across Egypt, Palestine, Syria, Iraq, a slice of Turkey, and descending through Iran to the Persian Gulf. But they were still close enough to learn and borrow from two high civilizations everlastingly at war. In time, those wasting wars were to make possible the sudden and improbable military ascendancy of seminomads from a corner of Arabia. These people moved with incredible speed into one of history's prime-time slots—but only after the two superpowers of Asia Minor had exhausted themselves in prolonged, mutual destruction. As fascinated spectators to what was, in effect, history's longest demolition derby, the tribes of the Arabian heartland found themselves holding one of history's winning tickets as protagonists almost by default in a new competition.

One cannot appreciate the Islamic rise to power without tracing the inexorable demise of these two great powers. Peace between Rome and Iran was an interruption rather than a normal state of affairs. Occasionally, of necessity, there was trade between them. Iran blocked the land routes to Asia. Rome was master in the Mediterranean. The Roman and Iranian upper classes were too busy fighting among themselves and consolidating territorial conquests to take much notice of each other until a century and a half before the birth of the Christian messiah. In 146 BCE, Rome plowed under a mortal enemy's North African capital and salted the surrounding fields so as to imbue with infamous meaning the finality of the peace inflicted upon the Carthaginians. "Before the destruction of Carthage, the people and the Senate of Rome together governed the Republic peacefully and with moderation," the historian Sallust regretted some eighty years later. "But when the minds of the people were relieved of that dread, wantonness and arrogance naturally arose, vices which are fostered by prosperity."[2] Now implanted on the African side of the Mediterranean, Rome the city-state marched in legionnaires' boots toward Asia Minor and into world-empire status.[3]

Some fifty-odd years later, the frontier forces of a relatively new Iranian empire encountered the Romans advancing into Mesopotamia from their North African beachhead. Latins and Iranians fought no major battles upon first contact in Mesopotamia, "the land between the [Tigris and Euphrates] rivers." The Parthian people of Iran were busy reclaiming the real estate lost after Alexander the Great's destruction in 332 BCE of the Achaemenid superstate created by Cyrus the Great.[4] Taking prudent account of the vast new Iranian empire bordered in the west by the Euphrates, in the east by the Indus, and to the north by the Oxus, the advancing Romans paused. Mithradates II (r. 123–88 BCE), Parthia's legendary empire-builder, was on a conquering roll. His eagle-eyed, hirsute profile on a 2,200-year-old coin from the royal mint at Seleucia, the Parthian capital, captures the archetypal profile of a master of the universe. With eastern Iran, Armenia, Turkey, Azerbaijan, and parts of Syria and today's Iraq subjugated or respectfully subservient satellites, Mithradates had every right to appropriate the ancient Persian title of *shahanshah* ("king of kings"). Taking the measure of Mithradates's vast land mass, Strabo, the great Greek geographer, marveled somewhat later that the Parthians ruled so much territory and so many peoples that they had become "in a way rivals of the Romans."[5]

Both powers formally agreed in 96 BCE, for the time being, to make the Euphrates River their common border. Rome's generals meanwhile laid claim to the Senate's favor as they apportioned Cleopatra, Egypt,

Palestine, and Syria among themselves. The first Roman-Iranian war finally began forty-three years later, just before Julius Caesar and Pompey plunged the Roman Republic into civil war and quasi-hereditary autocracy. Marcus Licinius Crassus took it upon himself to violate the territorial agreement. Crassus's wealth in slaves, silver mining, and real estate made him Rome's richest citizen. His real-estate practices gave the term *fire sale* its particular meaning. Owners had good reason to fear losing their property by arson if they refused a bid from Crassus. His loans enabled Julius Caesar to compete with the political and military maneuvers of his rival, Pompey. His role in suppressing the Spartacus slave rebellion was probably as significant as he claimed. A grateful Senate bestowed on him the title of consul and then, lubricated by *denarii*, elevated Crassus to the exalted rank of *triumvir*—one of the three rulers, with Pompey and Caesar—of the republic. Each of the Triumvirate's masters reserved a major portion of the known world to himself: Pompey had Spain; Caesar had Gaul; Crassus had Syria.[6]

Crassus intended Syria to be his springboard to easy military glory and even greater wealth. In the spring of 53 BCE, he took his seven legions (forty-four thousand men) across the Euphrates into Parthia. He was stern of mien, lean of physique, and in excellent health for a man in his late sixties, but Crassus lacked serious military experience in the field. The slaughter and crucifixion of seventy thousand rebellious slaves left him woefully unprepared to face an enemy on its own turf in the baked, exposed landscape of what is today western Turkey. When the local Parthian commander's horse archers attacked them at Carrhae (near modern Harran), the disciplined Roman infantry formed squares and hoisted shields to assume its classic tortoise formation, while wave after deadly wave of Parthian arrows rained over them. The Parthian camel corps (probably manned by Arab auxiliaries) not only kept the archers resupplied, but the archers' skill at over-the-shoulder arrow shots ("the Parthian shot"), whenever Crassus's cavalry forced a temporary retreat, took the heart out of the Romans. The Parthian commander, known to history only by his Suren-Pahlavi clan affiliation, timed the attack by his cataphracts (heavily armored cavalry) for the optimal moment of Roman fatigue and confusion. The slaughter was terrible, and Crassus was killed while trying to surrender. Some thirty thousand survivors were marched off into a lifetime of slavery at hard labor on Parthia's great network of highways. The debacle and the insult to their *triumvir* humiliated and enraged the Romans. Marcus Licinius Crassus had inaugurated history's longest war between two superpowers. In the grand gallery of folly and hubris that historian Edward Gibbon displays for our meditation, the Battle of Carrhae is a paramount case. "The conflict of Rome and Persia was prolonged from the death of Crassus to the reign of [Emperor] Heraclius," he wrote. "An experience of seven hundred years might convince the rival nations of the impossibility of maintaining conquests beyond the fatal limits of the Tigris and Euphrates."[7]

Two hundred fifty years later, Imperial Rome and Imperial Iran were still at it, although peace occasionally broke out and wars with others frequently distracted them. In the barely interrupted seesawing of conquest and defeat during the second century of the Common Era, Parthian heavy cavalry invaded Roman Armenia, and Marcus Aurelius (r. 121–80 CE), wisest and last of the "five good emperors," sent the legions trampling over the cataphracts in 164 CE to capture Ctesiphon, Iran's majestic capital, some twenty-five miles north of the spot on which Baghdad stands today. Thirty-odd years later, another Iranian *shahanshah*, Artabanus, even with formidable elephant cavalry, failed to oust Rome from Mesopotamia in such humiliating proportions as to cause the downfall of the Parthian dynasty. With the vast quantities of gold and silver stripped from its enemy, Rome was able to postpone the economic crisis of its hemorrhaging trade deficits for three decades. The last Parthian *shahanshah* was pushed off the scene after the dynasty had endured through forty-three royals for almost four hundred sometimes spectacular years.[8]

Then, in what the Romans came to call "the great crisis" in the third Christian century, Iran's new Sassanian rulers shook the Latin Roman Empire to its already-weakened foundations. Persian armored cavalry and well-disciplined infantry were probably the world's best military machine. In quick succession, the armies of Shapur I (r. 241–72 CE) humiliated three emperors and their legions. Seventy thousand captured legionnaires were put to work throughout his empire building roads, digging canals, and erecting the city of Veh-Andiokh-Shabuhr ("the better

Antioch of Shapur"), future cradle of Sassanian cultural and scientific production. But not only were two emperors outgeneraled and slain, a third, Publius Licinius Valerian (r. 253–60), was captured near Edessa in southeastern Turkey. For an emperor to be taken alive in battle against a foreign enemy was an affront to all that *Romanitas*—"Roman-ness"— stood for, a calamity incompatible with the Romans' ideology of divinely ordained invincibility. Valerian's captor inflicted upon him what to Iranian eyes must have seemed an exquisite comeuppance: Shapur I used the captured emperor as a human footstool. The great king's monument, carved into sand-swept ruins at Naqsh-i Rustan, near ancient Persepolis in southern Iran, is still visible.[9] Shapur looks down haughtily from his horse as a supplicating Valerian follows on foot. Shapur's was the imperious perspective from which successive Sassanid rulers regarded the Romans during the remainder of the Roman Empire's pivotal third century.

A hundred years after Shapur humiliated the Romans, the emperor known as Julian the Apostate would exhort his legionnaires, in full-throated resentment of Persian arrogance, to wipe out "a most mischievous nation, on whose sword blades the blood of our kinsmen is not yet dry."[10] But before the empire could face the Sassanians effectively, it desperately needed political reform and economic stability. Slow to recover at first from its plunge into anarchy, currency debasement, and civil war among the so-called barracks emperors, the Roman state eventually underwent a radical overhaul. A Greek soldier proved to be an extraordinary exception to the run of barrack emperors. Diocletian (r. 284–305) eliminated his competition, divided the empire into western and eastern halves ruled by a tetrarchy, and churned out a record number of transforming edicts. On paper, Diocletian's Tetrarchy was an elegant solution to political instability that had generated some twenty emperors and impostors in half as many years: he and comrade-in-arms Maximian as senior emperors (*augusti*) ruling in the East and the West, respectively, and two subaltern emperors (*cesari*) ascending to *augustus* status when the senior emperors retired or died. Milan became the administrative capital of the western empire. The town of Split in Croatia served as the capital of Diocletian's eastern half. Well before the end of his rule, the grieving Diocletian watched as the other *augusti* and *cesari* devoured one another.

Autocratic powers vested in the emperors made the hallowed motto *Senatus Populusque Romanum* ("the Senate and the People of Rome") hardly worth the marble entablature upon which it was inscribed. Since Diocletian had himself proclaimed a god, there was notable suffering among the empire's Christians for their reluctance to acknowledge the claim. Imperial edicts fixed prices and froze key commercial and bureaucratic professions in hereditary perpetuity. A confiscatory taxation system underwriting a vast bureaucracy transferred the remaining plebeian and equestrian wealth to the top tier of the patrician class and the military establishment. The empire's already large military force grew from thirty legions of 300,000 infantry to a total of 435,000 soldiers.[11] The great imperial innovator even pulled off a thirty-year peace with Iran. Even though the market economy and the agricultural base were seriously weakened—in ways that would become apparent toward the end of the next century—third-century Rome managed to survive some sixty years of Iranian challenges even as German tribes repeatedly pierced the Rhine and Danube defenses.

The empire deferred the barbarian deluge for a time. The options of the emperors, western and eastern, were seldom straightforward, and often a Hobson's choice—enough legions to checkmate Iran in Armenia, Macedonia, and Mesopotamia, but a risk meanwhile that the overstretched garrisons might not hold the Rhine and upper Danube boundary lines (*limes*) against the barbarians. The containment gamble failed disastrously in the summer of 378 CE. Pressed by a colossal population movement that had burst out of Asia three years earlier, the German tribes in Thrace (Bulgaria), along the lower Danube, desperately petitioned for permission to cross into the eastern edge of the empire. Valens (r. 364–78), the eastern emperor, cautiously assented. Mainly concerned with the Sassanian advance into Armenia under Shapur II, "The Great" (r. 309–79), Valens responded slowly as the surging Goths—joined by other tribes also fleeing the murderous Asiatic swarm—overwhelmed the imperial wardens and laid waste to much of Thrace. With every legion available from the east, Valens finally reached the Balkans, where, in the first week of August, 378, he lost his life and two-thirds of his army at Adrianople. Ammianus Marcellinus, the historian of this twilight age, moaned that the coming of the Goths was "the ruin of the Roman world."[12]

By the close of the fifth century, the Latin West had long since fallen out of the imperial competition. Diocletian's successor, Constantine the Great (r. 306–37), not only maintained the divided empire but even replicated the Eternal City as Constantinople on the site of the old Greek colony of Byzantium, a location strategic to the Danube and the Euphrates. The western half of the dual empire formally institutionalized by Constantine in 325 CE, and jointly ruled from Rome and Constantinople, ended ignominiously in 476, almost exactly one hundred years after the debacle at Adrianople. In the autumn of that year, a hulking, Romanized German warlord, Odoacer (Attila the Hun's brother-in-law), ordered the boy emperor, Romulus Augustulus, to leave the Eternal City. As good a date as any for the European Dark Ages begins with the unprotesting departure of Romulus Augustulus into pensioned retirement in Constantinople.[13]

Just shy of a century before Odoacer adjourned the western imperial office, the last emperor to rule over a united Roman Empire had promulgated a religious edict of extraordinary world importance. Theodosius I finalized the ecumenical triumph of an ideology that had spread steadily upward from the Roman world's underclasses. Although Constantine's Edict of Milan legalized Christianity in 313 CE, according the vigorous sect equal standing with the competing polytheisms and dualisms, it was not until Theodosius's decree in 380 that the new monotheism finally became the official faith of the Roman Empire. By no means had this outcome been a certainty, even some twenty-five years earlier. Mithraism was still the faith of choice in many of the legions. Manichaeism exercised a strong pull in the East. Powerful old senatorial families fought valiantly to preserve the pagan temples and maintain the festivals and Colosseum games. Their last best hope to save what they believed was the soul of their civilization from the Christian metastasis came with the brief, brilliant reign of the philosopher-emperor Julian the Apostate (r. 361–63). Until he was killed retreating with his army from a failed siege of the Iranian capital, the Apostate's policy of pagan restoration rallied Platonists and polytheists from Britannia to the Bosporus.

Theodosius not only ended any further public tolerance of the old idols and amusements (even abolishing the Olympic Games in 393), he made Christianity the sole legitimate faith in 391 and sought to settle with finality the essence of orthodox Christian dogma for the empire.[14]

Notwithstanding the foundational pronouncements at the Council of Nicaea in 325 CE, many agile Greek minds had continued lumping and splitting the degree of Jesus's divinity in the Trinity. There were the Nestorians, found in large numbers in Syria and Iraq, who insisted that the Christian messiah possessed two separate natures, human and divine. The Monophysites or Copts in Egypt and elsewhere in North Africa affirmed Christ's nature as singularly divine. However abstruse such ontological parsings rendered in Greek seemed, nothing could have mattered more to seventy million souls seeking salvation in Christ, and Theodosius had clarifyingly ordained in 380 CE that the Nicene Creed meant exactly and only what he said it said: The two natures of the Son were of the same (*homoousion*) "substance" as the Father. Nonetheless, ontological parsings of Arians, Monophysites, Nestorians, and other sects would compete with the orthodox Catholic doctrine for centuries to come. While Christological confusion persisted, Theodosius's imperial decrees settled the primacy of Christianity in the Western and Eastern Roman Empires.[15] In so doing, the emperors transformed the competition between the Roman and Iranian empires for glory, territory, slave labor, and riches into an ideological conflict for a monopoly on revealed truth.

❖

On the other side of the Euphrates, beyond the Syrian Desert and over the Armenian mountains, literate men and women were animated by another faith—one much older and more serene in its divine ordination. The established creed of the Sassanian state was the world's first revealed religion, a fourteen-hundred-year-old monotheism with strong dualist undercurrents that welled up from time to time into theological tsunamis that shaped credal contours across Asia Minor. Present at the dawn of the Axial Age—that pivotal time span from 800 to 200 BCE when the great world religions arose—Zoroastrianism emerged from the teachings of an Aryan priest, Zarathustra (Latinized as Zoroaster), history's first messiah. Zarathustra ("the one who owns camels") lived in ancient Bactria's high mountains, somewhere in the northwest of today's Afghanistan, but when he lived is uncertain—any time between 1200 and 600 BCE, though probably toward the earlier time period. This thirty-year-old seer had the earliest-known visions of a creation myth, of an end-of-time apocalypse, and of the promise of personal judgment and eternal afterlife once the uncreated creator of light, Ahura Mazda, vanquished the darkness and evil of Angra Mainyu. Zarathustra was believed to have commanded believers to pray upright five times daily in the presence of fire, symbol of purity, creation, and enlightenment. In Zarathustra's apocalyptic vision, Judgment Day (*Frashokereti*) arrived at the end of linear time (not cyclical time, as in the religions of Egypt, Greece, India, and Rome), and the believer walked across the bridge of death as his or her deeds were weighed and his or her afterlife decided.[16]

Little wonder that the religious and political elites of Iran took for granted their faith's intellectual and ethical superiority to Judaism, its near contemporary, and to the latecomer monotheism of the Romans. Darius the Great worshiped at Ahura Mazda's sacred fire. Parthian dynasts chanted the sacred hymns (*Gathas*) composed by Zarathustra himself. Sassanian *shahanshahs* prayed upright five times daily and extolled the austere values of the sacred scriptures (*Avesta*); a powerful priesthood kept the sacred-fire temples glowing and presided over the seven prescribed communal festivals—all of which served as ruling-caste glue and plebeian control.[17] Imperious, racially exclusive, and capable of great cruelty, the ruling classes were also masters of the politics of religious tolerance—up to a point. Shapur I, determined to do all he could to undermine the enemy, had encouraged Jews and the still-persecuted Christians in the second half of the third century to leave Roman rule and settle as taxpaying assets in his empire. It took the Sassanian kings another half century to be able to distinguish among their Christian subjects those for whom the imperial orthodox church held no appeal. Nestorians passed the Sassanian loyalty test, Monophysites less dependably so. Henceforth, the beliefs of peoples would be judged from un-Zoroastrian and un-Christian perspectives.

As the fifth century dawned, the two world empires, Graeco-Latin and Iranian met along the Mesopotamian divide as religious adversaries: Christian Rome versus Zoroastrian Iran. When an observant Egyptian businessman-turned-monk wrote his late-sixth-century memoirs, they exuded the righteous Christian imperialism that was typical of the age. "The Empire of the Romans thus participates in the Kingdom of the Lord Christ," wrote Cosmas, "seeing that it transcends every other power . . . and will remain unconquered until the final consummation. . . ."

Members of monastic orders fanned out across Asia Minor and Africa: Nestorian priests taking their version of Christianity over the Silk Road into China, Monophysite holy men carrying the gospel of the uncorrupted Christ up the Nile. If the mindset of this intensely sectarian Christian world seems today separated from the modern understanding by a great chasm of science and reason, there is yet a bridge of analogy from the theological opiates of the Eastern Roman Empire to the economic nostrums of the free-market present. To hear sixth-century Constantinopolitans parsing the Trinity sounds rather like twenty-first-century New Yorkers, Londoners, Muscovites, or denizens of Shanghai proffering stock-market tips or real-estate leads. "Everywhere, in humble homes, in the streets, in the marketplace, at street corners," sighed a bemused visitor to the imperial capital, "if I ask for my bill, the reply is a comment about the virgin birth; if I ask for the price of bread, I am told that the Father is greater than the Son; when I ask whether my bath is ready, I am told the Son was created from nothing."[18] Shapur II[19] was flabbergasted when the head of the Monophysite community refused to order his people to pay a special tax needed for another war with Rome. Hardly surprising, then, that a contemporary Sassanian source relates the widespread belief among the aristocracy and Zoroastrian clergy that "the Christians were all of them spies of the Romans. And that nothing happens in the kingdom that they do not write to their brothers who live [in Imperial Rome]." The *mobad* (high priest) of the Zoroastrian clergy, *Karter* or *Kirder,* policed religious thought and inveighed against Christians. His counsels influenced an otherwise-tolerant Shapur to order an un-Persian persecution that lasted until the end of his reign.[20]

✖

A hundred years after the institutional and cultural lights of Europe dimmed to barely a glow with the disappearance of the last western Caesar, Romulus Augustulus, a smoldering Asia Minor ignited in catastrophic war. The death of the great Justinian I in the winter of 565, the "last Roman emperor" of the Eastern Roman Empire, marked the end of four decades of dynamic leadership and sustained military expansion and the beginning of the final, suicidal phase of superpower confrontation. The *Corpus Juris Civilis*, a universal compendium of Roman civil law, was Justinian's foundational contribution to the reasoned rules and obligations that would inform future Western societies. *Las Siete Partidas*, the civil code of the Spanish-speaking world seven hundred years later, no less than the *Code Napoléon* for postfeudal Europe thirteen hundred years afterward, were inspired by Justinian's jurists. Constantinople's splendid Basilica of St. Sophia, acme of Hellenistic architectural audacity, was Justinian's legacy in brick and marble. That the great dome's sheer weight pushed the basilica's walls perilously outward until shored up by Isidore of Miletus was, said some, yet another sign of imperial hubris. "Solomon," Justinian was heard to murmur upon entering the completed structure, "Solomon, I have surpassed thee."[21]

The emperor conceived his awe-begetting house of worship as the material embodiment of the Apostolic Church, purified in doctrine against all deviancy and obedient to its august emperor. The opinions of the struggling bishops of Rome in such matters were deemed purely advisory. Monophysites and Nestorians, who exasperated Justinian with their stubbornly antithetical beliefs about the divinity of Jesus, were always a decree away from outright persecution. Jews, in fact, he persecuted with unusual harshness, forcing their conversions and expropriating their property. Justinian attempted to make one dogma fit all cases by upholding the Chalcedonian decree of 451, which stated that the two natures of Christ, divine and human, were actually one. Deviancy persisted even in the imperial household, however, where the Empress Theodora, the sinewy daughter of a "circus bear-keeper," according to waspish Procopius, historian of the regime, was accused of comforting and conspiring with Monophysites. Nestorians, stubbornly convinced of Christ's dual essence, departed in growing numbers for Iran's more accommodating confessional climate.

Above all else, this nephew of an illiterate Balkan soldier dreamed of a Rome reconquered, restored, reunited, and ruled from the center of the universe, Constantinople, the world's largest metropolis. If the "long peace" Theodosius I concluded with his short-lived Iranian counterpart, Shapur III (r. 383–88), had lasted yet longer, Justinian might have achieved much of his grand design. The exceptionally advantageous peace had endured more than a century—from 384 to 502—because of the havoc wrought on Iran in the middle of the fifth century by a nomadic people of obscure origins from northern China and Central Asia—the Hepthalites or White Huns. As the sixth century opened, however, the Sassanians' long period of internal preoccupation finally ended, and with it a resumption of war shortly before Justinian assumed the purple. For Justinian and his immediate successors, the nemesis was Khosrow I (r. 531–79), perhaps the greatest of the Sassanian dynasts, whose long reign and imperial ambitions paralleled Justinian's. Khosrow consistently opposed Justinian's every move for much of the sixth century. In retrospect, Justinian's geopolitical ambitions were far grander in conception than realistically sustainable, yet at the time they had seemed to need only imperial willpower, annual subsidies to the Persians, a few more forced loans, and a run of luck to succeed.

Two generals, Belisarius, loyal and uncomplicated, and Narses, gelded and scheming, served their emperor with such military genius that for an illusory season or two, Italia and Hispania had seemed secured. But the supply of Germanic barbarians was bottomless. The Iranians declared war just as Belisarius might have prevailed decisively in his Italian campaigns against the Goths, and the state tottered on bankruptcy. After almost twenty years of scorched-earth warfare, Italia was a virtual desert, but without peace. Never again would the rulers of the Second Rome nerve themselves for a herniating gamble to hold on to the lands lost to the Germanic barbarians by its dead sister empire in the West. Anemic holding operations at Ravenna and Benevento in Italy, and coastal garrisons in southern Hispania, were the best that could be ventured. Belisarius had won fame early in his career by clearing the North African breadbasket of the rampaging Vandals, securing it to the empire for another two generations until the Arab awakening. But in the end, the remorseless taxation and unmitigated indebtedness to pay for the great effort of imperial restoration seriously compromised the health of the Second Rome.[22]

Empress Theodora's political services were no less vital than those of the generals. Justinian's wife's web of spies and agents trolled the back alleys and bathhouses of Constantinople to report aborning plots and compromising gossip in minutest detail. Life at the top was always perilous in the world's biggest metropolis. The Hippodrome, Constantinople's outsize version of the Roman Colosseum, was home to the infamous Blues and Greens, two restive mobs steeped in political attitude and lethally intolerant of any imperial inattentiveness to their generous care, feeding, and amusements. Theodora's steel nerves once prevented her shaken husband from fleeing the city when the Hippodrome's regicidal rabble boiled over in turbulence that left much of the capital in ruins. Procopius, the historian who composed two accounts of Justinian's era (one, official and favorable; the other, secret and vicious), reviled Theodora as a scheming prostitute spawned from the city's underbelly. Although not born to the purple, she wore the robes of sovereign power with consummate authority. One look at her in Ravenna's Basilica of San Vitale, where the lifelike image both solicits and intimidates in mosaics, and the spectator takes away a sharp sense of Theodora's deadly guile. For better and worse, until her death at age forty-eight, few important decisions were made in the Great Palace without the counsel or approval of this Byzantine Eva Perón.

Justinian expired five years before the birth of the Prophet Muhammad, according to Muslim calendar reckoning. Fifty years later, Justinian's Graeco-Roman civilization (labeled "Byzantine" by nineteenth-century scholars) would be locked in a superpower death struggle that made possible—if, indeed, not inevitable—Muhammad's revolutionary overthrow of the old world order.[23] As the empire's cultural transformation accelerated under Justinian's successors, Latin would gradually cede to

Greek as the primary language of government and business. "Emperor" would eventually give way to the Hellenistic *basíleus* as the imperial title. Insanity, plain bad luck, bankruptcy, and assassination plagued those who came after Justinian. His young nephew and immediate successor, Justin II (r. 565–78), necessarily suffered in comparison with his illustrious uncle, whose statecraft (deftly assisted by Theodora until her death) appeared to operate from a precise calculus of force and finesse. Justin proved deficient in understanding on both counts.

The catalogue of imperial grief facing Justin was truly murderous: an aggressive new German tribe (the Langobards or Lombards) swarming into Italy; demands for ever-larger gold subsidies by the Asiatic Avars; uncertain relations with the Turks, making their first recorded appearance east of the Oxus River (Amu Darya); feuding Christian sects; appeals from Armenian Christians rebelling against their Zoroastrian Iranian masters. Arabs were more of a nuisance to commerce than a military concern, but their depredations were increasingly bold. Bedouin raids into Syria had started up under his uncle, and Justin was expected to continue the policy of paying extortion money to keep them away from the empire's trade routes and frontier communities.[24] The empire had been hollowed out by three decades of universal hostilities and confiscatory taxation. Even peace with Iran had been no boon to the economy because of the large annual indemnity and the reality that Iran remained largely in control of the Asian and Indian Ocean trade. Iran straddled the western end of the main overland route that arced out of China to northern Afghanistan's fabled Stone Tower at Tashkurgan, where Persian, Greek, and Semitic merchants exchanged their goods for jade, cloves, sandalwood, and priceless silk to carry back through Iran and west to Palmyra and Damascus in Mesopotamia. Sixth-century conflicts could be surprisingly market-driven, as by then the value and volume of intercontinental trade encouraged emperors and *shahanshahs* to think geopolitically.[25] Eventually, the Greeks could look forward to robust revenues from the first silkworm eggs secretly brought by two Nestorian monks out of China to Constantinople in about 550. But Justin's needs were desperately immediate.

⁑

Peace in the Middle East was war conducted by other means. In the vanished pantheon of Sassanian royals, Khosrow I, then in his last decade of life when Justin ascended the throne, had created a legacy both noble and sanguinary during his long reign. Khosrow Anushirvan's regnal name in Pahlavi meant "blessed, just or immortal soul," yet he mounted the throne with hands bloodied from repressing his own people. The Sassanian Golden Age began as a counterrevolution even before its progenitor attained the imperial dignity. In the early decades of the sixth century, a revolution swept across the Iranian plateau. It was so radical in its leveling aspirations as to prefigure the egalitarian passions of the French Revolution and the economic terror of the Bolshevik Revolution. The long-running conflict in the previous century with the Hephthalites had sapped much of the empire's life and treasure, and a stupefied people divined in the ensuing plague (horrifying bubonic), drought, and famine the malefic and apparently winning hand of the dark Zoroastrian god Angra Mainyu in the cosmic struggle of good and evil. At the same time, the high nobility and the high clergy, both exempted from taxes, were bent on exacerbating cosmic malice by extracting from the peasants and the common people what little wealth remained to them.[26]

Iran experienced an inspired attempt at social reform from the palace that gained in momentum to become a leveling revolution. Mazdak i Bamdad—an Iranian nobleman whose exact date and place of birth at the close of the fifth century are unknown—was a charismatic ascetic who had attained the rank of high counselor at Ctesiphon, the empire's monumental capital city, where he exerted unrivaled influence upon Khosrow's father, Kavadh I (r. 484–524). Mazdak was devoted to the egalitarian dualism of an earlier charismatic Persian prophet, Mani (210–76 CE), the martyred religious synthesizer whose Manichaean creed came close to official adoption in the late third century. Finding himself stymied at every turn by a reactionary nobility (and even chased into Syrian exile for two years), the beleaguered Kavadh embraced his counselor's program of peace, extensive tax reform, curtailment of the nobles' power, deflation of the Zoroastrian clergy, and welfare programs that opened imperial granaries to the poor.

Mazdak envisaged his royal disciple's reforms as only the starting point for a true societal transformation in which meat eating was abandoned and distinctions based on private property were gradually mitigated by common ownership. The high counselor was determined to bring about temporal social arrangements conducive to the victory of Light over Dark in the grand eschatological duel. As time passed, however, his peaceful vision of the good society morphed into the powerful ideology of Mazdakism, a radical gospel that seized the underclass imagination. During the long, violent, and profoundly destabilizing wars to evict the Hephthalites, thousands of peasants had deserted the land for the safety of the cities, forming something like an urban proletariat. Others, maddened by upperclass exactions and starvation, seized the property of the rich. Great numbers of Mazdakites went on rampages in Babylon, Ecbatana, and Persepolis, destroying fire temples, taking property from the rich, and distributing harem women as common possessions. Many thousands settled on lands belonging to the lords of the great estates.[27]

Counterrevolution also came from the top. No one now knows what Mazdak thought of the leveling Mazdakite firestorm—whether, like Martin Luther, enraged by the German peasants' revolting in his name, he denounced civil disobedience in the vilest terms or, instead, sought to mitigate the motives of the desperate. His imperial patron distanced himself from the movement as social upheaval and the aristocratic backlash gathered force. It had fallen to Khosrow to do his father's dirty work, hang Mazdak in about 528, and exterminate tens of thousands of Mazdakites in a class pogrom reminiscent of the Roman Republic's defeat of Spartacus and his seventy thousand followers in the last of Rome's three great slave revolts. Gibbeted peasants were silhouetted against the horizon and swarms of carrion birds darkened the skies. Thousands of the enslaved were distributed among the noble estates; others were sent to the galleys, the quarries, or quicker deaths in the mines, for which Khosrow's nobility and priesthood gratefully lauded him as *Anushirvan*.

Khosrow I masterminded a counterrevolution that actually achieved several essentials of Mazdak's agenda. Still, to the extent that his was an authentic golden age, it began as a violent reaction to radical ideals. As his first order of business, the *shahanshah* had reorganized the Sassanian war machine. A new nobility of service supplied a salaried officer cadre that supplanted the retainers of the old landed aristocracy. Serial victories racked up in Syria, Armenia, Cappadocia, and Georgia in the first years of his reign followed the enhanced discipline, morale, and money.[28] The *shahanshah* financed this mighty war machine by radical recalibration of the imperial tax system, a reform he imposed upon the bloated ecclesiastical caste as well as the great landholders, both previously exempt from taxation. All land in the empire was ordered surveyed and titles were revalidated after investigation. Taxes, collected triennially, were remitted directly to the imperial treasury. The proliferated privileges of the clergy were pared back. Twenty-five thousand salaried priests were created to tend the sacred fire temples, putting an end to priestly badgering for money. Tax reform, massive public works, a housebroken feudality, and a streamlined ecclesiastical establishment were antidotes that drew the poison from the stricken body politic.

A powerful army, dutiful royal servants, and, above all, redeemed clergy must serve the *Avesta*'s commandments. To that high purpose, Khosrow ordained that all the sacred Zoroastrian texts be transcribed from the old Avestan alphabet of twenty letters into the radical new Pahlavi alphabet of forty-six letters capable of sounding all vowels and consonants. Shapur's old city at Gondeshapur (his version of "the better Antioch of Shapur") in southwestern Iran became an intellectual center *sans pareil*, where Zoroastrian magi, joined by Nestorian theologians and Jewish physicians, studied and taught collaboratively. Khosrow endowed chairs at the university for Neoplatonic philosophers ousted from the venerable Academy at Athens, closed on Justinian's orders. At Gondeshapur, Indian and Greek literary masterpieces were translated into Pahlavi—among them the Hindu prototype of *The Book of a Thousand Nights and One Night* and the *Kalilah and Dimnah*, a collection of animal fables that served as fodder for parables thirteen centuries in the future.[29]

In this ethos of comparatively tolerant high culture, the religious scholarship of the Hebrew community excelled unprecedentedly, for it was roughly about then that the Mishnah, codifying religious and legal norms, and the Gemara, amplifying and explaining the former, were expanded and finally incorporated into the apodictic Babylonian Talmud. One of history's dismaying quirks is that this capstone of Hebrew law and learning would become celebrated as a remarkable achievement made possible under Islam, so complete was to be the submersion of Persian high culture under the Arabs. Yet more ironic was the fact that Zoroastrianism and its radical offshoots, the Indo-Persian literary canon, the formidable war machine and superb bureaucracy, the archetypal research university, and the Mazdakite socioeconomic experiment were the spores of much of Islamic science, culture, religious practice, and military organization.[30]

Balance had been restored. As the king of kings patiently explained to his people at the close of his glorious reign, progress came "not through discussion" but in thoughts, words, and acts in "full conformity" to the dogma of the Zoroastrian religion. Yet Mazdakites survived underground and in remote places for long years after the martyrdom of their prophet; Mazdakism survived much longer in the memory, myth, and inchoate aspirations of the Mesopotamian oppressed. That the political foundations of one of the world's two mightiest empires could be shaken by an egalitarian mass movement inspired by a religious seer was news that still resonated two generations later as far as the Hijaz homeland of Muhammad ibn 'Abd Allah ibn 'Abd al-Muttalib, a poor, twenty-five-year-old Arab herdsman in Mecca.[31]

⁘

Iran attacked the Eastern Roman Empire in the spring of 571. When Khosrow faced the Roman enemy in the last decade of his reign, he commanded what was probably the world's most tightly centralized state. Armenia was the *casus belli* waiting to happen, a religious powder keg wedged between the two empires. Iran's fifty-year peace with Justinian expressly forbade Christian proselytizing in the Sassanian Empire. The Iranians had become convinced, nevertheless, that the Greeks' evangelizing clergy, with the full assent of the increasingly mentally addled

Justin, was determinedly at work in Armenia. The Sassanian war machine was like a huge boulder in downhill motion. The Immortals were the tested best of the Persian nobility, ten thousand men encased in contoured body armor transforming their close-order cavalry charges into a solid wall of glinting bronze, ostrich feathers rippling from helmets. Behind the bronze wall came the rolling thunder of armored elephants that made horses gag and panic at their smell. Added to the Sassanian advantage of numbers and superior professionalism were the broad sympathy and much complicity garnered among the Eastern Roman Empire's religiously disaffected. No people showed greater determination to rid themselves of Graeco-Roman rule than the Jews, whose lot had become almost unbearable after Justinian's policy of forced conversion and property expropriation. To the dogged Nestorians, along with large numbers of suffering powerless and poor, the approach of the *kaviani*, the Sassanians' imposing gold, silver, and bejeweled rectangular battle standard, raised hopes of better days. Even Monophysites had become disaffected under Constantinople's sway.[32]

Faced with wars on several fronts and the gross wastage of material and human treasure in Mesopotamia, Constantinople finally sued for peace in 579, several months after death of the mentally unstable Justin II. Then, before negotiations could be finalized between Justin's successor and Khosrow I, the *shahanshah* died of natural causes in the forty-eighth year of his extraordinary reign. Three years later, Emperor Tiberius Constantine, Justin's militarily capable but spendthrift successor, dropped dead amid customary Byzantine rumors of poison. The imperial purple was draped over the shoulders of Tiberius Constantine's militarily cautious and administratively capable son-in-law, Maurice (r. 582–602), who was too proud to sue for a peace that left the empire no better off than at the start of the war. More to the point, his father-in-law had utterly depleted the imperial treasury by desperate stopgap expenditures. Biding his time, Maurice applied himself to the systematic overhaul of the army, dividing the empire into military districts (*themes*) commanded by prefects (*strategoi*), and writing *Strategikon*, a primer that became a military classic.[33]

There matters remained in stasis during his twenty-year reign: two decades of non-peace between the Eastern Roman Empire and Iran, a period of simmering ill will, border incidents and flare-ups, at least one significant confrontation, and proxy hostilities among satellites. In Maurice's ninth throne year, he overruled his counselors in a carefully calculated decision that ultimately proved to be as disastrous as it was objectively intelligent. The fifteen-year-old grandson of *Anushirvan* himself appeared on Byzantine soil seeking asylum and asked Constantinople's help in regaining the ancestral throne. The prince's father had perished in a *coup d'état* masterminded by the regime's senior general, a nobleman boasting descent from the last Parthian kings. The logic of the usurping general's dictatorship could only mean outright war with the Eastern Roman Empire. Khosrow II, dubbed *Parvez*, "the Victorious," hardly deserved his name in 590. Maurice embraced the prince's cause, supplying arms and scarce gold to the army of loyalists flocking to Syria on condition that, once in power, Khosrow's grandson would sign a treaty of perpetual peace and surrender of Armenia. The dictatorship collapsed within the year, and the new *shahanshah* conscientiously and gratefully ended the war with the Eastern Roman Empire. By the terms of the generous peace of 591, Persian Armenia and Syria, along with several major cities, were restored to the Greeks.[34]

❖

By the time Maurice of the Eastern Roman Empire and Khosrow II concluded the peace of 591, years of strident Graeco-Iranian competition since the death of Justinian and Khosrow I had forever altered the social, political, and commercial landscape of Arabia. It would have been the rare imperial counselor in the Great Palace at Constantinople or in the White Palace at Ctesiphon who concerned himself with the state of affairs in Arabia's inner peninsula. Then, as today, superpower panjandrums assumed the prerogative of optional notice of any collateral consequences of their policies. At the dawn of the seventh century, Arabs rated no more superpower attention than did late-twentieth-century Africans south of the Sahara. Pre-Islamic Arabia was a backwater tenuously tied to the great centers of Asia Minor by camel caravans and political alliances of secondary importance. Then, in the last third of the sixth century and the first twenty years of the seventh, Arabia was drawn into the Fertile Crescent's wars without end. Parthian Persia and Latin Rome were long gone. Sassanian Iran and the Eastern Roman Empire carried on in their names. For the tribes of the Arabian heartland, the Graeco-Iranian competition fiercely underway at both ends of their peninsula presented opportunities for enrichment, influence, and out-migration hitherto imagined by only the canniest among them. To be sure, out-migration to the edges of Jordan, Palestine, and Syria, where Arab clans assimilated the more sophisticated cultures, had been ongoing for centuries.

The *Sarakenoi,* as the Greeks called "the people of the tents" (*Saraceni* in Latin), in more recent times had begun to press harder against the frontiers of both empires. Bedouin raids on caravans and *razzias* for slaves and booty had accelerated during Justinian's reign. And in another of those characteristically principled but strategically questionable decisions, Justin II had provocatively terminated the Bedouins' protection money. But nothing tempted the Roman or the Iranian military establishments to consider invading Arabia proper, a sand mass nearly one-third the size of Europe, parts of which saw rain only every tenth year and for months were baked at 120 degrees Fahrenheit. A growing nuisance, the Arabs were still considered a backward people who merely featured in the peripheral vision of the superpowers, although Greek merchants and Persian importers became less risk-averse about turning a good profit at either end of the thousand-mile Arabian sand conveyor belt.

The Arabs of the Hijaz and the vast Najd watched as proxy wars raged in the peninsula's north and east, and conflict in the south spurted upward out of Yemen like ink on a blotter. The Romans had called Yemen *Arabia felix* ("Happy Arabia") because of its alluvial topography and rain-watered expanses. Once united by a powerful Arab state and ruled by a storied Hebrew king known to the Arabs as Dhu Nuwas ("the man with the hanging locks"), Yemen was partially conquered in 525 CE by an Ethiopian army from the kingdom of Axum, the Christian power-house in the Horn of Africa. Yusuf As 'as was the Hebrew name of the man "with the hanging locks." He was the scion of the founding Jewish dynasty of the great Himyarite kingdom of Yemen that the Axumite

Ethiopians invaded and subjugated. Legend holds that Yusuf As ʿas rode his horse suicidally into the Red Sea after losing his kingdom. With his disappearance, a curious chapter in Judeo-Arab domination closed in southern Arabia. Fifty years later, encouraged by Justin II's promise of money and manpower, the Ethiopian viceroy of Yemen felt strong enough to expand his control over southern Arabia. Yemeni Jews and local sheikhs who chafed under the Monophysite Ethiopians and remembered the golden age of the "hanging locks" man sent urgent appeals to Ctesiphon to act before it was too late.[35]

War reached the very gates of Mecca in 570. The Ethiopian viceroy, Abraha, approached with a large army and war elephants, beasts previously unseen in the desert. To plant Christianity deep in Yemen's soil, the Ethiopians had built a large church in Sanʿa, today the capital of Yemen. They intended the church to become a great pilgrimage center, a revenue source freed of competition from Mecca. The people of Mecca quaked behind their flimsy wattled fortifications as sand clouds on the horizon trailed the advancing Ethiopian host and its terrifying cacophony. That day fixed itself permanently in Arabia's racial and religious memory, an allusive phrase about "elephant people" inscribing itself in the Qurʾan. To the Arabs, Mecca had been miraculously spared, some said, by a flock of attacking birds. In reality, Meccans owed their deliverance to the sudden arrival of a Sassanian naval expedition, dispatched by Khosrow I to checkmate Graeco-Roman power in the Gulf of Aden. Iranian forces quickly routed the Ethiopians, who fled across the Red Sea to Axum. Yemen was enfolded into the Sassanian grand alliance. Three score years in the future, great significance would be divined in the fact that the Year of the Elephant, 570, was thought to be the very year of Muhammad ibn ʿAbd Allah's birth in Mecca. For Edward Gibbon, the Occident's cheerleader, 570 CE was another of history's lost opportunities. "If a Christian power had been maintained in Arabia," he reflected, "Mahomet must have been crushed in his cradle, and Abyssinia would have prevented a revolution which has changed the civil and religious state of the world."[36]

The political, commercial, and religious tremors visited upon Arabia by the superpowers were sudden, sharp, and unprecedented in force. Ethiopian elephants at Mecca's gates were but the seeming hallucinations of superpower geopolitics. When war came again in 571, Iran and Rome furiously pressed the game of checkmate by proxies across the Fertile Crescent. The proxy calculus was hardly new. At the top of the century, Constantinople and Ctesiphon had created the Lakhmid and Ghassanid kingdoms, now long forgotten. The Lakhmid kingdom, a Sassanian invention extending from the Persian Gulf to Iraq, was ruled by the Banu[37] Lakhm, an Arab clan that warred more or less on the side of the Iranians against the Graeco-Romans for three generations. The Ghassanid kingdom, a Graeco-Roman creation ruled by the nomadic Banu Ghassan, stretched across the top of Arabia from Sinai to the intersection of the Lakhmid territory with today's Jordan, Iraq, and Syria. The emperors suspected their Ghassanid potentates of collusion with the Iranians and, almost as intolerable, of genuine Monophysite convictions. In the first decade of the seventh century, Constantinople removed the Ghassanid leadership, whereupon several Ghassanid sheikhs defected to Iran. The Ghassanid kingdom, a considerable power blocking the advance of the hungry tribes of the Hijaz, all but disintegrated.[38] The loyalty of the Lakhmid kingdom's rulers also came under suspicion from their Persian overlords, and with a similar unintended outcome. The consequences were ultimately disastrous for the Sassanian and Eastern Roman Empires and liberating for the peninsular Arabs. By their own actions, the Greeks and Iranians opened an unrestricted channel to Syria for the desert Arabs.

❖

The people who soon flowed through those channels unintentionally created by the Graeco-Romans and the Iranians would come from the principal city of the Hijaz. Mecca was an economic powerhouse. It was the lodestone of al-jahiliyya ("the time before Islam"), the magnet drawing thousands of pilgrims from desert and oasis to perennial, spellbound circumambulation of the Ka'bah, the cube-shaped shrine housing "the great black meteor." The commercial city was dominated by the Quraysh, the most powerful tribe in the unforgiving Hijaz. Quraysh meant "shark," an eponym thought to have been based on the fish adopted long beforehand as the tribal symbol. The Quraysh were so numerous that an outsider might have wondered who was *not* a member of the tribe. Numerous, yes, but definitely all were not equal. At the top of the Quraysh social scale were such imperious clans as the Umayya family of the ʿAbd Shams clan, richer and more oligopolistic every year. They and their confederates had much improved upon the mundane practice of buying cheap and selling dear. They pooled capital and sold venture shares. They developed managerial procedures that rationalized caravan operations, hiring agents and dependable armed escorts and setting up well-provisioned caravansaries along the routes. They had optimized the advantages of crossroads geography and religious real estate with a vengeance. This was the clan as business cartel, something new in the way of Meccan affairs.

The emergence of the cartel had not boded well for the rough egalitarian simplicity that had characterized Arab life even in sprawling Mecca, Taʾif, Yathrib, and other good-size towns, to say nothing of its antithesis to the democracy of the desert. Disrupting and stimulating, continuous war meant commerce and trade for the well-capitalized and quick-witted Umayya. As the seventh century unfolded, the augmenting profits from the caravan trade and the revenues from the ancient tradition of the Kaʾbah pilgrimages accelerated the erosion of Mecca's social equilibrium, creating an environment in which the divide between haves and have-nots became as sharp as the edge where light meets the shadow of the palm tree. The mystical Kaʾbah was barely visible above encroaching rings of tents and stalls. The barter and purchase of goods and services around the holy spot even included a brisk and lewd sex trade. The city's population had exploded, bringing the adventurous, the unscrupulous, and the hapless, who reshaped and complicated the social landscape.[39] Many of Islam's first believers would come from the city's poor and dependent, increasingly alienated by new money and its accompanying ostentatiousness among the Quraysh. These were the mostly marginal, who warmed to a new message of equality in a new community of believers, an *ummah* of solidarity and compassion that welcomed even slaves.

To say, as one contemporary authority does, that Islam "developed as an answer to the problem resulting from Meccan commercial prosperity" seems somewhat facile, yet it holds much truth. Cracks along class lines caused considerable unrest in a number of caravan towns in the Hijaz and elsewhere—in Yathrib and Ta'if, for example—just as Meccan social unrest began to peak toward the end of the sixth century. Unprecedented prosperity made customary poverty seem cruel, unmerited misery—and were not both the special circumstance of mighty wars and calamities? The century lent itself to an all-pervading "end of days" ethos. Preachers and seers, *hanifs* and *kahins*, flourished among the Arabs. Among the Jews, a date certain—4291 of the Hebrew calendar and 531–32 of the Christian—was fixed (revised as required) for the coming of the Messiah. "When you see kingdoms fighting among themselves," learned men warned among the Jews, "then look for the footsteps of the Messiah."[40] The eschatological certainty appeared to be corroborated, as war, famine, and plague raked the Middle East. It seems clear that the sixth was one of those centuries vibrating, like the tenth, with chiliastic portents, an age of pivotal expectations.

Some of the exotic deities of the Fertile Crescent seeped even into the sands of the Hijaz. Nestorians were not unheard of there. Zoroastrian fire temples burned at the northeastern edge of the desert in Basra. Abraham and Moses were revered in oasis settlements such as Khaybar, not so distant from Yathrib. Tribes of Christian Arabs dwelled in the north. Mani, the third-century Persian aristocrat whose teachings only narrowly missed becoming the established religion of the Sassanid Empire, bequeathed a judgment of startling Middle Eastern prescience. "Wisdom and good works have been brought in perfect succession from age to age by the messengers of God," he told his contemporaries. "They came in one age through the prophet called Buddha in the region of India, in another through Zoroaster in the land of Persia, and in yet another through Jesus in the lands of the West." Mani was certain that his revelation "formed a great wisdom such as has not existed in previous generations."[41] The next messenger was about to receive such a revelation in a hillside cave near Mecca. In history's big picture, then, Muhammad and his new creed were incarnations of the Mesopotamian Zeitgeist and the new economy of the Hijaz.

2

"The Arabs Are Coming!"

MECCA'S caravans charged with dates, spices, perfume, and slaves ranged out of the desert, north and west to Judeo-Christian Palestine and Christian Syria, or south to Yemen and west across the Red Sea to Christian Ethiopia. One such camel train passing through the town of Bostra (Busra) on the Syrian border in about 582 carried eleven- or twelve-year-old Muhammad ibn 'Abd Allah out of Arabia for the first time, along with his guardian uncle, Abu Talib. Bostra was a big bustling town at the intersection of five trade routes. Its episcopal see had been authorized by the Empress Theodora, a Monophysite sympathizer, and the imposing Bostra Cathedral attested to the community's prosperous devotion.

As the story is variously recounted, an aged Monophysite monk named Bahira, observing the approaching caravan, noticed a small cloud moving above one of the riders and shading the boy when he dismounted and sat alone. Hurrying from his cell to ask about the background of this obviously very special young person, the monk learned from Abu Talib that his nephew was an orphan whose father died before Muhammad was born in the Hijaz. The excited monk sought out Muhammad in order to see if he possessed certain attributes foretold in an ancient book. Bahira found them on the boy's back. Muslim tradition holds that the monk affirmed Muhammad's special destiny to Abu Talib and insisted that the orphan's mission be kept hidden either from the Graeco-Romans or, in another version, from the Jews, who, "if they see him and get to know what I know about him they will try to harm him." One of early Islam's most astute Western interpreters reasonably regards the Bahira account as "primarily a way of reassuring people that Muammad was really a prophet."[1]

Thirteen years after his first caravan trip abroad, Muhammad set off again for Syria in 595 with a commission arranged by his uncle, Abu Talib, from a wealthy Meccan merchant. The Middle East was relatively quiet, as Emperor Maurice and *Shahanshah* Khosrow II had pledged their empires to a new era of peace four years earlier. Trade routes were open and fairly safe. Muhammad was about twenty-five then, of medium height and stocky build, by some accounts, with long russet hair and a kempt beard framing a large, round head. His gait was said to be wide and swinging, and his dark, piercing eyes and low, arresting voice caused people to take notice who might otherwise have been oblivious to someone of undistinguished social and material significance. The caravan commission not only would change the young loner's life, it also would set history on a radically new course and at a faster speed a hundred years after his death. By then, his special message would have garnered converts on a peninsula attached to the continent of Europe. Still, Muhammad was not exactly a nonentity before heading out of Mecca on the life-altering commission.

Muhammad's bloodlines as a member of the Hashimite clan, the Banu Hashim, were more than respectable. The Banu Hashim was a secondary subset of the proud, dominant Quraysh tribe. Moreover, his deceased father's brothers had standing in Mecca as successful merchants. Uncle Abu Talib, titular head of the Banu Hashim, was a person whose authority and protection could mean the difference of life, flight, or death in the event of a grave offense or misunderstanding in a society where people's nerve endings were always exposed. Grandfather 'Abd al-Muttalib's position as superintendent of the famous Zamzam well, a few miles outside the city, was one of the most important local services. Muhammad himself cut a fine figure, even as he shepherded and odd-jobbed in and about the hot, gray, lunar-landscape valley cradling the city. Had circumstances been different, his attractive young cousin would have accepted his overtures. She stayed his intimate friend for life, but Umm Hani married someone else. Orphaned by the deaths of his father, 'Abd Allah, and (five or six years later) his mother, Aminah bint Wahb, Muhammad's opportunities for self-improvement were hardly promising. In a society where tribal affiliation and social class were hierarchically fixed, an orphan's future dictated a veto from Umm Hani's family, even though the orphan was a relative.[2]

As even casual history students know, Muhammad married Khadija bint Khuwaylid, a wealthy forty-year-old merchant and a widow. Fifteen years older than Muhammad, she was related to the Banu Hashim but also to another clan higher up the social scale. Women who ran businesses in their own right were rarities anywhere in the late sixth century, and women of Khadija's affluence and prominence were almost as rare as snow in the Hijaz. That she was much impressed by her young agent's business acumen was not surprising. Muhammad had earned a reputation for skill and trustworthiness as an adult assistant to Abu Talib on caravan trips to Gaza and Damascus. Nor was it surprising that even a wealthy and obviously competent Arab businesswoman would need a husband as an able representative and manager in her patriarchal society. Muhammad, available and able, satisfied the role ideally and may even have been an emotional bonus for her.

It was Khadija who proposed, through an intermediary, in formulaic words praising Muhammad's "beautiful character and the truth of [his] speech." The orphan accepted, and Khadija gave him as a body servant a young slave, Zayd ibn Harithah, whom Muhammad immediately freed. Zayd, a precocious lad whose tribe, the Kalb, was partly Christianized, remained with his master for the rest of his life. Of Muhammad and Khadija's four daughters—Fatima, Zaynab, Umm Kulthum, and Ruqayya—Fatima's fingerprints on history would be largest by far. (Two males died in childbirth.) Khadija's gift to her husband of financial security and intelligent companionship mattered to posterity far more than progeny. Her contributions to Muhammad's growth as a seer would seem to merit considerably more speculation than has been hazarded so far. The Prophet of God is virtually inconceivable without the wealth, culture, affection, and connections of this exceptional wife. She would be Muhammad's first disciple, history's first *Muslim* (one who obeys).[3] As long as she lived, Muhammad had no other wife.

Now a man of independent means and much-enhanced standing, Muhammad might well have occupied himself exclusively with his wife's affairs and cultivating contacts among those with influence in the governance of Mecca. He did just that for the most part, although a certain malaise tugged at him through the years. At age thirty-five, we see fairly prominent Meccan Muhammad pitching in physically to help raise the Ka'bah walls and spruce up the numerous fetishes and minor deities surrounding the structure.

The severe monotheist hardly emerged overnight. One story honored by Muslims has adolescent Muhammad being roundly berated by a desert holy man—one of the many *hanifs* already transformed by visions of a single deity—for sacrificing a ewe to Al-Lat, goddess of the city of Ta'if. It would have been a perfectly natural thing for Muhammad to do at the time. Al-Lat, idol of the sun, was one of three principal deities venerated at Mecca. She hovered over the Ka'bah with Allah's other daughters: al-Uzzah, protector of the town of Nakhlah, and Manat, protector of Qudayt. Allah, all-powerful but remote and undefined, was the acknowledged but unaddressed supreme force, al-ilah—"the god," simply. Pilgrims came from every direction bearing tribute for Al-Lat, al-Uzzah, and Manat. As they circumambulated the Ka'bah, they chanted: "Verily they are the most exalted females/Whose intercession is to be sought."[4] As shepherd and man of affairs, Muhammad heard this incantation thousands of times.

Objectively, his situation as master of a successful export–import establishment and pillar of the religious status quo ought to have propelled him into the arms of the Quraysh oligarchs of Mecca. Instead, Muhammad's questing temperament and moral antennae, matched by Khadija's steadying personality, encouraged him onto another path, one of estrangement from and condemnation of the Meccan social order. He was often seen talking with outsiders passing through on the caravan conveyor belt: hanifs illumined by transcendent visions; Monophysites and Nestorians agitated by Trinitarian complexities; the odd Roman or Sassanian veteran or castoff with war stories to tell. Emperor Maurice's assassination, not so many years after Muhammad's marriage, had plunged the Fertile Crescent into another round of superpower conflict and wartime commercial opportunities for the resourceful and the connected. When the voice spoke that shifted forever the axis of his being, Muhammad had been subconsciously preparing to hear it for some time. Solitary wanderings about the rugged Meccan valley and in deepening, trancelike meditations in the hillside caves of Mount Hira, not far from the city, must have primed him for the extraordinary transmission. His first biographer, Ibn Ishaq (d. 767), writing more than a century after the Prophet's death, believes that Muhammad "grew to love solitude" and that he used to remain in a cave on Hira "engaged in acts of devotion for a number of days before returning to his family."[5]

The Godhead came like a clap of thunder. The year of the Christian calendar was 610—the same year that the mad usurper, Phocas, was assassinated and the Eastern Roman Empire emerged from a long nightmare of misrule and mayhem. Muhammad was in his fortieth year. The month was Ramadan, possibly the night of the 26th or 27th—"the night of destiny." The force seized him, compressing him three times. "Recite in the name of your Lord who creates!" an angel Muhammad identified much later as Gabriel (*Jibríl*) commanded with electrifying suddenness. "He creates man from a clot of blood." "Recite!" the voice boomed. "Your Lord is the Most Bountiful One, who by the pen taught man what he did not know." Muhammad had been standing, but he fell to his knees and, as Ibn Ishaq records him saying, "crawled away, my shoulders trembling. I went to Khadija and said, 'Wrap me up! Wrap me up!' "[6] Unsure of the reality of the message and the awesome imperative it bade him accept, he almost despaired of his sanity.

No Muslim would credit the pathological profile of Muhammad presented by the twentieth-century French biographer Maxime Rodinson, although, as Karen Armstrong believes, Rodinson's *Muhammad* is a masterpiece of Western scholarship by a self-proclaimed atheist. But if professions of divine revelations run against the West's grain of secular skepticism, they seem to have been no more congenial at first to Muhammad the Prophet—not because such communions were objectively improbable but because the common experience was that persons making such claims were more than likely deluded or demented. As commands by the unidentified voice assailed him—"You that are wrapped up in your cloak, arise and give warning"—Muhammad would take pains to be heard to say that he detested no one more "than a poet or a madman," an aversion finding chapter and verse in the Qur'an or the "Recitation" (rendered into English). The rich tradition of Arab poetry was to be greatly downplayed. *Kahíns* (soothsayers) and wandering versifiers deserved to have their words maligned and their sanity questioned. But he, Muhammad, was no *kahín*. His revelations would upend Arabia.

Khadija, believing his visions to be genuine, steadied her husband and sent him to a paternal cousin for guidance. Waraqah ibn Nawfal, an elderly man of some learning, knew the Bible and the Torah and may once have been a practicing Nestorian. The meaning of Muhammad's message was unmistakable to the holy man, who understood that Khadija's husband had received one of those epoch-changing revelations periodically vouchsafed to mankind by the Godhead. But Waraqah warned that Muhammad would be reviled and ostracized for it. Muhammad emerged from his crisis persuaded of the truth of his *barakah*, his spiritual destiny. Khadija, equally convinced that he was God's sounding board, became her husband's disciple. Gabriel's psychological opinion settled the matter: "By the grace of your Lord, you are not a madman. Yours will be an unending reward."[7]

The visions that came to him in ever-greater number and intensity in the hillside cave were dangerous, if true. There seemed to be no place in them for the old gods and demons in these visions of unique divinity. "Arise and warn!" the voice of destiny commanded again. "Glorify your Lord, purify your inner self." He was commanded to fight "until idolatry is no more and God's religion reigns supreme." The time had come for Meccans to wean themselves of superstition, to end usury, and to grant charity to the poor and justice to the enslaved. "As for the orphan," whose status was no better than a slave's, "be not overbearing." Not only did God ordain the right of women to hold property, Muhammad was told that their inheritances were sacrosanct ("whether it be little or much, they shall be legally entitled to a share") and that divorce, under certain circumstances, could be mutual between wife and husband, "for agreement is best." Despite Allah's permission "to forsake them [disobedient wives] in beds apart, and beat them," the sum total of prescriptions about women's rights and duties would make Muhammad's new religion the most enlightened among the revealed creeds in its time. His messages to his people were meant to lead them out of their "days of ignorance," the euphonious *al-jahiliyya,* an immemorial age of animism, polytheism, and blood-feud disunity stretching back into the mists of Arab origins.

The new prophet was soon seen as a nuisance by the proud Quraysh tribe, as a dangerous crank even, in the opinion of the politically astute 'Abd Shams, Makhzum, and Umayya clansmen, the richest and most influential of the Quraysh. Abu Talib's leadership of the Banu Hashim, together with Khadija's interlaced business arrangements, imposed a degree of tolerance of the Prophet's public statements. But there were murmurings in the marketplace, and evil eyes were cast upon him. Some of the revelations that came in trancelike meditations were easily vulnerable to misinterpretation, such as the rumor that Muhammad inveighed against the rich revenue trade from the Ka'bah pilgrimages. Veneration of the sacred stone was never in question, only the plethora of false spirits and *jinns* buzzing around it. Other revelations did carry disturbingly subversive implications, though, such as those early pronouncements about wealth. Their essence was that wealth must be used for the good of the many, that its ostentatious display—of which there seemed more each year in Mecca—was wrong. Woe betide the man who "gathers wealth and counts it over, thinking that wealth will perpetuate him!" Gabriel told Muhammad. "God will separate the wicked from the just." "He will heap all the wicked one upon another and then cast them into Hell." Judgment Day was pure Zarathustra. Those whose (good) deeds weighed heavily in the scales would dwell in bliss. "But he whose deeds are light, the Abyss shall be his home."[8] If the identity of the wicked seemed to match the profile of many Umayyas and Makhzumites, these oligopolists needed only mend their ways to spare themselves perdition.

Muhammad found many of his first recruits ("Companions of the Prophet," as they came to be called) among the city's poor and dependent. These were the mostly marginal men (and some women) from impoverished tribes or persons whose only communitarian significance, like the Banu Asah, was as an attachment to a powerful clan. They, together with several slaves, such as the gutsy Bilal, a dark-skinned Ethiopian, warmed to a novel message of equality in a new community of Believers, an *ummah* of solidarity and compassion. If Jesus of Nazareth's admonition comes to mind—that it would be easier for a camel to pass through the eye of a needle than for a rich man to get into the kingdom of heaven—so also does something of Mazdak's leveling ideal of common property. Social equality was at the heart of the message. Muslim lore relates the incident (late in his mission) of Muhammad reproaching a man beating a slave. "God made Adam in his [the slave's] image"—not, as the Christian interpretation holds, "in His image," the Prophet explained.

But not all the early disciples (of whom there were about forty) came from Mecca's social bottom or the marginal middle. A small, critical nucleus of Companions consisted of extremely well-born young anti-establishmentarians present in all societies, regardless of time and place, who were primed to press radical changes. Like Khalid ibn Sa'id al-As (older brother of the future conqueror of Egypt), some were Banu 'Abd

Shams. 'Uthman ibn Affan, whose admiration of Muhammad was almost romantic, belonged to a top-tier Quraysh family.[9]

As the illuminations came to Muhammad during a decade or more, they were memorized by followers; written on leaves, pieces of bone, and flat stones; and recorded by his scribe, Zayd ibn Thabit.[10] Muhammad's message was simplicity itself—spare, unambiguous commands, easily memorized and within every believer's ability to fulfill. Charity, tithing for the *ummah*, daily prayer, and the *shahada* affirming, "There is no god but God, and Muhammad is His prophet."

These fundamentals of belief emerged over time, of course, not all at once, and they were not completed until after the Prophet led the Believers north out of Mecca to welcoming Yathrib. Their propagation among the Meccans engendered controversy that hardened into political conflict along class lines. Abu Talib was warned to restrain his nephew. For his part, Muhammad entertained a temporary compromise strategy designed to placate Mecca's leading families. Compromise was alien both to temperament and message, but there were to be occasions when the Prophet demonstrated a saving grasp of mundane political necessity. The offer of common worship at the Ka'bah of Muslims with pagans was meant to propitiate the Quraysh and their dependents, the better to educate Meccans in the meaning of his new creed. The inducement for the Quraysh was that their three goddesses, Al-Lat, al-Uzzah, and Manat, were to be adopted by Allah as avatars—God's intermediaries. "Have you considered Allat and al-'Uzza/And Manat, the third, the other?" he mistakenly heard the true voice say.[11] Muhammad realized almost immediately, after a correction from above, that the revelations prompting the placatory devotional gesture came not from Gabriel but from Satan ("satanic verses," they would be called), that they were monotheistically so wrongheaded as to make a complete mockery of his calling.

The experiment proved politically fruitless as well. More than a few of Muhammad's less-fortunate followers must have wondered about the long-term advantages to themselves in this new regime of linked creeds and collaborating classes. When the Prophet declared the overture satanically inspired and immediately terminated, the Quraysh elite (*ashraf*),

suspected bad faith and soon concluded that they had no interest in seeing their goddesses play second fiddle to Muhammad's austere deity.
Nevertheless, Islam's newly minted monotheism was not at the heart of
the controversy, per se, since Arabia was home to great numbers of holy
men, *hanifs*, retailing inchoate concepts of an interventionist supreme
being, not to mention the ancient beliefs of the peninsula's many Jews in
a high god. It was to money, old and new, that Muhammad's Islam was
seen as a double threat: to the revenue stream flowing from idol shrines
at Ta'if, Nakhlah, and several other cities, including Mecca, as well as to
the vital, unquestioning deference the poor and lowly "owed" their bet-
ters. A telling description a century later that has the ring of actuality has
Qurayshite landowners from Ta'if marching into Mecca to find Muhammad: "They behaved violently towards him and showed their dislike of
what he said and so roused up those of its members who served them."
Soon it was reported that "every clan fell upon those of its members who
were Muslim, tormenting them, and trying to force them to leave their
religion."[12] When Muhammad's need of them was greatest, Khadija, the
first Muslim and his psychological compass, and Uncle Abu Talib, sympathetic buffer, died within months of each other in 619.

   Worse was in store for Allah's grief-stricken messenger. The new
sheikh of the Hashimites decided that his clan's continued protection of
Muhammad was inexpedient, an opportunistic decision taken after the
Prophet confirmed to a dismayed Abu Lahab the truth of the rumor that,
because 'Abd al-Muttalib had died an unbeliever, their common grandfather was in hell. Gabriel had a message for Abu Lahab: "Nothing shall his
wealth and gains avail him." With his own clan's elders standing aside,
Muhammad and his Believers found themselves facing ever-greater sanctions in a climate of increasing danger. The persecution foretold by
Waraqah, Khadija's relative, befell Muhammad. Many Meccans became
alarmed by his charisma, and they were offended by his moral presumptuousness and suspected his motives. Meccans were ordered to boycott
Muslim businesses and shun them individually in order to bring Muhammad to his senses. Slaves found to have converted were set upon with
particular harshness. One of them was exposed to the heat of the day in
a valley, a rock tied to his chest. "They asked him: 'Are Al-Lat and al-

Uzzah your gods, not Allah?" Ibn Ishaq reports. "And he said, 'Yes.' He had reached the stage where, had a beetle gone by . . . he would have said 'Yes' to that too."[13]

One likely inference is that, as the material circumstances became desperate for some and social pressures sharper for others, the Companions were riven by dissent and faltering resolve. In any case, the decision to send a score of disciples to Ethiopia had the effect of removing malcontents and relieving the desperate. The Axumites were major trade rivals of the Quraysh, and Muhammad may have briefly considered Ethiopian asylum for himself. In Mecca, a small band of Companions stayed by the Prophet's side constantly, on guard wherever crowds were too many in the souks and alleys. Several of these were Qurayshites who underwent sudden, powerful conversion experiences. Abu Bakr and 'Umar, somewhat younger than Muhammad, were experienced Qurayshite businessmen, physically strong and fearless in a fight. They were a study in contrasts: Abu Bakr was a contemplative man who demonstrated his religious sincerity by spending down his fortune buying slaves in order to set them free; 'Umar ibn al-Khattab a brusque mountain of a man with scant patience for the drawing of subtle moral distinctions. Both men became related through marriage to Muhammad, as his fathers-in-law. They, along with Ali ibn Abi Talib, the Prophet's cousin, second convert to the faith and first son-in-law (favored daughter Fatima's efficient husband), formed an inner circle later called the *rashidun*, the "rightly guided." One of the future "rightly guided," and also a son-in-law, 'Uthman ibn Affan, was a prized defector from the hostile Banu Umayya.

Over the next three years, the extinction of Islam became ever more certain, awaiting only the moment when the Prophet's enemies could kill him. After a depressing exploratory visit to nearby Ta'if and fruitless feelers sent to one or two other towns, his options seemed exhausted. He approached one of the Bedouin tribes visiting Mecca, but these desert pragmatists gave him no more than a cursory hearing before heading on. Meantime, Muslim ranks thinned, notwithstanding extraordinary tidings at about this time. Muhammad disclosed details of his breathtaking "nightly journey" from Mecca to Jerusalem and thence to heaven. How much Muhammad then knew of the sufferings common to prophets and messiahs—to Zarathustra, Moses, Jesus, or Mani—is unknown, but the last Meccan years before his flight fit the profile of martyrology. A bracing revelation came just as his spirits ebbed, a classic of the redemption-through-suffering genre: "Your Lord has neither forsaken you nor left you forlorn." It foretold an ending "better for you than the beginning."[14]

∷

If any history of Islam's beginnings is known to the non-Muslim, it is usually the phase during which the Prophet repaired to Yathrib in the 622nd year of the Common Era—the *hijra*, inaugurating an eight-year struggle to the death with the Meccan homeland. From the safety of Yathrib—known thereafter as Medina, *Madinat al-Nabi*, "the City of the Prophet"—Muhammad and his Companions built the first mosque and secured firm control of the government with the backing of the local converts (*ansars*). A verdant oasis town as old as Babylon, Yathrib was populated by two large and several minor tribes of inveterately feuding Arabs. The Aws and the Khazraj had probably migrated from Yemen, bringing their internecine misunderstandings with them. The Qurayza, the Nadir, and the Qaynuqa were three Jewish tribes that had been in Yathrib such a long time that the smaller Arab tribes had taken on many of their mores. Much of the city's prosperity was owed to the Jews, whose craftsmen, metalsmiths, and jewelers were renowned throughout the peninsula, as were the dates grown on their plantations. Of the many causes of enmities, ancient and recent, among the people of Yathrib, religion was not among them. All of the tribes, Arab and Jew, had finally agreed to consult an outsider to arbitrate mounting disputes that threatened the community's solidarity. After the second secret meeting at Aqaba outside Mecca, Yathrib's sheikhs and Arab elders not only offered Muhammad the position of tribal arbiter, several pledged themselves to Islam.[15]

With the coherence of purpose inspired and enforced by Muhammad and Abu Bakr, who were among the last to arrive, the Muslims transformed Yathrib in well under one year. Eleven Companions—including 'Umar and his wife Zaynab, Ali and Fatima, and 'Uthman and

Ruqqaya—were joined by seventy men and their families, the *muhajirun* (Meccan emigrants). Muhammad's household now numbered three wives, two of them widows, and Abu Bakr's six-year-old daughter, the sparkling, opinionated A'isha, with whom he would consummate their sexual union three years later.

Muhammad's position among the tribes, Arab and Jew, was still defining itself. His Meccan Muslims were a small minority, and many of the new converts were Muslims from expediency rather than conviction. Then there was the impressive leader of the Khazraj tribe, 'Abdallah ibn Ubayy, who was still taking the Prophet's measure and was decidedly wary of vesting too much authority in him. In this early period, Muhammad was on his best diplomatic behavior. The main elements in the parties' agreement made sense enough to allow him to solidify his role as ultimate adjudicator. All agreed to observe peace among themselves, to provide mutual support against enemies, and to submit all disputes to the Prophet. To the Qurayza, the Nadir, and the Qaynuqa, Muhammad made known the depths of his creedal affinity for Judaism. He had good reason in the first months to believe that the monotheistic Jews would find his preaching congenial. After all, he had imported from their religion some of the building blocks of the still-inchoate Islam.

But let there be no ambiguity about Islam's primacy. "The only true faith in God's sight is Islam," Zayd ibn Thabit recorded God Himself as saying in words dictated from his master. For the present, though, syncretism ruled. Jews were spiritual kinfolk, after all, the spawn of Abraham. Abraham's Egyptian slave girl, Hagar, was mother to Ishmael, the first Arab; Sarah, Abraham's aged wife, was mother to Isaac, the first Jew. Christians, too, shared descent from Abraham in common with Jews and Arabs. All, said Muhammad, were "People of the Book," worshippers of the same God whose revelations they had interpreted, each in their own way. Besides, the wealth and political support of the three Jewish tribes were much-needed assets. He was more than willing, then, to blend aspects of the two faiths. For a now seemingly implausible instant in its evolution, the Muslim feast of *Ashura* coincided with *Yom Kippur*, the tenth day of the Hebrew month of Tishri. Muslims were commanded to find the direction for prayers (the *qibla*) by facing Jerusalem. There was common Friday worship with Jews for the preparation of the next-day Sabbath. Circumcision and the prohibition of pork were adopted as requirements. The Jews of Medina were said to have long since lost touch with the main currents of orthodoxy. Even so, in his innovative enthusiasm, the Prophet failed to appreciate that the Nadir, Qurayza, and Qaynuqa, like all Hebrews, retained the ancient certainty of being God's chosen people whose tribal book told the history of creation. It was probably unavoidable that as Muhammad and his followers began to resent the condescension of their confessional partners, the groundwork was laid for harsh and blood-soaked consequences.[16]

The first blood spilled was Arab, however. In March 624, two years after the *hijra*, a few hundred Believers ambushed a much larger force of Quraysh at a place called Badr, a watering hole on the caravan route from Syria. The original objective had been that year's largest Meccan caravan, with a value estimated at 50,000 dinars. Its commander, Abu Sufyan ibn Harb, sheikh of the Banu Umayya and Muhammad's archenemy, was not the founder of Islam's future dynasty for lack of astuteness. His caravan cautiously veered away from Badr onto a secondary trail, even as a twelve-hundred-man Meccan relief expedition was speeding to give it more protection. Positioned behind the rise overlooking Badr, the Muslims set upon the unsuspecting relief expedition. With the advantage of surprise, Muhammad's force displayed more discipline than Arabs usually possessed in battle at the time. The Muslims were murderous. Several Quraysh sheikhs and more than fifty men were slaughtered, women chasing the defeated and shrieking as they killed and stripped the wounded. As front-line participants in those early, desperate matches, Muslim women were deservedly feared. Badr gave the Muslims confidence in warfare ("*Allahu akbar*"—"God is most great"—resounded in the desert for the first time), a fair amount of booty (150 camels and ten horses), hostages for ransom, various weapons, and an economic chokehold over the revenues from the northern caravan route.[17] The effect of the Battle of Badr within the Hijaz and as far as Yemen was immense. With their Red Sea caravan route no longer secure, Mecca's oligarchs were forced to use the longer one across the oasis-deprived Najd. Arabs even speculated that the center of power might shift permanently to Medina.

Muhammad's rising political stature was accompanied by a retooled Islam. After Badr, his religious ideas acquired a self-sufficiency that distinguished them from the companionate Judaism. Relations with Medina's Jews had continued to sour. The three tribes had taken no collateral part in the fighting. Their leaders, one elderly rabbi in particular, were believed to have shown disrespect for the Prophet's notions of commingled Judeo-Muslim rituals. Muhammad suspected, probably correctly, that the three tribes resented his augmented authority and were even more unhappy about their lost business with Mecca. He found worrisome the closeness of the Khazraj and the Qaynuqa—the former headed by the sheikh who increasingly resented Muhammad's authority, the latter a wealthy clan of goldsmiths and jewelers. He grew darkly suspicious of communications between the Qaynuqa and their business contacts in Mecca. Four weeks after Badr, the Prophet struck his first blow against the Jews of Medina. An incident at the market between a Muslim woman and one of the Qaynuqa escalated, with a Muslim male killed in the ensuing fracas. But rather than submit to Muhammad's arbitration, as required under the binding pact, the wealthy Jews haughtily withdrew behind their palisades at the oasis's southeastern perimeter. Muhammad ordered them to leave Medina within ten days, abandoning all their property. When they refused, Muhammad imposed a blockade to starve them into surrendering and then ordered them put to death. The sheikh of the Khazraj, the lordly 'Abdallah ibn Ubayy, objected, and he prevailed upon the Prophet to reinstitute the expulsion order. The heated exchange between the two is startling to read, as 'Abdallah seizes Muhammad's breastplate and the latter rages, "Let me go!" Not until you hear me out, "by Allah!" the sheikh rejoins, with a caveat that caused Allah's messenger to reconsider his awful decision. "Will you slay them all in the space of a morning? By Allah, in your place I would fear a reversal of fortune."[18] With the Qaynuqa death sentence lifted, the remaining Jewish tribes watched their coreligionists depart without recorded protest. When the year closed, Muslims no longer prayed facing Jerusalem; the *qibla* was oriented to Mecca. The fast of Ramadan replaced the fast of *Ashura*. Henceforth, Friday prayers were exclusive to Muslims. Rather than the model to emulate, Judaism had become the faith to censure. In fact, what he soon thought he had learned about the Judeo-Christian theological experience would impel Muhammad to make colossal claims about Islam's revelatory primacy and eschatological uniqueness.

That the Prophet had come north to be far more than an adjudicator was manifest in the "Leaf" or the "Writing," the foundational Islamic document known as the "Constitution of Medina," preserved by biographer Ibn Ishaq. Reza Aslan, the excellent contemporary interpreter of Islam, thinks that the Constitution of Medina, vaunted by Muslims as the world's first written constitution, must have been ratified several years after the *hijra*, as Muhammad's Muslims lacked the votes to ratify it in the first year or two. The period immediately after the Battle of Badr is highly likely. Whatever the timing of this historic pact, its significance as the will of the Prophet and the archetypal template of Muslim theocratic governance can hardly be overstated. "A document from Muhammad the Prophet . . . between the Believers, the Muslims of Mecca and Medina and those who followed them," it proclaimed. "They constitute an *ummah*, one community, excluding all others."[19] All were united against all enemies, pledging mutual support in warfare. *Zakat* (a percentage of an individual's total wealth) was imposed on the entire community for the benefit of orphans, the poor, and the sick. Ritual activity was made more systematic, with prayers five times daily, but, unlike the Zoroastrian model, prostrate rather than standing. Muhammad's unique authority as God's prophet was certified. The Jews were included in the pact and granted freedom to practice their faith and maintain their institutions.

It must have been during this period of antagonism with the Jews that the Prophet set down the imperative obligations of his now-liberated religion. In legend, the Five Pillars of Islam were spelled out one day in answer to a question from the angel Gabriel, posing as a traveler. In the memory of one who was with Muhammad on that day:

He sat down in front of the Prophet (may God bless and preserve him), rested his knees against [the Prophet's] knees, and placed his palms on [his] thighs. "Oh Muhammad, tell me about Islam," he said.

The Messenger of God (may God bless and preserve him) replied: "Islam means to bear witness that there is no God but Allah, that Muhammad is the Messenger of Allah, to maintain the [five] prayers, to pay the poor-tax [*zakat*], to fast [in the month of] Ramadan, and to perform the pilgrimage [*hajj*] to the House [of God at Mecca] if you are able to do so."[20]

The Meccans returned in full strength in March of the following year, determined to crush the Muslim center. Islam narrowly averted extinction in this second match near Uhud, a hilly area a few miles north of Medina. The discipline exerted at Badr gave way to bravura, with Muhammad allowing himself to be swept along by the younger warriors' clamor to take the offensive. Uhud proved a greater disaster than Badr had been a victory. Meccan cavalry commanded by Khalid ibn al-Walid, one of Islam's future generalissimos, sliced through the Muslims' left flank, disorienting the mass, while another sortie cut down Muhammad's guards. The sight of the Prophet, blood streaming from his face and climbing out of the hole where a Qurayshite lance blow had knocked him, utterly demoralized the Companions and the *ansars*. The Meccans cut down their retreating enemy to the vile exhortations of Hind bint Utbah, a high-clan widow who had lost a son at Badr and became famous as the harridan of Qurayshite vengeance. Abu Sufyan, the Meccan commander, could have finished off the Muslims that day had he pushed his men to carry the fight into Medina. He probably decided that the price of invading Medina was too great. In any case, Muhammad's defeat in March 625 must have seemed sufficient to discredit both the man and the movement. Medina's alliances with oasis towns hung in the balance. The Bedouin shunned the Muslims. The faith of the *ansars* dipped, even though a recent revelation had promised special consideration for all who died fighting for Islam. "They shall be lodged in peace together, amid gardens and fountains, arrayed in rich silks and fine brocade," was the desert-dweller's paradise conjured by Gabriel. "We shall wed them to dark-eyed houris."[21]

Medina's Jews had refused to fight again. Not only did they persist in their narrow interpretation of the Medinan covenant's requirement of mutual defense, Muhammad was convinced that they comprised a fifth column that could fatally undermine the city's resistance when the next attack came. If this conviction was empirically well grounded, another fateful assumption was susceptible of corroboration only by the Prophet himself. Although Muhammad brought an undefined fund of information about the religions, his knowledge of Judaism and Christianity greatly increased during the months immediately following the *hijra*. His revelations now told him that the Jews were a willful people who had dishonored the word of God. Theirs had been the highest honor bestowable upon a people—to be the custodians of God's universal plan. But the Jews had slipped twice: long ago when Moses brought the tablets; in the here and now by their insufferable condescension and tragic blindness before God's final revelation to mankind. "When they are told: 'Believe in what God has revealed,' they reply: 'We believe in what was revealed to *us*,'" the Prophet was told to recite. "But they deny what has since been revealed, although it is the truth, corroborating their own scriptures."

God was equally disappointed in the Christians, who misrepresented His being as threefold in nature ("Do not say: 'Three' ") and as fathering a son ("God forbid that He should have a son!"). Although the Christians claim "it is the Jews who are misguided," the Prophet was told that both lived in error. "The Jews and the Christians say: 'We are the children of God and His loved ones,'" yet Gabriel advised Muhammad to ask both these misguided peoples: "Why then does He punish you for your sins?" As for the Christians, God was especially insistent that they comprehend the fundamental error at the center of their faith—that the Messiah, "the son of Mary, was no more than an apostle: other apostles passed before him," as Mani had already iterated long ago. But there were no Christians with whom to come to terms in Medina. Six months after the debacle at Uhud, Muhammad commanded the Nadir tribe to leave Medina for the large Jewish oasis settlement at Khaybar, relinquishing their dwellings, goods, and date plantations to the *ummah*. Again, 'Abdallah ibn Ubayy of the Khazraj protested for a tense moment before yielding. The last tribe of Medinan Jews, the Qurayza, watched their brothers and sisters depart in silence.[22]

Two years later, in early March 627, a powerful coalition of three armies—the maximum might available to the Qurayshites—marched out of Mecca. Abu Sufyan, the Umayya chieftain, commanded a ten-thousand-man force of allied towns and Bedouin warriors. What was to become known as the Battle of the Trench tipped the scales for Islam, although the confrontation began inauspiciously for the Medinans. But Muhammad's response was ingenious. The oasis city was shielded from attack by hills and volcanic rock on three sides. The wide trench Muhammad ordered dug across Medina's northern approach was finished in six days, with all the tribes (the Qurayza included) participating. Abu Sufyan's men hurled insults and volleyed arrows and stones while frustrated horse and camel cavalry pawed at the trench's edge for almost a month. Close watch was kept on the Qurayza, who were suspected of conspiring with the enemy for an attack on the Muslim rear. The attackers' food supplies ran low, and the disgusted Bedouin pulled out of the offensive in the third week. The Battle of the Trench ended in fiasco and humiliation for the Quraysh. Muhammad the Prophet and his three thousand men had defied the most formidable Arab army seen on the peninsula in living memory.

Although the Battle of the Trench had gone in his favor, the Prophet was convinced of treachery on the part of Medina's last Jewish tribe. On the morrow of his great humiliation of the Quraysh, the Prophet received a terrible revelation that must have been fatefully intended for those who wished ill of his great mission. "As for the unbelievers," it announced, "neither their riches nor their children will in the least save them from God's wrath." 'Abdallah ibn Ubayy could not spare his Hebrew confederates this time. Muhammad's certitude about their hostile designs was unshakable. The men of the Qurayza were killed in Medina's central market just a few days after the Meccan withdrawal. Their headless bodies were tossed into the trench in a gruesome butchery of some seven hundred, lasting from sunup to dusk. Their women and children were enslaved and their property was spread among the Believers—after the Prophet's one-fifth share was set aside, as would become customary. Muhammad added one of the women, a strikingly beautiful captive named Rayhana, to his stable of concubines.[23]

The treatment of the Qurayza reveals much about the iron in the soul of the man who entered history as Allah's instrument. It was an act of retribution that sent a shiver across the sands of Arabia. By delivering an example in blood of his revelation, the Prophet meant to cower the people of a brutish, feuding Arabian society that had never imagined the rule of a single personality under a unique belief system. The high purpose of the terrible slaughter of Medina's Hebrews was to place tribal loyalty at the service of transcendent ideas—time-honored brutality at the service of a new morality of charity, ethical discipline, and social democracy.

There came a time, though, soon after the Battle of the Trench, when the Prophet's iron soul was shamefully tested in a personal matter. The "affair of the necklace" undermined the honor of the ruling household. When A'isha, Muhammad's thirteen-year-old wife, bounced into camp on a camel, clinging to a young warrior, just as the Believers' military expedition resumed its return march to Medina, eyes rolled and tongues soon wagged. The Prophet's wedding present—a necklace—had fallen off more than once, thanks to a defective clasp. When it happened yet again, A'isha had retraced her steps in search of the precious gift. She found the necklace, but the caravan was by then far out of sight. So slight was the girl-wife that her strong bearers had failed to notice the weight difference when they repositioned the enclosed litter atop the camel as the command to evacuate camp sounded. Alone with her necklace and the caravan nowhere to be seen, she was rescued by Safwan ibn Mu'attal, who rode up, innocently, in the prime of adolescence, averted his eyes until the Prophet's wife replaced her veil, and lifted her aboard his steed. They rode away in hot pursuit of the expedition.

That was A'isha's story, which she told with angry conviction. Muhammad became depressed. He questioned the women and fumed at the men with skeptical countenances. Then he cloistered himself, vainly awaiting revelations. "O A'isha, I have been told such and such a thing concerning thee," the fifty-year-old husband was heard imploring, "and if thou art innocent, surely God will declare thine innocence." The Messenger of Allah was still a man in a tribal society where the fastest glue was male honor. Finally, a revelation came that prescribed timeless Islamic rules in the matter of adultery: scourgings for all calumniators; and (with everlasting consequences intended or not for Muslim men and women) the requirement of four witnesses to corroborate the charge of adultery.[24] The Prophet's equanimity returned, at least for the time being.

As the wives and concubines multiplied, so did the Messenger of God's household troubles. There were revelations to come, for which he would be humbly grateful, that would allay and smooth over the domestic disputes. One such revelation, near the end of the decade, singularly exemplified Allah's abiding solicitude. The arrival of Mariya, a young Coptic concubine whose exceptional beauty drew the Prophet to her hut days and nights, occasioned public complaining by Hafsa ('Umar's daughter) and A'isha, (Abu Bakr's daughter) and a guilty Muhammad's promise of abstention. Mariya's baby, a son portentously named Ibrahim, compounded a fraught situation until Allah reminded His agent again of the uniqueness of his purpose. "Why do you prohibit that which Allah has made lawful to you, in seeking to please your wives?" Allah asked. The Prophet's God-given "absolution from such oaths" should have become clear.[25] Mariya's child died before his eighteenth month.

The Quraysh were stupefied by the news that reached them in the spring of 628. Muhammad and some seven hundred of his followers marching toward Mecca sent word of their determination to worship at the Ka'bah. The Prophet and his people approached without arms and promised to enter and depart in peace after three days. It was an inspired strategy that forced the Meccan leadership to honor the ancient status of their city as one of the major *harams* (sanctuary places) of Arabia—unless the problem could be liquidated before it reached the neighborhood. In the event, Quraysh and Muslims agreed to disagree peacefully at a place near Mecca called Hudaybiyya. While faithful 'Umar and others in the inner circle barely suppressed their indignation, the Prophet, with son-in-law Ali writing down what was said, agreed to a compromise: a ten-year truce of hostilities and the right to worship at Mecca for three days the following year. If many of the Companions and *ansars* thought that Muhammad had needlessly demeaned himself at Hudaybiyya, results that proved the political good sense of the armistice would eventually become manifest.

Within weeks after Hudaybiyya, the Prophet led more than a thousand men to surround the large oasis of Khaybar, the principal Jewish settlement in the Hijaz and the place where the Qaynuqa, his first Jewish victims, had found asylum. In a siege lasting a month, each of seven separate compounds was forced to surrender one by one with little or no bloodshed. Half of the harvests were confiscated and some of the women were distributed among the besiegers, the Prophet taking an unusually beautiful one for himself. Half of Khaybar's future harvests were to be surrendered to the Muslims. The slaughter of the Qurayza and capture of the Khaybar oasis effectively ended further possibilities of a Quraysh-Jewish coalition. Resistance to the Prophet began to fold in much of the Hijaz. Medina's control of the caravan trade, its wealth with which to hire the loyalty of the Bedouin, and its abundance of intimidating arms gradually drained away all but the most hardened enemies' enthusiasm for prolonging the unsettling situation. The conflict had been disastrous for trade. The Prophet needed only to play Hudaybiyya's last card. In accordance with its terms, Meccans were compelled to evacuate their city one year to the month after the armistice to allow the Muslims three days of ritual worship at the Ka'bah. The Quraysh elite suffered grievous deflation in the esteem of the people as all watched from the hills the silent, white-robed processional into Mecca of bareheaded Muslims led by a serene Muhammad with his swinging stride. Shortly after the three-day pilgrimage, though, one of the tribes allied with the Quraysh attacked one of the Hashimites' confederates. Turning a deaf ear to Abu Sufyan's anxious apologies and Abu Bakr's scruples, Muhammad declared the Hudaybiyya agreement annulled. The war was on again. "They have betrayed us and broken the pact," he told his followers, "and I shall attack them. But keep secret what I have told you."[26]

Twenty-one months after the armistice, the Prophet, at the head of four columns of sternly proud Believers, entered Mecca on January 11, 630 (20 Ramadan). He came as benign conqueror. Prompted by calculations of arms and ideological appeal, Abu Sufyan and the Quraysh elite had chosen negotiated surrender over war to the death. What the Muslims' most recalcitrant adversaries must have thought can be imagined as they saw Abu Sufyan hurriedly dismount before his house and summon all who could hear to embrace Muhammad and his army just outside the city gates. "O men of the Quraysh, Muhammad is here with ten thousand men of steel," the prince of the *ashraf* cried. "And he hath granted me that who entereth my house shall be safe." Hind, Abu Sufyan's wife, is said to have stormed out of their house in a rage, shouting to the Quraysh to ignore her "greasy, good-for-nothing bladder of a man." But the sounds that Meccans would recall the rest of their lives were of an endless tattoo of hooves, of the snap of yellow-and-red pennants as Khalid ibn al-Walid's column on the right, balanced by Zubayr ibn al-Awwam's on the left, trotted past them on their way to the Ka'bah, the Messenger riding at the head of an army come to secure God's final revelation. Enemies were amnestied and the supremacy of Islam proclaimed. Seven times around the Ka'bah on horseback in a ceremony of purification, the Prophet, intoning loudly, "*Allahu akbar, Allahu akbar,*" claimed the sacred enclosure for the God of Islam. He commanded the destruction of the 360 pagan idols on the shrine's perimeter. Lest any doubt his *barakah* and Allah's power, the Prophet entered the sanctuary and smashed Hubal, the fearsome Syrian fetish. Allah having foretold the day "when those who disbelieve will wish that they were Muslims," Muhammad, in an apotheosis of missionary confidence, commanded that letters and messengers be sent to the *shahanshah* of the Sassanid Empire of the Persians, the emperor of the Eastern Roman Empire, the rulers of Yemen, and the emperor of Axum in Ethiopia, bidding them embrace Islam.[27]

Compared to the grand preoccupations of the dynasts at Constantinople and Ctesiphon, and even Axum, Muhammad's conquest of Mecca and consecration of the Ka'bah as the spiritual epicenter of the new religion were rude parochial developments barely worthy of attention. The Middle East and Asia Minor had suffered a quarter-century of total war while Muhammad was busy building a religion and a polity in the Arabian cocoon. If the Graeco-Romans and Iranians even noticed the death of the sixty-two-year-old Messenger of Allah two years after his conquest of Mecca, they must have anticipated that the tribes of the Hijaz would fall back into ageless polytheism and fissiparous rivalry.

❖

Muhammad died of pleurisy at Medina on June 8, 632, nine days after receiving Allah's final message and without naming someone to lead the Believers.[28] 'Abdallah ibn Ubayy, sheikh of the Khazraj, the thorn in the Prophet's side, had died three years earlier. The Khazraj favored their sheikh's successor as the person most deserving of consideration for the mantle of leadership of the *ummah*. After all, the Khazraj had helped make possible the flight from Mecca and the years of productive asylum. The Companions could hardly deny the strength of the Medinans' claim, yet none of the Companions, to say nothing of the people of Mecca, really considered such an honor appropriate for one to whom the Prophet's great message had come late. Moreover, members of Medina's Aws clan were prepared to back almost anyone among the Companions rather than see themselves ruled by a Khazrajite. The Prophet's cousin, Ali ibn Abi Talib, and husband to his eldest daughter, Fatima, could well have been the Hashimite clan's premier contender. Ali's age (thirty-three) was to be one of the traditional explanations for the Companions' decision to bypass him—an admired battlefield commander, nimble negotiator, and either the second or third person to become a Muslim. Thirty-three was hardly too young an age in a time when life spans were short. Despite the belief of some that the dying Muhammad had designated Ali as his successor, the calculating Quraysh were adamant that this powerful Muslim movement must be controlled by them. They politicked to block a successor from the lesser Banu Hashim, whether Ali or another. Ability, personality, and obligations almost always mattered less in the final tribal analysis in the Hijaz.

Old Abu Bakr, Muhammad's father-in-law and three years his junior, was the consensus choice of the *shura*, the gathering of the elders, from which Ali was excluded. A member of the Banu Taim, one of the less important Quraysh subclans, he was not expected to occupy the office for more than a few years. The Meccan merchant would be the only one of the four *rashidun* successors—the "rightly guided" ones of Muhammad's inner circle—not to die a violent death. In the short time before his demise from natural causes in 634, Abu Bakr, calling himself *Khalifat Rasul Allah* ("Successor to the Messenger of God"), or caliph, made a start at gathering up the hundreds of bits of stone, bone, and leaf upon which Zayd ibn Thabit, Muhammad's scribe, had written the dictated words of God as delivered by the angel Gabriel to the Prophet.[29] Richard Bell's hypothesis that Muhammad reviewed and edited many revelations in his last year or two is blasphemous to Muslims, of course. In any case, the first caliph advanced the work of assembling what would become the Qur'an. This was vital work, for there was a raft of other messengers in Arabia whose growing prominence was due in great measure to the Prophet's success. Maslama of the Banu Hanifa near Yamama in the East foretold an ending that would commence a new order of things. In Yemen, the magnetic visionary al-Aswad prophesied an age of justice in the name of a deity he called Rahman ("merciful"). Khalid ibn Sinan, about whom less is known, spoke in the name of a transcendent entity.[30]

Nor was it any less significant that Abu Bakr enforced a rudimentary command structure and assembled the building blocks of the Believers' formidable military machine. Like the wily trader he was, Abu Bakr neutered the Quraysh aristocrats and other erstwhile enemies with lucrative military commands. The haughty Makhzumite and future *qa'id* (general officer) of the conquest, Khalid ibn al-Walid, was typical of the co-opted. The caliph sent them flying off on *razzias* with prospects either of riches and women or of a glorious death and eternal bliss. In these first years of caliphal consolidation, booty—*ghanima*—was the main revenue source for paying the Arab fighters. Abu Bakr fixed rules for divvying up booty (one-fifth to Allah) and enforced payment of the one tax demanded by the Five Pillars of Islam—*zakat*, 2.5 percent of each Believer's wealth. Ta'if and several oasis towns of the Hijaz, along with the huge northeastern towns of Yamama and al-Qatif which had never submitted, were brought under Medina's control by force of arms (the *Riddah* wars, or Wars of Apostasy) and the profitable tenets of the new faith.

After Abu Bakr's death, the second caliph preferred the less-regal title of *Amir al-mu' minin* ("Commander of the Faithful"). 'Umar ibn al-Khattab (634–44) was Muhammad's second father-in-law and Islam's great consolidator, both of scripture and territory. He towered over people and leaned into his gait as though riding a horse. He had a strong proclivity for acting before a moderating thought restrained him. 'Umar was vain and dyed his beard with henna. Yet because he was intelligent purpose hitched to muscular drive, the second caliph assured the continuity of the Islamic polity. What Abu Bakr had put in motion, 'Umar I vastly improved. It was he who ordained that the first year of the Muslim lunar calendar should begin on Muharram I, the date of Muhammad's arrival at Yathrib, or July 16, 622, of the Common Era.[31] He pressed forward nearly to completion the gathering of the revelations that they might be written down and arranged in what would become, in final scriptural form, the *suras* (chapters) of the Holy Qur'an.

Under 'Umar, the reports, recollections, and memories of Muhammad's words and deeds—*ahadith* (*hadith*, singular)—were assembled. *Hadiths* have sometimes proven profoundly problematic, however. In 'Umar's time, credit was given to a claim that the Prophet, Khadija's widower, had been heard to say that those who entrusted their affairs to women "will never know prosperity." But since 'Umar was a quintessential man of his time (a thoroughgoing misogynist, according to Reza Aslan) who instituted segregated worship of the sexes and compelled women to be educated exclusively by men, his decisive influence upon Islam may not have faithfully reflected the Prophet's best sentiments about gender. Curiously, the second caliph's prejudices received major reinforcement from a *hadith* corroborated by the third of Muhammad's eleven wives, the assertive A'isha, who claimed to have heard her husband say that adulterous women must be stoned to death. It was a curious claim for her to make, considering the backlash from the necklace affair. The greatest of the *ahadith*, the Hadith of Gabriel, ordaining the Five Pillars of Islam, was scripted from 'Umar's vivid recollection—that hypnotic catechism whose first commandment settles forever the claims of antecedent, infidel monotheisms: "*La ilaha illa-llah wa Muhammadun rasulu-llah*"—"There is no god but God and Muhammad is His prophet."[32]

The historical Qur'an's final complilation was completed by 'Uthman, the Prophet's son-in-law, in 656, the date of the end of 'Uthman's stewardship of the *ummah* as the third *rashidun* caliph. It was assembled into its 114 *suras* with little regard for chronology. The Recitation relates the word of Allah or God, beginning, after the short opening *sura,* with the longest *sura* and ending with the shortest. Although "measured out in stages," the effect of the ensemble was seismic. "This Book is not to be doubted," it proclaims. "It is a guide for the righteous." A great number of the proscribed and prescribed things the family head, merchant, Bedouin, or *imam* needed to know were contained, conveniently, in the second *sura*,"The Cow." Blasphemy, usury, wine, and "the flesh of swine" were forbidden. Fasting during Ramadan, the pilgrimage to Mecca, charity to the poor, and equitable bequests to family and relatives were ordained, as was observance of the property rights of wives, widows ("although men have a status above women"), and progeny. Elsewhere, the Qur'an stipulated the number of wives: "two, three, or four of them," but only if their keep could be adequately provided for. (Polyandry was unimaginable.)[33]

Among so much permitted and forbidden, there is a bellicose obligation in "The Cow" that contrasts with the Christian injunction to "love thy neighbor." Inescapably, it appears to conduce to the harshest treatment of the faith's enemies: "Slay them wherever you find them. Drive them out of the places from which they drove you. Fight against them until idolatry is no more and Allah's religion reigns supreme." A number of paragraphs later, however, in one of the Qur'an's most frequently cited injunctions, the *sura* forbids intolerance: "There shall be no compulsion in religion."[34] The patent message is that conversion to Islam was voluntary.

The Prophet disdained poetry and even seems to have made a point of mangling popular verse—such was his determination to dispel any suspicion that his visions partook of the imaginative license of versifiers. Yet the Qu'ran was poetry of the most ineffable intensity and beauty to Arabs hearing it recited for the first time. It was believed to speak in an Arabic more majestic, more euphonious, more mesmeric than had been known in the time before Islam, *al-jahiliyya*. To hear its *suras'* verses intoned or, for the able few, to read them was to know language that was a gift from the supreme source: "Who has not begotten, nor is He begotten, and there is no one comparable to Him."[35] The music of the message entranced, compelled attention that removed all doubt as to belief and obligation. Hearing it recited under the hot sun in a town square or shivering by an oasis in the cold night, the camel driver, the souk merchant, and the slave were uplifted by Allah's new commandments and commitments. Ancient tribal loyalties became loyalty to the greatest tribe of all— Islam. All whose *jihad* (struggle in the path of Islam) proved true at the end of their time were to be wondrously rewarded:

So Allah will ward off from them the evil of that day, and cause them
   to meet with splendour and happiness;
And round about them will go youths, never altering in age; when
   thou seest them thou wilt think them to be scattered pearls. And
   when
Thou lookest thither, thou seest blessings and a great kingdom.[36]

Yet, as much as the eudaemonia experienced in the hearing and the
reading of its scriptures, as much even as the confidence-building of their
clarity and rigor, the unique balm of Muhammad's message was that it
lifted the Arabs out of an aged inferiority complex. Ishmael's people had
languished in their *jahiliyya* of error and ignorance for centuries while
other peoples of the Fertile Crescent boasted in writing of God's special
favor. As if to sharpen the Prophet's learning curve, God placed the three
tribes of Isaac's arrogant descendants in Medina to trouble his path to
righteousness. The Qur'an reiterates the lesson learned, often caustically.
"Ask the Israelites how many conspicuous signs We gave them," God
prompts Muhammad to inquire. "Most of them follow nothing but mere
conjecture. But conjecture is in no way a substitute for truth." At last,
after more than a millennium of axial revelations, Ishmael's progeny had
been chosen to recite the truths that superseded the gospels of Zarathustra, Abraham, Moses, Mani, and Jesus. The "UnCreated Creator" chose
the Arabs as custodians of mankind's final covenant, for "the only true
faith in God's sight is Islam." The *sura* Al-Hijr assures Believers that "the
day will surely come when those who disbelieve will wish that they were
Muslims."[37] The truth of that prophecy was about to be tested.

3

"Jihad!"

"THE ROMANS have been defeated in a neighboring land," Gabriel told the Prophet on the eve of the *hijra*. "But in a few years they shall themselves gain victory: such being the will of God before and after." Muslims favored the Romans as kindred monotheists out of Abraham's fold. The news of reversals was accurate, but the victory prediction would have been received skeptically by many Graeco-Romans to whom military disasters had become the imperial norm. The promising treaty signed by Maurice and Khosrow II might have run many years more but for the stringent economies the emperor imposed upon his army. Demanding that the military do more with less, Maurice compounded its exasperation by ordering the northern army command to advance into Bulgaria in winter. An unsophisticated centurion risen from the ranks, one Phocas, marched to the capital at the head of an angry army, assassinated the emperor and his family, and seized the throne. Khosrow, professing outrage at the fate of his erstwhile protector, Maurice, sized up the situation in Constantinople as perfect for an invasion. Iran declared war on the Eastern Roman Empire in 603, six years after Muhammad assumed management of Khadija's affairs. Phocas—described by a contemporary as beetle-browed, depraved, and psychopathic—ineffectually defended the eastern frontier and continued to liquidate enemies, real and imaginary, among the Graeco-Roman aristocracy.[1]

Notwithstanding his armies' early successes, Khosrow II *Parvez* ("the Victorious") was not the man his grandfather was. More vain than intelligent, vindictively arrogant, and, when it might have saved him, heedless of advice, the *shahanshah* moved in a world of fabulous opulence and architectural grandiosity on the imagined scale of Iran's legendary founders, Cyrus and Darius. Tales of the majesty of his White Palace at Ctesiphon and the winter residence at Dastagard excited the cupidity of the Najd Bedouin and elicited wild calculations of their worth among Hijaz businessmen. In the end, his people would tire of the *shahanshah's* indifference to their suffering, his stubborn cruelty and hubris. Yet Khosrow would live on in his people's memory as the romantic king whose love of Shirin, a beautiful Christian wife, is immortalized in that marvelous epic of Iranian high culture, *Shahnameh* ("the Persian Book of Kings"). For him, divinity of person was more than a ceremonial attribute. Khosrow II believed himself to be a god. The success of his armies appeared to justify the conceit. His grandfather's sweeping tax reforms, creation of a service nobility, and modernization of the army had made the Zoroastrian state a military leviathan whose likes the Fertile Crescent had seldom known since Pompey's legions tramped into Egypt. By 604, Sassanian cataphracts had advanced across Armenia into the Balkans, after capturing Dara, the great fortress city on the Tigris, along with several other important towns. Much of Cappadocia (south-central Anatolia) was lost as Graeco-Roman defenses caved before the Sassanians over the next three years. Phocas's violent persecution of Jews and wholesale beheadings and dismemberments of Gentiles continued to do as much to undermine the Eastern Roman Empire's defenses as the enemy generals.[2]

As the Empire's center failed, Egypt responded. The powerful fleet sailing into the Sea of Marmara in the fall of 608 was commanded by the militarily experienced and politically adept son of the exarch, or viceroy, of Carthage, Flavius Heraclius the Younger. Father and son, having renounced their allegiance to the emperor, had spent the year raising a force in North Africa large and loyal enough to mount a credible threat to Phocas's control of the capital. Their control of Alexandria enabled them to deny Constantinople its vital Egyptian grain supply, almost a mortal blow to the homicidal usurper. As Heraclius's ships rode at anchor under the city walls, the starving, demoralized capital was riven by bloody factional conflict. Phocas, still feared by the citizenry, clung to the shards of power behind the doors of the Palace of the Archangel until conspirators finally gained enough courage to seize the berserk ruler. His end matched the brutality of his six-year rampage. Brought naked in chains to Heraclius's flagship, Phocas spat defiance as Heraclius ordered him to be slowly drawn and quartered. The headless trunk, minus arms and legs, was burned in the Ox Market. (The best that might be said of him was that by granting Pope Boniface IV [r. 608–15] permission to turn the Pantheon into a church, Phocas saved a gem of Roman architecture for posterity.) The purple robes of office over his shoulders, Heraclius set about reforming the civil institutions, rebuilding the army, halving state salaries, stripping the churches of gold leaf and silverplate, and sedulously avoiding the possibility of any decisive military confrontation with the victorious Iranians. The new emperor was then thirty-six, blond, handsome, muscular, of medium height, and possessed of a temperament three parts prudence and two parts audacity. In the spring of 609, prudence was desperately indicated.[3]

Somewhat to its own surprise, the veteran Iranian army under the western commander made a stunning breakthrough on the Graeco-Romans' eastern front. The breakthrough momentum smashed the defenses of Edessa and carried the Iranian armies across the Euphrates

and deep into Syria, leading to the capture the following year of Caesarea, stopping place of apostles Peter and Paul. At Ganzak, mountain
site of the great Zoroastrian fire temple in Azerbaijan, "the Victorious"
and his general staff mapped their campaign for the speedy dismemberment of the Eastern Roman Empire with a precision replicated some
thirteen hundred years later by the German *Blitzkrieg* campaign. In this
final conflict of the Asia Minor superpowers, the Sassanian regime had
gone to war served by two of the most gifted military talents in its history: Shahrbaraz and Shahin, Khosrow's Rommel and Guderian, respectively. Field Marshal (*Spahbodh*) Romizanes was known as Shahrbaraz,
"the Boar of the Empire," a terrifying handle he fully deserved.
Shahrbaraz's army conquered hallowed Antioch, the fourth great see in
Christendom, after a lengthy siege in 611; it took Damascus two years
later. The psychological shock to Christendom was as terrible as the loss
of life and lands. Besides the forty thousand or more men, women, and
children Shahrbaraz sent off to Ctesiphon for ransom and forced labor,
thousands of Syria's Christians (including Patriarch Anastasius) were
slaughtered by Jews exacting vengeance for three centuries of persecution and wild with joy at this Persian deliverance that evoked the deliverance of their ancestors by Cyrus the Great from the Babylonian
Captivity.[4] Massacres of Christians by Jews spread across Mesopotamia.

In some seven hundred years of warfare—not since Marcus Licinius
Crassus, the real-estate speculator, blundered into that Parthian hornet's
nest of a first encounter between Rome and Persia—there had not been
anything more disastrous to the "Romans" than Khosrow II's onslaught
after the breakthrough of 609–10. Two Sassanian armies moved across the
map—Field Marshal Shahin's rolling into modern Turkey, Shahrbaraz's
moving scythelike through Syria into Palestine. The Monophysite Ghassanids' kingdom, at the top of the Arabian peninsula, still loyal to Constantinople despite imperial mistreatment by Justin and his successors, fought
to the bitter end. Two of Field Marshal Shahrbaraz's generals perished with
their Arab auxiliaries trying to subdue the kingdom. At Mecca, where he had
just received Allah's first messages, a proud Muhammad is supposed to have
exclaimed, "This is the first time the Arabs have avenged themselves on the
Persians."[5] The Sassanian war machine was unstoppable, though, and the

Arab Ghassanids' power as a buffer state between the Hijaz Arabs and "civilization" was fatally weakened.

Crisscrossed by dislocating armies, already ravaged by drought and famine, and bereaved by the loss of Antioch and Damascus, the Christian world shuddered at the seeming fulfillment of the Apocalypse when Jerusalem fell in 614. Reverberations were felt in verse as far as the Hijaz, where the noted poet, al-A'sha, limned Khosrow's defeat of Heraclius. Steadied by its patriarch, Jerusalem's populace withstood two months of siege by Iranian sappers and Jewish auxiliaries before accepting what by some accounts were Shahrbaraz's generous surrender terms. For the first time since the destruction of the Second Temple and their expulsion by Titus in 70 CE, the Jews won the right to occupy Jerusalem. The horrific sequel is so overlain by partisan hyperbole that little more can now be said other than that the holiest city in Christendom was left a charnel house of smoldering ruins after several days of rape, pillage, and massacre. By one count, graves were dug for thirty-three thousand bodies. Some sources insist that the draconian punishment (somewhat uncharacteristic of the Sassanians) was inflicted after the Christians rose against the occupying garrison, slaughtering it to the last man, as well as all the Jews they could find.

At the site of the grand Church of the Resurrection—the tabernacle housing the True Cross—only rubble remained. This splendor of Hellenistic architecture was a gift from Constantine the Great, who commanded its construction in 326, fourteen years after the practice of Christianity was authorized in the empire. Helena, his remarkable mother, traveled to the Holy City to find the site on which to build the great shrine. Her reward was to find in a well beneath the Roman Temple to Zeus (erected on the spot of the obliterated Temple of Solomon) the beams of wood on which Jesus bled out on Gethsemane. Persian savagery was compounded by the news that the aged Patriarch Zacharias was sent to Ctesiphon as a war prisoner, along with the True Cross and the Holy Sponge and Lance as victory trophies.[6] As the awful news spread of the leveling of the church and the removal of the True Cross, Graeco-Romans high and low dreaded the withdrawal of divine favor.

If the withdrawal of divine favor seemed increasingly evident, the apathy of many of the empire's own people was a matter of comparable gravity. Decades of harassment and outright persecution visited upon heterodox Christians, great numbers of whom lived in the path of the Persians, left this population ill-disposed to the imperial government. With its Jews in open rebellion and many of the Monophysites willing to live under the Zoroastrian conqueror, the Second Rome's internal troubles vastly exacerbated its defense problems. The Zoroastrian regime knew how to play to advantage the Christians' passion for dogma-bashing. Ordering that they "come to a general assembly to confirm the right and reject the wrong," the *shahanshah* indulged the synod's review and interpretation of the pronouncements of Nicaea, Ephesus, and Chalcedon before terminating the raucous affair with a decree in favor of the Nicene Creed as understood by the Copts and Monophysites. "All Christians under my rule shall accept the [Monophysite] faith of the Armenians," Khosrow ordained. His Christian consort, the beautiful Shirin, was said to be much pleased by her master's official guarantee of freedom of Christian worship. Jews were made to pay a price, however, for the Sassanians' bid for Christian loyalty in the occupied territories. Their loyalty at Antioch and Jerusalem was repaid by the order to leave Jerusalem so that the Gentiles could speed the holy city's reconstruction undefiled.[7]

Field Marshal Shahrbaraz's veteran infantry advanced year by year into the Egyptian breadbasket, accepting the serial surrenders of Graeco-Roman garrisons from Carthage to Babylon (Old Cairo), until Alexandria surrendered in 619 after Iranian sappers finally breached the city's almost-impenetrable ring of walls. The odds against Heraclius began lopsidedly to favor an Iranian world with a rump Eastern Roman Empire consisting of little more than the impregnable capital, some heavily defended territory within sight of the city's Theodosian walls, and a sliver of Anatolia gamely fighting on against almost-certain extinction. A measure of these desperate days was the minting of a coin depicting Heraclius and his son Constans; on the reverse side was stamped the legend *Deus adiuta Romanis* ("May God help the Romans").[8] Although the new coin helped the Roman economy, God continued to leave the Romans to their enemy, for more catastrophes followed after the loss of the Egyptian breadbasket. Thirteen years after their brilliant breakthrough on the

Graeco-Romans' eastern front, Field Marshal Shahin's Iranians were only a few days' march from Chalcedon (today's Kadiköy, part of Istanbul), the ancient city on the Bosporus opposite Constantinople.

The Theodosian walls were Constantinople's longevity girdle. They bore the name of the fifth-century emperor who commanded their emplacement on a line running from the Golden Horn to the inland Sea of Marmara, a barrier of granite and brick behind which the proud metropolis, surrounded on three sides by water, had long wagered that it was all but impregnable. Twelve yards high and five yards thick, those walls would be scaled only twice in the twelve-hundred-year history of the Second Rome: in the thirteenth century and, mortally, in the fifteenth. In 622, however, Constantinopolitans' confidence was decidedly tested as they saw thirty thousand or more feral Asian Avars spread out before the Theodosian walls almost within sight of their basilica of Hagia Sophia. In a desperate ploy to wean the Avars from their Sassanian entente, Heraclius performed the hat trick of a bribe of two hundred thousand solidi. The Avars took the Greeks' money but also accepted Khosrow's refreshed retainer. Shahin's dispatches assured the *shahanshah* that the tightening siege on the Bosporus was certain to force—if not outright surrender of the citadel—humiliating terms upon the Greeks.

Twenty years after Khosrow II had used Emperor Maurice's assassination to justify a declaration of war, the Second Rome appeared to have barely a pulse. Shahin's armistice offer to permit Heraclius's capital an honorable capitulation was as mutually flattering as it would be proven wrong only a few years later. "This concord should be as profound as our empires are great," he graciously proposed, "for we know that no other state will ever appear to rival these our empires." As the walled metropolis held out against Shahin and his Avars, two Iranian armies scissored what remained of Graeco-Roman defenses in the Caucasus. News from Italy was also discouraging. The Lombards threatened to overrun the exarchate of Ravenna, where the empire kept an almost spectral presence. Yet it was about then, as the concatenation of Graeco-Roman woes mounted, that Muhammad received God's word that soon the Romans "shall themselves gain victory." The coincidence of sudden developments fifteen hundred miles away, and the accuracy of this Qur'anic revelation

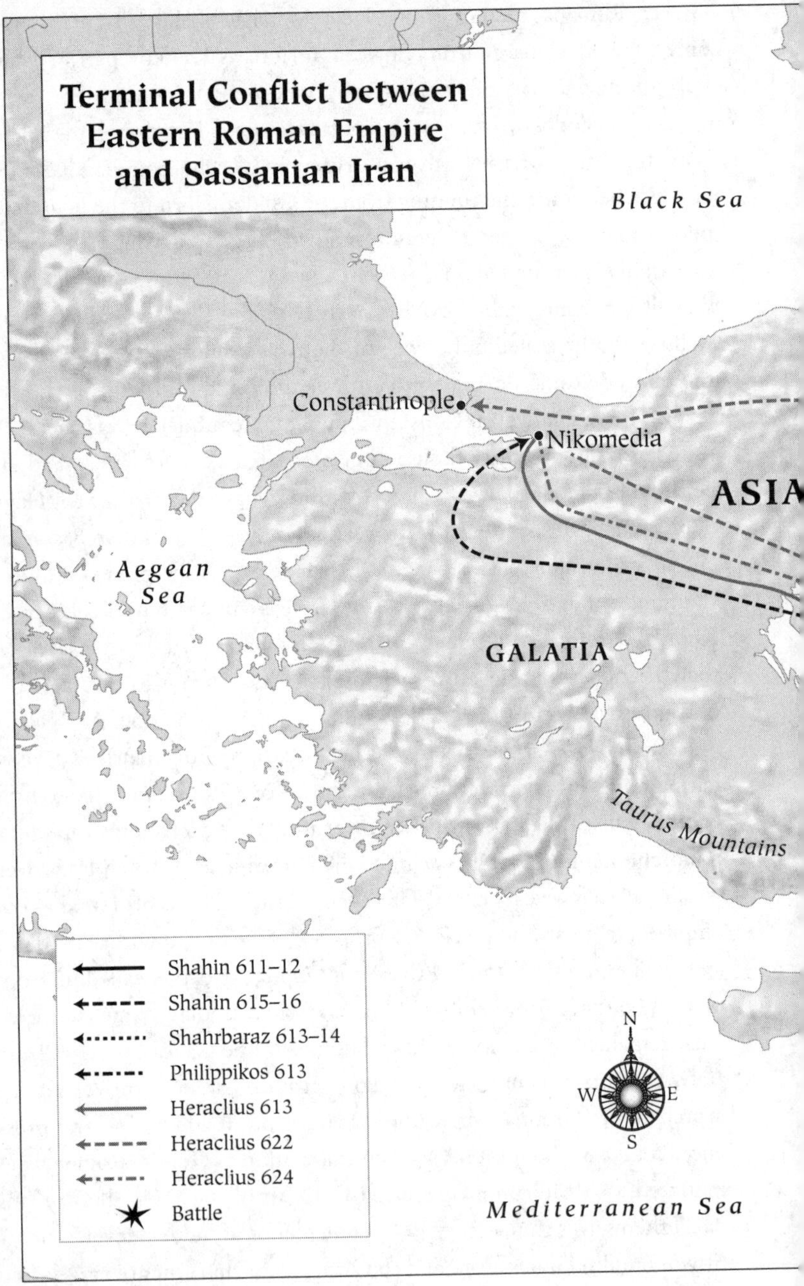

Terminal Conflict between Eastern Roman Empire and Sassanian Iran

Black Sea

Constantinople •⟵ ⟵ ⟵ ⟵ ⟵ ⟵
• Nikomedia

ASIA

Aegean Sea

GALATIA

Taurus Mountains

⟵———	Shahin 611–12
⟵----	Shahin 615–16
⟵········	Shahrbaraz 613–14
⟵-·-·-	Philippikos 613
⟵———	Heraclius 613
⟵----	Heraclius 622
⟵-··-··-	Heraclius 624
★	Battle

N
W E
S

Mediterranean Sea

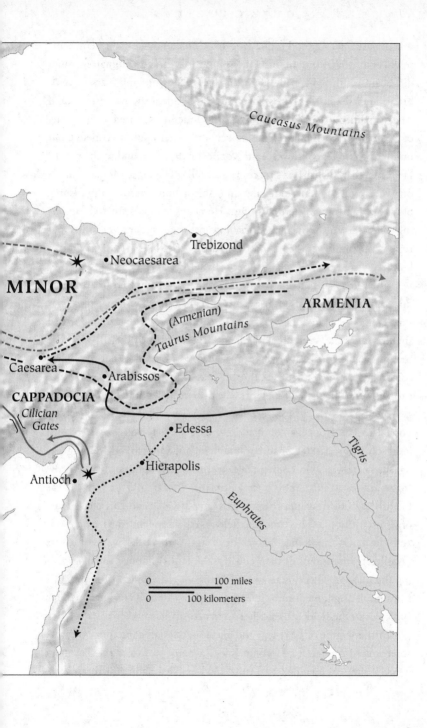

Caucasus Mountains

• Trebizond

• Neocaesarea

MINOR

ARMENIA

(Armenian)
Taurus Mountains

• Caesarea

• Arabissos

CAPPADOCIA

*Cilician
Gates*

• Edessa

Antioch •

• Hierapolis

Tigris

Euphrates

0   100 miles

0   100 kilometers

was remarkable. As the Prophet and his Companions established themselves among the contentious tribes in Yathrib, Graeco-Roman fortunes
did begin to lift. The army Heraclius had taken so many years to coax,
bribe, and shame into existence—as, simultaneously, he restructured
what remained of his shrinking empire—suddenly appeared in the spring
of 622 where the Iranians least expected to see it. Not in Armenia, but
hundreds of miles southwest in the opposite direction and to the rear of
Field Marshal Shahrbaraz's forces in Anatolia. The emperor had banked
on the capital's holding out long enough for him to strike a punishing
blow. Slaying Iranians left and right, Heraclius led his army to a smashing victory at a place in Cappadocia now lost to the record. It was his first
time commanding troops in battle, and the first time in more than two
hundred years that a Roman emperor had done so.[9]

The Graeco-Roman superpower regained momentum in a sudden,
upending streak of wins after 622. Two years after the first surprise victory, Heraclius routed the Sassanian forces in Armenia and then pursued
them as far as the Azerbaijan highlands, where he destroyed the great fire
temple near Ganzak, a desecration Khosrow regarded as personal. The
Sassanians claimed that Zarathustra had descended from Ganzak to
carry Ahura Mazda's gospel of salvation to mankind. The temple's
destruction was Heraclius's revenge for the Church of the Resurrection.
Forced to flee from his command eyrie, "the Victorious" reacted with
lethal outrage, ordering Shahrbaraz and Shahin to finish the draining war
or face death. All able-bodied males were conscripted in order to throw
three armies against the Graeco-Romans. In a replay of 622, it was
Shahrbaraz's turn to appear four years later at Chalcedon, in the shadow
of Constantinople. This time, the field marshal brought transport vessels
and the latest siege machinery. Once again, the tidal wave of Avars
(swollen by thousands of their cousins, the Huns) flooded the plain facing the massive Theodosian fortifications. As the Persian siege of Constantinople tightened into its second year, Heraclius continued his
successes in the field against Khosrow's new armies.

In the winter of 627, near the ancient Assyrian capital of Nineveh,
some miles from today's Mosul in Iraq, the emperor forced the Sassanian
Third Army, commanded by a third field marshal named Shahraplakan,

to a decisive match. Reports of eighty thousand Greeks and an equal number of Persians were typical exaggerations of the time. Probably, less than half that number slaughtered each other throughout the daylong battle, advantages seesawing wildly between the two sides, until the Persian center with its storied Immortals (or Golden Ones) finally caved in as night fell on December 12. A wounded Heraclius had rallied his men to victory when they saw the enemy commander's head on the point of their emperor's sword. Meanwhile, Sergius, patriarch of the Orthodox Eastern Catholic Church, had steadied his flock from Hagia Sophia's high altar with a success comparable to Heraclius's. God may have blessed their cause, as the new silver coin implored, but Constantinopolitans also fought their encirclement with the help of a secret weapon. Greek fire aboard hundreds of flame-throwing dromons (war vessels) destroyed wave upon wave of Shahrbaraz's ships and transport boats. Disease and dwindling food supplies as winter approached did the rest, forcing the Persians to lift the siege. Shahrbaraz's failure at Constantinople matched Shahraplakan's debacle at Nineveh.[10]

Twice, Khosrow had refused to consider a truce: after the first Roman victory and after the flight from Ganzak. Envoys from Constantinople's senate were thrown in jail without ever seeing the king of kings. The second embassy was contemptuously dismissed. "The Victorious" refused again after Nineveh, even though Heraclius's timely truce offer was desperately needed by the stunned Sassanians. With Heraclius in hot pursuit, "the Victorious" raced across Iraq for Ctesiphon, determined to raise yet another army. Counting the Arabs, Jews, Africans, Asians, and dozens of other subject peoples along with the Iranian levies, close to two hundred thousand men may have fought for the Sassanian demigod since the declaration of war in 603. They fought and many died in a ravaged war theater that extended from the Amu Darya to the Nile, from Macedonia to the Arabian Sea. Armenia was a cemetery. Cities lay ruined: Jerusalem was a shell under repair, Caesarea was impoverished, and Antioch would never regain its prewar size and prosperity. Famine raged because planting and harvest cycles were repeatedly broken by peasant conscription and infantry depredations. Disease and pestilence marched with the warring armies across Mesopotamia and Anatolia and on into

Asia. Around the rim of the Mediterranean, trade languished. The last levy of Khosrow's efficient tax farmers skinned the masses and sucked the great Iranian cities dry. The Fertile Crescent had become infertile and depopulated. The Eastern Roman Empire's shrunken possessions in Italia and Hispania were left to restrain the cupidity of various Germanic tribes by bribes and superior guile as best they could.

When Khosrow halted his magnificently caparisoned brace of Arabians before the ceremonial entrance to Ctesiphon's Great Hall (*Taq-i Kisra*), he realized too late that his aristocracy was not only done with fighting his wars but had decided to replace their megalomaniacal *shahan-shah*. Divinity was brought low with a brutal lack of circumspection. Seized on orders from his son, Kavadh-Siroes, whose own reign would last only a few months, Khosrow II, stricken with dysentery, was imprisoned, starved, and then killed as arrows were shot one by one into his torso. After a quarter-century of war, taxes, oligarchic oppression, universal conscription, and increasingly capricious behavior on the part of its exalted *shahanshah,* the Sassanid Empire imploded like a rotten desert cactus. A frenzied power struggle in the capital devoured four Sassanian royals pell-mell and Shahrbaraz himself in less than two years after Khosrow's execution. As his last service to the empire, the indispensable field marshal had handed over the True Cross to the Christians and ended the killing with a truce seven months after the Battle of Nineveh. The terms of the peace treaty ratified in 630 deprived Iran of virtually all that had been won after nearly thirty years of war. The Graeco-Roman reoccupation of Syria, Iraq, Palestine, Egypt, Anatolia, and Christian Armenia was well underway when Heraclius, the twenty-first emperor of the Eastern Roman Empire, arrived in Jerusalem in the spring of 630.[11]

Civilization, as Christian men and women knew it, had been saved. Like Salamis and Thermopylae, those epic fifth-century BCE battles between the Hellenes and the Persians that decisively shaped the Western Hemisphere's cultural identity, victory at Nineveh closed another chapter in the great competition for supremacy between the Occident and the Orient. Had they been victorious in Mesopotamia and at Constantinople, the Sassanians would have erased the Euphrates line dividing the Graeco-Latin-Germanic cultural sphere from the Afro-Semitic and Asian. Ownership of the Greeks' "wine-dark sea" and the Romans' *mare nostrum* ("our sea")—forfeited in war by the Persians and the Carthaginians—would finally have passed to Cyrus's and Hannibal's descendants. In the hypothetical hyperbole of an Edward Gibbon, Europe's political map would have been altered by Persian satrapies; fire temples lighting the night skies; Christianity and Judaism practiced at Rome and Cordoba with Zoroastrian sufferance. Whatever value judgment might be passed on such an outcome, that it is merely one of history's fascinating counter-factuals may be due to Heraclius's victory at Nineveh. That chapter was shut tight in the triumphant Roman spring of 630 as the emperor and his cortege of cavalry, archers, and lancers, "one blaze of gold and color," entered Jerusalem's Gate of Repentance from the city's eastern side. Come December of that same year, the Prophet Muhammad would enter Mecca in triumph and open a new chapter in world history.

Victorious in war and surpassed in achievement only by the great Justinian, Heraclius was the last Graeco-Roman emperor to visit Christianity's birthplace. Accompanied by his wife and their eldest son and heir, the *Autocrator* removed his gorgeous attire and walked the Via Dolorosa dressed as a simple pilgrim to carry the True Cross into the Church of the Resurrection. Christians throughout the empire had donated treasure so that the church might be quickly rebuilt. Blessed by Sylvester, patriarch of Jerusalem, Heraclius placed the recovered holy relic in the apse of the church that the Sassanian army had razed to the ground fifteen years earlier. The scene within the great house of worship on the thirtieth day of March was one of unbosomed thanksgiving amid welling tears and a *Te Deum* so full-throated it might have shattered the new stained-glass windows. Radiating contagious self-confidence in his fifty-fifth year, Heraclius experienced a most exquisite triumph as he knelt in the rebuilt church to receive the blessings of the patriarch that extraordinary day. Apologists would say afterward that only because of the adamant demands of the patriarch and the local clergy did the emperor rescind his pledge of amnesty and reluctantly authorize the forced baptism and massacre of the empire's Jews.[12]

Twelve years of life remained to Heraclius. They were to be blighted by the onset of a deteriorating mental condition never fully explained and by the appearance of an enemy never remotely anticipated. Yet the unanticipated may actually have made itself known two months after Heraclius and Shahrbaraz met in Cappadocia to hammer out truce terms. What may be nothing more than historical gossip claims that Heraclius was much bemused by Muhammad's temerity in sending a messenger bearing a letter inviting the emperor's submission to Islam. Having just vanquished the Persian Empire, it seems most unlikely that Heraclius would have noticed the presumptuousness of a desert holy man.* It is a matter of record, though, that the Prophet, much displeased by the treatment of his emissary, sent a thousand-man invasion force into Jordan in September 629, well armed and under the command of adoptive son and personal secretary Zayd ibn Harithah. Zayd and two other officers were killed, and the Muslims were sent flying back to Medina by a combined Graeco-Roman–Ghassanid frontier force. Mu'ta, east of the Jordan River, was the first bloodletting between Muslim Arabs and Graeco-Romans.[13] Not quite a decade elapsed after the skirmish at Mu'ta and the return of the True Cross to Jerusalem before the plates beneath history shifted violently, breaking one empire apart and reducing part of another to ruins. Not since Alexander of Macedon was so much real estate to be so rapidly conquered and reorganized as in the seventh-century Islamic onslaught.

⁘

The world's newest revealed religion seemed to roar out of the Arabian Peninsula like a cyclone, a force so irrepressible that nothing withstood the advancing faithful, motivated in their ferocity as much by the spoils of war as by religious zeal. *Jihad* was a new phenomenon. The Arabic word for the force that cracked apart the Middle East means "struggle" or "exertion"—struggle within oneself, exertion against enemies.[14] In less than a century after Muhammad's death in the 632nd year of the Common Era, and for the first time since Alexander the Great, an imperial belt of finance, trade, and commerce would stretch from Samarkand

---

*Khosrow ordered Muhammad's emissary slaughtered, then commanded his viceroy in Yemen to apprehend the Prophet and send his head to Ctesiphon.

toward China and Sind on the edge of India to Tangier on the Atlantic and Sijilmasa at the fringe of the Sahara. Sclerotic regimes and ancient cultures would be assimilated. Arab mastery of politics and economy, culture and technology sharpened in a century to an edge as fine as on the swords of tempered steel wielded by Bedouin cavalry. The Arab *jihad* swept aside kingdoms and empires with a speed that the bewildered clergy and chroniclers living at that time sought to explain as the consequence of moral transgressions visited by divine wrath. A millennium and three European centuries later, students of the Arab Conquest substituted the mystique of Holy War for the mystery of Providence as the reason for the defeat of armies arrayed against the Muslim host.

To one such Victorian scholar, the Arabs materialized as a cataclysmic infestation for which no antidote had then existed. Resistance had been all but useless: "Warrior after warrior, column after column, whole tribes in endless succession with their women and children. . . . Onward and still onward, like swarms from the hive, or flights of locusts darkening the land." Long the conventional explanation, the human-tidal-wave theory was abandoned in the early years of the last century, however, as new scholarship revealed the first Arab armies to have been dismayingly small—a few thousand at most to conquer Graeco-Roman Syria and fewer than twelve thousand, probably, to occupy Iran. The *élan* of the faith and the avarice of war, as well as the Arabs' very quickly acquired superior military organization, were supposed to have more than compensated for their relatively small numbers. Ancient greed soldered to a new ideology were said to have powered one of the most formidable military machines the world had ever seen. Much of this was true in detail, but it was only part of the reason for the world empire assembled in the blink of an eye, as history measures time. Muslims also won because their enemies had exhausted themselves.

In 636, four years after the Prophet's death, the Caliph 'Umar's armies commenced in earnest the conquest of the known world. "Fighting is obligatory for you, much as you dislike it," Allah had told Muhammad, and the tribes of the towns and the Bedouin of the desert fervently embraced the message. For had not Allah promised "rich booty" if they warred against the wicked and misguided, and had not that booty been delivered "with all promptness," as predicted early on in one of the Qur'an's 114 mystical sessions?[15] Now that the superpowers had all but destroyed the Ghassanid and Lakhmid Kingdoms—the firewalls that long blocked the Hijaz Arabs from bounding out of the peninsula—well-disciplined units of a few thousand Muslims began to chip away at Graeco-Roman positions in Syria. These were no tribal hordes thundering into battle with families and animal herds trailing behind, the locust swarm imagined later by Europeans. They had become fighting machines with command structures, battle tactics, and armaments that were much improved since the rout at Mu'ta of Zayd ibn Harithah. Some of their generals burned with the fire of the elected—smart and driven men certified by the Prophet as superior warriors. Sa'd ibn Abi Waqqas had helped win the Battle of Badr. Khalid ibn al-Walid had salvaged the day at Mu'ta. Abu Ubayda had that special ability to push men to do better than their best in battle. 'Amr ibn al-As, soon to conquer Egypt, was the personification of the *jihad* on horseback. The Commander of the Faithful shaped their armies. 'Umar inaugurated a rudimentary salary system that would become very quickly systematized under his successors, with the names and pay scales of every soldier inscribed in a master register (*diwan*).[16] To be sure, in the summer of 636, 'Umar's armies bore only the outline of their coming transformation.

The Battle of Jabiya-Yarmuk, as the Arabs called it, climaxed in late afternoon on August 20, 636, after three days of inconclusive engagements. 'Amr the One-Eyed's temporary taking of Damascus had been a shock to the Romans. From his headquarters in Antioch, Heraclius ordered his brother, Theodore, to join forces with the Armenian, Vahan, to expel the Muslim Arabs from imperial territory. Where the Yarmuk River flows into the Jordan, the best of Heraclius's army—some thirty-thousand veteran troops—were annihilated below the Golan Heights. General Vahan had positioned most of his army on the far side of a deep *wadi* (gully) at the confluence of the Yarmuk. A single span bridging the Ruqqad River served both to resupply and reinforce Vahan's men or as a corridor for orderly retreat to the well-defended camp in the Golan foothills. 'Umar's generals had never faced such a large army, but old Abu Ubayda ibn al-Jarrah, one of the Prophet's earliest and most able Companions (Muhammad had counted on Abu Ubayda to hold together the Believers sent to Ethiopia during the worst period of Meccan persecution), and young Khalid ibn al-Walid, once a fierce Meccan antagonist of Muslims (and much valued for having shown a cool head at Mu'ta), led the men—many of whom had been bloodied in Caliph Abu Bakr's fierce *Riddah* wars to impose Muslim unity on the Arabian peninsula. The Arabs knew the terrain better than the Graeco-Romans, but Vahan's battle plan conformed to the best principles in the *Strategikon*, Emperor Maurice's canonical manual of military tactics.

When Abu Ubayda pulled his men from their forward positions in a feigned retreat, General Vahan's infantry rushed to occupy the vacated positions and then pursued the enemy, paying little attention to Khalid ibn al-Walid's men hiding along the Ruqqad's embankment. A complicated maneuver by the imperial cavalry gave the Muslims an opening to drive a wedge between the infantry and the cavalry. In the ensuing confusion, Khalid's men captured the Ruqqad bridge, cutting off the Graeco-Romans' sole means of retreat. Panicked cavalry slid and rolled to death down the river's steep sides. Infantry piled on top of drowning cavalry, the rest fleeing in every direction possible, most cut down in the darkness and early morning by Bedouin who picked the fallen clean of weapons and valuables.[17] The emperor's brother and General Vahan were never found. Syria, Palestine, Libya, and Egypt would fall like dominoes by the early 640s. The Second Rome shriveled to a fifth its former size. When he died five years after the Battle of Jabiya-Yarmuk, Heraclius had become a listless figure seldom seen outside the Great Palace, his empire's defenses confined to the Anatolian high plateau straining to hold back the Muslim onslaught.

Persia was next. Sa'd ibn Abi Waqqas handed much of the Sassanian Empire to Caliph 'Umar the year after Jabiya-Yarmuk. Sa'd was famous for having drawn the first blood ever spilled in anger by a Muslim. As a new convert from the Quraysh, he had hotheadedly struck an idolater with a mule's jawbone after being mocked at prayer. Khalid excelled in tactical intelligence; Sa'd combined tactical intelligence with the command flair of a natural leader. Khosrow's grandson, Yazdegird III, last of the Sassanian *shahanshahs,* had ascended the ancestral throne after a string of succession homicides had seriously retarded Iran's postwar recovery. Doomed to face Arab armies intoxicated by seeming invincibility, he was forced to fight them defensively. He fielded perhaps as many as thirty thousand infantry and cavalry, the largest army possible. As the Arabs approached, the residual might of the Sassanian Empire stood athwart the west bank of the Euphrates near the village of al-Qadisiyya, not far from today's Baghdad.

Sa'd's six to twelve thousand cavalry matched themselves against the thirty thousand Persians. They charged repeatedly, but their fierce cavalry charges completely failed to dent the solid wall of cataphracts during the first day of a four-day engagement. Persian discipline and the weight of numbers carried the day. When the Sassanians released their attack elephants, the Arabs' horses panicked and Sa'd's forces fled from the field. A Muslim disaster was averted only after Khalid's experienced elephant fighters, arriving on the third day, sent wounded elephants crashing back through their masters' lines in a hail of arrows and shouts of "*Allahu akbar*"![18] "The Muslims had never been engaged in anything like it before," al-Tabari's great history of the conquest of the Middle East relates. "They first used up all the darts and arrows. Then all the spears broke, whereupon they resorted to wielding their swords and battleaxes. When it was time for the noon prayer, the fighters performed this by just nodding their heads." With backs to the river, the Persians' ability to maneuver and regroup was fatally handicapped once discipline began to give way. The Sassanian commander drowned with thousands of his men in a Euphrates River turned burgundy from slaughter. The Muslims even captured the dynasty's victory totem, its eagle-headed, bejeweled, golden battle standard, the *kaviani*.

Sa'd strode into Khosrow's White Palace as Khosrow II's grandson, the last king of kings, rode away from Ctesiphon, barely managing to fill enough chests with gold and silver to carry on the dynasty's fight. The desperate *shahanshah* headed for the Caspian Sea region, where he intended to build another army once the dispersed and demoralized nobility answered his calls to the colors. Meanwhile, the Arab conquerors paused. Mythic Ctesiphon, with its seven palace complexes—each a marvel of construction and interior appointments—mesmerized the Believers. Each man's share of the trove of gold, jewels, silver, silks, women, and weapons far exceeded all the booty won to date. Sa'd's report to Caliph 'Umar reads breathlessly. "How many gardens and springs have [the Persians] abandoned," Sa'd exclaimed, "how many sown fields and noble habitats, how many comforts in which they took delight[!]."

The general took up residence in the vaulted Great Hall, the *Taq-i Kisra,* from which he conducted mopping-up operations lasting many months. There was never much question of remaining long in such splendor, however. 'Umar kept his armies on the move, although the old Commander of the Faithful had grown more reflective and even somewhat uneasy about the perils of fabulous success. Once the basic terms of occupation were worked out and subject elites were deputized to run the particular province or city and collect the head tax (*jizya*) due from all subject peoples (the *dhimmis*), the caliph's *qa'ids* (chiefs) were expected to resume their conquering advance.[19] For men could go to seed in cities before a season ran its course, as alarming reports coming to 'Umar revealed, with warriors becoming "fatter while their vigor was on the decline." "Enlighten me," the caliph demanded of an informant at Ctesiphon, "as to what caused the complexion of the Arab tribesmen to change and their flesh [to become sallow]."

'Umar began the policy his successors would follow for a time of confining the Believers to garrison settlements outside great conquered cities such as Damascus or Homs, and even of letting these cities wither and die, as in the case of ancient Carthage and Ctesiphon. To keep the *muqatila* (regular infantry) trim for battle meant keeping their exposure to the fleshpots of an Alexandria or a Ctesiphon to a manageable minimum. 'Umar believed the solution was simple: "No land suits Arab tribesmen except that which suits their camels."[20] Obedient to their caliph's orders, Sa'd and his men soon abandoned al-Mada'in (as the Arabs called Ctesiphon) for an empty plain in Iraq near the Euphrates, where Sa'd founded al-Kufa, future capital of Iraq. He hauled there the Sassanians' enormous treasure, after sending the required one-fifth to 'Umar at Medina.

Sa'd had won less than half Yazdegird's empire. The long, rich history of Zoroastrian Iran effectively ended with the Battle of Nihawand, south of the old city of Hamadan, where Sa'd's cavalry, reinforced by Iranian deserters, destroyed its chances of survival. Enough of the Sassanian army reassembled for a final, game confrontation in 642, five years after the debacle at al-Qadisiyya. The Persian collapse opened the way to Armenia and Afghanistan, and Khurasan's endless spaces, and to the Asian steppes beyond the Oxus River (Amu Darya), where Islam soon clashed with Buddhism. Just short of ten years after that, a Muslim execution squad hunted down Yazdegird III near the old administrative center at Merv (Mary, in today's Turkmenistan). Deserted except for a servant, the last *shahanshah* fell on his sword in an unmarked hiding place in the far northeast of the dying empire. The religion and language of the Arab conquerors spread over the Iranian plateau like a prayer blanket, smothering an eleven-hundred-year-old civilization that would rebound, nevertheless, *mutatis mutandis* its Islamicization, slowly and almost stealthily in less than a century. An abiding sentiment of superiority prevailed long before *Shahnameh*, the Persian national epic, codified it in verse: "Damn this world, damn this time, damn this fate,/That uncivilized Arabs have come to make me a Muslim."[21]

⁘

Jerusalem (Aelia Capitolina to the Romans) was a Christian calamity and a Muslim apotheosis. 'Umar's best generals, the pride of the *jihad,* participated in the siege of the holiest of cities: Khalid ibn al-Walid; Abu Ubayda; Yazid ibn Abi Sufyan, brother of Mu'awiya, who would become the first Umayyad caliph—names emblazoned in the Muslim House of War, the *Dar al-Harb.* Behind their restored, strengthened walls, the besieged city's Christians received only the grimmest of news fragments: the Graeco-Roman defeats at Ajnadain and Jabiya-Yarmuk; the Iranian debacles at al-Qadisiyya and Jalula. From their ramparts, the Christian defenders could also see the Muslims' Jewish allies, those avenging Hebrews on whom Heraclius had declared a virtual open hunting season eight years earlier. Thousands of them, everlastingly hopeful of returning to Jerusalem, served as guides, supplied provisions, fought as auxiliaries, and followed in the wake of the Arab invaders. Khalid's men understood as yet almost nothing about siege machinery, so some six or seven months of stalemate elapsed while they "prowled round the walls," in the words of one Victorian authority on the conquest, "exchanging volleys of arrows and repelling sallies. . . ."[22] Starvation eventually forced the stern old patriarch, Sophronius, to ask Abu Ubayda for terms and then to demand that the Commander of the Faithful himself come to the walls to guarantee their scrupulous execution. At the first news of the Muslim onslaught, Sophronius had had enough prescience to send the True Cross and the Holy Sponge and Lance, together with other priceless relics, to Constantinople by sea. Sending ahead orders to spare the people and property, ʿUmar appeared before the city walls and waited for the gates to part.

The commander's visit is wreathed, on the one hand, in Islamic celebration and, on the other, in Christian consternation. Hosannas had resounded throughout Christendom when Heraclius restored the True Cross to its place in the rebuilt Church of the Resurrection. A mere eight years later, Jerusalem awaited ʿUmar's advent much as Paris, thirteen hundred years later, would suffer Adolf Hitler's inspection after the fall of France. A train of lamentations ran northward from Palestine to impregnable Constantinople and onward to ruined Rome in the Gregorian year of 638, after news spread that the Commander of the Faithful had entered Jerusalem on an ass (or perhaps it was a white camel), wearing an old ragged robe to receive Patriarch Sophronius's obeisance. The patriarch, newly elevated to the position of spiritual leader of the Holy City, was an old man who brought a young man's zeal to the detection and correction of religious error. Sophronius had labored righteously and lost bitterly in Alexandria against the majority Copts and Monophysites, who dared insist that Christ's divinity subsumed his humanity. Sophronius believed that for Chalcedonians alone—those who understood that Jesus had suffered as the son of Mary as well as the son of God—was there a true possibility of personal salvation.

To be compelled to open the Gate of Repentance to ʿUmar was tantamount in Sophronius's mind to spreading a red carpet for the Antichrist. They rode side by side through the narrow, cobbled streets from the Garden of Gethsemane up to the deserted, dung-covered hill known as the Temple Mount, above the Church of the Resurrection. It was there that what ʿUmar called the "Mosque of David" had once stood, the Second Temple destroyed by Titus. To offend the Jews, the Christians were using the Temple Mount as a garbage depot. On a night like none other in his life, Muhammad had ridden with Gabriel's guidance on a winged horse from Mecca to Jerusalem. There he ascended from a rock on the Temple Mount into paradise to meet figures from the Old and New Testament and to receive more instructions from Allah. 'Umar is said to have become enraged by the profanation of the Temple Mount and ordered Christian peasants rounded up to clear the place. As 'Umar walked pensively among the ruins of Solomon's Temple, legend holds that the patriarch finally lost composure and mumbled, "Behold, the Abomination of Desolation, spoken of by the Prophet Daniel, that standeth in the Holy Place."[23]

Apocryphal or not, the story must have been an accurate reflection of the patriarch's indignation and that of his community as their conqueror claimed this neglected piece of real estate for Islam. 'Umar commanded that a small wooden mosque be erected until the time when a suitable structure could be built. On that spot, to become known as the Noble Sanctuary, his successors would build the Dome of the Rock and, nearby, the al-Aqsa Mosque, two of Islam's most venerated structures. As wily as Sophronius was sophisticated, 'Umar politely accompanied the patriarch for an inspection tour of the Church of the Resurrection, but he declined the suggestion that he spread his blanket in the nave to pray. Were he to do so, he said, his men might claim the great Christian house of worship as a mosque for Islam. Jerusalem was now the property of the new Arab empire, but the sublease terms were generous. Future generations of Christians and Jews living under Islam would be grateful for the pragmatic pact putatively signed by 'Umar and Sophronius pledging, in accordance with what became verse 256 of *sura* 2 of the Qur'an, "There shall be no compulsion in religion."[24]

The irony was that, whatever the actual specifics of the pledge at Jerusalem, it was patriarchs such as Sophronius and his immediate predecessor whose persecution of Monophysite Christians and observant Jews had completely alienated the latter from Constantinople and predisposed most of the former to suffer Muslim domination. Word of

Jerusalem's benign treatment outpaced the Arab advance into Egypt and beyond, and as the ground rules under the Muslims became known, the willingness to die fighting against them declined steeply. The liberal surrender terms Sa'd is imagined (in al-Tabari's history) to have offered his enemies, although undoubtedly a reading back from later times, were faithful in spirit to the later tolerance practiced by Muslims. "There are three possibilities," Persians at Ctesiphon were told: "Embrace our religion [and] you will have the same privileges and obligations as we." Refuse, and "then you may pay the *jizya*," which meant being left otherwise to their own religion, laws, and mores, barring conflict with the overriding Islamic order. Reject both, said Sa'd sternly, and "you will have to do battle with us until Allah decides between us."[25]

Just as the Persian ruling classes eventually decided to sheathe their swords, pay the Muslim tax, and circumspectly practice their Zoroastrian faith, so the Egyptian aristocracy smartly calculated the mathematics of survival just as another Napoleonic engine of the Conquest, the intrepid 'Amr ibn al-As, marched on the Nile. 'Amr (not to be confused with his friend, 'Amr the One-Eyed) enjoyed the distinction of having been chosen as the Prophet's favorite commander. He was now in his midforties—a short, stocky, quick-witted Quraysh who had come to Islam only after a long period wrestling with doubts. Al-Tabari's history of the conquest quotes a Believer's praise of 'Amr, saying he had "never met a man who understood the Qur'an better, or had a nobler character, or was more honest and open in his dealings." Like Sa'd the conqueror of Iran and Abu Ubayda the conqueror of Syria, the conqueror of Egypt commanded warriors whose discipline and esprit de corps were at top pitch.

By 640, when 'Amr took Caesarea, Pontius Pilate's old prefecture on the Mediterranean coast, the army command structures had become routinized and pay scales were prescribed and recorded in the caliphal *diwan*. Learning as they conquered, elite cavalrymen (*mujarrada*) and ordinary Arab foot soldiers (*muqatíla*), saw more in one campaign than the sum of their ancestors' visual experiences. In the short time spent in Caesarea, the administrative capital of Palestine, 'Amr's soldiers bivouacked among a Judeo-Christian populace whose prosperity and cosmopolitanism were second to none in what remained of Heraclius's shaken empire. Caesarea had consumed a history tragic and glorious to both Gentile and Jew from King Herod to the Apostle Paul and the great theologian Origen. The city's library once housed thirty thousand manuscripts, the largest theological collection in the world. Perhaps most striking by far to 'Amr's soldiers would have been the great aqueduct, standard-issue Roman engineering but jaw-dropping to rubes. Arab acculturation to high civilization matched the speed of their military achievements in such places as Caesarea and Heliopolis and Misr.

Striking almost straight across the Egyptian desert from Caesarea a year later to capture the well-manned fortress at Babylon on the Nile (not the biblical Babylon), together with ancient Memphis and the Nile town al-Tabari refers to as Misr, the army of some twelve thousand rested briefly to prepare for the attack on Alexandria, the prize of the Conquest.[26] City sojourns were still anathema to 'Umar. On orders from Medina, 'Amr established the garrison city of al-Fustat, several miles south of today's Cairo on the Nile's east bank. It was during the laying out of al-Fustat that one of the most revealing cultural interplays of the *jihad* took place between "uncouth" Arabs and some very superior natives of the Nile Delta. The Coptic Christians of Misr were overheard disparaging their new masters' manners and questioning their capacity to rule. Alert to the risk of rebellion, 'Amr invited the Misr notables to observe his army eating camel meat and broth. If the story seems somewhat contrived, its very elaborateness makes it no less culturally significant. After watching the troops tearing meat with their teeth and slurping broth, "Arab fashion," the notables winced and departed, "their courage and ambition boosted." Invited to the Arab encampment the following day, the elders of Misr saw an entirely different display: "Erect figures dressed in Egyptian colors standing by, the Arabs eating Egyptian food, behaving in an Egyptian manner." The deflated Copts filed away, muttering that they had been "made fools of!" At the spit-and-polish maneuvers on the third day, the notables received a remarkable discourse about cultural adaptability from 'Amr—"aware," he noted, "that you were preening yourselves when you saw . . . the Arabs and their simple lifestyle." He continued:

Therefore, I wanted to show you what sort of people they really are, under what circumstances they lived in their own country, then what they have come to in yours, and how ready they are for war. They have defeated you, warfare is their life. They were anxious to take possession of your country even before they appropriated its customs as you saw on the second day. And I wanted you to realize that those you saw on the third day will not abandon the life you saw depicted on the second day, nor will they resume the lifestyle you saw depicted on the first day.[27]

The people of Alexandria were not to be so easily intimidated in the summer of 641. They held long memories of occupations from Julius Caesar's to Field Marshal Shahrbaraz's as recently as 619. Besides, citizens of the city whose architectural magnificence the Romans had imitated and whose artificial creation Constantinople had duplicated could be expected to keep their *sangfroid* when desert Arabs camped before expertly repaired and reinforced walls. The strength of those fortifications was utterly beyond the Arabs' capacity to penetrate. Nor could they attack from the sea. Alexandria seemed as impregnable on all sides as Constantinople. Indeed, the Roman garrison may have numbered fifty thousand men. The siege of Alexandria could have gone on much longer, therefore, than the five months that finally ended it in the liberal treaty signed between 'Amr and the scheming patriarch of Alexandria on November 8.

In the relatively short time since the victory at Nineveh, the goodwill of Egypt's Coptic or Monophysite majority had been squandered by Heraclius's fixation on religious orthodoxy. Taking a page from Justinian, but no more successfully, Heraclius attempted to impose on the Egyptian and Syrian Christians a Trinitarian solution that affirmed both Christ's duality and his uncorrupted divinity—what theologians call Monothelitism. Worse still, the emperor's man in Alexandria, the Patriarch Cyrus, was a fanatic persecutor of Monophysites. Bitterness of the mindlessly masochistic intensity that only religious hatreds can engender may well have roiled the populations' factions to such an intensity that Copts and Orthodox raced one another to make the best surrender terms. Moreover, Emperor Heraclius's death at the beginning of the year had plunged Constantinople into a family succession fight, making relief or resupply by sea of the empire's second city unlikely. History is fuzzy about the details of Alexandria's capture, but there was nothing fuzzy about Alexandria's powerful impression upon its conquerors.

"Are you not an Arab who can give a report of what you have witnessed?" 'Amr growled when the officer chosen to ride with news of Alexandria's surrender asked for a written report.[28] Because they had seen things unknown to all but a very few in Medina, the courier feared his words would be doubted. For who in the Hijaz could imagine the Pharos—the lighthouse of Alexandria—the ancient world's seventh wonder, rising perhaps as much as a vertiginous four hundred feet and equal to a fourteen-story skyscraper, its great mirror reflecting sunlight and fire thirty-five miles into the Mediterranean? The great statue of Poseidon no longer capped the summit, but when 'Amr's men saw the imposing structure in the winter of 641–42, it was substantially intact and functioning. Who would credit his description of "the pearl of the Mediterranean," he must have wondered, with a harbor big enough for two fleets at once? Who would believe not merely the outsize dimensions but the prodigious use of marble and granite with which Alexander the Great and Ptolemy I commanded the city to be built? Alexandria was white and bright night and day. By day, the glare from the marble blinded. By moonlit night, the city was bright enough that a tailor "could see to thread his needle without a lamp." The messenger had heard the saying attributed to Alexander that he built a city that needed a God, "but can do without people."

In fact, 'Amr did entrust the courier with a written report, after all. He had taken a city, it said, of four thousand palaces, four thousand baths, four hundred theaters, twelve thousand sellers of green vegetables, and "forty thousand tributary Jews." Neither 'Amr nor his messenger saw fit to mention the Serapeum (named for Serapis, the city's patron god), however. The fabled Serapeum, the Ptolemies' vast palace complex centered on the grid of palm-shaded boulevards, was a shell of its former glory. Once it may have housed the surviving portion of Alexandria's seven-hundred-thousand-volume library. Savage fighting between

Christians and pagans at the end of the fourth century, and the indignity of serving as a quarry for palaces of rich citizens, left it a marble carcass. That 'Amr and his officers neither knew of the Library of Alexandria nor seem to have heard talk of it while there is important to note, because it was later claimed by some Christian divines and scholars that the Arabs destroyed the library—antiquity's memory, no less. 'Umar is supposed to have sent this obtuse answer when asked whether access should be granted to the collections: "If what is written in them agrees with the Book of God, they are not required: if it disagrees, then they are not desired. Destroy them therefore."[29] 'Umar was not a large-souled man. In some ways, he was strikingly narrow-minded, especially about the role of women in public affairs. But he never ordered the destruction of the denuded library, for the very good reason that that terrible result had been all but accomplished in the last decade of the fourth century by fanatical Alexandrian Christians who travestied Emperor Theodosius's decree against paganism.

The Egyptian campaign climaxed with Alexandria's surrender, although a sidebar up the Nile in Nubia fared badly. So much momentum remained, nevertheless, that the conquering army swept west across Libya into the Maghreb, the "place of sunset," before it was braked by crises afflicting the caliphate. Other 'Amrs would carry Islam from the edge of Egypt westward along the North African littoral all the way to the Atlantic, even as a symmetrical *jihad* extended eastward across the Asian steppes to the T'ang Empire and the Hindu Kush. 'Amr ibn al-As was rewarded with the title of *amir,* or viceroy, of Egypt. Although soon relieved of the title, it would be restored to him after 'Umar's death and his decisive participation in the politics of caliphal succession.

'Amr, like Khalid, Abu Ubayda, and Sa'd, confronts the historian with an explanatory conundrum as old as Herodotus and Thucydides—the degree to which the man or woman makes history or history makes the woman or man. From one perspective, 'Amr and his peers are human projectiles sent shooting across a landscape by the shift of ideational and institutional plates under a civilization; from another, they indispensably determine whether or not the seism is merely catastrophic or primarily creative. Whether agents of history or its creators, their victories transformed the Eurasian landscape. Something like the Muslim plague described by the Victorians did indeed come to pass with the great Arab out-migrations after Yarmuk, al-Qadisiyya, Jerusalem, and Alexandria: "Whole tribes in endless succession with their women and children . . . like swarms from the hive, or flights of locusts darkening the land."[30] It was then that the Arabian Peninsula disgorged an enormous portion of its people from Yemen to the perimeter of Mesopotamia: a demographic belch of historic volume.

Much had happened since Muhammad and his Companions departed Mecca for asylum at Yathrib in 622. One superpower was deleted from history's slate: Iran had finally and fatally exhausted itself in war with the two Romes. The Second Rome lived on, a much-diminished though still-impregnable city-state at the top of Anatolia. Emperors from Justinian to Heraclius had matched themselves against *shahanshahs* from Khosrow I to Khosrow II, with the unintended consequence that both sides ceded the Fertile Crescent to a backward people inspired by a new religion and an ageless avidity. These results were as God had ordained in "Jonah," the tenth *sura* of the Qur'an:

> We destroyed generations before your time on account of the wrongs they did; their apostles came to them with veritable signs, but they did not believe. Thus shall We reward the guilty. Then We made you their successors in the land, so that We might observe how you would conduct yourselves.[31]

The Co-opted Caliphate
and the Stumbling *Jihad*

'UMAR, the stalwart of the Prophet Muhammad, was stabbed to death in 644 by a disgruntled Iranian slave who is recorded to have had no particular religious or political motivation. The fiery-tempered, sixty-five-year-old Commander of the Faithful with the henna-dyed beard was the first Muslim to preside over an empire. His ten-year reign as the second of the *rashidun* caliphs (from the Prophet's inner circle) had been more momentous than he himself had actually quite comprehended. His instinct had been to restrain his armies at first from fear of the military and moral disasters that come from overreaching. For a while, he resisted the occupation of Iran in favor of a Euphrates dividing line between the *Dar al-Islam* ("House of Believers") and the Sassanian Empire. As messengers rode into Medina with news of victories in Iraq, Syria, Palestine, and Egypt, followed by prodigious convoys of sequestered treasure, a weeping 'Umar is recorded to have explained to puzzled intimates that Allah "never gave [such as] this to any people without that giving rise to mutual envy and hatred."

As the empire expanded exponentially, 'Umar's attempts at reining in his tempestuous generals and enforcing a system of controls over the *ummah*'s rapidly amassing wealth created just the problems he had foreseen. A desert people were suddenly awash in spectacular riches accumulated in less than the span of a single lifetime. Tax revenues from Egypt during the first year 'Amr ibn al-As served as viceroy, for example, amounted to a staggering twelve million dinars. Since Allah's bounty was his responsibility, the Commander of the Faithful soon made extreme demands on 'Amr and other amirs to extract all they could from their subjects. "I am a merchant for the benefit of the Muslims," 'Umar became fond of saying.[1] When 'Amr showed reluctance to squeeze more out of the Egyptians, he was recalled shortly before 'Umar's assassination. The viceroy's replacement gratified Medina with a tax yield of fourteen million dinars. After 'Umar's assassination, avarice and nepotism became widespread.

Once again, the Companions passed over Ali, the Prophet's son-in-law, with his assent, and chose 'Uthman ibn Affan as the third *rashidun* caliph. His twelve-year reign (644–56) was also to end in violent death. 'Uthman, we recall, was the exceptional Quraysh who had rallied to Islam early in the Prophet's proselytizing, putting his considerable wealth behind the movement when every dinar counted. Marrying Muhammad's daughter and then, after her death, another daughter, he was appropriately called "the possessor of two lights." He possessed as well a phenomenal memory that was invaluable in assembling what stands today as the definitive text of the Qur'an. He, along with A'isha, the Prophet's child bride, and Zayd ibn Thabit, the multilingual scribe, could

claim to know what God had said to Muhammad better than almost anyone. 'Umar had ordered work begun on collecting Allah's commandments as imparted to his messenger. That his people had no compiled
book to compare with those of the Jews, Christians, and Zoroastrians
may have seemed an intolerable deficiency after 'Umar's experience of
Jerusalem, whose very hills above and stones within were the stuff of
imperishable scripture.

To be sure, neither for 'Umar nor 'Uthman was it a question of creating a national epic in the manner of the Hebrews or of combining the
narratives of five saintly Gentiles in book form. As the verbatim word of
God, the Holy Qur'an existed outside time—eternal, unchanging, and
uncreated—the transcribed emissions of a celestial wavelength, as it
were. Under 'Uthman, the gathering and authentication of materials
bearing the transmitted word of God were pressed to a conclusion by a
bevy of scribes who owed a considerable debt to Zayd's secretarial work.
The definitive Qur'an of 114 *suras,* or chapters, arranged more or less
according to length, materialized in 650.[2]

The finished Qur'an was 'Uthman's singular legacy to his faith, but it
also played a part in causing his death. On the one hand, dissent arose in
Egypt and elsewhere over the caliph's destruction of variant Qur'anic
texts; on the other, it provided scripture by which 'Uthman's enemies
could indict his unworthy conduct. On the latter score, there was much
for which to reprove 'Uthman. He was accused of flagrant nepotism, of
replacing dozens of ranking *amirs* for no other reason than preference for
his own Umayya clansmen. As the Umayyas accumulated prodigious
wealth, feelings ran high among the Quraysh's other elite clans, as well as
among the Bedouin and tribesmen. Qur'anic injunctions pertinent to
charity went largely unobserved, and the exclamation once uttered by
Umar would scarcely have registered: "How stupid is the Muslim who is
beguiled by material possessions!"[3] There were fine houses in Mecca and
the new garrison cities of al-Kufa and Basra. The caliph owned a thousand horses and a thousand slaves. Muhammad's criticism of oligarchy
had been central to the appeal of Islam. 'Uthman's cliquish sheikhdom
was seen by many common people as subverting the essence of the faith.

Soldiers from al-Fustat garrison rode into Medina from Egypt, furious about the tinkerings with the sacred book and the niggardly spread of the spoils of war and office. 'Uthman died shouting to the man who struck him down to let go of his beard. "Your father did not take hold of it!" he was recorded to have said. The man identified as Muhammad may well have been the Caliph Abu Bakr's son who led the mob into the palace where, in historian al-Tabari's vivid account of 'Uthman's last seconds, Believers "rushed upon him," some striking him with the iron tips of their scabbards while others battered him with their fists until the caliph lay a bloody mess on the floor.[4] The third caliph's success was part of his undoing. Al-Masudi's tenth-century universal history estimated 'Uthman's personal wealth at the time of death at one hundred thousand gold Roman dinars and a million silver Persian dirhams. When the caliph's unseemly exit occurred, the *Dar al-Islam* encompassed most of Iran (Yazdegird III had fallen on his sword four years earlier), much of the Caucasus, half of North Africa, along with Syria, Iraq, Palestine, and Cyprus. Allah's generosity in the short span of twenty-five years and three caliphs was truly unprecedented, yet, as sensible 'Umar had feared, an excess of success must lead to a plethora of troubles. Islam's first civil war was imminent.

Ali ibn Abi Talib was fifty-five at the time of his ascension to the caliphate in 656. He was the first Hashimite to hold the dignity and would be the last of the *rashidun* Commanders of the Faithful. The dutiful husband of Fatima, Muhammad's favorite daughter, Ali had twice been passed over by the elders, even though his supporters called him "the first male Muslim" (the honor of being the first Muslim convert went to Khadija).* This time, the hubris of the Quraysh, as reflected in 'Uthman's nepotism, disposed a cross section of elite and popular interests to favor a return to the old values of equality and doctrinal purity, which Ali, as the Prophet's son-in-law and blood relative, was believed to embody. It did not go unnoticed by the wealthy 'Abd Shams clan, however, that 'Uthman's principal assassin was probably A'isha's brother, Muhammad, son of Abu Bakr. He went unpunished. In the five tumul-

---

*Some accounts ascribe this honor to Zayd ibn Harithah, Muhammad's freed slave and adoptive son.

tuous years of his caliphate (656–61), Ali found himself embroiled in
family rebellion and civil war; as his star blinkered out, the star of the
murdered caliph's cousin, the powerful *amir* of Syria, Mu'awiya ibn Abi
Sufyan, rose brightly.

Family troubles came first. A'isha, Muhammad's third wife, disliked
Ali intensely. Ali's dead wife may have been the Prophet's favorite daughter, but, as she saw family matters, she, A'isha, had been the Prophet's
favorite wife. Besides, even though Ali was the first male Muslim, she
ceded her place among Islam's first authorities to no one. A'isha presumed to instruct the caliph in matters of the *ahadith* and even scripture,
her phenomenal memory serving as a fecund repository for much of what
the Prophet was supposed to have said and done. Rumors of a grudge
supposedly held by A'isha against Ali for the sexual improprieties whispered against her during the embarrassing "affair of the necklace" have
come down through the centuries. That incident had never been forgotten. It was lust for power, though, rather than the lusts imputed to A'isha
that disrupted the *ummah* in the winter of 656 in the first of the civil wars
(656–61), the bloody internal conflicts called *fitna*. Whether it was she
who initiated the revolt against her stepson-in-law or she simply found
common cause with some of the Prophet's resentful intimates, A'isha
rode her camel proud and high into battle alongside those who denied
Ali's right to rule. A'isha's was an egregious betrayal of the family and a
reckless assault upon the foundations of the theocratic state.

As resolved as A'isha was, Ali's forces prevailed in what came to be
called the "Battle of the Camel" in southern Iraq. Zubayr ibn al-Awwam
and Talha, the principal rebels, were killed. A'isha, captured and humiliated, was pardoned by Ali and then carted off to house arrest in Medina.[5]
Momentous consequences flowed from this slaughter near Basra. Not
only did it open the Pandora's box of civil war but it would encourage
Muslim men to justify the exclusion thereafter of Muslim women from
participation in public life. Muhammad's comparatively enlightened
ideas (as explained by Allah) about gender roles positively distinguished
the Qur'an from its misogynistic Mosaic and Pauline analogues. In the
last analysis, though, scripture is no better than the society through which
it lives, and the Prophet's ideas about women's rights cut across the patri-

archal grain of his race, place, and time. Muslim women had fought side by side with their men in the early battles, their ululations and fierceness often striking fear in the enemy and carrying the day. The Khadijas, Hinds, Hafsas, and other women of ability and initiative continued to exert a presence in the affairs of the *ummah*, but they would gradually be pressed under the weight of the traditions and institutions interpreted and constructed by men for whom honor and war were paramount values.

Having spilled the blood of the Prophet's intimates, the last of the *rashidun* caliphs had to decide a year later whether or not to spill even more Muslim blood. Ali purged 'Uthman's Umayya relatives from the emirates of al-Kufa, al-Fustat, and Basra, but the key post at Damascus was still occupied by Mu'awiya ibn Abi Sufyan, the ablest of his opponents. The viceroy of Syria not only flatly refused to step down but also had a large, loyal army of Yemenis at his disposal. He demanded justice for Uthman and placed his murdered cousin's bloody shirt on display in the Damascus mosque for all to see. Pretext or no, Ali's appointment of Muhammad ibn Abi Bakr, the man who may have struck the first blow on 'Uthman, as 'Amr's replacement in Egypt was seized upon as further justification for rejecting the fourth caliph's legitimacy.

The situation became increasingly tenuous. Among Ali's strongest allies were Bedouin who were implicated in the last caliph's demise. Lower-class Medinans who expected to see a reduction in the influence of the Quraysh regarded 'Uthman's assassins as honorable men. "It were easier to bail out the floods from the Euphrates," Ali is recorded to have complained, than to punish the regicides. Discussions between Medina and Damascus proved fruitless. Finally, in the spring of 657, Ali decided to move the capital from Medina to the more strategically centered garrison city of al-Kufa on the Euphrates. That May, he advanced up the right bank of the Euphrates with a force of some six to eight thousand toward a place called Siffin, near today's Raqqa. A Syrian army of ten thousand blocked Ali's march and refused the traditional battlefield courtesy of granting access to water from the river. The Syrian army's loyalty was pledged to Mu'awiya, viceroy of Syria and Egypt. The commander in the field at Siffin was none other than 'Amr, conqueror of Egypt, with 'Amr the One-Eyed as his second.

The *amir* (viceroy) of Syria had looked with jaundiced eye upon the anointing of a man brought to power by murderers as yet unpursued. Mu'awiya ibn Abi Sufyan, then in his mid-fifties, was the first Arab to "walk on water," in the sense that the earliest Muslim naval victories were in ships under his command and built by his shipwrights. He had taken Cyprus from the Graeco-Romans in 649 and defied all calculations six years later by destroying a Roman fleet of some three hundred vessels—thus ending virtually any chance of Constantinople's recovery of Egypt. He consolidated Muslim power in Egypt and sent an army blasting through Roman defenses deep into Anatolia. With all this, Mu'awiya was the scion of Mecca's most prestigious subclan, the Umayyas of the Banu 'Abd Shams of the Quraysh tribe. His father, Abu Sufyan ibn Harb, had humbled Muhammad at Uhud. His mother, the formidable Hind bint Utbah, had never truly reconciled herself to Muhammad's regime. It was, then, perfectly proper that the viceroy believed himself the rightful claimant to the caliphate.

The Battle of Siffin in 657 ought to have settled the dynastic collision between Hashimites and Umayyads decisively in Ali's favor. The caliph's forces withstood 'Amr's cavalry charge on their right flank, and then, as Ali rallied his center with exemplary courage, they outperformed the Syrians by sheer grit and deadly archery to clear a path to the river in a hard-fought, daylong contest. But instead of destroying the routed enemy, Ali elected to reason with it, sending plenipotentiaries to discuss terms with Mu'awiya and 'Amr that went on for 110 days without clear results. Perhaps the Prophet's interdiction undermined cold-blooded resolve: "He that kills a Believer by design," warns the Qur'an, "shall burn in Hell forever."[6] Yet there was always something Hamlet-like about the fourth caliph, a curious dyad of action and introspection.

Once again, though, Ali appeared to win the test of strength with the endlessly complaining and conspiratorial Umayyas when their armies clashed again near Siffin. Slightly outnumbered by Mu'awiya's army, the caliph's combined Bedouin, Kufan, and Medinan units withstood brutal cavalry and infantry onslaughts until nightfall and near collapse. Again, Ali's generalship and vanguard presence dramatically reversed the ratio of death on the third and final day. Mu'awiya saved himself and his army only after taking ʿAmr's desperate advice to have the men fix the Qur'an to their spear points, a ruse that disoriented some of Ali's deeply religious warriors. Both armies stopped fighting to shout together that Allah is great and that "the law of Allah shall decide between us!" Ali had had no choice but to agree to another truce.

An elaborate process of arbitration that went nowhere slowly undermined Ali in the eyes of some of his own allies. He was the Prophet's favorite son-in-law, father of al-Hasan and al-Husayn, the only direct (via marriage) male descendants of Muhammad, the duly chosen *Amir al-mu'minin* ("Commander of the Faithful"), yet Ali's purchase on the respect of his people slipped slowly away. The fierce but always unruly Bedouin, who supplied the bulk of his fighters, grew disgusted. The uncomplicatedly devout among the poor who revered his family ties became demoralized. Ali's negotiators were outclassed in the desultory public deliberations on the Siffin plain. ʿAmr, as alert to an advantage under a tent as on a battlefield, proposed that both leaders withdraw their claims in favor of a neutral candidate. Ali's old Bedouin representative, Abu Musa Ash'ari, agreed, and he publicly announced Ali's abdication to astonished observers, only to be utterly humiliated when ʿAmr praised his wisdom and proceeded to proclaim Mu'awiya the rightful successor.

Amid growing discontent, an enraged Believer plunged a dagger into Ali's chest on the steps of al-Kufa mosque.[7] The man who slew the last *rashidun* caliph was aflame with a puritanical understanding of his faith that would become known as Kharijism. Kharijites ("those who leave") held that family lineage or titles were irrelevant in deciding who should rule the community of Believers. Piety always trumped genealogy for the Kharijites. Ali's assassin was the first in the long line of fundamentalists who spread as sects from cradles in Iraq and Oman to congenial soil among the Berbers of North Africa. With the passing of Ali in 661 came the temporary breakup of the *Dar al-Islam* into warring clans in Mecca, Medina, Ta'if, Damascus, and al-Kufa. Ali had not long lain in his shroud when the overweight amir of Syria formally staked his claim to the caliphate in ʿUmar's wooden mosque on Jerusalem's Temple Mount.

The awe and adulation Mu'awiya ibn Abi Sufyan's name once evoked were to be replaced by contumely and silence in almost equal portions. To those for whom descent from the Prophet's immediate family is the ultimate legitimation of authority, the viceroy of Syria and his Umayyad successors were wily opportunists and even vile usurpers. Such people were *Sunnis,* those who believed that leadership of the *ummah* belonged to the most qualified, regardless of family heritage. As for Mu'awiya, his family ties to Allah's Messenger—the cousin of a son-in-law—were fairly remote. He was not one of the *rashidun.* The Abi Sufyan family had been at the heart of the early resistance to the teachings of Muhammad. Mu'awiya's embrace of Islam had come at just the point where continued resistance might have prejudiced his ambitions. Educated, clever, and politically apt, he had served as one of the Prophet's secretaries after the latter's return from Mecca. His organizing abilities justly earned him the rapid advancement that led to the Syrian governorship and much favor under cousin 'Uthman, the third caliph.

Mu'awiya worked hard, cleverly, and, as was often necessary, brutally to restore unity. He dispensed with Fatima and Ali's eldest son and heir with an offer of pensioned abdication that Hasan ibn Ali quickly understood would be unwise to refuse. His caliphate represented the aspirations of the Sufyanid family, which is to say the economic and political interests of the well-heeled *ashraf* of the towns, as opposed to the leveling ethos of the Bedouin and the fundamentalist impulses of the underclass and the Kharijites. As caliph, he had the authority to speak for the *ummah.* The Hashimite supporters of the slain caliph would sulk and gradually congregate at al-Kufa and spottily across Iran as the party of Ali—the *shiatu Ali*—Islam's minority sect of Shi'ism, in perpetual opposition to the Sunni. Kharijites nursed bitter grievances in Egypt and elsewhere against Umayyad impiety. Still, Islam advanced under Mu'awiya ibn Abi Sufyan, even though roiled from within by intraclan intrigue, Bedouin–town tensions, tribal mayhem, and religious enmities. Mu'awiya was said to be fond of repeating that he never used his sword "when the lash suffices, nor the lash when my tongue is enough."[8]

Booty was the balm of acquiescence, but lash and sword were the instruments of choice, nevertheless, and Mu'awiya and his clan waded to victory through a sea of blood whose stench would stay in Arab nostrils across the centuries. They established a caliphate by sword. It was a theocracy governed by warriors and merchants united by blood ties and pledged to uphold Sunni orthodoxy: the orthodoxy of pragmatism in politics and moderation in religion. The usurper's achievement was in knowing when and how to corral and divert Arabia's frantic bellicosity, in knowing how to master the process of state-building through war. Expansion therefore, became an essential part of the new regime with its capital at Damascus. The westward *jihad* into the Maghreb continued steadily, spearheaded most prominently during the late 660s by Uqba ibn Nafi, another charismatic proconsul on horseback. But the first caliph of the Umayyas turned his gaze intently north toward Constantinople, the great impediment to an enlarged *Dar al-Islam*.

Picking off one Aegean island after another—Kos, Chios, Rhodes—Mu'awiya's Saracens (as the Greeks called the Arabs) sailed into the Sea of Marmara in 672 and positioned themselves determinedly on a beachhead within sight of the walls of Constantinople for seven years. Heraclius, deranged and dying in the aftermath of Yarmuk, was long gone. Constantine IV now reigned in his place. For the second time in less than fifty years, the great citadel buckling two continents faced a well-led enemy supplied with seemingly bottomless reserves of manpower. In contrast to Shahrbaraz's campaign, launched with a mediocre navy, however, Mu'awiya's venture commanded an armada of stupendous size. Camel riders had become sailors virtually overnight. As many as a thousand ships matched themselves against the Greeks' fire-breathing dromons before the decision was made to reduce the great siege after two years of almost uninterrupted fighting. The Muslim navy ultimately succumbed to mysterious Greek fire, the ultimate secret weapon of Levantine science (probably a mix of naphtha, sulfur, and quicklime). Balked before walls of Constantinople that would spare Slavic Europe for another seven hundred years, the frustrated caliph finally abandoned the siege in 679. He agreed to evacuate the Aegean islands and pay a small annual tribute. Hardly pausing for breath, he redirected the momentum of conquest, propelling it around Anatolia and across the Oxus River into Bukhara, Fergana, and Samarkand in modern Uzbekistan, then on to Khwarizm, below the Aral Sea. Indian Ocean and Silk Road commerce trumped the riches to be had from the Maghreb, at Islam's western edge, where the inveterately independent Berbers contested the writ of the caliph.

The once-Spartan new garrison cities were supposed to remain unpolluted by infidel high culture and low morals, but city ways ineluctably seduced the Arabs. Persian affectation and Greek ritual would transform hard-bitten Bedouins, stolid camel drivers, and practical merchants into self-indulgent, overbearing masters whose lifestyles gainsaid the spirit if not the democratic letter of the Qur'an. The ruling Arab clans left the details of governing to conquered elites. Another fifty years would pass before the caliphs would entirely replace the old Graeco-Roman and Persian civil institutions at the start of the eighth century. They exacted tribute and taxes (*jizya*) from their new subjects (*dhimmis*) and kept themselves superior and apart not only from *kafir* (unbelievers) but also from their *mawali* (non-Arab) converts.[9] The conception of a universal Islam in which the highest positions of power and privilege were open to non-Arabs was more than a century away. Mu'awiya's Umayyad Empire was much like the old Roman one: a tax-collecting machine; tolerant of religious and cultural variety; merciless when challenged or betrayed; and a jealous guardian of the privilege of Arab citizenship.

Damascus, marvelously irrigated and arborescent, grew with the empire. The Greek and Roman architectural improvements adorning the oldest continually inhabited city in the world inescapably inspired imitation. The Street Called Straight, its grand avenue, ran nearly five thousand feet east to west, with a wide center lane flanked by a covered colonnade intersected by two arches. Soon after Ali's death, Mu'awiya proclaimed Damascus his capital and put Coptic craftsmen to work on an imposing stone palace topped by a large green dome, the Qasr al Khadra ("the Green Palace"). The Great Mosque of Damascus, one of the glories of Islamic architecture, awaited the turn-of-the-century command of Caliph al-Walid (or Walid I). Until then, as was the practice elsewhere in the first decades of the Conquest, Damascus's Muslims and

Christians shared the enormous Temple of Jupiter, renamed by the Graeco-Romans in honor of St. John the Baptist. Mu'awiya's Damascus was all that 'Umar had feared about the cities.[10] As the years passed, the Green Palace took on the trappings of a royal court fit to cradle a dynasty.

Sidestepping tradition through flattery, bribery, and nepotism, Mu'awiya succeeded in garnering the assent of tribal leaders for the appointment of his son Yazid as co-caliph and heir. Abu Bakr, 'Umar, 'Uthman, and Ali had been chosen Commanders of the Faithful by the process of *shura*, consultation of respected leaders after the incumbent's death. Mu'awiya's hereditary ploy was an extraordinary achievement that compromised the Prophet's democratic message, to say nothing of the Arabs' traditions of consensual leadership or Mu'awiya's pledge to Ali's senior son, Hasan, that the next caliph would be chosen through deliberation. When the self-proclaimed caliph passed peacefully from the scene in April 680 after nineteen years of well-managed despotism, Yazid—Yazid, son of Mu'awiya—assumed the title already assigned him by his father as a hereditary prerogative and promptly liquidated the competition, starting with Fatima and Ali's surviving family members. Hasan had departed the scene under questionable circumstances a few years earlier. His younger brother, Husayn, the great Hashimite hope, possessed charm, intelligence, and the courage of his principles, but his principles would prove fatal. Commanded to appear before Yazid's governor at Medina, where an oath of submission would be extracted, Husayn set out instead for al-Kufa, his father's capital and the Shi'ite stronghold in Iraq. The city's volatile mix of classes and contesting religious interests was held together as much by grievances against the regime as by loyalty to himself. Whether he was naive or not to trust the steadfastness of the people of al-Kufa, Husayn knew that his elimination was inevitable unless he raised a credible force with which to negotiate with the Umayyads.

The Prophet's grandson answered the Kufans' call as the call of a destiny whose outcome Allah alone could know. The populace had already been intimidated by Yazid's troops. Husayn's piteously small force of seventy was intercepted by several thousand Syrian cavalry at Karbala, some sixty miles from Baghdad. The five hundred Syrian archers made short work of their victims, decimating their ranks and wounding Husayn's infant son, who bled to death in his father's lap. The Prophet's grandson was among the last to fall with sword in hand. The man who killed Husayn cut off his head and presented it to his commander, later reciting the lines, "Fill my saddlebag with silver/For I have killed the well-guarded king/. . . . And when people trace descent his is the best."[11] Yazid commanded that the head of the Prophet's grandson be displayed in the Kufa mosque. With Husayn's martyrdom at Karbala on 10 Muharram 61 (October 10, 680), a generalized sentiment quickly hardened into the powerful and everlasting theological antithesis of Shi'ism, venerating Fatima and Ali's descendants as the true upholders of the faith.

Hardly had Husayn's headless remains been interred by inconsolable Shi'a than the Hijaz erupted in the second terrible *fitna*. In Mecca, the charismatic son of Zubayr ibn al-Awwam, one of the Companions of the Prophet whom Ali had killed at the Battle of the Camel, anointed himself the true caliph and raised a sizable army that almost carried him to victory. Until Zubayr's death in 692, there was always the likelihood of an anti-caliph riding to power on a wave of fundamentalist revulsion with the failings of an incumbent caliph. In an infamy their opponents never ceased to cite as typical of the Umayyas, Yazid sent his Yemeni cavalry from Syria to lay waste to much of the Hijaz, to Medina, and even Mecca itself, where his cavalry accidentally torched the Ka'bah. When Yazid I died suddenly in late 683 and Mu'awiya II, Mu'awiya's grandson, expired shortly thereafter, their deaths extinguished the direct family line of the Abi Sufyans and sent the caliphate into a free fall for the rest of the decade. In the summer of 684, following the death of the last Sufyanid, another branch of the Umayyas (the Marwanids) and its Yemeni forces met the Hijaz Arabs in battle at Marj Rahit near Damascus, one of the most savage encounters of the *fitna*. Arab memories are preternaturally long, and Marj Rahit is still remembered in the way that Sherman's flaming swath through Civil War Georgia once agitated white Southerners in the United States. The winner at Marj Rahit was Marwan ibn al-Hakam, who laid the foundations for the clan's restoration to power by seizing the caliphate as the fourth Umayyad (r. 684–85).[12] The conquering caliphate inaugurated in Jerusalem in 661 by Mu'awiya and rescued by ibn Marwan al-Hakam and his son, Caliph 'Abd al-Malik, was to survive some ninety mostly splendid years.

⁂

Uninterrupted expansion was essential to Islam in the eighth century. The staying power of the Umayyads depended on it. The dynasty and its ganglia of clans and dependents believed that as long as the energies of the empire were directed outward, as long as martial exuberance, political calculation, and economic gain were captured in the gigantic centrifuge powered by perpetual *jihad,* the authority of the center at Damascus was secure. But the perpetual motion of Islamic expansion also obeyed another internal dynamic—the demographics of religious conversion and its economic consequences. Like the first *rashidun* caliphs, Abu Bakr and 'Umar, the Umayyads also strove to keep the Arabs separate and superior in the new empire. An elaborate hierarchy of privileges and disabilities divided Arabs from *mawali* (non-Arab Muslims) and *mawali* from *dhimmis* (protected peoples of the Conquest). In the early years, they were simply uninterested as a warrior elite in the complexities of running an empire acquired in four or five decades that was as large as that of the Romans—uninterested and inexperienced.

Living apart in al-Kufa, Basra, Qayrawan, al-Fustat, and other numerous garrison towns, the ruling Arabs concentrated smartly on military organization and tactics to the exclusion of the mundanities of government, while clerks, scribes, accountants, tax collectors, and judges among the *dhimmis* managed such details and remitted the revenues from them. How rigorous and rigid the religious, sumptuary, and legal disabilities of non-Muslims were in reality remains uncertain, although they did become generally less onerous with the passage of time. Christians and Jews, when not forbidden new houses of worship altogether, were never to build them higher than the neighboring mosque or the tallest mosque of the town or region. Public processions and rites, loud singing and ringing of bells were restricted. Proselytizing was a capital offense. Giving evidence involving Muslims in court was not allowed, nor was bearing arms or riding or walking in the path of a Believer. A dress code distinguished by colors was required. On the other hand, the tolerance (or, rather more, the indifference) the ruling Arabs extended to the *dhimmis* was a considerable improvement over the sanctions and persecutions that people of different faiths, and, indeed, of variants of the same faith, experienced under contemporary Christian domination. The Qur'anic injunction, "There is no compulsion in religion," embodied in the Constitution of Medina and the putative Pact of "Umar, militated against the temptation and infrequent act of forced conversion.[13] All the more so, as the Umayyas preferred dutiful, taxpaying *kafirs* (unbelievers) to converts relieved of the *jizya*.

An Arab empire serviced by non-Arabs was inherently problematic, however, as Caliph al-Walid came to see clearly by the beginning of the eighth century of the Common Era. The high-speed incorporation of the Christian, Jewish, Zoroastrian, and pagan peoples of the Middle East, North Africa, and Asia Minor into an ecumenical imperium forced the transformation of conqueror and conquered. Arab knowledge in politics, economics, and technology sharpened by the close of the seventh century to an edge as fine as tempered steel. Damascus presided over what was virtually a free-trade zone from one end of the known world to the other. It was an ecumene in which Chinese silks, Ghanaian gold, Russian slaves, Persian fabrics, Arabian dates, Moroccan wheat, Egyptian cotton, and Damascene steel moved on camel backs and in ships' holds south from the Mediterranean to the Sahara, north from the Indian Ocean to the Black Sea, east from the Maghreb to the Mashriq, where the sun rose out of China, a fabulous swirl of commodities exchange that was somehow unhindered by the Qur'an's stern prohibition of interest on money. Less than a hundred years onward in the ninth century, the needs of traders and bookkeepers would benefit from the zero and the decimal system refined by the mathematician al-Khwarazmi. If the road to conversion had been well-trafficked from the beginning of the *jihad*, by the first decade of the eighth century the road to Islam had become a conveyor belt running at full throttle.

Year after year, more *dhimmis* became *mawali* and thereby obtained more of the rights, privileges, and exemptions possessed by their conquerors, many rising in status even to a level just below the *ashraf*—the Umayyad aristocracy. Neither Muhammad's recorded words nor the Qur'an as finalized in the reign of 'Uthman proclaimed Islam to be a proselytizing faith. As with the God of the Jews, Allah's message was primarily intended for His chosen people.[14] Yet if Islam's truths indeed trumped those of all other revealed religions—were universally and eternally valid—then the Arabs were to find themselves, as they did, logically and psychologically, forced to accede to their subjects' aspirations for religious citizenship. Al-Walid's attempted solution, like that of his father 'Abd al-Malik, was to make the religion and culture of the Arabs the glory of mankind—but as a glorious enterprise to be admired, served, and imitated in exchange for shares as second-class citizens (half-Arabs, as some said).

Al-Walid's Great Mosque in Damascus—with its astonishing vault, precious porphyry, and calligraphy in shimmering pearls—architecturally trumped any house of worship between Constantinople and Alexandria. His father's command that all official transactions be conducted in Arabic had marked the rationalizing of the empire's bureaucracy and cementing of Arab cultural imperialism. 'Abd al-Malik's elegant, hexagonal Dome of the Rock in Jerusalem, erected over the ruins of the Temple of Solomon by 691, asserted Islam's superiority in bold calligraphic effusions. "O, People of the Book, do not go beyond the bounds in your religion and do not say about Allah anything but the truth," trumpets the grandly condescending Qur'anic inscription on the southeast arcade. "So believe only in Allah and his messenger, but do not say 'Three' [Trinity] and it will be better for you. Allah is only one God. Far be it from His glory that he should have a son."[15] 'Abd al-Malik's mosque enclosed the very rock upon which God commanded Abraham to sacrifice his son. Looming above Jerusalem like some divine Rubik's Cube, the Umayyad Dome of the Rock symbolized Islam as God's capstone.

But to the degree that ideology succeeded in maintaining Quraysh-Arab hegemony, these policies worked even better to magnetize the *ummah*, transforming membership in it from a desirable option into an imperative that brought on a stampede to Islam and threatened to stop only when non-Muslims became a rarity in the *Dar al-Islam*. The consequences of an enlarging *ummah* were both politically troubling and, above all, fiscally debilitating as revenue from the *jizya* gradually declined. 'Umar II (r. 717–20), brother and successor to Sulayman, attempted to solve the problem of revenues lost through conversion. His solution was to increase the *kharaj* (tax on land paid by Muslim and non-Muslim alike). But his famous "fiscal rescript" seems only to have accelerated the urbanization of the empire, as thousands of Muslims and non-Muslims in Egypt and Iraq abandoned the land.[16] Pious, well intentioned, and the sole Umayyad caliph whose reputation survived the great revulsion to come, 'Umar II died before the unintended consequences of his fiscal "fix" became fully evident. Both his immediate successors—the inconsequential Yazid II (r. 720–24) and the imposing Hisham (r. 724–43)—were quick to see that more real estate filled with taxpaying infidels was a far more effective solution to the looming economic crisis. In the *Dar al-Harb* lay the fate of the *Dar al-Islam*—or "war is the health of the state," the caliphs might well have said.

⁙

As the close of the seventh Christian century approached, resistance appeared to be futile as everything in the Arabs' path seemed destined to be assimilated—with two adamantine exceptions: the Eastern Roman Empire, which would survive until 1453, and the Berbers of the Maghreb. Distributed across the plains and mountains from the edge of Egypt to the Atlantic, these ancient, blue-eyed people of undetermined origins— *Amazighen* or "free men," as the Berbers called themselves—were every bit as tough and proud as their new would-be masters. Their tribal confederations (Butr and Baranis, Sanhaja and Masmuda) had never been conquered, and only those on the plains had been touched by Phoenician, Greek, Jewish, Roman, and, most recently, Iranian religious influences.[17] If the Berbers found the Five Pillars of Islam congenial enough, they still expected the Muslims to respect their autonomy and ancient customs even after a formal profession of the *shahada* ("There is no god but God, and Muhammad is His prophet"). Mu'awiya's North African *jihad* had progressed brilliantly at first under the command of another of Islam's remarkable military talents. Uqba ibn Nafi, conqueror of the Maghreb, led his men out of 'Amr's al-Fustat across the Libyan Desert into Ifriqiya (today's Tunisia), where he founded the garrison city of Qayrawan (Kairouan) in 670, linchpin of the North African occupation.

Uqba's policy of paying scant attention to the Berbers' culture and institutions fomented armed resistance to Arab overlordship. Recalled for a time, then reappointed to his governorship by Yazid I, Uqba decided to finish the work of North African conquest and bring an end to these people's refusal to submit to the *Dar al-Islam*. Uqba is famous in the early Muslim histories for a famous boast. He is supposed to have knifed along the Mediterranean through today's Algeria and Morocco soon after Mu'awiya's death in 680. Barely stopping at Tangier, he and his army swept down the Atlantic coast to Agadir. They halted their splendid mounts saddle-deep in the tide, where Uqba is alleged to have proclaimed grandiloquently, "Oh God, if the sea had not prevented me, I would have carried on forever like Alexander the Great, upholding Your face and fighting all who disbelieved." The Arab chronicles report that Uqba's men, riding back to Qayrawan from the Atlantic, headed inland and up into the Middle Atlas, where they were ambushed and annihilated by the Berbers. As it turned out, Uqba never saw the Atlantic Ocean. The facts are that he died sometime in 682, somewhere in Ifriqiya, fighting a coalition of Berbers and Graeco-Romans led by a Berber chieftain known as Kusayla ("Lion of the Mountains").[18] His defeat resulted in a total collapse of Arab power in the Maghreb and a two-year rollback (682–84) of the *jihad*. Kusayla's forces took Qayrawan in 684 and pressed on almost to the ancient town of Gabés on the Mediterranean.

Worse was soon to come as the Arabs, distracted by the simmering *fitna*, attempted to regain a semblance of control over the Maghreb. During the next twenty years, Christian and pagan Berbers would check what had been until then an unstoppable juggernaut. Assisted by what survived of the Graeco-Roman garrisons at Carthage and Tripoli (reinforced by elite troops sent from Constantinople), and led, after Kusayla's death, by a fabulous Jewish resistance fighter known to history only as the Priestess (*Kahina*), or Queen, of the Aurès, they massed in overwhelming force against the Arab occupiers, ravaging their flanks and holding on to

Uqba's Qayrawan until either 688 or the following year. A massive infusion of forty thousand troops and the scorched-earth tactics of Amir Hassan ibn al-Nu'man finally cornered and killed the Priestess of the Aurès. Carthage was finally overrun in 690. Its capture ended forever the Graeco-Roman presence and consigned one of civilization's cradles to the indignity of desuetude. Not until 704 did the great caliph at Damascus, 'Abd al-Malik ibn Marwan (r. 685–705), receive assurances from the new *amir* of the new province of Barqa (as the Arabs called today's Libya) that Ifriqiya and Morocco were restored to the *Dar al-Islam*.[19] An embarrassing chapter in the *Dar al-Harb* closed—but not permanently, as Berber irredentism would embarrassingly reveal again.

Success in the Maghreb was largely due to yet another of Islam's master builders: Musa ibn Nusayr, viceroy of Barqa and Ifriqiya. Uqba had tried to impose Islam by fiat, with little care taken to have the new religion explained to the Berbers by *ulamas*, men wise in the subtleties of scripture. Musa ibn Nusayr used diplomacy, and his carrot-and-stick policies not only calmed the Berbers but also brought large numbers of them to Islam as warriors and officers of the caliphate. But Musa's was a loose-fitting Islam: observance of the Five Pillars minus payment of the 2.5 percent *zakat* obligatory for all Believers. Berber tribal customs, even traditional religious observances, were tolerated. Instruction in the language of the Qur'an necessarily lagged, for the good reason that the first Arabic grammar had only just been compiled. If circumcision was finessed, as it almost surely would have been, al-Tabari writes of otherwise-devout Arabs made queasy by the religious requirement. The empire learned that it was wise to adopt a certain delicacy in the care and conversion of the Berbers.

Musa ibn Nusayr was not only the finest military strategist in service to Islam west of Damascus, this Syrian warrior-politician, despite his seventy-odd years, was a visionary jihadist in the mold of Mu'awiya. He was also a perceptive judge of subalterns, one of whom, Tariq ibn Ziyad, he deputized to carry the message of the Prophet and the organizational genius of the Arabs to the cold land mass across the narrow strait separating Africa from Europe. No image of Tariq ibn Ziyad has come down to us. Some historians claimed that he was Persian, but it is almost certain that he was a convert from one of the major Berber tribes of the Maghreb, probably the Luwata. He is likely to have known something of the Greek and Arab scripts. He would have been not too old, a magnificent horseman, and almost certainly a born leader of men. Such reasonable speculations about him reach the limits of what can be ascertained, other than that Musa quickly discerned that Tariq ibn Ziyad's superb military skills, combined with his familiarity with the Maghreb's land and people, were invaluable assets. His reward in 708 was the vice-governorship of Tangier, capital of the restive Maghreb, and some ten thousand crack Berber warriors who were about to carry Islam to a continent where the civilizing legacy of the Roman Empire lay in ruins.[20] Islam was now positioned to leap a continent.

5

The Year 711

THE BELGIAN medievalist Henri Pirenne advanced a famous thesis in *Mohammed and Charlemagne* (1937), a groundbreaking book in its time, that the recovery of post-Roman Europe was stifled after the Mediterranean became an Arab lake in the eighth century. According to this reading of history, the political, commercial, and cultural affairs of the rest of the world carried on much as before around the southern rim of the "Arab" lake, but Europe, shut out and impoverished, tilted northward into backwardness as it sank on its Teutonic foundations.[1] It wasn't Pirenne's description of a dilapidated, Carolingian Europe that was wrong, but, rather, as the findings of medieval archaeology have shown, the cause he adduced for it: Islam. If anything, the Muslims' new civilization that Tariq ibn Ziyad and his few thousand Berber warriors were about to transfer from North Africa to Hispania held the promise of European revival.

The collapse of the West began at the end of the fourth century CE and became irreversible in the herniated sixth after Emperor Justinian's imperial overreaching. Almost two hundred years before Muhammad's birth, semicivilized Germanic peoples living in the southern bend of the Danube had ruptured the *limes* (frontier) set by Marcus Aurelius in the last third of the second century CE. Until that momentous development, these Goths (Greuthingi and Tervingi) in the Balkan pasturelands of Dacia had marveled at Roman technology, attuned their ears to Latin, puzzled over Roman law and Christian morals, and, above all, assimilated the tactics of the vigilant legions guarding the empire on the opposite bank of the lower Danube. Some sixty thousand infantry and a fleet of powerful triremes barred access to imperial territory the full length of the river. The great span across the Danube near the confluence with the Olt, an engineering feat ordered by Constantine the Great, existed primarily to shoot legionnaires to the other side—not as a conveyance for welcoming barbarians.

In the autumn of 376, Fritigern, chief of the Tervingi Goths, begged Valens, the eastern Roman emperor, for permission to enter the empire. He pledged his people's military service in return for land. Fritigern's Tervingi and their Goth cousins were scampering just ahead of the utterly savage Iranian Alans, who were also running west as fast as possible from the Hsiung-nu, or Hunnish scourge, erupting out of the Asian steppes. Valens granted permission, pleased by the prospect of a huge supply of soldiers and the bonus to the imperial treasury from the annual levy required of provinces in lieu of troops. Constantine's bridge was opened and river transportation, observed Ammianus Marcellinus, "went on night and day," permitting a hundred thousand of Fritigern's people, along with their tribal cousins, to settle in Thrace (modern Bulgaria). The local imperial officials, however, grossly mishandled their hearts-and-minds duties. If any single individual deserves the opprobrium of history's Romanophiles, it is Lupicinus, commander of the garrison at Marcianople. His corrupt exploitation of the barbarians was a major factor in bringing on the catastrophe of 378, mentioned all too briefly many pages ago. Lupicinus sold the Goths grain and winter blankets at sky-high prices and then ignored their pleas as famine and disease wracked their frozen encampments. The commander then attempted to silence the victims of his villainy by liquidating Fritigern and his fellow chieftains at a banquet. In the aftermath of Lupicinus's botched banquet plot, the Thracian infantry was intercepted and slaughtered to a man. Six months later, Thrace was on the verge of becoming a barbarian bastion inside the empire, a situation dire enough to demand a concerted response from both Valens and his western analogue, Gratian.

Valens marched from Antioch at the head of his finest troops in late summer of 378. He had reached a temporary understanding with Shapur II of Iran over Armenia. Simultaneously, Gratian readied the pick of his forces at Milan (administrative capital of the West) for a forced march to join the eastern emperor, only to be compelled suddenly to head north instead of south. The fierce Alamanni had punctured several of the Rhine defenses. Gratian's army made short work of the Rhine punctures and hurried for Thrace, where Valens had been waiting with mounting impatience. Even though the western emperor was only a few days' march away, the eastern emperor, seriously underestimating the enemy and urged by several fawning officers not to share the glory of victory, launched a precipitous attack. From Ammianus Marcellinus's contemporary account of that hot August morning, we can visualize the solid wall of shields glinting in the sun as the legionnaires advanced in lockstep on the barbarians' wagon circle, the Roman cavalry cantering on the infantry's right wing. The Goths' wagon circle shuddered under the ferocious Roman shock attack and appeared to cave in, only to be saved by their surprise cavalry attack that shattered the emperor's left wing. On a single day at Adrianople in early August 378, the Tervingi and the Greuthingi annihilated three Roman legions less than three hundred miles from Constantinople. Ammianus, Late Antiquity's best war correspondent, gives a chilling account of barbarian eyes "flash[ing] fire as they pursued their dazed foe. . . . Some fell without knowing who struck them, some were crushed by sheer weight of numbers, and some were killed by their own comrades." Emperor Valens, "the last true Roman," dutifully fell on his sword. It was a colossal disaster that trumped all Roman military defeats since three legions had evaporated nearly four hundred years earlier in a barbarian ambush in the Teutoburg Forest.[2] Fritigern broke the back of the Roman Empire.

Until the unthinkable outcome at Adrianople, the Teutonic hordes themselves had believed the Roman Empire to be invulnerable. Even then, instead of bloodying themselves on the walls of Constantinople, Fritigern and his people behaved as though at a loss for what to make of the future. For a few more years, they roamed and rampaged in the lower Balkans before accepting a deal in 382 for good farm land along the Danube, imperial subsidies, and service with the legions. Two decades later, they were still so awestruck by the might and majesty of the empire that Alaric I, their wily leader and aspirant to *Romanitas*, mostly demanded respect from the emperors (along with an annuity, a real-estate covenant, and a flattering Latin title). Failing to get the ultra-refined Emperor Honorius's attention, Alaric authorized a rather circumspect three-day sack of the Eternal City. Rome suffered extensive fire damage (the old Senate building burned). Temples, churches, and patrician mansions were cleaned out. Rape was *de rigueur*, and Honorius's half-sister, the versatile Galla Placidia, was hauled off to be married to Alaric's brother.

In Jerusalem, St. Jerome was inconsolable. "In one city," he wailed, "the whole world perished." St. Augustine began writing his great treatise on Christian therapy, *The City of God*, a few days after the sacking. Bad as it was, all in all, the sack of Rome in 410 paled in comparison to the dam-age that had been wrought by the Celts in 390 BCE. Honorius was safe in Ravenna, where the imperial capital had recently been moved from Milan. Confirming the curses put upon him, Alaric died before the year ended. The Goths never quite grasped that, sacked in 410 and cracked in 378, the empire they had only wanted to pillage and populate was slowly dying. The *Völkerwanderung*—the hundred-year "wandering of the peoples" from 376 to 476, when the last western emperor exited with a whimper—was, therefore, as much a trying-on of Roman culture and institutions by the Germanic hordes as it was a search for place.[3]

The Western Roman Empire went down swinging after Adrianople. To press the metaphor, it interrupted the final count of history time and again to rise from barbarian blows and fight a match to a draw and even to sustain an occasional victory. A mere decade after the sack of Rome, when the Rhine froze solid in one of the coldest winters in memory, more barbarians walked into the empire. They pressed on to cross over the Pyrenees in 409–10. Hispania, the complementary peninsula at the far end of the map, was the mirror image of Rome itself. Its provinces contained the empire's most Latinate populations outside Italy. Emperors Trajan (r. 98–117), Hadrian (r. 117–38), and Marcus Aurelius (r. 161–80) were natives of Hispania, as was a large percentage of the senators. Cordoba was the birthplace of the philosopher Seneca. Roman highways covered Hispania like veins in a membrane, circulating commerce, culture, and the legions to cosmopolitan cities such as Caesaraugusta (Zaragoza), Augusta Emerita (Merida), and Valentia (Valencia). The empire's great highway, the Via Augusta, ran two thousand miles from Cadiz to the Eternal City. A generation after Adrianople, memories had dimmed of that high noon of flowing exports of Iberian cereals rivaling the African granary, and of wines, olive oil, wool, and precious metals sustaining Italia's fortunes and lifestyles. Yet even what survived of that vital commodities lifeline threatened to vanish after the Alans, Suevi, and Vandals—marauders devoid of the Latin reinforcements of the Goths and altogether unamenable to imperial management—crossed the Pyrenees leaving behind a trail of rape and destruction.

Neither Honorius nor Flavius Constantius, his son-in-law and commander of the army, had much to work with in the way of manpower and wealth in those desperate days. Still, the Romans were usually smarter and certainly more devious than the unsophisticated invaders. Honorius recalled the legions from Britain for emergency duty in Hispania in 412 or 413, three or four years after the Germans entered the peninsula. Simultaneously (and now brother-in-law to a barbarian), he decided to make use of Alaric's Goths by brokering titles and lands in return for

their service in Hispania as *foederati,* or non-Latin imperial troubleshoot-
ers. Goths and Romans marched together for a half-dozen years to clear
Alans and Vandals from a large part of the peninsula and restore a
semblance of imperial rule. Their imperial commission substantially executed by 419, the Visigoths, as the Goths came to be called (nomencla-
ture historians now find meaningless), were granted territory in the
southern part of Gaul (Aquitania) in return for more housebreaking of
unruly cousins in the region.

Rome lost the African granary irretrievably to the Vandals in 460,
when the Vandals destroyed the fleet assembled at Cadiz to retake
Roman Egypt by Valerius Majorian (r. 457–61), the last western emperor
to show any determination. By then, Alaric's people had emerged under
one of his remarkable descendants as masters of the largest barbarian
kingdom carved from the moribund western empire. Euric (r. 466–84),
grandson of Alaric I, may not be associated in many minds today with the
likes of Julius Caesar or Charlemagne, yet in his capital at Toulouse this
Visigoth Bismarck united squabbling German tribes on both sides of the
Pyrenees, from the Loire to the Atlantic. His royal vita—what little we
know of it—impresses. Euric locked the North African Vandals out of
Hispania for good, pushed the fierce Suevi into the northwestern corner
of the peninsula, and obliged the spectral Julius Nepos, the penultimate
emperor of the West, to recognize his independence. [4] He was not only
able to read (albeit probably not to write), but even more extraordinary,
Euric was something of an intellectual among the Germans. The content
of his legal code is lost, but he was the first barbarian to codify his people's laws. From a pedestal in Madrid's Plaza de Oriente, his impressive
likeness appears to cast a satisfied gaze today upon the national achievements of sixteen centuries, for the Spain of the *Reconquista* owed him an
immense debt.

Had Euric's dynasty been luckier, the chiaroscuro history of medieval
Spain might have been painted in brighter colors. But his son, Alaric II
(r. 485–507)—dismissed by a French historian as a *"roitelet médiocre"*—
would die in a turning-point battle with the Germanic Franks a few miles
outside Poitiers without leaving a male heir. More will be said later about
this victory in 507 by the most successful German chieftain until Charle-

magne, Chlodowech (a.k.a. Clovis). The Battle of Vouillé decisively shaped Roman Hispania's future. Euric's vast Visigoth realm lost all of its real estate in Gaul except a sliver of territory in the southwest called Septimania. Whipped in Gaul and pressed over the Pyrenees into Hispania by the arriviste Franks, a humbled Visigoth nobility, deprived of a hereditary leader, repositioned itself in the remaining half of its kingdom and produced in the early sixth century a poor imitation of the imperial order they had helped to destroy.[5] Two hundred years later, one of Euric's unfortunate successors would lead his kingdom to disaster and obliteration in the first encounter between Christians and Muslims on the continent of Europe.

⁛

Sorting through the political sediment of Latin Christendom after the fall of Rome, the great medievalist Sir Charles Oman described Visigothic Spain as having been exceptionally opaque even for the so-called Dark Ages. Apollonius, archbishop of Clermont, who had firsthand dealings with Visigoths, depicted these hulking nomads as simpletons with a semblance of manners: "They will not come to you at dawn,/Breathing out leeks and ardour,/Big cheerful souls with appetites/Much greater than my larder." Notwithstanding the fragmentary chronicle by the monk John of Biclarum and the positive treatment of the subject matter in St. Isidore of Seville's great seventh-century history of their institutions, one is still unpersuaded that these ruling Visigoths had much improved since their forebears' mad dash for safety across the Danube.

The new rulers were a minuscule percentage of the total population by the end of the seventh century: at most, some four hundred thousand Visigoths among no fewer than five million Hispano-Romans, Jews, and Greeks, along with Galicians, Basques, and Celts.[6] Their great nobles installed themselves on lands that Latin speakers called *sortes Gothica*, and that they called (in guttural Gothic translation) *landa-hlauts* ("land lots"). Members of the lesser nobility made themselves useful to their superiors and troublesome to the native peasantry. The old Hispanic aristocracy, proudly Latinized and Roman Catholic in faith, held on to its estates and enriched itself with ecclesiastical benefices. The free and untitled masses desired, as immemorially, to be left alone at best or, when necessary, to be protected by the mighty from other mighties. The state of affairs in Hispania could best be described as tyranny restrained by anarchy, Teutonic tribalism proudly wedded to prejudices and disdainful of the brain-work imperatives of statecraft.

The Visigoth economy, such as it was, was built on slavery. Impressed by the ubiquitous slave labor in the Late Roman Empire, the Goths adopted and spread plantation slavery across northern Europe, where it had never flourished before, and they greatly reinforced the institution in those parts of the collapsed empire where previously, as in Hispania, it had served the Roman landholders. Several of the kings ordered silver coins struck, but the coins served more as a numismatic tribute to the reign than as a medium of monetary exchange in a barter economy devoid of all external trade except the importation of human chattel. Slavery in Europe reached its apogee in the sixth and seventh centuries, and Visigothic Iberia was one of its main engines. A supply line running from the Black Sea and the eastern Adriatic through Bohemia to Jewish and Christian merchants on Rhodes and in the port cities of Genoa and Marseille provided the warrior caste with an abundance of Slavic chattel. So many thousands of Slavs toiled under the lash and the Iberian sun on vast cereal and cattle estates (Visigoth versions of the Roman *latifundia*) that the word for *slave* in Spanish (*esclavo*) derives, like all European nouns for *slave*, from this servile population. Christianity countenanced slavery, as did Islam, although the Qur'an not only made it the Believer's duty to free the slave as soon as feasible, it forbade the enslavement of other Muslims. Christian authorities in Hispania, in keeping with the maxims of St. Paul and St. Augustine, regarded human bondage as a condition justified by original sin. Determined that nothing should complicate the assimilation of the barbarian aristocracies to Catholicism, the bishops of the Church, whether in Hispania, Gaul, or Italia, were more than content to ignore Christ's compassion for the underclass.[7]

The Visigoth order was hierarchical, but not consistently orderly. The great clans distinctly frowned upon any attempt at dynastic consolidation. "We are all kings in our own country," Tacitus had heard them boasting. Sir Charles Oman records "that of the twenty three Visigothic kings of Spain . . . no less than nine were deposed, and of these seven were murdered by their successors . . . and in only eight instances did a son succeed a father on the throne." Some kings were better than most others. Two of them, Leovigild and Sisibut, stabilized the kingdom politically. Another, Reccared, ended the division among Arian and Catholic Christians. Leovigild's relatively long reign (569–86) enabled him to unite most of the Iberian peninsula. The Basque northeast, which had never suffered the presence of a Roman legion, eluded Visigothic domination, but the great unifier succeeded in annexing the Suevian kingdom of Galicia. He had to abide the presence of Roman legions himself, however—Justinian and Justin's (re)occupation army. The king's undistinguished predecessors had devoted their energies to mutual homicide while the whole region south of a line from Valencia to Cadiz, including Cordoba, was lost to the Graeco-Romans.

Leovigild decided to abandon his capital at Narbonne on the Mediterranean for the security of Toledo. If the Toledo capital afforded protection from Constantinople's armies, Leovigild relished the elaborate protocol of the Constantinopolitan court and the exalted status enjoyed by Constantine the Great's successors. The great unifier's reign reinforced the Visigoths' complicated affinity for the culture of the Greeks even as it resisted their military and political sway. Twenty-five years later, Sisibut (r. 612–20), surviving his court's long knives, effected the final removal of the Graeco-Romans. His opportunity came when his contemporary, Heraclius, was beginning his life-and-death struggle with Khosrow II. Unable to maintain a credible military presence in the peninsula after the Sassanids resumed hostilities, Heraclius agreed to renounce the Roman claim to suzerainty over Hispania in return for Visigothic abandonment of claims to Ceuta, the Balearics, Corsica, and Sardinia.[8]

But if the royal crown of Iberia was seldom the exclusive property of a single family, kingship itself was racially exclusive. Only Visigoths need apply. Like all Germans except the Franks, Visigoths kept themselves apart as a closed oligarchy, a ruling caste, racially pure and, for 170 years until their pragmatic embrace of the Catholic faith, religiously distinct. Until the late sixth century, the integrity of caste was safeguarded not only by a ban on intermarriage but by the Arian creed to which almost all of the German tribes had originally subscribed during the fourth century. As Arian Christians who embraced the Nazarene's message but denied his divinity, the Iberian Visigoths held beliefs that were radically at odds with those of their Trinitarian subjects. Since the foundational Council of Nicaea in 325 CE, the Catholic doctrine of the Trinity had contended for preeminence over the Arian Christianity imported into the Western Roman Empire from the Eastern Roman Empire by one of the towering theological intellects of the early Church, Ulfilas, consecrated at age thirty as "Bishop of the Christians in the Gothic land." Indeed, for a disorienting interval in the fourth century, Arianism appeared to hold the upper hand among the clergy of the West, causing St. Jerome to exclaim, "The whole world groaned and marveled to find itself Arian."9 To be sure, the disparity between the Arian creed and confessional practice widened somewhat over time in Hispania, as members of the warrior caste took rich Hispano-Roman brides and solaced their souls with Catholic sacraments. Still, the divide between Arian and Catholic Christians nurtured two distinct, antagonistic confessional cultures on the Iberian peninsula, as it did elsewhere.

Reccared (r. 586–601), Leovigild's son, finally realized that religious conversion was a reasonable price to pay for a truly national monarchy. Biographies of these Visigoth royals leave much unexplained. In Reccared's case, his older brother's imprisonment and execution by their father for embracing his Frankish wife's Catholicism may have driven Reccared into filial defiance. The great unifier's sons cannot have been unaffected by their father's example of being the first king to break the intermarriage taboo. Leander, the Catholic bishop of Seville, was also deeply implicated in the conversion machinations. Reccared took the monarchy into Catholicism formally at the Third Toledo Council in May 589. Henceforth, Arianism was heresy in Iberia. The Seventh Toledo Council made the proscription chillingly unambiguous: "The King will tolerate no one in his kingdom who is not Catholic."10 The house that King Reccared and his successors built resembled a prison, however, more than a nation-state. Visigothic Catholicism was exceedingly mean-spirited and brutish, and not even St. Isidore had been able to discern much evidence of the spirit of the Gospels in his indulgent history of the regime.

Jews were now the only non-Catholic population of any significance after the regime's formal renunciation of Arianism. The Jews had lived in Hispania before recorded history, but their numbers had made a quantum leap after the brutal reduction of Judea by the Roman legions in 70 CE. Tens of thousands of Jews were dispersed to Hispania after the razing of the Temple of Solomon, decimation of the population, and obliteration of the name *Judea* from the imperial map. Not only were the Jews not amenable to voluntary conversion, their religion exerted more than a negligible appeal among the kingdom's common folk. Their existence outside what the Church fathers called the *societas fidelium* was both an affront to the consolidating exigencies of the monarchy and a troubling encouragement to recalcitrant Arian nobles, of whom there remained a considerable number after the Third Toledo Council. Since slaves provided a major source of wealth to the kingdom, the ownership of so many of them by Jewish landholders intensified official anti-Semitism. Jewish wealth in land and slaves meant relative independence, moreover: self-sufficiency *vis-à-vis* the Visigothic state and autonomy in religious matters. With the Catholic conversion of King Reccared, anti-Semitism became the official ideology of the regime, with the avaricious corollary of one monarch after another coveting the slaves and landed property of the Jewish communities in and around Toledo, Tarragona, Merida, and those long established in Baetica and Catalunya.

To King Sisibut, the existence of a large, prosperous Jewish population was utterly incompatible with the unitary Christian kingdom he was devoted to building. To that exalted purpose, he needed look only to Constantinople to find a well-tried formula for state-enforced religious conformity. How much influence Heraclius's treaty negotiators may have exerted on Visigothic anti-Semitism is impossible now to know beyond circumstantial inference. That there was much similarity between the policies at Constantinople and Toledo is clear. St. Isidore of Seville condoned Sisibut's conversion objectives on the canonical authority of Saints Paul and Augustine, though he was somewhat squeamish about the means, regretting that Sisibut "forced [the Jews] by power when he should have roused them by the doctrine of faith." Tens of thousands of Jews converted to Catholicism under Sisibut's terrible sanctions.[11]

The bishops of the Catholic Church of Hispania both promoted and acceded to restrictions upon the liberties of the Jews that ranged from inconvenient to outrageous. The Sixth Toledo Council in 638 CE promulgated the *Lex Visigothorum*, stating that Jews, "whether baptized or not baptized," were barred from giving testimony in court. Other councils followed, forbidding the celebration of Passover, observance of dietary laws, and the performance of marriage ceremonies. In addition to being disqualified from public service and the learned professions, they were even forbidden the ownership of Christian slaves or the hire of Christian servants. Still, enforcement of these and other such proscriptions was likely to have been inconsistently applied or widely ignored and evaded. Among the general population, unfriendly feelings toward Jews seem to have been casual rather than intense. The anti-Semitic resolve of the monarchy came to a feverish pitch, however, in the final two decades of Visigothic rule. A growing deference on the part of Hispanic prelates to the rites and prejudices of Greek orthodoxy contributed to the surge in extremism. Time frames for conversion or expulsion were announced.

King Egica's (r. 687–702) anti-Semitic virulence was remarkable even for a Visigoth. At the Sixteenth Toledo Council in November 695, his demands that the high clergy assent to the imposition of draconian measures presented Jews with intolerable dilemmas: emigration; forced conversion; impoverishment; and worse. Some emigrated, more converted (temporarily), while some of their leaders reached out to their coreligionists in North Africa and Mesopotamia. In ways that now elude precision, it seems obvious that Jews appealed to Arabs for relief from the Visigothic "final solution." "We can hardly doubt that the Jews of Spain looked upon the Arabs as liberators," the distinguished medievalist Richard Fletcher concluded. A furious Egica had reached the same conclusion and promptly instigated the Seventeenth Toledo Council, at which grave charges of treasonous plottings within and without the realm were drawn up against Jews. Evidence was presented of secret Jewish appeals for help in undermining the monarchy—those secret contacts with Jewish communities in Egypt and with the Muslims who were just then adding North Africa to the *Dar al-Islam*. It was recalled that Jews had sided with Muslims during the second *rashidun* caliph's siege of Jerusalem. The council's decrees were pitiless. Barring conversion, all adult Jews were to be sold as slaves and their children distributed among Christian families.[12]

Egica's death in 702 brought no reprieve. His successor, King Witiza, endorsed the final solution of "Toledo 17." Thousands of Jews would make their way across the Pyrenees into southwestern Gaul. To impugn these blond Teutons as the principal source of that Spanish fixation with purity of blood lines—*limpieza de sangre*—(which would become, by the end of the fourteenth century, the monomania of the *Reconquista*) would be much too simple, anachronistic. Still, the cultural clouds that were to form and re-form over the redeemed peninsula had certainly been seeded with Visigoth ethnocentrism.

⁙

Tangier was already old when the Greeks anchored ships there and the Phoenicians made it one of their principal entrepôts. Carthaginians, Romans, Byzantines, and King Gaiseric's migrating Vandals called at its port. From its beginnings in myth more than twenty-five hundred years ago, the fortunes of this ancient voluptuary at the confluence of the Mediterranean and the Atlantic ebbed and flowed with the tides that carried the great maritime empires of the ancient and classical world. By the time Tariq ibn Ziyad occupied the honeycombed city the Romans called Tingis, the once-vibrant capital of the imperial province of Mauretania Tingitana had become an underpopulated outpost on the edge of the known world. The legions of the Western Roman Empire had withdrawn from the western Mediterranean at the beginning of the fifth century CE. After the brilliant exertions and Pyrrhic dividends of Justinian's generals in the sixth century, Graeco-Roman sea and land forces had made only occasional, halfhearted attempts during the seventh to patrol and occupy the coastline where the Pillars of Hercules shot out of the Mediterranean. No longer the gateway to and from Africa—with galleys crowding the harbor and warehouses gorged with grain, dye, and spice— Tangier, like the Latin Roman Empire that had nurtured it for half a millennium, was now a decayed husk on the rim of the great sea—*mare romanum*—that once had seemed to abolish the distances between Europe, Africa, and the Middle East.

In the spring of the 711th year of the Common Era and the ninety-second of the Muslim calendar, Tangier's new governor received permission from his master at Qayrawan, Musa ibn Nusayr, the pacifier of the Maghreb, to cross the nine-mile stretch of blue-green water separating two continents. As Ifriqiya's viceroy, Musa answered directly to Caliph al-Walid ibn 'Abd al-Malik I at Damascus. But this proud old warrior-diplomat habitually arrogated the maximum possible latitude for independent operation. It will never be known beyond reasonable deduction what caveats the officials in the Green Palace sent Musa in the name of the aged al-Walid. The just-completed conquest of the Arab Far West had taken, on and off, some twenty-five years. It had needed forty thousand *muqatila* to kill Kusayla and the Priestess and subdue the Maghreb; thousands were still required for occupation duty. Meanwhile, the adjourned conquest of Constantinople had allowed Graeco-Roman military power to restrict somewhat the Arab expansion in the east. All things considered, taking on the Visigoths in Hispania was likely deemed ill-advised by the caliph's counselors. But Musa, whose navy had already driven the Graeco-Romans from the Balearic Islands, knew more about the confused political situation across the water than the advisers in the Green Palace. Jewish sources provided valuable intelligence about divisions among the Visigoths. Tariq was ordered to prepare an exploratory expedition.

The land mass on the other side, visible to the eye as a dark sliver on the horizon, would soon acquire its euphonious name *al-Andalus*, the Arabic rendering of *landa-hlauts*, that guttural Gothic translation of *sortes Gothica*. For the present, much of what Tariq knew of the Iberian peninsula came from reconnaissance gleaned the previous year by the first Muslim in recorded history to set foot on European soil. Tarif ibn Talib al-Mu'afire had landed in August 710 with some four hundred Berbers on the southernmost stretch of coast directly across the strait and a little to the left of Calpe Mountain, the Jurassic limestone outcropping that the ancients knew as one of the Pillars of Hercules. It is said that the local

Christians chose flight over resistance and divined apocalyptic omens from the unexpected appearance of Tarif and his men. Laden with booty and women after a few weeks of unhindered plunder, the expedition returned to Morocco with stories of riches to be had almost for the picking. The Andalusian village near the debarkation point still bears the expedition leader's name—Tarifa.[13]

History oscillates between meager fact and fabulous hypothesis at this point. The known facts are that the last but one Visigoth king, Witiza, expired of natural causes in 710, leaving an elder son, Akhila, whose claim to the throne was speedily usurped by the leader of one of the great clans, one Rudric or Roderic or Don Rodrigo. Akhila, duke of Tarraconensis and Septimania, and his two brothers refused to go quietly, so they called for family assistance. In late April or early May of the next year, Tariq and twenty Arab officers crossed to the Iberian peninsula from a point near the port of Ceuta with as many as twelve thousand and as few as seven thousand Berbers and perhaps seven hundred black Africans. From the perspective of sweeping historical forces, Tariq's invasion was part of the rolling Muslim barrage across the Eurasian land mass, a flange on the self-perpetuating *jihad* that seemed destined to fill completely the vacuum left by the Roman Empire.

In legends shared equally by Arab and Spaniard, it was not geopolitics that opened Europe to Islam in the first instance, however, but the gambit of an aristocratic father bent on avenging the violation of his tender daughter by the scoundrelly Roderic, illegitimate ruler of Visigothic Spain. These sources disclose that the governor of Ceuta sent his daughter Florinda to Toledo to be educated as a lady-in-waiting in the royal court. Shortly after arriving at court, however, old King Witiza died and the vulnerable maiden caught the eye of the usurper, Roderic, upon his return, brimming with vanity and testosterone, from a successful military expedition against the Basques. Deflowered and pregnant, Florinda reported her disgrace in piteous detail to her father, Count Julian, governor of Ceuta, who is supposed to have plotted a treasonous comeuppance with Duke Akhila (oldest son of dead King Wiltza), in alliance with Tariq of Tangier. The earliest Arab chronicler of the conquest of Iberia, Ibn 'Abd al-Hakam, imagines an appropriate soliloquy for the governor:

"I do not see how I can punish him and pay him back except by sending the Arabs against him."[14] Messages were then exchanged between Ceuta and Tangier; terms were agreed upon.

Analogous to the role played by Helen of Troy, Florinda's legendary disgrace is said to have launched a hundred ships, if not Helen's thousand, when Julian and his men rendezvoused with the Arab–Berber force assembled to invade Iberia. Arab sources unmistakably confirm the existence of someone in command of the garrison at Ceuta (a Julian or perhaps an Urban), who found it expedient to combine forces with the Muslims. As for the shamefully aggrieved Florinda, whose existence an older generation of Spanish historians only acknowledged in order to vilify as *La Cava* ("the Whore"), the sources are more problematic. Not all professional historians have dismissed the story of Count Julian with the withering pronouncement of one British authority—"purely unhistoric"—but nearly all have exercised a healthy skepticism about the interpretive value of Florinda as a *casus belli*. Julian recurs repeatedly in the sources, and the high probability that he was a real person does make it reasonable to suppose that the governor of Ceuta held one of those IOU's due the Witiza clan. Much ink has been expended, though, speculating about his authority: a Graeco-Roman official left high and dry by Constantinople as it receded from North Africa; a Berber usurper ready to strike the best deal (Ibn Khaldun's opinion); a Visigoth official offering booty in exchange for Muslim assistance to the rebel dukes?

The Muslim invasion of Europe began with a nighttime deployment on empty Calpe Mountain. Tariq built the brick fortress that still stands there, on what is now Gibraltar—*Jebel Tariq* ("Tariq's Mountain"). The names of two men on whom Tariq relied most heavily have come down to us: Tarif ibn Talib, leader of the previous year's Iberian sortie, and Mughith al-Rumi, a North African whose cognomen (Rumi) signified Graeco-Roman origins. A few days later, Tariq sent Tarif across the bay to secure a beachhead in the ruins of the old Roman settlement at Carteya (Qartayanna). From Carteya, where Tariq joined with the main force, the army advanced to a place on the coast some ten miles to the west that the Arabs called *al-Jazeera al-Khadra*—Algeciras, site of the famous international conference where European statesmen gathered in

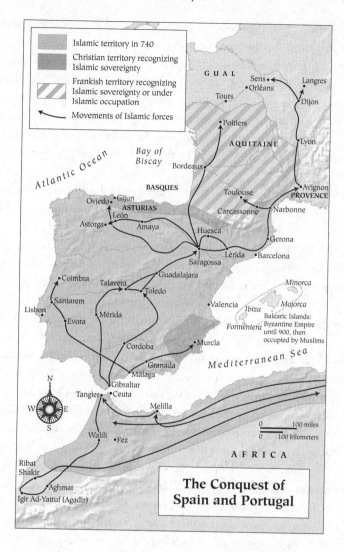

The Conquest of Spain and Portugal

Islamic territory in 740

Christian territory recognizing Islamic sovereignty

Frankish territory recognizing Islamic sovereignty or under Islamic occupation

Movements of Islamic forces

vain in 1906 to defuse tensions between France and Germany over North Africa.[15]

In the first days of July—the holy month of Ramadan—Tariq led his mounted force from today's Costa de la Luz into the mountains, the Berbers' small horses carrying them in a blur of speed past bewildered peasants as they headed due north out of the flange of coves and cliffs into dense inland pine forests. The account of an exhausted messenger bringing Roderic the first firsthand news at Toledo has the ring of verisimilitude, notwithstanding reports of Muslim coastal raids during the reign of Wamba (r. 672–80)—the "good King Wamba" of Spanish legend. "We do not know who these invaders are," he is supposed to have gasped. "We do not know whether they are from heaven or hell." In either case, they had come at a bad time for the king. There was trouble in the north with the Basques. In the southeast, Duke Akhila and his brothers persisted in their rebellion. Still, when the royal standard was raised, most of the nobles of the realm donned helmets and breastplates and galloped to the capital in numbers that seemed more than adequate to swamp the invaders.

In the third week of July 711, Tariq's cavalry and infantry encountered Roderic's much larger army near the Guadalete River. To Tariq, the moment was one of ultimate testing—either the end of a beginning or the certainty of a new order of things in this land across the strait. This Luwata Berber in his manhood prime was probably about the same age as Julius Caesar when Caesar set out to conquer Gaul. Like Caesar, Tariq was a gambler able to inspire his soldiers to die fighting almost gratefully against daunting odds. It is at least possible that these are Tariq's words, passed on orally and then in writing down the centuries until *The Sacred Books and Early Literature of the East* served them up in fourteen volumes of proper Edwardian translation in 1917. "Oh my warriors, whither would you flee? Behind you is the sea, before you, the enemy," was the likely essence of his battle command. "You have only the hope of your courage and your constancy. . . . The spoils will belong to yourselves." If hindsight permits us to cast the drama unfolding between the Rio Guadalete and the bishopric of Sidonia during Ramadan 92 as the hinge on which world history turned, neither the Muslim invaders nor the Visigoth nobility fully comprehended the epochal significance of the bloodletting about to begin. To speak of this moment as the moment of confrontation between Islamic civilization and Christian Europe would be somewhat of an anachronism, a reading back into 711 the history yet to be formed from its consequences. Although much of Europe, with the notable exception of the pagan Saxons and the even more petrifying Norsemen, was Christian, there were as yet no Europeans. The term itself awaited fabrication a hundred years in the future by an Andalusian priest.[16] With Tariq's incentives invoked in Allah's name, the Berber cavalry charged into history.

∷

The earliest surviving Arabic account records that the armies "met at a place called *Shaduna*," today's Medina-Sidonia. Sidonia is a hilltop town in the province of Cadiz. The Romans called this ancient Phoenician settlement Asido Caesarina; Christians renamed it Sidonia (Sidon). Lying about twenty-five miles inland from the Atlantic, it was the first town of any size in the path of Tariq's army as it advanced in a northwesterly direction from Algeciras. More than one fragmentary source claims the Visigoth force approached one hundred thousand men, although Ludhriq (as Tariq called Roderic, or Rudric) more likely commanded a third that number. Sidonia sheltered the Church of los Santos, one of Visigothic Hispania's holiest sites. It possessed strategic value as well because of its elevation. As word spread of the invaders' approach, it was natural, therefore, that frightened peasant folk headed for the hilltop refuge. From the old cone-shaped stone tower that still stands on a butte just above the town, sentinels, peering into the rugged, undulating landscape, fixed their sights on the southeastern horizon, just beyond which the match between Berbers and Visigoths unfolded on 28 Ramadan, the nineteenth day of July in 711.

What happened just over the horizon on that blazing-hot day transformed Visigothic Sidonia into the *madína* (city) of *Shaduna*, as Tariq's victorious Berbers would call the town. Yet no one can say with certainty today exactly where Berbers and Visigoths fought to the death. In all probability, there was a week of running skirmishes and inconclusive matches along or near the rim of Lake La Janda, with the armies repeatedly testing one another across the plain that stretches from the Rio Barbate to the Guadalete. The Visigoth host—ensconced in metal and mail flecked with gold, plumed helmets waving, shields arrayed—was a fearsome mass glinting in the noonday sun astride its stallions. Roderic divided his forces, entrusting the right and left wings to two of his dukes. Tariq's sandaled Berber infantry, in loose-fitting white tunics, stood bareheaded behind their lightweight shields reinforced by metal strips. His armored cavalry, the *mujaffafa* (perhaps more than a third of the total and readily identifiable by the ubiquitous *imama*, a turban over a metal cap), wore coats of light mail under leather or quilted jerkins.

Arab warfare was a lethal choreography of stunning speed and maneuver—*karr wa farr*, furious attack and withdrawal—in which initiative and improvisation were encouraged. Visigoth warfare was movement en masse from fixed positions; it was to Arab warfare much as American football is to soccer. There was disloyalty almost as soon as the two armies met. A cavalry wing secretly pledged to rebel Duke Akhila stood aside, giving the enemy an opening. Tariq's armored cavalry sliced through Roderic's front lines ahead of the foot soldiers and wedged into the mass—slicing, hacking, and spearing furiously until Iberian bodies heaped up like cords of wood. Notwithstanding their superior numbers and many displays of exceptional valor, the Visigoth host shattered and succumbed. But though dying and fleeing, it cost the Muslims dear. Three thousand of Tariq's men may have perished. "They fought a fierce battle," records Ibn 'Abd al-Hakam's *Narrative of the Conquest of al-Andalus*, "and God, glory, and greatness upon him, killed Roderic and those who were with him." The king either died in the final killing hour near the banks of the Guadalete or, as the *Chronicle of Alfonso III* claims, was overtaken in flight, killed, and stripped of his cloak and armor. In any case, the royal remains of the last Goth to rule Hispania were never found—only his magnificent white stallion, still saddled and dead in a ditch. A batch of heads, severed from the necks of ranking Visigoths, was collected and wrapped in camphor-soaked cloth to send along with bejeweled hilts and gold rings to Damascus as tributary proof of the scale of the Believers' victory.[17] Once again in history, a civilization's fate was determined by an encounter in which the objective factors of location, numbers, and equipment were decidedly not favorable to the winners.

Visigothic Hispania imploded with bewildering speed. Ironically, a proud warrior caste was also undone by the very separate, superior, and martial features that distinguished it. Excluded from the high calling of arms-bearing for some two centuries, the Hispano-Roman was neither expected to defend the land nor capable of doing so. For the most part, the people of Hispania were content to shut their doors and wait for the killing to end. The disappearance of the king, along with the cream of much of the nobility, need not have been an irremediable disaster, however, had the regime mobilized the remaining forces for well-organized, strategically placed defense. Having helped create the debacle through its own disunity, the warrior class was slow to comprehend the nature of the enemy. Part of the nobility even welcomed Tariq initially as a temporary necessity that would rid it of Roderic. The Visigoth oligarchy, bitterly divided as it was between Roderic and Witiza's two sons, may well have deceived itself with an assumption analogous to that held by Montezuma's Aztecs about the long-term residency plans of the first Spaniards. But Tariq and his people had come to stay—for more than seven hundred years.

Sevilla and two or three centers of serious resistance did emerge over the next year or so, but the overall lack of Visigothic resiliency fatefully determined the outcome of the invasion. After resting briefly at Medina-Sidonia and giving thanks to Allah, Tariq led his army nonstop across the province of Cadiz, wisely skirting well-fortified Sevilla and galloping through Moron de la Frontera to the old Roman town of Ecija, in the valley of the Rio Guadalquivir. It was in Ecija, the "frying pan" of the Andalusian summer, that new horses were rounded up and a no-return strategy of advance decided upon. Tariq's decision to press on for more than three hundred miles from Ecija to Toledo, after losing perhaps a fourth of his army, amounted to a remarkable throw of the dice. At this point, Julian of Ceuta reappears in some sources. Based on the count's advice, Tariq detached some seven hundred cavalry under the command of the Greek *mawla* (convert) Mughith al-Rumi ("the Roman") for a lightning run north to occupy Cordoba before the Visigoths could reorganize to the rear of the Berber line of advance. As Tariq and the bulk of the Muslim army made their way eastward along the old Roman road through Jaén toward Toledo, Mughith reached the banks of the Guadalquivir. They were greeted there by an unnerving panorama on the other side of the river. Engirdling Cordoba, capital of the old imperial province of Hispania Ulterior, were some of the most formidable fortifications built during the Roman occupation.

Had those walls been in good repair and manned by a garrison two or three times larger than the four or five hundred defenders, the Cordovans might well have kept their badly provisioned attackers at bay until the harsh Andalusian winter. When Mughith's men finally forced their way into the city through an old, unrepaired breach in the walls, they found themselves welcomed by a large portion of the populace, the Jews in particular.[18] The Visigoth governor, along with the notables and the garrison, had fled the city. Catching up with them on the Toledo road, Berber cavalry slaughtered them to a man, setting an example for the native population that Muslims had followed elsewhere: generosity toward those who surrendered; death to those who resisted. More severed heads and finely wrought weaponry were collected for the caliph's bulging Damascus consignment.

Returning to Cordoba immediately after the slaughter, Mughith established a precedent of historic political and religious impact. He assembled all of the Jews in the city and left them, "together with willing Christians and a small detachment of Muslims," in charge of Cordoba's defenses. Mughith's precedent established the conditions for the vaunted Muslim-Judeo-Christian interdependence that was to distinguish Islam in Iberia for several centuries. His collaborative precedent was also, to be sure, an astute response to the numbers on the ground—a Muslim force of infinitesimal size pragmatically manufacturing auxiliaries from the local population. King Egica's insensate proscriptions casting all unconverted Jews into slavery and confiscating their property had driven these people to save themselves by reaching out to the conquering Arabs. After so many years of living under the Damoclean sword of property expropriation, forced conversion, and expulsion, Jews throughout Hispania welcomed the Muslim invaders as deliverers.[19] Leaving this first large conquered city well pacified, Mughith saddled up and drove his cavalry due north to reunite with Tariq's main force, already at the gates of Toledo.

Toledo should have been an invading army's nightmare. Recognizing the outstanding strategic advantages of the location, the Romans had turned the granite mountain heights arcing above the encircling Tagus River into an aerial citadel that became the iconic signature of Castile. For similar reasons, Visigoth monarchs from Leovigild onward had made

Toletum their capital in the middle of the sixth century. The city loomed above its natural setting like a stone wreath fixed to the tip of an obelisk, a phenomenon both unreal and solid. The steepness of the approaches and the thickness of its stone defenses ought to have made the capital practically unconquerable by a few thousand cavalry without siege engines. Instead of finding a heavily defended bastion locked against an enemy, however, Tariq's Berbers rode into a city largely deserted except for its Jews. To safeguard the holiest symbol of their Catholic faith, the Toledo churchmen, escorted by a small cohort of armed nobles, had fled with the cathedral's high altar for a fortified place the Muslims would call *Wadi al-Hijara* ("river of stones)—Guadalajara—some three days' ride from the capital and but a few miles from the village of Madrid.

Tariq's cavalry raced out of Toledo onto the long Roman road running northeast across the peninsula. The Muslims had stopped long enough to water their horses and broker an arrangement with the city's leading Jews. "Solomon's Table," as they called the Toledo altar, intoxicated the pursuers, "for it was the table of Sulieman ibn Da'ud [Solomon, son of David], as is alleged by the People of the Book." With conventional exaggeration, historian al-Hakam reported that the table's value "was estimated at two hundred thousand dinars, because of the gems that were on it." Covering nearly eighty miles with incredible speed, Tariq's men overtook the fugitive clergy at *Qalat 'Abd-al Salam,* today's Alcala de Henares. For all the ritual thanks given to Allah and the Prophet Muhammad, the slaughter of the fleeing Visigoths exemplified the bloody avariciousness of the Muslim *Dar al-Harb.* "Tariq then took what was his from the gems, weapons, gold, silver, and table service," according to the *Narrative of the Conquest,* "and it amounted to the same value in money, the like of which had never been seen." [20]

The second invasion came the following year. Musa ibn Nusayr crossed the strait to Algeciras with eighteen thousand mostly Yemeni Arabs in Ramadan 93—June 712—a year to the month after Tariq's debarkation. *Jebel Musa,* the Moroccan mountain looming over Ceuta, bears his name today. The anonymous author of the *Mozarabic Chronicle of 754* laments the arrival of Musa ibn Nusayr as the end of civilization as he knows it: "Musa himself . . . entered the long plundered and godlessly invaded Spain to destroy it." The old proconsul brought his elder son, ʿAbd al-Aziz, as second in command. As the second act in the occupation drama, Musa's advent represented a significant investment of Muslim prestige as well as manpower. In addition to his ambitious son, the relatively large army included several officers whose forebears had been intimates of the Companions of the Prophet, as well as a (some sources insist) Ceutan contingent under Count Julian. Musa's character becomes difficult to assess from this point onward. In one version, the vanity of an old man caused him to resent Tariq's astonishing success and the besetting greed typical of many of the *jihadists* led him to accuse Tariq of misappropriating booty. Reports of viceregal conceits strained Musa's relations with the Green Palace. But there is another Musa ibn Nusayr, the driving visionary of some seventy years who acted consistently in the best imperial interests of the *Dar al-Islam*, and whose dynamism was misperceived and maligned by the panjandrums of the Damascus court. A worthwhile point to make is that as a fact of political life, Islam's great conquerors very often came to be regarded as liabilities by their caliphs.[21]

The second wave of some twenty cavalry units, each under its own regimental *raya* (flag), thundered into Cadiz province. A rendezvous at Toledo with Tariq was the ultimate objective, but reduction of Sevilla, the principal city of Roman Hispania, was a paramount priority. The Muslim army appears to have encountered about three months of stiff resistance from remnants of the Visigoth army, although accounts of the intensity vary. Once the city finally capitulated, sometime during the winter of 712–13, the invaders followed Mughith al-Rumi's precedent at Cordoba. Musa left the Jews to run Sevilla with the help of a small detachment of *muqatila*.[22] Before heading for Merida in early spring, the army veered west on a mopping-up campaign of Visigoth resistance near Beja, the garrison town founded by Julius Caesar in what would become Portugal. Musa entrusted somewhat less than half the army to ʿAbd al-Aziz, who pressed on in remorseless pursuit of the enemy deep into the southern end of the peninsula. The main force then headed in a north-easterly direction for Merida, the Visigoths' most heavily defended city.

Merida was a different story of prolonged resistance. The city held special meaning to the clergy and nobility, for one of the foundational works of Iberian Christianity, *Lives of the Holy Fathers of Merida*, had been composed under the protection of the Catholic bishops during the reign of King Leovigild, the last Arian Visigoth. Today's Merida, with its Roman bridges, amphitheater, and ruined temples and aqueducts cannot have looked much different when Musa deployed his army along the Rio Guadiana and cantered along its banks to take the measure of the impressive fortifications. For the first time on the peninsula, the Muslims were forced to tether their horses and build siege weaponry against well-guarded battlements. In another first, the Visigoth commander led his men out of the city in a massive combined charge of cavalry and infantry that took Musa's army by surprise and badly mauled it. The enemy's aqueduct-borne water supply presented the Muslims with the disheart-ening prospect of stalemate. After five months of siege, there was still no sign of the defenders' resistance slackening. 'Abd al-Aziz and his seem-ingly ubiquitous troops hurried to Merida in early July from the south-east, where they had managed a brilliant military success in the province of Murcia. Beards were dyed red to make the Visigoths think the Mus-lims were cannibals whose facial hair was clotted with human blood. The ruse failed, but once again the enigmatic Julian allegedly proved indis-pensable by lending his men to another Arab ruse. Pretending to be Christian reinforcements, a group of Ceutans deceived guards into opening a gate on the far side of the Muslim encampment. Merida fell in late July. Musa encouraged many of Merida's Christians to depart in peace, after which he spent several weeks carefully assembling and con-solidating a loyal municipal regime, much of it drawn from the old Jew-ish quarter.[23]

Father and son divided their forces again, the former setting off on the road to winter quarters in Toledo and the much-delayed rendezvous with Tariq. The latter headed for Sevilla to suppress a rebellion by the popu-lace. 'Abd al-Aziz made short work of the uprising, after which he con-ducted a furious return campaign in the territories that would comprise the future Portugal. Coimbra and Santarem were added to the *Dar al-Islam* in the spring of 714. If such feats were expected of the son of the last conqueror of the Maghreb, they were of a piece with 'Abd al-Aziz's hugely significant military-diplomatic triumph the previous year in Murcia. One of the last great nobles, Theodemir (or Tudmir), duke of Murcia, capitulated in April 713 after several hard-fought engagements with 'Abd al-Aziz. Like the Cordovan arrangement devised by Mughith, the treaty terms imposed upon Theodemir by 'Abd al-Aziz reconfirmed the Muslim policy of political and religious toleration—and of Realpolitik. The duke was allowed to keep the citadel of Orihuela and six other urban centers, including Lorca and Alicante on the Mediterranean. "His followers will not be killed or taken prisoner. . . . They will not be coerced in matters of religion, their churches will not be burned," the generous document decreed. As long as its terms were respected, much of Murcia would remain de facto self-governing. Considering that the Visigoth worthy was a defeated enemy, the quid pro quo—that "[Tudmir] will not give shelter to fugitives, nor to our enemies, nor encourage any protected person to fear us, nor conceal news of our enemies"—was hardly onerous. Tudmir also agreed to pay an annual poll tax (*jizya*) in money, grain, vinegar, honey, oil, and grapes.[24] A tradition of relative freedom in civil matters was to be especially honored in *al-Andalus,* with the felicitous result that many high-born aristocrats and their Catholic subjects were soon as ready to submit to Muslim overlordship as the Jews of Cordoba and Sevilla.

With the Trojan-horse capture of Merida in July 713, Islam had taken most of the southern half of the Iberian peninsula in three swift years. Exactly what transpired when Musa and Tariq finally met at the town of Talavera, west of Toledo, is unclear. The charge that Musa was angry enough to strike Tariq because Tariq had exceeded his orders seems not to make much sense, especially after their joint decision to round out the conquest of the peninsula. It is possible, of course, that the viceroy had supposed that his vassal would have conducted a limited holding operation after the Battle of Guadalete until Musa and his son arrived to reap most of the glory of the Iberian *jihad.* Grumbling over "Solomon's Table" and other baubles in Tariq's mountain of loot is likely enough. Musa busied himself distributing Tariq's booty among his officers. By the last prayer of the day, nevertheless, they had set aside whatever ill will existed. The next day, the two armies headed for winter quarters at Toledo.

Meanwhile, the faithful Mughith was on his way back from Syria, where, as instructed by Musa, he had presented a detailed report to Caliph al-Walid, who, as yet, had only a general appreciation of the scope of the invasion. Now in the twentieth year of his caliphate and assailed by poor health and scheming Marwan relatives, al-Walid's reaction to the Roman's news betrayed the indecision of a fatigued ruler faced with conflicting advice. To the caliph's brother, Sulayman, and some of the ministers, Hispania must have been an unwelcome distraction from their war plans for Constantinople, a dangerous enticement and a drain on critical manpower. Mughith headed for Ceuta carrying al-Walid's orders for Musa and Tariq's immediate summons to Damascus. Had Musa obeyed the caliph after the Roman caught up with him in the spring of 714, the course of Iberian history might have unfolded very differently.[25] Less than half the peninsula had been conquered. Beyond the Ebro and Duero Rivers, resistance groups of varying sizes were beginning to reorganize. Had the Muslim advance been stopped or curtailed for a considerable length of time, the inevitable Visigoth counteroffensive might well have upped the ante of conquest beyond the resources the caliphate was prepared to commit.

Rather than place the fate of *al-Andalus* at the mercy of an ailing ruler and the saturnine calculations of the caliphal court, the scarred old warrior and his protégé decided to flout their orders and, instead, to drive their armies hard to finish the conquest. Advancing on a parallel course across the vast, arid northeastern quadrant of Hispania into the province of Aragon, Musa and Tariq pierced the imposing defenses of Zaragoza, the old Roman center named after Caesar Augustus in the Ebro Valley. Where the Virgin Mary had appeared to James the Apostle, and where hundreds of the Christian faithful had been massacred on the orders of Emperor Diocletian, Musa commanded the building of the great mosque of Sarakusta, whose foundations today support the Cathedral of La Seo, one of Catholic Aragon's most venerable structures. Little more than a hundred miles due north of Zaragoza lay the Roman pass through the Pyrenees. For the present, the Muslims gave no thought to crossing the great mountain barrier. Tariq raced on into the provinces of Leon and Castilla (Castile), conquering the towns of Leon and Astorga in the far northwest, while

Musa's forces followed the Ebro into Asturias, taking Oviedo and sweeping as far north as the Bay of Biscay by the end of the summer. Islam had rolled across Iberia like a tsunami, gathering up the old order like flotsam and jetsam swept into the sea of history. "They placed prefects throughout all the provinces of Spain and paid tribute to the Babylonian king [caliph]," laments the *Chronicle of Alfonso III*. By ignoring temporarily the caliphal summons, the Syrian and the Berber had managed to round off the conquest of Hispania by the fall of 714. In a few months of summer, they had consolidated an *al-Andalus* running from the Atlantic and the Mediterranean to the Ebro in the northeast, the Duero in the northwest, and deep into central Portugal. As far as the Syrian viceroy and the Berber *amir* were concerned, Visigothic Hispania no longer existed.[26]

As officials in Damascus weighed the implications of the Iberian conquest, Musa staked the Muslim claim to the new lands with an act of audacious symbolism, based itself on an audacious precedent—the gold dinar minted by Caliph 'Abd al-Malik ibn Marwan in 694 in defiance of the exclusive prerogative to mint gold specie inherited from Latin Rome by the Graeco-Roman Empire. Musa's silver dirham, proclaiming God in Arabic and Latin as unique and Muhammad as His unique prophet, effectively placed the Roman legacy at the service of the Islamic future. By no stretch of the powers of clairvoyance could Musa have known that his numismatic twinning of Arabic to Latin aptly forecast the remarkable commercial prosperity of an *al-Andalus* that would cradle the philosophy, science, and architecture of a renascent continent.

❖

Musa and Tariq departed together for Damascus in September 714. Musa had chosen Sevilla as the capital of the all-but-conquered land mass soon to be known as *al-Andalus*. He appointed 'Abd al-Aziz as its de facto governor, or *amir*, just as Musa's second son administered Ifriqiya in his father's absence. The old proconsul and his young subaltern had pressed their Iberian luck month after month until inevitable disgrace and probable death awaited any further procrastination in answering their caliph's summons. But if success is the mother of indulgence, then the four hundred Visigoth prisoners, one thousand maidens, several thousand slaves, and sacks of treasure bulging on more than a hundred mules' backs were proof enough of these men's fabulous achievements and ought to have been profit enough to beguile critics. In early February, the enormous train was less than two weeks' distance from the capital when a courier brought instructions from the caliph's brother and designated successor, Sulayman ibn ʿAbd al-Malik, to delay its arrival until the old caliph's demise was announced.

The Caliph al-Walid's reign was in the final days of its illustrious decade. It had seen the pacification of the Maghreb and the occupation of Sind (Pakistan). Its architectural legacy was incommensurable. Al-Walid completed Jerusalem's al-Aqsa Mosque ("the farthest mosque"), begun by his father. It rose but a few yards from the Dome of the Rock, his father's iteration in porphyry, stone, gold, and calligraphy of Islam as God's final revelation. By al-Walid's time, so many subject peoples had embraced the Five Pillars of Islam that Islam's Arab core had come to seem smaller through the years. The caliph had responded wisely by ordaining Arabic (with its new grammar) as the official language of the Umayyad Empire. Second, he commanded that the Great Mosque of Damascus rise on the site where the Cathedral of St. John and, before it, the Temple of Jupiter, had stood, at the staggering cost of one million dinars. Damascus possessed four things that gave it superiority, he told the populace when the prototype of the Muslim world's great mosques was finished: "your climate, your water, your fruits, and your baths." To these he added a fifth—"this mosque." Rather than wait until the death of the Commander of the Faithful, whose writ he, Musa, had carried to one end of the earth, the pacifier of the Maghreb and coconqueror of Hispania hurried to present himself to the unwell ruler.

The caliph's brother wanted not only the glory of receiving an empire from the hands of its conquerors, he wanted the treasures they were bringing applied to his own account. The *Mozarabic Chronicle* enumerated fabulous spoils of war in the conquerors' train: precious gems stripped from "Solomon's Table"—"gold and silver, assayed by the bankers; a large quantity of valuable ornaments, precious stones, and pearls; ointments to kindle women's desire; and many others from the length and breadth of Spain that would be tedious to record"—more

than enough to stoke the caliphal heir's avarice. Within two months of
their arrival in the capital, al-Walid ibn 'Abd al-Malik, in whose reign
Shi'a insurgency was quelled, died. Sulayman promptly visited his displeasure upon the two conquerors. Accused of withholding Iberian spoils
for himself, Musa was "ignominiously removed from the prince's presence and paraded with a rope around his neck," claims the *Mozarabic
Chronicle*. One legend had the grand old warrior begging on the streets of
Damascus years later. Tariq, the general who brought Islam to Europe,
disappears completely from history.[27]

A rapacious ingrate, Sulayman meted out similar punishment to the
conquerors of Turkestan and Sind. In Musa and Tariq's case, however,
there was a major factor of conflicting imperial objectives at play, in addition to the caliph's cupidity and aversion to rivals. Although sanctioned
in principle by Damascus beforehand, Musa and Tariq greatly exceeded
whatever caliphal authority they were vouchsafed. Sulayman came to the
throne with a burning ambition to achieve what the great Mu'awiya had
failed to do: to send the *ahl al-Sham*, the elite Syrian troops, clambering
over the walls of the Second Rome. Until the Byzantine gambit had been
successfully played, the governance and settlement of *al-Andalus* was
something of a burdensome distraction. As the events across the strait
were sidebars to such calculations, Sulayman found it necessary to mar-
ginalize Musa and Tariq and to downplay their extraordinary victory over
the Visigoths, whatever his avarice about spoils of war. No other reasonable interpretation explains that curious and soon-disregarded caliphal
order to withdraw from the Iberian peninsula.

Sulayman's plans called for one of the largest military campaigns in
history, a double-pronged land and sea assault to remove the Second
Rome from the path of the Prophet's people—to smash, once and for all,
the world's largest, most impregnable city-state. To this epic end, he
invested his brother, Maslama, with the command of an army of eighty
thousand. This juggernaut rolled out of Syria and across Anatolia, almost
arrow-straight, crushing the Graeco-Roman defenses at Pergamum and
Abydos (in modern Turkey), and then spanned the Dardanelles into
Thrace, flanking the shore of the Sea of Marmara as it marched beneath
a cumulus of dust toward the Golden Horn. Maslama's army was the

acme in Muslim military evolution. The flower of Syrian manhood, the *ahl al-Sham,* riding under the white banner of the Umayyads, formed the vanguard—haughty Syrians who mocked the "lizard and gerbil eaters" of Arabia and Palestine.[28] Next came the Khurasan elite of northern Iran, followed by the thickly armored *mujaffafa* of Persia and the *mujarrada* cavalry of Iraq, Arabia, and Egypt, and then the *muqatila,* the fighting men, drawn from all corners of the empire—from the Oxus River to Ifriqiya and beyond. The great fortress metropolis of Constantinople lay hard and unmovable, like a nacre enveloped in the churning center of an expanding Islamic organism. Forty-odd years had gone by since Mu'awiya's thousand-ship fleet had filled up the Marmara like boats in a tub, only to burn and capsize by the hundreds as annihilating waves of Greek fire skimmed across the sea out of the Golden Horn.

On August 15, 717, General Maslama's legions encamped on the plain west of Constantinople, some fifty miles as the crow flies from Justinian's architectural marvel, St. Sophia—near enough that the muezzin's sundown chanting reverberated within some parts of the city. Twenty thousand tents in a hundred different colors carpeted the approach to the metropolis, a *madina* that stretched from the horizon to within a trebuchet shot of the Wall of Anastasius I, the so-called long walls forming the city's outermost protective ring. Two weeks after Maslama's army deployed before the triplex of walls forming the base of the Constantinople triangle, the caliph's armada sailed into the Marmara, eighteen hundred ships commanded by an admiral, *amir al-ma* ("chief of the water"), also named Sulayman. This was a display of military might out of Asia Minor not seen north of the Hellespont since Xerxes I at Thermopylae in 480 BCE. But it was not enough to have mobilized such awesome forces in order to reduce the impregnable world-city. Caliph Sulayman had reason to expect the collusion of the new emperor of the Second Rome.

Leo "the Isaurian," risen from the Syrian peasantry and invested with the governorship of Anatolikon province, had seemed to promise the surrender of the city if the caliph delayed his siege plans until the Isaurian seized power.[29] The Commander of the Faithful was one of the ablest of the Umayyads, but he was to be outclassed by the *strategos* (prefect) of Anatolikon, who could speak Arabic as convincingly as he

could dissemble. Supported by a cabal of insurgent governors in the early
weeks of 717, Leo had dispatched his feckless imperial predecessor to a
monastery and assumed the purple as Leo III (r. 717–41), not a moment
too soon—five months, to be exact—before the caliph's army spread its
tents before the long walls. Instead of finding a city poorly provisioned,
badly garrisoned, and disposed to accept generous surrender terms, General Maslama and Admiral Sulayman faced a populace and defense force
inspired by their new emperor. The great basilica of St. Sophia resounded
with the *Te Deum* as the Greeks knelt in prayer before their patriarch. The
city's granaries were stocked to outlast a three-year siege, its garrison
reinforced by the best units from all parts of the shrunken empire. With
no signal from Leo by the end of September, the supreme contest
between these two one-god faiths that had begun with Muhammad's surrender summons to Emperor Heraclius recommenced in earnest.

The siege of Constantinople in 717–18 turned out to be a disastrously premature dress rehearsal for a final act centuries in the future.
When the campaign aborted one month less than a year after Maslama's
deployment before the western land walls, his army had been decimated
by freezing weather, famine, pestilence, and a Bulgarian surprise attack
out of Thrace. Admiral Sulayman and tens of thousands of sailors had
perished in Greek-fire conflagrations on the Sea of Marmara. Humiliated, Sulayman expired from a dubious seizure of the digestive tract just
in time to leave the order to withdraw to his morose successor, 'Umar II,
who would prove to be one of the ablest of the Umayyad rulers.[30]

Defeat was a word seldom heard in Arabic. The standdown from the
Bosporus was written off by Damascus as a strategic reversal of temporary duration—as, indeed, it was. The Muslim empire's pressure on the
Graeco-Roman Empire's frontiers would be ongoing. For 'Umar II and
his *vizirs*, the strategic reversal posed a dilemma of considerable exigency
that would soon force the caliphate to reassess the geopolitical potential
of Musa and Tariq's conquest of *al-Andalus*. Finding the door to the land
of the Christians at the eastern end of the Mediterranean impregnably
battened, Arab strategists reassessed the continental entry point at the
western end—the beachhead across the water from Morocco.

Picking Up the
Pieces after Rome

THERE was a time when few of the foundational outcomes that
constitute European civilization as we know it were anything
but inevitable. On the eve of Islam's arrival on the European
continent, Europe the civilization was only—and, indeed, barely—a possibility. Institutions indispensable to cultural formation, political stability, and economic vitality either had yet to be invented or had become
degraded beyond viability and agency. The French nation and the papacy,

the future House of Europe's post and lintel, were entities *in utero* as the Muslim dawn broke over the Iberian peninsula. The logic of their future was as yet unclear to them, and, to the extent apparent, politically daunting. History can predict the past, however, and from that perspective it is evident that the logic of Europe's creation as a coherent culture and polity inhered in the commencing coordination and collaboration of the bishopric of Rome and the regime of the Catholic Franks. Absent history's hindsight, however, as Islam established its European beachhead and Arian Lombards their northern Italian kingdom, the early-eighth-century survival prospects of the Frankish people and the vicars of Christ were distinctly unpromising.

The Roman pontiffs lived in a world of brute force, sometimes draped in Roman livery but, nonetheless, elemental and vicious. In this world, the weak survived only by finding reasons for someone strong to protect them. In the collapsing scheme of things barbarian, the bishops of Rome were among the weakest. Yet, the See of Peter was no garden-variety entity. It believed itself to be the moral compass of the West, the rock upon which the Founder had commanded that a world religion be built. Fortunately for the bishops, the barbarians were, as were most Christians, deeply superstitious. Although the essence of their faith was the power to redeem sinners and the promise of eternal salvation, Christianity's reputed value as an insurance policy in war was what prompted some barbarians to test its efficacy. Almost any German chieftain who was serious about optimizing his conquests would have known of Constantine the Great's decisive victory at Rome's Milvian Bridge in 312. The future founder of the Second Roman Empire had invoked the favor of the Christian God, proclaiming as he led his men into battle under a crucifix, "*In hoc signo vinces*" ("In this sign shall you win"). Constantine won his battle and Christianity gained an empire—whether or not the legend itself is fact.

One hundred fourteen years before Muhammad heard Gabriel's command to recite for the first time, Chlodowech (Clovis), the tribal chieftain most responsible for making France possible, embraced Catholic Christianity on the eve of a fateful battle with the feral Alamanni, a tribe virtually untouched by civilization. Sir Charles Oman, the

English historian who found little good to say about the Visigoths, pronounced the Franks "one of the more backward of the Teutonic races, in spite of their long contact with Roman civilization." Backward, perhaps, but courageous in the informed judgment of a fifth-century Roman bishop. "If they are overcome by superior numbers or adverse terrain," said Sidonius Apollinaris, "they yield only to death and never to fear." They made excellent soldiers for Rome and, in time, credible Romans. Their mantle of *Romanitas*—"Roman-ness"—may have been roughly woven and badly torn, but they wore it with the pride of a people brushed by Latin civilization. When he commanded that his tomb's inscription proclaim, *"Francus ego civis, Romanus miles in armis"* ("I am a Frankish citizen, a Roman soldier under arms"), that Frank who was laid to rest in the late fourth century CE kept faith with his borrowed heritage.[1] In time came another heritage of which these Germans aspiring to become Romans were uniquely proud. The Franks made a great creedal leap forward late in the fifth century, causing the bishops of Rome to rejoice. Suddenly, from over the Alps, came reports of the existence of a vast Catholic kingdom stretching from the Rhine to the Pyrenees. Clovis, their long-maned chieftain, had brought the Franks to the Catholic faith en masse.

The sainted Bishop Gregory of Tours, a Gallo-Roman of formidable culture, relates the conversion experience of Clovis I in his monumental *Historia Francorum* (*History of the Franks*), a story that would become integral to the construction of Gallic identity and was once a staple of *lycée* instruction. A crucified god whose message was one of love, charity, sin, and forgiveness held no appeal to an evolved barbarian like Clovis. It was a creed unworthy of a powerful king who drank the blood of enemies and enforced obedience by smashing out the brains of miscreant soldiers as they stood in ranks. But marital politics, interpreted by Bishop Gregory as the work of the Lord, changed history. The Burgundians were a conquering German tribe that had gone soft after being assimilated by its much more sophisticated Gallo-Roman Catholic subjects. Consequently, Burgundy was all but absorbed by powerful Frankland through the union of Clovis with its Princess Clothilde. Clothilde appears in the Catholic Church's iconography as a willowy blonde, svelte by comparison to the typical large-framed females of her class. She was deeply religious and obviously courageous, because she risked her life in nagging her tempestuous barbarian to abandon the forest gods of his people.

At first, Clothilde appeared to have badly miscalculated when she overcame Clovis's objections to the baptism of their first-born son. Their child "died in his white baptismal robe." The furious, superstitious father embargoed giving any further offenses to the gods. Clothilde persevered, nevertheless, even after the death of a second child, and her persistence achieved its purpose at the close-run battle with the Alamanni in which the hard-pressed Franks faced disaster after a day's slaughter. At that instant, Clovis very likely thought that he had nothing more to lose when he finally appealed to the Galilean to work his magic. The *History of the Franks* vibrates with the elation of momentous closure as it describes Clovis's mass conversion of his people. "When he came among them, the power of God went before him," writes Bishop Gregory, "and before he had spoken all the people cried out together, 'We cast off mortal gods.'. . ." Like the great Constantine, whose bargain yielded a major military victory and Christianity's elevation as a legitimate imperial religion, Clovis's defeat of the Alamanni at Tolbiac in 496 put the Franks solidly in the Catholic camp alongside the Burgundians.[2]

For Gregory, the mass conversion was the Lord's work, but historians have noted that the bishop of Reims, the venerable Remigius, had acquainted the king with the power and glory bestowed upon Constantine the Great and other illustrious winners who had made well-timed conversions. The Franks' unanimous response on being summoned to Christ by their brain-bashing chieftain ought not have surprised Bishop Gregory. The ultimate consequences of Clothilde's piety were that they advantaged the cause of the bishops of Rome by establishing in the center of the continent, more than two hundred years before the arrival of Islam, a military auxiliary, as it were—the Frankish people—to which its creedal and political ascendancy were to become inextricably linked.

Faith and fate worked invincibly hand in hand thereafter. The king of the Franks led his Catholic folk out of the northern mists into Aquitania, the old Roman province of sunshine and vines, still deeply imprinted with Latin culture. This was the heart of Visigoth country, where Alaric's descendants ruled their enormous Arian kingdom from

Toulouse. In a dramatic encounter, details of which are long lost, Clovis appears to have surprised the enemy at Vouillé, not far from the cathedral city of Poitiers. The Franks decimated the Arian Visigoths with their massive throwing axes (*franciscae*), killed their king, Alaric II, and effectively ended their presence in all but a small portion of Gaul by driving them over the Pyrenees, where Tariq ibn Ziyad and Musa ibn Nusayr would eliminate them from history some two hundred years later. Clovis's defeat of Alaric II at Vouillé in 507 terminated one of history's major alternatives. It decided that post-Roman Europe was to be Frankish, not Gothic; Catholic not Arian; and that its rulers would be heritors of Clovis, not of Alaric and Euric.

Now, thirty-one darkening years after Odoacer had ordered Romulus Augustulus to vacate the western imperial throne, the eastern emperor, Anastasius, appointed Clovis honorary consul with insignia and uniform, in a gesture of far-reaching possibilities. The honorary consul returned the compliment by placing Anastasius's likeness on the coins of the realm. Bishop Gregory's *History* offers no speculations about Clovis's imperial ambitions, yet such speculations are irresistible. In the few years until his death in 511, at the then-considerable age of sixty-two, the lion-maned Clovis adopted the manner and policies of an aspiring *caesar*. There was just enough of the old imperial infrastructure remaining (more of it in the Gallo-Roman south and west) to try to build upon it a much-scaled-down, Frankish version of the Roman Empire. There was the new capital at Paris, in imitation of Constantine the Great's metropolis on the Bosporus; and, like Constantine at Nicaea, there was Catholic Clovis (instructed in the finer points of theology by Bishop Remigius) presiding over a great ecclesiastical council at Orléans. There was the new church dedicated to the Holy Apostles in Paris, however pitiable its comparison to the original Hagia Sophia dedicated by Constantius I. Finally, in the spirit of Theodosius I, there was the compilation and promulgation in writing of the *Lex Salica* in 511—the Salic Law, or laws of the Salian Franks.[3]

This remarkable document was to be transcendently important to the process of Gallic self-definition. It was the ideational script from which the Latin "race" would read down through centuries of self-construction, the *Ur*-text in Latin and German from which the Franco-Latin persona was gradually redacted. It told the Franks who they were and what they should become. They were among God's chosen people, Catholic, and "free of heresy," trumpeted the preface or preamble to the laws, "brave in war, faithful in peace, wise on their counsels, of noble body, of immaculate purity, of choice physique, courageous, quick and impetuous. . . ." Others had been housebroken, but the Franks "shook off the hard yoke of the Roman in battle."[4] Thus, the *Lex Salica* was nothing less than the founding charter of the evolving European mindset, of which the Salian Franks, as God's chosen people, were the anointed forerunners. In fact, the origins of the Franks (a "tribal swarm" somewhere between the Rhine and Elbe Rivers) were as inauspicious as the part they would play in the shaping of Europe was auspicious. They entered the Western Roman Empire in the early 260s, carving a deadly pathway with the double-headed axe from the Rhine south across Gaul. *Frank*, meaning "brave" and "free," was the name they gave themselves. They were inseminated from the beginning with the powerful germ of nationhood and its complement of obligatory *mission civilisatrice*. In the coming encounter of Franks and Muslims, theirs would be a meeting of expansionist *doppelgängers*.

The incomparable Clovis had rolled out an empire over the still-usable roads the Romans had cut into the northern quadrant of their empire. He reanimated the decayed Gallo-Roman bureaucracies in Burgundy, Provence, Languedoc, and other parts of Gaul, all the while mimicking the grandeur of the Caesars. Clovis glued together with sheer willpower and talent a simulacrum of the Roman Empire that his eponymous grandfather, Merovech (the first Frankish ruler noted by history), had fought to preserve. Unconquered by pagan Rome, but conquering for Catholic Rome, the people of the Salic Law proceeded to distinguish themselves from the other tribes emergent from the northern fastnesses. In contrast to all the other German warrior castes who kept apart from the original Celts and the Gallo-Romans, the Franks under Clovis abolished distinctions in law and practice between themselves and all Catholic inhabitants of the new kingdom, irrespective of ethnicity. Intermarriage with Gallo-Romans, tabooed by the Visigoths, became common. Saintly Bishop Remigius of Reims, by whom Clovis was baptized with the holy ampula brought from heaven by a white dove, deployed regiments of clergy to sow the Gospel of Christ's divinity among the peoples of the realm. Had the Merovingian superstate survived Clovis, the perilous predicament in which the Roman pontiffs soon found themselves surely would have been averted. The Franks would have stood like a firm dike between the rising tide of Gothic Arianism and the papacy. But as steep as was his learning curve, Clovis remained imprisoned in a congenitally Germanic conception of the State (an abstraction he may even have dimly grasped) as family property. With his death, the unlikely empire of the king of the Franks was sundered by sibling mayhem and tribal conflict.[5]

The Indian summer of early sixth-century institutional restoration and political progress under Clovis, as recorded (if more allegorically than historically) in Bishop Gregory's still-correct Latin, was followed by a long winter of crude substitutes, exhausted forms, and internecine strife. Only some sixty years after Clovis's death, the cradle of Clovis's Catholic confession, the bishopric of Rome, was again menaced with extinction by one of the deadliest barbarian infestations yet to sweep across the Italian peninsula: the Langobards ("Long Beards") of Scandinavia. The Catholic kingdom built by Clovis, for which the bishops had rejoiced mightily, was a shadow of itself by that time. The Eastern Roman Empire was locked in another long, wasting struggle with its Iranian nemesis. The few thousand troops it was able to spare for the protection of the Eternal City and the exarchate at Ravenna merely served as red flags to the Langobard (or Lombard) bull, this latest Germanic intruder. In that hour of mortal peril, as a sea of hostile Arianism rose ever higher, the bishop of Rome found himself virtually deserted. The Holy Father had few illusions about the efficacy of scripture, crucifixes, or holy relics to turn away the threatening horde. Practitioners of the true Trinitarian faith abounded in the old Gallo-Roman provinces of the south and west, but their military value to the pontiff was much diminished—not merely by distance but by chronic decline in martial ardor. As for Christian Hispania, the situation of true Catholics under the heel of Arian Visigoths was to remain parlous until the late sixth century.

For a good many decades, it seemed that the decline of Catholicism and the rise of Arianism was as inescapable as had been the fall of Rome. Drowning in a hostile sea with no hope of rescue from the Arian Lombards by the Second Rome, the Roman pontiffs anxiously scanned the confessional horizon for an ally among the multitudinous wild men beyond the Alps.[6] It was an alarming *tour d'horizon* during much of the sixth and seventh centuries after the collapse of Clovis's Merovingian kingdom. Even if, as the holy fathers certainly believed, the Gospel of Christ was imperishable, they knew there was nothing imperishable about the physical church. Of the five original patriarchates, only Constantinople and Rome survived. The apostolic sees of Antioch, Jerusalem, and Alexandria were in the Muslim empire.

⁛

As turbaned *mujarrada* were about to sweep around the eastern end of the Pyrenees in ever-greater numbers in the early years of the eighth century, a remarkable scribe finished writing the history of his dark and deadly times. It is not known who he was or where he wrote, although the best evidence points to the Abbey of St. Denis, a few miles north of Paris. Papyrus was no longer available to write on in his world, only animal-skin parchment. Perhaps he sweetened a carafe of rough wine with honey or cinnamon while he shivered near the fire in a smoky room, his eyes straining in the penumbra as the stylus incised momentous events on the page. We know that the year was 727 when this scribe finished the *Liber Historiae Francorum,* known in English as *The Book of the History of the Franks* and abbreviated by medievalists as the *LHF.* He was a Salian Frank, and his homeland, Neustria ("New Lands"), the smaller but richer of the two Germanic kingdoms (Austrasia, or "East Lands," was the other), formed part of the core of Francia, or Frankland.[7]

This scribe, who devoted his life to keeping score of royal winners and losers, had almost finished his undertaking just as the Muslims began their probes into southwestern Gaul. The shock waves set off by the Islamic irruption nearly a century earlier were sweeping the rim of the Mediterranean at high tide. Yet the chronicler has nothing to say about the menace of Islam, which seemed a far-off happening in another world, even though he must have heard something of Islam's unwonted defeat by Duke Odo at the great Battle of Toulouse. The inhospitable corner of the world known to him had come about after the disintegration of the Merovingian superstate created in the fifth century by Clovis. He knew little else, and even what he knew came from shards randomly recovered from a stretch of history that had been violently trampled. The *LHF* is claustrophobic and suffers from memory loss, a perfect reflection of the historical consciousness of the Dark Ages—a dull mirror of an imploded civilization. To the scribe at St. Denis, the kingdom of the long-haired Clovis was by that time nearly as much the stuff of legend and mystery as was the fallen empire of the western Caesars.[8]

Between the lines of the *LHF*'s degraded Latin and royal deference can be read the free fall of Frankish civil society into jaggedly antagonistic fragments. As contradictory as it sounds, it was chaos in slow motion, for, as one student of this obscure period has written, "life crept rather than ran." The *LHF* chronicled a nadir. It was the story of the end of the line of what had begun as one of history's *tours de force*: Clovis's Merovingian Frankland. At the end of this line was the late-seventh-century beginning of another *tour de force*: Carolingian Frankland, or Francia. Where *The Book of the History of the Franks* ended, the *Chronicle of Fredegar,* also anonymously composed, carried forward into the late eighth century a story begun more than a hundred years earlier. Between these two foundational sources for the Dark Ages falls a time span from Clovis I (ca. 466–511) to Charles Martel (686–741), at which latter point the challenge of Islam evoked a world-historic response.

The downward spiral in Merovingian Gaul had compounded the misery of the bishopric of Rome. By the close of the sixth century, the Eternal City was moribund, a crepuscular near-wasteland of weeds and wolves and a mere twenty thousand dispirited, malarial residents eking out livings among monuments stripped of marble, public buildings cannibalized for their brick and bronze. Constantine I's great basilica, erected over the remains of the Apostle Peter in the swampy cemetery below Vatican Hill, sheltered the popes in monumental space by then beyond their resources to maintain. St. Peter's bones gave the bishops enormous moral authority, both real and potential. The bishops found their ecclesiastical power greatly restrained, however, by the autonomy and competition of a high clergy appointed by local synods responsive to local magnates. That the southern foundations of St. Peter's Basilica were slowly sinking into landfill might rightly have been divined as an augury of the papacy's imperiled future. The unevenly talented and often corrupt procession of bishops who occupied the great basilica struggled not just for authority but, periodically, for physical survival.[9]

To the north of Rome, those fiercest of the Germanic peoples, the Lombards had carved out a kingdom that would prove almost impervious to Latin institutions for more than two centuries. Compared with the Lombards, the Franks were cosmopolites. The Lombards arrived in northern Italia in the middle of the sixth century, a killing machine that pulverized the Ostrogoths to the west and the Byzantine enclave at Ravenna to the east.* Their great king, Alboin, established a capital at Pavia in the late 560s. Alboin and his successors applied themselves to slicing off pieces of the Roman patrimonium as they marauded into the south, pushed along by the even fiercer Avars. Lombard depredations had a sharp Arian edge. Hunting down Catholic clergy of whatever station was an act of faith for them. Virtually defenseless, the hierarchy and citizenry of Rome existed on borrowed time. Some thirty years earlier, Emperor Justinian had dispatched an army under the military genius Belisarius just large enough to wrest a portion of Italia from the barbarians. It was altogether insufficient, however, to arrest the tribal carving-up and general unraveling of the Italian peninsula. Indeed, when Belisarius's army marched from Ravenna to Rome, the neighborhood Ostrogoths had inflicted a terrible wound to the city in that fateful year of 537. They destroyed the aqueducts supplying hundreds of gallons of water to every man, woman, and child and to all the fountains and baths on Rome's seven hills.[10] Until the demolition of the splendid aqueducts, the Eternal City had rolled with the punches of the *Völkerwanderungen*, repelling or absorbing the serial predations of the German tribes while its citizens remained buoyed by their august heritage as the "first Romans."

Byzantine and *Byzantium* will be used from here onward.

An analogous entropy was underway about six hundred miles over the Alps. The Merovingian empire had dwindled after Clovis, but the dynasty would endure some ten unbroken generations, a succession of Chilperics, Dagoberts, Clothaires, and Sigiberts, as politically impotent in their final decades as they were symbolically indispensable—"*les rois fainéants*," the "do-nothing kings," as French historians labeled them with unforgiving severity.[11] Not all the monarchs were content to remain hirsute ciphers trundled to their few ceremonial duties in ox-drawn carts. Even so, their power slipped irretrievably away, decade by decade, into the hands of their chief ministers—the mayors of the palace of Austrasia and Neustria, the men without whose seals no official document was valid. Not for another quarter-century after the *LHF* chronicler concluded his work, however, was the last Merovingian to be tonsured, shorn of his traditional body-length beard, and sent to a monastery. Until that day came, the semidivine descendants of the illustrious Clovis continued to serve as pawns in the power contests among the two dozen or so great noble families of Frankland, who seldom lost a day scheming, murdering, and betraying one another.[12]

❖

As far back as the 650s, one family's display of royal ambition was so naked that it had alarmed its Dark Ages peers and come within an ace of destroying the clan. Grimoald I was mayor of the Austrasian palace and a master schemer whose family originated in a corner of Western Europe recently familiar as the Benelux countries. Grimoald's father, Pippin of Landen, a major magnate, and his uncle, Arnulf, archbishop of Metz, were exemplars of deviousness. Arnulfings or Pippinids, as the family line was known, were men and women on the move. Grimoald's bald maneuver was to inveigle the royal nonentity of Austrasia into adopting Grimoald's son as heir to the throne in place of the pious cretin's own infant son. Grimoald's ploy infuriated the magnates of Neustria, whose king was the Austrasian royal's younger brother. Details from these ill-lit times can be maddeningly elusive, but Grimoald's machinations appear to have caused a general consternation in both kingdoms, and ultimately, after his unhappy fate, a decade of mayhem, murder, and tonsurings (once tonsured, the victim was forced to enter a monastery) among the Austrasian nobility.[13]

Grimoald had been premature. His nephew would accomplish his *coup d'état* not quite a century later. Resolving not to suffer more chaos, the Austrasian magnates appealed to the palace mayor of Neustria to take charge of their affairs. This able worthy was none other than Pippin of Landen's grandson and Grimoald's nephew, Pippin of Heristal—calculating, avaricious, audacious, and battle-worthy. Added to these attributes was the enormous wealth of his wife, the equally calculating Countess Plectrude. Her dowry brought a broad swath of territory that stretched from Alsace to Cologne, and it paid for her husband's creaky war machine, soon needed to repel Austrasia's enemies. At the village of Tertry, near the Ardennes Forest, Pippin's horsemen pulverized the Neustrian army in 681, after which he settled enough scores to ensure his rule as palace mayor and de facto sovereign of both kingdoms for twenty-seven years. He and his court rotated among Metz and Paris and the family estates at Landen and Heristal—although *estates* sounds much too grand for low-slung, timbered structures and a few crude stone buildings.

Pippin II, mayor of the palace (*maior domus*) of Austrasia and true founder of the dynasty, expired of natural causes in December 714. Three months earlier, Musa ibn Nusayr and Tariq ibn Ziyad had sailed from Sevilla for their appearance before Caliph al-Walid. The mayor's oldest son and heir, Grimoald, had been murdered in church not long before that. This Grimoald's six-year-old son, Theudoald, was too young to ascend to the dignity of mayor of the palace. Drogon, Pippin's second son and *dux* (duke) of Champagne, was long dead. Grimoald and Drogon were sons of Pippin's legitimate spouse, Plectrude, a convention-defying Frankish noblewoman who upended the political order of her time. There was a third son, twenty-seven-year-old Karl, or Charles the Bastard, in every respect other than maternal descent an ideal successor to his father. His contemporaries found him to be a warrior who was "uncommonly well educated and effective in battle." Yet Charles's father had passed over him for the preferments of office. No summons had come when Pippin lay dying without a suitable adult heir. In a later time, it would be said that Charles's succession problem was illegitimacy. His mother, Alpaide, an uncommonly beautiful woman, had been one of Pippin's mistresses. She was born of undistinguished parentage in a village near Liege. Despite the Church's conscientiousness in the matter of marital vows, however, bastardy was not yet a disability for high office among the Franks.

Charles's problem was his ambitious mother and his aggrieved, strong-willed stepmother, Plectrude. Plectrude was grandmother/guardian of Grimoald's boy, Theudoald. Pippin's treatment of her had been callous. In the first throes of passion for Alpaide, he banished Plectrude from the circle of family and intimates. His public concubinage had brought thunderous reproach from the bishop of Maastricht and other high clergy. Plectrude bore the indignity with the prim grace of her caste. Her generous dowry included Echternach, a once-magnificent Roman villa near Trier that Pippin consented to transfer to the Benedictine order, so she repaired to Echternach to devote herself to good works and knowledge. Echternach became a powerhouse of learning under her sage patronage, a point of light piercing the age's omnipresent opacity. Meanwhile, Alpaide and her relatives decided to ensure Charles the Bastard's inheritance of the mayoralty by murdering Grimoald as he knelt praying. The scheme failed when the ailing mayor, who lay unconscious, unexpectedly regained his senses. Pippin had the culprits killed and then lapsed into a terminal coma.[14]

Plectrude's failure to take religious vows permitted her to take hurried leave of Echternach in order to promote her grandson's claims. She conceived an audacious gambit to which her husband's illegitimate son was an obstacle. Dispatching her emissary to Paris to demand acknowledgment of her six-year-old grandson as Austrasian palace mayor, whom she herself appointed, Plectrude threw Charles into prison and set out to rule Frankland and another inconsequential Merovingian principality through her grandson.[15] A Frankland ruled by a powerful woman ran against the German grain—to say nothing of tribal sentiments elsewhere. Her temerity united an aghast Neustrian nobility within six months of her coup. The first weeks of 716 saw a large force of Neustrians, commanded by their king and palace mayor, advancing on the Meuse River. Saxon raiding parties menaced Austrasia from the north. The duke of the

Frisians, with his strong contingent, marched on Cologne. Austrasia faced certain defeat in a classic pincer movement. Within the kingdom, much of the nobility showed itself disinclined to fight for its Pippinid mayor and his grandmother. The confused situation enabled Charles the Bastard to escape his cell and raise a band of warriors among his mother's people, who welcomed him as the hope of the family and as Austrasia's only chance of independent survival.

For a few weeks, it looked as though Plectrude had bought a second chance for herself by handing over the treasury to the Neustrians and relinquishing authority over the Austrasian mayoralty. Charles had raced to overtake the Neustrians, pouncing on them without warning as they retired with carts overloaded with valuables. His victory at Amblève in April 716 was a serious reversal for an independent Neustria and the allied duchy of Burgundy. It was also the beginning of the end for the Merovingian monarchy. Hard on his victory at Amblève, Charles proceeded to crush Plectrude's lackluster forces in the spring of 717, before again chasing down the Neustrian palace mayor and his reorganized army on their own territory. The scribe of the *Early Annals of Metz* has nothing to say about what Charles did with Plectrude, but he roundly reviles her for overweening ambition and hapless scheming.[16] Her unnerving example would serve the cause of female exclusion from politics among the Franks in much the same way that A'isha's example had been censured among the Arabs. Countess Plectrude was dead by the end of the year.

In Paris, they still regarded Charles as an upstart who had no right to the office of mayor. The Neustrian king and palace mayor rejected his peace offers out of hand and proceeded to assemble a powerful coalition of Burgundians and Duke Odo's Aquitainians. "The Bastard" was outnumbered, but the enemy was outsmarted. He smashed the Neustrians and the Aquitainians at Cambrai and Soissons in 719 and pressed on to occupy Paris. The Neustrian *roi fainéant* was forced to abdicate in favor of Charles's own Merovingian cipher, one Clothaire IV, which finally brought Ripuarian and Salian Franks under a single, omnipotent Pippinid mayor.[17] No longer "the Bastard," the new palace mayor displayed the qualities of initiative and ruthlessness that awaited the sobriquet by which history would know him—Charles Martel, "the Hammer."

In the opinion of the Neustrian author of the *LHF*, whose country-men and -women Charles had trounced, Charles the Bastard was "uncommonly well educated." Minimal literacy might have been a desir-able family attribute for the job of palace mayor, the one person in the kingdom without whose affixed seal no royal document was valid. For Charles, a semblance of literacy and a fair amount of rote learning may have been survival tools growing up in the shadow of his stepmother's sons and preferred heirs. Keeping a safe distance from Countess Plec-trude, he appears to have taken advantage of his ambiguously privileged status to improve himself under the tutelage of the extraordinary Bene-dictines in his father's service. These sojourners from Anglo-Saxon Northumbria made their unbidden appearance in Frankland sometime in 690. There were but two in the beginning: Willibrord and Wynfrith, among the most learned priests in Western Christendom. The six-foot Wynfrith would be immortalized as St. Boniface, one of the great institution-builders of the Dark Ages. Charles profited from his expo-sure as a boy to the intellectual culture of these Benedictines, although it is unknown how much Latin he mastered, how well he could write, and how many numbers he could count.

Very probably, what he possessed of these capacities was very mini-mal, but what he did possess was managerial acumen, a grasp of political design, a logic of statecraft that would decisively advance the construc-tion of the infant French state. Benedictine reforming zeal and drive for order, of which Boniface was the embodiment, would have nurtured the triumphant Pippinid's innate qualities. Whatever the long-haired stu-dent owed to mentoring Benedictines, however, the twenty-eight-year-old new mayor of the Austrasian palace owed even more to the school of cold-blooded cunning. From the pinnacle of power to which he had risen against the odds, Charles envisaged himself the builder of a kingdom that would stretch from the Rhine to the Muslim Pyrenees—a Clovis without even a third of the resources Clovis had possessed.

Charles came late to power but early in the Dark Ages to the process of building a strong kingdom. If the time was not yet right for a change in dynasty, this ruthlessly calculating Pippinid ruled as though Clothaire IV and Thierry IV, the *rois fainéants* he installed at Cologne, were nonexistent. The task ahead was objectively just short of impossible. After forcing several distinguished enemies to enter religious orders, the young duke promptly began rearranging the map of Gaul. Charles's kingdom of the moment was little more than a faint reminder of the sixth-century Frankish superstate. The centrifugal forces of the times militated fiercely against the most heroic efforts at gathering-in of resources, of consolidating and enlarging central institutions, of simply finding the wherewithal to assemble and sustain a war machine. In the two hundred years since Clovis's death, the economy of Frankland had spiraled downward to the point that it responded barely, if at all, to the Mediterranean engine that had once quickened it.[18]

Westward from the Rhine to the Seine, north to the English Channel, and as far south as Alsace and the upper Loire, an ad hoc zone of barter, payment in kind, self-sufficient agriculture, and accelerating serfdom prevailed. Gold specie had disappeared, although silver coins had begun to circulate again. Even in the Ile-de-France, the historic core of Neustria and richest of Charles's newly acquired provinces, olive oil had given way to wax produced through beekeeping and animal fat. Spices, jade, tinted silks, and carved ivory were dimmest memories, as was the papyrus long ago supplanted by expensive parchment. Women wove and spun rough cloth and embroidered it with bone needles. Food, however, was plentiful. The people grew barley for its heavy dark grain and beer-making properties, rather than wheat. Improved breeds of cattle, along with much brine-preserved fish, made for an energy-fueled diet sufficient to grow the big-boned frames of the typical blond Frank warrior.[19] Pippinid Frankland was a place where the adapted Roman water mill was the sum of cutting-edge technology.

Had satellite imaging existed, those distinguishing features of civilized life—towns, roads, cultivated expanses—would have been mostly invisible to the camera eye under their canopy of primeval growth. Beneath the green scrim, millions of wolves roamed the twilit forests; packs prowled the rutted streets of Compiègne, Soissons, Quierzy, Aisne, and the other skimpily peopled settlements, and even of Paris and Orléans. The clearing of the great forests was yet six hundred years away. Charles's was an age mainly of wooden buildings; walled enclosures and stone castles would proliferate some 150 years later, in response to the Viking infestation. As with the Great Wall of China, said to be visible from the moon, satellite imaging would have detected two Roman highways laced across Charles's realm. From the wooden longbridge over the Rhine, a northern route ran to the Pyrenees from Magdeburg through Cologne to Paris, Orléans, and Tours to Bordeaux. The southern road continued on from Reims via Nîmes, Narbonne, and Gerona to Barcelona—the route that had brought slaves from Slavic lands to the Iberian Visigoths. More deadly than wolves, though, were packs of brigands along the crumbling, unpoliced Roman highways, as well as the dreaded Basques at the terminus of the northern route.[20]

By the time Tariq ibn Ziyad crossed the Gibraltar strait, the Gallo-Roman peoples in Septimania and Provence, around the northern rim of the great sea, were an arrested economic force, locked in slow-motion imitation of the agricultural and commercial activity of their Roman prime. Twenty years later, the Muslims pouring into the plains of Septimania (the Catalan region) and northward over Aquitania came as the forward wave of a civilization that was, by comparison with that of its enemies, an organic marvel of coordinated kingdoms, cultures, and technologies in service to a politico-cultural agenda incomparably superior to the primitive force pulling itself together at Metz and Paris.

**

Muslims came to Europe because of the plight of a woman, as some of the sources would have it. In a similar vein, their troubles in Hispania were said to have begun with the pretensions of another woman. Obedient to the immemorial conventions of misogyny, the *Narrative of the Conquest of al-Andalus* blames the misfortunes of 'Abd al-Aziz, Musa's son, on Egilona, King Roderic's daughter. As her story has come down to us from men whose *raison d'être* was to make history the record of other men's significance, the significance of the Egilona of legend is reputed to have been woeful. Entrusted with the reins of power by his absent father, the middle-aged governor of *al-Andalus* was soon reproached by the no-nonsense Berbers and proud sons of the Prophet's Companions for the royal affectations of the court at Sevilla, where it was alleged that Egilona set the tone and etiquette of her husband's establishment. Egilona badgered 'Abd al-Aziz to adopt the court etiquette she had known well at Toledo (a poor imitation of Constantinople's ceremonial pomposity) in order to comport himself with the dignity befitting a great sovereign. Why did she not see his people "glorifying you," she is supposed to have asked haughtily. "They do not prostrate themselves before you as the people of my father's kingdom glorified him." Soon those granted audience at Sevilla were obliged to bow in the presence of the *amir* of *al-Andalus*, now a browbeaten Visigoth version of a Caesar. Rumor spread that his wife had even secretly converted 'Abd al-Aziz to Christianity. Rising impatience became consternation, with regicide as the predictable outcome. 'Abd al-Aziz died either from poison taken with his meal or, as the *Narrative of the Conquest* vividly relates, from assassins' knives as he recited scripture in Sevilla's Friday Mosque.[21]

In reality, Musa's son died from an acute case of what might be called "caliphatitis." That the real culprit in the story was not Roderic's daughter, assigned the role of proverbial temptress, but, rather, the Commander of the Faithful, becomes obvious at the end of the rather fanciful story when al-Hakam describes Sulayman's morbid pleasure at receiving 'Abd al-Aziz's severed head "in the presence of the murdered man's father." Elimination of any possibility of competition appears to have been the signature of Sulayman's short reign. Centers of semiautonomous proconsular power were anathema to him. As for Princess Egilona, her objective importance is in what it represents in the rapid interracial commingling of Arabs and Berbers with Visigoths and Hispano-Romans well underway in the early Conquest. Having crossed the strait without women, the conquerors found wives and concubines among the conquered of all classes.[22] Egilona's sister, Sara, became the matriarch of a distinguished Andalusi Muslim clan. Moreover, since the early conquerors were but a numerical drop of Berbers in an indigenous ocean, they could hardly have duplicated the haughty *ashraf* exclusivity practiced elsewhere.

After 'Abd al-Aziz's assassination at the end of 714, a prolonged period of political turbulence ensued in *al-Andalus*: forty years of discontinuity, due partly to power politics swirling around the caliphate and partly to ethnic and tribal conflicts among the Andalusi Berbers and Arabs. Hardly had Musa and Tariq reported to Damascus when the Butr and Baranis Berbers, and as many Arabs from Yemen, Jordan, and southern Palestine, began crossing the strait in a flow that would bring their numbers to more than one hundred thousand in the first few years after the Conquest. With the Arabs came an almost congenital factional enmity that still defies explanation, the blood feud between northern and southern Arabs (Qays and Yemeni, respectively) tracking back to the second *fitna* and the bitter battle at Marj Rahit (684–85).[23] Although the weak central authority during the "period of dependent governors" allowed fairly steady commercial and agricultural prosperity, the seeds were planted for tribal and regional conflict that would flourish disastrously at some of the most critical moments in the future. Twenty-two *amirs* succeeded one another in *al-Andalus* at an average rate of one every two years.

Musa's grandnephew, Ayyub ibn Habib al-Lakhmi, who moved the capital from Sevilla to the more central Cordoba in 717, displayed considerable statecraft while he lasted, but he, too, was soon undone by the machinations of Damascus. He had time enough, however, to found the town of Calatayud on the northern perimeter of the Muslim realm. Calatayud—"quarter of the Jews" (in Arabic, *Kalaat al-Yahud*)—evidenced the ongoing Andalusian mutuality of Arab and Jew. Of secondary importance at the time, although of momentous future significance, were the pockets of Visigothic resistance in the far north beyond the Duero River. Al-Lakhmi took anxious note of these developments and ordered a military sweep through restive Asturias, a region into which many tens of thousands had trekked after Musa's army crushed the last fragments of organized resistance. Neither Romans nor Visigoths had ever come close to taming the people of this heavily forested region in the massifs of northernmost Cantabria and Asturias. At the very moment of Arabo-Berber victory, a nation in embryo formed of Visigoths, Latinized Iberians, and original peoples, the most determined of whom took refuge in the Picos de Europa, made inaccessible by swift rivers and snow-capped cordilleras. Pelayo, a fugitive Visigoth nobleman from the Battle of Guadalete, rallied the local people (the Asturis), who elected him prince of Cangas de Onís.

Possibly, as Spanish sources believe, Pelayo was Roderic's nephew. Ironically, the feat that was to immortalize the "king of Cangas de Onís" in Spanish history almost escaped the Arab chroniclers' notice. The skirmish at a place called Covadonga, between Pelayo's few hundred followers and the Berber force sent to eradicate them in 717 or 718, was a mere sidebar to the latter. "A despicable barbarian . . . rose in the land of Galicia," sniffed one historian of the Conquest. "Thirty barbarians, perched on a rock," were of no consequence. For the Spanish, though, Covadonga would serve as the founding myth, the shining moment from which to date the rebirth of the Christian nation. "The slings were prepared, swords flashed, spears were brandished. Arrows were shot incessantly," records the *Chronicle of Alfonso III* portentously. "But on this occasion the power of the Lord was not absent."[24] At Cangas de Onís, suspended above the vertiginous Los Beyos ravine in the Sierra de Covalierda, Spain, mythical and *reconquistadora,* emerged virtually undetected.

While Caliph Sulayman's war machine revved up and then sputtered out before Constantinople in the fall of 718, small groups of mostly Berber Muslims had already begun to cross the Pyrenees above Pamplona or to pivot past them along the Costa Brava. These raiding parties into Aquitaine and Languedoc, led by warriors whose names are long forgotten, were not much more than sorties, *razzías* in quest of booty rather than invasions for the purpose of settlement. But Muslim penetration beyond the great eastern mountain range eventually altered dramatically in scale and design when Damascus sent new instructions to al-Samh ibn Malik al-Khawlani (718–21), one of the ablest of the early governors-general. He lost no time putting reliable fellow Syrian *wazírs* in charge of the principal cities, recruiting the *dhimmis* for state service, building mosques and converting churches to Muslim houses of worship, and devising carrot-and-stick policies for the restive Berbers.[25] Damascus had decided to send armies sweeping through Gaul and Italy into Macedonia and Greece, until Muslim power completely rimmed the ancient, common lake—"thus to make the Mediterranean a Moslem sea," as J. F. C. Fuller, the eminent British military historian asserted half a century ago. If old Musa ibn Nusayr was alive in the summer of 719, he must have seen al-Samh's invasion of southwestern Gaul, the "Great Land" (*al-*

Ard al-Kabirah), as bitter personal vindication. The large, disciplined army of Berbers, reinforced by crack Syrian and Yemeni units, streamed into Septimania, that sliver of territory still ruled by the Visigoths, pillaging along the Golfe du Lion as it bore down on Narbonne. The old seaport capital of the Roman Empire's first colony in Gaul, Narbonne was the first prize to fall. Once the hub of the Gallo-Visigoth kingdom, and still an imposing shell of its former administrative and commercial importance, Narbonne was a major center of Arian Christianity. Arianism's appeal among the Goths had survived as a potent force east of the Pyrenees long after Reccared's embrace of Roman Catholicism.

Al-Samh followed 'Abd al-Aziz's precedent and granted the Narbonnais unfettered religious freedom. Carcassonne, on the Roman road heading northwest from the sea, was taken next. In Roman times, Carcassum had been a major diocese of the new Nazarene religion, a distinction it continued to hold under the Arian and then Catholic Visigoths in southern Gaul. Granting religious freedom seldom interfered with lucrative brigandage, however. The Muslims sacked Carcassonne, pillaging the tombs of Saints Paulus and Rusticus, appalling desecrations in Gallo-Roman eyes. When the bulk of the army returned to *al-Andalus* early the following year, flush with treasure and women, a portion remained as a permanent garrison in Narbonne, now the capital of Muslim Septimania.[26]

Al-Samh reappeared in the spring of 721, commanding an even larger army reinforced by more northern and southern Arabs and massive siege machinery. This was a full-scale *jihad* designed to level the strongest fortifications and settle the Prophet's servants in the vast sweep from the Pyrenees to the Loire. Aquitaine stretched from the Garonne River to the Loire. Roughly a fourth the size of Roman Gaul, it was the richest province and retained much of its Latin culture. The invaders marched northwest from Narbonne on the old Roman road toward Toulouse, Aquitaine's stout-walled capital. The mail-coated Arabs and their barefoot Berbers, halting in unison to pray prone on the Roman highway, were apparitions outside the experience of any Aquitainian peasant or lord. Toulouse was bursting at the seams with asylum-seekers when the *amir's* many thousands deployed before its battlements, but the duke (*dux*) of Aquitaine wasn't among them. Odo (Eudo or Eudes, as he was later Gallicized) had ridden off to assemble a relief army while the Toulousains held on long enough to make the gambit successful.

Odo was a Frank by heritage, but his family had resided in Aquitaine long enough to have become thoroughly identified with his Latinized and largely Celtic people. The duke was in his late fifties when al-Samh invaded his duchy, a *grand seigneur* in full possession of his faculties and in superb physical condition. Because he had joined the losing side in a power struggle among his Frankish cousins a few years earlier, Odo now faced the gravest crisis of his life, with no prospect of assistance from outside Aquitaine. The siege of his capital was in its third month, with only a few weeks' worth of provisions, before Odo managed to assemble his nobility for a masterful surprise attack on the Muslim rear. Simultaneously, the city's gates swung open for a frontal attack by several thousand pike men, archers, and lancers—a rare feat of coordination that spelled disaster for the *amir*'s men. The Aquitainians' heavy horses plowed through the enemy mass as it surged into a narrow strip of land between the walls and the encircling cavalry. The slaughter on the narrow strip, where the Syrians and Berbers found themselves unable to maneuver, was terrible. More than half the Muslim army was destroyed on the blood-soaked plateau.* The mortally wounded governor-general's second in command steadied the bruised remnant enough for it to fight its way through the encirclement and escape to Narbonne.

Duke Odo was the first Christian ruler east of the Pyrenees whose command of mounted men in the field proved more than a match for the invaders.[27] The Battle of Toulouse registered as a footnote in the Arab accounts when it was mentioned at all. It was hardly a bump in the *jihad*, though. The Andalusi would require a decade of recovery and preparation before resuming their advance beyond the Pyrenees. When that occurred, 'Abd al-Rahman ibn 'Abd Allah al-Ghafiqi, the officer who salvaged part of al-Samh's army, would lead the invasion force. Odo's vic-

---

*Most sources do not refer to al-Samh's defeat as the *Balat al-Shuhada* ("Path of the Martyrs"). That distinction is generally, though not always, confined to the Battle of Poitiers in 732.

tory was a dress rehearsal for a confrontation a few years later upon which historians have lavished epic significance. His success retarded an advance that might otherwise have acquired a reinforced momentum that became unstoppable. When the Muslims returned to the charge, Gallo-Romans and Franks bowed to the necessity of cooperation.

Arabic sources describe Hisham ibn 'Abd al-Malik as a particularly avaricious and tightfisted caliph, most probably because the empire's declining tax revenues necessitated more taxable subjects and much tighter tax collecting—and war. Hisham's caliphate (724–43) was one of the longest of the Umayyads, a nineteen-year reign of almost uninterrupted expansionist, revenue-driven *jihads* in which Islam pushed its frontiers forward mightily at virtually every compass point. The caliph ordered his new governor-general at Cordoba to carry the holy war over the mountains. Four years after Toulouse, the anonymous author of the *Chronicle of Fredegar* bewailed the reappearance beyond the Pyrenees of the "mighty race of Ishmael, who are now known by the outlandish name of Saracens."[28] The scribe who "continued" the fourth book of *Fredegar* had reason to moan. *Amir* Ambasa ibn Suhaym al-Kalbi rolled up the Gallo-Roman hosts who dared face his "Saracens," exhorting his men straight across the southern flange of Gaul at breakneck speed. *Saracens,* an ancient Greek generic term (*Sarakenoi*) for "nomadic peoples," now came to signify "terrifying Arabs." The Saracens recaptured Carcassonne, took Nîmes, and thundered upward out of Languedoc into the Rhone Valley. At Arles, the Gallo-Romans stood and fought to the death at the river's edge until the Rhone flowed crimson. Ambasa's *mujarrada* advanced along the river upward past Lyon to Autun, the capital of Burgundy, which they sacked. A mere 180 miles southeast of Paris, seven-hundred-year-old Autun, with its temples, monumental arch, amphitheater, and baths, had been the pride of Roman Gaul. Although the bulk of the Muslim army withdrew before winter set in, nearly a fifth of Gaul remained under occupation by the race of Ishmael.[29]

The Myth of Poitiers

THE Battle of Poitiers was fought at a place about a third of the distance from Poitiers to Tours. Besides this now generally accepted fact, however, little else was agreed upon for many years about what Edward Gibbon called "an encounter which would change the history of the world." The persistence of Tours as the name of the battle is explained by the British determination to give pride of place to the 1356 victory over the French at Poitiers of Edward the Black Prince. There is consensus about the month of October. A more careful examination of the Arabic sources has now definitively fixed the year as

732, not the following year. Until the last half of the twentieth century, the exact location of the battle between the Saracens and the alliance of Franks and Aquitainians was also a subject of debate—so much so that one authority wrote of it simply as having been fought in a place "that historians have failed to identify with precision."[1] Like Tariq ibn Ziyad's victory near Medina-Sidonia twenty-one years earlier, Poitiers was an event in search of its battlefield.

Eleven years earlier, Duke Odo had led his cavalry to withering victory over Amir al-Samh and his forces at Toulouse, mortally wounding the governor-general and forcing the invaders to fall back on Narbonne, the coastal linchpin of Islamic power in Septimania.[2] Much had happened since this first Muslim defeat on the continent of Europe. Pippinid hegemony crystallized in those crucial eleven years after 721—temporal space available for evolving Frankish institutions. From the perspective of the era of nation-states formation, Toulouse was the battle that saved Western Christendom. Not that the Christian players in this historic confrontation could even have understood the meaning of such an outcome. Duke Odo would have just as soon seen both the Pippinids of Austrasia and the *amirs* of Cordoba perish. The duke had fought the Muslims in order to save his position in the scheme of things and to keep his estates. For a *grand seigneur* of the eighth century, the high stakes at Toulouse involved personal honor and territory—family and lands. By no stretch of imagination was Odo fighting to preserve the Catholic faith presided over by the bishop of Rome. Even less so was he animated by any notion of fidelity to a Roman imperium sustained by the emperor at Constantinople. For Odo and his warrior caste, whatever existed beyond the limits of a generously endowed Aquitaine was either foreign or foe or both. Well before there was feudalism the institution, there was feudalism the state of mind. No conception of Greater Gaul (or *Francia Magna*) as yet existed—nor, for that matter, would such an abstraction have been welcome to Aquitainians or Burgundians.

At Toulouse, Odo had fought for honor and independence. His Aquitainian magnates had responded to the peril, rallying behind their valiant overlord. That peril they had forestalled, only to see another menace on the eastern horizon. Odo had earned Duke Charles's enmity two years before the Battle of Toulouse when he joined forces with the Neustrians and Burgundians at Soissons to overthrow the Austrasian wonder. Soissons was a major humiliation, with Odo having to surrender Chilperic II, Neustria's refugee king, and his treasure and swear fealty to Charles the Bastard.[3] Neustria united with Austrasia under the belligerent Charles posed a terrible danger. Odo and the magnates of Aquitaine faced dismal choices: subjugation by Muslims or annexation by Franks.

Odo's solution to Aquitaine's annexation/subjugation emergency was ingeniously cynical and guaranteed to precipitate the problem it was designed to mitigate. In a phrase, the duke's solution was half again too clever. When not fighting together, Arabs and Berbers in al-Andalus fought among themselves. Whenever the central government at Cordoba was weak, the sub-emirs and walis, or governors of the distant provinces (many of them Berbers), exploited the situation in order to institutionalize their independence from the center. Whenever Cordoba attempted to exercise a centralizing authority, those same entities bridled at the merest interference. It was this restive situation at the edges of the Andalusian emirate, especially along the Pyrenees, that encouraged Odo to propose an astonishing Christian/Muslim alliance. High in the Catalan Pyrenees, where some of Europe's best ski slopes exist today, the Berber wali of Cerdanya chafed from the reins of Cordovan overlordship. Cerdanya's location at the southwestern tip of Gaul made it both a potential buffer state between the Cordovan jihad and Aquitaine, as well as a partner in the Gallo-Roman struggle to stop the Austrasian steamroller at the Loire.[4]

Once he learned of the wali's determination to escape the centralizing pull of Cordoba, the duke of Aquitaine rolled the geopolitical dice by offering his daughter in consideration for a compact of mutual defense. The wali of Cerdanya's name comes down to us mangled in the various sources as something like 'Uthman ibn Abi Nessa (or Tessa)—Munuza to the Christians. The daughter was Lampegie. Nothing more than her name has survived the entropy of history. What Lampegie thought of her father's deal as she was transported to Munuza's qasr (palace) is unrecorded. If she bore the deep imprint of her Catholic faith, as was likely for a high-born female, she faced the anguish of conversion to an alien creed. She knew well that contemporary nuptial politics reduced the personal qualities of the husband her father had chosen to irrelevancies. Yet if Lampegie had a care for manly courage and firm convictions, she may have perceived early on that her *wali* lacked these virtues. Clearly, her father was unfazed by the anomalous religious and cultural implications that would appall a much later generation of Christians.[5]

The consequences of the union of Lampegie of Aquitaine and Munuza of Cerdanya were as momentous as the marriage of another Aquitainian noblewoman of the future, Eleanor. To Odo and a critical mass of similarly alarmed notables, the nuptial ploy of an independent Catalunya allied to an autonomous Aquitaine was an inspired checkmate to Arab and Frankish subjugation. In Metz and Cordoba, predictably, there was great consternation. In late spring of 731, an angry Charles the Bastard led his Austrasian heavy cavalry into Burgundy, rolling over Burgundian levies and advancing westward to visit comparable punishment on the Aquitainians. On their way to a battlefield reckoning, the Franks wreaked havoc across much of Aquitaine as they pillaged peasant villages and vacuumed up grain and livestock to fuel some five thousand veteran killers. When Charles found Odo near Toulouse toward the end of the summer, the duke found himself compelled to give battle without his son-in-law's help. Appeals for troops had been met with silence from Cerdanya, where Lampegie's husband, Munuza, had suffered a nervous breakdown.

The duke of Aquitaine lost much more than a battle to the mayor of the palace of Austrasia on a summer day in 731. Austrasia had been at war almost uninterruptedly since its ruler's decisive victory at Soissons twelve years earlier. Stolid, disciplined Frankish infantry went into battle supported by more heavy cavalry than enemies were capable of fielding. Odo's forces were disastrously outmatched, his infantry ground up somewhere near the Garonne, and his horse sent flying for safety. He was compelled to acknowledge King Theudoald IV, Charles's Merovingian puppet, and place his domain under the protection of the Austrasian/Neustrian powerhouse (although without intending to honor his pledge one season longer than necessary).[6]

Odo's defeat carried an even larger penalty, however. He was to be deprived of his rightful place in history. What better corroboration of the aphorism that winners write history than the portrait of the duke that has come down to us from the *Continuations of Fredegar* and the *History of the Lombards* of Paul the Deacon? The unknown author of the fourth *Fredegar* was a Burgundian who read the politics of the times accurately. For him, as for Paul the Deacon later, Charles of Austrasia saved Christendom, and the duke of Aquitaine was an arrogant fool who jeopardized the future of Europe by inviting the Muslims into Gaul. Odo's victory at Toulouse in 721 (without which much of Gaul might have disappeared into the *Dar al-Islam*) almost disappears from the record.[7] It served no purpose to the partisan chroniclers of Duke Charles's achievements to observe that his 731 intervention in Aquitaine invited disaster for Gallo-Romans and Franks alike.

Meanwhile, as Gallic scores were being settled across the mountain range, a new governor-general of *al-Andalus* assembled a large army to eliminate the renegade Munuza, the Berber *wali* of Cerdanya. In this era of "dependent governors," *Amir* 'Abd al-Rahman 'Abd Allah al-Ghafiqi stood high above his peers. Charismatic, the new governor-general possessed special status in the Umayyad hierarchy because of his mentoring by a son of one of the Prophet's earliest disciples. Intelligent, eloquent, and an accomplished administrator, al-Ghafiqi commanded unprecedented deference among *al-Andalus*'s original Muslims—the *baladiyyun*, as they were called. When the *amir* advanced on Cerdanya with some fifteen thousand troops in the fall of 731, Munuza ran for the mountain heights, his situation now desperate after the sharp setback suffered by his Aquitainian father-in-law. In one account, he committed suicide by leaping from a mountain; in another, Munuza perished at the hands of al-Ghafiqi. In any case, his camphored head was packed in brine and sent as a trophy to Damascus, along with Lampegie, who vanished into the maw of a harem.[8]

Elimination of the *wali* of Cerdanya restored the *jihad*'s line of advance. Twenty years after the destruction of Visigothic Hispania, a determined Muslim commander fully intended to duplicate Tariq ibn Ziyad's feat at Guadalete on the rolling plains of Aquitaine. Once winter passed, 'Abd al-Rahman planned to swoop down into Gaul from the western end of the Pyrenees, following the old Roman highway from

Pamplona. The caliph, Hisham ibn 'Abd al-Malik, expected results from this far-flung region of his empire. In Damascus, al-Ghafiqi was thought to be the commander finally capable of drawing the Mediterranean circle (from Gaul's Golfe du Lion to Italia's Tyrrhenian Sea) almost, if not completely, to a close—writing, as it were, the penultimate chapter in the capture of Constantinople and the conquest of a continent.

⁑

In the northeastern corner of the Iberian peninsula, the shortest distance between two points is a curved line. The paved Roman road from Sarakusta (today's Zaragoza) undulates across Navarra to Pamplona and then shimmies into the Pyrenees until it swerves out of Roncesvalles down into the Basque region of Aquitaine below. This was the route 'Abd Allah al-Ghafiqi, the much-admired *amir* of *al-Andalus*, chose for the conquest and occupation of southwestern Gaul in 732. In numbers unseen in the living memory of Gallo-Romans, no fewer than thirty thousand, and perhaps as many as fifty thousand, Arabs and Berbers swarmed over the landscape of Aquitaine. Fifteen thousand were campaign-hardened warriors—*muqatila* hungry for booty and primed for martyrdom. They came with their women and their families, a small nation of people on the move. The caliph had spoken. Across the cold English Channel, news of the *amir*'s massive incursion inspired apocalyptic forebodings in the Einstein of the Dark Ages, the Venerable Bede, as fires rained from the heavens. "Two comets appeared around the sun, striking terror into all who saw them," the great Anglo-Saxon mathematician and chronicler noted. "A swarm of saracins [sic] ravaged Gaul with horrible slaughter. . . ."9 Another contemporary described the invaders as like "a brush fire fanned by the winds" as they swept across Aquitaine.

This time, Odo and his men failed to stem the Andalusian torrent. Nor was their failure surprising, in light of their mauling by the Austrasians the previous summer. They fought a disciplined, motivated army whose commander possessed a special connection to the Prophet Muhammad; and they were outnumbered two to one. 'Abd al-Rahman's men drove the Aquitainians to the banks of the Garonne near Bordeaux, where the latter were disastrously bloodied. The duke fled for his life with the terrible sounds of the sacked city in his ears. "Only God knows how many died and vanished," lamented the scribe of the *Mozarabic Chronicle of 754*.[10] Poitiers, on the old imperial highway, came next. One of the oldest Gallo-Roman towns, it lay directly in the path of the Muslims, north by northeast from Bordeaux.

As the people watched from their stone battlements, the Arabo-Berber legions approached unopposed, the white banners of the Umayyads snapping in the autumn breeze. In the fourth century, one of the holiest priests and wisest theologians of the Catholic faith had drawn about himself at Poitiers a pious cadre of fearless proselytizers. This venerated priest, St. Hilary (St. Hilaire), lay entombed just outside the city walls in an impressive basilica raised by the *Poitevins* to honor their bishop's incomparable ministry. 'Abd al-Rahman's army slowed its swath of fire and destruction just long enough to plunder the basilica, stripping St. Hilary's tomb of its overlay of gold and precious stones and torching the building's interior.

Sixty miles farther up the Roman road lay the holy city of Tours—"*la ville sacrée de la Gaule chrétienne*." Not only had it served as the episcopate of St. Gregory, author of the *Historia Francorum* (*History of the Franks*), Tours was the resting place of St. Martin, the fourth-century Roman centurion who "found Jesus" while on duty in Gaul and became Hilary's most illustrious protégé. As the patron saint of soldiers and the favorite of Clovis, St. Martin was the object of the most intense veneration. Because of the saint's steadfastness, Aquitaine had been cleansed of Arianism. The destruction of Tours and the defilement of St. Martin's richly endowed basilica would have been a catastrophe rivaling the advent of the Antichrist. An even more terrible prospect impended once Tours had been taken. The *amir*'s trajectory would follow the course of the Loire out of the city, pressing on to Orléans and onward into the heart of the Frankish realm. No Frank—least of all the Neustrians—could forget that one of 'Abd al-Rahman's predecessors had charged up the Rhone to within a hundred or so miles of Paris seven years earlier and put Autun to the torch before retreating. But that predecessor, Ambasa ibn Suhaym al-Kalbi, had retreated. 'Abd al-Rahman ibn 'Abd Allah al-Ghafiqi had come to stay.[11]

Duke Charles was campaigning far away on the Danube when news of the Muslim invasion reached him. It came with a desperate appeal from Odo for assistance. Fredegar the Continuator had no doubt that Charles's military prowess was due to Christ's help—"*Christo auxiliante*"—but Charles also helped himself by setting his men an example of personal valor and hard-nosed concern for their welfare that enabled him to extract remarkable feats on the battlefield. With several thousand men already mustered and more summoned to the colors, he force-marched his army across the map of Frankland into Aquitaine. His cavalry and infantry almost certainly numbered ten thousand, the bulk of it infantry. Odo awaited the mayor's arrival at Tours, where the former had managed to replace some of the losses suffered on the banks of the Garonne, so that Aquitainian manpower swelled the ranks of the defenders probably by another two or three thousand.

Duke Odo had humbly reaffirmed his vow of fealty to Charles. He could do no less, and this time the mayor demanded high-born hostages to seal the bargain. The Muslim army was only a few days from Tours, marching fast up the Roman highway and confident of yet more glory in the name of the Prophet. It is an assumption, a reasonable one, that al-Ghafiqi planned to quarter his army in Tours for the winter. The autumn weather was still dry and clear, but winter chills were beginning to be felt. Grave Christians in Tours accoutered themselves as though for Armageddon. Somber, with heads uncovered, the men of Austrasia and Aquitaine followed their admired leaders, Charles and Odo, into the Basilica of St. Martin, where chain-mail tunics and oiled leather jerkins shone and glowed in the suffused light of the tapers. Wafted incense, hymns by sweet-voiced boys, verses of the *Te Deum laudamus*, and vows to die for Christ must have momentarily exalted many of these veteran killers, adventurers, aspiring panjandrums, and a few honorable men. On, or soon after, October 15, 732, the revictualed armies set out from Tours for the old town of Châtellerault, more or less due south.

Although hilly in places, the region south of Tours is fairly flat—good country for cavalry. Even today, industrial development is still insignificant in this part of the Touraine, where the hectares are given over to wheat and the Vouvray grape. Much of the present-day landscape within the triangle of Châtellerault, the Vienne River, and Poitiers—especially the sparsely populated space just below Châtellerault—probably looks as it did when Charles and Odo led their forces into the triangle to meet al-Ghafiqi's Arabo-Berber army as it marched on Tours. The Roman road, still paved with the original tightly fitted stones, bypasses Moussais-la-Bataille, a tiny settlement barely eligible to be called a village, and runs on past the second-century Roman amphitheater just below the undistinguished village of Vouneuil-sur-Vienne. Some French scholars believed the conflict had unfolded on the banks of the Boivre, a small river south of Poitiers. Most were inclined to favor Moussais-la-Bataille, north of Poitiers, even though for many years none could say anything more specific about the actual site.[12]

Until the end of the last century, Moussais-la-Bataille was little more than a historian's place name, a village found either within or at the bottom of the page of a scholarly text, but of vague and undetermined actual location. In *Charles Martel et la Bataille de Poitiers,* Maurice Mercier and André Seguin set out in 1944 to re-create the Battle of Poitiers in its exact locus by meticulous scrutiny of the ancient texts—a scrutiny that arrived by process of elimination at Moussais-la-Bataille, which looks today much as it did nearly thirteen hundred years ago. Building on their meticulous extraction of facts from the morass of Arabic and French sources, other medievalists, notably Jean-Henri Roy and Jean Deviosse, gradually pieced together a vivid narrative of the historic combat as it may have unfolded over a seven-day period that climaxed on a tilted plain just outside Moussais-la-Bataille.[13] From a slightly elevated plateau, whose sight lines offer an unobstructed, 180-degree sweep of the gradually sloping terrain, today's visitor to the village is positioned almost on the exact spot where Duke Charles weighed his chances for victory as he watched the approaching Saracens.

❖

If, as choirs of Eurocentric historians were to intone, the fate of the West was truly decided at Poitiers, it was not decided all in a day. Warfare in the eighth century (and for nearly seven hundred years afterward) almost always took its time building to bloody finales. Combatants on foot and horseback armed with spear, sword, and arrow engaged one another with far less lethality and choreographed precision than would become typical during the bloody tumult of the sixteenth century, when gunpowder multiplied the destructive power armies could inflict upon each other. The eighth century saw feints, tentative encounters, hesitant pursuits, time-outs for foraging, eleventh-hour crises caused by titled egos, and victories snatched from melées that might have gone either way. That said, Muslim military organization and tactics had progressed apace since Caliph Umar's preliminary reforms. The Believers organized themselves into standard infantry units and bannered squadrons of armored and light cavalry led by a general officer, or *qa'id*. They advanced in crescent formation or *hilali*, the right and left wings pivoting from the center in order to envelop an enemy. The shield-bearing vanguard, or *muqaddima*, were infantry shock troops, while the main force of iron-helmeted, mail-wearing *muqatila* (fighting men) followed, usually after unleashing a volley of arrows but always wielding a length of steel tempered to a fine edge.[14]

From the first moment of contact during the third week of October, Poitiers fairly well followed the pre-gunpowder scenario. Gibbon's *The History of the Decline and Fall of the Roman Empire* presents a cautious Charles telling Odo to take his advice not to "march nor precipitate your attack." The Saracens were "like a torrent, which it is dangerous to stem in its career," he explained. "Be patient till they have loaded themselves with the encumbrances of wealth."[15] This advice to a man who knew the enemy from firsthand contact reads more like sagacity after the fact. In any case, Charles followed his own advice and left much of the harassing action to the Aquitainians. The Christians harassed them and fell back. The Muslims rolled on, a juggernaut that brushed aside the enemy as it moved up the Roman highway toward the town of Cenon-sur-Vienne.

On the third or fourth day of sporadic engagement, the defenders forced the Muslims to take them seriously. At Porte-de-Piles, a landscape feature long since vanished, the invaders encountered the Franks ranged in force along the banks of the Creuse, a minor tributary of the Vienne transecting the Roman highway. Surprised by the ferocity of the enemy's well-executed cavalry and infantry attack, the Muslims halted, falling back along much of the length of the highway. Dusting himself off, 'Abd al-Rahman repositioned his army by crossing to the right bank of the Vienne, where it pitched camp in the valley. Thinking that his men were protected by the river separating them from the Franks, the *amir* only exposed himself to another surprise. Crossing the Vienne downstream with his main force of Austrasians, Charles attacked 'Abd al-Rahman from the rear, a maneuver lauded with superlatives by Fredegar the Continuator: "*Super eosque belligerator inruit, Christo auxiliante, tentoria eorum subvertit*" ("With Christ's help, he overturned their tents and slaughtered them").[16]

But the *jihad* continued to run the next day, a Friday, advancing up the Roman highway in high gear. The loss of booty had not been great, but the invaders had lost not only comrades—wives, family, and concubines had been wounded and slain. When al-Ghafiqi and his general staff espied the serried rows of Franks and their Gallo-Roman allies on the rise off to their right of advance, they promised Allah to put an end to the infidel interference once and for all. The definitive settling of scores began at noon on Saturday—"*l'épisode final de cette semaine de manoeuvres et d'accrochages*" ("the last act in this week of maneuvers and skirmishes").[17] The plateau at Moussais-la-Bataille served as the stage for the final testing of the armies. Charles chose the spot for the advantage of its gradient above the Roman highway, and he force-marched his men to Moussais-la-Bataille in order to position them above and along the route taken by the ancient artery.

Seen from the plateau, the Roman highway is like a thin line drawn by a piece of chalk straight across a green slate. The plateau afforded the Franks the advantage of wide-angle vision and downhill engagement with the enemy. On this chilly October day, Charles ordered his men to lock their shields together so as to form tight, compact rows of infantry stretching the width of the gradual incline and in parallel with the Roman road. If nothing else, a week of fighting and following the Saracens had made one fact plain to the mayor: His troops were no match for the speed and maneuverability of the enemy. The solidly built Austrasians made a virtue out of a deficiency and presented themselves as an adamantine force. Obedient to the Prophet's injunction, al-Ghafiqi gave the order to engage the enemy after noon prayers. The heavily armored cavalry, his *mujaffafa* in hauberk and conical helmet, commenced the attack in a chorus of "*Allahu akbar*," tearing up the hill from the Roman road in a nimbus of nostril steam from their mounts behind volleys of arrows, the *mujarrada* (light cavalry) following hard on. The tactic was tried and true *karr wa farr*, with its waves of high-speed cavalry swarming and re-forming and charging again, the whole nimble mass crashing into the enemy's front to turn its flanks.[18]

Jihad met its match on the slopes of Moussais-la-Bataille as wave after wave of al-Ghafiqi's horsemen caromed off the Austrasians' human berm. Eventually, momentum tipped, and the Franks pressed forward in lethal lockstep like a giant scythe slicing through high grass. A Catholic monk somewhere in *al-Andalus* left a fitting description of the astonishing situation of the day. "The men of the north stood as motionless as a wall," wrote Isidore Pacensis in the *Mozarabic Chronicle of 754*. "They were like a belt of ice frozen together, and not to be dissolved as they slew the Arabs with the sword. The Austrasians, vast of limb and iron of hand, hewed on bravely in the thick of the fight." By one account, the battle turned decisively in favor of the Christians after Odo hurled his Aquitainian cavalry upon the enemy camp a league off in the distance, endangering women, children, and the Muslim treasure hoard. A large mass of Berbers broke away to secure the camp. Franks and Gallo-Romans grappled furiously with Arabs and Berbers as a vortex of hand-to-hand combat sucked in wave after wave of slashing, grappling cavalry and infantry.[19]

Charles had kept his cavalry hidden until the right moment. Now it thundered into the maelstrom, and the Muslim center began to collapse. Spurring his horse to the front to steady his men, 'Abd al-Rahman al-Ghafiqi had begun to succeed when he was slain by an arrow. His death demoralized the troops and gave the hard-fought battle to the Franks, although some of the Berbers appear to have kept on fighting until sundown. At first light, the winners were surprised to find the enemy encampment deserted. With ranks thinned, the bruised, shaken Saracens had gathered up their dead silently in the night and set upon a course to outpace the rising sun. The eleventh-century Andalusian historian Ibn Idhari described the waste of life on the Roman road as the "*Balat al-*

Shuhada—another "Path of the Martyrs." Arab chroniclers actually speak of two "path[s] of the martyrs": the 721 debacle at Toulouse and the one eleven years later at Moussais-la-Bataille. The Believers were badly stung by both defeats, and Western historians have characterized the Battle of Poitiers as a Muslim reversal of virtually incommensurable significance. Objectively, however, Poitiers was certainly less of a disaster to the advancing Arabs than their great crisis a half-century earlier in the Maghreb when Uqba and Musa battled to housebreak the Berbers. In Cordoba and Damascus, plans were already under way for a new *jihad* in *al-Ard al-Kabirah*, "the Great Land."[20]

⁕

Accepted versions of history are written by the winners. Fredegar limned the victory at Poitiers in prose that was to resound down the centuries: "Prince Charles boldly drew up his battle line against them, and the warrior rushed in against them. With Christ's help he overturned their tents, and hastened to battle to grind them small in slaughter." Charles's apotheosis commenced from that day forward, although the *nom de guerre* of Martel—"the Hammer" may not have become officially recorded as his sobriquet until the early ninth century.[21] In that same historical instant, the people who prevailed at Moussais-la-Bataille obtained a new and prospectively potent identity. In calling the victors at Poitiers "Europenses" for the first time, Isidore Pacensis's neologism introduced a holistic concept that transcended (definitionally, at least) the savage particularisms of his century, a meta-category to replace the lost, lamented *civitas romanum*. The inhabitants living in a part of the planet whose post-Roman world resembled a river of piranhas would gradually come to be known after Poitiers as Europeans. Europe the continent—*ereb,* meaning "land of sunset or darkness" in ancient Semitic— becomes home to a new people in history: Europeans. As Catholic and European became synonymous in the mythopoeia of the coming decades, the Austrasian Franks and their Neustrian cousins were credited with having "saved" Christian civilization—or, more aptly, of having made possible the invention of a Europe of Europeans.

Contemplating Europe's narrow escape from a supposedly terrible fate, Gibbon still shivered in relief after a thousand years: "Perhaps the interpretation of the Koran would now be taught in the schools of Oxford, and her pulpits might demonstrate to a circumcised people the sanctity and truth of the revelation of Mahomet." François Guizot, King Louis-Philippe's prime minister and a prolific historian of immense authority, certified that the Franks had delivered civilization from an unspeakable fate. "Poitiers," proclaimed Henri Martin in his nineteen-volume *Histoire de France . . . jusqu'en 1789,* was the moment when "the world's fate was played out between the Franks and the Arabs."[22] Poitiers was Europe saved by the Franks from "Asiatics and the Africans," one of the arbiters of early twentieth-century historiography, Ernest Lavisse, reiter-ated. The great German military historian Hans Delbrück, writing in the early twentieth century, declared: "There was no more important battle in the history of the world." Smarting from the deep humiliation of World War II, many a twentieth-century French historian uncritically commended the balm of Poitiers. Writing at the beginning of the next century in *Carnage and Culture: Landmark Battles in the Rise of Western Power* (2001), American military historian Victor Davis Hanson was of the same opinion. Today, Charles Martel's defeat of 'Abd al-Rahman ibn 'Abd Allah al-Ghafiqi is buried deep in the collective memory of the West, a marker of an important happening seldom recalled with the hyperbole typical of an earlier, more culturally self-aggrandizing age. Apart from a few academic specialists, however, it probably occurs to few, if any, of the contemporary descendants of the "Europenses" to credit the existence of the European Union to the Battle of Poitiers.

An occasional scholar has asked a more philosophical question about Poitiers, one that eschews considerations of nationality and religion. Deferring value judgments to the degree possible, they have invited spec-ulation about the cost benefits of the bloodletting some sixty miles from the Pyrenees. Had 'Abd al-Rahman's men prevailed that October day, the post-Roman Occident would probably have been incorporated into a cosmopolitan, Muslim *regnum* unobstructed by borders, as they hypothe-size—one devoid of a priestly caste, animated by the dogma of equality of the faithful, and respectful of all religious faiths. Curiously, such specula-tion has a French pedigree. Forty years ago, two historians, Jean-Henri

Roy and Jean Deviosse enumerated the benefits of a Muslim triumph at Poitiers: astronomy; trigonometry; Arabic numerals; the corpus of Greek philosophy. "We [Europe] would have gained 267 years," according to their calculations. "We might have been spared the wars of religion." To press the logic of this disconcerting analysis, the victory of Charles the Hammer must be seen as greatly contributing to the creation of an economically retarded, balkanized, fratricidal Europe that, in defining itself in opposition to Islam, made virtues out of religious persecution, cultural particularism, and hereditary aristocracy.

Whether or not Poitiers had indeed ensured the future of Western civilization, the victory guaranteed in short order both the ascendancy of the Pippinid clan and the hegemony of the Frankish tribe. Odo, worn down by his Austrasian entrapment, retreated to a monastery three years after Poitiers. His sons, Halto and Hunald, outmatched by the Austrasians, acknowledged Charles's suzerainty. Hunald also soon trooped off to a monastery. Exalting the mayor as the savior anointed of Christ, the *Historia Langobardorum* of Paul the Deacon even gave much of the credit to the mayor for the great repulse in 721 by placing Charles at Odo's side when al-Samh was slain. When Theudoald IV, the cipher king of both Austrasia and Neustria, expired in 737, Charles simply left the throne vacant. The shape and meaning of Poitiers, therefore, served the vaulting ambitions of the house founded by Pippin of Heristal and imparted to the Frankish people a special identity in great measure derived from both the victory and the victors' narrative. "Frankland—the greater part of modern France and western Germany—would be transformed," writes the Carolingian historian Pierre Riché, "from an outpost of Mediterranean civilization to the center of a new Christian civilization."[23]

Christian chroniclers of the late eighth and ninth centuries naturally divined the hand of their God in the outcome at Moussais-la-Bataille. Yet on the morrow of the great slaughter on the "path of the martyrs," it would have been an unnaturally credulous monk who believed that Allah had failed the sons of Ishmael for good, that the *jihad* into Gallic Christendom had expended itself against Isidore Pacensis's Austrasian "belt of ice." The impressive magnitude of the victory was indisputable, but the true weight of Poitiers on the scales of history was to remain uncertain another half century and more, for the compelling reason that the Arabs and Berbers would keep coming. Not quite two years after Poitiers, a good-size army commanded by the new *amir* of *al-Andalus,* one 'Abd al-Malik of the powerful al-Fihri (a subclan of the Quraysh) streamed down the mountains into Aquitaine bent on avenging Poitiers. Odo's army caught the Muslims at the foot of the Pyrenees, mauling them so badly that the *amir* was recalled to Damascus in disgrace. It was Odo's bravura farewell.[24]

⠶

But the rhythm of holy war was unbroken. Far from bringing an end to Islamic incursions, the Battle of Poitiers accelerated them. For almost the entire decade after the slaughter on the slopes of Moussais-la-Bataille, Franks and Latins of the Great Land were pressed nearly to the breaking point by ever-larger and strategically more venturesome attacks from *al-Andalus.* Instead of being the definitive terminus, 732 represented a significant spike on the Islamic invasion graph. The patience of Hisham I had worn thin. Damascus ordered Cordoba to resume the march against the infidels. It was a time both of general tightening-up of the empire and of expanding the walls of the *Dar al-Islam* in order to add more tax-payers to the ranks of the *dhimmis.* The next *amir* at Cordoba after 'Abd al-Malik ibn Qatan al-Fihri lost no time leading an army into the Dauphiné and Burgundy, taking Lyon in the process. This *amir* was another Uqba, unrelated to Uqba ibn Nafi, conqueror of the Maghreb, but possessed of similarly superior military acumen. In sending him from the governor-ship of Ifriqiya to *al-Andalus* in 734, the caliph made his will clear to Uqba ibn al-Hajjaj al-Saluli. The Frankish impediment to the empire's advance had to be liquidated and the cost necessitated by new military units defrayed by increased tax revenues.[25] Uqba implemented a two-pronged, coordinated attack into Gaul. On his orders, Yusuf, the governor of Narbonne, charged out of Septimania, the corner province on the Mediter-ranean that was an appendage of the Cordovan amirate, and again captured Carcassonne and Nîmes. Uqba invaded Aquitaine.

For the Franks, the danger was magnified by Yusuf's success in cor-ralling Christian collaborators in the *jihad.* Maurontus of Provence, who styled himself duke of Marseille, was typical of the coastal magnates who, like Odo of Aquitaine, understood that the Catholic Franks were a greater immediate threat to their freedom than the Muslims. Mauron-tus's collusion made possible a Saracenic condominium of allied and con-quered towns and cities that curved around the Mediterranean from Narbonne to Marseille and beyond. The littoral beyond Marseille seemed destined to serve as the causeway to a Muslim Italia—the north-ern pincer in Damascus's grand design for cracking "fortress Constan-tinople." Heading up the Rhone Valley, Yusuf's expedition pillaged across Burgundy on a northward course that threatened the old Roman jewel, Arles.[26] Meanwhile, Uqba had advanced across the map, through Burgundy and into Dauphiné, capturing Valence on the Rhone and lay-ing waste to the towns and villages around Vienne. Much of Gaul verged on collapse.

Charles the Hammer was tied down at that awkward moment cam-paigning against the Frisians just as Yusuf of Narbonne advanced across the lower half of Gaul. Assembling his Austrasians in force in late sum-mer of 737, Charles and another of his father's illegitimates, Duke Childebrand, led separate armies into the Rhone Valley to repel the invaders. Childebrand, about whom little more is known than that he was a skilled campaigner, liberated Avignon after a brief siege and hur-ried to connect with Charles for the invasion of Septimania. Seeing his rear menaced, the hard-driving Yusuf fell back on his capital. Uqba with-drew to the Pyrenees as well, carrying into slavery thousands of women and children whose husbands and fathers the Muslims had put to death. Once in Cordoba, he lost no time responding to the Franks' encir-clement of Narbonne by sending a naval squadron to relieve the garrison. The Franks cut the relief force to pieces in the marshland between the coast and the Berre Lagoon. Charles and Childebrand's men were able to ring Yusuf's capital completely, cutting off Narbonne from relief by water and land. But Narbonne withstood the Franks' arsenal of siege machin-ery, and once again the "wild men of the forests" forced Charles to race to the north with his army. Not only did Narbonne hold, it would remain a Muslim stronghold for twenty years more.

The *jihad* of 739–40 far surpassed Poitiers and the reprises of the late

730s in scale and strategy. We know that, but without knowing many of the specifics. We do know that Charles Martel regarded the invasion as so ominous as to send messengers to Pavia with an appeal for Lombard manpower. Until then, there had been little contact and less affinity between the two Germanic peoples, Franks and Lombards. The army that Uqba led from the Ebro in the fall of 739 was larger and more battle-hardened than any previous Andalusian invasion force. It bore down on Lyon, recapturing it, and went on to menace Dijon as it laid waste to much of Burgundy. Once again, Yusuf of Narbonne and his Christian confederates charged up the Rhone into the Alpine province of Dauphiné and hurtled on toward the Italian Piedmont. The gravity of the situation brought the anxiously awaited positive response from the Lombards. Their king, Luitprand, brought his men from the Alps to join the Franks in Dauphiné, where they were deployed in the path of Yusuf's hard-charging Saracens. Beyond its apparent success in forcing the Muslims to turn back to Septimania and the ousting of Maurontus from his dukedom, enragingly little else is known about this singular interception of the enemy. The abrupt Islamic withdrawal behind the Pyrenees requires an explanation, which is shortly to be provided. What seemed certain at that time, though, was that the return of the Arab-Berber legions to the Great Land was an imminent certainty.[27]

In *The Fields of Gold*, a remarkable tenth-century history of the known world, al-Masudi makes note of the Franks' fearful bellicosity but finds nothing to say about the Battle of Poitiers or its immediate sequels. An understandable aversion to recording defeat is not the main reason for the Arab sources' relative silence, however. Nor would it be accurate to infer from such silences, as some have, that Damascus dismissed Poitiers as merely a low-stakes operation at the margins of empire. Poitiers and its analogues were humiliations that mattered. Yet even so, in the immediate aftermath of these defeats, and for several decades to come, the Arabs had little military reason to grasp the full, fateful meaning of al-Ghafiqi martyrdom on the Roman road. Poitiers and its footnote sequels were seen as jarring speed bumps across the path of an unstoppable ultramontane advance blessed by Allah. Later, when the loss of the Great Land was understood to be permanent, Muslim historians such as al-

Masudi would pass over Poitiers with minimal commentary. But in doing so—unlike the enemy Franks who took all the credit for saving Europe—the Muslims would rightly blame their own internecine preoccupations as the real reason for Christian Europe's survival.[28]

⠶

Looking back at Poitiers eleven hundred years later, a school of nineteenth-century German historians spun a formidable theory about the role of stirrups in the evolution of European society and politics. Stirrups were unlikely to have reached *al-Andalus* before the middle of the eighth century. Even so, the opportunity that was missed in reality, historians have recaptured *ex hypothesi*. Heinrich Brunner and his disciples (of whom the twentieth-century American Lynn White was the most original) imagined Charles Martel and his magnates debating on the morning after Poitiers the value of the newfangled Muslim implement, the rapid adoption of which supposedly brought about a reconfigured Frankish social order whose characterization awaited its precise seventeenth-century definition by the term *feudalism*. "Few inventions have been so simple," the pioneering medievalist Lynn White wrote of Duke Charles's putative reorganization of his military structure, "but few have had so catalytic an influence on history." Sitting tall in their saddles, the lance's recoil absorbed by their stirrups, the horsemen would come to look down from a great height of hierarchical command that turned Europe into a vast protection racket wherein the strong obliged the weak to pay for being protected. The scholarly quip that "it is impossible to be chivalrous without a horse," captured the phenomenon perfectly.[29]

Charles Martel built a powerful Frankland and a transformed church. But cavalry equipped with stirrups, despite much scholarship to the contrary, was not part of his legacy. The Frankish military establishment continued to depend primarily on its infantry of stolid, foot-slogging freemen and peasants, as well as on the artillery's sappers and technicians who manned the catapult, trebuchet, and other formidable siege machines. Still, warfare and horses clearly did alter the pace and complexity of Frankish society in the wake of Poitiers. Charles's Franks went to war on horseback in unprecedented numbers. Franks were as much cowboys as were Americans of the nineteenth-century West; and they were even fonder of their mounts. A fallen warrior was buried with his horse. "Kill my mother, I don't care!" a typical notable shouted. "Never will I give up to you the horse you demand. He was never made for the reins of a wretch like you!"[30] Under the Pippinids, the proportion of saddled combatants to foot soldiers grew significantly. Charles's Austrasian *caballarii* thundered onto battlefields accoutered in iron-laced (*spangen*) helmets and iron-plated tunics or leather *brunia*. Oval wooden shields reinforced with metal were slung over the left shoulder, a quiver of arrows on the other shoulder, barbed javelin *angos* in the right hand, and, strapped to waists, were those double-edged broadswords the Franks prized as secret weapons.

All this horseflesh, leather, wood, iron, and tempered steel was a far cry from the axe-throwing savages the Byzantine historian Procopius described from erroneous hearsay. The milk cows, oxen, slaves, parcels of land, and crop yields that Charles needed in order to put hundreds of armored men in the saddle filled ledgers and made for towering calculations. Forty *sous* (which a serf would almost never see) or eighteen cows bought a cavalry horse; twelve *sous* for an iron-laced leather tunic. A pair of greaves (shin armor worn by heavy cavalry) might cost in excess of forty solidi, roughly the value of twenty cows; a good *spangen* helmet, *brunia*, and a buckler to go with a horse ran to fifty-five *sous*, about twenty-five cows.[31] The escalating costs of the military enterprise had to be financed through extraordinary means and devices. Pippin of Heristal had developed the rudimentary means to do so by exploiting the property of the Church through intimidation, legerdemain, and even sword-point, in order to pay for a greatly expanded military and bureaucracy.

Banks are robbed because they hold money. His father's son, Charles robbed the Church from the same motive. Frankland and territories immediately adjacent were studded with more than a hundred bishoprics—from opulent benefices in the Ile-de-France and the Rhine Pfalz, with their thousands of hectares worked by scores of peasant villages, to modest sees of a hundred acres tucked away in the foothills of the Vosges or virtually forgotten in the far north. In the Rouen diocese in the northwest, the monks of the St. Wandrille and Jumiège abbeys had drained swamps and cleared leagues of forests to create virtual kingdoms of Benedictine prosperity.[32] Truly enormous quantities of deeded land passed in perpetuity to the religious orders and the dioceses. It certainly seemed to Charles that he ruled as palace mayor over a country much of whose real estate belonged to another power. That this was an intolerable situation the duke was determined to remedy was evident from one of his first acts upon assuming power.

He sent packing the powerful, unfriendly bishop of Reims and handed over the great diocese to a supporter of notorious morals who also held the strategic archbishopric of Trier. Bishoprics and abbeys were doled out to clansfolk and cronies with little or no regard for ecclesiastical worthiness—or even whether they had taken Holy Orders. Ecclesiastical offices fell vacant due to convenient deaths. Seeding bishoprics with allies was one tactic. More common was the forced lending of land—the involuntary lease of property. Alienation or outright expropriation of Church property was by far the exception. The duke deprived the Church of the *use* of some significant portion of its enormous wealth, not legal title to it. The principal device used to achieve his objective was the once-much-misunderstood *precarium*—precarial tenure—a legal instrument granting access to ecclesiastical wealth but not ownership of it. Instead, priors of abbeys and monasteries, finding themselves intimidated and "protected" in ways that twentieth-century *mafiosi* would have admired, entered into lease agreements with Charles's agents that amounted to temporary confiscation. Depredations followed in a widening circle until Boniface, Charles's ethical preceptor, complained that his pupil was packing bishoprics with partisans as given to fornication as to fighting and either woefully ignorant or cynically indifferent to the tenets of the faith.[33]

The policy ordained by the crown at the great ecclesiastical Council of Estinnes in 743 perfectly expressed Pippinid *raison d'état*. "Because of the wars which threaten, and on account of the hostility of the rest of the peoples who surround us, we have decided, with the advice of the servants of God and of the Christian people, to keep for a while longer a portion of church property." These were not Charles's words. They would be pronounced two years after his death by his son, Carloman. They spoke, however, to the essentials of his father's politics. Two centuries later, relying on the plaints of Boniface and the even-angrier charges of one Hincmar, archbishop of Reims, high Church officials would consign Charles to the fires of hell for having stolen Church lands. "Of all the kings and princes of the Franks," Hincmar fumed, he was "the first to take property away from the Church and to divide it up."[34]

The benefits of the *precarium* to Charles's war machine were invaluable, but both the great Frankish clerics and the Benedictine reformers stood to gain much from reciprocated royal goodwill: emoluments of office and other preferments for the former; synods to reform the Church and protection of missionary work among still-untamed Germans for the latter. Having gradually converted a critical bloc of the wild men of the forest from the late fifth century onward, the Frankish Church increasingly bent before Pippinid power as the price to pay for protection and collaboration in its mission to convert the wild men of the forest. Much as St. Isidore and the Iberian clergy had found it expedient to legitimize by scripture and practice the exploitative excesses of the Visigoth regime, so the evangelizing priests who crossed the channel from Northumbria trimmed their sails to catch the rising Pippinid wind. Willibrord, the learned master of Echternach, and his fellow Northumbrian, Boniface, the "Apostle of Germany," colluded in the buildup of royal authority by Pippin II and Charles in exchange for hunting licenses for souls—all the while reproving royal immoralities and improprieties. The royal synods convened under Charles's protection were a boon to both sides—if more to *regnum* than to *sacerdotum*, to call State and Church by their contemporary terminology: On the one hand, the edicts and regulations the synods issued on standards, practices, and morals for the clergy were implements with which dedicated Benedictines could reform the Church; on the other, the reforming synod was the vehicle through which royal power was augmented.

The duke of the Franks effected a consolidation of power in which a Roman patriarchate, menaced by Lombards on its doorstep, had not much choice other than one of cagey approval. The model the Church would in time impose upon Christianity—an imperial papacy whose commands an obedient hierarchy enforced upon the faithful on pain of excommunication—was still only the ambitious design of the Sergiuses,

Johns, Gregorys, and Stephens who fretted in the dilapidated Lateran Palace. Centers of ecclesiastical power lay not with the See of Peter but in Constantinople, Pavia, Metz, Paris, and elsewhere. Frankish bishops, like those elsewhere on the continent and in the British Isles, were confirmed by their fellow bishops and served for life unless deposed by a council of neighboring bishops. As a political fact, Frankish ecclesiastical confirmation lent itself to Pippinid manipulation. The modicum of deference owed the bishop of Rome counted for less when measured against the power of the mayor of the palace. More than coincidence was to be read in Pope Gregory III's presents to Charles Martel in 739, the same year in which Franks and Lombards joined to fight the Saracens. Fredegar gushed that "such things had never been seen or heard of before," when the keys to St. Peter's tomb and a portion of the saint's chain arrived in Quierzy-sur-Oise. In fact, these relics were papal staples strategically dispensed where politically useful.[35] A struggling papacy salivated at the prospect of winning the prince's political sympathy and thereby a much-augmented influence upon the Frankish Church.

With the clergy of Frankland used for his reins, so to speak, Charles thundered across his enemies' borders with murderous trains of regiments whose large mounts and costly equipage had been bought with Church wealth. Ducal dominoes fell one by one to the Austrasian mayor: Bavaria, again in 728, where the prince took the accomplished Suanehilde, one of its princesses, for his mistress; Alamannia, in 730, with the decisive subjugation of its resilient duke, Lantfrid. Illustrious or petty, fealty was exacted and elaborate oaths spoken in the name of God, saints, family honor. Minor nobles were swept up like metal shavings in the path of a magnet. A rhythm of aristocratic life settled in under Charles: the grand muster of fighting men from March to May, depending on weather, on the Marchfield; the campaign lasting perhaps until the onset of winter; slaughter, conquest, rape, booty, ransom, and distribution of estates; winter under smoke-filled eaves with howling wolves outside and indiscriminate copulation within; helmet, shield, lance, and sword again to the Marchfield.*

---

*Marchfield was the traditional muster of the Frankish army, in spring.

Greater Frankland—the evolving Francia—was now a possibility to be formed out of a mystique, itself an evolving one, of providential uniqueness sustained by war. Charles Martel, leader of a special tribe, had saved Christian civilization, which could mean nothing less than that he and they must be the vessels through which God worked His wonders. But Frankland immensely benefitted from a vessel through which Charles himself worked with adroitness. The duke co-opted the men and women and machinery of the Catholic Church to serve as substitutes for the secular government that had long ago disappeared.[36] With the sometimes censorious help of the two Northumbrian Benedictines, Willibrord and Boniface, Charles left his sons a greatly consolidated realm served by a somewhat reformed ecclesiastical establishment free of any Arian traces. The *jihad* of 740 was Charles's valedictory in the saddle. A year later, as he wintered in the royal village of Quierzy-sur-Oise, the once-fabled constitution of the fifty-three-year-old ruler began to fail. He passed his days bedridden in feverish flotation in and out of consciousness until the twenty-second day of October. "741. Charles, mayor of the palace, died," the *Royal Frankish Annals* announced not long after the *Continuations of Fredegar* had fallen silent.[37] Pippinid Frankland at the close of his rule was the second most powerful political force in Christendom after Byzantium. Austrasia, Neustria, and Burgundy now composed a solid core for the kingdom, with Aquitaine and Provence chained to the center.

Uqba, the sixteenth *amir* of *al-Andalus*, was laid to rest in Cordoba a few months before Charles Martel received the last rites. None of his five successors would command military expeditions into the Great Land where the *jihad* had several times been derailed.

The Fall and Rise of the Umayyads

CHARLES Martel—the Hammer—expired in the winter of 741, nine years after his great victory at Poitiers. His mortal remains were interred in the Abbey of St. Denis, resting place of the kings of France since the fifth century. Although he shared space with the venerable Clovis, Charles had entered eternity not as a king but as mayor of the palace and duke of the Franks. Chilperic III reigned in law as sovereign of the united kingdoms of Austrasia, Neustria, and Bur-

gundy. This was a mere legalism, however, when weighed against the significance of all that Charles had accomplished in twenty-two years of
actual rule. In the greater Frankland being built on Austrasian and Neustrian foundations arose a confidence—albeit one shaken from time to
time by Saracen incursions—that grew steadily more certain of God's
providence.

Yet what made that growing confidence a prudent belief rather than
the dangerous illusion it might otherwise have been was not the bloody
outcome at Moussais-la-Bataille but political disruption in *al-Andalus* and
the faraway Maghreb. When the ferocious Uqba ibn al-Hajjaj al-Saluli
took up the banner of his martyred predecessors and charged into Burgundy in the late 730s, the Muslim advance into Aquitaine and along the
Mediterranean littoral into Burgundy and Provence appeared destined
to continue with gathering strength. Until the Berber revolt that swept
across the amirate more than a year before Duke Charles's death, the
Great Land of the "Europenses" seemed destined to become part of
the Muslim imperium. But the powerful invasion force assembled in the
summer of 739 never descended into Aquitaine from the western Pyrenees. Berber unrest at Zaragoza had compelled Uqba to turn the
Andalusi *jihad* in its tracks.[1]

Not only had Berbers come over from Africa with the "original
Arabs" of the Iberian Conquest, the *baladiyyun*, it was Berber swords and
spears that made the *baladiyyun* gamble a paying proposition. And among
the gamblers, the greatest of them was Tariq, the Luwata Berber. In an
al-Andalus where centrifugal and centripetal forces were constant and
widespread, the Berbers were vital for policing the realm. The
governors-general had learned from experience that if Berbers were difficult to rule, ruling *al-Andalus* without them would have been almost
impossible. They had come in much larger numbers than the Arabs—an
advantage they continued to hold as more crossed the strait to settle the
highlands and serve the Cordovan military establishment.[2] Some made
their homes in the Almaden mountains in the west, high terrain resembling their Atlas Mountains homeland. The great majority settled in the
north beyond the Meseta Central (the "great table") and above and
below the Duero River, whose long course from east to west carved the

frontier separating greater *al-Andalus* from the hostile Christian north.
The first Arabs and Berbers combined were but a tiny one or two percent of the total population. The Arab overlords had kept most of the
best real estate for themselves and positioned the Berbers more or less
along the perimeter of the amirate to serve as the first line of defense.
Many Berbers were settled in the Lerida region of the northeast, a short
march to the Pyrenees.

As time passed, the Berbers contrasted bitterly the niggardly division
of Iberia's victory spoils with the Qur'an's edifying promises often
intoned in the Friday Mosque. Thirty years after Tariq ibn Ziyad's annihilation of the Visigoths in 711, the warriors from the Maghreb were still
awaiting the fruits of full membership in the *ummah*. The Prophet
ordained that all Believers were equal, yet Berbers had good reason to
feel that theirs was an equality that was separate and distinctly second
class. What could have spoken with more relevance to the Andalusian
Berbers than the *sura* aptly entitled *Al-Anfal* ("The Spoils")? "Those that
have embraced the Faith and fled their homes and fought for the cause of
God," announced the Qur'an, "they are the true believers. Forgiveness
and a gracious provision await them."[3] But the "gracious provision"—the
fertile valley of the Guadalquivir, with its three major cities (Cadiz,
Sevilla, and Cordoba)—was distributed among the lordly Arabs. Berber
resentment deepened over the years as one governor-general followed
another, each one almost invariably accompanied by a retinue of Yemeni
Arabs who were given prime lands in the Guadalquivir Valley or on the
Meseta. The curious alliance of the *wali* of Cerdanya and Duke Odo of
Aquitaine had been a cautionary example of the extremes to which alienated Berber rulers could go.[4] As the years went by, the substrate of broad-
based Berber disappointment and frustration thickened.

While the patience of the Berbers was more and more tested, the
rulers of *al-Andalus* pursued a policy of civil pluralism permitting a latitude
in mores, beliefs, and institutions unmatched in the West since Augustan
Rome—a policy whose success depended on cohesion within the political class of high-born Arabs, complemented by deference paid by Berbers
and other Muslims of inferior pedigree. As long as the great Yemeni clans
felt secure in the land and the Qur'an went publicly unchallenged, the

dhimmis were left to their own pursuits; religious and social institutions were respected. No pressure was exerted upon the Catholic majority, so most of its members remained faithful to the Church in the decades immediately following the Conquest, yet in culture and Arabic-inflected speech it began to assume what was called "Mozarabic character." For several years after the Conquest, conquerors and conquered had spoken Romance, but squads of *imams* soon succeeded in enforcing Arabic as the tongue of commerce, government, law, and learning.

By the 740s, as Frankish hegemony asserted itself on the other side of the Pyrenees, a small percentage of Andalusis began to embrace Islam. As *muwalladun* (Iberian non-Arab converts), they were released from the *jizya* and admitted to a semblance of the privileges of the old *baladiyyun* elite. For all the Qur'an's welcoming of converts and tolerance of the sacred books of others, however, Arab pride of lineage invariably trumped the *ummah*'s vaunted solidarity. It even seemed that Allah had slipped a subtle qualifier about community status into the eighth *sura*: "They too are your brothers; although according to the Book of God those who are bound by ties of blood are nearest to one another."[5] Some of the *baladiyyun* boasted descent from the *rashidun*, if not from the Prophet himself—claims no Berber could make.

In the autumn of 741, after a good many months of premonitory rumblings, *al-Andalus* was struck by the Berber earthquake that was to undermine the Umayyad Caliphate. Destruction of the amirate seemed certain. The end of Ifriqiya—of the Arab Maghreb—seemed equally imminent. Berbers on both sides of the strait rejected the writ of Damascus with swords and arrows. It was those early tremors in the Zaragoza region populated by Berbers and Basques that had caused Uqba to postpone his Aquitainian invasion two years earlier. Revolt in the far northwest swept across the Cordillera Central and sent Arab forces tumbling out of the Meseta Central and into the south. The column of advancing rebels shaved their heads as a sign of defiant distinction and rejection of the regime.

The predicament of the Andalusi Arabs was exacerbated by the change in leadership after Uqba's departure for police duty in North Africa. The new governor-general was a popular leader of the *baladiyyun* and a member of the distinguished al-Fihri. Inheriting the worst of two crises, a tax revolt and an insurrection, Uqba's replacement faced a three-pronged Berber advance with few soldiers and a demoralized people. The Berber steamroller had halted for the winter. It regained momentum in the spring, flattening whatever obstacles it encountered on a triple course of slaughter set for Toledo, Cordoba, and Algeciras. Precisely what Amir 'Abd al-Malik ibn Qatan al-Fihri had attempted to accomplish after three or four months in office is unclear. By spring of 742, however, the overthrow of the Arab regime in *al-Andalus* had become all but inevitable.

Caliph Hisham's determination to end the special tax exemptions of Berbers and other groups in the *Dar al-Islam*, a well as to rationalize the fisc and increase extant rates, sparked a rolling barrage of tax revolts aggravated by deep ethnic resentments and religious fundamentalism that sundered the very foundations of the Muslim imperium. Hisham's tax edicts had enormous consequences in and beyond *al-Andalus*. Although the Franks could hardly be expected to acknowledge the fact, rebellious Berbers were their best allies.[6]

Grievances against Arab rule in Ifriqiya and Morocco derived from much the same causes as those across the strait. In the Maghreb, as elsewhere, revenues from the *jizya* declined as conversions increased. To compensate, Damascus tightened up collection of the *kharaj* (the land tax paid by Muslim and non-Muslim alike) and the assessment of 2.5 percent of movable goods throughout the empire. But in North Africa, festering resentments and a special brand of Islam made for a volatile mix primed to explode from the spark of tax collection. Kharijism, that stern version of Islam whose debut in history began with the assassination of Ali, the fourth *rashidun* caliph, had implanted itself early among the Berbers of North Africa. Berbers of the Atlas Mountains had always been a hard sell for the *imams,* and, once converted, they infused their new faith with the doctrinal rigor of the Kharijism imported by fugitives from Oman and Iraq.[7]

Kharijism spoke to the ancient peoples of the plains and mountains of North Africa—the Sanhaja, Masmuda, and Zanata Berbers and a dozen more tribal confederations from whom the Arabs expected dutiful service in exchange for the Prophet's message and a share in the spoils. According to the Kharijites, who lived and died by the dictum, "Judgment belongs to God alone," neither Sunni nor Shi'a had kept the true faith. All who obeyed the strict letter of the Qur'an, Arab and non-Arab alike, were equal in the *Dar al-Islam* and equally qualified to teach as *imams*, to judge as *qadis*, or even to rule as Commanders of the Faithful. Kharijites paired radical egalitarianism with rectitude of conduct. If they transgressed the faith, caliphs—even those who claimed descent from the Prophet—had no more right to rule than a beggar in Mecca. Believers of weak virtue were deemed to be as unworthy as those who willfully transgressed—the former were punished by ostracism, the others by death.[8] Kharijism was the stem of Islamic fundamentalisms to come.

From the beginning, Berbers and Bedouin coexisted in a flammable symbiosis, and when the former rose up soon after their incorporation into the *Dar al-Islam*, their resistance was so well organized by the confederation chieftain Kusayla and the mysterious Priestess (*Kahina*) and her sons that the Arabs lost control of the territory for more than a decade after 680. Fumbling through the trial and error of co-optation, Uqba ibn Nafi's military rule, Musa ibn Nusayr's diplomacy, and the teaching of *imams*, Damascus gradually regained the upper hand by the end of the seventh century. Economic necessity in time caused the Arabs to unlearn the lesson of carrot and stick. Caliph Hisham, stern and inflexible, answered protest and resistance by sending a massive army of thirty thousand to the Maghreb in the fall of 741. The commander was the pick of the generals, his thirty thousand Syrians the seasoned elite of the Umayyad war machine, the formidable *ahl al-Sham* ("people of Syria"). But once again, disaster struck Arab might in the Maghreb. The Syrians fell by the thousands that October, in what was called the Battle of the Nobles. The Berbers boxed them in on the banks of the Sebou River in northern Morocco. The Syrian commander was killed, and his deputy ran for Ceuta with a ragtag remnant of some ten thousand. The Berber siege tightened like a noose around the enclave in the fall of 741.[9]

Repeated appeals to Cordoba from Balj ibn Bishr al-Qushayri, the surviving second in command, for permission to ferry his starving troops across the strait went unanswered by the governor-general. This was the same governor-general who was staring Berber disaster in the face at that moment—'Abd al-Malik of proud al-Fihri pedigree. No love was lost between Arabs of the Hijaz and Syrians, the former still rubbing the wounded memory of a savage defeat at Syrian hands during the civil-war conflicts of the early 680s. As far as the Medinan governor-general cared, Balj and his Syrians could face their fate as best as Allah provided. As the Berbers bore down on Cordoba, Amir 'Abd al-Malik ibn Qatan suppressed his sixty-year-old animus and summoned Syrian assistance, much as the Visigoth rebels had welcomed Tariq ibn Ziyad thirty years earlier—as allies whose sojourn was supposed to be well compensated but brief. The desperate Syrians pledged to return as a unit to a secure part of North Africa. Balj and what remained of his army crossed the strait to Algeciras in the spring of 742.

The relatively young man who came to save *al-Andalus* from the Berbers was to play a brief role as an agent of major political and social change. His al-Qushayri pedigree made him a prince among the Syrian *ashraf*, and his coolheadedness in the field brought him the solid loyalty of the men in his command. Able and ambitious, Balj ibn Bishr, son of Qushayri, was unlikely to fulfill the repatriation conditions of the contract with the governor-general. His veterans discharged their commitment to rid *al-Andalus* of the Berber menace. The combined force of Syrians and *baladiyyun* rolled back the main Berber advance at Toledo and quickly neutralized the rest. The fate of the elderly governor-general might have been predicted. He was powerless to hold the Syrians to their promise or to placate the bitter factionalism stimulated by their increasingly presumptuous presence. 'Abd al-Malik ibn Qatan al-Fihri was taken from his palace and hanged from the old Roman bridge spanning the Guadalquivir River. In a gesture of supreme contempt, the old *amir*'s head was exposed between a hog and a dog, animals despised as unclean by Muslims.[10]

In a repeat of Iberian history, Balj installed himself in the amiral palace and proclaimed himself the new ruler. Then the Syrian usurper had to fight Ibn Qatan's sons and the Cordovan establishment to keep his position, a contest he won in the summer of 742, only to die of his wounds soon after a fierce battle near the capital. Balj's Syrians altered the political culture of *al-Andalus*. Their coming brought the inveterate tribal feuds of the terrible second civil war—the *fitna* of the 680s—to *al-Andalus*. Geographically bewildering and historically so complicated as almost to defy summarizing, the feud between the northern and southern Arab tribes—the Qays/Mudari of the north and the Kalb/Yemeni of the south—was like a recessive gene, an inherited disposition inducing unpredictably recurrent outbursts of seeming group irrationality. The *baladiyyun*, with their distinctly South Arabian and Yemeni tribal character, bitterly resented the northerners, these Syrians they called *al-Shamiyyun* ("people of Syria"), from the Tigris and Euphrates steppelands, who intimidated by their large numbers and war skills.

The transplanting of the old enmities of Qays and Yemenis caused a period of disastrous martial strife. The exhaustion of all the parties made it possible for the new *amir*, a Yemeni aristocrat, to impose a solution of elegant practicality: that parties unable to live together should live apart. Legend has it that Count Ardabast, a Visigoth who switched sides after the Battle of Guadalete, advised the new governor-general as to the most satisfactory geographical dispersal of Balj's Syrians. Syrian military formations were organized by provinces called *junds,* rather like British formations bearing such territorial names as Warwickshire or East Surrey. On the Visigoth's advice, the Damascus *jund* was dispersed to Elvira, the Jordanian *jund* to Malaga, the Palestinian *jund* to Medina-Sidonia, and so on. Even as the dispersal saved the center from being overwhelmed by the Syrians, it embedded a troublesome sectionalism in the Andalusian state. The record is unclear, yet it seems highly likely that the Muslims finally nullified 'Abd al-Aziz's exemplary 713 Treaty of Tudmir during this period, expropriating more than a third of the rich lands of the old Visigoth duchy for Syrian settlers.[11]

At the close of 743, death from old age removed the longest-reigning Umayyad caliph, Hisham I. Money-grubbing and luxury-loving though he was said to be, Hisham I had been a commanding personality. He was a despot, but an enlightened one who promoted the arts and the translation of scientific works. During his long caliphate, the Muslim empire surpassed the Roman one in size. In Hisham's time, Muslim world trade moved along an interlaced, crescent-shaped network running from the silks of the Mashriq ("the place of sunrise"—China) to the gold from the Maghreb ("the place of sunset"). The empire soldered the vast economies of the Indian Ocean to those of the Mediterranean. His attention to the details of state might have seemed compulsive had not the seams of his sprawling monster of a world empire necessitated a tireless tailor to hold it together. Even then, the seams repeatedly ripped. Hindus rebelled in the Sind. Berbers ousted their overlords from the Maghreb. Restive Shi'ites in Iraq's far northeast were primed for sedition whenever the situation permitted. The eternally renascent Byzantines opposed his best armies. The killing fields of Aquitaine claimed four of his Andalusi *amirs*. Finding the revenues to keep the *Dar al-Islam* upright had proven more difficult by the decade as the rate of religious conversion accelerated. Until his last years, nevertheless, Hisham's forceful personality, integrity, efficient intelligence service, and insistence on strict adherence to *Sharia* (Muslim law) kept the seams joined.

He was followed by a succession of weak rulers. Plague and famine followed rebellion in the Maghreb at the end of the decade. If the caliph's ministers of the *diwan* had risked fomenting widespread distemper by universalizing the *kharaj* (as in the case of the Berbers), the policy had been fiscally prudent if not politically well considered. Deprived of the Berbers, some of the best manpower, the Umayyad war machine lost momentum and cohesion. Gone were the heady days of the great Andalusian pincers into Gaul. The Muslim garrisons in Septimania and in striking distance of Marseille were now no more than holding operations virtually cut off from a homeland whose Berber reservoir was all but depleted.[12] If the Berbers shook *al-Andalus* to its foundations, their Maghrebian rebellion sundered the very foundations of the Islamic state.

■■

An age was ending. The reign of the Umayyads was reaching its term. They had ruled the Muslim world since 661, the year in which the legendary Mu'awiya ibn Abi Sufyan was formally invested with the title *amir al-mu'minin*, Commander of the Faithful. Commencing with Hisham's cousin, the versifying al-Walid II, three short-lived nonentities succeeded one another from year to year. Caliph al-Walid was known as *al Naqis* ("the Inadequate") before his ascent to the throne. *The History of the Prophets and Kings* speaks well of al-Walid's successor, the pious Yazid III. In an edifying mosque sermon on the obligations of the caliphate, Yazid proclaimed that a caliph who disobeyed God "deserves to be disobeyed and killed. This is what I have to say, and may God forgive me and you." So saying, he pledged reforms but dropped dead four months later.[13] Bedouin simplicity had long since given way to an opulence imitative of the imperial court of the Byzantines and the Sassanids. The better to indulge their sensual appetites unobserved by the pious and the poor, the Sunni caliphs repaired to Rusafa, a magnificent desert retreat many miles from Damascus. Umayyad corruption in fact and fiction was broadcast covertly and, lately, it was even censured in mosques.

Four years after Hisham's death in 743, in what had seemed an eleventh-hour reprieve for the Umayyads, the *amir* of Armenia or Transcaucasia (a member of the junior branch) led his troops into the Syrian delta and proclaimed himself caliph at Damascus. Marwan ibn Muhammad was an able administrator and an innovative military commander. Enthroned a few years sooner, the middle-aged Marwan II might have arrested the rot his three indifferent predecessors had only succeeded in accelerating. The situation was already beyond his control, however, as simultaneous revolts in Iranian Khurasan and Transoxiana (Uzbekistan) complicated the new caliph's unsteady hold on Syria itself. For the third time since the death of the Prophet, the *ummah* was riven by civil war.[14]

Muslim Khurasan, a province of illimitable space and multiple races, commenced in eastern Iran and ended somewhere beyond the Oxus River. Khurasan ("where the sun rises" in Persian) was a place made for unreconciled sectarians. Shi'ite and Kharijite creeds found purchase there among subject Persian, Turkic, Kurdish, and Scythian peoples, who retained many ancient beliefs and found good reason for new grievances. This simmering stew was the elixir of overheated minds like that of a portentously named leader of a breakaway sect called the *Hashimiyya*. Abu Muslim rode into Merv, the administrative capital (in today's Turkmenistan), in Ramadan 129 (747 CE) and unfurled the black banner of

revolt. By the close of 749, when his forces captured Kufa, the administrative capital of Iraq, Abu Muslim's egalitarian brotherhood had
attached itself to the cause of a descendant of Muhammad's uncle, al-
'Abbas. One Abu'l-'Abbas, lineal descendant of al-'Abbas, was acclaimed
spiritual leader and caliph in the Kufa mosque.[15] Abu'l-'Abbas (749–53)
took the caliphal title of al-Saffah I ("the Shedder of Blood") in Kufa
and, as his first command, ordered the annihilation of the Umayyads. If
the *Hashimiyya* and their sympathizers believed that the new thousands
who rallied to their cause shared their radical egalitarianism and veneration of Ali and Husayn, then they committed the common fallacy of
zealots. A charismatic and militarily accomplished figure, as resourceful
as he was brutal, talked his way to supreme command of Abu Muslim's
troops. Once 'Abd Allah ibn Ali took control, the Shi'a lost purchase on
their revolution.

The Muslim world not only changed dynasties in 750; it annulled
ninety years of Islamic history. Caliph Marwan II lost his army and his
empire at Tell Kushaf on January 25, 750, and, seven months later, his
head in an Egyptian backwater where an Abbasid flying squad found him
virtually alone. The founding dynasty of Islam was to be covered with
obloquy and buried beneath the rubble of its own destruction. Abbasid
wrath had already shown itself to terrible effect after a month-long siege
of Damascus. After excoriating the family in the Great Mosque that had
been al-Walid I's pride, General 'Abd Allah ordered the tombs opened
and the remains exhumed, violated, burned, and cast to the winds. An
exception to the desecration was made for the pious Umar II (717–20).
Execution squads ran down prominent members of the old political class.
The hand and foot of an Umayyad grandee were cut off and the victim
was paraded across Syria with a crier shouting, "This is Aban ibn
Mu'awiya, the best horseman of the Banu Umayya." Umayyad property
was burnt or confiscated.

The last chapter in the dynasty's obliteration was to be unscrolled on
the banks of the Tigris. The brother and successor of al-Saffah, the first
Abbasid caliph, literally turned his back on Damascus. Abu Ja'far 'Abdallah ibn Muhammad al-Mansur (754–75) moved the capital eastward to
a temporary site in Iraq. The abandonment of Damascus became final

once the building of *Madinat-al Salam* ("City of Peace") commenced in 756.
The great, circular, sixteen-gated capital of the Abbasid Empire (Baghdad, as it came to be called) rose on the banks of the Tigris in Iraq in the
first years of the Caliph al-Mansur.[16] Over time, Persian cultural influences became markedly pronounced in the new caliphal order. As the axis
of the Muslim ecumene shifted eastward and away from the Mediterranean basin, not only was nearly a century of history from Mu'awiya I to
Marwan II officially vilified, but the historical record sanctioned by the
Abbasids found little to say about the Berber revolts that had caused the
Dar al-Islam to be turned upside down. Similarly, distant *al-Andalus* receded
from the imperial priorities of the court at Baghdad.

The egalitarian ideals of the Kharajites also receded from the concerns of the Sunni regime. While it became true that the citizenship discrimination practiced by the Umayyads greatly diminished, and the
offices of state were opened to non-Arabs, the Abbasid Caliphate nevertheless was a family autocracy even more regal than its predecessor. In
this new universe of imperial arrangements and concerns, little or no
thought was given to the emergent "Europenses."

⁝

ʿAbd al-Rahman ibn Mu'awiya ibn Hisham, prince of the house of Abi
Sufyan and grandson of the Caliph Hisham I, in whose household he was
raised, was born one year before the Battle of Poitiers. He was nineteen
years old when the avenging Abbasids came to power. Palm trees ringed
the palace compound of his childhood at Rusafa. They shaded the cool
courtyards where fountains burbled musically and inlaid floor tiles
described delicate geometric patterns. He never forgot the palms of his
youth. Years later, as the ruler of a foreign country, he composed a touch-
ing poem about those palms, and legend insists that he planted the first
ones in that land. "How like me you are, far away and in exile," he would
muse. "In long separation from family and friends./You have sprung from
soil in which you are a stranger;/And I, like you, am far from home." In
the foreign land, he would be called *al-Dakhíl* ("the Immigrant"). He had
no memory of his father, who died when ʿAbd al-Rahman ("Servant of
the Merciful") was a child. His mother, Ra'ha, was a Berber concubine of

the Nafza tribe, but her personality and direct influence on her son (which may well have been considerable) are unknown.[17]

The royal complex at Rusafa lay northeast of Damascus and beyond Palmyra, the oasis city of magnificent ruins punished by Rome for rebellion. Instructed guesses place Rusafa on a tributary of the Euphrates near the contemporary border with Iraq, although no trace of it remains today. During Hisham's long residence, the complex served as the empire's center of government as well as the Umayyads' secluded Xanadu of sybaritic indulgences, where forbidden wines and meats were consumed and hanging silks displayed voluptuous human forms. Versions conflict in detail, but the anonymous *Akhbar majmu'a* has the ring of plausibility. It would have been soon after the debacle at Tell Kushaf that an Abbasid contingent raced into Rusafa to torch the palace and liquidate the occupants. Years later, 'Abd al-Rahman recalled that instant almost as sharply as when he experienced it. Sitting under a tent and playing with Sulayman, his four-year-old son, he was drawn into the open by loud distress sounds. "I saw the whole village in confusion. . . . I went a little farther on and saw the black banner [of the Abbasids] fluttering in the wind." Suddenly, his excited younger brother ran toward him. "'Away! Away with thee, O brother! For yonder black banners are the banners of the sons of 'Abbas.' Hearing this, I hastily grasped some dinars . . . , and fled precipitately out of the village with my child and my younger brother, taking care to apprise my sisters of my departure, and the road we intended to take."[18]

'Abd al-Rahman and his younger brother escaped the compound together, along with the prince's faithful servant, Badr, while the shrieks of the massacred filled the desert air. The princes reached the nearby river with the assassins galloping a few yards behind them. A poor swimmer, the younger brother hesitated and was immediately cut down and killed. There is no further mention of the fate of four-year-old Sulayman. 'Abd al-Rahman and Badr reached the river's far side and eluded the search parties, motivated by the huge bounty on his head. "My feet scarcely touched the ground," he wrote. He flew, "rather than ran." The facts at our disposal are minimal. We know that he was hidden by Umayyad loyalists in Palestine for a time. From there, the tall, redheaded prince with the high cheekbones reached Egypt, whence began a five-year odyssey across North Africa. 'Abd al-Rahman's Berber lineage enabled him to survive in the breakaway Maghreb, where he eventually made contact with his mother's Nafza tribe. He settled in the Moroccan coastal village of Nakur, under the protection of his uncles.[19]

His unique fate as the Muslim world's most marked man might have unmanned the prince, paralyzing willpower and instilling a furtive nature that craved anonymity. Instead, as the years of Maghrebian refuge passed, this hunted survivor of an illustrious dynasty acquired a powerful sense of *kisma* (destiny), matched by an instinct for command. As he learned more each year about the political possibilities a few miles across the Mediterranean from Morocco, he came to believe that *al-Andalus* was the future. Balj's Syrians in Jaén province across the strait might well respond to his person. Many of the *baladiyyun* owed their social positions and prosperity to favors bestowed by his ancestors. In his twenty-fifth year, he decided to cross the strait. With the entitled confidence of the anointed, he sent his servant, the astute Badr, to stake his claim to the amirate of *al-Andalus*. But the situation was complicated.

The notable who had served some eight years as governor-general was Yusuf ibn 'Abd al-Rahman al-Fihri, the Yusuf of Narbonne fame whose *jihads* had terrified Provence and Burgundy twenty years earlier. He was an old man now and had borne the title of *amir* longer than all his predecessors—more than eight politically adroit years. The old Syrian military formation in Jaén, the *jund*, was pledged to Yusuf al-Fihri. The Syrian *vizir* pungently rejected the pretensions of Hisham's grandson. "He comes from such a people that if one of them peed on this peninsula," said he, "all of us, and all of you, would drown in his urine." Badr had much better luck with the Yemenis at Almunecar, who were happy to see troubles visited on Yusuf, the Qays sympathizer. Steadied by the courage and calculation that had kept the odds against him at bay since the escape from Rusafa, 'Abd al-Rahman crossed the North African Rubicon, stepping ashore with a thousand or more Berber cavalry at Almunecar on the Granada coast on I Rabi 138 (August 14, 755).[20]

Prince 'Abd al-Rahman moved west for Medina-Sidonia almost immediately, his forces growing by a third as Yemeni horsemen signed on in eager desire to punish the hated Qaysi and Mudari—the Syrians. But Yemenis notwithstanding, as the weeks went by, loyalties of lineage drew significant support to his cause from Syrian *junds*. By spring of 756, much of Jaén province had transferred allegiance to "the Immigrant." Taking the measure of this capable Umayyad interloper, Amir Yusuf offered a generous bargain: position and wealth in Cordoba and the hand of his daughter in exchange for the prince's formal renunciation of political ambitions. According to the predicable treacherousness with which the power game was played, the prince knew that poison or an assassin's dagger awaited him once under the protection of al-Fihri. The end game came in the middle of May, within sight of Cordoba, on the same day (Friday) and month that had brought his ancestors their great victory in 684 in Syria—at Marj Rahit, where the Arab north-south split between Syrians and Yemenis had been sealed.[21]

The prince took the *amir*'s larger army by surprise and forced it to fight off balance along the banks of the Guadalquivir. Cordovans heard the muezzin broadcast the defeat that Friday evening of the fourteenth as Yusuf ibn 'Abd al-Rahman al-Fihri and his demoralized remnant retreated across the Roman bridge into the city. Two months later, the twenty-five-year-old victor entered the capital to accept al-Fihri's formal surrender and to proclaim himself master of *al-Andalus* from the Friday Mosque. The Umayyad dynasty, disgraced and decimated in its Syrian homeland, was positioned in 756 to create on the Iberian peninsula a political and cultural experiment of unique brilliance that would have no counterpart on the other side of the Pyrenees. Yet there were changes underway in the Great Land as significant in their own way as those portended by the regime debuting in Cordoba. Chilperic III, the last of the Merovingians, had been deposed and sent to a monastery five years earlier.

When news reached Baghdad that an Umayyad prince now sat in the house of government in *al-Andalus*, the great consolidator of the Abbasid Caliphate, Abu Ja'far al-Mansur, roared his displeasure. No investiture of office was ever to be sent from the spanking-new caliphal city on the Tigris. To be sure, formal rupture with Baghdad was more than a century and a half in the future, when the third 'Abd al-Rahman would assume the title of caliph for himself. Until then, the prince's descendants found it advisable to follow his policy of formal deference to Baghdad. The new *amir*'s situation was anomalous. The man he pushed aside, the valorous old Yusuf, had governed with tacit or implied Abbasid assent after the destruction of the Umayyad Caliphate. No such fiction could apply to 'Abd al-Rahman's seizure of power. He settled for the title of *amir*, but the sources note that, astutely advised by a member of his inner circle, the prince soon dropped all reference to the Abbasid caliphs in public prayers at the Friday Mosque.[22] Despite his dubious legitimacy—even because of it—'Abd al-Rahman I commenced his reign with a clear-headed, reforming resolve that would in time earn a half-admiring al-Mansur's flustered characterization of him as "the Falcon of the Quraysh." What the Berbers had begun, Umayyad Andalusia institution-alized. Not since the conquest of Mecca by the Prophet had the political unity of the Muslim world empire been as profoundly compromised.

Survival was the game plan. Hedged about by tribal treachery of all stripes—Berber, Syrian, Yemeni—hobbled by a state apparatus schooled in disloyalty and skilled at procrastination, outlawed by the supreme authority in Islam, the immigrant prince seemed, nevertheless, to own a saving patent on recruitment of the best and brightest to his cause. Umayyad clansmen reporting for service in Cordoba were the fittest sur-vivors of the liquidating Abbasid dragnets throughout Syria. Al-Walid ibn Mu'awiya, a brother of his, and two sons of the Caliph Hisham reached safety in *al-Andalus*. A distant Marwan cousin excelled at political calculation and became indispensable counselor and *hajib*, or virtual prime minister. A brother of the Caliph Umar II served in the inner cir-cle of counselors. Then there were *baladiyyun* such as the grandsons of old Mughith al-Rumi, one of the 711 conquerors, who rallied, as did a criti-cal mass of *muwalladun,* or non-Arab free-people (Christian converts), who owed their place and prosperity to Umayyad favor and protection.[23] The regime 'Abd al-Rahman began to build was of necessity nontribal. It was a mosaic of loyalties, with the prince at the center. If the scant sources mention somewhere that the prince made one or more strategic unions in marriage with the daughter of some powerful notable (as almost certainly he must have), names and particulars remain elusive.

But 'Abd al-Rahman's authority was only as good as the army he could raise to enforce it. He was soon tested. The failure to be able to send enough troops to help Narbonne in the final months of the Frankish siege of 759 was a bitterly significant defeat. Charles Martel had been compelled to abandon his siege of the city thirty years earlier in frustration. As long as the Narbonne beachhead stood, the resumed *jihad* had purchase. Narbonne's loss was due in part to a simultaneous emergency nearer home. The deposed Yusuf al-Fihri (of Narbonne fame, ironically) slipped away from Cordoba to raise the standard of revolt among Syrian and Berber loyalists in the West. 'Abd al-Rahman's regime met its first grave test near the old Roman provincial capital of Merida. Al-Fihri was hunted down and killed after his army had been smashed and scattered by the prince's generals in the winter of 759. But the al-Fihris, entrenched in Extremadura and southeastern Portugal, were a large clan, well endowed with political and military talent. In some respects, the Banu Fihri constituted a breakwater to the nascent power of the Umayyad state analogous to the Aquitainian dukes in aborning Francia.[24]

Now that construction of the majestic Abbasid capital on the Tigris was well along, the great Caliph al-Mansur turned his attention to what he deemed as an intolerable situation in *al-Andalus*. An Abbasid agent landed on the western coast in late March 763 with the black insignia and the investment of office. They were presented to a local notable, who promptly established himself at Beja, in southern Portugal, as the rightful *amir*. Assembling an army of Yemenis, he marched straight across the peninsula to occupy Sevilla. Anointed by the caliph and in possession of the Andalusian southwest, the contender, one al-'Ala ibn al-Mughith al-Yahsubi, posed a deadly double threat. It was a threat to which 'Abd al-Rahman's limited military resources prevented an effective response for several years. For the present, the *amir*'s response to Baghdad was his creation of an army of slaves tied to the regime's fate. One remembers that, in contrast to Christian ambiguities on the subject, the Qur'an condemned enslaving Muslims and People of the Book but approved of enslaving those captured in war or captured and/or purchased outside the *Dar al-Islam*.[25] The *amir* tapped into the old chattel network left by the Visigoths. The slaves—*saqaliba* (*siqlabi*, sing.)—who formed the prince's elite army units were blond, blue-eyed Slavic aliens whose sole *raison d'être* was to protect 'Abd al-Rahman, who, in turn, protected them. Caucasian infantry was complemented by the prince's bodyguard of dark-skinned Africans, whose status may have been superior to that of the Slavs. Since manumission of slaves was a virtue under Islam, many of 'Abd al-Rahman's *saqaliba* would rise to prominence in state affairs and eventually form a powerful separate class.

By the end of his first decade in power, 'Abd al-Rahman felt confident enough to lead his slave army in person against the Yemeni pretender at Sevilla. By then, his natural gifts of command had been refined by almost-unbroken war in the saddle. Contemporary sources, which invariably inflate numbers, give the modest figure of seven hundred Cordovan soldiers involved in the match with the pretender—perhaps to magnify the *amir*'s victory. The Battle of Carmona was a make-or-break confrontation whose outcome was uncertain until the end. A short distance east of Sevilla, the citadel of Carmona then stood, as it stands today, walled and high above the Guadalquivir plain, levitating like some nineteenth-century dreadnought transported back in time. The approach to the fortress from Sevilla followed a road almost arrow-straight until it loses confidence as it ascends the sharply angled landscape. The fortress's reputation for impregnability was self-evident and well documented.

'Abd al-Rahman assured himself a considerable strategic advantage. The Cordovan army, secure behind its battlements, waited until the frustrated enemy was about to call off its siege. Suddenly descending from the citadel, the steep terrain in its favor, the combined force of *saqaliba* and *muwalladun* decimated the Yemeni. "The battle lasted long until God did His marvelous work," one of the later Arab chroniclers reported.[26] 'Abd al-Rahman ordered all the prisoners executed, personally presiding over the slicing-off of Ibn al-Mughith's hands and feet before the decapitation. Labeled and pickled in brine, the leaders' heads were dispatched to Mecca, where, it is reported, the *amir*'s agent left sealed packages in one of the public spaces. When Caliph al-Mansur received the gory details, he is said to have expostulated, "God be praised for placing a sea between us!" The following year, 764, the *amir* ended the long standoff at Toledo and broke the power of the Toledan Banu Fihris and their Berber auxiliaries. The camphored head of Hisham ibn 'Urwa ibn al-Fihri took its place in the amiral palace beside that of the elder Yusuf al-Fihri. From that time onward, 'Abd al-Rahman was even better known by the sobriquet of "the Falcon of the Quraysh."[27]

※

'Abd al-Rahman I brought a uniting vision of community. It is hardly surprising that one whose survival into young adulthood had depended greatly on native intelligence would prize such a quality over caste and class. An era of relative stability commenced in Andalusia. Since the murder in 716 of 'Abd al-Aziz, the redoubtable Musa ibn Nusayr's son and heir, a score of governors-general had come and gone, most of them departing after no more than two years in power. To this chronic problem of Andalusian disaffection, 'Abd al-Rahman addressed a civic ideology that found space, in law and public practice, for community above race or tribe (except at the pinnacle of power), a regime increasingly congenial to justice and liberality for all Muslims whether *baladiyyun*, *Shamiyyun*, Berber, or *muwalladun*.

The *dhimmis*, the protected Iberian majority of Mozarabs, were guaranteed their separate rights and privileges under the old Visigothic codes, the *Lex Visigothorum*; Jews were served by rabbinic law. If his social contract was, from the vantage point of doctrine, really a restatement of Qur'anic first principles, it greatly mattered that 'Abd al-Rahman I intended that those principles govern the public lives of his people. "Fulfill your duties to Allah and bear true witness," the Prophet had commanded and 'Abd al-Rahman reiterated. "Do not allow your hatred of a people [to] incite you not to act equitably." This vision of societal comity the *amir* himself preached on regular occasions from the *minbar* of the Friday Mosque.[28]

From these enlightened policies would flow in good time the fabled *convivencia*, an ethos of storied tolerance and mutuality in which Muslims, Christians, and Jews long enjoyed (if not with the prodigious success too often romanticized ex post facto) civilized coexistence that might have served as a model for the continent. It was not social equality that distinguished the *convivencia*, but tolerance secured by restrictions. Infidels were not allowed in the first years of the Conquest to erect new houses of worship nor repair old ones; nor were Christians and Jews to hold public religious processions, pray too loudly, or proselytize. The homes of the *dhimmis* (Jews in their quarter, Christians in theirs) were not to rise higher than Muslims' dwellings. Sumptuary laws required that non-Muslims display badges and that clothing worn by the *dhimmis* be distinguishable from that worn by Arabs. The bearing of arms was forbidden. For a non-Muslim to strike a Muslim was a grave offense. Riding horses not only required a permit—riding them saddled was forbidden.

As time passed, many prohibitions fell away and others were seldom enforced. Muslim tolerance was based more on condescension than on generosity. As a people uniquely vouchsafed God's final revelation, the conquerors of Hispania looked upon their Christian and Jewish subjects as people stunted by a failure of theological understanding. In marked contrast to the Frankish rulers beyond the Pyrenees, for whom religious conversion and conformity would become policy imperatives, the Andalusian *amirs* believed that it made good social and political sense to let infidel conversions proceed, as it were, naturally. Enforced conversion was alien to Islam in *al-Andalus*, as it was elsewhere in the *ummah*. Moreover, the tax benefits of slow-rate conversion always remained compelling.

In contrast to the amirate's often-demeaning treatment of its Berber population, a paradox was discernible in 'Abd al-Rahman's continuation of liberality to the Jews. Their strategic value in the consolidation of Muslim rule had been enormous. From the first moment of contact, the Jews of Sefarad (Spain) had collaborated with the Arab conquerors. In places where their numbers were significant, such as Cordoba, Merida, Ecija, Jaén, Toledo, and Cuenca, that collaboration had sometimes been crucial to Muslim success. Entire regions of the newly conquered realm were later secured by wholesale relocation of Jews to sparsely populated places along the Mediterranean coast (Malaga, Granada, Almeria, Alicante) and to urban centers whose Catholic character they diluted by their numbers (Murcia, Pamplona, Guadalajara, Salamanca, Zaragoza).[29]

In close contact with other Jewish communities thriving in the

Mesopotamian watershed, distributed across North Africa, and positioned along the Mediterranean littoral, Andalusian Jews possessed unique assets for their Muslim conquerors. Indeed, the quintessentially urban Jews contributed more than loyalty, wealth, and numbers to the amirate; they showed the Muslims how to run it—so competently, indeed, that as time passed, several would rise to the high office of *vizir* and, in at least one spectacular instance, *hajib* (chancellor) of an Andalusian principality. The Arabs—desert warriors to whom the minutiae of governing had initially been less than congenial—found Jews to be indispensable as scribes, clerks, physicians, and court officials. Berbers fought like tigers, but their administrative skills were almost nonexistent.[30]

The topography of 'Abd al-Rahman's peninsula, a platform of crisscrossed cordilleras, has always resisted the power of the center. It would take several generations of Umayyad *amirs* before *al-Andalus* became a cohesive realm where Cordoba's writ ran generally unsubverted and uncontested. Beyond the outer limits of effective control were the embryonic Catholic kingdoms of Galicia and Asturias and Navarra, bordered by the Duero and the Ebro, of which all thought of Muslim conquest had long since faded. Wisely, rather than attempt to change the Andalusian structure of governance, the prince was content to reinforce the realm's administrative parts and prudently to shore up the authority and power of the center. Appropriately, one of his first acts was to abolish the nettlesome Syrian *junds*. In the beginning, he could do little more than hope that his carefully selected cadre of loyal, able governors and judges (*walis* and *qadis*) might be acknowledged or at least tolerated by the notables beyond the Cordovan core: in the Upper March, with its capital at Zaragoza; the Middle March, centered on Toledo; and the Lower March, encompassing Extremadura and Portugal and administered from Merida.

The Upper March, with its Berber population and converted Visigoth ruling clan, the Banu Qasi, remained problematic. Still, at the close of the first decade of his reign, with power buttressed by his formidable *saqaliba* military, 'Abd al-Rahman cowed or replaced unreliable governors. It was then that those special arrangements struck during the Conquest appear finally to have been abrogated. Whatever may have survived of the Treaty of Tudmir after the Syrian influx under Balj ibn Bishr was canceled. Similarly, another Visigoth nobleman who had bargained to keep his estates, the illustrious Count Ardabast, was relieved of his possessions.[31] Much like Charles the Hammer, the Falcon took what real estate he needed in order to endow a class of dependents.

The peace and order that prevailed in the Guadalquivir Valley and soon spread to the marches was a boon to the agriculture and trade that, in turn, bolstered the tax revenues of the state. What had been done by previous *amirs* to restore the extensive Roman irrigation system, ʿAbd al-Rahman accelerated and amplified. Canals laced large stretches of the southern plain. Thousands of distinctive Arab waterwheels, the *qanat* and the *noria*, raised water and milled grain. Like some giant, modern Erector set, one of the waterwheels that fed Cordoba still towers today above the banks of the Guadalquivir. From the plateau to its north, the city was plentifully supplied with corn, beef, and sheep from the Sierra Morena. Giving the finest wool in the world, the merino may have been introduced to Andalusia by Berbers during the Falcon's time, although possibly somewhat later. Like the merinos, the indispensable olive migrated across the Mediterranean at about this time. From the Campiña plains to the south, wheatfields, alternating with olive plantations and vineyards, stretched beyond the horizons. The Prophet did indeed disparage the consumption of wine, but the cultivation of vineyards for Christian consumption and export proceeded apace in *al-Andalus*, as did the consumption, even among some cosmopolitan Muslims, of the yield.[32]

In truth, the introduction of exotic plants was to be one of the Falcon's enduring legacies in his adopted land. Rusafa, his suburban villa outside Cordoba, built from boyhood memories, was both family retreat and botanical laboratory. There ʿAbd al-Rahman not only wrote wistful poetry about palm trees, he also brought them from Syria to plant them as the peninsula's first date palms. The palace retreat was the chrysalis of the future Spain's flora and fauna, the well from which so much of its ecological character was drawn. Flora from far-off worlds sprouted in the *amir*'s botanical gardens. Lemons, limes, and grapefruit were Rusafa introductions, along with almonds, apricots, saffron, and mulberry trees for silk cultivation—not to omit henna for hair care. The orange-blossom fragrances wafting over countless generations of Alhambra visitors figuratively emanated from the tree's first home at Rusafa. Sugar cane and rice also came to Andalusia, all part of the vast east-to-west migration of crops out of monsoon India that—thanks to the Cordovan state's irrigation program—became cultivable in Hispania's different climate.[33]

In a symbiosis unseen since the high noon of Roman colonization, Cordoba, as well as Sevilla at the western end of the Guadalquivir plain, waxed richer and larger as its market enriched the countryside that fed it. Cordoba was transformed. 'Abd al-Rahman I commenced its ascent from Visigothic dilapidation to a cosmopolitan splendor that would eventually make the old Roman capital of Baetica the urban marvel of tenth-century Europe. The city walls were repaired, as was the Roman bridge spanning the Guadalquivir, soon after he took up residence in the amiral palace. He commenced work on the city's great aqueduct that would continue almost to the end of his reign. The city would attain its unique pinnacle of commerce and culture, science and architecture during the reign of 'Abd al-Rahman III (912–61) and his son, al-Hakam II, but the foundations of greatness were laid by the Falcon. Emblematic of that future greatness was the exquisitely designed silver dirham minted late in the *amir*'s reign (the second silver coinage of the Conquest). Less than a century after 'Abd al-Rahman's death, the city on the Guadalquivir would grow to one hundred thousand, its population rising by the decade on a wave of trade and commerce. No other city in the West came near it in size. Cordoba, the economic and cultural acme of the Falcon's achievement, was to become an urban wonder.[34]

Organized by religion into economic guilds, Jews, Christians, and Muslims bought, sold, imported, and exported in a robust, wily competition that poured profit into the city. 'Abd al-Rahman's dirham was part of the remonetizing of world trade, a dynamic phenomenon made possible by the Arab ecumene's control of and access to vast sources of silver and copper. By contrast, Pippinid Francia was almost entirely bereft of specie. In an essay in the incomparable *Legacy of Muslim Spain*, the Islamist scholar Olivia Constable re-creates this sustaining international trade nexus. She imagines an Andalusi Muslim trader purchasing indigo, wool, or grain from a North African colleague who sells Spanish silk, timber, or "singing girls (captured from the Christian north) in return." From

Egypt, a Jewish trader arrives with a "cargo of flax, pearls, and brazilwood (a red dye), with perhaps a packet of eastern medicines as a gift for his Spanish partner's family."[35]

Lest *al-Andalus* be mistaken as a Dark Ages argument for laissez-faire capitalism, however, it must be noted that its economy operated under price controls set by the state. It was also an economy without interest charges on loans, *ríba* (banned by the Qur'an, as was usury in Christianity). Custom and biblical proscriptions operated in a somewhat similar manner under the Pippinids—the major difference being, however, that there was much less to be regulated in Francia. At the geographical margin of the empire, 'Abd al-Rahman's Cordoba was a piston in the economy of the Muslim universe; and although the relations between Umayyad *al-Andalus* and Abbasid Iraq often just barely skirted open warfare, mutual political animosities had little or no impact on trade relations.

Cordoba's goal of stealthy centralization advanced almost with the regularity of the seasons, and to some of the *baladíyyun* nobility and the ever-restive Berber notables, the winter of their power was fast approaching. Hotspots of resentment and resistance were most intense along the Andalusian perimeter—at Zaragoza, administrative capital of the Upper March, and at Huesca, the garrison town in the far northeast. The ruling families in these parts—possibly motivated by the calculus of political autonomy—professed themselves to be faithful clients of the Abbasid Caliphate. Baghdad encouraged their sedition with much alacrity. Among these notables was one Sulayman ibn al-A'rabi, *walí* of Barcelona and Girona, a consummate schemer and the architect of an audaciously complicated rebellion against the central authority. Sulayman's machinations, involving Franks, Abbasids, and Hispanic Catholics, had the potential to destroy the Umayyad regime. This unexpected saga would soon unfold.[36]

By any and all apparent measures, the Andalusian future dazzled. Well might the Falcon, as his people now called him, boast, as was his wont, "I came fleeing hunger, the sword, and death, attained security and prosperity, and gathered together a people. No one has done as I have," he reminded his followers. "Inspired by noble indignation, baring a double-edged sword, I crossed the desert and traversed the sea." Three young sons capably assisted their father in running the state. Hisham, the oldest, governed Merida. Sulayman ruled Toledo. The youngest, 'Abd Allah, appears to have been 'Abd al-Rahman's eyes and ears in Cordoba.[37] After more than twenty years of continual warfare, political machinations, and assiduous attendance to the architecture of grandeur, 'Abd al-Rahman I, still hard-driving in his mid-forties, soon faced his regime's greatest threat. For in the eyes of many who chafed under the weight of taxes, the force of laws, and the presence of agents and soldiers, the Falcon had succeeded all too well in building a strong state. The new Frankish kingdom had taken envious notice of the Andalusian phenomenon.

9

Saving the Popes

WHILE the West was learning to live with the suspense of another *jihad* after the Battle of Poitiers, the See of Peter faced imminent extinction. For better and worse, the bishops of Rome had been constrained to fill the power vacuum created by a much-weakened and preoccupied Eastern Roman Empire. Avars and Bulgarians menaced Constantinople from the northwest, Turks from the southeast, and the armies of the caliphs pressed unremittingly against the desperately defended Anatolian frontier. The Byzantines maintained a spectral presence in the Eternal City through a *magister militum* ("master of the soldiers"), the imperial representative theoretically responsible for defending the municipality and surrounding territory called the *Ducatus Romanum* (Duchy of Rome). The Master of the Soldiers had few soldiers to master, however, and those he did turned out for ceremonial occasions. After the tragically well-intentioned Emperor Maurice made a stab at reorganizing imperial authority near the end of the fifth century, the Exarchate of Ravenna on the Adriatic became the viceregal capital of Italy. Like the *magister militum* in Rome, the exarch in Ravenna commanded little more than a phantom garrison some 150 years later. He disposed of more troops at Bari on the Adriatic, some 150 miles south of Rome, on the eastern side of the peninsula—too far away to be of any use to the Holy Fathers, who expected to hear the hooves of Lombard horses on the Lateran steps any day.

These Lombards were as deadly a threat to imperial authority as they were to pontifical survival. Yet, repeated and increasingly urgent appeals from the Lateran Palace to Constantinople for military assistance, money to purchase mercenaries, or diplomatic initiatives among the Franks had been answered evasively or by silence. The evasions and silences were mainly an unacknowledged admission of Byzantine impotence to do anything to protect their Italian possessions. Yet even if the Byzantine treasury and military had been more robust, imperial policy dictated a fierce hostility to the bishops of Rome in their hour of greatest need, notwithstanding the perilous situation of the empire's own Ravenna exarchate. It was the cruelest of ironies that Leo "the Isaurian," the very emperor who saved the Eastern Roman Empire in 717–18 from Caliph Sulayman's attack by land and sea (the caliph who ordered Musa and Tariq to abandon *al-Andalus*), had seemed to go berserk over an issue that sundered the doctrinal unity of East and West for a century. Whether due to some dormant prepossession in his Syrian-peasant past that suddenly overrode political reason, or due to strong currents of Jewish and Muslim religious aesthetics within the empire, Leo banned the artistic representation of holy figures and thereby provoked the so-called Iconoclastic Controversy. Opposition in the West to Leo's edicts was overwhelming. Pope

Gregory III excommunicated the patriarch, and Rome recalled its representatives. Constantinople reciprocated.[1] A punitive Byzantine fleet, sailing to Ravenna, sank in a storm. Leo "the Isaurian," savior of Byzantium, died in June 741, five months before the death of Charles Martel, savior of Europe. The war of the icons continued unabated, nevertheless, under the emperor's son, Constantine V. Relations between the calculating bishop of Rome and the libertine *basileus* of Byzantium were poisoned beyond the balm of antidote. The Romans had to save themselves.

The Langobards (Lombards) were the last of the Germanic invaders. A quarter of a million of them stormed over the Alps in the late sixth century after a roundabout migration through the Balkans. Killing machines whose martial skills had improved with service as imperial mercenaries, they swept aside the Latins of the upper peninsula and outmatched the Ostrogoths. The Lombards had contracted the so-called German disease, the Arian creed endemic to the early Goths. Church property was fair game and the hunting season on priests was permanently open. Like the Goths, their racial pride was to keep them from adapting to the customs of the conquered for a considerable length of time. Alboin, their superchief, established a capital at Pavia and a concept of kingship distinguished by the possession of a sacred bejeweled iron crown. The Lombards' formal renunciation of Arian Christianity at the beginning of the seventh century was unmatched by any lessening of their insatiable appetite for papal territory, however. Nor were the kings and their dukes constant in their Catholicism.[2]

At the beginning of the eighth century, the iron crown of Lombardy passed to King Luitprand, a strong personality and a sovereign whose Roman and Christian improvements to the Lombard Code made him something of a lawgiver. Although the evidence for it is poorly supported, he could have brought his army into Provence in the summer of 737 to join Charles Martel's Franks in turning back the Muslim advance from Septimania. On the minus side, however, was Luitprand's policy of undermining the bishops of Rome in their disputatious dealings with Constantinople around the Iconoclastic Controversy and questions of apostolic prerogatives. Popes Gregory II, Gregory III, and Zacharias were taxed sometimes to distraction by the intricate dance steps demanded by Lombard diplomacy. When the feral Aistulf became the Lombard ruler in 749, papal wariness gave way to outright alarm. Aistulf's religion was war, and he was good at it. In 751, his army captured Ravenna, the major outpost of Byzantine power. The exarch died fighting. Aistulf's army then headed south to the Duchy of Rome, with the clear design of incorporating it into the Lombard realm.

Zacharias and Stephen II, Gregory III's successors, had shuffled the Vatican corridors as men who knew their leases, barring divine intercession or a rescuing army, were in imminent danger of being canceled. The end impended on Stephen's watch. In what appeared to be the twilight of its independent existence, the Roman episcopacy reached out to the tribe with the strongest army in Latin Christendom—the Franks, Catholic by the grace of God and Clovis. A sophisticated Greek and master manipulator, Zacharias in the last year of his life devised the scheme to replace the last Merovingian cipher with a family indebted to the papacy for its throne. For three centuries, the soul of the Franks had been preserved incarnate through the unbroken Merovingian line from Merovech to the last Childeric. No matter that they had passed their last undistinguished hundred years or so as manipulated figureheads, as marginalized Clothaires, Thierrys, or Dagoberts—long-haired totems in political service to virile, scheming Austrasian and Neustrian palace mayors. By their very existence, Frankland (Francia) was sustained in perpetuity, and no act had validity that impugned their ultimate authority. True enough, Charles the Hammer had audaciously prorogued the royal succession in 737 after the death of Thierry IV, but that no one supposed Pippinid sovereignty to be other than de facto was shown by the elevation of Childeric III to the vacant throne soon after the great mayor's demise.[3]

The majestic Boniface (Wynfrith) was assigned a crucial part in the scheme to replace the three-hundred-year-old Merovingian line. This wise holy man, selflessly devoted to improving the education of priests, restoring the integrity of the episcopate, and converting the heathen forest people, was no political naif. After some thirty years of ministry to the pagans of Upper and Lower Hesse, and Thuringia, of building churches and founding monasteries with pious helpmates, and of elevating clerical standards by sheer power of personal example, the giant Englishman received papal appointment as archbishop of Mainz and primate of Germania. Boniface's exemplary ways were often compatible with temporal machinations, for the astute priest believed that God was disposed to condone whatever arrangements served Mother Church's higher interests. The pontiffs regarded the priest's influence over the Pippinid princes as key to the Roman Church's survival. His was a considerable influence, as Charles Martel had entrusted the education of his sons, Carloman, Pippin, and Grifo, to Boniface at St. Denis. On the Hammer's death in 741, Carloman, pious and temperamental, and Pippin, wily and steady, had divided the spoils of palace mayor between them: Austrasia and Alamannia to the former; Neustria and Burgundy to the latter. Grifo, issue of a different mother, was marginalized.

As their preceptor and spiritual uncle, the future saint had imbued the dukes—Carloman in particular—with religious sentiments notably absent in their father. Although a first-class warrior who cooperated with his brother to stanch the perennial ducal rebellions in Aquitaine, Alamannia, and Bavaria, Carloman was of a distinctly spiritual cast of mind. Soon after the Hammer's death, Boniface had written to urge, "In the event of your coming to power," that Carloman "help the clerics, priests, monks, nuns and all the servants of God in Thuringia, and that you will protect the Christians from the hostility of the heathens."[4] Charles Martel had cowed and alienated the clergy in order to pay for armies to enforce political unity. Carloman's gambit was to foster national unity by cultivating the high clergy and espousing ecclesiastical reform, the better to bind the Church to Pippinid authority and territorial consolidation. The lawless souls who came to God became dutiful subjects of the king.

Boniface proposed rules that received Carloman's active commendation on the governance and training of priests, the enforcement of celibacy and banning of participation in warfare, and the dispatch of missions to pagan regions. At the first of several religious conclaves during the 740s, Carloman presided over the great reform synods in April of 742 and in March of the following year at Estinnes (in what is now Belgium), with Boniface in attendance. Yet, though a faithful son of the Church, Carloman's deference stopped short of secular folly. The prelates assembled at Estinnes were told, as already mentioned, that the unsettled conditions of the kingdom forced him to keep for a while longer "a portion of Church property." Four years after Estinnes, the introspective Carloman surprised his people by abdicating as palace mayor of Austrasia and ruler of Alamannia to take religious vows. The Catholic prince who could have led a relief army of veteran Frankish infantry against the heretical Lombards went to Italia instead as a humble, tonsured monk to reside in the Benedictine monastery dramatically sited on Monte Cassino.[5] Carloman's motives are purest mystery. Sensitive and educated, he may have judged that a life of ceaseless warring from a saddle was the vanity of Ecclesiastes. He must have seen the hard choice soon to be made between the Lombards and the popes. On the one hand, there was his father's pro-Lombard policy and his own partiality to the court of Pavia; but on the other, the welfare of Christ's vicar and the prospects for his own salvation tormented him. Better to seek answers from God in a mountaintop monastery figuratively halfway to heaven. Two years after Carloman's retirement, the predatory Aistulf became king of Lombardy and two years later terminated the exarchate of Ravenna.

Pope Zacharias vented his frustration in letters to Boniface and died within the year. Papal appeals to Constantinople for military assistance continued to go nowhere. The Franks were the last resort. Pippin, now ruler of the united kingdom, weighed the large dynastic implications of Zacharias's predicament in consultation with Boniface. Pippin—known to history as "the Short," the sobriquet befitting his stature—was the Hammer's second son and the third Pippinid, or Arnulfing, to bear that name. There was nothing diminutive about Pippin the Short's political ambitions. Undistracted by his older brother's otherworldly concerns, this squat figure with the large Pippinid head was his father's son in physical strength, military science, and political calculation. With Carloman gone, he had quickly and brutally checkmated what was left of the competition. By the end of the 740s, Pippin III was master enough of his rambunctious realm that Bavarian dukes, Saxon chieftains, Frisian warlords, and Septimanian *amirs* looked with increasing concern to their defenses. There was more than enough to keep him busy consolidating the hard-won gains of his father and brother in the lands between the

Pyrenees and the Alps without taking on the murderous Lombards. Lombard cavalry would be worth a great deal more than papal blessings when the Saracens came again in force. Pippin may have been the first politician to pose the question, "How many divisions does the pope have?" Not that Pippin III needed much prompting from his inner circle of magnates and bishops to ponder regime change, but circumstantial evidence points to Boniface as the one who broached the possibility of papal sanction for the overthrow of the Merovingian dynasty in exchange for an army of Franks to stop Aistulf. Duke Pippin's elation may have been matched by trepidation. If politics and logic commended such a gambit, hallowed tradition denounced it.

Pippin the Short approved of the special mission suggested by Boniface. Off to Rome went the bishop of Wurzburg and the chaplain of St. Denis to ask the momentous question the new pope, Stephen II, was waiting eagerly to answer. Asked "whether it was good or not that the King of the Franks should wield no royal power," Stephen replied that the situation in Frankland was unwise, that he who held the power in fact should be king in law and in the eyes of God. Pippin's emissaries returned from Rome with the pope's historic recommendation that, because it was better to have a king able to govern "by apostolic authority," Stephen II bid Pippin the Short "be crowned King of the Franks." The high prelates of the realm solemnly declared that regime change was sanctioned by God. He who was "falsely called King" was consigned to oblivion. In 751, almost ten years to the month after Charles the Hammer died at Quierzy-sur-Oise, the last Merovingian king, Childeric III, twenty-second in his line, was deposed. "His hair was cut short and he was shut up in a monastery," wrote a near-contemporary. The magnates clashed their shields in approbation, and Boniface officiated at the coronation of the new king in the Abbey of St. Denis.[6] Duke Pippin III, palace mayor of Austrasia and Neustria, became King Pippin I in his thirty-seventh year. Bertrada, the legitimate wife and mother of the king's several children, became queen.

Nothing in the records from those heady days suggests any awareness in Austrasia of the almost-simultaneous overthrow of the Umayyad Caliphate. With Pippin's election by the high nobility and elevation to the purple, the Carolingian dynasty, so named for the Carolus who united Frankland and repelled the Muslims, formally took center stage in the history of the West. Pope Stephen and his successors resolved to perform the role of stage manager. A cultural fact of decided significance to people at that time, but whose importance history has elided, is that the ascendancy of the Pippinid-Rhineland Franks of Austrasia measurably diminished the Gallo-Latin character of Merovingian Francia with its Paris-Soissons-Reims orientation. The German-speaking Carolingians, with their preference for Metz, Cologne, and Frankfurt retarded the spread of Francia's Romance language and ensured a bulwark of Frankland's Nordic speech and mores beyond the Moselle River. Not so many centuries in the future, cultural chauvinists would cite the coronation of Pippin I as a marker for the submergence of the Gauls by the Germans.[7] For the Church of Rome, 751 marked the moment when its future as the purveyor of the "universal" faith of the West was ensured.

⸬

The Lombard peril forced Pope Stephen II to risk a heroic journey into alpine altitudes and through dead-of-winter snows to plead for King Pippin's help in person. His unprecedented arrival pushed ecclesiastical leverage to a maximum just a few months after Boniface's martyrdom at the hands of heathens in the Frisian woods. The first pontiff to travel voluntarily beyond Italia, he and his coterie of tired priests reached eastern Austrasia via a lifeline of monasteries extending from Turin through the Great St. Bernard Pass and then across the Rhine Pfalz into Francia in late December 753.[8] The pope had risked wolf packs, bandits, accidents, and hypothermia in a high-stakes gamble to broker a formal, offensive alliance with the first Carolingian royal.

Pope Stephen's mission came at the most parlous moment facing the Holy See since the menace of Attila and his hordes. Aistulf was nearly at the gates of the Eternal City. Stephen's was the mission of a man without options. Messengers reached the king at Ponthion, the royal village in the Lorraine somewhere north of Metz. Pippin I was resting for the winter in the wooden palace compound with his wife and family. Queen Bertrada's present dynastic contribution was as mother of the kingdom's adolescent heirs, Charles and another Carloman, but she was to show herself a woman of even more ability and political initiative than the Countess Plectrude, wealthy consort of the first Pippin. As a mark of respect, the king sent the older boy, nine-year-old Charles, or Carolus (the future Charlemagne), to welcome and escort the Holy Father from the town of Thionville. Rocking unsteadily in his saddle, Stephen was heard to mutter repeatedly, "*Mefandissimi Langobardi, mefandissimi Langobardi*" ("Most evil Lombards, most evil Lombards").

According to the *Royal Frankish Annals,* when Pippin and Stephen finally met face-to-face on January 6, 754, the king dismounted and walked on foot for a mile or so, leading the pope to his palace by the horse's bridle. It was a gesture pregnant with meaning for the coming struggles between popes and emperors for temporal supremacy. Cautious, complex negotiations occupied them over the next weeks as the two men took full measure of each other. One was a king who had usurped his throne with papal blessings, the other a pope come to collect a debt to save the See of Peter. Of the two, Stephen, relatively young and an orphan raised in the papal court, was the more adroit politically. Pippin the Short was five feet of dynastic ambition and a natural leader of fighting men. The high-stakes negotiations unfolded amid bearskins, stacked weaponry, snoring dogs, cluttered bones, and upturned wine jugs as high nobles and papal notables shivered near an open fire and the sizzle of a spitted pig. The timbered scene was likely to have been pure *Beowulf*: "Benches were pushed back, bedding gear and bolsters/spread across the floor. . . ."9

The palace compound at Ponthion vanished without a trace more than a thousand years ago, a curious fate for a place where preliminary decisions were taken that laid the foundations for the first nation-state in history, the supremacy of the bishop of Rome, the irrecoverable alienation of the Latin West from the Greek East, and the emergence of religious fanaticism and chronic, reciprocated hostility of Islam and the Occident. The immediate consequences of the lengthy deliberations of Pippin and Stephen were politically dramatic; the long-term consequences were world-determining. In an imposing ceremony of incense, pageantry, and Latin staged in the Abbey of St. Denis, Pippin was anointed with holy oil and pronounced king in June 754 by virtue of the authority reposed in the pope by St. Peter. From that moment, the divinity of the first Carolingian surpassed even that of the semidivine Clovis, blessed though he was by a great bishop, St. Remigius of Reims, but no pope. But Pippin I may not have been fully conscious of the implications of his coronation—the transforming of kingship based on the Germanic principle of hereditary election into monarchical succession based, above all, on the legitimation of papal sanction.

In recognition of the Lombards' ferocity, Pippin's Italian invasion was of an unprecedentedly ambitious scale. As the Franks were to fight to protect the papacy and uphold its territorial claims, the campaign was also devoid of the usual incentives of real estate and domination—a distinct disincentive to many of the great nobles. To all such concerns, Stephen had brought a remarkable answer in his saddlebags: the *Donation of Constantine*. A lengthy document in Latin worthy of the Caesars, it was supposed to have been composed in the early fourth century at the behest of Emperor Constantine I on the eve of his departure from Rome for the new capital on the Bosporus. As Stephen and his bishops patiently explained to Pippin, Constantine deeded to the bishops of Rome all the imperial property of Italia and rights thereunto: "And we did hand it over, to be enduringly and happily possessed, to our most blessed father, Sylvester, the supreme pontiff and universal pope, and, through him, to all the pontiffs his successors, God our Lord and our Savior Jesus Christ consenting." If the founder of the Second Rome had vested the Holy See with the safekeeping of the First Rome, then the hoary Latin mumbo jumbo surely made the dispossession of the Lombards an obligation of faith and law. Pippin readily assented to defend the material interests of the papacy against all threats. The *Donation of Constantine* presented a powerful argument, one of the most famous forgeries in history. Although the exact time and place of its conception has been long disputed ever since a cynical Renaissance papal secretary established it as a fraud, its presentation to Pippin I on the occasion of Stephen's heroic visit is most likely.[10]

With the pope riding in a baggage wagon, King Pippin led an invasion force over the Alps in late summer of 754 to attack the Lombard stronghold at Pavia. Aistulf had little stomach for the Frankish style of war to the last-standing man. The Lombard sued for peace, withdrew from the Duchy of Rome, and pledged to hand over the exarchate of Ravenna and other lands to the papacy. Imitating Constantine, Pippin issued his own donation justifying his refusal to honor the Byzantine emperor's enraged demand that Ravenna be returned to imperial control. Faithful to the supposed rights granted to the Church by the *Donation of Constantine*, the king of the Franks decreed the former Byzantine territory forfeit to the See of Peter. Nor had the pope emptied his saddlebags of dazzling documents. Stephen transferred to the king of the Franks the resonant honorific of *patricius Romanorum*—"patrician of the Romans"—the title reserved exclusively to the Byzantine emperor's representative.[11] With all this, Aistulf's chastisement was only temporary. As soon as Pippin crossed the Alps for Frankland, Aistulf reneged on most of his territorial pledges. The patrician of the Romans had to mount a second campaign in 756, when Aistulf pledged to surrender the promised possessions as well as Spoleto and several other choice parcels.

The ferocity of the battle over images reached frightful intensity during Stephen's papacy, with Byzantine refugees arriving in Italy seeking asylum from imperial persecution. With Pippin's territorial donations of 754 and 756, papal deference to Constantinople ended for good, and the bishop of Rome became a secular sovereign as well as the spiritual pastor of Christendom. Acclaimed throughout the Christian world for having saved the papacy, Pippin the Short set forth to match his father's great achievement against the Saracens. In the summer of 757, as 'Abd al-Rahman I was locked in desperate struggles with powerful enemies, the king assembled a large army for the invasion of Septimania and capture of Narbonne, the Muslim canker lodged in the southwestern corner of Francia. To the relief of Pippin and the immense satisfaction of Pope Stephen, King Aistulf had died in a hunting accident a few months earlier, just as the incorrigible Lombard's army was assembling for another attack on Rome.

When Pippin the Short died of dropsy in September 768, the building blocks of the post-Merovingian order were solidly in place. The Narbonne redoubt in Septimania had been reconquered from the children of

Ishmael and the pagan Saxons punished, if far from subdued. Frankland
had experienced what its people believed was a providential breathing
spell in the thirty-odd years after the Battle of Poitiers. But it was a
breathing spell due far more to Berbers than to God. The time span of
that reprieve had in fact begun in 740 with the rolling rebellion across *al-
Andalus*, rather than in 732 at Moussais-la-Bataille. Pippin, the first
Arnulfing king of his line, had taken full advantage of the interrupted
jihad in order to make the sum of royal power greater than the parochial,
bickering parts. During his seventeen-year reign, the realm's dukes and
counts were tamed by a combination of force, manna, and religion.

The profitable codependency between Pippin and the Church had
shifted decidedly in his favor. Not only did he appoint bishops, the king
ventured to mediate fundamental theological deliberations at a historic
conclave convened in 767. Western men and women of faith had been
sorely troubled by Byzantium's on-again, off-again prohibition of any
depiction of holy personalities, an imperial edict that threatened to
extinguish what little solidarity remained between Rome and Constantinople. "The Lord King Pepin then held a great council at Gentilly with
Romans and Greeks about the Holy Trinity and the image of the saints,"
according to the *Royal Frankish Annals*.[12] Pippin's assumption of the role of
theological coadjutor was appropriate to one who bore the resonant titular distinction *patricius Romanorum*. His pragmatic involvement in the
Iconoclastic Controversy, wily interventions in the religious politics of
Italy, and numerous military victories brought recognition from the
Byzantine imperial court in his last years. In calculated tribute to the
king's new importance in the scheme of world affairs, Emperor Constantine V sent the first pipe organ ever seen in the West to the Frankish
court. Abbasid Baghdad took similar note of Pippin as a significant
player by inviting an exchange of embassies for the obvious purpose of
isolating the Umayyads of *al-Andalus*. Muslim emissaries arrived at Metz
with the returning Franks just as the king expired.

With its evangelizing clergy protected by the crown, the much-
reformed Frankish Church penetrated the daily life of the common people as never before. The people were fine-tuned to the routine of
worship and rehearsed in the mysteries of the flesh-and-blood Holy

Communion and other sacraments. They were discouraged from deeply entrenched polygamy and incest, awed and subdued by visions of hellfire and the imperative of the confessional. Vows of priestly chastity, poverty, and obedience began to be enforced from above. Pagan accretions and Arian corruptions were assiduously pursued and extirpated in villages and remote habitats. The liturgical regime was tightened and a pre-scribed minimum of Latin was ordained. Pity the priest who, like a late-eighth-century Bavarian, baptized his parishioners *in nomine patria et filia* ("in the name of the nation and the daughter")! Indeed, because so many priests were educationally challenged—especially when it came to Latin—bishops ordered elementary homilies distributed among them. There must be no "inventing or recounting to the people [of] new things . . . uncanonical and according to their own taste rather than the Holy Scriptures," a typical injunction read.[13] Clergy were subjugated to the absolute authority of bishops, with the trade-off that priests exercised unquestioned patriarchal authority over their flocks.

Frankland was now the largest Roman Catholic community in the West. It served as the proving ground for the rise of a hierarchical, mili-tant religious caste whose interpretive monopoly of the sacred texts of the Christian faith was virtually absolute—a holy bureaucracy interposed between God and the believer. Boniface and his indefatigable servants succeeded in making the acceptance of clerical authority the ideal order in secular society. From crib to grave, no possibility of salvation for the humble Frankish believer existed without the intercession of the regular and secular priesthood. At the ecclesiastical pyramid's apex sat the pon-tiff in Rome—more than a millennium from the papal encyclical of doc-trinal infallibility, true, yet a mere two centuries' distance from papal absolutism. The Christianizing of the "Europenses" became, thanks to the Boniface revolution among the Franks, the Roman Catholicizing of those "Europenses." The octogenarian martyr's lasting legacy was a refur-bished clergy duly responsive to the Holy See and possessing enough political clout to help the popes calibrate and enforce the collaboration of an increasingly powerful Carolingian monarchy.[14]

The Pippinid realm was now an immense geographical mosaic extending from the Rhine west to the Pyrenees and from the North Sea south to Bavaria—a structure replicating Clovis's stupendous achieve-ment. It remained relatively underpopulated for its vast size, with the parts that had formed Roman Gaul containing a population probably reduced to half the number in the last imperial census. As with the Merovingian state, the Pippinid body politic turned on a northeasterly axis between the Seine and the Rhine. It was also a heterogeneous mess, a Babel of tongues congealing beneath a scrim of formal Latin into the Romance languages of *oïl* and *oc* and into Germanic dialects of Flemish, Dutch, and others. Beyond the Austrasian/Neustrian/Burgundian core were semiautonomous dependencies peopled by Aquitainians and other Gallo-Romans who clung to what little remained of their old Roman ways, along with tribal Thuringians, Bavarians, Frisians, and Swabians in varying stages of Christian acculturation. The realm's exiguous spheres of commerce and culture were virtually unpenetrated by energies from the Arab or Byzantine Mediterranean. The economy was local, agricultural, and virtually moneyless. About the only commerce that could be described as transregional was the robust slave trade.[15]

After fifty-three good years, Pippin I expired in 768, leaving the kingdom to his two intelligent, battle-seasoned sons, Carolus and Car-loman, both of whom Pope Stephen II had crowned with their father at the start of the monarchy. They came into their inheritances ready for the tests of strength certain to come out of the mountains in the West, where the Falcon of the Quraysh was building a powerful state. Other tests awaited the new royals, however—tests beyond the Alps equally as momentous for Europe's political and cultural future. Carloman, the younger brother, was given the kingdom's more peaceful portion, an unbroken block of territory stretching from Septimania to the Rhine that included Frankland's heartland, with many of the largest towns. The share held by the twenty-year-old Carolus (the future Charlemagne) was a thin, crescent-shaped domain (slicing through the western and north-ern portions of Austrasia, Neustria, and Aquitaine) that enveloped his brother's in an arc from east to west. The crescent not only formed something of an outer protective rim for his brother Carloman's posses-sions, it positioned his own kingdom so that portions of it abutted the

Franks' obstreperous neighbors. As had happened so often before with Germanic rulers, the partition of the kingdom ordained by Pippin was conducive to fratricidal conflict. Little or no love had ever been lost between the two brothers in any case. Less than three years after Pippin I's demise, Frankland was on the verge of civil war.[16]

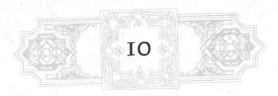
An Empire of
Force and Faith

ALTHOUGH his biographer used Suetonius as the model for his *Vita Caroli Magni* (*Life of Charlemagne*), Einhard, the Frankish scholar who served as adviser and architect of Carolingian learning, is a disappointing gossip. Not nearly enough is said about the flesh-and-blood subject. Charlemagne exuded native intelligence and affected a cordial ease with intimates, we are told. "His eyes very large and animated," observes Einhard. "Nose a little long, hair fair, and a face laughing merry." The young king's voice is said to have been somewhat curious, in fact, because it was "too high-pitched." Morever, he was given to stuttering when he spoke rapidly. Charlemagne's extraordinary height was definitively settled in the mid-nineteenth century when the emperor's tomb was opened and his six-foot, three-and-a-half-inch measurements were taken. His muscular torso was well proportioned and would remain so, except for a slight paunch in middle age.[1]

An early misreading of the *Vita Caroli Magni* assumed that Charlemagne was illiterate and that he spent his life in an unsuccessful struggle to master his letters. A once-popular description limns the monarch as a dumb giant reaching under his bed for writing tablets for the purpose of alphabet practice. What Einhard probably meant, however, was that the king never mastered the complex and delicate script known as Carolingian minuscule (containing, unlike the Roman, lowercase letters) and introduced into Frankland after Charlemagne reached adulthood. But if so, then the official biographer was more than generous. The king of the Franks never mastered writing in any form, as his mark on state documents, two crossing lines, shows. But literacy's meaning in the Dark Ages rarely implied a command of script. In an oral age in which most of what people wanted and needed to know came by way of the voice rather than the stylus, writing was hardly a skill expected of the warrior class, even of a ruler of Charlemagne's importance. For that purpose, there were priests aplenty. Reading was marvel enough for any member of the warrior class, although hardly regarded as essential to the performance of his professional duties.

Charlemagne spoke Latin easily ("as well as his own native tongue," said Einhard), was able to understand spoken Greek, and was especially fond of having St. Augustine's *City of God* read to him.[2] There was, however, virtually no comparison between his cultural sophistication and that of the exquisitely educated Umayyad prince whose rule over *al-Andalus* had already run a dozen years when Pippin's oldest son inherited the Austrasian kingdom. We don't imagine Charlemagne composing a wistful poem like the Falcon's "Palm." Nor should we expect to hear him deliver a polished public address in Latin in the manner of one of 'Abd al-Rahman's sermons in elegant Arabic from the *minbar*. Yet, the king of the Franks and the *amir* of *al-Andalus*, the most powerful and politically astute rulers on the European continent, were a study in contrasts aspiring to each other's strong suit: the Frank dreaming of an economically and culturally dynamic kingdom; the Arab needing military invincibility in order to secure a remarkable economic and cultural base. Charlemagne's literacy has fascinated historians for the good reason that the not-quite-literate future emperor of the West was himself profoundly fascinated by the power of the written word. He was a barbarian more deeply impatient with the intellectual poverty of his fellow barbarians than perhaps any other well-positioned German since the collapse of the Roman Empire.

How Charlemagne came to be that way, what the influences and epiphanies may have been in childhood and adolescence, can't be descried without the peril of leaping speculation. Einhard could have been expected to offer at least the rudiments of events of Charlemagne's early years. Instead, he begins the biography with an almost suspect disclaimer, protesting that it would be "folly . . . to write a word concerning Charles's birth and infancy, or even his boyhood, for nothing has ever been written on the subject." Do we really believe him when he adds, "and there is no one alive who can give information of it"? No relatives among the extended family and its branches? No fireside stories about the early years of the Franks' greatest state-builder and military commander? Unlike his younger brother, Carloman, Charles was almost certainly born before his royal parents were united by the Church. Pensioned handsomely in 828 after almost forty years of indispensable service that helped build the Carolingian order, Einhard conceived the value of his biography in the spirit of the hagiographer: Charlemagne's Parson Weems.[3] But vacuums will be filled, and the *Life of Charlemagne* has invited more than enough circumstantial evidence, deduction, and tribal memory to harden suspicions that Einhard knew things about his royal ideal's pubescent youth that were better left undisclosed.

The sin of incest, for instance—the extirpation of which the educated clergy regarded as a top priority—was common practice among the

Germans. When Carolus was becoming Charlemagne, few aristocratic parents, to say nothing of his peers, yet fully grasped the awfulness of the transgression that caused such despair in the Willibrords and the Bonifaces. Tribal memory, mediated through the *Karlamagnus Saga*, a thirteenth-century Norse epic based on "lost" fragments of Dark Ages derring-do, remembers Charlemagne's sister, Gisela, who, after bearing her brother's child, is locked away in a religious establishment for life. That he never allowed any of his daughters to marry but kept them close by (even Einhard found that a bit odd) nourished the underground legend of familial kinkiness. A better reason may well be that Charlemagne was loath to share his kingdom with sons-in-law and generations of consanguineous claimants. Certainly, Einhard would have found the rumored circumstances of Gisela's confinement uncongenial—demeaning details to be deleted from the exemplary record of the father of a civilization. Gisela's story, if true, signified the increasing success of the Church in setting the standards for the moral behavior of the ruling class. Einhard's Charlemagne was domestically virtuous, a sovereign uncontaminated by ecclesiastical taboos of incest or polygamy, the faithful husband of five wives serially acquired and six dutiful concubines enjoyed between the deaths of the breeding wives.[4]

Carolus was three years older than Carloman and somewhat more tested in combat, although Pippin had taken both boys on many campaigns. Carolus possessed in exceptional degree the attributes that mattered above all others in Frankland's martial society: courage and a powerful sword arm. Since the *Royal Frankish Annals* were written in praise of Carolus after he became Charlemagne, a degree of skepticism about the negative portrayal of his brother is in order. Carloman had no Einhard to gild his life, and it seems obvious that his personality bore little resemblance to his namesake uncle's spirituality. Relinquishing power for the cloister was assuredly not in his constitution. However competent as a commander of men in battle, Carloman would have suffered by comparison with a sibling who was—as virtually every account since the eighth century affirms—one of the world's greatest military geniuses. Ingratitude and treachery are the qualities imputed by the *Royal Frankish*

Annals to Pippin's second son; and, since even his mother came reluctantly to favor the cause of her oldest boy, almost nothing in the sources gainsays the impression of an ungrateful, headstrong conniver.

It seems fair to say that Carloman's sibling competitiveness pushed him into hasty decisions and caused him to believe that his older brother plotted to deprive him of his father's legacy. Carloman's inheritance was the richer, as it comprised most of Roman Gaul as well as a portion of Aquitaine. He contested minor property claims and resented Carolus's prior claim to burial rights at St. Denis. Two centuries after Clovis, German succession rights were still uncertain: older sons were not automatically privileged. Signaling to the world that his family should have parity with his brother's, Carloman and Gerberga baptized their first son with the talismanic name of Pippin. Carolus and Himiltrud, daughter of a minor magnate, had just named their first-born Pippin. In the midst of these complaints and machinations, a realm crisis emerged. Hunald, Duke Odo's humiliated son, left his cloister and raised the standard of revolt in Aquitaine. From his seat at Laon, Carloman declined his brother's appeal and left him to fight the renegade duke alone. No sooner had Aquitaine been adequately policed than rumors spread of an alliance in the works between Carloman and the king of Lombardy.[5]

Whatever their truthfulness, the rumors angered Carolus and stupefied the Holy Father. Frankland, the continental power that future popes would fondly call "the eldest daughter of the Church," was the cornerstone of the Catholic Church's foreign policy—an insurance policy for the papacy's very survival. Relations between the pope and the Greek patriarch were then at one of their low points. Three months before King Pippin I's entombment in St. Denis, Pope Paul I, his pontificate pressed to the ropes by the everlasting Lombards and manipulative Byzantines, had passed away after ten desperate years, leaving the Eternal City engulfed in civil strife. As the ally of Desiderius, the bullying Lombard ruler, Carloman would acquire wealth and men sufficient eventually to force his brother from the throne and steal the other half of his father's bequest. For the papacy, Carloman's alliance with Desiderius, Aistulf's successor, would mean Lombard overlordship and much worse.[6]

The contest of power between the brothers was the stuff of grand opera, with scheming royal parents, petulant siblings, nuptial ploys, suspiciously convenient deaths, and cameo appearances by papal courtiers, Bavarian dukes, and scurrying emissaries. Had Charlemagne's mother's scheme succeeded, the course of European history-in-the-making might have been altered. Queen Mother Bertrada, daughter of the count of Laon, was known to contemporary sources as Bertrada or Bertha. The people of Frankland called her "Queen Goose Foot" or "Bertha of the Big Foot" because of her large feet and manner of walking. She was a resourceful woman in the mold of Countess Plectrude, that remarkable predecessor whose political machinations as Pippin of Heristal's widow had unwittingly brought Charles the Hammer to power in Austrasia. Whether she was finally more swayed by a mother's affection or the pitiless dictates of Realpolitik remains ambiguous, but once she sided with her oldest boy, her mastery of the game of high-stakes diplomacy was unrivaled. A hostilely divided kingdom appeared to be inevitable, so she must have concluded that Carolus's political survival was imperative. Bustling off in the early summer of 770 to try brokering a compromise between her sons, the queen mother found Carloman in Alsace, determined to trump his brother by an alliance with the Lombards. She hurried to Bavaria to whisper preemptive inducements into the ear of its duke, Tassilo, son-in-law of the Lombard king, then headed for the alpine passes to confer with King Desiderius in his capital at Pavia.[7]

Bertrada's Lombard proposal was inspired. She pledged Charlemagne in marriage to Desiderius's thirteen-year-old, willowy, blonde daughter whom several sources erroneously claim to have borne the fetching name Desiderata, although no trace of her real name survived the patriarchal indifference of her age.* She cared little that her son already possessed a legal wife, Himiltrud, by whom Charlemagne had been given an heir—the child Pippin, called "the Hunchback" because of a spinal deformity. The future master of most of Europe did as his mother told him. Himiltrud's divorce was accomplished by diktat,

---

*Alessandro Manzoni famously called her Ermengarda in his 1822 play *Adelchi*, but the record is utterly blank about the Lombard princess's real name. Desiderata, a copyist's mistake, is used here for convenience.

despite the union's having been consummated under Church law. The queen's nuptial gambit on behalf of her oldest son, therefore, dumb-founded the Holy See. A Lombard queen for a Frankish kingdom and a Frankish king as a Lombard son-in-law realigned the stars in Christen-dom. Stephen, the third pontiff to bear the name, was quite beside him-self as he fulminated by circular letter against Bertrada's consorting with "the faithless and most vile Lombard people which do not count among the ranks of the peoples and whose members have certainly brought forth the lepers."[8]

The pope had every reason to vituperate. Stephen III's papacy had survived unprecedented calamities. Paul I, Stephen's legitimate prede-cessor, had been followed by two antipopes, Constantine and Philip. The first was the creature of the Tuscans, the second of the Lombards. Ais-tulf's territorial aggrandizings had unleashed a stampede among Italia's titled brigands. The major polities no longer saw the point of an inde-pendent Duchy of Rome. The duke of Tuscany, Toto of Nepi, galloped into Rome with his men and installed his brother on the papal throne at sword point. Lombard cavalry arrived immediately in answer to desper-ate appeals from papal dignitaries and Rome's anti-Tuscan partisans. Duke Toto died fighting King Desiderius's troops on Vatican Hill. Toto's brother, "Pope" Constantine II, an ecclesiastically ignorant layman, was dragged from the Lateran Palace, blinded, and then imprisoned, where he was brutally murdered. Farce followed tragedy with the Lombards' imposition of a humble priest named Philip to do Pavia's bidding.

Stephen, a Benedictine monk of Sicilian origin, was the candidate of the traditional papal establishment and the Romans. He waited offstage until the Lombard cavalry left. The Roman mob and Stephen's Lateran supporters immediately dispatched the hapless Philip. Thereafter, by conciliar decree, only Roman cardinals and priests were to be eligible to elect a pope. Desiderius was apoplectic. Stephen's ascent to the fisher-man's throne was a Lombard humiliation, a literal palace coup in the summer of 768. With the feeble militia of Rome scattering out of the way, Lombard cavalry again clattered through the streets of the Eternal City on a rampage. Desiderius ordered that no harm be visited upon the distraught Stephen III, "a pitiable cipher" (in the judgment of one medievalist), but his men murdered the papal chamberlain and his son for their part in the coup before withdrawing.[9] To an inconsolable Stephen, then, Bertrada's scheme of Franks consorting with Lombards appeared to be the work of the Antichrist.

Suddenly, Bertrada "Goose Foot" was in Rome, waddling past startled officials at the Lateran door. This energetic facilitator had sped from Pavia with a trio of conciliatory proposals. She reaffirmed her oldest son's loyalty to the Roman Catholic Church and pledged the guarantee of her own special influence upon Carolus. She revealed that Desiderius was willing to respect the Church's rights in central Italia in return for papal acquiescence in the union of her oldest boy and the Lombard's daughter. The secret was known far and wide that the outsize young Austrasian king deferred to his strong-willed mother. In effect, the pope was presented with a *fait accompli* demanding he make the best of it. Stephen decided that Desiderius, restrained by sympathetic Frankish in-laws, might, after all, not be the disaster he had at first feared. But the strain of Bertrada's gambit told on the fifty-two-year-old pontiff, and he would die within a few months. Meantime, Carloman appeared to have been neatly checkmated: his brother's realm, together with the Lombards, flanking him to the northeast; the Bavarians on his left flank. But Carloman's sudden, mysterious death, near Laon in the winter of 771, just as every sign portended civil war, altered the math of Bertrada's power equation. "God has preserved you from the wiles of your brother," a contemporary prelate fawned in a letter to Carolus.[10] Carloman's exit changed the relationship between dutiful son and imperious mother.

As for Bertrada, it is possible to say much about what she tried to accomplish. About Desiderata of Lombardy, nothing can be said other than that the fates were cruel. She had arrived in Thionville to meet her husband-to-be in her future mother-in-law's caravan. The bride's pedigree was impeccable. Her ancestors had been kings far longer than the royals of the House of Arnulf, the iron crown of Lombardy having passed from one virile king to the next for more than two centuries. She was sister-in-law to the proudest of German dukes, Tassilo of Bavaria. Her hand might well have been offered to a son of the imperial house of Byzantium. What she felt about Bertrada's son is a question contemporaries seldom if ever asked. Indeed, until the age of Eleanor of Aquitaine four hundred years later, it was almost impossible that such a thought would even occur to anyone. Still, the man to whose bed Desiderata was consigned was a thirty-year-old marvel. It is possible that she may have thought herself fortunate in the beginning. Carolus's lustfulness was notable even for his lusty times, yet his Lombard queen bore him no children nor seems even to have become pregnant. She seems to have meant little to her husband beyond being a valuable chess piece on the board of continental power politics. In any case, in little more than a year, she was gone—packed up by Charlemagne and sent home to her father. Pope Stephen was pleased to pose no objection.

Queen Mother Bertrada objected strenuously to her son's decision to rid himself of his wife, and reproachful murmurs were heard from relatives and high magnates at the Thionville court. Einhard leaves it to us to divine the king's inner thoughts. Of great weight must have been the teachings in his youth of Boniface and the Benedictines. He began to grasp, if but dimly, the formula by which a social order within an empire was to be created: a hierarchical religious institution obedient to a supreme pontiff dependent upon and defended by the king of the Franks. Whatever he felt about his Lombard spouse, Carolus decided that a strong and friendly papacy offered greater political advantages. He certainly knew enough about the reestablished Umayyads of *al-Andalus* to be concerned about the dangers they posed in the south. 'Abd al-Rahman had several times tested the defenses of Narbonne, but Carolus calculated that Lombard military help was no longer indispensable against the Muslims. Ultimately, his mother's geopolitics would mean the incorporation of the papacy into an even mightier Lombardy. Hers was a scenario of collaboration that ran not only against the logic of superpower politics but also sharply against the grain of her son's vaulting ambitions. Desiderata's return was the opening move in a deadly new chess match.[11]

Hardly had his younger brother been interred in the royal vault at St. Denis than Charlemagne descended on Laon to lay claim to the other half of Frankland for himself. Carloman's widow, Gerberga, and two sons in direct line of inheritance joined Himiltrud and Desiderata on the king's list of discarded inconveniences. After the magnates approved the appropriation of her children's inheritance, Queen Gerberga slipped away with her infant boys to Lombardy. Neither the *Royal Frankish Annals* nor Einhard's *Life of Charlemagne* ventures much about the personal aspects of a painful policy disagreement that marked the emancipation of Charlemagne from his mother's tutelage. After he rejected her counsels, the king of a now-unified Frankland relegated his mother to the sidelines—she who had made the hard choice between siblings and whose uncommon physical energy and diplomatic virtuosity were largely responsible for his success. Carolus had truly become Carolus Magnus, Karl der Grosse, Charlemagne. From that moment forward, the giant redhead's grand, inspired enterprise of consolidation and modernization moved apace, only occasionally hindered by significant rivalry among the Franks or a mother's idea of statecraft.

⁙

The crystallized concept of the *imperium Christianum*—the "Christian Empire"—was still several years in Charlemagne's future, as was his regime's official motto, *Renovatio Romani Imperii* ("Restoration of the Roman Empire").[12] Charlemagne's political ideas were refined on battlefields. Expeditions into Saxony and Lombardy took the young king down the road to the future Christian Empire at a fast gallop. Saxony—independent, pagan, and territorially contiguous—mocked the emerging Carolingian design for a Frankish superstate. Saxons were ferocity personified. Allergic to civilization and immune to Christianity in their veneration of the gods of Walhalla, the Saxon people were virtually unchanged three hundred years after the fall of Rome. The tribes lived in a kind of Teutonic cocoon in the north of today's Germany, between the Rhine and the Elbe Rivers. After losing three veteran legions in the Teutoburg Forest in 9 CE, a devastated Caesar Augustus fatefully decided to pull back from the Elbe and fix the empire's frontier at the Rhine. The Saxons and their cousins had crossed the North Sea to occupy parts of Britain after Roman withdrawal in the early fifth century. Clovis had conceded their independence. Charles the Hammer had warred against them with little success. Pippin the Short managed one or two Pyrrhic victories at best. Theirs was a feral heathenism that withstood the best efforts of Willibrord, Boniface, and the Benedictine missions, for, as Einhard regretted, "They did not consider it dishonorable to transgress and violate all law, human and divine."[13] The premier chieftain among them was the leathery, scarred Westphalian freedom fighter, Widukind, brother-in-law to the pagan king of the Danes.

Charlemagne mustered his men on the Marchfield almost immediately after acquiring a replacement for Desiderata. The new wife, thirteen-year-old Hildegard of Swabia (for whom he showed genuine affection), was Tassilo of Bavaria's cousin, a nuptial arrangement designed to mitigate the duke's wounded family honor and preclude a Lombard-Bavarian alliance on Frankland's northern flank. In the summer of 772, he attacked the Saxons with a large force. He crossed the Ems River with a surer knowledge of the forest than the Roman legions had. His army chased Widukind, the canny chieftain, snarling and cursing to the Danish frontier. It was the first of a half-dozen encounters with the dogged Westphalian. At Eresburg, the Saxons' forest settlement a hundred leagues or more beyond the last Frankish outpost, stood their totem Irminsul, the giant oak tree that connected earth to heaven. Sacrifices, beast and human, were offered to Irminsul. Charlemagne proceeded to chop down and burn the totem. The people were forced to embrace Christ and swear fealty to the king of the Franks. This first Saxon campaign, in what was to become a thirty-year conquest, yielded considerable benefits, at least in the short run. Piled at the base of the totem were the precious stones, hides, old Roman coins, and assorted items of silver and gold that the Saxon people had dedicated to their gods through the decades. From this trove, the king rewarded the magnates who had assembled with retainers and serfs on the Marchfield in answer to his war summons.[14] Carolingian aristocrats expected to be well compensated for the dangerous work of converting heathens.

Upon his return to Frankland from the Saxon victories in the fall of 772, the twenty-four-year-old monarch was challenged to make his biggest decision when the elimination of an independent papacy appeared inevitable. From Bergamo in the north to Benevento in the south, much of Italia was Lombard country. But for those obdurate bishops of Rome and their claims upon the broad swath of towns and villages across the country's middle (a swath annoyingly reconfirmed as papal territory by King Pippin), all but the peninsula's southernmost tip would have been under the iron crown of the Langobards. Papal relations with the Lombards went from bad to worse after the death of Pope Stephen III in January 772. Whatever the depths of his religious convictions, Desiderius was perfectly clear about his geopolitical imperatives. From Alboin to Luitprand and the impetuous Aistulf, wearers of the iron crown understood that an independent Roman patriarchate was incompatible with Lombard state planning. The precondition for an Italia united under Lombardy was a neutered Roman patriarchate. Nearly eleven hundred years later, the great Italian novelist Alessandro Manzoni expressed his contemporaries' regrets, in his play *Adelchi*, that Desiderius's Lombards failed to unite the peninsula.[15] He and they would have wished that Bertrada's counsels had been respected by her son.

Desiderius anticipated that Pope Stephen III's successor meant trouble for Lombard primacy. Adrian I (772–95), from the old Roman aristocracy, a tall, leonine cardinal of considerable culture and matching political acumen, would enjoy one of the longest tenures as pope in Church history. He moved aggressively against Lombard influences within the Curia, imprisoning the powerful chamberlain whose agile service to Desiderius had intimidated Stephen III. The Lombard response was decisive. Ravenna, now theoretically the property of the bishops of Rome, was besieged. Once again, the Lombard army bounded into papal territory. A certain amount of theatrical axe-brandishing was *de rigueur,* but Desiderius had recently demonstrated a chilling readiness to settle papal scores with tempered steel. Lombard cavalry circled the walls of the Eternal City while the new pope threatened excommunication and sent another life-or-death appeal to Charlemagne. Desiderius, for his part, cleverly sought to undermine the legitimacy of his former son-in-law and new master of united Frankland. Carloman was dead, but his widow, Gerberga, and her two sons resided in Verona under Lombard protection. Desiderius demanded that the besieged papacy acknowledge their claim to Carloman's legacy as preeminent. The king of the Franks had good reason to be concerned. His own rights in the matter of Carloman's estate might have proven none too solid if subjected to scrupulous examination under either German customary law or the Theodosian Code.[16] Pope Adrian's refusal to acknowledge Desiderius's petition was an invitation to be removed from office.

Such was the crisis in Christendom among Desiderius, Charlemagne, and Pope Adrian in the winter of 772: papal territory invested by a hostile army; the Holy Father menaced with removal from office and worse; Frankland's territorial integrity overshadowed by hereditary conflict; the king of the Franks embarrassed by his powerful, cunning erstwhile father-in-law. In a virtual replay of the desperate mission of Pope Stephen II to Pippin the Short nineteen years earlier, Adrian's emissaries trooped into Thionville at the beginning of 773 to secure the protection of the Franks "for the sake of God's service and the rights of St. Peter." The demeaning treatment of his daughter notwithstanding, a Lombard embassy arrived at Charlemagne's court to present Desiderius's side of the dispute a few weeks later.

Desiderius's ambassadors dismissed the Roman bishopric's legal claim to Italian territory as dubious, if not an outright fabrication. The bishop of Rome might be beyond challenge in claiming spiritual supremacy as the steward of Western Christendom, they asserted, but where was it written that the Holy See had legal claim to temporal sovereignty—to ownership of towns and ports and rule over lords and serfs? By what train of logic or what precedent of law did the pope arrogate the right of *sacerdos et rex*—priest and king—in central Italia? The papal response at Thionville to Lombard protestations came in Latin on hoary parchment. Charlemagne's father had been happy to accept the authenticity of the *Donation of Constantine*. As the king and his magnates deliberated the controversy of papal territorial rights in late spring of 773, piety, precedent, and politics argued for Rome over Pavia—as did the lure of treasure.

The army summoned to the Marchfield in June 773 was one of the largest Western armies assembled in three centuries, probably as many as three thousand cavalrymen and eight thousand foot soldiers. Aquitainians barely reconciled to subordinate status; Austrasian and Neustrian Franks divided by a common history; and Alamanni, Burgundians, and Rhenish tribes of dubious loyalty comprised this formidable, heterogeneous invasion force. Charlemagne's attention to equipage and enforce-ment of rules excelled anything seen since the standards of the Late Roman Empire. All free men in the kingdom were ordered to service on pain of a heavy fine of sixty *sous* (about twenty mares or thirty cows). Vas-sals were commanded to arrive on the Marchfield punctually "on the fif-teenth calends of July [June 17] with all your men, well armed and equipped with arms and baggage and all the furnishings of war. . . . Each knight is to have a buckler, lance, longsword and short sword, a bow and a quiver full of arrows."[17] The Frankish *spata* (longsword) was one of the Dark Ages' major secret weapons. It was a double-edged, hundred-centimeter shank of pattern-welded iron and steel whose manufacture was carefully guarded and sale outside the kingdom strictly banned.

Charlemagne pushed into the alpine passes in late June as the last snows melted. *Caballarii* or *scara*—the heavy cavalry ("the queen of battles")—led the invasion. At Geneva, centuries old when Julius Caesar first entered its name into the written record, Charlemagne divided his forces, placing the other half under the command of his uncle, Duke Bernhard. It was a measure of Charlemagne's supreme self-confidence and unique ability to project a persona both incorporating and tran-scending Frankland's disparate parochialisms that he was able to conduct war almost with the organizational sophistication of a Roman general. Dividing the army into two wings became his signature strategy, some-thing no previous Dark Ages chieftain had dared try. Splitting his forces reduced the volume of wastage to the countryside.[18] Charlemagne knew better than anyone the cruel devastation of an army passing through like a hurricane of locusts—the pillaged huts, devoured livestock, violated women.

Einhard heaves Bernhard's forces up through the Great St. Bernard Pass and over the Alps with descriptive economy as the invaders climb "trackless mountain ridges, the heaven-aspiring cliffs and ragged peaks" in a mere half-dozen sentences. Charlemagne's thousands descended from Mont Cenis into the Valle d'Aosta, where they were rejoined in mid-August by Bernhard's wing.[19] Desiderius's army awaited him near the old Roman citadel town of Susa. Comparable in numbers and pos-sessing the great advantage of home terrain, Desiderius's troops should have proved a terrible test for the Gallo-Frankish invaders. The outcome disappointed their reputation—in part, it seems, because a portion of the Lombard nobility resented its king. Charlemagne's men broke through the enemy lines with such force (the *furia francese* famous in a later time) that Desiderius's infantry collapsed, and with it all will to fight. Smashed and routed, the Lombards retreated to Pavia and locked themselves behind Roman and Gothic walls that were thought to be impregnable. Many miles farther to the northeast, Desiderius's son and heir, Adalghis (a.k.a. Adelchis), shut the gates of Verona in preparation for a siege.

Pavia was better fitted to survive a lengthy siege than the besiegers. Its deep cellars were gorged with the harvest of the Po River plain. A curious raconteur (to be reencountered), the Monk of St. Gall—presumed to be Notker "the Stammerer" (Notker *Balbulus*)—fictionalized a lively account of the siege that, nonetheless, delivers the flavor of this pivotal contest as Desiderius and a turncoat Frank supposedly watch from a tower while the Franks deploy below:

> Baggage trains appeared that would have been worthy of the campaigns of Darius or Caesar, and Desiderius said to Otkerus, "Is that Charles in that vast army?" He replied, "Not yet." Seeing then the army of simple soldiers gathered by the immense empire, he said confidently to Otkerus, "Clearly Charles must be standing proudly among these troops." Otkerus replied, "But not yet, not yet." . . . "You will see when he comes. As for us, I do not know what our fate will be."[20]

Charlemagne sustained his siege at full strength from September 773 until a few days after Christmas, when he took a portion of the army across the peninsula's upper spine to capture Verona. Prince Adalghis and the Veronese were caught off guard by this unlikely, audacious attack in the dead of winter, even while Pavia was ringed by siege machines. As the king of the Franks entered the fallen city, Desiderius's son escaped out the back gate, heading for the Adriatic coast and a ship bound for Constantinople. Queen Gerberga and sons surrendered to Charlemagne and disappeared from history. The Italian campaign advanced from surprise to surprise. In April 774, Charlemagne appeared just outside the gates of the Eternal City with a quarter of his army.

Rome—reduced in size to perhaps a tenth of its Augustan Age population, its public buildings and monuments scavenged and stripped to indecent nudity—was still the incomparable site where the universe had found its Archimedean center. "So long as the Colosseum stands, Rome will stand," its citizens said.[21] The drama attending Charlemagne's entry into Rome on Easter morn 774 prefigured the legendary ascension on Christmas Day twenty-six years later, when the king of the Franks would become the first emperor of what was to become the Holy Roman Empire. With the nobles and militia come out to do homage and lead his vanguard the last twenty miles, Charlemagne passed through the city's great ceremonial portal wearing his billowy blue cloak, astride a massive white stallion. The diminutive Romans lining his progress hailed him as *imperator* ("emperor"). It was as if deliverance had come in the person of a giant blond divinity. As Charlemagne dismounted before St. Peter's Basilica and then ascended step by kissed step on his knees to humble himself before Pope Adrian I, he may already have envisaged the re-created Rome that was to become a reality under his aegis a quarter-century in the future. Although Einhard's biography is silent, hearing himself proclaimed successor to the Caesars must have had an intoxicating effect upon Christendom's most evolved German warrior.

On that Easter morning, and during a week of worship and celebration in Rome, the king, in close conference with the pope, attained the substance of an ambition. The form would come later. To imagine the notes of their St. Peter's discussions revealed under subpoena is to be privy to one of the greatest deals in history. Removal of the Lombard polity was an existential imperative for the papacy and a strategic necessity for the coming Carolingian superpower. Charlemagne promised to eliminate the hated Lombards and to restore the papacy's stolen towns and lands in accordance with the *Donation of Constantine*, along with the terms of his own father's 756 donation. Both of these grants were incorporated into the historic *Donation of Charlemagne*, for eleven centuries "the

Magna Charta of the temporal powers of the Popes," according to the arbitral *Catholic Encyclopedia,* but, in all likelihood, another forgery.[22]

Charlemagne's alliance would answer all future questions about the number of divisions available to the pope. The bishops of Rome were assured temporal sovereignty in Italia as the prince-popes of what were to become the Papal States. For his part, the Holy Father decreed the Carolingian monarchy to be divinely ordained, a pronouncement that sacralized hereditary kingship among the Franks once again, as when Stephen II anointed Pippin, thus modifying the rough-and-tumble old tribal principle of elective rule. Whether or not the Frankish king was actually granted the extraordinary privilege of nominating popes and investing bishops (strenuously denied by the papacy later), Adrian's need of Charlemagne's immediate and future assistance was certainly acute enough to make for an unusual concession or two. The king departed Rome for the besieged Lombard capital consecrated as the first champion of the Catholic Church, his luster as *patricius Romanorum* reaffirmed.[23]

Pavia fell in June 774, its numbers hollowed out by a plague caused by putrescent bodies the Franks catapulted over the walls. With its surrender, the two-hundred-year-old line of Lombard kings ended. Desiderius was accorded the fate of fortunate royal losers—banishment to a monastery for life. Yet, just as this portentous new chapter in the power politics of Christendom opened, the pope and his ally were struck twice by near-fatal disaster. While the siege of Pavia hung in the balance, the Saxons had laid waste to villages and even the great monastery of Fritzlar, east of the Rhine, to avenge the destruction of Irminsul. Until the Lombard capitulation, barely enough troops were found to stabilize the situation. Leaving Pavia securely garrisoned, Charlemagne bounded over the Alps with his best troops to organize a formidable Saxon invasion force in the first weeks of 775. At Quierzy, the angry king announced a final solution at the great assembly of magnates that would, as a Frankish scribe later reported, "overwhelm in war the infidel and faithless Saxon people and continue until they either had been defeated and subjugated to Christianity or were completely annihilated."[24] During the remainder of that year, the Saxons were subjected to an ethnic cleansing so remorseless that news of it sent chills down the spines of the gentle monks in distant Northumbria. Saxon resistance wilted in the heat of a savage Carolingian retribution that, but for developments in Italia, would have achieved its terrible objective.

But the Lombards were no more reconciled to defeat than were the Saxons, and Charlemagne found himself confronted by simultaneous liberation struggles. Moreover, the Byzantines were equally unreconciled to the new Italian order. Constantinople had vociferously protested Charlemagne's formal annexation and transference of Byzantium's Italian possessions. Pope Adrian's extinction of Byzantine influence at Ravenna, and elimination of all imperial references in papal documents, infuriated the emperor. The capable if rather narrow-minded Emperor Constantine V financed a serious anti-Frank coalition comprising the dukes of Benevento, Spoleto, Friuli, and Tuscany. Plans were finalized for Desiderius's son, Adalghis, to command an invasion fleet from Constantinople. Two years after the fall of Pavia, then, Charlemagne was back in Italia with a large army to suppress a rolling rebellion in the North and in the distant Campania. Leaving a band of devastation and famine that forced thousands to sell themselves into slavery, Charlemagne's lightning campaign across the Italian peninsula became a textbook model for what military tacticians of a much later age would call *Blitzkrieg*. Leaping from the Brenner Pass and sweeping down the peninsula into the Campania in the summer of 776, he forced Desiderius's relative, the duke of Benevento, to recognize the new status quo.[25] Constantine V conveniently obliged by dying, which caused the Byzantines to abandon the anti-Frank coalition. The bishops of Rome were assured temporal sovereignity in Italia.

Charlemagne's return to Italia was a culminating development in the redefinition of power relations between Christian West and East, a finalizing of the Germanic reordering of the post-Roman Western world. The king's alliance would answer all future questions about the number of divisions available to the pope. Carolingian steel guaranteed that the See of Peter was out from under the frightening shadow of conquering Lombards and delivered as well from demeaning subordination to iconophobic Byzantine emperors. It is one of history's singular paradoxes that in order to survive as the supreme custodian of the emergent Occident's spiritual kingdom, the papacy found it necessary to acquire and rule a territorial kingdom among men and women. Adrian I now became prince-pontiff and actual ruler of a broad territorial belt across Italia's midriff. His successors would rule the Papal States from the Vatican for a thousand years.

The interrupted conquest of Saxony resumed in the autumn of 777. Five years had elapsed since Charlemagne had chopped down Irminsul, the great oak, and used it for firewood in a Westphalian clearing on the Pader River. The clearing at Paderborn now served as anchor for Carolingian military power in Saxony. Charlemagne, his magnates, and the high clergy had a terrible score to settle with these people. A policy of systematic colonization of northwestern Germany got underway as tempered steel outmatched the iron axe. The king of the Franks had added the crucifix to his arsenal with a vengeance. Thousands of Eastphalians and Westphalians, clamped in the fire-and-steel vise of the advancing Franks, were forced to swear fealty to Charlemagne and embrace Christ on pain of death. Widukind eluded capture once again, but pacification of Saxony had appeared to succeed. Franksih nobles were settled among the conquered, their military service rewarded with handsome land grants.[26] Benedictine priests went forth with crucifix and sermon to explain mysterious concepts of sin, salvation, and the Trinity to the bewildered vanquished. Houses of worship were built in which to confess sins, administer the miraculous host, and baptize the newborn. Trinitarian Catholicism had been very good to Frankish sovereigns from Clovis to Pippin the Short, but Charlemagne transformed what had been a mainly dynastic asset into a crusading ideology mandating enforced religious conversion. It was not until the Saxon Wars (the anti-Semitism of the Hispanic Visigoths excepted) that Christian conversion in the West became not just a prescription for spiritual salvation but the *sine qua non* of group survival itself. Surrender alone no longer sufficed; the defeated were obliged to renounce all that was heretical and heathen under pain of sanctions whose extreme harshness Charlemagne himself helped devise. The Qur'anic injunction that religion must be free from compulsion would, had he known of it, have made little sense to the king of the

Franks, for whom State certification of confessional practice was a prerequisite.

A brilliant chapter thus opened in the history of Charlemagne's family. They gave their name to an era, to more than a century of European stewardship lasting from 732 to 843—from the Battle of Poitiers to the Treaty of Verdun—in the process reshaping the political and cultural map of the continent. Charlemagne formally annexed two-fifths of the Italian peninsula, inventing for himself the sonorous title *rex Francorum et Langobardorum*—king of the Franks and the Lombards. He expropriated the prodigious treasury at Pavia, along with the iron crown of its monarchs.[27] Carolingian Frankland's core pretty much resembled the hexagonal France of today, a northern fringe or so excepted. With its annexation of northern Italia, Helvetia (Switzerland), and large swaths of the Rhineland, the eighth-century superstate was about half the size of Imperial Rome north of the Mediterranean. To be sure, the new Carolingian realm was still a work in progress. Because its political cohesion depended on two parts royal leadership and three parts military success, not a single year would pass that the king and his men were not on campaign. Warfare, to paraphrase a twentieth-century American pacifist, was the health of the Carolingian State. The fall of Pavia marked the beginning of a special use and abuse of religion by the secular order that would leave a deep, subsisting imprint upon post-Carolingian Europe. Henceforth, the Carolingian *regnum* acted as proselytizer for a militant Catholicism whose dogmatic and punitive strictures it both inspired and readily enforced at the point of a sword.

◼

Victorious in war against the Lombards and all but the most obdurate of the Saxons, Charlemagne had summoned his nobility and clergy to the groundbreaking Diet of Paderborn in Westphalia in the spring of 777. In a cavernous wooden structure erected for the occasion, the great assembly set about deliberating the religious and secular rules of the new Carolingian order. The great secular and ecclesiastical magnates were confidently deliberating the future of occupied Saxony when three Saracen notables arrived at Paderborn, having traveled under protection the breadth of Frankland. The Saracens and their retinue must have been an astonishing and doubtless alarming apparition as they rode their splendid Arabians into the lands of the forest people, past simple peasants and villagers. A generation had elapsed since the last Muslims had been sighted. Hulking Germans of virtually every tribe—Franks, Frisians, and Burgundians, Alamanni and Saxons—together with the sophisticated Gallo-Romans, would have leaned forward from rude bearskin-covered benches to grasp the purpose of this extraordinary trio's business before them.

Sulayman ibn al-A'rabi, Abbasid *amir* of Barcelona and Girona, along with his coconspirators, al-Husayn ibn Sa'd ibn Ubada, *wali* of Zaragoza, and the unidentified *wali* of Huesca, were in a desperate state of mind about the aggrandizing statecraft of 'Abd al-Rahman I. The *amir* of *al-Andalus* had grown so powerful, said the three Saracens in translation, that all regional independence, Muslim and Christian, would soon disappear from Hispania. Now in the forty-second year of his amirate, the Falcon of the Quraysh had succeeded in spreading his authority over a good two-thirds of the Iberian peninsula. Unless some means were soon devised to arrest or blunt its magnetic pull, these men knew that perimeter cities like theirs—Zaragoza, Huesca, Girona, Barcelona—once secure in their de facto autonomy, would be captured in Cordova's force field.[28]

The Andalusis proposed an ambitious military alliance. In return for protection from a consolidating Cordoba, Sulayman and al-Husayn promised to secure the approaches for an invasion and occupation of northern Hispania by Frankish armies. Al-Husayn promised to clear the western passes over the Pyrenees to Pamplona and to throw open the gates of Zaragoza, that site of chronic sedition. Sulayman promised to exert influence at Barcelona and elsewhere beyond the Ebro River. The Saracens told the great assembly that Muhammad al-Mahdi (775–85), the almighty Abbasid caliph at Baghdad, was similarly disconcerted by the Umayyad prince's political designs. He promised an invasion force.[29] To the magnates, the Muslim rebels' proposal could only be a signal from the Lord, working, as was His wont, in mysterious ways. Here were the means and moment to carry the fight against the infidels to their own country, to preempt *jihad* by crusade. In taking the Cross over the mountains into the land of the Ishmaelites, there was also the considerable incentive of booty. Tales of teeming cities and irrigated croplands tantalized the imaginations and stoked the cupidity of the peoples of the North. To Charlemagne and the lords of the Holy Church, the proffered alliance carried the additional incentive of ameliorating the lot of Catholics living in the geographical limbos of the Iberian peninsula.

The time between the Berber destabilization and the Battle of Pavia measured a thirty-four-year *jihadic* hiatus in Islam's advance beyond the Pyrenees, an interlude that had created space for the strong, ruthless regime that operated as a perpetual war machine. But the alliance consummated at Paderborn can hardly have meant the same thing to all parties. The Muslims of Barcelona, Zaragoza, and Huesca expected the Gallo-Franks to help them repel the Falcon's *mujarrada* in return for occupation of the Pyrenean northeast.[30] For Sulayman and al-Husayn, the deal was a classic *quid pro quo* between realists—security for Barcelona and Zaragoza, some treasure and a slice of territory for the Franks. For Charlemagne, however, the deal meant the opportunity to repeat the success of Italia in Hispania. Otherwise, the decision to invade *al-Andalus* before finishing the domestication of Saxony makes little sense. The imperial stakes justified the risk, even with the keening of the Saxon people still audible and an avenging Widukind on the loose.

To French scholars, Charlemagne's Spanish campaign of 778 remains a somewhat embarrassing sidebar. The little attention paid by them has centered on the famous ambush of Roland in the mountain pass at Roncesvalles or Roncevaux. In reality, the king was of a mind to save the Andalusis in the same way the Franks aspired to spread the True Faith among the Saxons and bring regime change to the Lombards. To Charlemagne's vaulting ambitions, the symmetry of a Frankland flanked by two conquered peninsulas proved irresistible—*rex Hispanicum* added to the title *rex Francorum et Langobardorum*. He envisioned *al-Andalus* with its Muslim rulers defeated and converted, its subject populations of Gentiles and Jews pledged to himself in a splendid empire that far surpassed the achievements of Justinian I. His fascination with "Espaigne" had begun in the first months of co-kingship with Carloman, when he defeated Odo's son's rebellion and then pursued the renegade deep into Gascony-

Navarra. The duke of Gascony had denied Hunald asylum, surrendered the Aquitainian, and pledged Gascony's service to Charlemagne. The king retained an inflated conviction from this experience of an *al-Andalus* ringed with Visigoth Pelayos awaiting the opportunity to march against 'Abd al-Rahman. If Saxons were too benighted to appreciate salvation when it presented itself on horseback, surely, he believed, Hispania's persecuted would see the Lord's hand in the coming of the Franks.

In striking contrast to the generalized disorder of the times, the huge Carolingian war machine excelled in complexity and discipline. The taut, fast-moving line of march, stretching over the countryside for leagues, was possible because foraging was kept to a minimum. Not only was the mandatory three-month food supply each man brought to the March-field piled into covered ox wagons by the army's efficient commissary, but additional supplies were requisitioned and stockpiled along the routes of march weeks in advance. Einhard says that Charlemagne headed for the Pyrenees "at the head of all the forces that he could muster" in the summer of 778. It was one of the largest musters since the time of Merovech, eponymous founder of the Merovingians—perhaps as many as twenty-five thousand cavalry and infantry. "To Saragossa came his men from Burgundy, Austrasia, Bavaria," wrote the amazed *Royal Frankish Annals* scribe of what was really Europe's first international military operation, "as well as [from] Provence and Septimania, and part of the Lombards."[31] Charlemagne brooked no indiscipline. Looting was severely punished.

As in Italia, Charlemagne divided the command with Duke Bern-hard, whose wing left Austrasia on a southern course for the eastern Pyrenees. Bernhard's route brought the additional dividend of battening down Carolingian rule in Frankland's southwestern quadrant. The king assembled the main wing in Neustria for a northerly advance to the western end of the mountain range. Charlemagne's plan was to pierce Andalusia at both ends of the Pyrenees—west via Pamplona across Navarra, east through Girona across Catalunya—with the deadly pincers closing at Zaragoza, where Sulayman's Abbasid troops and al-Husayn's Berber levies were supposed to join them. The counts of Bordeaux, Bourges, Toulouse, Limoges, Clermont, Narbonne, and more joined up with their levies as the stupendous hosts rolled across the early summer

An Empire of Force and Faith

fields of old Roman Gaul. Of the few officers whose names have come down to us, Eggihard and Anselm rated mention by Einhard along with the mythic Hruodland (Roland), commander of the elite Breton *scara* (cavalry).[32] On schedule and with morale high, the Franks and their allies crossed into *al-Andalus* in the last days of June 778.

Muslim sources often affected a studied indifference to their Christian adversaries, but it was impossible to ignore them completely. The fighting ferocity of the Franks had been duly, if briefly, acknowledged soon after the debacle of Moussais-la-Bataille in 732. *Franks* had become the generic term for all Western enemies of Muslims, just as *Moor* and *Saracen* were applied indifferently by Christians to Arabs, Berbers, or Muslim Persians. Whether the cry—"The Franks are coming"—actually ricocheted in their narrow streets, it is certain that Cordovans heard their muezzin sound some similar alarm in summer of 778. The shock of Christian armies bent on occupying their cities galvanized the Andalusian political class. For the first time in history, part of the *Dar al-Islam* was under significant attack from the people of the Christian Book—infidel, primitive Franks. Whether Duke Bernhard's wing gave battle as it moved north from Catalunya is unclear. Inferential evidence points to something like a concerted response by the Umayyad amirate. The reinforcements promised by Baghdad appear to have been intercepted and repulsed near Barcelona after one of the Falcon's spies poisoned the commander.[33] As Charlemagne and Bernhard converged on Pamplona, the *amir* assembled his elite corps of Balkan and black African *saqaliba*, supported by a large amalgam of *baladiyyun*, Syrians, and *muwalladun* for the advance to Zaragoza. The odd *wali* intent on playing both sides or wanting to remain neutral soon found the Falcon or his generals at his *alcazar* portal demanding a renewed loyalty pledge. The very survival of *al-Andalus* was in play.

Christianity had progressed slowly and unevenly among the pagan Basques of Navarra, another primeval people like the Berbers, of mysterious origin and language. The high-walled city of Pamplona was the jewel of missionary success in a part of Hispania that neither Romans and Visigoths nor Muslims had colonized with any staying power. The people of Pamplona were Catholic Christians, but the independence of their land was the vital creed by which they passionately lived and willingly died. When the two armies came together beneath their walls in July, Pamplonans raised their gates to admit Charlemagne and Bernhard with a hesitancy that was insulting. Sulayman of Barcelona kept his commitment, bringing an army of undetermined size to join the king and the duke on the Roman road from Pamplona to Zaragoza.

Ahead lay Zaragoza, where al-Husayn, in command of more friendly troops, was supposed to be waiting to welcome the invaders. The crusaders had force-marched more than nine hundred miles, expecting to participate in a rolling rebellion against the authority of 'Abd al-Rahman. Pontoons and heavy siege machines hadn't been included in the inventory. As the armada of allies deployed across the landscape, however, doubts about the long-term objectives began to assail other rebel leaders. Well-grounded suspicions arose that the great caliph of Christendom had concluded an alliance with Alfonso II, the Catholic monarch of Asturias, an additional good reason to wriggle out of collaborating with the Franks.[34] Charlemagne's Muslim partners had no intention of exchanging eventual subordination in a Cordovan hegemony for immediate incorporation into a Carolingian imperium.

French chroniclers of a later time imagined the king of the Franks at the head of Jehovah's hosts, the oriflamme banner shimmering in red and gold, as Ishmael's accursed children quailed before him on the road to Zaragoza.[35] In truth, this sacred oriflamme banner (presented in legend to Charlemagne by Pope Adrian I) was the fabrication of a later time. Its legendary existence was to become an indispensable element, nevertheless, in the creation of a protonational saga of uniquely encompassing religious and cultural potency. But the reality awaiting the Franks and their allies at Zaragoza spelled the beginnings of a disaster. Zaragoza's surviving Roman fortifications still impress today's visitor—a gray mass of stones forming a protective rim along the Ebro's winding course. The defenses presented formidable engineering challenges to an enemy approaching, as the Franks were, from the north. It had been one thing for al-Husayn to conspire with the grand caliph of Christendom in the forests of faraway Saxony, quite another to hand over the keys of *al-Andalus* to twenty thousand enemies of the True Faith massed on the banks of the Ebro. Nor had the *wali* anticipated the speed with which 'Abd al-Rahman could mobilize a counteroffensive. Reports came to him of an army of tens of thousands assembled at Cordoba in preparation for the occupation of the Upper March.

In a fit of indecision or regret, al-Husayn barred the gates of Zaragoza to the Franks and their allies. A month into the siege, it became clear that the city would never fall without a lengthy undertaking that taxed the ingenuity of the king's artillery and the reserves of the quarter-master corps. Still, the reduction of Pavia had gone on for many months before the Lombards capitulated, although it was also true that the arid, rocky Aragonese countryside was a far cry from the verdant topography of Tuscany. Moreover, it was only a matter of time until the Falcon's forces arrived to support the feckless al-Husayn. Whether or not Charlemagne would have attempted to press the reduction of Zaragoza to a successful end, his decision to lift the siege and return to Frankland was to be made for him by others. As the *Royal Frankish Annals* sighed, "The Saxons rebelled again as usual and some Frisians along with them."[36] Their rebellion enraged Charlemagne beyond measure and caused him to feel humiliated in the eyes of much of Christendom. As couriers brought news in greater detail, he understood that the stability of his realm was threatened. Not only had Frankish military and ecclesiastical outposts been swallowed up in the Saxon firestorm, depredations were underway well west of the Rhine. News of the Saxon uprising came just as the wary Basques shut the gates of Pamplona.

All thought of sustaining the campaign ceased once the invaders were denied Pamplona as a base for winter quarters. In no mood to suffer more embarrassment, the king of the Franks turned his wrath on Pamplona. The Christian city was destroyed, along with the walls, and its people were harshly chastised. The deed was a stain upon his reputation that made ecclesiastical Europe shake its head in sorrow and disbelief. As for the point man of the cabal, one version of Sulayman's fate has him accompanying the retreating Franks; another has him falling into the hands of al-Husayn and being executed.[37] The combined armies of the king and Duke Bernhard barreled up the Roman road toward the pass through the western Pyrenees.

Einhard exaggerated when he claimed that "all the towns and castles that [Charlemagne] attacked surrendered," but the booty Charlemagne's Franks amassed in their Andalusian campaign was still quite considerable. Rather like the *ghanima* accumulated by the warriors of Amir 'Abd al-Rahman al-Ghafiqi advancing along the Roman road to Poitiers nearly half a century earlier, Charlemagne's men exited *al-Andalus* gorged with spoils of war that would affect the dénouement of his Spanish campaign. The passage of the Franks' baggage wagons piled high with silks, precious stones, exquisite carvings, Damascus swords, silver coins, women, and hostages was entrusted to the commander of the Breton cavalry—Hruodland or Roland, the "bravest of the brave," limns the *Song of Roland*. As the bulk of the king's forces precipitated from the Pyrenees into Aquitaine, Count Roland and his rear guard waited their turn in order to thread the baggage wagons through the narrow mountain pass at Roncesvalles. They began their approach to the summit on the morning of August 15, 778.

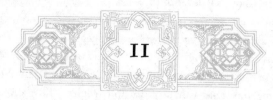

II

Carolingian *Jihads*: Roncesvalles and Saxony

THE road of march taken by Charlemagne's retreating army is today a two-lane highway that rises steeply beyond Burguete, an ancient, somewhat mournful Basque village remembered in travel guides for its prominence in Ernest Hemingway's *The Sun Also Rises*. Because it serves as a branch of the pilgrimage route to Santiago de Compostela, one of Catholicism's holiest sites, the road is especially well traveled in July, when the feast day of St. James occurs. Just short of the pinnacle, signs in Euskara (the Basque language) announce the approach at 3,862 feet above sea level of Orreaga, the Basque name for Ronces-valles (Roncevaux in French). A large, gray rectangle known as the *Iglesia de la Real Colegiata de Santa María* (the Royal Collegiate Church of St. Mary) hugs the mountainside on the right. It is part of a collection of historic structures dating from the twelfth century. Religious and royal relics and remains, together with works of art and trophies, fill the chapel, the museum, and the Gothic chamber. A war hammer ascribed to Roland, putative commander of the Frankish rear guard, stands near the sarcoph-agus of Sancho VII ("the Strong"), the great Navarrese victor at Las Navas de Tolosa. In this epic battle between Christians and Muslims in 1212, the *Reconquista* took on the deep tincture of religious fanaticism that became official Western ideology three years later when Pope Innocent III ordained the crusade against heretics, Jews, and Muslims at the Fourth Lateran Council.

Some distance apart, and distinctively un-Gothic in appearance, stands a squat, whitewashed building in the shape of a box that covers a pit into which legend holds that the bleached bones of Roland and his fallen comrades were eventually interred on Charlemagne's orders. The summit a few yards ahead offers a magnificent panorama of the Navar-rese plain, which would have seemed to stretch into infinity as Roland's men reached the top on a warm late afternoon in August 778. A massive block of rough-hewn granite stands upright on a mound in the swerve of the road as it descends sharply into the mountain's forested haunches. The inscription on it, "ROLDAN, 778," is a twentieth-century contribu-tion memorializing this as the spot where the valiant Frankish paladin drew his final breath in valiant defense of his king's property. Although legend, plausibility, and national pride favor the actual existence of Hruodland or Roland, history disputes the accuracy of his Orreaga mon-ument's location.[1] The destruction of the rear guard commanded by Roland occurred not at the summit but far down the slope of the moun-tain, under a torrent of boulders and in a hailstorm of arrows.

The primeval Basques, who had kept Romans, Visigoths, and Arabs at bay, were intimidated at first when Charlemagne's colossal army arrived at the gates of Pamplona in the summer of 778. Their welcome was correct, but the Basques hardly disguised their relief when the king and his men headed south to rendezvous at Zaragoza with the renegade Berber *wali*. But the *wali*, who had been so resolute the summer before in his enmity at Paderborn, no longer wished to offend his *amir*, 'Abd al-Rahman. Charlemagne stared at the barred fortress city with his encamped fighters for four infuriating weeks, until news of the Saxon uprising precipitated a headlong march for the Rhine. Pamplona closed its gates to them this time, and the Franks destroyed the city in an act of departing malice that roused the Basques to a fury of reprisal. Roland and his men were fatally trapped between the swarming natives above and the groaning baggage wagons clotting the narrow trail below. "The Basques forced them down into the valley beneath, joined battle with them and killed them to the last man," Einhard records, his stylus quickening at this point. "They then snatched up the baggage, and, protected as they were by the cover of darkness, which was just beginning to fall, scattered in all directions." Among the prominent dead mentioned by Einhard were Eggihard, "in charge of the King's table, Anselm, the Count of the Palace, and Roland, Lord of the Breton Marches, along with a great number of others."[2]

Hispania in the summer of 778 was no replay of Italia in the summer of 774. The grand strategy that was supposed to coordinate the Franks' advance with an Abbasid invasion from North Africa foundered either from Muslim dissension or from robust response by the Andalusi—or, perhaps, from both. Had Charlemagne's invasion been successful, it would have accelerated the armed confrontation with Islam by four centuries. Instead, the army, assembled from virtually every corner of the realm, failed to conquer a single hostile Muslim city. (Barcelona and Girona opened their gates in accordance with Sulayman's Paderborn pledge.) Instead, it had leveled the walls of the only Christian city along the line of march. The aborted campaign set an exceedingly grave precedent for the Carolingian regime. It was a humiliating reversal of fortune whose consequences were potentially calamitous in an age where the loyalty and obedience of egocentric vassals (*vassi*) were prone to disappear whenever bad omens and misfortune befell a powerful leader. A careful reading between the lines discloses the care Charlemagne's contemporaries took to mitigate the Spanish failure. The *Royal Frankish Annals*, written some fifty years after Roncesvalles, fudged the facts and hurried past the episode, merely mentioning the destruction of Pamplona and speciously boasting of the subjugation of the "Spanish Basques and the people of Navarre." Einhard wrote with similar evasiveness of the king's triumphant march across Spain, glossing Roncesvalles and its "Basque treachery" as "a brief moment on the return journey."[3]

The business in the Pyrenees became a mere sidebar as the chroniclers shifted attention to the king's Saxon campaign. Although Frankish sources leave little sense of panic and disorientation, in reality Charlemagne scrambled with his army out of Hispania into another crisis that nearly scuttled his regime. Had the king's empire-building strategies failed in the aftermath of the retreat from Zaragoza, there would have been no *Chanson de Roland,* no literary transmuting of a military embarrassment into a nation-molding epic of unique, perdurable potency. Roncesvalles's evolving mystique was to Saxony's killing fields what justification is to homicide. The historic and brutal Carthaginian peace eventually inflicted on the forest tribes living between the Rhine and the Elbe was ennobled over time as the work of selfless, Christian knighthood exemplified by Roland's imagined martyrdom.

A twentieth-century interpreter has called *The Song of Roland* "poetic history" ("*histoire poétique*"), a distinction whose meaning, while obvious to the modern reader, would have been far less evident to the man and woman of the Early Middle Ages. To minds of the Dark Ages and of later times, the ambush at the summit of the western Pyrenees unfolded literally as related by the author of the greatest *chanson de geste* ("song of deeds"). Whoever he was, Turoldus put into decasyllabic verse near the close of the eleventh century (at about the time, probably, that the Bayeux tapestry was woven) a story that became, first, the national epic of France and, soon thereafter, one of the great constitutive myths of Christendom. *The Song of Roland* placed the West's future at the service of the Frankish nation, a chosen people charged to seek and destroy the Muslim Antichrist and build the new Jerusalem with sword and cross, in that order. Distilled from a dozen or more analogously heroic tales sung in the evolving tongues of Europe (the Norse *Karlamagnus saga*, the Middle

High German *Ruolandsliet*, the medieval Welsh *Can Rolant,* the Middle English *Song of Roland*), this foundational document, written down three centuries after Roncesvalles, was to be a superordinate factor in the European sense of self and of otherness—of what Europeans were and others were not. Though much of it was a fabrication of history, it possessed the higher truth of folk myth.[4]

❖

Some three hundred years in the future, the *Chanson de Roland* would remember Charlemagne's leave-taking from *al-Andalus* as a voluntary departure at the end of a long, triumphant military campaign. Turoldus, its probable author, about whom little or nothing can be known, tells us in Anglo-Norman French that the king intended that his exit be unopposed, an honorable farewell to be negotiated between warriors. *The Song of Roland* begins thus: "*Carles li reis, nostre empere magnes/Set anz tuz pleins ad estet en Espaigne.*" "Charles the king, our great emperor,/Has been in Spain for seven long years. . . ." It boasts that Charlemagne has conquered this proud land "as far as the sea." No more battles need fighting, therefore. "The Emperor says that his war is over," and rides toward the "fair land of France." Turoldus sends the honorable Franks and their allies homeward over the western Pyrenees. The huge army's rear guard is commanded by Roland, count of Brittany, the "bravest of the brave," whose exhortation to fight on until Spain is totally subdued was rejected by his fellow magnates. Roland's stepfather, Ganelon, the villain of the epic, calls him mad, and says, "Nothing pleases him more than combat." Ganelon feels he has good reason to ridicule the count. He blames Roland that he, Ganelon, has been chosen by Charlemagne to risk his life negotiating a truce with the deadly devious Saracen king Marsile. In revenge, Ganelon plots his stepson's death with Marsile by pledging to manipulate his fellow Franks into choosing Roland to command the rear guard that is to be ambushed.

Charlemagne has "generously" granted the Saracen king "half of Spain as a fief," yet the unprincipled ruler of *al-Andalus* is ready to betray his pledge. Well advised by Count Ganelon, Marsile bides his time until savage retribution can be inflicted upon the unbelievers. "In three days," says Turoldus, the Saracen chief assembles four hundred thousand men who "hoist Muhammad on high in the tallest tower. . . . Then they ride with great zeal." Once the great coalition of Christian knights has filed through the high pass at Roncesvalles into the valley below, Muslim perfidy, as Roland foresaw, behaves true to infidel form. When the bulk of the Christian army is thirty or more leagues' march beyond the mountain, the Saracens in the epic spring their trap and attack Roland's rear guard as it files with baggage wagons through the Puerta de Ibañeta, the ancient mountain pass at Roncesvalles that the Muslims called *Runshafala*.[5]

Turoldus changes the incomparable Roland—"never [to] be vanquished by mortal man"—from a Breton magnate to a Frank who is a nephew of the great king. Not only does the royal relationship assigned to Roland up the military ante and redound to Frankish valor, the blood tie may have been a subliminal trace of a dark Carolingian secret transmitted to the new "eye literature" from the old "ear literature." Some believed those curious silences in the *Royal Frankish Annals* and Einhard's *Life of Charlemagne* about Charlemagne's adolescent years concealed the sin not uncommon among the Franks that the Church was fiercely intent upon suppressing. The old "ear literature" hinted strongly that Roland would have been the fruit of incest. If Charlemagne's incestuous relations with his sister are speculative at best, the hint of speculation reveals, interestingly, the slow progress of the new domestic morality among the Franks. Hard on the heels of the Church's ban on unions of seven kinship degrees or less had come the institution of marriage as a sacrament and, still more intrusive, the imposition of monogamy. Turoldus says that Roland has pledged to marry his best friend Oliver's sister, the suicidally faithful Aude, a monogamous limitation Turoldus's listeners would have known Roland's Saracens were not obliged to observe.

Ganelon's perfidy, as Turoldus relates, is ingeniously conceived to undermine his king and countrymen. Roland's death in the Roncesvalles pass would, as he assures the Saracen king, demoralize the Christians. Of the "twelve peers of France," Roland's unique knightly virtues inspire the Franks to "hail him as their protector." With Roland's death, the king of the Franks "would lose the right arm from his body." Fully persuaded, Marsile attacks the twenty thousand Franks in four waves of a hundred thousand each, figures of pure Gallic imagination. "Never has any man on earth seen more," broadcasts Count Oliver, one of the boldest of the twelve peers and prospective brother-in-law to Roland, as he races along the tight line of march to alert his alter ego.[6]

To Oliver's three appeals that he blow the Oliphant, an ivory horn whose reverberations in the valley below would bring reinforcements, Roland retorts spiritedly, "Do not speak of such an outrage." Having promised the king to lose not "a single palfrey or war-horse,/Nor a mule or jenny, which is fit to ride," Roland refuses to dishonor family and the "fair land of France." Oliver insists that he can see "no blame in this." If the ivory Oliphant is sounded, the Franks are saved, he protests. In a single sentence, Turoldus defines the two paladins and the values they incarnate: "*Rollant est proz e Oliver est sage*" ("Roland is brave and Oliver is wise"). Roland's famous refusal to sound the Oliphant at Roncesvalles guarantees one of world literature's most memorably disastrous and titanic bloodlettings. The dispensable Basques, whose role as principals was frankly acknowledged in Einhard's *Life of Charlemagne* and in the *Royal Frankish Annals*, are banished from the epic. Turoldus, who would have known the available Latin translation of the *Iliad*, serves up the biggest clash of civilizations since the Greeks and the Trojans, with Islam as the enemy.[7]

The emergent Church Militant, whose tonsured warriors marched into Saxon history with crucifix and sword beside the avenging Franks, steps forward in the character of Archbishop Turpin to sanctify the imminent carnage. Twenty thousand doomed Franks are vouchsafed the same salvation of which the Muslim foe is assured. If they die, they will be "blessed martyrs/And take your place in paradise on high." In the final carnage hour, and reduced to the last thousand or so, Roland does sound the Oliphant—so strenuously, indeed, that he bursts the blood vessels in his head. "Clear blood gushes forth from his mouth." Bitter reproach comes from Oliver for what seems an impulse of enormous capriciousness, and yet another deed to provoke generations of literary and cultural scholars. Oliver, the anti-Roland, protests his friend's perversity, saying through gritted teeth, "Roland," had reason prevailed rather than the dictates of personal honor, "we should have fought this battle and won it." "*La prudence est plus importante que la bravoure*," says the exasperated

Oliver—"Prudence is more important than valor." His disgust makes him regret even that his sister, Aude, was ever affianced to Roland.[8]

Roland's final, anticlimactic horn burst turns Charlemagne from his homeward course, despite Ganelon's insistence that nothing is amiss in the mountains. Fighting to the last man, Roland, Oliver, the archbishop, and the other magnates perish with the flower of Frankish chivalry. The superior justice of the Franks' cause requires the Muslims to die in the hundreds of thousands. Some are said to be even as brave as the Franks: "Had he been a Christian, he would have been a worthy baron." When the Saracen king matches himself against Roland, the outcome is foreordained. The count's gleaming weapon of mass destruction, Durendal, slices off Marsile's right hand. Roland continues to hold off the enveloping enemy. He is the last of the twenty thousand to die. France's incomparable warrior lifts his right glove to God, who sends Saints Gabriel and Michael. "They bear the count's soul to paradise," Turoldus solemnly relates. In the telling of the poet, Roland and his men set the bar for aristocratic valor, for fidelity to king and class, and for militancy of faith that would gradually come to define the ethos of Europe.

But Turoldus hadn't finished his tale. Charlemagne's return to the mountain pass raises the curtain on a vast sequel. Turoldus describes the wrenching scene affronting the great king and his nobles as they regain Roncesvalles just as night begins to fall in the epic: "There is no road or path there,/No open space, no yard or foot,/Not covered with either Franks or pagans." Though devastated by the carnage, the Franks soon compose themselves and get ready to ride in search of the Saracens. The emperor "prays for a divine favor in the thickening dusk." Turoldus tells us that "God performed a great miracle for Charlemagne,/For the sun remained where it was." By the time the miracle expires, Frankish mayhem has cleansed the territory of Muslim warriors from Roncesvalles to Zaragoza. "Striking powerfully they keep on killing them," while many thousands more drown in the Ebro. Nor is the Muslims' god worth much in a pinch, Turoldus duly notes. Cowering behind Zaragoza's battlements, the maimed Marsile, his wife, and his courtiers are made to denounce Muhammad: "Anyone who serves you well receives a poor reward."[9]

Having avenged their comrades, whom they now gather up at Ron-

Emperor Justinian I, Bishop Maximianus, and attendants. Detail of mosaic (ca. 547 CE) from the north wall of the apse. Basilica of San Vitale, Ravenna, Italy.

Cameraphoto Arte, Venice / Art Resource, NY

Empress Theodora and attendants. Detail of mosaic (ca. 547 CE) from the north wall of the apse. Basilica of San Vitale, Ravenna, Italy.

Cameraphoto Arte, Venice / Art Resource, NY

The victory of Shapur I over the Roman emperors Valerian and Philippus the Arab, 260–72 CE. Sassanian relief in Naqsh-i-Rustam, Iran.

SEF / Art Resource, NY

Ctesiphon: Capital and palace complex of the Parthian and Sassanian empires, located twenty miles southeast of Baghdad. The main portico, or great vault, of the Sassanian audience hall (*Taq-i-Kisra*).

David Nicolle, Historical Atlas of the Islamic World. *Permission granted by Thalamus Publishing*

Dome of the Rock. Erected by Caliph 'Abd al-Malik ibn Marwan between 685 and 691 CE. Located within the Muslim Noble Sanctuary, known to Jews and Christians as the Temple Mount, Jerusalem, and the spot from which Muhammad ascended to heaven.
Wayne McClean

Santa Maria la Blanca. Synagogue erected in classic Mudejar style in 1180 CE. Converted to a Christian church in the fifteenthth century.
Walter B. Denny, Islamic Art Slides Archive

Late-Roman or early-Byzantine "iron crown" of Lombardy (also known as the crown of Theodelinda). Fifth-century Chapel of Theodelinda in the Duomo, Monza, Italy.

Scala / Art Resource, NY

Vatican equestrian statuette of Charlemagne. From the treasury of Metz Cathedral; Carolingian, ninth century; bronze with traces of gold. Location: Louvre, Paris, France.

Réunion des Musées Nationaux / Art Resource, NY

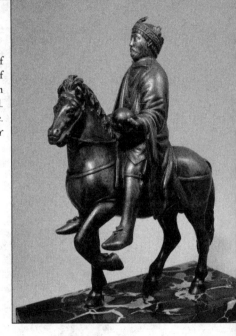

Coronation sword of the kings of France, called "sword of Charlemagne," inside its sheath. From the treasure of Saint-Denis; gold, lapis lazuli, steel, glass; tenth–fourteenthth century. Location: Louvre, Paris, France.

Réunion des Musées Nationaux / Art Resource, NY

Alhambra Lion
Court in Granada.
*Walter B. Denny,
Islamic Art Slides Archive*

Interior of Cordoba's Great Mosque.
Walter B. Denny, Islamic Arts Slides Archive

Detail of *The School of Athens*, fresco painted by Raphael in 1509–10 for the Stanza della Segnatura in the Apostolic Palace, Vatican City. Averroës, turbaned, observes Pythagoras from the far left.

Courtesy of the Vatican Museums

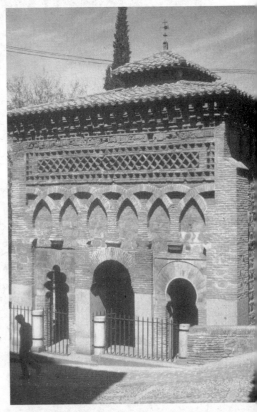

Church of Cristo de la Luz: Mosque built in Toledo in 999 CE. Converted to a Christian church by Alfonso VII in the twelfthth century.

Walter B. Denny,
Islamic Art Slides Archive

Madinat al-Zahira, Salon Rico, Cordoba.
Walter B. Denny, Islamic Art Slides Archive

Carolingian ewer with Persian, perhaps Sassanid, enamel plaques fixed to a Carolingian gold base and spout; ninth century. Location: abbey treasury, St. Maurice, Switzerland.
Erich Lessing / Art Resource, NY

Statue of Maimonides in the Cordoba ghetto.
Pronin, Anatoly / Art Resource, NY

Great Mosque of
Qutubiyya, Marrakesh,
late twelfth century.
Walter B. Denny,
Islamic Art Slides Archive

Carmona.
Ruth Ann Stewart

Giralda.
David Levering Lewis

cesvalles and accord fitting obsequies, the Franks again prepare to leave Spain. But the *Chanson de Roland* serves up yet another clash between Occident and Orient, this one also of titanic scale. Baligant of Babylon, the aged, grand *amír* of the Muslim world, having finally resolved to end the Christian threat to Andalusia, "summons his men from forty kingdoms" for an invincible *jíhad*. At this point, the Roland myth becomes a global contest. "Below Alexandria there is a seaport;/There he made ready his entire fleet;/Then in May on the first day of summer,/He set sail with all his forces." Riding ahead of the advancing legions, the *amír*'s messengers carry orders to Zaragoza:

> "And on my behalf inform Marsile
> That I have come with help against the Franks.
>
> I shall go to France to wage war against Charles;
> If he does not kneel at my feet, at my mercy,
> And should he refuse to forsake the Christian faith,
> I shall seize the crown from his head."[10]

Stanza follows stanza as the opponents mass and maneuver. The hosts of light and darkness are frozen for dramatic effect as they face one another in the hours before combat commences. "Vast are the armies and handsome the divisions," the fabulist intones. "The helmets glitter with their gold and precious stones/And the shields and saffron byrnies." Ten divisions, representing the tribes of Europe (Bavarians, Danes, Bretons, Flemings, Burgundians, Normans, and more), await Charlemagne's command, "*Monjoie!*" Many more Muslim divisions assemble behind the *amír*'s pennant—the tribes of the *Dar al-Harb* on the march. "The smallest division had fifty thousand men," writes Turoldus: Syrians, Avars, Huns, "the sixth of Armenians and Moors/The seventh of men from Jericho." Then begins the great battle, and the Franks and the Arabs "strike fine blows;/They smash their shafts and their furbished spears."[11] Charlemagne slays Baligant. The Carolingian allies decimate the enemy. Marsile dies brokenhearted, and his queen opens the gates of Zaragoza to Charlemagne and converts to Christianity.

Roland's proud obduracy has generated an industry of interpretation, the "splendid folly" thesis long predominant among them. Roland is the warrior of archetypal subjectivity whose sacrifice of himself and others is seen as the essence of knightly virtue. A knight's *armor propre*, his good name gloriously and impetuously vindicated, persistently trumps corporate mission. The sum is never greater than the parts in the calculus of Roland's mental space. His kind personify honor in battle over expediency in victory, the noble death above safety in mere strategy. He is, in this view, a precursor to the great superhero of the Western world, so to speak—but a distinctively upperclass superhero. Thundering to its death, plumed and bemetaled in a hailstorm of English longbow missiles, French chivalry at Agincourt in 1415 was a classic example of Roland's much-admired, catastrophic courage. Or was that the only lesson the ruling caste learned from *The Song of Roland*? Others argue that its impact was contrapuntal over time, with one tradition flowing from Roland's audacity, the other inspired by Oliver's intelligence. To the assured contention of one Middle Ages scholar that the *Chanson de Roland* represents a "swansong for the reckless *fortitudo* of its defeated hero," much contrary evidence commends the view that, even though these two traditions long continued in problematic coexistence, it was Roland's example that infused the West's dominant ethos of heroic individualism.[12]

The heroic individualism prized by the *chansons de geste* was not a right possessed by the European Everyman—or Everywoman. Aude, Roland's intended and Oliver's sister, elects to die rather than contemplate life without Roland—not from romantic regret, however, but in fidelity to a masculine ideal of feminine virtue. It was the privilege exclusive to a class, a *privilege* in the etymological meaning of that word—private or personal law. Because it was the sword-bearer's special role to defend the Christian commonweal, the role was said to be best suited to the special personality exemplified by the likes of Roland. Not all Franks were Rolands, of course. Most were peasants, priests, merchants, and common folk; but all Rolands were Franks. Since the best of the Franks were Rolands, and stars, therefore, of a warrior class that was fast becoming a warrior caste, Franks in general imbibed and propagandized the virtues spilled at Roncesvalles. In time, then, the Franks became Europe's archetypal swordbearers. Much, much more time elapsed until the logic of Frankish privilege played itself out in the consolidation of the French nation-state and its concomitant nationalism, but the line of descent from Roland to Francis I is fairly discernible.[13]

The *Roland* saga presses on beyond the martyrdom of the rear guard to frame the contact of Christianity and Islam as an epic struggle that can never end until Muhammad's legions will have been run to ground, defeated, and converted to the True Faith. The elimination of the Basques from the saga permits the transformation of a costly sneak attack on a mountain trail into a Manichaean standoff between two civilizations, one of which the Almighty Himself ordains the merciless destruction.

Turoldus's "great, shaggy, uneven masterpiece" running some four thousand lines became—in content, style, and form—the template of a civilization. What lasting emotions of fear and enmity must its stanzas (*laisses*) have inculcated in devout eleventh-century lords and ladies, simple priests and peasants, and aspiring Rolands young and old? Sung at summer fairs or in a thousand badly heated great halls as the Dark Ages brightened into the medieval, the "Europenses" relived the Battle of Poitiers through stories from the *Chanson de Roland*. It was a *chanson de geste* of Christians versus Saracens that generations of *jongleurs* (minstrels) would sing. From the earliest versions in song, the *Chanson* possessed extraordinary psychic clout for the men and women of the West, a powerful mythopoeia engirdling their understanding of class, marriage, and gender, of order and obligation, and above all else of the martial imperatives of the True Faith.

In the century of its written composition, eighty or more *gestes* (songs of deeds) were known in various Germanic and Romance languages. Beowulf of the full-throated cry, "Let whoever can win glory before death," is plainly one of Hruodland's spiritual forerunners. From the "matter of France"—a reservoir of Franco-Gallic folk memory saturated with the tribulations and triumphs of Charlemagne, Oliver, and Roland—medieval poets and writers bottled mythic tales of Christian instruction, as in the Norse *Karlamagnus Saga* of the thirteenth century and the Italian *Orlando Furioso* of the sixteenth. But it was the *Roland*, featuring the Franks as God's anointed and France as His special domain, that trumped the competition in a remarkable synthesis of saliency at the service of the most dynamic of the "Europenses." As best as can be determined, the earliest written version of the epic appeared about fifty years before Pope Urban II summoned the First Crusade in 1095 to expel the infidel from the Holy Land. In the apt phrase of one erudite literary scholar, the *The Song of Roland* served as "inspiration for the *gesta Dei per Francos*" ("works of God through the Franks")—*Ur*-text for the West, in a word. Nor is it reductionist to underscore that Turoldus's epic embedded the "otherness" of Islam deep in the memory banks of the West.[14]

⁜

The world of the real Saxony was as sanguinary as the carnage of the imagined "Espaigne." As the historical king of the Franks pondered the altered state of affairs after Roncesvalles, his fictional counterpart also reflected upon troubled times. Commanded by the angel Gabriel to don armor once again in God's name and smite enemies of the true faith, Charlemagne of the *Chanson de Roland* utters the epic's final line: " 'God,' said the king, 'how wearisome my life is.' " Had the flesh-and-blood Charlemagne's soothsayers dared predict that the final pacification of Saxony after 778 would take twenty-five years more, even he might have sighed fatefully at the heavy honor of being the Defender of the Faith. Whether he would have recoiled from the scorched-earth brutality and price to be paid in lives is doubtful, however, because his Saxon campaigns were to become infused with an unprecedented religious fanaticism.

Charlemagne decided that the Saxon people deserved unmitigated punishment not only because they rebelled against his law but also because their unyielding, recidivist heathenism was intolerable to God. The campaigns after 778 differed from the previous Saxon chastisements by the religious fanaticism that nearly transformed the good-natured king into an avenging angel of death. Papal blessings upon the Saxon war came as a matter of course. The Benedictine abbots Sturmi and Willihad, two of the Church's most effective servants in the mold of the untiring

St. Boniface, had long since departed on missions deep in the "frightful wilderness" of Hesse and Thuringia, leaving a trail of crude chapels and imperiled converts likely to be destroyed any day by Widukind and his Saxon guerrillas. Still, as military expeditions followed each other pell-mell, Charlemagne hardened his heart against the Saxons to such a degree that his collaborator, Pope Adrian, sometimes winced at his pre-cocity for defining astringent rules governing un-Catholic activities.

Sometime in June 779, the largest-yet Frankish invasion force moved with remarkable speed out of Duren, a stockaded settlement on the Rhine, and managed to take Widukind's camp by surprise. The West-phalian fox escaped to sanctuary among the kindred Danes again, but Charlemagne led the army (much of it on horseback) to the banks of the lower Elbe for the first time. "No war ever undertaken by the Frank nation was carried on with such persistence and bitterness," says Ein-hard.[15] The king broke the people's resistance—temporarily. Saxons embraced Christ by the thousands, albeit in the glint of hovering broadswords. His was a hard policy of conversion or extirpation. Sturmi, the abbot beloved of the king, had died leading soldiers in battle, but Charlemagne institutionalized St. Sturmi's missionary work by dividing Saxony into missionary districts, each with its own bishop. Sturmi's part-ner in the hazardous work of saving Saxon souls, Willihad, became the first bishop of Bremen. From 780 onward, the soldiers of the Church fanned out across Westphalia under the protection of the crown. Pope Adrian's letters to Charlemagne overflowed with gratitude for the treas-ure expended by the crown and nobility for the building of churches and monasteries. To be sure, the magnates were generously compensated for their participation. They became enormously wealthy after receiving large parcels of territory, much of it Saxon real estate made available through Charlemagne's policy of forced relocation.

In the summer of 782, Charlemagne, now a commanding figure among kings and leaders of peoples living within the general boundaries of the old Western Roman Empire, convened a show assembly inside Saxony. He meant the world to see the success of his pacification policy. Indeed, he had made some significant alterations to Europe's political map shortly after the Spanish campaign. The first order of business was a purge of nobles who had performed poorly during the invasion, among them the counts of Bordeaux, Toulouse, Poitiers, and Limoges. Their fiefs were either forfeited to the crown or assigned to loyal *vassi* (as they were beginning to be called). He had taken sons Carloman and Louis, issues of third wife Hildegard, to Rome for a grand twin coronation on Easter Monday of 781. Carloman rose from his knees to accept from Pope Adrian the new name of Pippin and anointment as king of the Lombards. Oldest son Pippin the Hunchback remained in the shadows at Thionville. Louis became monarch of the new Kingdom of Aquitaine. Charlemagne created new vassals to police these realms.

The summons to Charlemagne's assembly of 782 was a command to attend an A-list event. A full complement of Frankland's and Italia's potentates, together with such unwonted pagan participants as emissaries of the king of the Danes and the *khagan* of the Avars, came to the assembly. Saxon chiefs reported as ordered. The large wooden meeting hall throbbed with the self-importance of titled panjandrums who flattered the king of the Franks, who in turn flattered many of them by the mere proximity of his six-foot-three majesty. The great assembly was obviously intended as the precedent for deliberations of supreme continental importance to be resolved in the presence of the supreme Carolingian. The apparent success of the summer assembly was a costly deception, however. Widukind slipped back into Saxony and called the tribes to the largest revolt yet. A crack Frankish army was annihilated on the lower Elbe River after its commanders acted with the classic imprudence of a Roland. The king's chamberlain and constable (equivalents of the modern-day prime minister and defense minister) were killed. Trusted Saxon auxiliaries slipped away during the waning months of 782 to join the seemingly ubiquitous Widukind. The fierce Frisians and the Slavic Wends came to the aid of their tribal cousins. Many churches were torched, and the monks of Fulda were forced to run for their lives, carrying the remains of St. Boniface to safety.

A second army commanded by Charlemagne in person finally succeeded in cornering the main Saxon fighting group near Verden, a Saxon settlement deep in the woods near the Weser River. Once again, the foxy Widukind eluded capture and headed for the Danish refuge. The punishment Charlemagne inflicted on the Saxon people was intended as a permanent cure for what he regarded as a chronic deceitfulness, which the tribes saw as a fight for their way of life. During one long, infamous day (whose exact date is unknown), the giant Frank watched as his men slaughtered forty-five hundred Saxon prisoners of war on his orders.[16] Some of the arms-bearing priests looked on approvingly, and Charlemagne probably thought he was following the Old Testament examples of Joshua and David. It would have been impossible for him to reflect upon the fact that his version of justice most closely resembled the Prophet Muhammad's appalling sanction of the Qurayza at Medina. As the news of their terrible fate spread across Christendom, sensitive souls professed shock at what had been done to the prisoners at Verden. Pope Adrian disassociated the Church from all complicity in what he called an act of misguided zeal. (That priests had borne arms in Saxony in violation of canon law was an impropriety to be ignored.) The atrocity was elided in Einhard's *Life of Charlemagne* with a reference to the necessity to "wreak vengeance and exact righteous satisfaction."

The Verden bloodletting of 782 was followed by a resettlement program on a scale sufficiently massive to evoke comparisons with twentieth- and twenty-first-century ethnic cleansings. Of one such relocation, the ever-discreet Einhard notes that Charlemagne "took ten thousand of those that lived on the banks of the Elbe, and settled them with their wives and children" in Gaul and Germany. Two years after Verden, Charlemagne was in the saddle continually, coordinating what were almost blanket sweeps of his divisions through Westphalia and the rest of Saxony. Ten years after the wars began, any thought of winning Saxon hearts and minds had become perverted by mutual and unceasing perfidy and barbarism. Saxons were devil worshippers who "transgress[ed] and violate[d] all law, human and divine," moaned Einhard.[17] Whatever the charitable disclaimers of the papacy, powerful members of the Frankish clergy, such as the bishop of Mainz (St. Boniface's successor), invoked the wrath of God upon these people and cheered on the patrols of homicidal Saxon hunters. In truth, the Saxon pacification was a model collaboration of Church and State, in terms of both manpower and ideology.

By 785, three years beyond the Verden massacre, major Saxon resistance had been worn down and "sometimes so much weakened and reduced," Einhard wrote, "that they promised to renounce the worship of devils." The wrap-up phase of pacification came in the autumn, when Widukind's luck finally ran out. Cornered and vastly outnumbered, he may have allowed himself to be captured in order to spare his people further misery. Widukind had no Einhard to chronicle his exploits, so he survives as one of history's caricatures of misguided obduracy brought to Christ in the end. Charlemagne's tender treatment of this most obdurate of adversaries reflected the cross-and-sword calculations of his Saxon policy. In the waning weeks of the year, the redoubtable old guerrilla leader was brought to the royal chapel at Attigny to be baptized, with the king of the Franks acting as godfather. News of the Attigny conversion elated Rome. Pope Adrian ordered three days of litanies and thanksgiving. Verses composed by the bishop of Mainz rejoiced that the Saxons had been driven to Christ by force. Widukind's embrace of Christianity was imitated by most of his followers, although a rump group of the unconverted faded into St. Sturmi's "frightful wilderness" to fight on for another fitful decade.

Never one to practice half measures, once he abjured pagan ways, Widukind surrendered his axe for good and appears to have ended his days as a faithful son of the Catholic Church. Their leader's departure from the scene marked the beginning of the definitive end of the Saxons' independence. It also marked the definitive beginning of an aggressive Catholicism that came to dominate the West—not only because of its edifying creed of sins forgiven and life eternal, which an often-exemplary clergy ubiquitously disseminated, but even more because it became the doctrinal building block of a regime whose imperial ambitions were fiercely hostile to varieties of religious belief. The moment in history when un-Christian activities were incised in granite comes sometime soon after the climactic developments of 785. Charlemagne's so-called Saxon Capitulary (or Capitulary of Paderborn) was promulgated as a series of edicts of unequivocal severity: punishments stipulated for thirty-four religious practices among the Saxons ranging from death in eleven cases to sizable fines.[18]

What the capitulary proscribed for the Saxons would set the standard for correct Christian conduct and the definition of un-Christian activities in non-Muslim Europe well into the coming centuries. Thereafter, "any one of the race of the Saxons" who "scorned to come to baptism" was to be killed. The range of capital crimes covered such predictables as infidelity to the king, killing of clergy, rape of high-born daughters, and desecration of churches, as well as what may seem the more arbitrary theft of Church property and the elastic "conspiracy with pagans against the Christians." Cremation of the dead and burial in unhallowed ground were capital offenses. Likewise, pagan practices involving devil worship, sacrifice of witches, and eating of human flesh were "punished by death," as was the eating of meat during Lent. Edict fourteen offered an escape clause from the thicket of "mortal crimes": Those whose guilt was undiscovered were spared death if they confessed to a priest who testified on their behalf in consideration of a penance. "Prohibited or illegal" marriages (incest), worship of "springs or trees or groves," and failure to baptize an infant "within a year" were among the sins expiated by fines to be paid in rare silver coin.

Punishment by death and fines were grim exactions in a web of ecclesiastical proscriptions and obligations designed to subordinate the Saxons to a hegemony that became the model for the coming quasi-theocracy in the West. All royal receipts derived from "any penalty of any kind" were to be shared with the parish church and priest. Notwithstanding large-scale relocations and the deadly blanket of religious sanctions and strictures spread from the Rhine to the Oder, the Saxons would revolt repeatedly until the first decade of the ninth century. Thus, Saxony was never far from becoming a quagmire, which explains, though hardly excuses, the bloody-mindedness of Charlemagne's policy of scourging the Saxons in order to bring the benefits of faith and order. The consequences of the Saxon Capitulary were to be profound and long term. As one scholar of the period solemnly judged, the document "stands as a blueprint for the comprehensive and ruthless Christianization of a conquered society."[19]

The Great Mosque

ᶜABD al-Rahman I—the Falcon of the Quraysh—had ruled Andalusia nearly a quarter century when Charlemagne heaved his powerful army over the Pyrenees in the summer of 778. The *amir* had been taken by surprise. Whatever serious thought he had given to the crude infidels east of the Pyrenees was colored by a well-justified assumption of cultural superiority and military parity. He and his Andalusis had never attached tremendous significance to the embarrassment at Moussais-la-Bataille, the *Balat al-Shuhada* ("Path of the Martyrs") of 732. In the Falcon's reading of history, Charles the Hammer's victory was an aberration of short duration that should have been avenged by a reenergized *jihad.* Nevertheless, the *amir's* analytical mind must have understood why and how this unexpected and grave menace from the land of the unbelievers at the end of the 770s had come about. He blamed the Abbasid caliphs, who rode to power over his ancestors' burnt bones, for the *Dar al-Harb's* arrest at the Pyrenees after 740. No Umayyad grandee could think otherwise of that time of troubles beginning at the top of the 740s in the Maghreb and in Iranian Khurasan. The *ummah* had been fractured at the very time when the Christians in the Great Land were still vulnerable to attack. Without that *jihadic* pause, no Frankish invasion of Andalusia such as this massive Carolingian incursion could ever have happened. It had been the pause that saved civilization as the "Europenses" came to know it.

Things were never to be quite the same again after Roncesvalles. Galicians and Basques went on the offensive, according to al-Masudi, "and snatched the towns located near the Franks' frontier from the Muslims."[1] Perturbations in the invasion's wake would grow deeper as the eighth century wound down. Basque nationalism, to speak anachronistically, had been inflamed. Unrest among the *amir's* Christian populations above the two great rivers in the north and east, the Duero and the Ebro, augured badly for the long-term stability of the frontiers. There were enough instances of Christians' rallying to the Franks in the Upper March as well as in the southeast to induce a certain wariness among Muslims after some seventy years of uncontested and relatively gentle overlordship. Of actual religious persecution, there were only a few instances, but an era of tightened policing of the frontier Christians began. Muslims began to be more suspicious of their Christian subjects, a bit more imperious in their interfaith dealings. Unfortunately for the health of the amirate, Muslims of the Upper March remained deeply suspicious and resentful of Cordovan policies. Ahmed ibn Mohammed al-Makkari (Maqqari), the indispensable historian of *al-Andalus,* offered a wistful judgment on this pivotal period: "Whilst the Muslims of al-Andalus were thus revolting against their sovereign and striving to overthrow his empire, the people of Galicia were gathering strength, and their power greatly increased."[2]

Christian out-migration to Aquitaine and Septimania, once negligible, accelerated greatly after Charlemagne's Franks came charging back in 785 to capture Girona, the strategic Catalan valley city with a large and loyal Sephardic population. A territorial tug-of-war ensued, with Muslims regaining and losing Girona and smaller towns in the region. Christian forces put Muslims on the defensive. Meanwhile, Carolingian pressures from the northeast stimulated religious and political particularism in the petty Catholic kingdoms of Asturias, Castile, Leon, Aragon, Catalunya, and parts of Navarra, where Visigothic culture and institutions survived beyond the effective reach of Cordoba. Little more than a decade beyond Roncesvalles, Alfonso II (759–842), king of Asturias and grandson of the legendary Visigothic resistance fighter Pelayo, began leading his people south into the valley of the Duero. Alfonso, called "the Chaste," exerted more realm-building initiative than did a long line of successors. Even though his nobles resented any flexing of monarchical muscle, Alfonso had welcomed Charlemagne's invasion and sought an alliance with the Franks.[3] The result, then, of the Franco-Abbasid entente was a double Muslim calamity of unintended consequences: First, the Frankish invasion stimulated an inchoate Visigothic irredentism that would propel the *Reconquista,* the reconquest of the peninsula from the Muslims; second, the Carolingian attack was a dress rehearsal for the religious crusades to come out of the Latin West two centuries later.

At forty-seven, an age well beyond the average male life span at the time, 'Abd al-Rahman showed no signs of diminished intellectual or physical capacity. His counselors had finally been able to persuade the *amir* to cease strolling about the city in his distinctive white jellaba and turban unaccompanied by guards. He worshipped with his people in the Friday Mosque and frequently spoke to them from the *minbar.* 'Abd al-Rahman spent much of his time now at Rusafa, his estate outside Cordoba. We know almost nothing of his domestic arrangements, of wives or the size of his harem. One of the *amir*'s favorites survives as little more than a name—Da'ja, in *The Ring of the Dove* or *The Dove's Necklace* (*Tawq al-Hamama*), Ibn Hazm's eleventh-century treatise on love. Two of his three

sons—Sulayman, the elder, and Hisham—served as provincial governors;
the other, 'Abd Allah, seems to have acted as his father's eyes in Cordoba.
The *amir* was served by a well-run cadre led by Umayyad relatives and
staffed by Syrians, *muwalladun*, Jews, and Mozarabs who penetrated the
farthest towns and cities in stealthy enforcement of Cordoba's authority.
White slaves (*saqaliba*) supplied by the network of Jewish merchants,
made up the bulk of the professional army.[4] The *shurta*, a highly disciplined black African police force, guaranteed the Falcon's personal safety
as well as the security of the denizens of one of the world's greatest and
often-volatile cities.

Sevilla, chronically rebellious, had been subdued by the mid-770s
and had been given to a faithful cousin, 'Abd al-Malik ibn Umar ibn Marwan, to govern. 'Abd al-Malik was a vigilant taskmaster who ordered his
own son beheaded for having failed to stand his ground before a large
contingent of armed Yemeni rebels. In distant Extremadura, as well as in
several borderland regions, the Banu Fihri descendants of old Yusuf of
Narbonne, still unreconciled to their political dispossession, stood ready
to exploit any weakness in the regime. Like the Banu Fihri, the old settler families who governed Zaragoza jealously guarded their patrimony
from the Falcon's encroaching agents. Cuenca, located in the Sierra de
Cuenca, had been roiled since the late 760s by the guerrilla resistance of
a fanatic Berber convert to Shi'ism. Andalusis of the region evinced little
interest in the fanatic's religious exuberance, but they indulged Shaqya
ibn 'Abd al-Wahid's resistance to central authority.[5] In a sense, political
disloyalty in Andalusia was a tribute to the statecraft of the Falcon and
his ministers. A weaker ruler would have been readily accorded the for-
malities of deference by those who had little to fear from a potent central government.

A heightened awareness of his mortality turned 'Abd al-Rahman I to
concerns about legacy, even as resources were committed to stabilizing
the frontiers. The incomparable grandeur of the Abbasids' city of Baghdad, its greatly ornate Ozymandian construction completed before
Caliph al-Mansur's death—with additions and refinements ongoing
within circular walls enclosing a hundred square miles of palaces, schools,
inns, hospitals, parks, and more—may well have been a factor in the tim-

ing of 'Abd al-Rahman's decision in 785 to erect the Friday Mosque of Cordoba. The great Caliph Abu Ja'far al-Mansur (754–74) described the shape of his world-class capital in the sandy plain beside the Tigris with the point of his sword, after which a hundred thousand laborers, architects, engineers, and masons were put to work to finish the city in four years. Constantinople excepted, nothing on the scale of Baghdad, *Madinat al-Salam* ("City of Peace"), with its caliphal Palace of the Gilded Gate and outsize mosque had been seen before in history. Fifth-century BCE Persepolis and first-century BCE Ctesiphon, imperial cities created *de novo* by fiat, paled by comparison. St. Petersburg and Versailles would be puny imitations. Thirty-odd years after it was finished, Baghdad had a population approaching one million.[6]

The Falcon was determined to safeguard the political independence of *al-Andalus* from the Abbasid Empire, and at this he succeeded. Cultural independence was quite another matter. The high wall of political enmity between Baghdad and Cordoba was as porous as a sponge when it came to money, trade, culture, and regal example. The Abbasid Caliphate presided over the most powerful economy since Rome—a free-trade zone from China and India to the Atlantic of goods and manufactures, money and services, science and philosophy. The Mediterranean was now a Muslim sea from Gibraltar to the corner at the Bosporus where the formidable Byzantine defenses still held. The spectacular monumentalism of Abu Ja'far al-Mansur and his successors was an example to be envied. Baghdad was infinitely beyond 'Abd al-Rahman's means to replicate, but improvement decrees had planted a mosque in Algeciras and an *alcazaba* (fortress) in Malaga, repaired walls by the banks of the Guadalquivir at Cordoba, and erected a new amiral palace (*dar al-imara*) within the city. The new palace, finished in 784, stood near the Muslim baths (one of which is still extant) and close by the church and monastery of St. Vincent. In the shadow of the new palace was the densely populated Jewish quarter, the *madinat al-Yehuda*. The following year, the Falcon commanded the building of the new Friday Mosque, what he called "the Ka'bah of the West," after the votive cube at Mecca.[7]

At the time of the Conquest of 711, Cordoba's Visigothic church and monastery of St. Vincent had been divided by treaty to serve equally

Muslims and Christians. Muslim and Christian worshipped under the same roof, but separated by a wall. The *amir* honored his religious duties scrupulously, and it was a rare Friday when he failed to speak to the Prophet's devotees regarding matters moral and civic. To be sure, his sermons no longer asked the Prophet's blessings upon the usurpers in Baghdad. That the master of the Iberian peninsula and his flock continued to worship in a Catholic church built over a Roman temple spoke volumes for the Qur'anic injunction to respect all "People of the Book." The precedent was Damascus before the building of the Great Mosque by 'Abd al Rahman's great ancestor, Caliph al-Walid. Yet, if not for reasons of confessional superiority, the arrangement was no longer satisfactory due to the great increase in Believers.

Although it must have been an offer they knew better than to refuse, the Christians agreed to some eighty thousand dirhams in fair value for St. Vincent. The Falcon then leveled both the church and the monastery, after which the Catholics erected a new cathedral on the city's outskirts. Work on the mosque commenced in 785, and it rose in less than a year on the foundations of the old Visigothic house of worship a few steps beyond the Roman bridge.[8] Few accomplishments exemplified the innovative prowess of the Arab-dominated *Dar al-Islam* after 150 years of conquest and assimilation. Had 'Abd al-Rahman I failed in all other undertakings, his Great Mosque of Cordoba (*la Mezquita* in Spanish) would have redeemed ancestral pride, glorified the regime, and ensured a permanent legacy.

The oldest still-standing Muslim structure on the peninsula, the Great Mosque became, by virtue of its purity of form, the architectural archetype for three cultural zones: Muslim Andalusia, Christian Spain, and Hebrew Sefarad. Its builders devised the art and science of transmuting matter into light and form that medieval Christendom was the poorer for its general inability to comprehend. Some accounts attribute the structure's harmonious design to a Syrian master builder or an architect sent from Constantinople, others to the equally likely hand of the *amir*. His ancestors' architects, after all, had built two of Islam's most venerated structures—Jerusalem's al-Aqsa Mosque and the great Umayyad prayer hall in Damascus. The influence of the former on Cordoba appears to be echoed in the placement of the arcades perpendicular to the rear wall. In any case, the basic plan was simplicity itself, a perfect square whose sides measured (within inches) 242 feet each. Half of the square, the *Patio de los Naranjos*, was given over to an open courtyard with rows of orange trees whose seasonal fragrance caressed the contemplative at prayer and those at postprandial repose. The courtyard fronted the prayer hall comprising the other half of the square and pierced by four entrances ornamented by Arabic calligraphy.[9]

Eighth-century buildings were more often than not scavenged from impressive Roman ruins in the neighborhood: columns from pagan temples; pillars from abandoned buildings; granite from downed walls. The large number of columns demanded by the prayer hall must have denuded many Visigothic structures still standing in the city as well as distant Roman sites, perhaps as far away as Italica, birthplace of Emperors Hadrian and Trajan, northwest of Sevilla. Not a single column was newly carved, and few were topped with identical or even similar capitals. Some were of the rare porphyry no longer quarried, giving credence to the story that they were politically inspired gifts from Constantine VI of Byzantium. These 152 columns, with their various cornice styles, were arranged along eleven aisles facing south and perpendicular to the *mihrab*, the niche in the wall aligned (but not quite exactly in this case) toward Mecca. Because no other pillars were available, the prayer hall's ceiling height would have been limited by the Roman columns' regulation length, likening the resulting gloomy interior to a tunnel. The unprecedented innovation of the Great Mosque's master builder was to loft the coffered ceiling to a height of forty feet by means of an upper tier of semicircular arches that appeared to be clamped to the bottom tier of horseshoe arches supported by columns.[10]

The famous horseshoe arches atop the columns were themselves not unique, as frequently claimed. The Visigoths had developed a crude prototype, and the Friday Mosques in Damascus and in Qayrawan in Ifriqiya featured arches and window designs almost as pinched. But the distinctive horseshoe arch was perfected at Cordoba. Since the horseshoe arches were not load-bearing, the function of their alternating sandstone and brick voussoirs, fitting like pie wedges pressed together, was largely aesthetic. Structurally ingenious, the visual effect of the double arches has been from the moment of completion one of the world's distinctively edifying aesthetic experiences. It was as if the muezzin's call to prayer drew the Believer through a flood of light into a nursery of soaring marble palm trees whose fronds were made of red and yellow voussoirs. As measured in historical time, 'Abd al-Rahman I's Great Mosque overnight became one of the wonders of the world. It graced the Iberian Muslims with an iconic tabernacle of faith the likes of which Europe's Christians would go without until Chartres Cathedral three hundred years later. 'Abd al-Rahman commanded these words to be inscribed in the exuberant elegance of the Arabic script: "It embodied what came before. Illuminated what came after."

The embodiment in ashlar and stone of the True Faith, the Great Mosque was also the vehicle of literacy, a virtue integral to Islam in contrast to Roman Catholicism at that time. Calligraphy ran like filigree around the great doors and like latticework across the walls inside. It repeated God's words, the faithful believed, recited by His Messenger Muhammad and recorded in the Holy Qur'an. Muslims had known of the Deity's linguistic preference for nigh 150 years, as the inscription proclaimed in the Great Mosque and ubiquitously in prayer halls and public buildings throughout the *Dar al-Islam*: "We have revealed the Qur'an in the Arabic tongue," God makes eternally clear, "so that you may grow in understanding."[11] Christians had received no such assurance from God about the revelatory primacy of Latin—or Greek, for that matter. Moreover, in Charlemagne's rough-and-ready kingdom, Latin, like Hebrew, was intelligible only to the learned few who were secure from malnutrition in well-endowed centers of learning such as Echternach or Jumiège. The unwashed many could read no Latin and spoke the new tongues of the continent: proto-French, proto-Italian, and proto-Spanish, along with an evolving Anglo-Saxon, German, and Sephardic Ladino. Rather than a vehicle for instruction of the people, as was Arabic, ecclesiastical Latin congealed into a formulaic mumbo jumbo that served far more to mystify, intimidate, and humble the faithful. If Arabic was the language understood by all who prostrated themselves toward Mecca, Latin was the exclusive vehicle of a priestly caste whose interposition between God and His children provided a running translation of the moral meaning of life and afterlife.

"Veneration of text and language thus went hand in hand in Islam," observed a perceptive student of the competing histories of Judaism, Christianity, and Islam. It was true that in Judaism the same veneration of text and language prevailed, but with the vital difference that Hebrew dropped away over time from the living experience of most Jews of the diaspora. Arabic was always to be a sacred language in daily use by the whole community of Believers. Moreover, because it was God's language, the leap-forward language of the Qur'an was seen to possess a beauty, complexity, and precision insusceptible to complete rational explanation. Written and spoken, Arabic conveyed a distinctive connection between sound and content, what one particularly keen northern European described as an inner unity of word and deed "run[ning] like a scarlet thread through all its word formations." Indeed, Arabic calligraphy did run across all the public surfaces in the Muslim world like a scarlet thread. The result, as gloriously attested by the Qur'anic phrases incised like fine veins in the skin of the Great Mosque, was the alphabetical meld of beauty and knowledge. Literacy and religion were indissolubly linked.[12]

To be able to read the prose of God was to live in a state of grace that was as much civil as it was spiritual. Although Muslims did not care to force their faith upon others—believing their religion required only that God's final revelation be available to all who wished to know the truth— they charitably warned that the fate of those who knowingly rejected Islam was terrible to contemplate. The Prophet's words, on public display everywhere, admonished: "The day will surely come when those who disbelieve will wish that they believed that they were Muslims. Let them feast and make merry; and let their hopes beguile them. They shall learn." Those who could read would surely learn. From Mu'awiya to Marwan II, Umayyad caliphs had deemed it their duty to encourage literacy among the people.[13] If rote memorization and recitation formed the basis of instruction for the great mass of Believers, the Sunni *ulamas* also taught the many their *alif, baa, taa*'s.

What percentage of the Arabic-speaking population could read and write in 'Abd al-Rahman's day is unknowable. Even less is it possible to know how many Christians and Jews, whose principal tongue was not Arabic, could read the language of the conquerors. Outside the large cities, the percentage of the literate must have been infinitesimal. As has been the case throughout history, literacy was, as in *al-Andalus*, the privilege of elites. Nevertheless, many more people other than rich men and women read and wrote in Toledo, Sevilla, Jaén, and Girona, and a dozen other urban places, than was the case in Latin Christendom. But not only were their numbers significant, a significant number of literate *dhimmis* preferred Arabic to Latin or Romance. The archbishop of Cordoba had good reason to worry that a trend toward Arabic on the part of educated Catholics threatened to become a convention by the end of the century. The good prelate lamented the reading of "verses and fairy tales of the Arabs." Worse still, he declared, his fellow Christians read "not in order to refute them, but to express themselves in Arabic ever more correctly and elegantly. . . . Alas! All talented Christians know only the language and the literature of the Arabs."[14] The archbishop's lament, if probably somewhat overstated, anecdotally corroborated the accelerating, if impossible to quantify, Arabization of Iberia's non-Muslim population.

'Abd al-Rahman I died peacefully in the first week of October 788, two years after the sun caliph, Harun al-Rashid, began his opulent reign in Baghdad. Work on Cordoba's Great Mosque was carried on by 'Abd al-Rahman's son Hisham. The *amir* was fifty-eight, twelve years older than Charlemagne, who would live another quarter century. He left twenty children, "eleven of whom were sons."[15] The Falcon's rule had lasted just shy of a generation, a crucial thirty-two years. His passing represented not an end but the end of a beginning. Islam had come to Iberia as an alien civilization, its conquest significantly advantaged by dissension among the ruling Visigoths, indifference on the part of the common people, and assistance from the kingdom's beleaguered Jews. Eight decades later, as 'Abd al-Rahman took his last breath, Islam, its language, and its culture were indelibly stamped upon the racial face of Iberia. The Falcon of the Quraysh had shown himself a superbly worthy descendant of the Muslim world's first dynast, the great Mu'awiya ibn Abi Sufyan. By dint of his extraordinary achievements in politics and war, Umayyad rule was ensured in *al-Andalus* for an additional 243 mostly illustrious years. More than the Romans and far more than the slow-learning Visigoths had ever done, the Falcon's regime brought a degree of cohesion to a peninsula whose transverse mountain ranges and ecologically disparate basins defied political centralization.

That 'Abd al-Rahman had succeeded in holding together *al-Andalus* was due to his pragmatic understanding of limitations and possibilities, his balancing act of autocracy and laissez-faire. There were never enough Arabs and Berbers on the peninsula to enable the *amir* to enforce a rigorous, rigid Islamic theocracy, even had he unwisely wished to do so. *Al-Andalus* was still overwhelmingly Christian at the end of the eighth century, although the rate of Islamic conversion was accelerating. The objective reality was that demography was the handmaiden of the legendary Andalusian tolerance. The Falcon adopted a pragmatic approach to the management and manipulation of his predecessors' regional structure of government. His Cordovan heartland, now divided into units called *kuwar*, obeyed the orders of a civilian administrator (*wali*). He greatly rationalized the three marches—Upper, Middle, and, Lower—subordinating them to the appointed military official, *qa'id*, who governed from Zaragoza, Toledo, and Merida, respectively. His professional army of slaves, *saqaliba*, freed the *amir* from overdependency on the old and often prickly Syrians, Yemeni, and original settlers, along with the risky Berbers.[16] His ministers counted it a major success that the troublesome *junds*, those Syrian military formations brought over during the Berber troubles, were disbanded. As for the Berbers, a large but undetermined number had simply quit the peninsula for the Maghreb during the middle of the century. Thousands decided that the lands they had been ordered to settle were too arid, too alluvial, or too alien. Their departure created large vacuums in the northern regions that were gradually filled by the Christian people who had retreated above the Duero and Ebro Rivers in the aftermath of the Battle of Guadalete.

In the decades to follow, Jews, *muwalladun*, and Christians would ascend to high office, as in the famous case of Hasdai ibn Shaprut, Sephardic counsellor to 'Abd al-Rahman III, and the learned Racemundo, Catholic bishop of Elvira and Cordoba's ambassador to Constantinople. Under 'Abd al-Rahman I, however, the upward mobility of non-Arab talent was restricted to the middle rungs of state service. The ruling inner circle was, with few if any exceptions, an Arab aristocracy whose major players were Banu Umayya, whose counsels the *amir* might seek but whose subordination was supposed to be unconditional. Sometimes, though, the relatives caused him pain enough for public outbursts "when we grant them security; and surround them with every comfort and luxury. . . ."[17] There were exceptions to the Arab ceiling, such as the powerful Visigoth families in Huesca and Zaragoza who had converted to Islam at the time of the Conquest and occupied high positions of service and command. Mughith al-Rumi's descendants were indispensable, for instance, despite their ancestor's Greek origins. Muslims, especially those of *baladiyyun* pedigree, insisted on maintaining certain distinctions in dress and civic prerogatives as marks of superiority to non-Muslims.

Still, a fair amount of relaxation of the sumptuary requirements and discriminatory building codes imposed upon the *dhimmis* occurred under the Falcon, although the actual gap between law and practice is now impossible to determine. As was the case elsewhere in the *Dar al-Islam,* the Falcon's amirate left subject populations to the governance of their own leaders under their own religions: Christians under the guidance of priests and the Bible; Jews obedient to rabbis and the Torah. In the ordinary run of affairs, the *Forum Judicum* and the Talmud served Gentiles and Jews, respectively, unless there was a conflict with the superior laws of the Muslim state. Exceptions to the rule of tolerance happened only along the northern and eastern borders of the state, or *dawla,* where incidents of friction—even hostilities between Muslims and Christians—were on the rise. Gascony-Navarra especially concerned the Falcon's generals because of the Gallo-Frankish military operations there. Yet, overall, religious and cultural variety were almost seamlessly accommodated in *al-Andalus* by an official ideology of pragmatic tolerance.

The contrast between the money economy presided over by the Falcon and the barter-and-services arrangements available to Charlemagne was almost incommensurable. The economies of both were based on agriculture, but in *al-Andalus* farmers and herders serviced the growth of cities, whose reciprocated mercantile and commercial wealth worked to the profit of the countryside. In Frankland, cities were anemic Roman leftovers or permanent fairs located where the flow of road or river traffic sustained them. Insofar as the term applied, the Carolingian State derived no direct revenues from the economy. What mattered most to 'Abd al-Rahman, as it did to the caliph in Baghdad, and as it had to the Caesars whose system served as model, was the bottom line—tax revenues into the *diwan*. To the *amir* and his government, what taxpaying people believed was a matter of respected indifference. The introduction into *al-Andalus* of only one of Islam's four major (Sunni) legal systems— the Malikite school of jurisprudence—at the end of the Falcon's rule placed a virtual embargo on the kind of divisive legal controversies that soon roiled and divided the educated in Baghdad.[18]

'Abd al-Rahman understood the weaknesses of his oldest son, Sulayman, his governor in Toledo. Second son Hisham, as governor of Merida, possessed a more serious disposition than his brother. A favorite story of the Cordovan *ashraf* was that whenever the *amir* asked about Sulayman, the invariable answer was that Sulayman's quarters were always crowded "with sycophants, fools, and cowards." Hisham, on the other hand, was reputed to spend his time in quarters "thronged with learned men, poets, and historians."[19] The Falcon's illness must have been brief, otherwise both brothers surely would have been present to hear his deathbed wishes. Hisham and Sulayman reached Cordoba nearly a week after their youngest brother, 'Abd Allah, had supervised the preparation of and interment of the *amir*'s body at Rusafa. Hisham arrived first and was immediately proclaimed the new *amir* of *al-Andalus* by 'Abd Allah, supposedly in accordance with the deceased's wishes. Seniority alone was no guarantee of succession among the Arabs, but Sulayman, the superior military talent of the three, protested. The leading families, however, insisted that Hisham succeed his father. Even so, the new *amir* had to fight Sulayman for almost two years before military engagements, diplomacy, and money settled affairs decisively in his favor. Three years after his father's death, Hisham I (788–96) completed the Great Mosque and erected the minaret that stands today as a bell tower.

Well might 'Abd al-Rahman "the Immigrant" boast, as was his wont,

"I came fleeing hunger, the sword, and death, attained security and prosperity, and gathered together a people." 'Abd al-Rahman I left unmentioned one of the most important things he was never able to accomplish as a devout Muslim: the pilgrimage to Mecca. In his mid-ninth-century reckoning, Ya'qub ibn Ishaq al-Kindi, Islam's first philosopher-historian, found nothing to gainsay the Falcon's appreciation of himself. "It is said," wrote al-Kindi, "that when 'Abd al-Rahman took over the reins of government, *al-Andalus* was a glowing coal, a spluttering fire, with overt and covert resistance seething between its borders. Through his fortunate hand and strong power, God pacified the country."[20] In resurrecting the Umayyad Caliphate (in all but name) at the edge of Europe's Dark Ages, Mu'awiya's descendant not only thrust his dynasty centuries into the future; his achievement made *al-Andalus* the channel through which the science and philosophy of classical antiquity, preserved and augmented in the *Dar al-Islam*, would flow steadily into the Occidental void.

The First Europe, Briefly

A S THE eighth century wound down, the Franks came closer each year to achieving continental military and political hegemony. Greater Europe was a Carolingian work-in-progress, and the king of the Franks and the Lombards now had an ally whose weaponry no competing secular ruler could match. Papal power to loose and bind mere temporal power-holders was a unique asset. That power, combined with the Marchfield muster of twenty thousand Franks, made the team of Charlemagne and Adrian virtually invincible. The battlefield victories of the one advanced the ecclesiastical ascendancy of the other in a symbiotic union. The old Lombard-hater, Pope Stephen II, would have rejoiced at the fulfillment of the mission that had propelled him through the alpine snows to Pippin's Ponthion: the complementarity of papal and monarchical politics. Complementarity did not necessarily mean symmetry, however, as would become evident in time.

Charlemagne's dominions stretched from the Pyrenees to the Danube and the Oder, from the North Sea to Sicily. Pockets of Saxon resistance survived, but the endgame was certain. Tassilo III, duke of Bavaria and son-in-law of old Desiderius, was as determined to keep the Franks at bay as once were the dukes of Aquitaine and Burgundy. His determination finally brought matters to a head with his nominal overlord when he formed a defensive alliance with his Avar neighbors, some of the continent's most dreaded pagans. The duke's intransigence came to an end in the summer of 788, after Pope Adrian threatened excommunication. The king of the Franks and the Lombards forced Tassilo III to undergo judgment at the hands of the Frankish magnates. The duke of Bavaria was allowed to keep his title and his head, but the king of the Franks helped himself to Tassilo's country. Widukind's tribal cousins, the pagan Danes, were a more serious matter. Their incessant frontier raids threatened to destabilize the always tenuous Saxon peace. Einhard reported that Godefroid, their king, "was so puffed up with empty ambition that he planned to make himself master of the whole of Germany." In the end, Godefroid dropped dead just as his warriors massed for a decisive match with Charlemagne's levies. The Danes turned to coastal raids and then occupation of England. An uneasy truce held with the Franks, but missionaries would make no headway among the Danes until the tenth-century conversion of King Harold Bluetooth (Harald Blatand).[1]

The Avars of Hungary, nomads from the Asian steppes whose threat to Byzantium had been contained since the sixth century by annual subsidies as high as one hundred thousand gold solidi, were as pagan as the Danes and as ferocious as the Saxons, with one consequential asset denied Saxons or Danes—stirrups. The stirrups that made Avar cavalry so stunningly lethal on the Pannonian (Hungarian) plain finally impressed their enemies, who had somehow failed to take notice of them on Saracen horsemen.[2] Charlemagne planned a monster campaign in which he and his son Pippin (the rebaptized Carloman), along with the housebroken Tassilo, coordinated a joint invasion of Hungary by Frankish, Friulian, and Bulgarian cavalry and infantry, together with a flotilla up the Danube. The two Avar campaigns of 791 and 795 beggared even the Spanish in size and complexity of execution, with Charlemagne imposing his strategic will upon what was virtually a huge army of nations. The king ordered thousands of peasants to try digging a canal between the Rhine and the Danube in order to move his forces swiftly by water across the endless Pannonian plain. The pigtailed Avars manipulated ten-foot lances on fleet ponies and fought a merciless guerrilla war against their well-equipped adversaries.

Once again, Charlemagne had chosen an enemy whose capable leader, the *khagan,* and his people were willing to pay the ultimate price for their liberty. Systematically ground down year after year by a steady influx of settler-soldiers accompanied by soul-saving clergy, the Avar kingdom was all but erased from history after 795. Christianity and civilization triumphed once more by the sword as pagan Avars reported en masse for baptism as ordered. These were "irrational and unlettered people," sniffed a Frankish missionary bound for conversion duty in Pannonia, which would be a repeat of Saxony. Fifteen ox wagons piled with gold taken from the Avars' prodigious hoard not only handsomely compensated Frankish magnates and their peers and enriched the papal treasury but also went to pay for the completion of Charlemagne's royal capital near Mainz.[3]

But the peninsula on the other side of the Pyrenees still defied the Franks. If the Umayyads confounded Charlemagne's imperial ambitions, however, it was equally true that the Frankish military establishment had bulwarked Islam and Africa at the Pyrenees. The Spanish campaign of 778 had ended badly as a military venture, but it marked the all-but-final end of the Muslim advance into the European heartland. In 793, when the Falcon's son and successor, Hisham I, dispatched two armies into Septimania and Languedoc, besieging Narbonne and Carcassonne and carrying off much treasure and hostages to complete Cordoba's Great

Mosque, Charlemagne recognized the incursion for what it was, a demonstration of defensive strength rather than a genuine *jihadic* reprise. Two years later, 795, came the Spanish March (*Marca Hispanica*) the Carolingian response—the strip of territory straddling the Pyrenees from Aquitaine to Septimania.[4] As a barrier to significant Muslim military incursions, the Spanish March worked well enough. As a firebreak against unwelcome religious ideas, however, results were poor from the beginning, as unsettling and heterodox concepts leached into the Christian West out of the tolerant, eclectic Muslim purlieus of Toledo and Cordoba.

A perfect case of the Christological license permitted in *al-Andalus* was Adoptionism, a theological deviation that had become almost unthinkable east of the Pyrenees yet unsurprising among Arab monotheists whose founder had dismissed the Trinity as illogical. "Unbelievers," admonished the Qur'an, "are those who say, 'God is one of three.' There is but one God." No less a personage than the Catholic archbishop of Toledo, Elipandus, together with the bishop of Urgel, Felix, were among the Andalusian clergy tainted by Adoptionism, the creed of those hyperanalytical Nestorian Christians from Palestine granted refuge in *al-Andalus* from Byzantine persecution. Adoptionists contended that "Christ as man is son of God only by adoption and grace"—the adoptive and not the natural son of God—thereby undermining the foundations of the Trinitarian faith as defined at the first Council of Nicaea. While Pope Adrian and his successor remonstrated in shrill pastoral letters, Charlemagne presided either in person or through his representatives at synods in Narbonne in 788, Ratisbon in 792, Frankfurt in 794, and, finally, Aachen in 799 that seemed oddly patient in their condemnatory dealings with Adoptionism (also referred to as *Hispanicus error*). As a faithful son of the Church, Charlemagne abhorred the Adoptionist heresy. As protector of the Spanish March, however, he preferred to avoid the outright alienation of Hispania's theologically deviant Catholics.[5] The politics of empire occasionally trumped confessional rectitude. The real significance of Adoptionism was that it was a harbinger, one of the first in a steady flow of unsettling ideas from *al-Andalus* into an intellectually impoverished and rigid Christian Europe.

⁘

The new Carolingian order, therefore, was religiously intolerant, intellectually impoverished, socially calcified, and economically primitive. Measured by these same vectors of religion, culture, class, and prosperity, 'Abd al-Rahman's Muslim Iberia was at least four centuries more advanced than Western Christendom in 800 CE. An ironic intelligence from another planet might have observed that if Carolingian Europeans believed that Charles the Hammer's victory at Poitiers made their world possible, then it was a fair question to ask whether or not defeat might have been preferable. From the plains of Pannonia to the crest of the Pyrenees, the peoples of the West were obliged to accept the governance, protection, exploitation, and militant creed of a warrior caste and its clerical enforcers, an overlordship sustained by a powerful military machine and an omnipresent ecclesiastical apparatus. The European shape of things to come was set for dismal centuries following one upon the other until the Commercial Revolution and the Enlightenment molded new contours.

A thousand great families—such as the Niebelungs, the Welfs, the Unrochids—enriched by benefices carved from continual conquest and bound by fealty oaths to the king, occupied the top of the Carolingian pyramid. There was an undeniable upswing in the consolidation of holdings by powerful families such as these that portended profound changes in the social order. Everywhere, the species *potentes* emerged—"men of power," of mixed German, Celt, and (occasional) Roman origins—united, says an unfailingly perceptive religious scholar, "by tenacious bonds of a shared Catholicism and a shared avarice." Class lines hardened as the scale of estates, benefices, and *mansi* (freeholds) expanded. The hierarchical elaboration of classic feudalism, with its monarchical primacy, its three rigid social orders, its mystique of Christian knighthood, its vassals enfeoffed to protecting lords—a pyramid of interlocked, unequal obligations resting on the mortared base of serfs and slaves fixed in perpetuity to manors and abbeys—was still perhaps two centuries off.[6] Whether the institution ever attained the pyramidal elegance described by the much-respected F.-L. Ganshof (a fusion of elements from the

Late Roman Empire and the German conquests) or remained a messy patchwork that defies the historian's schematics, "feudalism"—whatever it was or became—surged ahead during Charlemagne's watch.

"Carolingian society," in the summary judgment of one medieval scholar, "comprised . . . three groups: those who fought, those who prayed, and those who labored."[7] He could have added that, among those who labored, a great many were slaves. West of the Pyrenees, Islam, the newest world religion, ordained the equality of the faithful as the objective of civil society, not as a beatitude reserved to the afterlife. Nor, in stark contrast to Christians, could Muslims enslave other Muslims— although, with equal explicitness, the Qur'an condoned the enslavement of non-Muslims. Christian doctrine looked to Aristotle, St. Paul, and Isidore of Seville to justify enslaving other Christians. To be sure, the literate Christian few who possessed even cursory knowledge of the Gospels could have found verses with which to deplore the buying and selling of their confessional brothers and sisters. Yet whatever the congruences of Muslim and Christian ideals, Frankland's emergent social order was shaped by realities of caste and exploitation. A representative inventory of several large estates or villas listed about a third of the workers as slaves. Large numbers of them were pagan Slavs—Bohemians and Wends, especially—captured in campaigns in the East or imported into the kingdom for sale principally by Jews.[8] Many others were desperate Christians who sold themselves into slavery in order to survive. Another hapless percentage comprised criminals, persons kidnapped on the dangerous roads of the realm, and men forced by powerful local magnates to alienate their holdings.

Gradually at first, and then accelerating to a peak near the close of Charlemagne's century, free men and women—Franks, in the etymological sense of the word—all but disappeared, most into serfdom but others into the maw of bondage. The finite number who climbed and clawed to the top of the economic and political pyramid joined the magnates or *potentes*, lay and ecclesiastical, whose multiple estates sustained the Carolingian war machine and the complementary seigneurial lifestyle. Voices of conscience speaking in Latin, German, and Romance sincerely deplored cruelty, cupidity, and corruption. "Do justice fairly, correctly, and equitably to churches, widows, orphans, and all others, without fraud, corruption, obstruction or abusive delay," was the well-intentioned highmindedness ordained in one of Charlemagne's last capitularies. The best of the Benedictines honored St. Boniface's exemplary solicitude for the poor and the weak. Almsgiving was a Christian imperative, just as *zakat*, the Third Pillar of Islam, dictated that a percentage of each Muslim's wealth go to charity. Despite occasional grumbling from powerful bishops who looked askance at their free movement within the kingdom, Jews enjoyed the king's protection and were almost never molested because of their religion.[9] It was not that compassion and Christian morality were meaningless, but rather that their potency was inherently constrained by the exploitative structure of things, by an institutionalized rapacity that enforced its lethal logic in an economy of agrarian subsistence that was virtually devoid of innovation. Wealth meant ownership of land stocked with servile animals, human and domestic, neither of whom, people or beasts, were fed well enough to plow and harvest optimally.

An agrarian civilization dominated by warriors and prince-bishops was inherently disinclined to value tradesmen, merchants, and moneylenders. It was the likes of Roland of Roncesvalles who set society's tone and direction, looking down from their mounts with a contemptuous indulgence upon what there was of an entrepreneurial class. Except for payment of fines, tolls, and purchases at fairs, the role of money was almost nil where the medium of exchange was labor service, grain and livestock quotas, and bartered goods. The innovative three-field system of cultivation was still more than a century in the future, although crop rotation would make a tenuous beginning in the Paris basin at century's end. Elsewhere, though, lords still pressed their serfs to clear and plant more forest land while the exhausted old fields lay in fallow recovery. All but cut off from the enlivening economic and cultural energies of *al-Andalus* and the Arab lake—the Mediterranean—the Carolingian North began to prosper inequitably in the 790s on the beer, meat, butter, and furs of the Rhine and the North Sea. But missing the critical urban stimulus, the magnates and the high clergy enriched themselves as in the past with more land and more peasants—land that became available in great quantities as a result of serial, bloody conquests.

Magnates became wealthier, the realm less so. Since it was little more than a hierarchical arrangement based on extortion, the Carolingian "State" deprived itself even of the conception of anything resembling the *diwan* (national treasury) of the Andalusian Umayyads. No national tax levy—like the universal *jizya* required of all *dhimmis* or the *kharaj* imposed on Muslim property holders—existed. In exchange for the real-estate bonanza distributed by the crown, dukes and counts took an oath to arrive at the Marchfield equipped and ready for war. When not fighting for king and faith, they were supposed to police the realm in accordance with their sovereign's instructions. The economic order that Charlemagne assembled with no grand a priori design confined inherited wealth and high social standing to the spiritual descendants of Roland. Peasants need not apply. The Oath of Loyalty of 793 required all who socially mattered to assemble in churches and villages throughout the realm to swear before God their fidelity to Charlemagne. Slaves and serfs were excluded.[10]

"*Renovatio*" was the Carolingian mantra. Magnates and scribes at court often heard the expression in the king's high voice—"*Renovatio Romani Imperii*" ("Restoration of the Roman Empire"). The campaigns, punitive expeditions, and police actions conducted year in and year out across three decades had accomplished much. Aquitaine, Bavaria, Saxony, Italia, Austria, and Hungary had been pulled into a rough, viable federation. Nevertheless, it was an empire carved by swords, a league of extortioners far more than a political and social order bound together by uniform laws and competent servants of the crown. The contrast with the centralizing institutions of *al-Andalus* or Byzantium was stark, and a cause for more than a little Frankish resentment. The diminished empire, ruled from Constantinople, shone on Metz or Aachen or Paderborn like a sun at high noon. Charlemagne would never be able to retire Joyeuse, his great longsword, but the end of the 780s saw him apply his energies to important reforms and innovations in governance, many to outlast him and his descendants by centuries. A raft of capitularies bearing the king's monogram attests to growing resolve to build an orderly, organic body politic.

Like the Saxon Capitulary, which did much to militarize the faith of the Catholic West, the ambitious General Admonition of 789 fixed standards of behavior for a clergy whose morals were too often indistinguishable from those of its parishioners, and occasionally scandalous. If it was no longer quite as true as when St. Boniface accused them of sleeping with four or five concubines a night, the nocturnal habits of Frankish priests decidedly still needed policing. Clerical celibacy was essential to the disposition of property that could not be individually owned and inherited. Observing Sunday as a holy day of rest and worship became a requirement whose violation by priests and laity was henceforth severely punished. Some years earlier, an illustrated manuscript called the Godescalc Lectionary was compiled in order to equip the struggling, poorly educated priesthood with a calendar of holy days and a uniform text from which to conduct Mass on Sundays, feast days, and Easter.[11]

Monogamy had always been problematic among the Franks and the other Germanic tribespeople. Charlemagne set a fine example that few of his nobles would have wished to emulate. His five unions blessed by the Church were contracted serially only after a death. The General Admonition, supplemented by capitularies, reinforced ecclesiastical proscriptions on incestuous unions, polygamy, and divorce: one wife and one husband at a time and separated by seven degrees of consanguinity; no divorce except on grounds of adultery; remarriage allowed only after the spouse dies. And there was more. Concubines were denied property rights. Children born out of wedlock were barred from inheritance if there were legitimate offspring. The social ramifications for Western society could hardly have been more profound. Selection of exogamous mates imposed patience, discipline, and discernment. Though valued as property and for procreation, women of the upper classes gradually acquired greater influence as mothers in marital decisionmaking. Relieved of the intraspousal competition for respect, power, and resources that characterized polygamous arrangements, Western women—notwithstanding the oppressive realities of patriarchy—achieved in time the potential for personal freedom that would set them apart from most of their sisters elsewhere in the world. With a fine sense of the blunt, Bishop Hincmar of Reims told Frankish men where things were heading. "Whether she be a drunkard, irritable, immoral, luxurious, and gluttonous, a vagabond, cursing and swearing," said he, "whether you like it or not, you must keep her."[12] For all the cultural superiority of their situation to their Carolingian peers, Andalusian women were given no such guarantees by the Qur'an.

The decade of the 790s saw more precedents. A corps of royal emissaries, *missi dominici*, was created to canvass the realm annually, hearing complaints and righting abuses. A capitulary establishing a fixed monetary standard was the first in the West since the end of the fifth century: one pound of silver was valued at 20 shillings or 240 pennies (or dinars); 12 pennies equaled 1 shilling or solidus. The right to mint coins was henceforth exclusive to the crown. In reality, however, the land-service–barter economy vastly reduced the practical utility of specie (some gold solidi and the penny were struck); the real value of Charlemagne's monetary system was to serve as a contemporary means of calculating values and, far more significantly, to bequeath a vigesimal basis for currency in much of Europe that was to endure a thousand years after the Carolingian order was merely a memory.

The *Capitulare de Villis,* promulgated by the king in the late 790s, prefigured the remarkable *Domesday Book*, compiled three centuries later in Norman England. *De Villis* was a game project worthy of Roman administrative efficiency, an annual inventory of stores, livestock, and laborers, and an itemized record of all consumption and expenditures on the royal estates that "by Christmas informs us of everything, subdivided and categorized."[13] Much of this royal centralizing had scarcely more than a parchment reality in a world of near-universal illiteracy, deep suspicion and resentment on the part of the nobility, and a crippling disparity between resources and objectives. Far too ambitious for his own age, Charlemagne's admonitions and capitularies were to serve as templates for the future European civilization.

❖

Charlemagne had the good fortune to encounter a wandering English priest during one of his lightning rides into Italia, this one during Easter week of 781, when Pope Adrian baptized his sons Pippin (Carloman) and Louis as kings of Lombardy and Aquitaine, respectively. He met the wandering priest at Parma. Alcuin of York was already an old man of fifty— not the most original product of the remarkable Northumbrian ecclesiastical "think tanks" inspired by St. Aidan of Lindisfarne and the Venerable Bede, but one of its most versatile. Alcuin possessed what passed for an encyclopedic knowledge adorned with apt Latin quotations and ready anecdotes—qualities, along with a capacity for hard work and geniality, that hit their mark immediately with Charlemagne. Even as the king annexed nearly as much real estate as Julius Caesar, he began to see the urgency not only of the glue of law and bureaucracy but of a culture of literacy and learning if his creation was to endure. He could count on the custodians of the Church for moral validation. The requisite intellectual armature was his own responsibility and safeguard.

As he and a few of his more inquisitive magnates took the full measure of conquered Lombardy, they acquired an appreciation of Imperial Rome's surviving urbanism and cosmopolitanism in cities such as Bologna, Modena, Parma, and Vicenza. The Italian peninsula had been a revelation for Charlemagne. After repeated rebellion on the part of the Lombard high nobility, he had decided to seed more than thirty duchies with his own dukes and counts. A significant portion of this transplanted Frankish aristocracy began to acquire the sensibilities, if not quite the culture, of the conquered. They could not but compare their own still-crude mores with those of some of their Lombard subjects, who, after 250 years on the peninsula, had become rough approximations of Roman patricians. Italia shaped a new conception of royal leadership and soon jump-started the Carolingian Renaissance, that cultural mirage whose hold on European memory has been as strong as its reality was anemic.[14]

The jovial Alcuin served as a sort of chancellor of knowledge to the king of the Franks from their meeting in 781 until his well-provisioned retirement fourteen years later. He devised a program for the advancement of learning, recruiting a cadre of philosophers, educators, and

scribes and presiding over what became the Palace School. During those
first years, however, Alcuin and his crew had no fixed address; they traveled, yawing and bouncing, in the train of ox wagons with Charlemagne
on campaigns and among the numerous royal residences. One of the very
few descriptions of this remarkable academy-on-wheels comes from the
famous stammering Monk of St. Gall, Notker *Balbulus*, a source often as
unreliable as it is colorful. In *De Carolo Magno*, which appeared seventy
years after the king's death, Notker's intellectually avid Charlemagne
takes every possible opportunity to improve himself during the hiatuses
between slaughtering Saxons and Avars and breaking the proud spirits of
Bavarian and Friulian dukes. To believe Notker, an impatient Charlemagne once exclaimed after a tutorial session with Alcuin that he wanted
"a dozen churchmen as wise and as well taught in all human knowledge
as were Jerome and Augustine!"[15]

It was true that the king felt genuine admiration for those who could
not only read Vergil and Suetonius but also could record what they knew
on vellum or parchment. He put the matter straightforwardly some years
later when his aspirations were proclaimed in one of the capitularies.
"We are concerned," said he, "to restore with diligent zeal the workshops
of knowledge which . . . have been well-nigh deserted." To serve this tall
ambition, the priest recruited some of the best scholars in Western
Christendom: Peter of Pisa, master grammarian and pedagogically so
able that Charlemagne redoubled efforts to learn to write; Paulinus of
Aquileia, an immensely learned Benedictine interpreter of the scriptures;
the Andalusian Visigoth Theodulf, a sophisticated prelate the king
appointed to the bishopric of Orléans; and Dungal of Ireland. The basics
of the Palace School's instructional program Alcuin explained in *On
Grammar*, a seminal book that synthesized educational ideas reaching back
to Rome and Greece with particular indebtedness to Magnus Aurelius
Cassidorus, Isidore of Seville, and Venerable Bede. Learning commenced, according to Alcuin, with the mastery of the "science of letters"
imparted by the curriculum of the three liberal arts—the foundational
trivium comprising grammar, rhetoric, and dialectic or logical disputation.
If the *trivium* was the course of study leading, as it were, to the
Romanesque GED, the four remaining *artes liberales* of the *quadrivium*

(arithmetic, music, geometry, astronomy) were the pathway to postgraduate learning.[16]

It would be the rare Benedictine who essayed the *quadrivium* as a course of study, to say nothing of high-born aspirants. The *trivium* proved daunting enough. Encouraged by the king, who set an example of occasional attendance with his sons and daughters, the sons of magnates trooped into Alcuin's or Peter of Pisa's lectures to sit cross-legged and copy the rules of Latin grammar on wax tablets. The experience was clearly not suited to all or even most young aristocrats, whose class education had never before required more than expert familiarity with the implements of war, horsemanship, and a smattering of manners and liturgical practice. Notker relates an incident where one of Alcuin's laggard pupils was physically disciplined by Charlemagne, who roared as he wielded the rod, "By the King of Heaven, I take no account of your noble birth. . . ."[17]

What came to be called the Carolingian Renaissance struggled against the grain of its society. There was nobility and much long-term gain in the effort. Its Latin translators (Greek was still a mystery) and copyists performed the invaluable archival service of ferreting out and preserving a vital portion of the Roman past, of compiling and stockpiling legal, medical, historical, and geographical information for the ages. The library of the grand monastery of St. Riquier in the Somme, with several hundred manuscripts, represented the scholars' ideal, even though its small holdings were deemed pitiful by Gibbon when compared with the holdings of libraries in *al-Andalus*. Alcuin's semiofficial edition of the Bible enforced greater uniformity in the interpretation of the Gospels. In a time when double Easters were still being celebrated—as in Britain, with one Catholic and one Celtic holy day—the palatine scholars' preparation of a liturgical calendar for the kingdom was another notable advance toward a common religious culture. A final decision on how time was to be measured enlisted Charlemagne's full support with an appropriate capitulary. In the *Ecclesiastical History of the English Nation*, the Venerable Bede had proposed that the hourglass start with the birth of Christ—*anno Domini*, the first year of our Lord. The adoption of Bede's Christian time, near the close of the eighth century, settled a vital question of dating the past that Islam had resolved under the first *rashidun* caliph.

The Palace School over which Alcuin presided with unflagging devotion never reached its potential. Dialectical discourse tended to bore the sons of hard-charging magnates. Geometry was the Romanesque equivalent of nuclear physics. "How few care about such things!" the priest observed in retirement. He had done his best to advertise his pedagogical wares on a famous sign displayed at Strasbourg: "Choose, O traveler; if thou wilt drink thou must also pay money, but if thou wilt learn thou wilt have what thou seekest for nothing." A leading Carolingian historian suspects that a regular course in the *trivium* and the *quadrivium* was "probably never given."[18] The king, his *missi dominici,* and the palatine scholars instigated game efforts at implementing the grand scheme of public instruction at Fulda, Tours, Mainz, Metz, and a dozen other religious centers. Foundations for free public instruction were laid with the remarkably ambitious series of capitularies issued from 787 onward and later called Charlemagne's "Charter of Modern Thought." Stipulating that no charges be assessed against its pupils, the capitulary of 789 commanded that "every monastery and every abbey have its school, in which boys may be taught the Psalms, the system of musical notation, singing, arithmetic, and grammar." Unquestioning patriarchy excluded girls from an education that was otherwise designed to be free and open to males from all classes, each one "according to his ability and the Divine assistance."

"In this way," as Notker exaggerated, "the most glorious Charlemagne saw that the study of letters was flourishing throughout the length and breadth of his kingdom."[19] If what were in truth modest and fragile accomplishments destined to peter out in the political confusion and massive invasions of the bloody, terrifying ninth century, their example was not lost to the European future in which they proved an incommensurable legacy.

Almost twenty years after 'Abd al-Rahman's Great Mosque of Cordoba rose near the bank of the Guadalquivir, masons laid the last granite

blocks for Charlemagne's Royal Hall (*Aula Regia*) and residential palace at
Aachen—or, as the French know it, Aix-la-Chapelle. The palace complex
at Aachen would become the king's permanent residence in the mid-
790s, a ten-year work-in-progress designed to emulate the Caesars.
There were notable advantages to the location. A day's ride west of
Cologne, it was roughly at the geographical midpoint of his huge, jig-
sawed realm. Aachen's thermal springs had been channeled by the
Romans to make a large, colonnaded bath whose waters stayed at a comfortable sixty-five-degrees. Charlemagne was an avid bather—unusual
among his contemporaries (clergy were notoriously averse to water) in
drawing an intuitive connection between cleanliness and health. "It was
for this reason that he built his palace at Aachen," Einhard opined, and
remarked that the king was in the habit of inviting "not only his sons to
bathe with him but his nobles and friends as well."[20] Einhard might also
have mentioned that the forests of the Aachen Valley were home to an
abundance of rabbit, boar, and deer for hunting parties.

The Franks had gone without a fixed capital for centuries. Warrior
tribesmen of a culture formed in the dense northern forests, their kings
and palace mayors, from Clovis to Pippin the Short, had roamed endlessly
between the Rhine and the Loire. Depending on the political geography
at the time, the business of government, such as it was, was transacted in
Metz, Thionville, Worms, or and elsewhere in Austrasia—or, alternatively,
in the centers of Paris, Quierzy, Soissons, and several others in Neustria.
Charlemagne was much drawn to Attigny and especially to Heristal, the
ancestral cradle in modern Belgium. But peripatetic sovereignty had
begun to seem increasingly incompatible with the dignity befitting a king
of the Franks, who now also carried the sonorously empowering titles of
rex Langobardorum and *patricius Romanorum*. A king whose family had twice
rescued the papacy from political irrelevancy, a king whose supremacy in
Italia obliged the haughty Byzantines to entreat his goodwill and propose
the mating of a daughter with the imperial heir, a *rex Francorum* with
impressionable visits to the Eternal City under his belt—such a king was
prone to think of himself as the legatee of the Caesars.

As he turned his attention increasingly to his palatine city at Aachen,
Charlemagne experienced sadness and betrayal in his personal life. In the

year after he slaughtered the Saxons at Verden, he lost both his wise mother, Bertrada "Goose Foot," who died at the ripe age of sixty-three in her ancestral home in Laon, and his respected wife of twelve years, Hildegard. Hildegard died in childbirth after producing three sons who reached maturity and several of Charlemagne's eleven daughters. The king took as his next-to-last wife the daughter of a Frankish count, the strong-willed Fastrada. Einhard's *Life of Charlemagne* and the *Royal Frankish Annals* disclose serious domestic troubles that may have been factors in the establishment of the permanent capital. Fastrada was much maligned by her contemporaries for bringing troubles to the family. She was said to have had such grandiose notions (all the more outrageous in a woman) of the privileges and powers of kingship as to have caused revolts that forced the king brutally to repress them in 783 and again in 786. The conspiracy six years later involved Pippin the Hunchback, supposedly driven by Fastrada's haughtiness into self-pitying manipulation. Already denied the Lombard crown and forced to share his name with half-brother Carloman, Pippin was understandably bitter. He would die blinded in a monastery as punishment for supporting the 792 plot against his father.[21] Bitter himself and henceforth much more on his guard, the king seems to have decided that placing his large, rambunctious family and relatives under a single well-observed roof was eminently prudent.

In much the same way that Cordoba's Great Mosque was the physical embodiment of the spiritual and cultural energies of Andalusia, the palatine complex at Aachen was to be symbol and anchor of a renovated world order, the king's own Second Rome. Like the Falcon with his master builder, Charlemagne was partner with Einhard to his architects, one Odo of Metz in particular, suggesting changes in design, closely monitoring the work on the ten-year project. Nothing remains today of the Royal Hall (*Aula Regia*), the two-story stone structure where embassies were received and large assemblies were held. The Royal Hall was the largest stone structure north of the Alps. Here was a space, finally, grand enough for Harun al-Rashid's gift of a live elephant, Abu'l-'Abbas, which the caliph's emissaries delivered to Charlemagne in 801. It was a hall not to be despised by supercilious Byzantine ambassadors. Abu'l-'Abbas was a whimsical feature of Abbasid geopolitics: a compliment to Carolingian aggression, for the Franks had finally taken Barcelona from the Umayyads in that same year.

At the southern end of the fifty-acre compound were religious buildings grouped together in the shape of the Latin cross. At the center of the group was the *Pfalzkapelle* or Palace Chapel, the octagonal structure Einhard knew as Holy Mother of God Church—in his estimation, "a really remarkable structure." The Octagon Chapel (as it is more commonly known) was solid, massive, and dynamic, like the Frankish people themselves. The octagon was a structure meant for the ages. And like the Christian society it served, the tall church divided the high from the low. 'Abd al-Rahman's Great Mosque welcomed all in a common space. In Charlemagne's Palace Chapel, the king and his magnates worshipped God in the gallery above the people. Among the models for the structure were Ravenna's San Vitale and Constantinople's imperial Great Palace, with its fabulous octagonal inner chamber—the tongue-twisting *chrysotríklinos*, a combination chapel and golden throne room.[22] The throne of the emperor of the east, the *basíleus*, occupied the easterly space conventionally reserved for the altar. The *basíleus* of Byzantium was God's representative on earth, the Christian world's ultimate spiritual and secular authority.

The king of the Franks admired the *chrysotríklinos* enough to have it reproduced (albeit diminished in scale and opulence), but with the telling variation that he placed the throne in the Octagon Chapel's choir, west of the altar. The variation was no little matter, for it spoke to an Occidental quintessence that would work in another eight centuries to the hegemonic advantage of the civilization made possible after Moussais-la-Bataille. As the king said in explanation of the location of the throne, it "gave to God what was God's." Germanic kings were not gods, however godlike their powers might become. About that distinction Charlemagne permitted himself no confusion. But what was left to Charlemagne as earthly ruler begged the question of secular authority. It was a foundational question about dual sovereignty—one uniquely fundamental to Western Christendom, one that would have been meaningless to a Muslim ruler such as 'Abd al-Rahman I. Was the king of the Franks and the Lombards beholden to the Holy Father in Rome for his authority—the shield and servant, therefore, of Christ's vicar, whose power to loose and bind was beyond challenge? Or was the bishop of Rome at best only the equal of the king in matters secular and civil—if not, indeed, his subordinate?

In a real sense, the king of the Franks and the pope had made each other historically viable by a mutual-aid compact religiously sanctioning a dynastic putsch. On the one hand, the dominion of the bishops of Rome in their Italian real estate was guaranteed by Pippinid and Carolingian military supremacy; on the other, the papacy placed the seal of divine legitimation on a dynasty on the make and destined for continental hegemony. But popes and Pippinids had yet to address the conundrum embedded in their common history—the crucial implications of the relationship of secular to sacral power. It was one thing to bring Saxons and Avars to Christ with the sword and to plant a crucifix on the Pyrenees heights. It was quite another to claim the sovereign prerogative of appointing bishops, of apportioning conquered real estate to the clergy, to say nothing of arrogating the right to determine ecclesiastical practice (as Charlemagne did in the General Admonition of 789, regulating clerical standards) or even deciding high matters of dogma, as he ventured to do without papal consultation three years later in the *Libri Carolini*, four books (ghostwritten by Alcuin) rejecting the iconoclastic compromise of the Second Council of Nicaea.[23]

Because of its near-monopoly on knowledge, its evolving clerical bureaucracies and spreading matrices of propertied abbeys, convents, and monasteries, the Church was, if not the very political order the Carolingians were trying to resurrect, unquestionably a parallel civil universe. Nor did doctors of canon law intend for any confusion about parallel orders to lead to confusion about primacy. Centuries earlier, Pope Gelasius I (492–96) and St. Isidore of Seville—enormously reinforced, subsequently, by the forged *Donation of Constantine*—had served up preemptive canonical strikes demolishing any presumed equality of the two orders. Humankind was ruled by two powers, but one power was inferior to the other, Gelasius had informed an incredulous Emperor Anastasius I. "Although you take precedence over all mankind in dignity," Gelasius had lectured, "nevertheless you piously bow the neck to those who have charge of divine affairs and seek from them the means of your salvation." Four centuries after Charlemagne's death, Gelasius's ideas triumphed in the papal autocracy institutionalized by that maestro of theocracy Innocent III. The king of the Franks would have been dismayed by such an outcome. He may not have seen the pope "as his chaplain," as a contemporary medievalist suggests, but Charlemagne's thinking about the bishop of Rome (particularly encouraged by Alcuin's treatise *Rhetoric and the Virtues*) had evolved by the 790s to a presumption of his own supremacy.[24]

⁘

Adrian I—aristocratic, learned, politically astute—was the pope of Charlemagne's maturity. He deserves either tribute or censure, according to interpretation, as the effective founder of the temporal sovereignty of the papacy. Theirs was a symbiosis whose remarkable intimacy is reflected in their correspondence. The pope had been much vexed one time by the king's presumption to lecture him on fine points of theology when Charlemagne's advisers mistranslated the text of convoluted Greek explaining the tenuous iconoclastic compromise between Rome and Constantinople at the Second Council of Nicaea in 787.[25] Squabbling over arcane Greek proved a minor discord in a success story of codependency. The pope's death on Christmas in 795 deeply affected the king. Not only did Adrian's departure deprive the king of an admired collaborator, it handed him the papacy's greatest institutional crisis since Pope Stephen II's frantic appearance at Ponthion to beg for Pippin the Short's intercession somewhat more than four decades earlier.

In the spring of 799, just shy of four years after Pope Leo III's ascension, grave charges of adultery and perjury were lodged against the pope by his predecessor's relatives and partisans. Besieged in the Lateran Palace and fleeing Rome for his life, Leo hurried to Paderborn for protection, preceded by the terrible news that his eyes and tongue had been torn out of him. A miracle restored the papal tongue and eyes, the victim himself explained to the king and the likely skeptical magnates. Royal arbitration restored Leo to Peter's throne after months of negotiations, threats, and Charlemagne's eventual decision to settle the controversy in person. Once again, Christ's vicar owed his lifetime position to a king of the Franks. And once again, when the debt was claimed, it altered Western history. On Christmas Day 800, the king of the Franks knelt before St. Peter's tomb as the third Mass concluded. The *Royal Frankish Annals* described the momentous scene:

> Pope Leo placed upon his head a crown and the whole Roman people acclaimed him: Life and victory to Charles, Augustus, crowned by God, the great and peaceful Emperor of the Romans! And after the laudation he was adored by the Pope in the manner of ancient princes and instead of Patricius he was now titled Emperor and Augustus.[26]

In that instant, the West was sundered from the East, now politically as well as religiously.

The Christmas Day coronation of Charlemagne annulled the last scintilla of primacy remaining to the Byzantine emperor and the patriarch in Constantinople. Decades of spluttering Byzantine protestations were to come, but at the time, Constantinople ostentatiously ignored the event. Nor would the oft-ridiculed Holy Roman Empire come into formal existence until the time of Emperor Otto I in the early tenth century. Charlemagne's title was king of the Franks and emperor of the Romans—*rex Francorum* and *imperator Romanorum*. Einhard's *Life of Charlemagne* famously claimed that Charlemagne was both surprised and annoyed by Leo's gratuitous act—"He would not have entered the church if he had known beforehand the Pope's intentions." Out of the blue, as it were, the scheming pontiff had sprung an epochal *fait accompli* on the humble servant of the Faith and the peoples of Christendom, according to Einhard. An edifying fable, and a gross misrepresentation of the facts. Alcuin's advice, written from retirement in Tours during the heated dispute between Leo and his Roman enemies, faithfully conveys the mindset at Paderborn and Aachen. "Up to this point, three people have held the highest position in the world," the pope, the emperor, the king of the Franks, Alcuin lectured Charlemagne. "You are more noble in your wisdom. You are more awe-inspiring in the dignity of your kingdom. The well-being of the churches of Christ rests on you alone."[27] So much for the theocratic pretensions of a Gelasius.

By his action, then, the emperor bequeathed to the political culture of Europe a more-than-millennial duality that was unique among the world's manifold models of sovereignty. Out of this competition and conflict between "Church" and "State" emerged a monarchical, secular, and constitutional theory of the State "as a deliberate product of human reason and will." An ambiguity embedded in the relationship of Church and State from the start was destined to nourish an increasingly strenuous contest for secular supremacy that would emerge as a major theme in the power politics of the European nation-states. The consummation of this contested interaction grafted the separation of the sacral and the secular upon the European body politic. For the European person, there would be the permanent possibility of defining oneself in opposition to either the Church or the State, or both. True enough, this permanent possibility was almost entirely the privilege of the people at the top, those who, like Roland of Roncesvalles, existed as first-person pronouns.

When Charlemagne departed for Italy in the spring of 800, he had finally decided, with Leo's complicity, to become in law what he had in reality been for a decade: supreme ruler of the Christian West. In a sense, the Western Roman Empire had gone into papal receivership in 476 after the inglorious departure of the boy Caesar, Romulus Augustulus. Three hundred twenty-four years of imperial absence had caused even people who could remember an age of Caesars to forsake any thought of a restoration. Only the finite number of men and women whose ideational culture was formed, like Charlemagne's, in the two dozen or so pockets of literacy throughout the West lived with a sense of ruptured history, of time interrupted by the fall of the Western Roman Empire.[28] Most people knew no history beyond the village events of seasons past. To them, the very thought of an emperor rising in the West was meaningless. Yet there it was, embodied in a single person and appearing as suddenly as a nova—a new Rome created by the descendants of those who had pushed the original one aside. Circumscribed by fierce parochialisms of tribe and place, the powerful and the powerless of this Europe forged in blood and faith were not at all sure what to make of their empire. The Homeric joke was that the Carolingian Empire would fall apart much too quickly and completely for the "Europenses" to learn to exist as Europeans. At the end of the eighth century, Europe was militarily strong enough to defend itself from Islam, thanks in part to Charlemagne and his predecessors. The question was whether it was politically, economically, and culturally better off for being able to do so.

14

Equipoise—
Delicate and Doomed

THE late-eighth-century world outside Hisham I's Cordoba palace (*qasr*) might as well have existed on another planet from the one seen by the magnates at Aachen. The *qasr* was new, completed just as the Falcon ordered the foundations laid for the Friday (Great) Mosque. Not many steps away were the public baths. Nearby was the central market, where basic commodities of bread, vegetables, fruit, oil, and lamb at regulated prices were upstaged by Persian carpets,

Damascus metalware, China silks, fine leather and jewelry, slaves, and much else supplied on demand by the Muslim world economy. From the *qasr*'s windows, Hisham and his son and successor, al-Hakam I (796–822), surveyed a landscape dominated by ongoing social progress and economic prosperity. The capital's streets, following no particular pattern from the long wall beside the gray Guadalquivir River, linked neighborhoods where Jews, Berbers, Catholics and Orthodox, Arabs and *muwalladun* lived as though in their own separate worlds. Sephardic apothecaries, Visigoth blacksmiths, and Greek surgeons offered services in these long, narrow arteries. With Cordoba as the envied model, Sevilla, Malaga, and Karnattah (Granada) also gave themselves impressive Friday Mosques. Those public gardens that lent a distinctive seasonal fragrance of lemon and orange trees to Muslim urban spaces became standard features. The long Guadalquivir plain, abundantly irrigated by waterwheels, was carpeted with cereal plantations of wheat, rye, and barley, and olive trees forever. The Cordovan core, then, was the showplace of *al-Andalus*.

Even though *al-Andalus*'s military strength was overmatched by the growing power of Frankland, the amirate's market-fed entrepreneurship and virile mix of creeds, cultures, and classes put its capital city on a ninth-century path of messy cosmopolitanism unseen in Europe since the fall of Rome. A century after 'Abd al-Rahman I's death, Cordoba's narrow streets would be paved and lighted by torch. Many who walked these streets wore comfortable, cork-soled shoes, the latest footgear imported from the East. An abundance of inns and hostelries would accommodate travelers on business. Chess, a favorite pastime of Harun al-Rashid, would be taken up by Andalusians in the 820s. Precisely when chess underwent its startling revolution on the Iberian peninsula is uncertain—when, that is, the "queen" would displace the "vizir" as the most powerful piece in the game, empowered to move unrestricted in all directions.[1] In any case, the fact that the chess game played among the Andalusi Arabs would keep to the old rules along with the traditional pieces, while Christians and Jews accepted the "queen," raises enough thoughts about the politics of gender in early Islam and Christianity to fill many books.

Ninth-century Cordoba was a prefiguration of modernity in every sense. Its professional classes, in addition to *ulamas* (religious scholars), priests, and rabbis, were manifold: lawyers, architects, astronomers, physicians, bureaucrats, tailors. The pursuit of too many of its citizens ranged from conspicuous displays of wealth to conspicuous displays of arcane learning. Nor were the eccentric and the dogmatic in short supply: mystics; Muslim purists; Catholic fanatics. Mosques abounded, their architecture typically modeled on that of the Falcon's Great Mosque. The first Arabic translations from Greek were made by a Falcon ancestor, Prince Khalid Yazid ibn Mu'awiya of Syria, at the top of the eighth century.[2] Though their numbers were quite small, high-born Cordovan women participated in the flow of knowledge. One of them is reported to have amassed her own good-size library.

By the time he died in 804, at the advanced age of about seventy, Alcuin, Charlemagne's indispensable adviser, had heard something of the dazzling scientific and philosophical efflorescence well underway over the Pyrenees and far beyond in the Fertile Crescent ruled by the Abbasids. The secret of making paper had come from China after the Battle of Talas and the capture of a T'ang frontier post in 751 by one of the new Abbasid armies. He could have known of the remarkable precursor to the personal computer that would have been a boon to Charlemagne's *missi dominici*, the abacus then in fairly common use in Cordoba and elsewhere. Perhaps he also heard about the "Hindu numbers" recently introduced in Caliph Harun al-Rashid's Baghdad. A mere score of years later, the great caliph's successor endowed a center of learning that would be unimaginable in Western Christendom for centuries, the *Bayt al-Hikma* ("House of Wisdom"), the great "think tank" of the Muslim world.[3] The existence of such a place, along with the scientific and technical advances fueled by it, beggared the most visionary ambitions of Alcuin's Palace School enterprise.

For all his optimism, Alcuin had become apprehensive about the prospects of revived learning in the West. It became only too evident just how endangered the Carolingian Renaissance was in 793, the fateful year the heathen Danes sacked and burned Lindisfarne Monastery, the island cradle of Dark Ages learning. Jarrow and Iona off the Northumbrian coast were incinerated, along with their priests the following year. Within a span of two solstices, emergent Europe suffered the modern equivalent of the destruction of Oxford, Cambridge, and the Bibliothèque Nationale. *Al-Andalus*, however, was to be spared the worst of the Scandinavian catastrophe that rolled over England and Ireland and across much of France, Russia, and southern Italy, causing most of Europe to crash in the late ninth century.[4] A comparatively few Scandinavian episodes occurred west of the Pyrenees. The first Norsemen would appear in the coastal waters off *al-Andalus* only some forty years after the master of the Palace School had gone to his rest.

❖

When Hisham I succeeded 'Abd al-Rahman I in 788, his powerful rival across the mountains was a vigorous forty-six and still completely in command of his faculties and his vassals. Hisham's people knew him to be devout. Examples of the *amir*'s religious convictions were many. He fed the poor with his own hands and often paid nocturnal visits carrying the Qur'an and medicines to the sick. Although he was exceptionally devout for an Umayyad, Hisham was also more than enough of his father's son to put the Faith to excellent political use. Rebel defiance was endemic. The *amir*'s declaration of *jihad* was the first in many decades. Hisham, whose watchword was caution and whose temperament was distinctly pacific, believed that Charlemagne had made a serious blunder in committing most of his armies against the Avars in the summer of 791. Toledo was perennially on the cusp of armed resistance. Zaragoza's Berber notables simmered. Hisham's aim was to mobilize the nation for Holy War against the Franks and the petty Christian states, as had not been done since the days of al-Ghafiqi and Uqba ibn al-Hajjaj in 732. Besides, *jihad* was the ordained obligation of the Commander of the Faithful.

The proclamation of war was displayed in his father's Great Mosque. "Oh, true Believers, fight against the infidels who are near you, and be hard on them," Hisham enjoined the Believers from the *minbar* of the Great Mosque in the winter of 792. Victory in the name of the Prophet was a blessing, but Allah assured all that death was equally noble. "He has reserved for you in your after-life a happiness which eye has never seen, ear has never heard, heart has never felt," preached the *amir*. "Make yourselves worthy then of such blessings."[5] Although amiral recruitment efforts fell significantly short of their goal—perhaps because the incentives of religion and war counted for less in a settled society of productive farmers and prospering city dwellers—Hisham's *jihad* was still impressive. In the spring of 793, two large armies commanded by two of Mugith al-Rumi's descendants advanced simultaneously on the Catholic kingdoms of Asturias in the north and Navarra in the northeast. The first fell upon Asturias with a ferocity to be remembered as an object lesson by its people for decades. The second veered into Septimania and Languedoc after 'Abd al-Malik of the Mughith line, Hisham's *vizir* and army commander, sized up Navarra's unbreachable defenses.

Charlemagne and his armies were fighting the Avars in Hungary. Count William of Toulouse, prefect of Septimania and one of the Franks' ablest generals, hurried to intercept the invaders, positioning his men across their line of advance. William "Short Nose," as his men called him, lost his life and his army on the banks of the Orbieu, a river about midway between Narbonne and Carcassonne. What was left of his army shambled in retreat to the safety of Narbonne. The psychological impact of the Saracens' victory was terrifying to "Europenses." Frankland—or Francia as it was coming to be called—was almost defenseless. People said Mass in parishes a thousand leagues from Septimania in order to catch the intercessory attention of a busy Deity. The *vizir* 'Abd al-Malik and his staff decided to withdraw behind the Pyrenees before Charlemagne dispatched a major force against them. The victors streamed into Cordoba with groaning baggage wagons of hostages and treasure roundly worth seven hundred thousand gold francs. In *al-Andalus*, mosque attendance validated Hisham's person and policies with an unprecedented exuberance. The *amir* added the muezzin's tower (minaret) to the Great Mosque and improved the city's fortifications with the victory proceeds.

Charlemagne's reaction to Hisham's 793 *jihad* was characteristically deliberate. Eight years earlier, he had sent his son Louis of Aquitaine charging over the western Pyrenees with enough momentum to capture Girona briefly and extend Frankish influence almost to the Ebro. Two

years after the Muslim victory in Septimania, Charlemagne formally created his Spanish March and claimed part of Iberia. Each year, Francia's
frontiers pressed beyond the mountains deeper into Navarra and Catalonia. In 799, Louis's army occupied Pamplona. The anticipated consequences of these well-executed invasions between 785 and 799
stimulated territorial ambitions among some of the petty counts and
kings of the region. The king of Asturias, Alfonso II "the Chaste," had
been emboldened to march beyond the Duero and bring back Christians
to populate the emptiness between *al-Andalus* and Asturias. Alfonso's
audacity had played a causal role in Hisham's ambitious offensives in 793.
Alfonso's capital at Oviedo was burnt to the ground.[6]

The threat posed to the amirate by the king of Asturias was not military, but rather one of rebellious example. He and other titled aspirants
in Navarra, Aragon, Leon, and Galicia owed their existence to the unfinished business of the Conquest. Seventy-five years earlier, Pelayo, the
fugitive Visigoth nobleman from the Battle of Guadalete, had rallied the
local people (the Asturis), who elected him as their prince. For the Spanish, Pelayo's skirmish at Covadonga served as the shining moment from
which to date the rebirth of the Christian nation. The marriage of the
duke of Cantabria's son, Alfonso, to Pelayo's daughter, Ermesinda, sealed
an alliance whose bloodlines would inseminate the *Reconquista*. Pelayo and
his son-in-law, the future Alfonso I "the Catholic" (r. 739–57), would
transform the petty kingdom of Cangas de Onís into a Christian realm
that embraced Cantabria, Asturias, and part of Galicia.[7] The Carolingian
design was to draw these self-important, fiercely squabbling power centers of the far northeast into the Spanish March.

Frankish designs on Catalunya (Catalonia) went back to the fall of
Narbonne in 759, when Christians living within the city surprised the
Muslim garrison. In the four decades since, hardly a year had passed
without a Frankish-inspired incursion into Catalunya from Christian
Septimania. A large coalition commanded by Louis of Aquitaine and
drawn from the minor nobility of Gascony, Navarra, and other Catholic
feudatories besieged the old Carthaginian port city of Barcelona for
almost two years, until famine and plague forced its surrender in 801.
Hisham had died of natural causes five years earlier, and his son al-

Hakam I lacked the capacity to break through Louis's iron-ring siege. As with Charlemagne's invasion of 778 and the fall of Girona in 785, Barcelona's capture offered a lesson in military preparedness, in that it belatedly mobilized Muslim and Mozarab under al-Hakam's leadership.

Al-Andalus during al-Hakam's vigorous, twenty-eight-year rule (796–822) was to become a much more centralized realm. Hisham had found strength in prayer and meditation and upright private conduct. He believed there was no gift more useful than a copy of the Qur'an bestowed upon a needy soul. His tall, sophisticated, and militarily capable son was an epicurean and an indefatigable lover whose progeny would number more than twenty sons. It was common knowledge among Cordovans that their *amir* kept a cellar of fine wines in violation of the Prophet's proscription. Al-Hakam also fancied himself something of a poet. Of necessity often hardhearted in public, he wrote poetry that showed a softer side. When five young and beautiful harem women defied him by denying their services, the Umayyad grandee "told them of my right, yet they persist/In their disobedience, when mine has ceased," he sighed. "A king am I, subdued, his powers humbled/To love, like a captive in fetters, forlorn." By contrast, public resistance to his will—such as two insurrections in the capital, a seven-year rebellion in the Merida region, and several tax-driven revolts—al-Hakam overcame with condign severity.[8]

The two Cordoba uprisings were genuine socioeconomic revolutions in the making. In order to equip *al-Andalus* with a standing army of mercenaries, the *amir* imposed new taxes in addition to the traditional ones based on the Qur'an. The seeming arbitrariness of new taxes, together with simmering disapproval among the pious of the *amir*'s libertine lapses, provoked a major uprising at the end of his first decade in power. In 805, the community legal authorities (*fuqaha*) plotted with merchants, students, and craftsmen in the teeming suburb south of the city and across the Guadalquivir to replace al-Hakam with a pliable cousin. Called *al-Rabad* ("the suburb"), this quarter was on the left bank, interestingly, and appears to have been a ninth-century approximation of the nineteenth-century's volatile, barricade-building quarters in Paris, Frankfurt, and Vienna. Although the disparate parties were mobilized by anger at the *amir*'s supposedly unjust taxes, some of the leaders were fundamentalists animated by visions of a purified community of Believers. The plot aborted in betrayal and crucifixion of seventy-five ringleaders on the city's walls.

The conspiracy hatched in *al-Rabad* by the same groups thirteen years later nearly succeeded. It held greater social significance because of the support of several prominent jurists and some of the old settler families (*baladiyyun*). The jurists (*fuqaha*) were disciples of Malik ibn Anas of Medina, founder of one of Islam's four major schools of jurisprudence, a school impatient with the subtleties and levels of meaning inherent in other legal traditions. Led by the revered jurist, the *faqih* Yahya ibn Yahya al-Laythi, the conspirators overwhelmed the *shurta*, the city's police force, and stormed the palace. Their revolt would have been a revolution had it succeeded, for its aim was to make Cordoba more like Medina. Al-Hakam escaped capture, kept his nerve, and quickly prevailed at the head of his special Negro guard. Fifteen thousand rebel Cordovans were expelled from *al-Andalus,* most of them settling in Fez in Morocco, where their presence is still marked. Yahya, his life spared by al-Hakam, was eventually allowed to return to Cordoba from his Toledo exile. The conspiracy failed to replace the *amir*, but it definitively displaced the previous Andalusi legal principles with the far more literal Malikite *Sharia*.[9]

Repression accompanied progress under al-Hakam. The last barriers were finally being relaxed to permit non-Arab Muslims, *muwalladun*, to fill top positions of service and command at court, in the judiciary, and in the army. Mozarabs and Sephardim served the regime in increasing numbers, augmenting the reservoir of trained Arabs. Military service continued to be borne by the Syrian settlers, the old families, and those whose taxes were forgiven in exchange for service, but al-Hakam established the precedent of an elite corps of Negro mercenaries, a major innovation upon which his successors would expand. The *amir*'s legacy was mixed. Crucifixions and expulsions were regrettable aspects of nation-building. Enlightened despotism was the alternative to rule by the consensus of classes or rule by the oligarchy of affluent families—or subservience to *ulamas* and *fuqaha*. As with his successors, al-Hakam's challenge was to preserve and enhance the authority and power of the *amir*—the better to guide his heterogeneous, independent, and volatile population. The loss of Barcelona to Louis the Pious in the winter of 801 was the *amír*'s greatest military defeat. He died in 822 without further loss of significant territory to the new Christian kingdoms emerging from a distintegrating Carolingian empire. Al-Hakam stipulated in writing that his oldest son, another 'Abd al-Rahman, should succeed him.[10]

❖

'Abd al-Rahman II (822–52) watched with much satisfaction, as had his father, as Christian Europe collapsed. The news from the land of the Franks generally pleased him. The great king of the Franks was no more. The Frankish realm was falling apart, and fierce men from the Far North had begun to wreak destruction across much of the continent. Charlemagne had outlived Alcuin by ten years. His reign lasted almost half a century—from the joint coronation in 768 with his outmaneuvered younger brother, Carloman, to a quiet death from fever on January 28, 814. The king-emperor had lived without a legal mate after the unremarkable Luitgard died in 800. (She became his wife shortly after the 794 demise of Fastrada, his controversial fourth spouse.) He died in the sprawling palace complex at Aachen, surrounded by eight doting, unmarried daughters and a concubine or two. He had allowed none of the daughters to marry—mainly, undoubtedly, to preserve his empire's territorial integrity from divisive spousal claims against it. Just for a season or so, Charlemagne had seriously considered pledging daughter Rotrud to Constantine VI, the doomed son of Empress Irene of Byzantium. But Irene decided to win the support of the Catholic West against her enemies by devising a compromise formula ending the Iconoclastic Controversy, after which she blinded and murdered her son. The daughters' morals scandalized the clergy and even evoked a telling warning from Alcuin to a student to take care that the "crowned doves" flying about the palace "do not come to your window." The daughters were their father's comfort at the end, but their brother, the emperor designate, Louis the Pious, banished them from Aachen as one of his first official acts.[11]

Charlemagne's fifty military campaigns, faithful cadre of literate servants, and divisions of spiritual police in service to an increasingly dogmatic monotheism had patched together a new social and economic order out of the detritus of the Roman Empire. As Charlemagne's six-foot-three remains were placed in his recycled Roman sarcophagus beneath the floor of the Octagon Chapel, Louis the Pious, lone survivor of illnesses that had felled his brothers Charles and Pippin, assumed the title *rex Francorum* and *imperator Romanorum* and possession of the equivalent of modern France, Germany, the Benelux countries, Switzerland, Austria, most of Italy, and much of Hungary. Louis inherited his father's title, but he was far from the mythmaking stuff of the founder of Europe. Had Charlemagne's favorite, Charles the Younger, lived, the weak Louis almost certainly would have carried on as king of Aquitaine in accordance with Charlemagne's *Divisio regnorum*, drawn up eight years before his death.[12] But Pippin and Charles had died within months of each other in 810 and 811, respectively, and the king of the Franks made the final determination of succession at Aachen in September 813, four months before his own death. Louis's sons were to serve as kings under their imperial father: Lothair of Italy; Pippin (now Gallicized as Pepin) of Aquitaine; and Louis of Bavaria. Amost immediately, the three brothers displayed their dominant trait, squabbling among themselves—except when they united to dethrone their father temporarily. The consequences of sibling rivalry on such a grand scale were soon fatal to their grandfather's legacy but a vital boon to Muslim Iberia.

Meanwhile, the Viking onslaught began in earnest beyond the Pyrenees. The first Norsemen appeared in the coastal waters off *al-Andalus* twenty-two years into 'Abd al Rahman II's amirate, when eighty Viking longboats sculled up the Guadalquivir in 844 and plundered Sevilla. These petrifying visitors had come ashore in the Christian north of the Iberian peninsula before they singed the Mediterranean's north shore. The universal horror these warriors from the bleak North evoked is preserved in an account by a monk who witnessed their depredations at Lindisfarne Monastery. "They came from the sea. Heathens! They plundered, and they murdered," he moaned. "Blood flew in the altar. Christians were trampled under foot like filth in the streets. Some of the brothers were carried off. We did not believe that such sea voyages were possible." 'Abd al-Rahman II mounted a vigorous, coordinated response from Cordoba. After these blond raiders were intercepted and defeated, and the survivors converted to Islam, a stout wall was built around Sevilla. A crash shipbuilding program in Lisbon, Sevilla, and Valencia equipped the amirate with two of the largest fleets in Europe, one for the Mediterranean and the other for the Atlantic.[13] By then, Charlemagne had reposed in his sarcophagus beneath the Octagon Chapel for thirty turbulent, inglorious years. By the time the walls went up around Sevilla to fend off the Norsemen in 844, his empire would be as dead as he, formally dissolved the previous year by three acrimonious grandsons in the watershed Treaty of Verdun.

In accordance with the Treaty of Verdun of 843, Emperor Louis's three sons carved up their patrimony into France, the Low Countries, and Germany with its Italian dependencies. The partition was as much linguistic as political: Latin ceded more and more to Romance and German in the affairs of its French, German, Italian, and Flemish peoples. By dismembering itself at the worst possible moment—just as the Scandinavian pestilence arrived—Carolingian Europe squandered its future to the chaos of invasion and the slow-motion anarchy of feudalism. The result was to be a classic historical *déjà vu*. Just as the Battle of Poitiers in 732 marked a rupture in the political and cultural advance of Islam on the continent of Europe—a temporary halt in the *Dar al-Harb* that turned out to be permanent—Verdun and the Vikings after the 840s would wreck the Spanish March and plunge Christian Europe into four hundred years of civil war, knightly mayhem, protonational consolidation, and homicidal crusades in the Middle East, Spain, and the south of France.

❖

The second 'Abd al-Rahman merited his Roman numeral. He was an Umayyad cut from the Falcon's cloth. Under his skilled, prudent, and lucky guidance, Andalusis knew a generation of steady, robust prosperity and political progress. Historians as prophets in reverse, however, may signal developments whose seeming insignificance or eccentricity at the time are adumbrations of revolutions to come. Even as the military threat posed by the Carolingians receded during the second 'Abd al-Rahman's reign, new, analogous military and religious perils arose on the Iberian peninsula and within *al-Andalus* proper. In great measure, these new internal disturbances were directly traceable to Charlemagne's appearance with Roland at Roncesvalles in 778. The Falcon's grandson would have lain in the family crypt two centuries and one generation when the full consequences of an obscure military defeat and an aberrant religious provocation that occurred on his watch came to pass. Charlemagne's double-pronged invasion of 778 and the ongoing Spanish March disturbances stimulated the Christian statelets on the Duero-Ebro flange—Galicia, Asturias, Castile, Leon, and Aragon—to commence tentative probes into Muslim lands.

⁛

In the same year that Norsemen probed the Guadalquivir, 'Abd al-Rahman II ordered a punitive invasion of Castile at a point on the Duero below the ancient town of Tordesillas. The *amir* was resolute in policing the frontiers of the Upper March. Outnumbered by an army commanded by one of the *amir*'s experienced generals, the king of Castile, Ramiro I, decided to stand and fight. If the hilly terrain favored the defenders, little else did until James, brother of John and one of Jesus's twelve apostles, appeared in King Ramiro's dream before dawn broke over the rugged Clavijo terrain. The saint's bones had but recently been unearthed in the wild Galician remoteness at a place thirty miles from the Atlantic illumined by a star. *Campus stellae*, the Spanish *Compostela* ("field of the star"), was an astonishing resting place for St. James, whose last known address, until then, had been in Jerusalem, where King Herod I Agrippa beheaded him in 44 CE. The Church soon clarified the matter by explaining that the apostle had preached the Gospel in Hispania on a side trip before going on to his Jerusalem martyrdom.[14]

With the assurance of St. James vouchsafed, Ramiro buckled on his armor and led his troops into a battle that amazed both armies. St. James, who also buckled on armor, materialized on a white horse, brandishing a splendid sword and scattering scallop shells. As Gibbon relates in his monumental narrative, "a stupendous metamorphosis was performed in the ninth century when from a peaceful fisherman of the Lake of Gennesareth, the apostle James was transformed into a valorous knight, who charged at the head of Spanish chivalry in battles against the Moors." On that day in 844 at Clavijo, *Santiago Matamoros* ("St. James the Moorslayer") entered the ideational matrix of Catholic Hispania. To the future legions of the *Reconquista*, his many reappearances in the heat of close-run battles (accompanied by cries of "Santiago! Santiago!" as at Valencia in 1094, Alarcos in 1195) were to be received not as apparitions but as the flesh-and-blood presence of unique providence—"given by God to Spain," said Cervantes's *Don Quixote*, "for its patron and protection." To 'Abd al-Rahman and his ministers, Clavijo was nothing more than another unmemorable clash like that of Pelayo at Covadonga. Yet, ten years after King Ramiro survived his contest at Clavijo by the grace of St. James, the spirit of *Santiago Matamoros* confounded the interfaith comity of 'Abd al-Rahman II's Cordoba.[15]

In *al-Andalus*, Christians assimilated the new Muslim learning in the sciences and humanities with an almost-untroubled alacrity, which was hardly surprising, seeing that their accommodation to the language and culture of their Arab masters continued to accelerate throughout the ninth century. Estimates derived from village tax returns indicate that almost forty percent of the Andalusian Christian population became Muslim less than a century after the Falcon's demise. True enough, a declaration of faith was also a tax statement that brought release from or alleviation of sumptuary, conjugal, and legal restrictions. But it was also the case that compulsory conversion to Islam under the Umayyads was virtually unknown. The rate of Christians converting to Islam undoubtedly alarmed the Church. Besides the outright converts, there were the Mozarabs, the Christians who adopted Arab speech, names, dress, and foods. The rules of the game of religious coexistence dictated that the Catholic Church keep a low and prudent profile. Proselytism was proscribed and capital punishment was inflicted upon any Muslim who converted to Christianity. Despite such restrictions, the Catholic hierarchy took subtle care to discourage the growth of Mozarabic-Muslim religious affinity. The very idea that Islam might be "a 'new religion' was in the strict sense of the term unthinkable" to sincere Christians.[16]

It was in desperate reaction to the success of the "unthinkable" that a small group of Andalusian Christians, whose fanaticism appeared to represent only themselves, defied the full authority of the Muslim regime in the middle of the ninth century. Christians as well as Muslims, not to mention bemused Jews, regarded the actions of these "martyrs" as aberrant, a senseless spike in religious provocation that just as suddenly dissipated seemingly without a trace. By the end of the 860s, the *al-Andalus* of 'Abd al-Rahman II's successor, Muhammad I (852–86) had already begun to forget about them. While it lasted, however, the fever that seized the "Mozarab martyrs" achieved a sensational intensity that might have deserved the success of a great religious awakening. Toward the closing decade of 'Abd al-Rahman's amirate, and forcing dismayed concern in the first decade of his son's, individual Christian priests and laypersons publicly insulted the Muslim faith. The monasteries of Tabanos and St. Zoilus near Cordoba served as crucibles for exalteds who publicly disrespected mosques, the Qur'an, and the Prophet's name. Soon the blasphemy of one Isaac, who resigned from the *amir*'s service, followed by a soldier named Sanctius, and, in the weeks ahead, a dozen more troubled souls, forced the reluctant hand of Cordoba's *qadi* (chief judge). Muhammad I approved his *qadi*'s death sentence in 851–52 for thirteen Christians for whom clemency was impolitic if not impossible under Malikite *Sharia*.

The intellectual heavyweights of this religious movement made their debut with the publication of a polemical book about apostasy among the Christian faithful. Paul Alvarus's *The Unmistakable Sign* (*Indiculus Luminosus*) was a confessional alarm written in 854. Alvarus wrote his book not in the Arabic read by all educated non-Muslims but in the Latin that everfewer Andalusis read or spoke. Alvarus wrote in a time of accelerating social and demographic changes that disturbed many Andalusis, regardless of faith. Christian conversion to Islam was roaring ahead. Jews were rising in intellectual and political influence. Muslim fundamentalists were exerting greater pressure upon the regime to hew faithfully to the Qur'an. Alvarus, the learned Cordovan Christian, eloquently inveighed against the proliferating Mozarab dilettantes who thought, talked, read, and wrote only in Arabic. "The Christians love to read the poems and romances of the Arabs; they study the Arab theologians and philosophers, not to refute them, but to form a correct and elegant Arabic," deplored the seminary-trained layman with feigned incredulity. Alvarus especially regretted the fascination exerted upon his educated coreligionists by Persian tales refined in Baghdad. "They have forgotten their own language," he charged, and Christian culture was fast dissolving in the Arab solvent. "There are a thousand who can express themselves in Arabic with elegance, and write better poems in this language than the Arabs themselves."[17]

Alvarus's good friend and fellow seminarian, Eulogius, who had taken religious vows (Alvarus had not), took up the call to awaken the Mozarabs while there was still time. Small of stature yet so imposing in intellect that Alvarus claimed that he "surpassed in knowledge all his contemporaries," Eulogius belonged to one of the most distinguished families of the surviving Hispano-Roman aristocracy. A brother served on the palace staff of 'Abd al-Rahman II. As is the way with such figures, Eulogius emerged from a conversion experience believing himself designated to challenge the legitimacy of Islam. In panic and disapprobation, the Catholic hierarchy distanced itself from Eulogius and his movement and joined the regime in efforts to defuse the inflammatory scandals. The Christian militants were deaf to all pleas, nevertheless, and the *qadi* finally imposed more death sentences in accordance with the Malikite *Sharia*. Public beheadings and bodies displayed on the walls followed. Twenty or so "Mozarab martyrs" were dispatched in 853 or the year following, and a dozen more afterward. In another wave of Christian blasphemy in 859, thirteen more were executed, along with two daughters of a prominent Muslim family living in distant Huesca who defiantly disclosed their secret Christian conversion. Eulogius, whose admiration by the clergy had nudged the Church to appoint him archbishop of Toledo, was brought to Cordoba for trial that same year. His public decapitation in Cordoba would be celebrated in a biography by his friend Alvarus. Sanctification in Rome soon followed.[18]

A poll taken of Andalusians of all faiths would have shown an overwhelming disapproval of the "Mozarab martyrs." These Christian extremists were an aberration not because they acted outside history but because they were premature—three centuries ahead of the history whose intense cultural nationalism and religious intolerance were incul-

cated in the decades after the Battle of Clavijo. It would have been a
clairvoyant subject of the amirate who could have divined that the aberrant religious exhibitionism encouraged by Eulogius and Alvarus was a
harbinger of the deep, savage, religious intolerance that would engulf
Muslims and Christians alike some four hundred years in the future.

⁘

When 'Abd al-Rahman III assumed the amiral title in 912, *al-Andalus*
had barely survived as an intact polity after a quarter century of chaos
under *Amir* 'Abd Allah ibn Muhammad, his grandfather. Morose, misan-
thropic, and vindictive, 'Abd Allah became *amir* by either chance or fratricide. His older brother, the militarily capable and popular *Amir*
al-Mundhir (r. 886–88), died suddenly after a brief reign. 'Abd Allah (r.
888–912) inherited a state somewhat weakened by economic crises,
regional separatism, and rebellions—two of which raged out of control
during the final decade of their father's long reign. The economy, separatism, and rebellions overwhelmed 'Abd Allah and caused a "slide into
anarchy," in the apt phrase of one authority.

The economic crises stemmed from an irreversible demographic
reality: *al-Andalus's* Christian majority of the eighth century would comprise a minority of the total population by the end of the tenth because
of conversion and out-migration to the Christian kingdoms. The old
story of regional separatism among the Basques of the Upper March and
of Berbers in various provinces acquired some new chapters. One major
rebellion concerned 'Abd al-Rahman ibn Marwan al-Jalliq of Merida's
Arab aristocracy, who formed a breakaway state at Badajoz with enough
military power to threaten Sevilla. Then there was 'Umar ibn Hafsun,
the ex-Christian *muwallad,* who set up a lair of brigands, criminals, and the
disaffected near Ronda in Malaga province in the 890s. This religious
chameleon would humiliate and defy the central authority for decades
from his hilltop bunker at Bobastro in Malaga's El Chorro Gorge. When
'Abd Allah finally expired in the winter of 912, his anointed heir and
twenty-one-year-old grandson inherited a realm at its nadir.[19]

'Abd al-Rahman III would rule as *amir* from 912 to 929 and as caliph
from 929 to 961—one year shy of a glorious half century. The time of

troubles at the beginning of his rule would become history in short order. His success was reminiscent of that of Heraclius before fate unhinged the Byzantine emperor. Indeed, 'Abd al-Rahman's physical description—short and muscular, with fair hair and blue eyes—recalled that of the savior of the Eastern Roman Empire. His precocity impressed. Ahmed ibn Mohammed al-Makkari, the chatty source for *al-Andalus*'s history, says 'Abd al-Rahman was noted for his meekness, "his generosity, and his love of justice," which were proverbial. He was a patron of the arts, loved science, and, adds al-Makkari, loved to converse with scholars and intellectuals.[20] His time as 'Abd al-Rahman III *al-Nasr li-Din Allah* ("Champion of the Religion of God") was the apogee of Umayyad *al-Andalus*. The situation beyond the mountains enabled the *amir* to channel his resources to the mastery of challenges within the peninsula. His nearest external enemy was France, the recent kingdom formed not long after the divvying-up at Verdun of Charlemagne's superstate by his larcenous grandsons. Charles III ("the Simple"), the French monarch, exemplified how far the apple had fallen from the Carolingian tree when he was forced to sign away a wedge of his kingdom in 911 to Rollo the Norwegian, whose Norsemen had carved out a region they called Normandy.

The Norsemen, or Vikings, wrought such terrible damage to the feeble and primitive economic and social infrastructure that wolves had taken over great swaths of transmontane Europe. Hordes of marauders preyed on those rich or desperate enough to risk travel. Walled settlements and castles anchored timorous villagers and peasants driven from their lands by fear of swift Norse longboats that appeared with deadly suddenness. Blackened silhouettes of abbeys and monasteries outlined the horizon. An Abbasid ambassador who encountered a Viking expedition on the banks of the Volga River sent a vivid report to Baghdad on their manners. "They are the filthiest race that God ever created," winced the caliph's ambassador. "They do not wipe themselves after going to stool, nor wash themselves after a nocturnal pollution any more than if they were wild asses."[21]

In the eastern part of the dismembered Carolingian Empire, where the German language prevailed and the imperial crown held on to its mystique, Europe faced the Magyars, its newest scourge. They were so wanton in their ferocity as to be mistaken for returning Huns when they poured across the Danube at the end of the ninth century and plundered as far as Burgundy. People called them Hungarians and later believed themselves delivered by a miracle when the Hohenstaufen king of the Franks, Otto I (r. 936–62, emperor 962–73), finally halted the Magyars at the Lech River, a tributary of the Danube, in August 955. Had Europe been struck by plague during these brutal times, it would have seemed but another sign of the certain "end of the world" widely predicted to happen with the millennium.

During the next two centuries, then, the ninth and the tenth, Muslim Europe and Christian Europe faced each other in a delicate equipoise at the great mountain range, adversaries in a declared war for which there was no net advantage to either. Europe east of the Pyrenees was now *hors de combat*—out of the running—as far as any meaningful threat it posed to the amirate. The significant threats came from within the Iberian peninsula and from North Africa. 'Abd al-Rahman ("Champion of the Religion of God") gave priority to the securing of borders and sending of routine military campaigns into the checkerboard Christian statelets to the north and east that rimmed the Duero and Ebro Rivers within the peninsula. Relatively small and congenitally fractious, the counties and kingdoms of Asturias, Leon-Castile, Navarra, and Catalunya won occasional battles against the Muslims (as at Pamplona and Clavijo) but remained mostly on the defensive. 'Abd al-Rahman III was no Charlemagne in the saddle, but he personally commanded five expeditions, four of them attaining the desired strategic and mythical success. Neither his great-grandfather nor his grandfather had solved the humiliation of Umar ibn Hafsun, the brigand ruler of Bobastro. [22]

Bobastro was a castle literally built in the air, a mountaintop ashlar fortress above the gorge of the Guadalhorce River not many miles from Ronda, future cradle of bullfighting. For almost fifty embarrassing years, from the 880s until its surrender, Bobastro defied Cordoba. It held rapacious sway over much of the region from Malaga north to Ronda. 'Abd al-Rahman finally assembled a force sufficient to blockade all approaches to the fortress and starve its garrison into surrender after a siege of several months. The fox of Bobastro had died ten years earlier, but his four sons

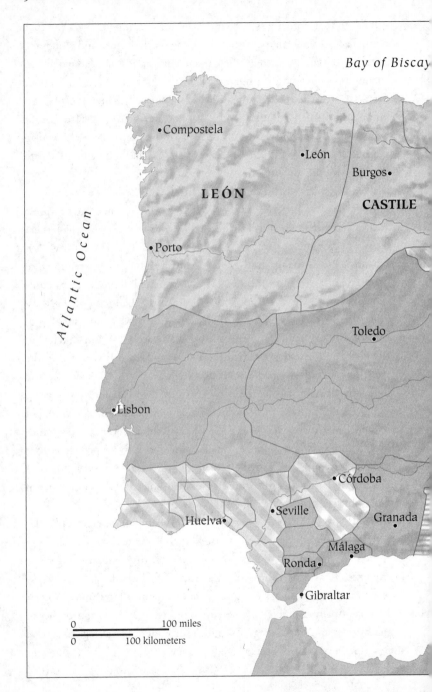

The *Ta'ifa* Kingdoms of Iberia

FRANCE

AVARRE

ARAGON

CATALONIA

• Gerona

Saragossa
•

• Lérida

• Barcelona

Tortosa

Balearic Islands

Minorca

• Palma

Majorca

• Valencia

Ibiza

• Denia

Formentera

Mediterranean Sea

• Murcia

N
W   E
S

Christian states

ta'ifa states ruled by dynasties of Berber origin

ta'ifa states ruled by dynasties of Slav origin

other *ta'ifa* states

honored the family tradition. Success came on the fourth expedition in 928. An Umayyad chronicler captured the moment when the last missing piece was inserted into the jigsaw puzzle of central power as "the Champion" destroyed Bobastro, "reducing its fortifications, pulling down its walls and razing everything standing in it of palaces, dwellings, storehouses, and buildings, returning it to a bare mountain. . . ."[23] A decade later, Ceuta was occupied and a considerable Umayyad military presence was planted in the Maghreb that would last for some fifty years.

The danger from Muslim fundamentalism in North Africa went to the heart of everything the Umayyads represented. The once-mighty Abbasid caliphs in Baghdad had become pawns politically manipulated by their Turkish slave-soldiers, a Praetorian guard of their own creation. As the caliphal center weakened, other power centers arose and pulled away from Baghdad. One of them, the Fatimid dynasty of Ifriqiya, proclaimed its independence in the fateful year of 909 as the first Shi'a regime. The new Tunisian ruler, the *imam* Ubayd Allah, claimed direct descent from Fatima, wife of Ali and daughter of Muhammad. The Fatimids were expansionists who invaded Sijilmasa, the gold entrepôt on the edge of the Sahara. At long last, the divisive issue of legitimate leadership of the *ummah*—an evaded, muted, and repressed perennial—confronted all Sunni regimes. Shi'ism, with its dogma of the lineal purity of the ruler and its religious literalism, was a reproachful reminder to the *Dar al-Islam* of Sunni illegitimacy and wickedness. Twenty years after the creation of the Tunisian Fatimids, and on the crest of the Bobastro triumph, Sunni *al-Andalus* became a formal caliphate in prophylactic reaction to the Shi'a Fatimids. 'Abd al-Rahman III chose 929 as the propitious moment to transform *al-Andalus* into a caliphate. "Allah has favored us," the caliphal proclamation trumpeted. "He has shown His preference for us, He has established our authority and has allowed us to realize His success with ease."[24] *Al-Nasr li-Din Allah* ("Champion of the Religion of God") serenely reaffirmed his dynasty's claim as the exclusive inheritor of the Prophet's mantle. To mark the new caliphate's advent, he struck the continent's first gold dinar since the fall of the Damascus caliphate 150 years earlier.

'Abd al-Rahman III not only arrogated the title of caliph but also matched the architectural grandeur of the Falcon's Friday Mosque. The cinnamon-colored Great Mosque had already been widened under 'Abd al-Rahman II and Muhammad I, with two symmetrical galleries for female worshippers and an eighty-foot extension of the oratory with eighty columns. The new caliph's palace city, *Madinat al-Zahra,* which rose on the slopes of the Sierra de Cordoba three miles northwest of the capital, was an architectural hyperbole. The scale and magnificence of the excavated and partly reconstructed ruins of this palace city astound the modern visitor. Although an appealing legend confers the honor of the palace's name, *Zahra,* upon 'Abd al-Rahman III's favorite wife, the more plausible etymology derives *Zahra* from "blossom" or "flower."[25] What remains of the caliph's royal compound still beggars Versailles as, in the caliph's time, its colonnaded great halls, geometric gardens, and cascading fountains humbled generations of ambassadors and awed subjects.

'Abd al-Rahman III wished that his *Madinat al-Zahra* paralyze the first-time visitor's vocal chords: approaching royals, ambassadors, distinguished foreigners, *walis* from the marches, and subjects bearing gifts and petitions. Its incommensurable magnificence symbolized the power and imperishability of the Umayyad dynasty. Nowhere on the continent was there an experience comparable to ascending the palace's long, rising approach to present credentials or receive the sovereign's command or pleasure. Charlemagne's official residence at Aachen was a hovel by comparison. A Muslim observer recorded the presentation of credentials by the Holy Roman Empire's ambassador as he advanced three miles under a double rank of soldiers, "their naked swords, both broad and long, meeting at the tips like rafters of a roof. . . . The fear that this inspired was indescribable."[26]

When the regent of the Christian kingdom of Navarra brought her afflicted son, Sancho I of Leon (r. 956–60), to Cordoba for medical treatment, this politically savvy woman was mesmerized by the opulence of *Madinat al-Zahra*—the cupolas cast in stucco that filtered sunlight through lacy roof panels onto the walls covered by brilliant tiles. Magnified and intensified, the light was reflected back upon the walls from mercury-filled pools in the floor. Cured by court physicians of the obesity that caused his dethronement, Sancho "the Fat," with his mother's blessing, gratefully reaffirmed Navarra's fealty to 'Abd al-Rahman and departed with a Muslim army charged to restore Sancho to power.[27] Sancho paid his medical bill with ten towns. Old Count Borrel of Barcelona, along with youthful Count Garcia Fernandez of Castile, followed by other Catholic worthies of the North, shared Sancho's memorable audience experience at *Madinat al-Zahra*: the thousand guards lining the ceremonial esplanade; the symphony of fountain waters; the ether of roses and orange blossoms; and, finally, the Pharaonic stage set of the grand reception hall, where 'Abd al-Rahman received them in splendor.

Caliphal Cordoba, as befitted a world capital, dressed itself up spectacularly during the Champion's golden reign. The seventy-odd libraries of Cordoba would amaze modern scholars almost as much as they stunned literate Christians of the late tenth century. There would be nothing at all comparable elsewhere in the West to Cordoba's main library of four hundred thousand volumes of mostly paper manuscripts. The great Benedictine abbey of St. Gall in Switzerland numbered a mere six hundred books, all of them in vellum (calfskin) or parchment (sheepskin). The availability of paper in the Arab empire greatly enhanced the diffusion of knowledge and made large library holdings possible. Paper—made from bark, linen, and hemp rather than the papyrus of pressed reeds of the Egyptians—would have an impact on Muslims similar to that of the printing press on Europeans seven hundred years later. Andalusia's own paper factory was finally established in the early eleventh century at Jativa, a valley town south of Valencia. Gibbon delighted at the book worship of Cordoba's citizens, a bibliophilia he disdainfully contrasted to the paucity of written works in the Christian West.[28] Cordoba's narrow streets were lined with thousands of small shops and workshops where weavers produced brocades, silks, and woolens; craftsmen shaped crystal and tooled the famous Cordovan leather. Hroswitha of Gandersheim, a Saxon nun of rare learning and extraordinary influence for her gender and time, would describe the Cordoba of 'Abd al-Rahman III as "the brilliant ornament of the world," in an epistolary effusion that became famous.[29]

City-ruled, agriculturally productive, its trade globally powered, its commerce transacted in silver and gold coinage, *al-Andalus* passed through its ninth and into its tenth century as a country whose *jihadic* origins exerted much less intrinsic appeal to its heterogeneous peoples. Decisions were made about national defense during the reign of 'Abd al-Rahman III that reflected one of the perennial problems all successful societies face over time. The warrior was honored by *suras* from the Qur'an, his profession limned in song and story audible in the *Song of the Cid* (*Cantar de Mío Cid*) two centuries later. Yet his was the one class, paradoxically, increasingly underrepresented. Despite the esteem of the soldier's profession in creed and rhetoric, the reality of Muslim Andalusia was that most people had little desire to go to war—even Holy War. To a large extent, the business of *al-Andalus* was business, in great contrast to Carolingian Europe, where warfare comprised most of the business and the *raison d'être* of a specific caste was the perpetuation of war. The Andalusi—Muslim, Christian, and Jew—preferred to pay taxes (*jizya, zakat, kharaj*) for others to fight *jihads*. Under 'Abd al-Rahman III, then, trends and policies that had begun with the Falcon's *saqaliba* soldiers were finalized with the creation of a paid, highly professional military establishment manned largely by Berbers, Africans, and Slavs supplied by the ceaseless warfare in Europe's eastern lands. In Francia, all free men reported to the Marchfield. In *al-Andalus*, they made themselves available, generally, for the tax collector.[30]

⁝⁝

Christians adopted Arab speech, names, dress, and foods, but Jews and Muslims found high-level collaboration even easier to come by. That collaboration, as we know, began even before the Arabs and Berbers came ashore at Algeciras. Through Ibn Hayyan, indispensable for insight into the tenth century, we meet a remarkable personality whose services to the new caliphate encapsulated the unique contribution of learned Jews to the transmission of knowledge to the stubbornly dark and intellectually shuttered universe beyond *al-Andalus*. Hasdai ibn Ishaq, Ibn Hayyan's

"Jewish scribe," represented 'Abd al-Rahman III at Barcelona in either 939 or 940. Barcelona had been embedded in Charlemagne's Spanish March in 801, after Louis the Pious's tenacious two-year siege. The city (and territory) had since remained largely outside its former Andalusian orbit, while guarding a healthy autonomy from the new kingdom of France. Ambassador Hasdai negotiated a turnkey treaty with the son of Wilfrid "the Hairy," founder of the Frankish dynasty of the counts of Barcelona. "Hasdai called upon the nobles of Barcelona to obey *al-Nasr li-Din Allah* ["Champion of the Religion of God"] and to make peace with him," records Ibn Hayyan.

Hasdai's treaty with the count of Barcelona guaranteed his subjects freedom "to engage in trade wherever they wished" in *al-Andalus*, on condition that they "terminate assistance to or friendship with all Christians who are not at peace with *al-Nasr li-Din Allah*."[31] The occasion was singular enough that Christian magnates from territories somewhat distant came to observe the deliberations. The count of Arles asked for a guarantee of safety for various kinds of merchants of his land "to conduct business in al-Andalus." According to Ibn Hayyan, "a group of their kings agreed to this," and "from that time on," thanks to Hasdai ibn Ishaq's treaty negotiations, "the profit increased because of it." But the profits, such as they were, from improved relations between the Barcelona counts and the Andalusian regime were not exclusively commercial. The balance sheet for knowledge was also significant. Barcelona was Catholic enough for the popes yet was no firewall committed to safeguarding the Catholic West from Muslim heresies. Rather, especially after its treaty with *al-Andalus*, it was on its way to becoming a way station between two Europes, Muslim and Christian.

A few years after the treaty negotiated by Hasdai ibn Ishaq, Gerbert of Aurillac arrived in Barcelona in the retinue of a French nobleman. Gerbert's was the sort of Dark Ages success story that would have gratified Charlemagne. Through the force of a brilliant intelligence recognized by all who met him, he rose from poverty through mastery of the *trivium* and *quadrivium* to instructorship at the prestigious cathedral school at Reims. He then became abbot of a well-endowed abbey, archbishop of Ravenna, and expositor of canon law at synods before being tapped as adviser to the boy emperor Otto III. Those distinctions came after Gerbert's student days in prosperous and relatively cosmopolitan Barcelona, where he commenced the difficult mastery of the Arabic numerals and the new methods of calculating. He continued his studies under Muslim masters in Caliph al-Hakam II al-Mustansir's (961–76) Cordoba and Sevilla, even though he found the toil so daunting as to be "almost impossible." In 980, the priest published his revolutionary four-page textbook on the new mathematics. It was a pivotal moment in the intellectual history of the West, reminiscent of the four physics papers published by Albert Einstein in 1909. Henceforth, Christian Europe could not only dispense with XXIV + XLIII = LXVII but could conveniently represent large and complicated multiples and dividends arrived at by universal rules of reckoning. The nine "Hindu numbers" and the Arab zero were potential magic.[32]

Some of Gerbert's educated contemporaries were bewildered by his mathematical learning. He braved their suspicions of demonic powers as the source of his awesome accomplishments. After February 999, his contemporaries kept their suspicions to themselves. Gerbert was elected to the papacy as Sylvester II, the first French pontiff. This man of science, and therefore of the future, occupied St. Peter's chair at the historic millennial moment when much of Western humanity waited for the end of time in a frenzy of thanksgiving. As pope, he used his office to introduce to the Catholic West the new numbers from India and the mathematical science advanced by them. His reputation as one of the greatest minds of Europe, together with his educational reforms and mathematical writings, garnered the sobriquet "Scientist Pope." In reality, though, Pope Sylvester's putative numerical and mathematical revolution turned out to be a centennially slow evolution, a revolution that hurt too many people's heads to proceed rapidly. One of Gerbert's pupils flinched when remembering years later the "great sweat" he spent with a band of others on mathematics.[33] That pupil neglected to mention that his labors were simplified by the abacus Gerbert brought from *al-Andalus*. It did more to promote the culture of numbers beyond the Pyrenees than any textbook.

The likes of Gerbert of Aurillac could be placed on the head of a pin in the tenth century. But if the assimilation of Andalusian knowledge and high culture by Christians east of the Pyrenees was rare, it was also not so impressive among the Mozarabs, who by the end of that century comprised only some thirty percent of the Andalusian population. The fact that the beheaded Bishop Eulogius's potboiler of a book, *Apología for the Martyrs*, detailing the final agonies of the "Mozarab martyrs," still circulated in the tenth century was a measure of ongoing alienation among literate Christians. After having been a numerical majority during the eighth century, Mozarabs were reduced to political and social inferiority. The steady rate of conversions to Islam and a rising out-migration across the Ebro and Duero left the tenth-century Mozarabs a demographic minority. Also, Mozarabs were disproportionately peasant folk, living considerable distances from the major cities. The Mozarabic bishop of Elvira, Racemundo, who would serve as the caliph's ambassador to Constantinople and the court of Otto I, was an outstanding example of interfaith comity; yet the Muslim-Mozarabic parallel would never quite seem to match the qualitative interaction of the Muslims and Jews in al-Andalus.[34]

❖

The Golden Age of Muslim Iberia and the Golden Age of Sefarad (Jewish Iberia) were something like two sides of the same coin—two centuries, the tenth and the eleventh, during which the Andalusian wellsprings of Jewish intellectual and political contributions appeared, on the one hand, to be almost inexhaustible, while, on the other, the imprint of Arab culture and science upon Sefarad was transformative and unmistakable. Jews comprised no more than one percent of the total population—some sixty thousand, primarily in the cities. The term *convivencia* ("coexistence") would gain currency in a later chapter of Iberian history, but its meaning would be exemplified by the illustrious career of Hasdai ibn Shaprut (915–60), the *nasi* (prince) of Cordoba's Sephardic community. He was a born diplomat and learned physician whose antidotes for poisons were especially valued in his politically treacherous country. His medical learning was brought to the attention of 'Abd al-Rahman III, who was sufficiently impressed by Hasdai's suavity and judgment that he eventually made the physician chairman of the medical council and official emissary abroad.[35] Giving a Jew or Christian authority over Muslims ran against the grain of tradition and Qur'anic interpretation; only a secure ruler could choose to do so. Hasdai's role in the exchange of ambassadors with Constantinople, like that of his namesake's in Barcelona, was a diplomatic success that yielded lasting scientific benefits.

Just as Harun al-Rashid's elephant was meant to encourage Charlemagne's Spanish aggression, Constantine VII's mid-tenth-century gift to 'Abd al-Rahman III was designed to encourage Andalusia's antipathy toward the Abbassids. The *basileus*'s ambassador presented the caliph with a lavishly bound and illustrated gift, the *De Materia Medica* of Dioscorides, in the original Greek. This foundational work of Greek science existed in Arabic only in a poor translation undertaken at Baghdad's House of Wisdom a century earlier. At Hasdai ibn Shaprut's suggestion, Constantine's ambassador returned to Cordoba with a Greek monk to assist in producing a definitive translation. No such translation enterprise as that led by Hasdai ibn Shaprut—in which a Jew, a Byzantine, and several Arabs collaborated for more than a year to identify and classify the ancient pharmacology—would have been conceivable in the Catholic West, or in the Greek Orthodox East, for that matter. It gave powerful stimuli to botanical and agronomical investigation and the development of medical therapies. Four centuries passed before the Latin version of *De Materia Medica* reached Christian Europe, where it remained the standard reference work until the Enlightenment. Successful proctorship of the *De Materia Medica* enterprise ended as well the necessity for Andalusian medical students to take the equivalent of an internship in Cairo or Baghdad. Cordoba, along with Palermo (then part of the *Dar al-Islam*), became the premier medical center in Europe.[36]

Hasdai ibn Shaprut's public life was exceptional, yet what would later seem even more remarkable is that it was merely one among many such exceptional examples. When he died at the age of fifty-five in 970, the Golden Age of the Sephardim would last almost another century. His death occurred nine years after that of his master and patron, 'Abd al-Rahman III. The "Champion of the Religion of God" had succumbed to a "paralytic fit" in October 961. He bequeathed a tranquil, confident empire to his scholarly heir, al-Hakam II (961–76), that would have been the envy of Croesus, says Mohammed al-Makkari. State revenues amounted to a fabulous 6,245,000 dinars annually: 5,480,000 dinars from the *kharaj* and 765,000 dinars from duties and indirect taxes. "As to the sums which entered the royal coffers, being the fifth of the spoils taken from the infidels, they were beyond calculation," Makkari gasped, "and cannot be estimated, as no precise account of them was kept in the treasury books." The caliph and the *nasi* died without equal among their contemporaries.

In the remarkable run of his life, 'Abd al-Rahman III can have had few profound regrets. Nevertheless, there had been one exception to the victories in the field that covered his regime with glory. Leading one of the largest expeditions yet assembled deep into the kingdom of Leon in 939, the caliph exposed his flanks to an ambush in mountainous terrain. His army was decimated by King Ramiro II's troops at a place called "the Ditch" (*al-Khandaq; Alhandega* in Spanish), and the caliph only managed to escape capture by making a frantic gallop from the field. After the debacle at *al-Khandaq*, 'Abd al-Rahman never again led armies into battle.[37] The northern statelets posed no significant offensive threat as yet to the caliphate, but *al-Khandaq* was an omen.

15

Disequilibrium, Pelayo's Revenge

AS THE tenth century ended, two European civilizations occupied the continent—one Muslim, one Christian. As Andalusis waited in 976 for their new caliph to be announced from the *minbars* of a thousand mosques, none among them, save perhaps a few embittered Christian visionaries, envisaged the imminence of a future in which these two social orders were no longer fated to exist side by side. Little had happened to alter the balance of the struggle between the two

True Faiths since the two major Holy Wars of the eighth century. In the version of history sacralized in Christendom, Europe had been saved in 732 by Charles the Hammer and his Franks, who turned back the demonic Saracen onslaught. In Islam's version of that baleful week in October, the *Balat al-Shuhada* ("Path of the Martyrs") merely interrupted temporarily the momentum of a *jihad* that would have proved irrepressible but for civil wars racking the *Dar al-Islam*. As for the Carolingian crusade of 778, Muslim chroniclers ceded the mythologizing of Christendom's first Holy War against Islam to the perpetrators themselves. Charlemagne's embarrassment before the walls of Zaragoza and his loss of the rear guard in the Pyrenees were reversals that Turoldus spun into the shining triumphs of the aristocratic and martial European spirit. In al-Masudi's *Fields of Gold*, by contrast, the coming of the barbarous Franks had no significance other than to cause a general tightening-up of Andalusia's borders.[1]

Nearly 270 years had passed since the pivotal Battle of Poitiers. More than 250 years had gone by since the founding of Carolingian Frankland and Umayyad Hispania—249 years, to be exact, since Pippin the Short had formally ended the Merovingian monarchy in 751. Precisely 244 years had intervened since 'Abd al-Rahman I, "the Immigrant," installed himself in the Cordoba *alcazar* in 756 as hereditary ruler of a de facto kingdom independent of the Abbasid Caliphate. By early in the ninth century, it became increasingly apparent that Muslim Europe and Christian Europe were mutually checkmated at the Pyrenees. The last real effort at *jihad* had come from Hisham I, when he ordered two large armies into Francia in 793. The Carolingian siege and eventual capture of Barcelona in 801 pushed the Spanish March to its limits. In the seventy years after Poitiers, the Frankish war machine grew in size and efficiency until it was more or less unbeatable in the field. But the empire built by the king of the Franks and the Roman emperor was more a fighting machine than a society, a fraternity of the saddle-ready that slaughtered and robbed in the expiatory names of saints and divinities. Its economy was still little better than Late Neolithic when Charlemagne expired at Aachen in 814.

The state the Umayyads built tended to delegate national defense to slaves and the hired help, with sometimes-unimpressive results in the field. But *al-Andalus*, notwithstanding its fractious mixture of Arabs, Berbers, Goths, Hispanics, and Jews, and the splintering cordilleras, was an intact creation by the end of the tenth century. By contrast, the seams of Charlemagne's Europe—once it was deprived of its animating, aging genius—began to loosen badly. The center failed to hold and the avaricious parts turned on one another while even more fierce Scandinavian and Slavic intruders tested their defenses and ravaged the countryside.[2] If anything, the situation in 976 portended a long, antipodal continuity of the two Europes—one secure in its defenses, religiously tolerant, and maturing in cultural and scientific sophistication; the other an arena of unceasing warfare in which superstition passed for religion and the flame of knowledge sputtered weakly.

When al-Hakam II al-Mustansir died in October 976, the assiduous patron of learning and the arts had given his country fifteen years of stable government and sustained economic growth that augured an eleventh century no less brilliant than the expiring tenth. Exports leaving the great, high-walled port of Almeria on the Mediterranean rose year after year: olive oil, figs, leather goods, raisins, almonds, and timber—not to omit wine sent to the Christian North. Ghanaian gold to buy those products flowed into *al-Andalus*, part of it minted for the gold dinar that served as the caliphate's standard currency. Of *al-Andalus*'s six million inhabitants, more than seventy percent were Muslim. Cordoba boasted ninety thousand denizens, and more people lived in Zaragoza, with a census of twenty-eight thousand, than in any of the cities of the Christian West. The frontiers were mostly secure, although the Duero Valley, where the scrappy counts and kinglets of Galicia, Castile, Asturias, and Leon sometimes tried to push their borders southward, bore watching. Also worrisome were the expansions of dogged Christians in the hardscrabble far side of the Muslim *thagr* (line of control)—*repoblacion*, as the Spanish called it.[3] The Upper March had been strengthened with a new military command at Medinaceli, an old Roman hill town at the axis of the main roads into the Ebro Valley and the Upper Duero.

Yet between 976 and 1009, a span of a fateful generation, the decline of Umayyad *al-Andalus* took hold. Caliph Al-Hakam II, so attentive to the details of governing and solicitous of his people's welfare, had behaved like a sentimental father rather than as an astute dynast in choosing his heir. Hisham, a delicate boy of twelve and an innocent in warfare and statecraft, was deemed temperamentally unsuited to serve as caliph by all within the inner circle of power—especially so by the cabal headed by the *hajib* (chancellor), who cynically engineered Hisham's ascension in order to preserve his own power. The palace Slavs who proposed the deceased caliph's brother, al-Mughira, as the capable substitute and mistakenly believed they had the assent of the *hajib*, were outmaneuvered. Ja'far ibn 'Uthman ibn al-Mushafi, the *hajib*, seized the moment to rule through a puppet. Ordering the Slavs sequestered by a detachment of soldiers, the chancellor entrusted the dirty work of the assassination of al-Hakam's brother to a quick-witted subaltern known to be free of scruples.

The man al-Mushafi chose returned quickly from the intended victim's house shaken. Understandably, the assassin had hesitated in the presence of al-Hakam's brother. Killing an Umayyad prince in line for the throne was the gravest of crimes. "If you don't like the commission, I will send another to execute it," the chancellor snapped when he heard his agent's misgivings. Cordovans, told of the accidental death of the caliph's brother, were not slow to hear that al-Mughira had been strangled by Muhammad ibn Abi Amir, an ambitious servant of the state whose ancestor had fought with Tariq at the Battle of Guadalete. Muhammad ibn Abi Amir was about thirty, handsome, golden-voiced, a gifted intriguer, and very likely the lover of the deceased caliph's favorite wife, Subh the Navarrese. (Al-Hakam II was rumored to have had bisexual preferences.) From a position as steward of the favorite's finances, Ibn Abi Amir rose to become the comptroller-general of finances for the caliphate's African army in Morocco. With the blood of an Umayyad prince on his hands, he understood that there was no room for error in the game of power into which he had entered.[4]

Presented to his people in late October 976 as Caliph Hisham II, the teenager afterward was almost never seen outside *Madinat al-Zahra*, except to deliver the Friday prayer in the Great Mosque. The conscientious Slav eunuchs were sent away. Power resided with the unscrupulous chancellor and the efficient Muhammad ibn Abi Amir, now appointed to the council of *vizirs*. Theirs was an inherently fragile arrangement, unlikely to survive the Umayyad clan's resentment of the caliph's enforced impotence and the people's discontent with a sham government's rampant nepotism. The chancellor's prospects for political survival darkened, and Ibn Abi Amir's anxiety about keeping his own head inspired a risky scheme for a military diversion. Reports of Christian border raids served as justification for an invasion of the north. Cordovans watched a quickly assembled but well-equipped expedition gallop off for Leon under the command of Ibn Abi Amir, who had never commanded troops or even seen action. Leon's monarchy was troubled at the time, its nobles more practiced at internecine slaughter than at organized defense. Muhammad ibn Abi Amir returned in Holy War triumph, loaded with booty from the ruins of Salamanca. The chancellor rewarded his accomplice with the chieftaincy of the military police, *wali* of the *shurta*.

The police chief turned *al-Andalus* into a dictatorship. The palace Slavs were gone, the army's officer corps purged of Umayyad loyalists, the elite cavalry and infantry units filled with the Sanhaja Berbers steadily imported by the police chief. The novice general conducted several more lightning campaigns against the petty northern kingdoms, gilding an already-formidable reputation as a military commander. The caliphate's ranking military officer, Ghalib ibn 'Abd al-Rahman, was a *siqlabi* veteran of numerous campaigns and commander of the Upper March at supreme military headquarters in Medinaceli. Ibn Abi Amir used flattery and generosity to disarm whatever institutional concerns the general might have had. Better still, he married the general's daughter. The nuptials were celebrated on New Year's Day, 977, in *Madinat al-Zahra* in Hisham II's presence, "with unusual pomp and magnificence," as described by an observer.[5] As guardian of public order and law, Ibn Abi Amir exploited his access to the caliph to convey privileged information, to seek the Commander of the Faithful's opinions, or to present small gifts. Imprisoned in the magnificent palace and pitifully grateful for the police chief's attention, Hisham II was persuaded that the chancellor's departure would be in everyone's best interests. His seal upon the chief's decree removed Chancellor al-Mushafi from office and sent him to prison and death. Ibn Abi Amir was invested with the *khil'ah* ("dress of honor") by his caliph, whom he now served as *hajib*. By 981, five years after Muhammad ibn Abi Amir strangled the caliph's uncle, his and the caliphate's transformation were complete, the caliphate now a shadow of its former, tolerant self.

"Meanwhile [Abi Amir] filled the functions of his offices in so satisfactory a manner that the citizens of Cordoba had no reason to regret the loss of their former governors and magistrates," Ahmed ibn Mohammed al-Makkari, the chatty seventeenth-century Arab historian, writes of this fabulous adventurer who might be described as the Andalusian Napoleon. The new *hajib* brought order to the great city. The administration of justice was swift and unvexed by nuance under the literalism of Malikite jurisprudence.[6] The sometimes-dangerous denizens of *al-Rabad*, the suburb on the Guadalquivir's left bank, became unexceptionally law-abiding. "All this he accomplished with the help of [General] Ghalib," al-Makkari adds. His father-in-law was the *hajib*'s next target. General Ghalib commanded the best units of the traditional army at Medinaceli, many of whose officers belonged to the first families of the Conquest or were descended from the Umayyads of the Falcon's era. His son-in-law's new army of rough-and-ready Sanhaja and Zanata Berbers, new to the refined ways of the Andalusis, all too obviously threatened to replace the last pillar of the old order. The wily old general attempted to trump the *hajib* in an alliance with the rulers of Castile and Navarra.

Ghalib faced his son-in-law with the help of several thousand Christian troops commanded by King Sancho II of Narvarra's son and the promise of additional support from the count of Castile, Garcia Fernandez. This Christian-Muslim battlefield combination was by no means the first ('Abd al-Rahman III had lent Sancho the Fat an army to regain the throne of Navarra), nor was it to be unusual in the future. The bloodletting near Medinaceli in July 981 was another of those turning points in history whose long-term consequences only became evident to a later generation. Muhammad ibn Abi Amir led his Berbers to a smashing victory in the name of the Prophet. The heir to the Navarrese throne died fighting, and General Ghalib surrendered to his son-in-law and was never seen again. Cordovans received their deliverer with panegyrics and festivities. Hisham dutifully bestowed the suggested title by which history has ever since known Muhammad ibn Abi Amir. He became *al-Mansur* (*Almazor* in Spanish)—Muhammad "the Victorious." In twenty-two years of de facto and formal rule, al-Mansur would conduct fifty-two military campaigns in person—as many as Charlemagne in about half the time. Proclamations of *jihad* became routine, as did the tax increases to pay for them.[7]

Al-Mansur's new order offered war, morality, and prosperity. He won virtually every campaign, returning with aristocratic hostages for ransom, baggage wagons crammed with valuables, and harem supplies. His social policies were applauded and he made a great show of religious piety, consulting his Qur'an ostentatiously before going into battle. The spirit of intellectual inquiry symbolized by al-Hakam II's great public library of four hundred thousand volumes faded away. Ten thousand supposedly questionable books were removed from the shelves and publicly burned. The opinions of *fuqaha* and *ulamas* were regularly recalled to the citizenry to encourage proper Muslim conduct. Moral slackness in public was firmly discouraged and punished. Little or no explanation was thought necessary of the disappearance of caliphal institutions, prominent Umayyas, long-tenured servants of the regime, and all possible rivals to power. Andalusis were told that their caliph's lack of visibility was due to Hisham's intense devotion to Qur'anic study and prayer and the bibliophilic compulsions inherited from his father. The people of *al-Andalus* surrendered virtually all the traditional restraints on power—one-man rule replaced divinely sanctioned authority. Not only was the lonely bachelor Hisham made to vanish, Muhammad the Victorious upstaged *Madinat al-Zahra* with an even grander palace complex of his own on the other side of Cordoba called *Madinat al-Zahira*. Believers were ordered to offer up a prayer in his name "after the usual one for the Caliph Hisham."[8]

As impressive as al-Mansur's military and political triumphs were, they proved eventually to be fatally counterproductive. His success masked a fundamental weakness in the long-term soundness of the Andalusian body politic that would emerge with a paralyzing suddenness when his successors stumbled on the high wire of tyranny. Meantime, the ruling classes in the four or five Christian kingdoms along the Ebro and the Duero were kept perpetually off balance and divided among themselves. On the surface, it seemed that all was well. Berber cavalry blazed across the land, laying waste to towns and fields, annihilating armed resistance, transporting tens of thousands into harems and captivity for ransom, exacting tribute and submission from the kings and counts of Leon-Castile, Aragon, Navarra, and Catalunya. Barcelona, the prize acquisition of the Carolingian Spanish March, was retaken in 981 by al-Mansur after 180 years of Christian occupation. The revolt of Sancho Garcia of Castile against his father in 997 was typical of the mischief instigated among the infidel nobility by al-Mansur's agents. Distracted by his family problems, the aged Count Garcia Fernandez lost his army and his life in a hurried encounter with al-Mansur and his invading Berbers.

What befell the defeated, disoriented Castilians next in the late summer of 997 was an outrage that was to register in Spanish memories for a millennium. Riding westward in a wide circuit of fire and destruction through the peninsula's upper end into Galicia, the Victorious and his Berbers fell upon the third holiest city in Catholic Christendom. When they rode out of Santiago de Compostela on August 10, only the bones of St. James remained unmolested beneath the smoldering devastation.[9]

Given the unrelenting viciousness of al-Mansur's attacks in the North, it was hardly surprising that the counts and kings of the region began to respond collectively to a degree. The uncustomary solidarity of the Catholic sovereigns at the battle of Pena de Cervera signaled a learning curve that was sharpening against the Muslim whetstone. Three summers after the destruction of Santiago de Compostela, the nobility of the North steeled themselves against one of the largest Muslim incursions of record. Al-Mansur had brought over new North Africans to double his forces at Medinaceli. Rebel son Sancho Garcia of Castile stood with his men beside those of Leon's King Alfonso V, together with Navarra's Garcia Sanchez II, pinned with the sobriquet "the Cowardly." Al-Mansur kept his record of brilliant wins at Pena de Cervera, pulverizing the three infidel armies and charging on to Burgos to destroy that city's Romanesque cathedral. This was the next-to-last victory. Muhammad ibn Abi Amir al-Mansur, *hajib* of *al-Andalus* and founder of the Amirid dictatorship, died of unspecified causes in the spring of 1002 as he returned to Medinaceli from campaigning in Castile's La Rioja. His men buried him at Medinaceli, where his remains still lie. His Andalusis bitterly mourned him in 'Abd al-Rahman's Great Mosque, whose size al-Mansur had nearly doubled with an extension illumined by lamps cast from the melted bells of Burgos Cathedral.

To those who asked themselves the question, the answer was that the net gains of dictatorship were not so reassuring. By fighting the Christians on their own ground, some argued that Andalusis had been spared fighting them at home. On the other hand, endless wars of offense began to produce opposite results as the small Catholic kingdoms reluctantly collaborated and improved their fighting tactics. After more than two decades of hostilities, not only had the borders remained much the same but the number of Christian emigrants to the contested regions had increased greatly.[10] If it seemed mysterious at first that neither al-Mansur nor his oldest son and successor attempted to resettle indigenous Muslims or Berber veterans in the wide spaces south of the Sierra de Guadarama, the probable reasons were the climatic extremes of rain, bitter cold, aridity, and searing heat in the regions above the Duero that no Berber would find congenial. The contrast of six million people versus one million in the North was impressive, but *al-Andalus* boasted no surplus of Muslims to induce to become pioneers for the Duero borderlands. No doubt a *jihad* in the caliph's name, well funded and mobilized by *ulamas,* could have repopulated portions of the borderlands. Such a policy would have facilitated resettlement, but it would hardly have been politically astute in a realm in which most people were pleased with themselves and felt little appetite for *jihads*.

Al-Mansur's able son succeeded him as *hajib*, an office that was now understood to be hereditary, in the same manner as the Merovingian palace mayoralty became Pippinid family property. 'Abd al-Malik al-Muzaffar ibn al-Mansur carried on his father's policy of heavy taxation to maintain a Berber-dominated military establishment that he used to lay waste to the kingdoms of the North in almost perpetual *jihad*. Al-Muzaffar ("the Conqueror") maintained the fiction of caliphal deference. His younger half-brother possessed the family aptitude for war and served as al-Muzaffar's second in command. The two brothers gave every evidence of mutual respect for one another and, more important, an appreciation for their father's calculus for managing a popular dictatorship: efficiency, religion, and war. When "the Conqueror" died suddenly in the prime of life, six years after taking power, strong suspicions of foul play abounded, suggesting that 'Abd al-Malik had died of an apple sliced with the poisoned blade of his brother's knife.[11] Hisham II immediately appointed the younger brother the third Amirid *hajib*. 'Abd al-Rahman al-Sanchol's pedigree was significantly curious. He was the grandson of the king of Navarra, who had presented his daughter in tribute to al-Mansur, who married her as a Muslim. *Sanchuelo*—"Little Sancho," as he was familiarly called—was a fine example of the fusing of faith and race long under way even as Muslims and Christians geared up on the Iberian peninsula for the series of decisive battles that would determine ownership of the majority shares in world history.

The new *hajib* performed well in battle but with fatal unwisdom in politics. With unmitigated gall, Sanchuelo prised the caliphal succession from the limp hand of the forty-five-year-old Hisham II, who designated him heir to the throne of the Umayyads. What a troubled witness called "a very solemn ceremony" transpired in the *Madinat al-Zahra* before a cowed assembly of notables in the dead of winter in 1008. What thoughts may have disturbed the caliph's mind that November day as he signed his own death warrant and terminated 240-odd years of Umayyad hegemony in *al-Andalus* are unknown. Sanchuelo kissed his cipher sovereign's ring after Hisham read the extraordinary assigned script. "After searching, therefore, high ranks as well as low," intoned Hisham from Sanchuelo's document, "the Caliph Hisham has found none more deserving to be appointed his successor or to become the heir of the Caliphate after his death, than the trustworthy, honest and beloved . . . son of Ibn Abi Amir."[12] Mu'awiya, the first Umayyad caliph, had seized power from the Prophet's cousin and son-in-law, Ali, the sole legitimate claimant in Shi'ite eyes to the mantle of the Messenger. But Mu'awiya was a Quraysh, the supertribe in Muhammad's Mecca. He was the second cousin of 'Uthman, the third *rashidun* Commander of the Faithful. The Amirids were mere upstarts—masterful warriors and politicians though they were. They lacked even a scintilla of legitimizing historical connection to the Prophet's family. Sanchuelo had fatally overreached.

The new *hajib* assumed that another successful sweep through the Christian North would cement his authority with the populace. The days of the old army at Medinaceli appeared to be numbered, as were those of the much-diminished cadres of aristocratic or old-line functionaries. He augmented the power and prestige of the Berbers to new heights. Believing himself secure in his new dignity, Sanchuelo departed with his Berbers for the Duero.

⸬

The Umayyad Caliphate of *al-Andalus* ends like silent film footage in a runaway old projector. Jerky actions by protagonists leading or fleeing a cast of thousands flit past. Scenes of triumph and tumult alternate with a suddenness fatal to an understanding of original plot line. Flickering images disappear to snapping sounds and leave the screen of history momentarily blank. On the night of February 15, 1009, just as Sanchuelo and his army crossed into Castile, an audacious young Umayyad aristocrat whose family had been persecuted by al-Mansur gave the signal for which his followers had been waiting. This was more than rebellion. It was revolution. The large crowd, most of whose leaders belonged to the Arab well-born, stormed out of Cordoba for the *Madinat al-Zahra*, where, encountering barely token resistance from the *saqaliba* sentinels, it unceremoniously forced a cornered Hisham II to abdicate in favor of the young, aristocratic ringleader. An almost-contemporaneous account of these developments describes Hisham as behaving, for once, with stoic dignity as the mob acclaimed a new caliph. The new caliph was Muhammad ibn Hisham ibn 'Abd al-Jabbar, etc., whose name was longer than his nine-month tenure on the throne. A grandson of 'Abd al-Rahman III, Muhammad proclaimed himself Caliph Muhammad II al-Mahdi ("the Expected One"). As his second decision of that singular night, he countenanced the destruction of *Madinat al-Zahira*, the ostentatious preserve of the Amirids outside Cordoba—an act of pillage and obliteration so thorough that no trace of the complex survives today outside Cordoba.[13]

When Sanchuelo reversed course for the capital after news of the uprising, he found the new caliph's surprisingly large force of *shurta*, palace *saqaliba*, and citizen-soldiers blocking the approach to Cordoba. The wily Berbers gauged the situation and left al-Mansur's impetuous son to the murderous care of his adversary's troops. They slaughtered Sanchuelo on the spot, extinguishing the upstart Amirids, who had managed a run of thirty-two years. Their political theory was inherently toxic to themselves and the state they abused, a perfect illustration of the axiom that unchecked power corrupts absolutely. But instead of finding himself in the enviable position of winner, Muhammad "the Expected One" had to throw himself into a coalition beyond his capacity to manage. He needed the Berber army to consolidate his power and project military strength on the frontiers. Not only did his core of Umayyad supporters hate the North Africans, but Cordoba's common people resented them as alien mercenaries. The officers of the old army at Medinaceli were also adamant. How many years had faithful Slav soldiers watched and seethed as the Berbers received preference? Medinaceli pledged to uphold the new regime if the men from the Maghreb were marginalized. After some three months of worsening relations and officially sanctioned anti-Berber discrimination in Cordoba, Muhammad II ordered the Berbers out of the city in June 1009.[14]

Aggrieved and denied the security and income of caliphal patronage, the Berbers glowered in their tents at Calatrava, a Praetorian guard without an emperor. And, like any Praetorian guard, they were ready to back a replacement for an inconvenient ruler. The new Caliph Muhammad's cousin, one Sulayman, offered himself to the Berbers. With Berber allegiance pledged to cousin Sulayman—self-anointed as Sulayman *al-Musta'in* ("the One Who Is Aided")—both caliphal claimants reached for Christian manpower: the Medinaceli army and the Catalonians behind Muhammad the Expected One; the Berbers and the Castilians behind Sulayman the One Who Is Aided. Muhammad racked up a surprising defeat of his cousin, only to have the results nullified months afterward when Sulayman's Berbers smashed Muhammad's mixed army of citizen-soldiers, professional military, and mercenaries a few miles outside Cordoba in the winter of 1009. Sulayman celebrated victory in the Falcon's *qasr* with

Count Sancho Garcia of Castile standing by, demanding his compensa-
tion. Muhammad II retreated to Toledo, regrouped with the help of the
Catalans, and soon surprised Sulayman and his Berbers near Cordoba.[15]

The fortunes of both caliphs seesawed until the summer of 1010.
Reoccupying the capital after defeating Sulayman's troops, Muhammad
reinstalled himself in *Madinat al-Zahra*, only to see his influence slip away.
His exasperated plebeian supporters blamed him for the aggrandized
role of the aristocratic Medinaceli officers. Meanwhile, starvation and
disease wracked the city as his cousin Sulayman's Berbers and Castilian
auxiliaries surrounded Cordoba and tightened the noose. In a desperate
sleight-of-hand to retain the tolerance of the people, Muhammad II
renounced his title and plucked Hisham II from hiding to restore this
spectral figure to his former station—a maneuver that failed abysmally.
The enraged Cordovans killed him. The abused Hisham tried to break
Sulayman's siege with generous offers of gold to the Castilian counts, but
the besiegers expected to have more than enough treasure once the
starved Cordovans succumbed. When the city gates finally opened to
admit Sulayman and his Berbers, the "ornament of the world" had held
out through famine and plague for three brutal years, from 1010 to April
20, 1013. "A general massacre ensued," al-Makkari records. The Berbers
sacked the city, violated the women, pillaged and destroyed the homes of
the wealthy, and razed Cordoba's grand buildings—though, of course,
sparing the Great Mosque. They burned and leveled the Falcon's Rusafa,
and al-Hakam's wondrous library must have disappeared at this time.
Hisham was executed secretly, and no source reveals the manner in which
his arrested, manipulated life ended.[16]

The thread of legitimacy was broken, and replacement caliphs came
thick and fast. Sulayman's comeuppance came in the person of a Berber
wali from Ceuta, who arrived with an African army pledged to avenge
Hisham's murder. Sulayman was defeated in a sharp encounter south of
the capital. The Ceutan *wali* publicly decapitated him in mid-July of 1016.
Sulayman's executioner himself was soon executed, to be followed by
flickering images of a fourth and fifth 'Abd al-Rahman, a Muhammad
III, and, finally, a third Hisham (a genuine Umayyad), who reigned more
or less in absentia from 1027 until his enforced abdication in 1031. On

November 30 of that year, Cordoba's governing council formally abolished Andalusia's Umayyad Caliphate. The last frame on the reel had run. Still Europe's most splendid metropolis, the violated and diminished capital of a moribund empire proclaimed itself a self-governing polity, something like an oligarchical republic. The three years during which Muhammad and Sulayman had tried to rule *al-Andalus* were enough to alter irreversibly the political structure of Muslim Iberia.[17]

Since the power of the central government had waned after Sanchuelo's elimination, much of the national real estate was claimed by local Arab clans, *muwalladun* governors, *saqaliba* commanders, Berber tribes, and assorted adventurers. Sulayman had formalized these irregular or illegitimate developments so as to reward his legions of Sanhaja and Zanata Berbers and placate powerful enemies. As a result, Granada fell to the Zirids, a branch of the Sanhaja Berbers, while the new Berber clan that controlled Toledo presided over a brilliant period of cultural and architectural development. Zaragoza's long-sought autonomy was sealed under the Berbers of the Huddid clan.[18] The formal dissolution of the Umayyad Caliphate in 1031 merely recognized in law the city-state reality of an Andalusia without the Umayyads, a tesselated political landscape devoid of a core.

❖

A new era stumbled on stage, that of the *ta'ifas*, leaders of city-states in a vacuum. They were the "party kings" or "petty kings" (*muluk al-tawaif* or *reyes de ta'ifas*) of Toledo, Badajoz, Sevilla, Granada, Valencia, Zaragoza, and more than a dozen other locales. It would be a comparatively brief age of vibrant cultural innovation and political dysfunction.[19] As the eleventh century came to pass, an altered Cordoba bled talent as well as blood. Some of its most productive and cultured citizens departed for new beginnings, seeking either security in quiet places or arenas where their talents would be readily recognized.

Members of the Naghrela family were among the prominent émigrés. The Naghrelas of Cordoba went back generations: physicians, rabbis, businessmen, and advisers to the court. They were already an old Hispanic family when the Visigoths had arrived, their lineage reaching back to the ancient Levites of the Temple of Jerusalem. They had been part of the brilliant circle that gathered to read poetry and discuss ideas in the salon of 'Abd al-Rahman III's minister and ambassador, Hasdai ibn Shaprut. The head of the family, Isma'il (Samuel ha-Nagid) ibn Naghrela, also known as Samuel ibn Naghrela (993–1066), was *sui generis*. Added to the customary medical, philosophical, political, and literary credentials of a Golden Age paladin were Samuel ibn Naghrela's military achievements, which would compare not unfavorably with those of the *Cíd*, the fabulous knight of the *Reconquista* who fought for both sides and inspired Catholic Spain's Roland-song, *Cantar de Mio Cid*. He served as an adviser to the court of one of the last would-be Umayyad caliphs before the dynasty's extinction.

After political chaos and Berber violence terminated the caliphate in 1031, Samuel and his family relocated themselves and the family spice-import business to Malaga. They were notably proud of themselves, and the exquisitely educated, professionally accomplished Samuel especially so. Claiming descent from King David, he had much of which to be proud. Politics was second nature to Samuel, and the Sanhaja Berber *ta'ifa* of Granada welcomed the services of the forty-year-old physician. These were early days in that city's history. The ruling family, the Zirids, had just begun to shape Granada's magnificent architectural landscape. The brick fortress atop Sabika Hill was only a rudimentary anticipation of the Alhambra of fable and architectural perfection—the incomparable *al-qal'a al-hamra* ("red citadel"), which Granada's next dynasty, the Nasrids, would erect over several family generations in the thirteenth century.[20]

Samuel ibn Naghrela, a Jew, became Granada's *hajib* in 1037 after deft management of the winning older brother's campaign for the Zirid throne. The next year, the *nagid* (prince) commanded young King Badis ibn Habbus's army in the field to repel the Muslim army of the *ta'ifa* king of Almeria, the impressively walled port city at the eastern end of *al-Andalus*. The Almerians were badly trounced at a place called Alfuente. Their king died fighting, his *hajib* was beheaded in Granada, and a large indemnity was exacted from Almeria. Even in ethnically diverse Andalusia, a Jew at the head of an army of Believers was thought somewhat irregular by Muslims on the winning side and an insult to the Qur'an by the losers and their sympathizers. To hear the "new David's" version of events, as set to poetry in rhymed Hebrew after the battle by Samuel himself, Alfuente was a vendetta centered on Samuel:

> [T]hey felt resentment over my high rank,
> Resolved to see me overthrown at once;
> For how (they said) can aliens like these
> be privileged over Muslim folk
> And act like kings legitimate?

The Almerians surely went to war from motives other than his prime ministership, but vanity never ceases to arouse envy and hatred. "I am," said Ibn Naghrela, "the David of my age." Ibn Hayyan, the major historian of the period, paid Samuel the Nagid (as he became better known) a memorable backhanded compliment. "This cursed man was a superior man," he conceded, "although God did not inform him of the right religion."[21]

Granada prospered under Samuel ibn Naghrela in the mid-eleventh century. He was the model for the quintessential "rabbi-courtier"—invaluable to his superior because of intelligence, expertise, and material resources, but he was only as powerful as his protector allowed. His achievements would have ensured legendary status, but Samuel the Nagid added to them a new genre of poetry. There had already been novel applications of Arabic rhyme and meter to Hebrew verse in Hasdai ibn Shaprut's salon of rarefied Sephardic and Muslim literati in Cordoba in the mid-tenth century. Rather like those late-twentieth-century African-American lyricists who jazzed Gospel music, these Sephardim skirted the profane with their wine-women-and-song motifs. Samuel the Nagid pressed the experiment in his Granada palace on Sabika Hill. Before the license taken by him and his experimenters, Hebrew was the austere, dignified language of the synagogue. A typical verse of the Nagid's called attention to itself in a Hebrew that used Arab meter and rhyme for the first time in the history of that sacred language:

> Friend, lead me through the vineyards, give me wine
> And to the very brim shall joy be mine;

Perchance the love you pledge me with each cup
May rout the troops around my care's ensign.[22]

"For the first time in a thousand years," Maria Menocal lyricizes in her luminous *The Ornament of the World*, "Hebrew was brought out of the confines of the synagogue and made as versatile as the Arabic that was the native language of the Andalusian Jewish community."[23]

There was never quite a Christian parallel to the political and cultural symbiosis achieved between Arabs and Jews. There were few Gentiles whose professional accomplishments placed them near the center of power in *al-Andalus* in the manner of the elite Sephardim around Hasdai ibn Shaprut and his friends Solomon ibn Gabirol (Avicebron) and Dunash ben Labrat, philosopher and poet, respectively. Yet just as the Nagid's career was one of spectacular rise, it was also illustrative of spectacular descent, for there were dangerous limits to the symbiosis of Islam and Israel. Not only did the touted *convivencia* have its flaws, its relative success contained within it the seeds of its own destruction. Derived power in a time of growing factionalism invited scapegoating. In *The Book of Tradition*, Abraham ibn Daud, the twelfth-century historian of Sefarad, understandably judged that the Granadan *hajib* had been "good for Israel in Spain." But the truth of Daud's observation inspired spilling of ink in caustic personal reproach symptomatic of much deeper tensions by the Nagid's Muslim contemporaries Ibn Hazm and Abu Ishaq (the former a fellow Cordovan exile of the same age, the latter a defeated rival at court).[24]

Muhammad ibn Sa'id ibn Hazm (994–1064) was hardly a mediocrity like Abu Ishaq, belonging as he did to one of the foremost Arab families of *al-Andalus* and possessed of one of the finest intellects of Muslim Iberia. Ibn Hazm wrote prolifically on theology and law, an *oeuvre* distinguished for its comprehensiveness but somewhat marred by vindictive tendentiousness. "On the Inconsistencies of the Four Gospels" (*Al-Fasl fi al-milal*), his hair-splitting deconstruction of Christian dogma, concluded on the splenetic note that "the Christian community is altogether vile." When Ibn Hazm and Samuel ibn Naghrela crossed forensic swords as admired symbols of their respective causes, both were living in exile.

Both men were then in their mid-thirties; both were paragons of Andalusian high culture; both played high-stakes politics as kingmakers (Ibn Hazm was *hajib* during the brief Umayyad restoration of 'Abd al-Rahman V); and, in singular similarity, both were major literary innovators. *The Ring of the Dove* (*Tawq al-Hamama*), a blend of sensibilities nurtured by a harem education in his youth and the prudery of a scholar's Qur'anic ideals, was Ibn Hazm's masterpiece of courtly love—love Platonic, exquisite but unrequited, adulatory yet ennobling.[25] Europe's troubadours imbibed the *Dove* like a fine wine.

But no love was lost between the philosopher and the Granadan David. A Muslim thinker of Ibn Hazm's stature was not pleased to find his writings matched by those of an equally opinionated Jewish intellectual who ventured a critique of the contradictions of the Qur'an in much the same spirit as Ibn Hazm's of the Bible. Then, too, whereas the Nagid thrived in the shifting sands of *ta'ifa* politics, the Muslim theologian and jurist bewailed the parochialism that thwarted the restoration of his beloved caliphate. That Granada had played a part in the defeat of 'Abd al-Rahman V's bid to return to Cordoba merely exacerbated Ibn Hazm's ill will, even though his own imprisonment in Granada occurred before the Nagid became its chief minister. Ibn Hazm made certain that his bilious advice to the city-state's ruler about his arrogant minister was widely known. The king should "stay away from these impure, evil-smelling, unclean people upon whom God has inflicted curse and malediction."[26] When Ibn Hazm died in his family retreat near Sevilla in 1064, the Nagid had two years more in which to enjoy acclaimed success and prosperity in Granada.

Abu Ishaq outlived the Nagid by just a year, but before dying he composed a rant against the Jews of Granada and Ibn Naghrela in particular. The power and conspicuous wealth of the Naghrelas and Jews in general had grown considerably in a city whose Jewish population was large. Nevertheless, Ibn Hazm's old aspersions were still remembered in the city. A great wrong had been done Islam, Abu Ishaq charged. "Through [the Nagid] the Jews have become great and proud and arrogant—they, who were among the most abject . . . and how many a worthy Muslim humbly obeys the vilest ape among these miscreants." Ibn Hazm and

Abu Ishaq's writings must surely have helped incite the Muslim and Mozarab populace against Joseph ibn Naghrela, the Nagid's much less adroit son and successor. When Joseph's ploy to block Sevilla from annexing Granada by an alliance with Almeria (and the establishment there of a Sephardic principality) became known, prejudice and politics fused disastrously. His assassination and the pogrom that murdered hundreds of Granada's Jews in 1067 marked the beginning of the end of the Golden Age of Sefarad.

⁂

As political and military power became fragmented in *al-Andalus*, an opposite phenomenon finally began to materialize north of the rivers. On October 18, 1035, the most powerful of the northern Catholic rulers died. The caliphate had been abolished four years before sixty-five-year-old Sancho III *el Mayor* ("the Greater") of Navarra received the last rites. The king of Navarra had accomplished what none of his fellow rulers had ever imagined possible, and indeed, several had no desire to see happen. Through the jigsaw of nuptial politics and the wielding of a stout broadsword, King Sancho III had united all but two of the significant counties above the Duero and the Ebro under the crown of Navarra. The nobles of Aragon, Castile, and Leon were Sancho's vassals; only gray, wet Galicia and temperate Catalunya were outside his ring of feudatories. While the almost interchangeable Alfonsos and Garcias, Fernandezes and Ramirezes of the North passed the decades fighting among themselves, with the frequent instigation of Muslim agents, the king of Navarra had exploited the Andalusis' political distress to expand his frontier to the caliphate's border.

Sancho the Greater's political creation might have advanced the *Reconquista* by almost a century, a united Christian realm positioned to march against the collapsed *al-Andalus*. Looking back, Spanish historians regretted 1035 as the year of an impossible possibility. Sancho the Greater's testament disassembled the grand polity that he had never understood as anything other than his personal property. Leon, Castile, Aragon, and Navarra were bequeathed to Sancho's four sons. The old cycle of fratricide, parochial agendas, and endogamous assassinations resumed. Sancho's will bequeathed the county of Leon to the son most like himself in ruthless calculation—Ferdinand, the second oldest, who lost no time eliminating his brother royals. He slew Ramiro of Aragon and Garcia of Navarra and fused Leon and Castile to make himself king of Leon-Castile (1037–65) and "high king" of the North.[27]

Ferdinand I's breathtaking geopolitical ambitions were to have great significance. He warred against the Badajoz *ta'ifa* in Portugal (eventually capturing Coimbra, expelling its Muslims, and conquering two-fifths of that country). Almost simultaneously, he fought the Navarrese and forced the Zaragozans to pay protection money (*paria*). He humiliated the Valencians on the battlefield after a bold southern sweep in alliance with Toledo's risk-taking king or *amir*. Toledo's balance-of-power strategy was one of buying off the Christian kings and using their armies to advance the city-state's territorial ambitions. Still, the view from Toledo grew ever more threatening as Ferdinand's own territorial ambitions became more obvious. The view from the South was even more disconcerting for the Toledans. Sevilla had emerged as the strongest of the city-states after the fall of the Umayyad Caliphate, swallowing up most of the others in the lower Guadalquivir Valley by the 1060s. Sevilla's ruling Arab clan, the Banu Abbad, built its power on the son of the city's chief *qadi*, one 'Abbad *al-Mu'tadid* ("the Supporter"), who earned a reputation for cruelty in an arena crowded with competitors for the distinction.[28] Balked in his designs on Granada, Sevilla's *amir* had devoted himself to on-and-off warfare with just about every other *ta'ifa,* but with the primary ambition of conquering Toledo.

In 'Abd al-Rahman III's era, only ninety years earlier, northern kings and counts had paid homage at *Madinat al-Zahra* and entreated the great caliph's assistance in their serial territorial scrapes. Muslim gold and Muslim steel had arbitrated the power outcomes north of the two rivers. That time was a bitter memory for the Muslims, for the roads to power led north to Christian kings ready to hire out their armies for generous allotments of Andalusian territory. *Amirs* and *muluks* (kings) who, like Toledo's or Valencia's, aspired to replicate the caliphate, had to rent Christians to do the fighting; increasingly, they had to pay their Christian protectors for the privilege of keeping their *ta'ifas*. But the roads from the North had also begun to introduce a different species of Christian into the peninsula, men whose ideas could excel the power of Navarrese knights and Castilian infantry on the battlefield. Sancho the Greater had already welcomed the first monks of the reformed Benedictine order of Cluny to his kingdom near the end of the tenth century.

The Cluniac movement was French in culture (Duke William the Pious of Aquitaine had endowed the first abbey on his property in 910), zealous in faith, celibate, and unexcelled in scientific enterprise. The Cluniacs were already well installed in Leon-Castile when Ferdinand invaded the Muslim region of Galicia in the 1040s. The self-abnegating Cluny monks radiated probity, propagandized superbly, and practiced consummate court politics in obedience to Rome. They embodied the militant Catholic ideals for which Eulogius and the "Mozarab martyrs" had given their lives. They followed the advancing armies into the South, establishing outposts and recharging or reawakening the faith of the Mozarabic peasantry. Cluniacs and Cistercians were formidable opponents. Muslim *al-Andalus* had no standing army of priests obedient to a hierarchy; of more relevance, what *imams* preached and *ulamas* interpreted could never properly be imposed on nonbelievers. The business of the Cluniacs in *al-Andalus*, and of the Cistercians coming after them, was the imposition of the True Faith until its creed was universal. [29]

The power of the Cluniacs and their analogues inhered in their exemplary conduct and efficient packaging of doctrine. The power of crusading knights, also coming from the roads north, lay in their sword arms. In the summer of 1064, three thousand Norman, French, and Italian knights, under the nominal command of Duke William VIII of Aquitaine and William of Montreuil, commander of the papal cavalry, rumbled though the Pyrenees pass at Roncesvalles and headed for the fortress city of Barbastro in the province of Huesca. This international force of freebooters, second sons without prospects, and grimly motivated penitents was the perfervid response to the appeal by Pope Alexander II (1061–73) to carry the message of Christ to the land of the infidel. Occurring a generation before the First Crusade of 1095, the siege of Barbastro was a practice flexing of muscles by the new papal imperialists in Rome. Pope Adrian I's successors were building a new superstructure above the Carolingian dynasty's broken and scattered remains—a house in which political power devolved to the Lateran Palace incumbents, whose determined goal was universal religious conformity. A certain Christian fundamentalism took hold that would define much of the eleventh century. Pope Alexander II and his immediate successor, Hildebrand (Gregory VII), were pledged to impose radical reforms that would have dismayed Charlemagne—challenging the authority of counts, kings, and even Holy Roman Emperor Henry IV (1056–1106) to invest the clergy with the ring and staff of ecclesiastical service.

The Christians who besieged Barbastro under the pope's standard for forty days in 1064 were the unbathed, larcenous forerunners of a hundred thousand holy warriors whose sins would be forgiven in advance and salvation certified by Christ's vicar. The people of Barbastro surrendered their prosperous trading center in late July, after its water supply failed. Six thousand Muslims were slaughtered in a festival of violence, and twice as many women were enslaved under the command of the Aragonese Count Armengol IV of Urgel. The Normans assimilated the culture of the conquered with a zest that their Muslim contemporaries reported with aggrieved curiosity. The Christian knights were entranced by the lyrics of the *qiyan* (singing girls) and seduced by the manners of their wealthy hostages. A Jewish intermediary sent to bargain for the release of the dead commander's daughter found her ex-Viking master dressed as a *qa'id* and enjoying the daughter's lute-playing. The Norman dismissed the ransom money and, as the historian Ibn Hayyan reported, grandly declared that her singing was worth all the world's gold.[30]

When the *amir* of Zaragoza, al-Muqtadir, arrived the following year in strength sufficient to reclaim Barbastro, he put the entire garrison to the sword. Many of the original crusaders had wisely slipped over the Pyrenees with women, boys, and valuables before the *amir*'s angry army arrived. After word of the rapine and butchery perpetrated by the Christians at Barbastro spread across *al-Andalus*, the *ta'ifas* had rallied to al-Muqtadir's *jihad*. It would be one of the last to be mounted by the Andalusis. Pope Alexander's authorized massacre was a travesty of the *Song of Roland,* but Barbastro was the myth of manly heroics and religious arrogance as it would play out in reality many times again. Barbastro's significance was an early example of Christian Europe's acculturation through violence of Islam's more advanced civilization. History remembers that Duke William VIII of Aquitaine, who delighted in the company of Barbastro's lute-playing *qíyan,* was father to William IX, founder of France's wandering troubadours.[31]

The *amír* of Zaragoza reclaimed Barbastro from Pope Alexander's crusaders in 1065, just as Ferdinand I *el Magno* ("the Great") died that summer. He left his sprawling possessions to three sons and two daughters. The ensuing scenario, complicated and murderous in its familial particulars, produced the usual crowned strongman, middle brother Alfonso, who reunited the possessions that the paternal bequest had divided. In less than two years, 1071–72, Alfonso's brothers had been eliminated—the youngest, Garcia of Galicia, by Sancho and Alfonso acting together. Alfonso fled to asylum in Toledo ahead of senior brother Sancho of Leon's headhunters. But Sancho was pushed off a cliff over the Duero River by his sister, Urraca, most probably in compliance with instructions received from brother (and perhaps lover) Alfonso, in hiding in Muslim Toledo. Alfonso VI "the Brave" (r. 1065–1109) emerged from his asylum triumphant as the twenty-five-year-old king of Leon and Castile, but under fairly plausible suspicion of fratricide.

Although Alfonso swore his innocence on an oath before the magnates and knights of Leon-Castile, Rodrigo Diaz of Burgos, famous as *el Cid Campeador* ("the Champion")—Christian Spain's Roland—almost certainly believed that Alfonso was implicated in Sancho's murder.[32] The *Cid*'s suspicions were no bar, however, to his pledging his services to Alfonso.* Nor did Alfonso's religion, regicide, or territorial ambitions much bother Toledo's *amír,* Yahya al-Ma'mun (1043–75), the most lavish builder in the city's history. Three years after Sancho's assisted exit, al-Ma'mun required Alfonso to redeem his debt for Toledo's grant of asylum. Castilian soldiers marched with Toledo's to attack and occupy Cordoba, fallen from its commanding heights several years earlier to

---

Cid, from Arabic *sayyíd,* meaning "sir" or "lord."

become a satellite of Sevilla. Even after its long gamut of assaults, insults, and occupation by the Sevillians, the city was still impressive in its ruination, still unsurpassed in size by any city beyond the Pyrenees.

Cordovans had had to endure subjugation by Sevilla, and although they put up a proud fight against the behemoth of the South, Hroswitha's "brilliant ornament of the world" finally capitulated in 1069. The Sevillians had stayed six years, but Cordovans' historic rivals, the Toledans, were gone in less than two years. When the great builder, Yahya al-Ma'mun, suddenly died the year after his Toledans bivouacked in the shadow of the Falcon's Great Mosque, Sevilla's army raced again to the gates of Cordoba. Sevilla's reoccupation of Cordoba was a preparation for the conquest of Toledo and the restoration of an *al-Andalus* dominated by a single power center. Toledans certainly understood the danger, and they soon became disenchanted with their new incompetent and malevolent *amír*. Al-Ma'mun's heir, Yahya ibn Ismail *al-Qadir* ("the Capable"), inspired little confidence in his people and even disgust for his petty vindictiveness and fascination with clocks, to the neglect of the city's affairs. He appeared to have no policy for Toledo's independence other than a pricey Castilian insurance policy. Not only had al-Qadir lost Cordoba in 1075, three years later the Sevillians took Valencia from Toledo. An exasperated populace finally erupted and expelled the erratically brutal ruler. The ostracized al-Qadir fumed in nearby Cuenca, the elevated town impressively fortified by his compulsive builder of a grandfather, and plotted with the Castilians.[33] The people of Toledo reached for the protection of Badajoz, one of the strongest of the *ta'ifa* city-states. Soldiers from Badajoz occupied the *alcazar* high above the Tagus River in the summer of 1078.

Neither the *amír* of Sevilla nor the king of Castile felt he could tolerate the presence of Badajoz's army in Toledo. Sevilla's thirty-five-year-old ruler, Muhammad ibn Abbad al-Mu'tamid, was that aggressive city-state's third Abbadid ruler and a complex personality. Poetry was a passion, but al-Mu'tamid was a political realist of the highest order. Cosmopolitanism was in al-Mu'tamid's blood, along with romantic sensibility. When he was out walking one day and reciting some unfinished verse of his own, a girl washing clothes by the Guadalquivir overheard him and offered to finish the stanza. After she did so, he married al-Rumaykiyya and made her his favorite wife and the object of more poetic effusions. His poetry divagations in the elaborate *Qasr al-Mubarak* ("the Blessed Palace") were disrupted by King Alfonso's transparent designs on Toledo. On a personal level, the two rulers, who were the same age, found they had much in common. Neither allowed religion to spoil an appetite for intellectual inquiry and both prided themselves on the liberality they accorded their subjects to observe their religious practices. Al-Mu'tamid's domestic life was likely to have been more fulfilling than Alfonso's. The king's two French wives—the first an Aquitainian, the second a Burgundian—had produced no sons. The delicious irony that Alfonso's only son and heir, Sancho, was the issue of a union with al-Mu'tamid's former daughter-in-law was years in the future. On the political level, the Sevillian and the Castilian found a great deal to divide them.[34]

###

The fall of Toledo was the beginning of the end of Islam's long sojourn in Europe. Toledo was the first domino. Once it fell to the Christian kings, the retreat of Muslim Iberia before the cumulative power of the advancing northerners was a matter of time and a question of military asymmetry. With the map of Spain before us, the course of history might even appear to reveal a partiality for gravity, as the line of conflict dropped steadily toward the Mediterranean after 1085, when the mightiest efforts of the Muslims—the Moors or the Saracens—were capable only temporarily of retarding their enemies' descent. But inevitability is the perspective, after all, of hindsight. From the surrender of Toledo to Alfonso the Brave on the morning of May 25, 1085, to the evacuation from Granada of the last *amir* on Spanish soil on January 2, 1492, it's a run of 407 years. In the span of nearly half a millennium, human and material features of the political map could and did sometimes dramatically alter as a result of sudden and unforeseen developments. If the fall of Toledo meant the inevitable overthrow of Muslim Iberia, certainly few of the protagonists of the *Reconquista* drama knew it at the time, or even for

more than a century afterward. Certainly, neither King Alfonso VI of
Leon-Castile nor *Amir* Muhammad ibn Abbad al-Mu'tamid of Sevilla
believed that he was witnessing the end of history as he had known it.

When the Badajoz cavalry squadron streamed through Toledo's main
gate in the fall of 1078, a race to the Tagus had commenced between al-
Mu'tamid and Alfonso, with the Castilians advantaged by the deposed *Amir*
al-Qadir's money. The *amir* of Badajoz, a descendant of the founding Slav,
had surrendered his claim to Toledo the next year, after Alfonso's heavy
cavalry punished him near the old Roman town of Coria in the mountains
of Extremadura. In 1080, the king sent a regiment of Leon cavalry to
Cuenca to return the unprepossessing al-Qadir to power in Toledo. Castilian garrisons had set up quarters in two towns north and south of Toledo,
their cost borne by al-Qadir. This phase of the *Reconquista* was mainly about
money and territory. Religious feelings were still to come powerfully to the
fore. Al-Qadir had gladly remitted Alfonso's protection money (*paria*) and
waited to learn the size of the Castilian's final bill.

Al-Mu'tamid had discerned where the ineluctable trajectory of
Leon-Castile's increased power would carry the king. When Alfonso's
Sephardic minister came to al-Mu'tamid for his king's *paria* to finance
more Christian ventures, the *amir* had attempted to pay in debased coin
and then killed the emissary for daring to protest. Their relationship
reached bottom the next year, when Alfonso repaid al-Mu'tamid's insult
by quartering his army before Sevilla for three menacing days in 1083.
That summer, the king had blazed across much of *al-Andalus*'s southern
half, intimidating minor *muluks* and collecting protection money. When
he reached Tarifa, where Tariq ibn Ziyad's scouts had come ashore 373
years earlier, Alfonso rode his horse into the Mediterranean and, legend
insists, exulted, "This is the last land in Spain, and I have trod it!" In legend, Uqba ibn Nafi, conqueror of the Maghreb, had voiced a similar
boast across the strait when Islam was only fifty years old. Alfonso's
horseback bravura had made it obvious to al-Mu'tamid that the fate of *al-
Andalus* was desperate. Possibly, as some chronicles claim, al-Mu'tamid
went in person to Morocco immediately after Alfonso's grandstanding
for a parley with a charismatic personality with whom he shared nothing
other than Islam. Far more likely, the *amir* had sent plenipotentiaries to

Morocco to negotiate with a Berber whose North African followers called him the *Murabit*.[35]

In Toledo, the situation had deteriorated suddenly the previous year—for Alfonso. Al-Qadir's hard-core opposition nearly succeeded in eliminating him. Whatever this faction's ultimate designs, loathing for their *amir* and unhappiness with de facto Castilian rule pushed them into a failed attack upon the *alcazar* in May 1082. An advance contingent of King Alfonso's army encircled Toledo in the winter of 1084. His representative drafted *in camera* with al-Qadir the treaty by which the narcissist would hand his city to Alfonso VI. The *amir* was guaranteed a safe lifetime retirement in sunny Valencia. Throughout the spring of 1085, some twenty-eight thousand Toledans watched as more Castilian cavalry and infantry camped in the bend of the Tagus. By the beginning of May, they numbered more than three thousand. The show of force was more than sufficient for a proper surrender and al-Qadir's *armor propre*. The ruler's baggage was packed and ready, his precious clocks secured for the trip. When Alfonso arrived on a splendid white stallion to conclude the farce on the morning of May 25, 1085, the gates of Toledo were flung open and history changed religions in much of *al-Andalus*.

Alfonso VI called himself "king of the two religions" and guaranteed the Muslims of Toledo the right to worship in their Friday Mosque. All who wished to leave with their property had the king's permission; those remaining would pay a special tax comparable to the *jizya*. The favorable status of Jews, about fifteen percent of the population, remained unchanged.[36] As a sure sign of troubles ahead, however, the new archbishop appropriated the mosque and converted it, as "a tabernacle of celestial virtue for all Christian people," into Toledo's principal cathedral. Alfonso's devout second wife, the daughter of the duke of Burgundy, was blamed for the violation of the surrender terms. In any case, because of Queen Constance's piety, Toledo's Mozarabs would be obliged to adjust to the Roman ritual that replaced the ancient one devised by St. Isidore of Sevilla. Al-Makkari rendered a solemn encapsulation of that fateful day:

> The tyrant Alfonso took the city of Toledo from the Muslims; . . . for
> . . . perceiving the weak and helpless state to which the Arabs had

been reduced by their sins, he overran and plundered the flat country, and so pressed al-Qadir that he obliged him to surrender his capital . . . , on condition, however, that [Alfonso] should assist him in
gaining possession of Valencia; which he did. There is no power or
strength but in Allah, the Great! The High![37]

Fifty years earlier, the *ta'ifa* potentates had hired Christians to do their
fighting. With the capture of Toledo, they sought salvation from the
Almoravids (*al-Murabitun*) of North Africa. The man to whom the *amir* of
Sevilla turned for help was an eighty-year-old Sanhaja Berber of the most
rigorous religious orthodoxy. Al-Mu'tamid's emissaries in Marrakesh proposed an alliance with Yusuf ibn Tashufin, of the *Murabitun*. Some thirty
years had elapsed since the *Murabitun* had roared out of the Sahara with a
ferocity that overwhelmed, first, the Zanata Berbers who controlled Sijilmasa, fabled entrepôt of the Sahara gold trade; then the puissant Negro
kingdom of Ghana at about the same time, in 1055. Twenty years later,
under Yusuf ibn Tashufin's inspired generalship, they captured Fez in
Morocco, then, in 1082, Oran and Tlemcen in Algeria. *Al-Murabitun*, "men
of the *ribat*" (militant retreat), swept other Berbers from the High Atlas,
where Yusuf founded Marrakesh as capital of the new Almoravid
dynasty.[38] When Sultan Yusuf finally answered al-Mu'tamid, he declined
the alliance offer. But that was before Toledo fell to Alfonso.

The contrast between Yusuf, the *Murabit*, and al-Mu'tamid, the versifying cosmopolite, could hardly have been more extreme. Yusuf ibn
Tashufin, leader of a fundamentalist Islamic sect with origins in Mauri-
tania, was an ascetic who wore the blue veil still worn today among the
Tuareg people. He dressed in wool and supped only on barley, camel
meat, and camel milk. The creed he espoused was of an undeviating
Qur'anic literalism bent on the propagation of "righteousness, the correction of injustices, and the abolition of unlawful taxes." Yusuf commanded the absolute obedience of a people so fierce that other Berber
tribes quailed before them.[39] Al-Mu'tamid's was the quintessential *ta'ifa*
heritage: fabulous wealth and tolerant religious beliefs. Al-Mu'tamid was
a better poet than a warrior, though he gave a good account of himself on
both scores. The *amir* of Sevilla detested Christian military victories, not

Christians, some of whom were among his best acquaintances, while Yusuf ibn Tashufin hated non-Believers. There was no place in his thinking for pragmatic dealings with such unworthy people, to say nothing of the abomination of cosmopolitan intercourse between privileged Muslims and Christians.

The most famous observation al-Mu'tamid is known to have made was not in a poem. Told of the loss of Toledo, *al-Andalus*'s most historic city, he said that he "would rather be a camel-driver in Africa than a swineherd in Castilla."[40] The options available to an Arab panjandrum in a Christian kingdom were not that dire in the short term, but, among his bickering *ta'ifa* brethren, he alone seemed to grasp the apocalyptic fate ultimately awaiting Muslims after the *ta'ifa* polities were no more. In the *al-Andalus* of Umayyads and *ta'ifa* potentates, swineherds could profess the faith of Muhammad or Jesus or Moses. Whether or not Spain of the *Reconquista* would be congenial to any but Catholic swineherds was a risk al-Mu'tamid resolved not to take. He succeeded in enlisting Zirid Granada and Aftasid Badajoz in his new appeal to the Almoravids. Yusuf at that moment was busy besieging Tangier and Ceuta, but he was receptive to a strategic real-estate offer and a guarantee of Christian spoils of war, holy warrior though he was. After al-Mu'tamid ceded Algeciras, on the southernmost coast, Yusuf ibn Tashufin disembarked four thousand Almoravid cavalry and infantry on the beach there on July 30, 1086. A few days later, in Sevilla's Friday Mosque, the *Murabit* summoned the faithful of Andalusia to a *jihad*. Yusuf and al-Mu'tamid received a tentative response. Valencia remained loyal to Alfonso. There was silence from Murcia and Almeria. Zaragoza would have joined the coalition, but it was fighting for its autonomy at that moment against Alfonso's best forces.[41]

After a two-month wait for the peninsula's Arabs, Berbers, and *muwalladun* to join him, Yusuf led his men out of Sevilla. The Berber ruler of Badajoz, al-Mutawakkil, welcomed the *Murabit* and the Dependable, adding his own forces to make the numbers of the army of holy warriors respectable. As King Alfonso hurried to meet the Almoravid invaders, he was compelled to leave a sizable portion of his army in position at Zaragoza. Yusuf had the advantage of numbers—probably three times

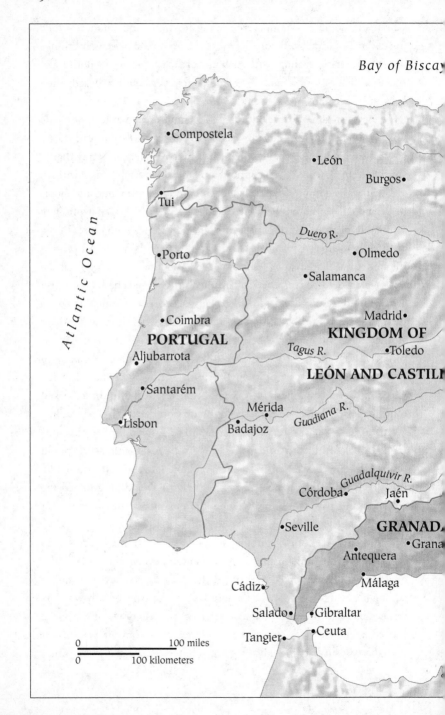

Bay of Biscay

Atlantic Ocean

•Compostela

•León

Burgos•

Tui•

Duero R.

•Porto

•Olmedo

•Salamanca

•Coimbra

Madrid•

PORTUGAL

KINGDOM OF

Aljubarrota

Tagus R.

•Toledo

LEÓN AND CASTILE

•Santarém

Mérida•

Guadiana R.

•Lisbon

Badajoz•

Guadalquivir R.

Córdoba•

Jaén•

•Seville

GRANADA

•Grana

Antequera•

•Málaga

Cádiz•

Salado•

•Gibraltar

Tangier•

•Ceuta

0 _____ 100 miles

0 _____ 100 kilometers

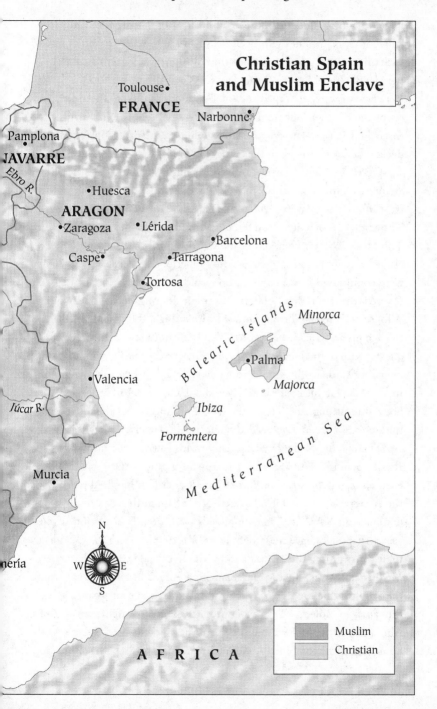

Christian Spain and Muslim Enclave

Toulouse
FRANCE
Narbonne
Pamplona
NAVARRE
Ebro R.
Huesca
ARAGON
Zaragoza   Lérida
Caspe   Barcelona
Tarragona
Tortosa
Balearic Islands   Minorca
Palma
Valencia   Majorca
Júcar R.   Ibiza
Formentera
Murcia   Mediterranean Sea
N
W   E
S
nería
AFRICA

Muslim
Christian

larger than those under Alfonso's command after the arrival of King 'Abd
Allah of Granada and the pick of his small army. The two armies faced
each other at a place near Badajoz that Muslims would call *Zallaqa* ("slip-
pery land"), the Christians' Sagrajas. Of King Alfonso's 2,500 men, 750
were heavy cavalry, stirruped and steel-encased. Faithful to the precedent
set by the Prophet Muhammad, Yusuf sent a messenger to offer Alfonso
three alternatives: convert to Islam; submit to the protection of Islam;
decide their differences on the battlefield.[42]

On that October day in 1086, the Spanish Muslims won a crushing
victory over the Spanish Catholics. Alfonso attacked first, putting his
trust in his heavy cavalry, which charged while the enemy was at prayer.
The cavalry's momentum and ferocity carried it deep into Yusuf's center.
The Muslim center bent and nearly buckled until the *Murabit* ordered a
classic crescent advance. Enveloped by superior numbers, the Castilians
were compressed into a compact body and slaughtered. So much blood
covered the field that soldiers lost their footing and slipped. King
Alfonso, who repaired from the field with a thigh wound and less than a
third of his army, made his way to Toledo. Within a few months, the conquests south of the Duero by the king of Leon-Castille were erased. Not
long afterward, al-Mu'tamid wrote a poem about his part in one of history's most fateful contests: "Never did I charge into battle/with the
hope of returning safe./This is the way of my ancestors./The roots beget
the stems."[43] The *Murabit* headed home as Alfonso mended in Toledo.

The coming of the fanatical Almoravids rewrote the history of the
Iberian peninsula. Al-Mu'tamid's successful appeal to Yusuf ibn Tashufin
ensured Islam's presence in Europe for another four hundred years. But
the Almoravid advent introduced a form of Islam that had never been
dominant in *al-Andalus*. The Almoravids were fired by a version of the
ummah that might have chastened the *rashidun* caliphs. With the Qur'an as
their constitution, the *Murabit* and his disciples had created a latter-day
Medina at Marrakesh, a Maghrebian state purged of all deviation from
the Prophet's message. Two years after Zallaqa, Yusuf came again to press
the *jihad* to Toledo. The expedition of French knights answering
Alfonso's 1087 appeal for reinforcements had grown bored and returned
home just as the combined Almoravid-Andalusi army set out for Toledo.

But Yusuf read the signs as unfavorable and decided to depart for Morocco. Two years passed before the old Berber fundamentalist returned. This time, in the summer of 1090, Yusuf came in response to urgent, anguished pleas from *ulamas* and *fuqaha* who spoke for the common people, the poor, and a significant percentage of the Andalusi establishment. The *muluks* and *amirs*, they reported, had reverted to balance-of-power politics and checkbook diplomacy.

After the Battle of Zallaqa, four years were more than enough to inspire a profound aversion in Sevilla's poet-ruler for the Murabit's rustic manners and fanatical beliefs. Maybe, after all, it might be better to be a swineherd in an *al-Andalus* shared with the practical, cultured Alfonso. Al-Mutawakkil at Badajoz and the Banu Zirids of Granada chafed at the Malikite extremism engendered by the Almoravids. The feelings, as they say, were mutual. Yusuf returned in 1094 with a *fatwa* from his great teacher in Alexandria, Muhammad al-Tartushi, legitimizing the overthrow of the *ta'ifa* kingdoms. The *Murabit*'s army broke through Sevilla's defenses after the city fought fiercely to save its independence. Granada and Almeria surrendered. Once again, Yusuf veered away from strongly defended Toledo, where King Sancho Ramirez I of Aragon and his army had joined Alfonso's. When the *Murabit* headed for Marrakesh this time, he took al-Mu'tamid with him as his prisoner. He left behind much of his army, under the command of a viceroy who was ordered to wipe out the *ta'ifas* and enforce proper Muslim behavior throughout *al-Andalus*. Al-Mu'tamid died in captivity in Morocco a few years later.[44]

Yusuf ibn Tashufin's Almoravids pressed the Christians across the peninsula, retaking part of Portugal and expelling their armies from Huesca and Cuenca in the northeast. Three years after the incomparable *Cid*'s death, Valencia fell to the Almoravids after a fierce siege in 1102. When Alfonso VI died in 1109, he had outlived the *Murabit* by three years and his only son and heir, Sancho, by fourteen months. Sancho, the issue of Alfonso's marriage to Zaida, al-Mu'tamid's daughter-in-law, died in a headlong cavalry charge worthy of Roland against Almoravid infantry at the Battle of Ucles, yet another Christian debacle.

Convulsed by another fundamentalist movement, this one inspired by the Masmuda Berber Ibn Tumart (1080–1130), the Maghreb exchanged the intolerant Almoravids for the mystical Almohads—*al-Muwahhidun* ("the Unitarians"). Within a thirty-year span after 1130, Ibn Tumart's principal disciple had crushed the Almoravids in their capital at Marrakesh and led the victorious Masmudas out of the Atlas Mountains to conquer North Africa from Morocco to Egypt. The Almohads crossed to Algeciras in 1147, displacing their confessional rivals in short order, after which they established Sevilla as their empire's capital. Along with their formidable military prowess, the Almohads brought to *al-Andalus* a curious mixture of intrusive fundamentalism (persecution of Jews) and evolving intellectual curiosity. The third Almohad caliph, Abu Yusuf Ya'qub al-Mansur (r. 1184–99), evoked memories of the third 'Abd al-Rahman. He commanded the building of Sevilla's great Friday Mosque, with its neck-craning minaret of 320 feet (today's Giralda), then the world's tallest tower.[45]

Like the great Umayyad caliph, who matched architectural triumphs with military ones, the Almohad caliph dealt a humiliating blow in 1195 to the Castilians at the Battle of Alarcos, near the Guadiana River, sending Alfonso VIII scrambling for his life. Ya'qub al-Mansur ("the Victorious") died in Morocco four years after his great victory, never imagining that Alarcos was Islam's last great victory on the Iberian peninsula.

Knowledge Transmitted, Rationalism Repudiated: Ibn Rushd and Musa ibn Maymun

WAS THERE such a place in ninth-century Baghdad as the *Bayt al-Hikma* ("House of Wisdom"), a corporate body sponsored by the Abbasid caliphs with faculties and students of philosophy, jurisprudence, medicine, and astronomy? Shapur the Great's Gondeshapur, generously patronized by Khosrow I, could have served as an obvious precedent for what has sometimes been described as the pro-

totype of the European university. The famous *Bayt al-Hikma* may have
been in actuality a time and a milieu, not a physical academy: an imposing name given to one of mankind's most fecund periods of cross-cultural
intellectual and scientific production—with Baghdad as its magnet and
fulcrum from about 760 to 900 CE.[1] By that same token, the Umayyad
Caliphate's own House of Wisdom was the metropolis of Cordoba itself,
Baghdad on the Guadalquivir. The flow of science and philosophy from
the Fertile Crescent into *al-Andalus* increased in volume even as the Iberian peninsula became politically fractured and increasingly war-torn in
the eleventh century.

In the mid-ninth century, 'Abd al-Rahman II and Muhammad I had
lavished favors on men of learning and amassed rare manuscripts in
proud rivalry with Baghdad. Cordoba never surpassed Baghdad, with its
two million souls, as the seat of Islamic scholarship, but it would eventually achieve a second-to-none prominence in its own right.[2] The signature of Arabic philosophy (*falsafa*) was synthesis and commentary whose
prototype came with the Persian-inflected writings of Ya'qub ibn Ishaq
al-Kindi during the middle of the ninth century.[3] A star of Baghdad's
House of Wisdom, al-Kindi professed to be able to harmonize Greek
philosophy with the precepts of the Qur'an. His *Treatise on Intellect* won
him renown as "the first philosopher of Islam" and respect or reproach
(according to theological prejudice) as the original source of the Neoplatonic and Aristotelian ideas that flooded and perturbed the Christian
West four centuries later. The principles of good and evil were independ-
ently demonstrable through logic as eternal realities, according to him,
for the mantra of the House of Wisdom held that no conflict existed
between "the work of God and the word of God."[4] Rudimentary algebra
would reach Cordoba from Baghdad sometime in the early ninth century,
when the first book to use the term *al-jabr* crossed the Gibraltar Strait, al-
Khwarazmi's *Kitab al-Jabr w'al-Muqabala* (*The Book of Compulsion and Comparison*).[5] Its meaningful discovery on the far side of the Pyrenees had
another three centuries to run.

Andalusians assimilated the new learning in the sciences and
humanities with an almost-untroubled alacrity, thereby creating a basis
of knowledge that would provide the foundation for the Renaissance in

Christendom certain to come. In the polarized twelfth century, the flow
of knowledge gave way to a virtual flood. Muslim learning, having seeped
into the Christian West for decades from Andalusia, commenced a tor-
rential outflow. It was a process mimicking osmosis at first and, later, a
conveyor belt. Hasdai ibn Shaprut's tenth-century translation project of
De Materia Medica more than doubled the medical and pharmacological
corpus available in Europe. In truth, by the first quarter of the twelfth
century, philosophy and science fairly tumbled out of "occupied" Toledo
into Christian Europe. The seepage of early times had yielded the writings of Ibn Hazm, historian, jurist, and Platonist; of al-Zarqiyal (Zar-
qallu), Toledan astronomer (whose *Toledan Tables* shaped the development
of Latin astronomy); of Solomon ibn Gabirol, Sephardic philosopher and
poet of Zaragoza, influential in the Latin West as Avicebron.[6] The
impact of Gerbert of Aurillac's mathematics textbook, as has been seen,
was far from widespread east of the Pyrenees; its influence was still more
prospective than real even by the thirteenth century.

A man of science and philosophy who became well known to literate
Christians was a Persian who never traveled to *al-Andalus*. His Latinized
name was Avicenna. A child prodigy born in a remote corner of the Muslim empire at the end of the tenth century, Abu Ali ibn Sina had assimilated the entire contents of a sultan's library by the age of eighteen. Ibn
Sina the philosopher caused the doctors of the Church much worry
about his synthesis of Platonic pantheism and Aristotelian rationalism.
Ibn Sina the physician was eventually received almost with veneration,
however. *Al-Qanun* (*The Canon*), his *magnum opus*, was a *summa* of all Graeco-
Arabic medical knowledge, systematically described and logically
explained. Its classification of contagious diseases and description of the
progression of tuberculosis made Avicenna's *Canon* the principal authority in the medical schools of Europe and Asia for centuries.[7]

The literate culture of poetry, reason, and science cradled in Baghdad
and nurtured in Umayyad *al-Andalus* would be the retarded Latin West's
academy. As the long experiment in confessional tolerance from 900 to
1100 faded, Toledo experienced, nevertheless, its remarkable "Indian
summer" of prodigious interfaith collaboration. Welcomed by Castile's
Alfonso VII, and their activities encouraged by Archbishop Raimundo

(1130–80), many of the finest Christian, Muslim, and Jewish intellects in Europe assembled there in order to interpret, debate, and translate. The Toledo conveyor belt delivered a volume of translated data that significantly lifted the cultural level of the West. Herman of Carinthia translated the astronomical tables of al-Khwarazmi, as well as the *Planisphaerium* of Ptolemy. Gerard of Cremona produced a new translation of Aristotle's *Physics*, Euclid's *Elements*, al-Kindi's *De Intellectu*, and some seventy more "lost" or poorly rendered works. The first solution of a quadratic equation published in Christendom, based on the calculations of Abraham bar Hiyya, came from the indefatigable Plato of Tivoli, who translated a small library of Muslim astronomical and trigonometric data. Other missing books by Ptolemy became available: the *Almagest*, the *Quadripartitum*. Robert of Ketton, assisted by Herman of Carinthia and an unidentified Muslim, was commissioned by Peter the Venerable, head of the Cluniac order, to produce a true Latin translation of the Qur'an, which appeared, the better to document "the heresy of Muhammad," in 1143.[8] For their part, literate Muslims in Baghdad and *al-Andalus* had possessed Arabic translations of the Christian scriptures for more than two centuries. Another hundred years of such rarefied Judeo-Christian-Muslim collaboration as that at Toledo would produce the entire corpus of the recovered ancient learning known today.

⁂

Both thinkers were born in Cordoba ten decades after the humiliating departure of the last Umayyad ruler in 1031. Ibn Rushd (b. 1126) and Musa ibn Maymun (b. 1135) are vintage representatives of the old *al-Andalus* of cultural eclecticism and creedal forbearance—men who were to find themselves profoundly out of place in the radically altering political, cultural, and religious circumstances of their times. Ibn Rushd saw the uncongenial future reserved to his enlightened Muslim kind in the Spain being united by war cries of "*Santiago Matamoros!*" ("St. James the Moorslayer!"). Musa ibn Maymun observed with dismay the accommodating Islam of his youth close its door to Jews.

Aristotelian philosopher, physician, and jurist like his father and father's father (*qadis* of Cordoba), Ibn Rushd served *al-Andalus*'s new

Berber rulers (the Almohads, who had pushed aside the Almoravids) as a consummate physician-bureaucrat. The conquering Almohads arrived in Andalusia in 1147, just as the novice physican reached his twenty-first year. They halted and reversed the *Reconquista* only somewhat more effectively than they persecuted Jews and proscribed deviations from their fundamentalist interpretation of the Qur'an. Many in his class lost positions and influence, but Ibn Rushd's abilities eventually attracted attention. As chief *qadi* of Sevilla, appointed to the post in his midthirties, Ibn Rushd (also known as Averroës) moved in the regime's highest circles. The time would come when he was recognized and seconded by Andalusia's new masters to duty as royal physician to the caliphal court at Marrakesh, the mountain capital of the new Almohad dynasty. It was a risk wrapped in an honor, however. Ibn Rushd was a finer philosopher than a medical man or jurist.[9] Written in Arabic, his *Commentaries* on Aristotle—though based not on the original Greek but on a Syriac translation—reached the Christian West via the translation industry established in conquered Toledo.[10] The earliest recapture of Aristotle beyond the Pyrenees was due to thirteenth-century readings of Ibn Rushd in Latin. The rise of Scholasticism has been said to have been inconceivable without the profound impact of Averroës. St. Thomas Aquinas respectfully referred to him simply as "the Commentator"—no further identification necessary—and modeled his own expository style on the Cordovan's summary elucidations.[11]

By the end of the eleventh century—notwithstanding the *ulamas'* fierce and increasingly effective condemnation—the schools of speculative philosophy had produced a muscular, variegated body of work that tested Islam's revealed truth and hallowed tradition in the light of Greek philosophy. For al-Kindi and his disciple al-Furabi (d. 950) of the *Bayt al-Hikma*, as well as the Persian polymath Ibn Sina (Avicenna), reason and divine truth were compatible, the truth of the Qur'an ascertainable through the power of intellect and dialectics. One such school of religious science, the Mu'tazilite, not only maintained that the Qur'an was created in time, but also ventured to interpret it metaphorically. Caliph al-Qadir, who ruled Baghdad from 991 to 1031, had thought to put an end to Mu'tazilism by decree.

Not quite a hundred years after the caliph's death, Ibn Rushd, the greatest exponent of a modified Mu'tazilism, had drawn his first breath in Cordoba. In contrast to Ibn Sina and his philosophical companions, no Platonic pantheism or Sufi mysticism infected Ibn Rushd's writings. His intensely rationalist philosophy reiterated Aristotle's insistence that existence preceded essence, that science trumped theology—that essences were mental abstractions. The immensely learned Andalusi refuted Islam's premier theologian of the late eleventh century, Abu Hamid al-Ghazali (d. 1111), whose arbitral book, *The Incoherence of the Philosophers* (*Tahafut al-Falasifa*), purported to prove that causality was an illusion and rational philosophy, therefore, futile. Ibn Rushd rejoined that God had created a logical universe of cause and effect. "He who repudiates causality," he stipulated in his audacious book *The Incoherence of the Incoherence* (*Tahafut-al-Tahafut*), "actually repudiates reason."[12] There were three paths to knowledge, he dared to contend—a threefold system of truth: rhetorical (religious); dialectical; and philosophical (empirical). The former served the needs of the unsophisticated; the latter was the tool of the educated. All were serviceable, he noted, but Ibn Rushd left no doubt as to which was superior.

When Ibn Rushd's reputation as a physician brought him to the Almohad caliph's attention, he was yet to make his name as the Muslim world's most unorthodox and, arguably, most brilliant philosopher. His new master, Caliph Abu Ya'qub Yusuf (1163–84), was a complex personality—guardian of the regime's rigid Ash'arite school of theology in public, yet patron of enlightened philosophical speculation within palace walls. The caliph unnerved him by posing perhaps the most dangerous question for a Muslim scholar: "What do the philosophers believe regarding heaven?" he asked Ibn Rushd at their first meeting. "Is it eternal or created in time?" An affirmative answer to the second possibility would have betrayed dangerous Mu'tazilite ideas, but, when Ibn Rushd feigned little philosophical knowledge, Abu Ya'qub astonished him by expounding on Plato and Aristotle. The physician was told he was free to hold controversial thoughts. A relieved Ibn Rusd confided to a friend that the caliph possessed an unsuspected "profuseness of learning."

The caliph's call for a document encapsulating the essential principles of Almohad belief resulted in the '*Aquida*, the remarkable Almohad Creed of 1183, a triumph of rationalism mobilized in support of Qur'anic authority. "It is by the necessity of reason," proclaimed the first sentence of chapter two, "that the existence of God, Praise be to Him, is known." The author of that Aristotelian maxim is believed to have been Ibn Rushd, the court physician. As long as the Almohad grip on the Iberian peninsula remained firm, the melding of Aristotelianism and Islam was sanctioned from the palace. As the power and fury of the *Reconquista* redoubled, however, caliphal authorities were forced to gin up the religious passions of the people.[13] Ibn Rushd's philosophical speculations attracted the angry suspicions of conservative *ulamas*, and the less sophisticated. The next caliph, Abu Yusuf Ya'qub al-Mansur, withdrew his favor from Ibn Rushd. In 1195, he was banished in disgrace to Lucena, a village near his beloved Cordoba. The sentence of exile was lifted in 1198, less than a year before his death. He received a dignified funeral in 'Abd al-Rahman's Great Mosque, but his philosophical ideas had been proscribed and many of his books were consigned to the fire and permanently lost.[14]

The Maymun (or Maimon) family had long been prominent in Cordoba's professional and cultural life as physicians, teachers, and merchants. Indeed, they were model members of the *dhimma*, people whose Arabized culture was second nature. Precocity in the sciences would have secured young Musa ibn Maymun an honored post in the Cordovan establishment in earlier times. Born after the Golden Age of Sefarad, however, his was the mixed blessing of a uniquely perceptive existential perspective upon what it meant to be an Arabized Jew in an age of religious fanaticism. Almohad treatment of Jews was barbarous. Thousands had been massacred in the Maghreb after the Almohads fought their way to power over the Almoravids.[15] When the Almohads established control over Cordoba in the late 1140s, Musa and his family left for the port city of Almeria, one of the last centers where something of the bygone ethos of Umayyad *al-Andalus* survived. It seems that Ibn Rushd, then in his late teens, was taken to Almeria with his family at about the same time. *Qadis* who had served the Almoravids were also an endangered species. Musa and Ibn Rushd's predicaments made for an uncanny pairing of destinies.[16]

Both these extraordinary minds, Ibn Rushd, with all his old family reinforcements among the high *baladiyyun*, and Musa ibn Maymun, possessed of an illustrious pedigree as an Arabized Jew, had become splendid twelfth-century anachronisms in a world energized by two hostile monotheisms. As men of culture and principles, they came to be regarded as liabilities at best and dangerous subversives at worst. Ibn Rushd served Muslim rulers on two continents and observed from a privileged professional perch the close-mindedness enveloping his faith. His remarkable *The Distinguished Jurist's Primer* (*Bidayat al-Mujtahid wa Nihayat al-Muqtasid*) is still today serviceable in Islam. Nor have his Aristotelian meditations been entirely ignored. But his influence in the Christian West has been immense—much greater than his philosophical influence upon Islamic thought. "Rationalism," declared the great French intellectual historian Etienne Gilson in his authoritative *Reason and Revelation in the Middle Ages* (1938), "was born in Spain in the mind of an Arabian philosopher as a conscious reaction against the theologism of the Arabian divines."[17]

When Ibn Rushd's work was translated into Latin under the name Averroës at the beginning of the thirteenth century, the ensuing controversies among the Scholastics provoked several ecclesiastical condemnations. Trouble with the Greeks, as interpreted by the Arabs and Arabized Jews, would bring things to a boiling point when theologians used the writings of Ibn Rushd and Musa ibn Maymun as brickbats. Although Averroës and Maimonides were as much misunderstood as understood in Paris and Rome, neither exponents nor adversaries misperceived the core premise of their thought that eternal truth was to be ascertained through reason—that logic led to salvation. In Paris, the reading of Aristotle's *Physics* and *Metaphysics* was banned in 1210, and again in 1231 by Pope Gregory XI, until Averroistic heresies could be safely identified, classified, and proscribed. Peter Abelard, Duns Scotus, Siger of Brabant, Pierre de Bois, and many more Scholastics were deemed to be desperately in need of interpretative correction. St. Thomas Aquinas's *Treatise on the Truth of the*

Catholic Faith (*Summa de Veritate Catholicae*), written in Rome explicitly to refute the "Jews and Moors of Spain," would arrive in 1264 just in time.[18]

While Ibn Rushd was being rewarded as *qadi* of Sevilla and then of Cordoba, the Maymuns kept a low profile in Almeria and other less-threatening places until Almohad emigration restrictions were lightened. Wandering to Fez and Palestine, they settled in Fatimid Egypt among the large Jewish community of Alexandria and, finally, in 1168, among those of al-Fustat (also in Egypt). The sojourn in Fez might have been fatal. Musa ibn Maymun was arrested by the authorities on the charge of relapsing into Judaism—an accusation, his excellent biographer Sherwin Nuland reveals, he escaped only because a Muslim friend attested to Musa's good Muslim character. He was never given to converting genuinely to Islam, but he had embraced the culture. Moreover, in the *Epistle on Martyrdom,* he justified formal conversion to Islam as a worthy alternative to pain and death under Almohad fanaticism. "Let him set it as his objective [under persecution] to observe as much of the Law as he can," Musa insisted. "Utter the formula and live."[19] He soon came to regret, as a cruel deception, the long cultural coexistence of his people with Islam. Urban class conflict, Berber armies invited from Morocco to fight the advancing Christians, and two Crusades to the Holy Land (1095 and 1147) had transformed an increasingly less tolerant Muslim Iberia into a gradually more intolerant Catholic Spain.

When the Sunni Ayyubids displaced the Shi'a Fatimids as Egypt's rulers, the Shi'a of Yemen set upon the Jews, and Musa was moved to write of his own embrace of the Muslim culture with a seared bitterness. *Letter to Yemen* bade farewell at age thirty-four to the person who was Musa ibn Maymun—or almost did so, for Maimonides wrote his refutation of Islam's claim to final revelation not in Hebrew but in Arabic. "No nation has ever done more harm to Israel," he lamented. "None has matched it in debasing and humiliating us."[20] The "Rambam," as he had come to be known acronymically, prophesied that Israel's oppressors would have a fitting comeuppance. "Be assured, my brethren, that our opponents . . . will vanish. They may continue to prosper for a time, but their glory will shortly disappear."[21] Indeed, in the *Letter to Yemen*, Maimonides ventured to predict the date of the return of the Messiah, a Messiah who would restore the Jewish nation in 1216 CE (4976 AM).

Aristotelian, Talmudist, physician, and poet, known by his Hebrew name as Moshe ben Maimon (Maimonides), Moses produced most of his writings in al-Fustat, where he served for a period as physician to the court of the great Sunni sultan Salah al-Din (Saladin; r. 1174–93) and leader of the Jewish community of the Ayyubid sultanate of Egypt.[22] It was, then, one of history's ironies that Maimonides, always writing in Arabic except for the *Mishneh Torah*—his incomparable digest and commentary in Hebrew of all Jewish law—composed the book that would represent the highest triumph of Arabic Aristotelian scholarship, his exquisitely subtle *summa,* the *Guide for the Perplexed* (1190).[23] To those who found themselves mentally and spiritually perplexed by the seeming divergence of scripture and reason, the *Guide for the Perplexed* offered cogent assurance that God played by the rules of logic, that He did not, as it were, play dice with the universe.[24] Unlike Averroës, Maimonides modified his Aristotle with a Neoplatonic bias, to which he added a distinctive biblical component. His *Commentaries* postulated the absolute concordance of faith and reason.

Picking and choosing carefully from the dangerous Maimonidian *oeuvre,* Europe's Scholastics—Albert the Great, St. Thomas Aquinas, and others—helped themselves to what was theologically safe and serviceable for their purposes. The medical knowledge Maimonides assembled was assimilated over time with much less controversy in the West, superstition notwithstanding. That no less an authority than St. Bernard had inveighed against medical training for monks and that, in 1135, the Council of Reims forbade the practice of medicine by clergy as a violation of God's design, would be well forgotten. Maimonides's medical tracts would remain standard reading in Europe's medical schools well into the Renaissance.[25] Medical schools in Salerno, Montpellier, and elsewhere in late-Renaissance Europe utilized the Maimonidean medical oath.[26] In this usually bowdlerized, much contested, and frequently obscurantist manner, the men and some few women of the Latin West eventually acquired the knowledge of the ancients as mediated by the encyclopedic and rationalist Andalusian thinkers.

When the Renaissance learned to live with the risks of reason, a turbaned Averroës would find a place of honor standing behind Pythagoras in *The School of Athens,* Raphael's masterpiece in the Stanza della Segnatura in the Vatican. What Ibn Rushd thought of the Christians' Third Crusade of 1188 to recapture Jerusalem can only be imagined. He died two years shy of the new century and six years after the failure of that disputatious, lumberingly lethal cavalcade commanded by Richard the Lion Hearted, Philip Augustus, and the ill-fated Frederick Barbarossa.[27] Moshe ben Maimon's death in Cairo happened in the same year, 1204, in which the Fourth Crusade would turn upon its Byzantine hosts, pillaging and raping the people of Constantinople and destroying the imperial regime. The two humanists died, beleaguered, as representative heirs of a social and political order, and the cluster of ideas integral to it, that were unique to *al-Andalus* founded by 'Abd al-Rahman I in the crucial eighth century.

Eight years after the death of Moses Maimonides, Pope Innocent III, remorseless pursuer of heresy and architect of the religious unity of Europe, commanded the kings of Christian Spain and the knights of France and the Holy Roman Empire to take up the cross and expel the Muslims. This pope's conception of the Deity's design for continental peace and salvation was, in its own way, quite as fanatical as the fundamentalism animating the Almohad *ulamas.* To Innocent, suppression of errors not only was compatible with elimination of perpetrators, dogma made it imperative more often than not. The pope's militant creed owed much to the spirit and practice of the Carolingian conversion of the Saxons and the Avars. What Pope Urban II had begun at the Synod of Clermont in 1095 with electrifying sermons that sent Europeans crusading to the Middle East on the first of many such excursions to come, Innocent invested with greater ideological and institutional power.[28] Here was Charlemagne's Saxon Capitulary applied to all of Christendom. Uniform, undeviating, militant Catholicism he sought to impose and enforce by ideas in action. The religious orders installing themselves on mountaintops and near well-trafficked roads throughout the continent—the Cluniacs, Templars, Cistercians, and others relatively new—exemplified and catechized correct thought and right action that affected both nobility and common people.

Papal exhortation was backed by papal treasure and blanket indulgences, as Castile's Alfonso VIII, Navarra's Sancho VII, and Aragon's Pedro II raised battle standards in the summer of 1212. Templars, Calatrava, Santiago—three of the Church's most famous fighting orders—reported for duty and the blessings of Toledo's Muslim castigator, Archbishop Rodrigo. Contemporary accounts estimated the three Catholic kings to have ridden out of Toledo at the head of a hundred thousand cavalry and infantry. The actual number was probably two-thirds smaller. The Muslims awaited them at Las Navas de Tolosa, not far from Jaén and in sight of the Sierra Morena. Seventeen years earlier, Alfonso had lost his army and barely escaped martyrdom at the Battle of Alarcos. The army deployed by the Almohad caliph Muhammad III *al-Nasr* (1199–1214), son of the victor of Alarcos, surpassed numbers ever seen before in the peninsula, even in Roman times: tens of thousands of Tunisians, Algerians, Moroccans, Mauretanians, and Senegalese. Since the end of the caliphate, Muslims and Christians had fought one another (separate or blended) primarily for control of real estate and its resources. The battles fought by the iconic *El Cid* (Rodrigo Diaz of Burgos), alternating with and against the Muslims, were of this nature. Las Navas de Tolosa was the first war fought by Christians and Muslims exclusively *as* Muslims and *as* Christians—a war between civilizations. Alfonso's surprise flanking maneuver through the Despenaperros Pass gave the day to Christianity in 1212 and amassed a slaughter of real Muslims that beggared the imaginary massacres of the *Chanson de Roland*.[29]

Las Navas de Tolosa changed Spanish history. "Certain it is that this defeat may be regarded as the real cause of the subsequent decline of Western Africa and Andalus," al-Makkari mournfully pronounced. Three years afterward, Pope Innocent III convoked the most important council of the Middle Ages in order to declare war against abuses in the Church, war against heretics, and war against unbelievers. The pope's Fourth Lateran Council authorized crusades for the Holy Land, Muslim Spain, and Albigensian France and prescribed a compulsory dress code for Europe's Jews and Muslims. "Jews and Saracens of both sexes in every Christian province, and at all times," the council ordained, "shall be marked off in the eyes of the public from other people through the character of their dress." Difference, immemorially accommodated for better and worse among Western Europe's peoples as the way of the world, was institutionalized henceforth as unassimilable "otherness." In the words of a contemporary American Catholic historian, "the main elements of the Catholic culture as we know it" were perfected: the seven sacraments; transubstantiation; the seal of confession; clerical discipline; a refurbished Nicene Creed—and the exclusion of Jews and Muslims from the *societas fidelium*.[30]

Thirty-two years after Maimonides's death and thirty-eight after Ibn Rushd's, Muslim rule in a diminished Cordoba would end with the triumphant entry into the city of Ferdinand III of Castile in 1236. One must wonder what the king may have thought of the Arabic legend on the wall of 'Abd al-Rahman I's Great Mosque, *la Mezquita*. The brief inscription on this most perfect structure whispered an oracular subtlety that lingers in the mind. Before the House of Islam became possible, two world empires—the Roman and the Iranian—had struggled seven hundred years for primacy. After the construction of the Great Mosque of Cordoba, Islam would wax and wane in Europe seven hundred years until its definitive suppression. *La Mezquita*'s Arabic spoke of itself thus:

It embodied what came before. Illuminated what came after.

More than ever before, light needs to be shone on the long Andalusian aftermath that is pressingly with us now.

Acknowledgments

CONCEIVED SIX MONTHS before September 11, 2001, a small book that was supposed to be finished quickly became a larger one that took considerable time to write. Some of those thanked below anticipated a different book; others probably never quite knew what to expect. Whatever satisfaction or disappointment this book evokes, the final product has benefited from individual and institutional assistance that any author would envy. To such assistance much of the text's interpretive clarity and factual accuracy is indebted. The failures are mine alone.

Among those who countered the author's earliest conceptual enthusiasms with patient expertise was UCLA's generous Nikki Keddie. From a cautionary conversation struck up at the 2001 *Los Angeles Times* Book Fair ensued e-mail exchanges of inestimable benefit with this pioneering scholar of Iranian history, Middle Eastern studies, and Muslim women. Similarly, on a memorable autumn afternoon in Princeton that same year, the learned Bernard Lewis summed up centuries of Islamic history for my benefit in his garden. Medievalist William Jordan, another Princeton fixture, entertained hypotheses about stirrups, heresy, and the Carolingian bureaucracy. Chouki El Hamel, Arizona State University, provided a Western-trained historian's deep knowledge of his native Morocco.

Those who read evolving versions of this book in whole or in part will merit special status if there is truly a day of judgment: Reza Aslan, University of California–Riverside; Lauren Benton, Katherine Fleming, and Francis E. Peters, New York University; Jonathan Berkey, Davidson

College; Matthew Guterl, Indiana University; S. Wamiq Jawaid, Columbia University. The material read was continually improved by the much appreciated responses to the author's many questions from Bernard S. Bachrach, University of Minnesota; Rudy Bell, Rutgers, the State University of New Jersey; Olivia R. Constable, University of Notre Dame; James Fernandez, New York University; Richard Gerberding, University of Alabama; Hugh Kennedy, emeritus, University of St. Andrews; Maria Rosa Menocal, Yale University.

Comment and criticism on papers I presented in the following fora proved immensely beneficial: the New York Humanities Institute, February 2005; the Spanish Department's "Unusual Suspects' Lecture," NYU, March 2005; Phi Alpha Theta / Organization of American Historians' Distinguished Lecture Program, Fordham University, April 2005; Dinner with the Provost, NYU, April 2007. Also very beneficial were the insights of the exceptional NYU students enrolled in Europe in Africa and Africa in Europe, my 2005 and 2006 freshman honors seminar.

The prodigious resources of the New York Public Library's Asian and Middle Eastern Division and of the Dorot Jewish Division facilitated much of the research for God's Crucible, as did the library's indispensable Wertheim Room, where a considerable portion was written. The Wertheim Room, access to which the amiable Wayne Furman has dispensed over the years like Solomon, is a writer's nirvana. New York University's Elmer Holmes Bobst Library, with its obliging, resourceful staff, complemented the great holdings at 42nd Street and Fifth Avenue with convenient sufficiency in Washington Square.

Library use was optimized by three superlative NYU graduate research assistants, consecutively: Stacey Pamela Patton, Lisa Westerbeek Viscidi, and Kendra Taira Field. Without their resourcefulness at finding photographs and reproducing illustrations, their e-mail diligence in obtaining positive responses from staffs at university and national libraries in other countries, their astute suggestions and sometimes reservations about a given line of thought, and, *mirabile dictu*, their cybernetic dexterity with maps, glossary, chronology, and those endless endnotes (Lisa Viscidi), this larger book would have taken even longer to write. Farida Jaber's Arabic language tutoring was invaluable.

The John D. and Catherine T. MacArthur Foundation astonished me in July 1999 by awarding one of its five-year fellowships. This good fortune was supplemented after 2003 by research funds attached to my NYU Julius Silver University Professorship. The sustained and generous interest in the research and writing of this book shown by NYU president John Sexton, arts and sciences dean Richard Foley, provost David McLaughlin, graduate faculty dean Catharine Stimpson, and history department chairperson Michael Gomez are deeply appreciated and, one hopes, justified by the printed product.

Friends have indulged the author's enthusiasms and despairs over the years with unfailing goodwill and even as conscripted researchers and editors. Sandra Masur suggested the title of the book; husband Victor Schuster concurred. Susan Butler Plum and Irwin Gellman read every page, critically. Carol Ann Preece relived her graduate student days in Franco's Spain and had an uncanny capacity for recommending brand new pertinent publications a preoccupied author had yet to notice. Joni Maya Cherbo listened and advised, as did dinner and traveling companions Robert and Patricia Curvin, Richard and Carolyn Thornell, and Paula Giddings, Fred Plum, Kenneth Wheeler, and Stephen Banker. Amanda and Larry Hobart offered summer shelter in Maine, and Carl and Clare Brandt winter relief in the Caribbean. Soyo Graham and Karl Horwitz insisted that research sojourns in Paris be leavened with fun and food, as did Barbara Chase-Riboud and Sergio Tosi. The Ehrenkranzes, Anne and Joel, have monitored the book's vital signs with flattering assiduousness.

W. W. Norton and Company calls to mind a paraphrase of the old Buick commercial: when better books are written, Norton will publish them. Drake McFeely, Norton's president, liked the idea of the book. Robert Weil's enthusiasm matched my own. The combination of critical enthusiasm and total engagement Bob Weil brings to manuscripts is matchless. Kathleen Brandes's copyediting of *God's Crucible* was superb. The capable assembly of the book by the Norton production team of Tom Mayer, Lucas Wittmann, Debra Morton Hoyt, and Anna Oler appeared to be seamless. The unflappable Carl Brandt—editor, therapist, and family friend—is a literary agent *sui generis*. This book owes Carl a grateful great debt.

As always, I am thankful for the presence in my life of daughters, Allison and Allegra, and sons, Eric and Jason. Ruth, although this book is dedicated to our first grandchild, my dedication to you is timeless.

Notes

Note: Citations from the Qur'an come from The Holy Qur'an, *with Arabic text, English translation, and commentary by Maulana Muhammad Ali (Lahore, Pakistan: Ahmadiyyah Anjuman Isha'at-e-Islam Lahore, 1995; orig. ed. 1917). For clarity, preference has occasionally been given to the fourth revised Penguin edition of* The Koran, *translated with notes by N. J. Dawood (London: Penguin, 1999; orig. ed. 1956).*

Preface

1. Edward Gibbon, *The History of the Decline and Fall of the Roman Empire.* 8 vols. (London: The Folio Society, 1983; orig. eds., 1776–88), vol. 7, p. 34.
2. David Levering Lewis, "In Morocco," in *The American Scholar* (winter 2002), pp. 38–40.

Chapter One

1. *Iran,* meaning "Land of the Noble" in Proto–Indo-European, replaced *Persia* as this nation's official designation in 1935. Properly speaking, Persians were the people of the province of Pars. All Persians were Iranians, but not all Iranians were Persians. The two terms are often used here interchangeably.
2. Sallust (Gaius Sallustus Crispus), quoted in Finley Hooper, *Roman Realities* (Detroit: Wayne State University Press, 1979), p. 178.
3. On Rome's expansion after Carthage: Hooper, *Roman Realities,* chs. 5, 6; Tom Holland, *Rubicon: The Last Years of the Roman Republic* (New York: Doubleday, 2003), chs. 1, 2.
4. On the rise of Parthia: Josef Wiesehöfer, *Ancient Persia from 550 B.C. to 650 A.D.* (London: I. B.Tauris Publications, 2006; orig. ed. 1995), pp. 3–117; Percy Sykes, *A History of Persia.* 2 vols. (London and New York: RoutledgeCurzon, 2004; orig. ed. 1915), vol. 1, chs. 26, 27.
5. Strabo, quoted in John P. McKay, Bennett D. Hill, John Buckler, eds., *A History of World Societies,* 3rd ed. (Boston: Houghton Mifflin, 1992), p. 214; Sykes, *History of Persia,* vol. 1, ch. 29; Wiesehöfer, *Ancient Persia,* ch. 6.
6. Hooper, *Roman Realities,* p. 223; Sykes, *History of Persia,* vol. 1, p. 30.
7. Profile of Marcus Licinius Crassus and his Parthian campaign as related in Hooper, *Roman Realities,* pp. 223–71 Holland, *Rubicon,* pp. 250–60. See also, for Arab participation, Jan Retsö, *The Arabs in Antiquity* (London: RoutledgeCurzon, 2005), p. 395; Sykes, *History of Persia,* vol. 1, ch. 30. "The conflict of Rome and Persia was prolonged.

. . .": Edward Gibbon, *The History of the Decline and Fall of the Roman Empire*. 8 vols. (London: The Folio Society, 1983; orig. eds., 1776–88), vol. 5, p. 335.

8. On the downfall of the Parthian dynasty, see Sykes, *History of Persia*, vol. 1, ch. 34; Mary Boyce, *Zoroastrians: Their Religious Beliefs and Practices* (New York: Routledge, 2001; orig. ed. 1979), pp. 79–83, 117–18.

9. On the great Roman crisis in the third Christian century: Peter Heather, *The Fall of the Roman Empire: A New History of Rome and the Barbarians* (New York: Oxford University Press, 2006), pp. 60–66. On the Persian victories at Antioch and over Valerian: Hooper, *Roman Realities*, pp. 482–98; Sykes, *History of Persia*, vol. 1, pp. 401–2; Wiesehöfer, *Ancient Persia*, pp. 160–62.

10. "A most mischievous nation. . . .": Emperor Julian, quoted in Hooper, *Roman Realities*, p. 519.

11. On Diocletian's reforms: Hooper, *Roman Realities*, p. 493; Heather, *Fall of the Roman Empire*, pp. 62–66; James Carroll, *Constantine's Sword: The Church and the Jews* (Boston: Houghton Mifflin, 2001), pp. 166–70.

12. On Emperor Valens and the disaster at Adrianople: Hooper, *Roman Realities*, p. 524; J. F. C. Fuller, *Decisive Battles of the Western World and Their Influence Upon History* (London: Eyre & Spottiswoode, 1954), pp. 275–76; Heather, *Fall of the Roman Empire*, pp. 177–81.

13. Departure of Romulus Augustulus: Heather, *Fall of the Roman Empire*, pp. 427–29.

14. On the competition of the faiths (Mithraism in the Roman Empire), see Richard C. Foltz, *Spirituality in the Land of the Noble: How Iran Shaped the World's Religions* (Oxford: Oneworld, 2004), p. 33; Desmond O'Grady, *Beyond the Empire: Rome and the Church from Constantine to Charlemagne* (New York: Crossroad Publishing, 2001), pp. 1–19, 27–28; Carroll, *Constantine's Sword*, p. 167; Boyce, *Zoroastrians*, p. 119.

15. John Julius Norwich, *Byzantium: The Early Centuries* (New York: Knopf, 2001), pp. 148–56; O'Grady, *Beyond the Empire*, pp. 27–28.

16. On the religions of the Axial Age: Jonathan P. Berkey, *The Formation of Islam: Religion and Society in the Near East, 600–1800* (New York: Cambridge University Press, 2003), pp. 4–28; Karen Armstrong, *The Great Transformation: The Beginning of Our Religious Traditions* (New York: Knopf, 2006), pp. 8–12; Wiesehöfer, *Ancient Persia*, pp. 94–98; Foltz, *Spirituality*, pp. 25–28; Boyce, *Zoroastrians*, pp. 18–20; Sykes, *History of Persia*, vol. 1, ch. 9.

17. On Darius and Cyrus and Zoroastrianism: A. T. Olmstead, *History of the Persian Empire: A Historical Pageant of the Greatness of Ancient Persia* . . . (Chicago: University of Chicago Press, 1948), pp. 24–37. On Zoroastrian scriptures and practices: Boyce, *Zoroastrians*, pp. 17–67.

18. "If I ask for my bill . . ." (visiting businessman quoted): Stephen O'Shea, *Sea of Faith: Islam and Christianity in the Medieval Mediterranean World* (New York: Walker, 2006), p. 14.

19. Shapur II is believed to be history's only king who was crowned *in utero*: Sykes, *History of Persia*, vol. 1, p. 411.

20. On Nestorians and Monophysites among the Iranians: Foltz, *Spirituality*, pp. 80–84; Boyce, *Zoroastrians*, p. 111; Berkey, *Formation of Islam*, p. 31. The Egyptian businessman Cosmas, quoted in Maxime Rodinson, *Muhammad* (New York: New Press, 1968; Eng. ed. 1971), p. 2. "The Christians were all of them spies . . .": Sassanian source quoted in Wiesehöfer, *Ancient Persia*, p. 202. On the role of the Zoroastrian *mobad*, *Karter/Kirder*. Boyce, *Zoroastrians*, p. 111; Berkey, p. 31.

21. "Solomon, I have surpassed thee" (Justinian quoted): Norwich, *Byzantium*, p. 204.

22. Justinian and Theodora, and Procopius's views of them: Procopius, *The Secret History*

(London: Penguin, 1966), ch. 2, esp. pp. 80–84; Norwich, *Byzantium,* pp. 204, 247. On the campaigns of Belisarius and Narses against the Goths in Italy: Peter Saris, "The Eastern Roman Empire from Constantine to Heraclius (306–641)," p. 53 in *The Oxford History of Byzantium,* ed. Cyril Mango (New York: Oxford University Press, 2002).

23. Citizens of the Eastern Roman Empire never referred to themselves as Byzantines but rather as Romans and/or Greeks; their corner of the Middle East to them was not Byzantium but rather Rome, the Second Rome, or the Eastern Roman Empire. The editor of *The Oxford History of Byzantium* (2002), p. 2, puts it nicely: "Byzantium, then, is a term of convenience when it is not a term of inconvenience." *Graeco-Roman* is my inconvenient term of convenience.

24. On the empire after Justinian, especially Justin II's difficulties: Steven Runciman, *Byzantine Civilization* (London: Methuen, 1975; orig. ed. 1933), p. 111; Saris, "The Eastern Roman Empire," p. 19; Norwich, *Byzantium,* ch. 13; Rodinson, *Muhammad,* p. 34.

25. Byzantine/Iranian geopolitics: Runciman, *Byzantine Civilization,* p. 132; Norwich, *Byzantium,* ch. 13; McKay, Hill, and Buckler, eds., *History of World Societies,* p. 215.

26. The Iranian crisis and the Sassanian Golden Age: Boyce, *Zoroastrians,* pp. 130–33; Wiesehöfer, *Ancient Persia,* p. 173.

27. Mazdakism and Khosrow's counterrevolution: Foltz, *Spirituality,* pp. 103–13; Boyce, *Zoroastrians,* pp. 130–33; Sykes, *History of Persia,* vol. 1, pp. 442–44, 461–65.

28. Khosrow's counterrevolution: Boyce, *Zoroastrians,* pp. 130–31; Foltz, *Spirituality,* pp. 112–13; Sykes, *History of Persia,* vol. 1, pp. 449–50; Wiesehöfer, *Ancient Persia,* pp. 173–74.

29. Intellectual ferment at Gondeshapur: Wiesehöfer, *Ancient Persia,* pp. 162, 217–25.

30. Persian high culture and the Babylonian Talmud, and Persian high culture and the Arabs: Rodinson, *Muhammad,* pp. 7–8; Foltz, *Spirituality,* pp. 53–54; Richard N. Frye, *The Golden Age of Persia: The Arabs in the East* (London: Weidenfeld and Nicolson, 1975), pp. 18–22; Sykes, *History of Persia,* vol. 1, ch. 41.

31. "Mazda-worshipping religion" (Khosrow quote): Boyce, *Zoroastrians,* p. 133. Mazdakite influences on Islam: Foltz, *Spirituality,* pp. 112–18.

32. The Sassanian attack on the Eastern Roman Empire: Norwich, *Byzantium,* p. 272; Saris, "Eastern Roman Empire," pp. 53–54; Sykes, *History of Persia,* vol. 1, pp. 476–78.

33. Emperor Maurice's mindset and his classic *Strategikon:* Runciman, *Byzantine Civilization,* p. 110; Norwich, *Byzantium,* p. 273.

34. Emperor Maurice's policies and Khosrow II: Runciman, *Byzantine Civilization,* pp. 142–45; Sykes, *History of Persia,* vol. 1, pp. 478–80.

35. The spillover of the Iranian/Byzantine conflict into Arabia: Jan Retsö, *The Arabs in Antiquity: Their History from the Assyrians to the Umayyads* (London: RoutledgeCurzon, 2005), pp. 17–18; Boyce, *Zoroastrians,* pp. 29–33. On Dhu Nuwas, "the man with the hanging locks": Rodinson, *Muhammad,* p. 30.

36. The Ethiopian invasion of Mecca and Muhammad's birth: Abu Ja'far Muhammad ibn Jarir al-Tabari (839–923), *The History of the Prophets and Kings [Ta'rikh al-Rusul wa'l-Muluk]:* Vol. 6, *Muhammad at Mecca,* trans. and annotated W. Montgomery Watt and M. V. McDonald (Albany: State University of New York Press, 1988), p. xiii; Bernard Lewis, *The Middle East: A Brief History of the Last 2,000 Years* (New York: Simon & Schuster, 1995), pp. 43–45; Retsö, *Arabs in Antiquity,* p. 17; Rodinson, *Muhammad,* p. 33; Fred McGraw Donner, *The Early Islamic Conquests* (Princeton, NJ: Princeton University Press, 1981). "If a Christian power had been maintained": Gibbon, *Decline and Fall,* vol. 5, p. 206; Reza Aslan, *No god but God: The Origins, Evolution, and Future of Islam* (New York: Random House, 2005), p. 18.

37. *Banu* is Arabic for "clan."
38. The collapse of Lakhm and Ghassan: Donner, *Early Islamic Conquests*, pp. 45–47; Rodinson, *Muhammad*, pp. 27–28.
39. Muhammad's Mecca and the origins of the Quraysh: al-Tabari, *Muhammad at Mecca*, pp. xxviii–xxix; Rodinson, *Muhammad*, pp. 35–39; Donner, *Early Islamic Conquests*, pp. 51–52; Lewis, *The Middle East*, pp. 42–43; Aslan, *No god but God*, pp. 24–31.
40. Islam "developed as an answer to the problem. . . .": al-Tabari, *Muhammad at Mecca*, p. xxix; Donner, *Early Islamic Conquests*, pp. 51–52. "When you see kingdoms fighting . . .": quoted in Rodinson, *Muhammad*, p. 66.
41. The Mesopotamian Zeitgeist and Muhammad: Aslan, *No god but God*, p. 22; Wiesehöfer, *Ancient Persia*, pp. 210–15; F. E. Peters, *Judaism, Christianity, and Islam: The Classical Texts and Their Interpretation*. 2 vols. (Princeton, NJ: Princeton University Press, 1990), vol. 1, pp. 188, 194, 274. "Formed a great wisdom such as has not existed in previous generations . . .": Mani, quoted in Berkey, *Formation of Islam*, p. 31.

Chapter Two

1. Meeting of Bahira and Muhammad: Ibn Ishaq, *The Life of Muhammad: Apostle of Allah*, ed. Michael Edwardes (London: The Folio Society, 2003), pp. 23–24; al-Tabari, *Muhammad at Mecca*, pp. xxix–xxxi; Martin Lings, *Muhammad: His Life Based on the Earliest Sources* (Rochester, VT: Inner Traditions International, 1983), pp. 19–30; Maxime Rodinson, *Muhammad* (New York: New Press, 1968; Eng. ed. 1971), pp. 46–48; "Primarily a way of reassuring people that Muhammad was really a prophet": al-Tabari, *Muhammad at Mecca*, p. xxix; Reza Aslan, *No god but God: The Origins, Evolution, and Future of Islam* (New York: Random House, 2005), p. 21.
2. Muhammad's coming of age: Ibn Ishaq, *Life of Muhammad*, pp. 1–25; Aslan, *No god but God*, p. 232; Rodinson, *Muhammad*, pp. 38–42.
3. Muhammad and Khadija: Lings, *Muhammad*, pp. 34–36. Muhammad's "beautiful character . . .": Khadija in Lings, p. 35; al-Tabari, *Muhammad at Mecca*, pp. xxii, xxxi; Rodinson, *Muhammad*, pp. 51–54.
4. Mecca's deities: Aslan, *No god but God*, pp. 6–8. "Verily they are the most exalted females . . .": Ka'bah chant in W. H. McNeill and Marilyn Robinson Waldman, eds., *The Islamic World* (New York: Oxford University Press, 1973), p. 9; F. E. Peters, *The Monotheists: Jews, Christians, and Muslims in Conflict and Competition*. 2 vols. (Princeton, NJ: Princeton University Press, 2003), vol. 1, p. 12.
5. The path to early revelations: Muhammad "grew to love solitude . . .": Ibn Ishaq, in al-Tabari, *Muhammad at Mecca*, p. 67.
6. "The night of destiny": Ibn Ishaq, *Life of Muhammad*, p. 36; Rodinson, *Muhammad*, p. 73; Lings, *Muhammad*, pp. 43–44. "Wrap me up!": Muhammad, quoted in al-Tabari, *Muhammad at Mecca*, pp. xxxvii, 67–68. "Recite!": *The Koran*, trans. N. J. Dawood (London: Penguin, 1999; orig. ed. 1956), 96:1; *The Holy Qur'an*, trans. and commentary Maulana Muhammad Ali (Lahore, Pakistan: Ahmadiyya Anjuman Isha'at-e-Islam Lahore, 1995; orig. ed. 1917); Rodinson, pp. 72–73.
7. Muhammad reassured: Rodinson, *Muhammad*, p. 148. "A poet or a madman": al-Tabari, *Muhammad at Mecca*, p. 71. "Yours will be an unending reward": *Qur'an*, 68:2. Waraqah ibn Nawfal in Rodinson, p. 73.
8. The first commandments and end of the *al-jahiliyya*: "That wealth will perpetuate him": *Qur'an*, 104:3. "He will heap all the wicked one upon another": *Qur'an*, 8:36. "The

abyss shall be his home": *Qur'an,* 101:9. Other *suras*: "Glorify your Lord": 74:2, 3; ". . . until idolatry is no more . . .": 2:193; "As for the orphan . . .": 93:9; ". . . legally entitled to a fair share": 4:7; ". . . for agreement is best": 4:35; ". . . and best them": 4:34.

9. Egalitarian principles and class tensions in Mecca: Lings, *Muhammad,* p. 113; Rodinson, *Muhammad,* pp. 100–101. "God made Adam in his [the slave's] image": Muhammad in al-Tabari, *Muhammad at Mecca,* p. xviii. Critical nucleus of Companions: Rodinson, p. 100.

10. The scribe's full name was Zayd ibn Thabit ibn al-Dahlak, born at Yathrib in 611 and soon orphaned. Recognizing his precocity, Muhammad instructed Zayd to master Syriac and Hebrew.

11. Fundamental and false steps: al-Tabari, *Muhammad at Mecca,* pp. xliv, xxxiv. "Have you considered Allat . . .": *Qur'an,* 53:19.

12. Opposition hardens: F. E. Peters, *The Monotheists,* vol. 2, p. 94; Rodinson, *Muhammad,* p. 106; Ibn Ishaq, *Life of Muhammad,* pp. 47–48; al-Tabari, *Muhammad at Mecca,* p. xxxiv. "They behaved violently towards him": Rodinson, p. 108. "Every clan fell upon those of its members . . .": al-Tabari, *Muhammad at Mecca,* p. 97.

13. "Nothing shall his wealth . . .": *Qur'an,* 111:2. "He would have said 'yes' to that too . . .": Ibn Ishaq, *Life of Muhammad,* p. 48; Rodinson, *Muhammad,* p. 110.

14. Ethiopia, Qurayshite hostility and the "rightly guided": Rodinson, *Muhammad,* p. 116; Lings, *Muhammad,* ch. 27. The "nightly journey": al-Tabari, *Muhammad at Mecca,* p. xli. "Better for you than the beginning": *Qur'an,* 93.

15. Medina arrival: Rodinson, *Muhammad,* pp. 139, 152; Aslan, *No god but God,* p. 59; Lings, *Muhammad,* pp. 113–14.

16. The party's agreement: Lings, *Muhammad,* pp. 111–12, 56. Muhammad and the Jews: Rodinson, *Muhammad,* p. 159; Peters, *The Monotheists,* vol. 1, p. 101. "The only true faith in God's sight": *Qur'an,* 3:18, 19; Michel Abitbol, *Le passé d'une discorde: Juifs et Arabes du VIIe siècle à nos jours* (Paris: Perrin, 1999), p. 14.

17. The Battle of Badr: Rodinson, *Muhammad,* pp. 165–70.

18. Expulsion of the Qaynuqa: Lings, *Muhammad,* pp. 161–62; Rodinson, *Muhammad,* p. 173. "Will you slay them all?": Rodinson, p. 17; Peters, *The Monotheists,* vol. 1, p. 101.

19. The Constitution of Medina: Aslan, *No god but God,* p. 55; Azim Nanji, ed., *The Muslim Almanac: A Reference Work on the History, Faith, Culture, and Peoples of Islam* (Detroit: Gale Research, 1996), p. 6.

20. "He sat down in front of the Prophet": John L. Esposito, ed., *The Oxford History of Islam* (New York: Oxford University Press, 2000), p. 75.

21. The Battle of Uhud: Rodinson, *Muhammad,* pp. 180–83. "They shall be lodged in peace together": *Qur'an,* 44:51–55.

22. Muhammad's conflict with the Medina Jews: "We believe in what was revealed to *us*": *Qur'an,* 2:89. "God forbid that He should have a son!": *Qur'an,* 4:171. "Why then does He punish you for your sins?": *Qur'an,* 5:18. "We sent other apostles before you": *Qur'an,* 13:38. Expulsion of the Nadir: Rodinson, *Muhammad,* pp. 191–93.

23. The Battle of the Trench: Rodinson, *Muhammad,* pp. 208–12. "Save them from God's wrath": Rodinson, p. 311. Muhammad's Rayhana, the beautiful captive: Rodinson, p. 213. Massacre of the Qurayza: Rodinson, pp. 213–14; Lings, *Muhammad,* p. 214.

24. The necklace affair: "And if thou art innocent . . .": Muhammad, quoted in Lings, *Muhammad,* p. 245. Rodinson, *Muhammad,* pp. 199–204. The resolution of adultery as a result of the necklace affair: "Those that defame honorable women and cannot produce four witnesses shall be given 80 lashes": *Qur'an,* 24:4.

25. The Prophet reproached for Mariya: "Why do you prohibit that which Allah has made

lawful . . .": *Qur'an*, 66:1; Lings, *Muhammad*, p. 277; Rodinson, *Muhammad*, p. 283; Abu Ja'far Muhammad ibn Jarir al-Tabari (839–923), *The History of the Prophets and Kings* [*Ta'rikh al-Rusul wa'l-Muluk*]: Vol. 13, *The Conquest of Iraq, Southwestern Persia, and Egypt*, trans. Gautier H. A. Juynboll (Albany: State University of New York Press, 1988), p. 58.

26. On Hudaybiyya: Lings, *Muhammad*, pp. 280–81. "They have betrayed us": Lings, p. 292.

27. Muhammad enters Mecca: "O men of the Quraysh, Muhammad is here . . ." (Abu Sufyan quoted) and "greasy good-for-nothing bladder of a man" (Hind quoted): Lings, *Muhammad*, p. 298. Destruction of Hubal and the idols: Lings, p. 300.

28. Scholars differ as to the content of Allah's final message. Among the most likely is *sura* 5:3: "This day have I perfected for you your religion and completed my favor to you and chosen for you Islam as a religion."

29. Death of the Prophet; his successor: al-Tabari, *Muhammad at Mecca*, p. xli; Aslan, *No god but God*, pp. 112–19.

30. Consolidating Islam: Rodinson, *Muhammad*, p. 241; Fred McGraw Donner, *The Early Islamic Conquests* (Princeton, NJ: Princeton University Press, 1981), p. 85. Other prophets in the Hijaz: Jonathan P. Berkey, *The Formation of Islam: Religion and Society in the Near East, 600–1800* (New York: Cambridge University Press, 2003), p. 71; Rodinson, p. 67.

31. The Muslim lunar calendar: al-Tabari, *Muhammad at Mecca*, p. xlvi.

32. The *ahadith*: "Will never know prosperity" (a Companion quoted): Aslan, *No god but God*, p. 69. A'isha's *hadith* on adulterous women: Paul Fregosi, *Jihad in the West* (Amherst, NY: Prometheus Books, 1998), p. 63; Nikki Keddie, *Women in the Middle East: Past and Present* (Princeton, NJ: Princeton University Press, 2006), ch. 1.

33. Qur'anic pronouncements: "This Book is not to be doubted": *Qur'an*, 2:2, "The Cow." Blasphemy, usury, wine, and "the flesh of swine" forbidden: *Qur'an*, 2:173. On the number of wives ("two, three, or four of them"): *Qur'an*, 4:3.

34. "There shall be no compulsion in religion": *Qur'an*, 2:256. "Slay them wherever you find them": *sura* 2:191.

35. "Who has not begotten, nor is He begotten": *Qur'an*, 112:1, 4. On Muhammad's animus against versifiers: Rodinson, *Muhammad*, p. 149.

36. "And round about them will go youths": *Qur'an*, 76:19 and 76:11–21.

37. "Ask the Israelites . . .": *Qur'an*, 2:211 and 10:36. "Those who disbelieve will wish that they were Muslims": *Qur'an*, 15:2.

Chapter Three

1. "The Romans have been defeated . . .": Muhammad quoted, *Qur'an*, 30:2; Walter Kaegi, *Byzantium and the Early Islamic Conquests* (Cambridge: Cambridge University Press, 1992), p. 33. On the fall of Phocas: John Julius Norwich, *Byzantium: The Early Centuries* (New York: Knopf, 2001), p. 279; Alfred Butler, *The Arab Invasion of Egypt and the Last Thirty Years of Roman Dominion* (Brooklyn, NY: A & B Publishing, 1992; orig. ed. 1902), pp. 2–4.

2. On Khosrow II and the Byzantine Empire: Walter Kaegi, *Heraclius: Emperor of Byzantium* (Cambridge: Cambridge University Press, 2003), p. 39; Kaegi, *Byzantium*, pp. 66–67. On Nestorian Christianity in Iran: Fred McGraw Donner, *The Early Islamic Conquests* (Princeton, NJ: Princeton University Press, 1981), pp. 168–69.

3. Heraclius removes Phocas: Kaegi, *Heraclius*, p. 50.

4. The Iranian *Blitzkrieg*: Kaegi, *Byzantium*, pp. 33, 45; Kaegi, *Heraclius*, p. 75; Cyril Mango, ed., *The Oxford History of Byzantium* (New York: Oxford University Press, 2002), pp. 53–55; Donner, *Early Islamic Conquests*, pp. 7–9.

5. "Avenged themselves on the Persians . . .": Muhammad quoted in Maxime Rodinson, *Muhammad* (New York: New Press, 1968), p. 65; Mango, ed., *Oxford History of Byzantium*, pp. 53–55.

6. The Iranian sack of Jerusalem: Butler, *Arab Invasion of Egypt*, pp. 59–64; Norwich, *Byzantium*, p. 285; Kaegi, *Byzantium*, p. 45; Percy Sykes, *A History of Persia*. 2 vols. (London and New York: RoutledgeCurzon, 2004; orig. ed. 1915), vol. I, pp. 482–83. Arab poet al-A'sha: Kaegi, *Heraclius*, p. 131.

7. Persian exploitation of the Eastern Roman Empire's religious divisions: Norman A. Stillman, *The Jews of Arab Lands: A History and Source Book* (Philadelphia: Jewish Publication Society of America, 1979), pp. 19–22. "All Christians under my rule . . .": Khosrow II quoted in Butler, *Arab Invasion of Egypt*, p. 65.

8. "May God help the Romans": Kaegi, *Heraclius*, p. 93.

9. Iranian siege of Constantinople: Butler, *Arab Invasion of Egypt*, p. 70; Kaegi, *Heraclius*, p. 84; Rodinson, *Muhammad*, p. 59. Field Marshal Shahin's quote: Kaegi, *Heraclius*, p. 84. "Shall themselves gain victory": Muhammad quoted: *Qur'an*, 30:2, 3. On Heraclius's victory: Norwich, *Byzantium*, p. 290; Rodinson, p. 266; Mango, ed., *Oxford History of Byzantium*, p. 55.

10. Events leading to the Battle of Nineveh: Kaegi, *Heraclius*, pp. 128–32; Norwich, *Byzantium*, p. 293; Butler, *Arab Invasion of Egypt*, pp. 120–25; Sykes, *History of Persia*, vol. I, p. 485.

11. Khosrow's military defeat and the collapse of the Sassanian Empire: Mango, ed., *Oxford History of Byzantium*, pp. 55–56; Kaegi, *Heraclius*, pp. 174–88; Rodinson, *Muhammad*, p. 266; Kaegi, *Byzantium*, pp. 66–67; Sykes, *History of Persia*, vol. I, p. 486.

12. Heraclius in Jerusalem: "One blaze of gold and color": Butler, *Arab Invasion of Egypt*, p. 131. Church of the Resurrection: Butler, p. 131; James Carroll, *Constantine's Sword: The Church and the Jews* (Boston: Houghton Mifflin, 2001), pp. 196–99; Kaegi, *Byzantium*, p. 117. Heraclius's persecution of the Jews: Yitzhak Baer, *A History of the Jews in Christian Spain*. 2 vols. (Philadelphia: Jewish Publication Society of America, 1961–66), p. 19; Butler, p. 134; Steven Runciman, *The First Crusade* (Cambridge: Cambridge University Press, 1980; orig. ed. 1951), pp. 12–13.

13. The decline of Heraclius: Kaegi, *Byzantium*, pp. 64–65. Muhammad's invitation to Heraclius: Kaegi, p. 69; Runciman, *First Crusade*, p. 12, Rodinson, *Muhammad*, pp. 255–56.

14. *Jihad*, struggle or exertion within oneself or against enemies: John L. Esposito, *What Everyone Needs to Know about Islam* (New York: Oxford University Press, 2002), p. 184.

15. "Warrior after warrior, column after column . . .": Donner, *Early Islamic Conquests*, p. 3. On the size of the Arab armies: Donner, pp. 4–8, 126–32, 205. "Fighting is obligatory for you": *Qur'an*, 2:216. "Rich booty": *Qur'an*, 48:20.

16. 'Umar's *diwan*: David Nicolle, *Armies of the Muslim Conquest* (London: Osprey, 1993), pp. 18–19; Abu Ja'far Muhammad ibn Jarir al-Tabari (839–923), *The History of the Prophets and Kings [Ta'rikh al-Rusul wa'l-Muluk]*: Vol. 13, *The Conquest of Iraq, Southwestern Persia, and Egypt*, trans. Gautier H. A. Juynboll (Albany: State University of New York Press, 1988), p. 177.

17. On the Battle of Jabiya-Yarmuk: Kaegi, *Byzantium*, pp. 119–27; Hugh Kennedy, *The Armies of the Caliphs: Military and Society in the Early Islamic State* (London: Routledge, 2001), pp. 4, 11; Donner, *Early Islamic Conquests*, p. 133.

18. On the Battle of al-Qadisiyya: "They first used up all the darts . . .": al-Tabari, *Conquest of Iraq*, p. 41; Sykes, *History of Persia*, vol. I, pp. 495–96. 19. On the Iranian collapse: "How many gardens and springs . . .": Sa'd ibn Abi Waqqas quoted in al-Tabari, *Conquest of Iraq*, p. 23.

19. Bernard Lewis, *The Middle East: A Brief History of the Last 2,000 Years* (New York: Simon & Schuster, 1995), pp. 56–57.

20. "Fatter while their vigor was on the decline": al-Tabari, *The Conquest of Iraq, Southwestern Persia, and Egypt*, pp. 62–63. "That which suits their camels": al-Tabari, *Conquest of Iraq*, pp. 63, 66.

21. End of Yazdegird: Sykes, *History of Persia*, vol. I, pp. 501–2. "Damn this world . . .": Persian saying from the *Shahnahmeh (Book of Kings)*.

22. On besieging Jerusalem: "Prowled round the walls": Butler, *Arab Invasion of Egypt*, p. 166. Leaders of the *Dar al-Harb*: Donner, *Early Islamic Conquests*, pp. 178–202.

23. 'Umar enters Jerusalem: Butler, *Early Islamic Conquests*, p. 165; Kanan Makiya, *The Rock: A Tale of Seventh-Century Jerusalem* (New York: Pantheon, 2001), p. 30. "Mosque of David": Makiya, p. 308, Norwich, *Byzantium*, pp. 306–7. "Behold the abomination of desolation": Norwich, p. 307.

24. "There shall be no compulsion in religion": Qur'an, 2:256; Stillman, *Jews of Arab Lands*, p. 25.

25. On the rules of the game: Norwich, *Byzantium*, pp. 306–7. "There are three possibilities": al-Tabari, *Conquest of Iraq*, p. 16.

26. 'Amr's conquests: Butler, *Arab Invasion of Egypt*, pp. 257, 368–69. "Never met a man who understood the Qur'an better": Butler, p. 204; Kennedy, *Armies of the Caliphs*, p. 71; Muzaffar Iqbal, *Islam and Science* (Burlington, VT: Ashgate Publishing, 2002), p. 7.

27. On Arab display of sophistication at Misr: al-Tabari, *Conquest of Iraq*, p. 174.

28. On the conquest of Alexandria: Butler, *Arab Invasion of Egypt*, pp. 156, 194–221. "Are you not an Arab?": Butler, p. 329.

29. Occupied Alexandria: "Could see to thread his needle . . .": Butler, *Arab Invasion of Egypt*, p. 369. "But can do without people": al-Tabari, *Conquest of Iraq*, p. 169. "Forty thousand tributary Jews . . .": Butler, p. 368. "If what is written in them agrees with the Book of God . . .": 'Umar quoted in Butler, p. 402.

30. Advance into the Maghreb: Butler, *Arab Invasion of Egypt*, ch. 26. "Whole tribes in endless succession": Donner, *Early Islamic Conquests*, p. 3.

31. "We destroyed generations . . .": Qur'an, 10:13.

Chapter Four

1. 'Umar's concerns: Allah "never gave [such as] this . . .": Abu Ja'far Muhammad ibn Jarir al-Tabari (839–923), *The History of the Prophets and Kings* [*Ta'rikh al-Rusul wa'l-Muluk*]: Vol. 13, *The Conquest of Iraq, Southwestern Persia, and Egypt*, trans. Gautier H. A. Juynboll (Albany: State University of New York Press, 1988), pp. 46, 43. "I am a merchant for the benefit of the Muslims": Alfred Butler, *The Arab Invasion of Egypt and the Last Thirty Years of Roman Dominion* (Brooklyn, NY: A & B Publishing, 1992), p. 459.

2. Zayd ibn Thabit, the scribe: Reza Aslan, *No god but God* (New York: Random House, 2005), p. 126.

3. "How stupid is the Muslim who is beguiled": al-Tabari, *Conquest of Iraq*, p. 33; Butler,

Arab Invasion of Egypt, p. 463. 'Uthman reproached: Aslan, *No god but God*, p. 125. G. R. Hawting, *The First Dynasty of Islam: The Umayyad Caliphate, AD 661–750* (London: Routledge, 2000; orig. ed. 1986), pp. 27–28.

4. Death of 'Uthman: "Your father did not take hold of it!": W. H. McNeill and Marilyn Robinson Waldman, eds., *The Islamic World* (New York: Oxford University Press, 1973), p. 76; Bernard Lewis, *The Middle East: A Brief History of the Last 2,000 Years* (London: Weidenfeld and Nicolson, 1995), p. 63.

5. Ali's caliphate: Nikki Keddie, *Women in the Middle East: Past and Present* (Princeton, NJ: Princeton University Press, 2006), pp. 27, 29, 209; Hawting, *First Dynasty of Islam*, pp. 30–32.

6. Competition between Ali and Mu'awiya ibn Abi Sufyan: Butler, *Arab Invasion of Egypt*, pp. 492–93. "He that kills a Believer by design": Qur'an, 4:93.

7. Ali's martyrdom: Ignaz Goldziher, *Introduction to Islamic Theology and Law* (Princeton, NJ: Princeton University Press, 1981; orig. ed. 1910), pp. 170–72; Butler, *Arab Invasion of Egypt*, p. 492; Hawting, *First Dynasty of Islam*, p. 32.

8. The rise of Mu'awiya: Hawting, *First Dynasty of Islam*, ch. 3. Sunnis: John L. Esposito, *What Everyone Needs to Know about Islam* (New York: Oxford University Press, 2002), p. 178. "When the lash suffices": Hawting, p. 42.

9. Umayyad expansionism: John Julius Norwich, *Byzantium: The Early Centuries* (New York: Knopf, 2001), pp. 323–24; Lewis, *Middle East*, pp. 64–66; Hugh Kennedy, *The Armies of the Caliphs: Military and Society in the Early Islamic State* (London: Routledge, 2001), pp. 35–51. Taxes, *jizya, dhimma, mawali*, and *kafir* explained in John L. Esposito, ed., *The Oxford History of Islam* (New York: Oxford University Press, 2000), p. 13.

10. Mu'awiya's Damascus: Abdulqader Rihawi, *Damascus: Its History, Development, and Artistic Heritage* (Damascus: self-published, 1977); Finbarr Barry Flood, *The Great Mosque of Damascus: Studies on the Makings of an Umayyad Visual Culture* (Leiden: E. J. Brill, 2000).

11. Umayyad-Hashemite conflict (Ali ibn Abu Talib): "Turn aside from what will cause your death": Abu Ja'far Muhammad ibn Jarir al-Tabari (839–923), *The History of the Prophets and Kings [Ta'rikh al-Rusul wa'l-Muluk]:* Vol. 19: *The Caliphate of Yazid ibn Mu'awiyah*, trans I. K. A. Howard (Albany: State University of New York Press, 1988), p. 73. "Fill my saddlebag with silver": al-Tabari, *Caliphate of Yazid*, p. 76; 'Abd al-Ameer 'Abd Dixon, *The Umayyad Caliphate, 65–86/684–705: A Political Study* (London: Luzac & Co., 1971), pp. 3–83; Jonathan P. Berkey, *The Formation of Islam: Religion and Society in the Near East, 600–1800* (New York: Cambridge University Press, 2003), pp. 65–78; Aslan, *No god but God*, p. 177; Hawting, *First Dynasty of Islam*, pp. 51–54.

12. The savage encounters of the *fitna*: Hawting, *First Dynasty of Islam*, pp. 46–51.

13. Organizing the *jihad*: Hawting, *First Dynasty of Islam*, p. 37; Lewis, *The Middle East*, pp. 56–57. "There is no compulsion in religion": Qur'an, 2:256.

14. Hawting, *First Dynasty of Islam*, pp. 4–5.

15. "So believe only in Allah . . .": Qur'an, 4:112.

16. 'Umar II's "fiscal rescript": Hawting, *First Dynasty of Islam*, pp. 77–79.

17. The Berbers of the Maghreb: Salma Khadra Jayyusi, ed., *The Legacy of Muslim Spain*. 2 vols. (Leiden: Brill, 1992), vol. 1, pp. 12–14; Hugh Kennedy, *Muslim Spain and Portugal: A Political History of al-Andalus* (London: Longman, 1996), pp. 5–7; Abdulwahid Dhannun Taha, *Muslim Conquest and Settlement of North Africa and Spain* (London: Routledge, 1989), pp. 19–22; Richard Fletcher, *The Cross and the Crescent: Christianity and Islam from Muhammad to the Reformation* (New York: Viking, 2003), pp. 39–42.

18. "Oh God, if the sea had not prevented me . . .": C. R. Pennell, *Morocco: From Empire to Independence* (Oxford: Oneworld, 2003), p. 24. On Kusayla, "Lion of the Mountains":

Roger Collins, *Visigothic Spain, 409–711* (Oxford: Blackwell, 2004), pp. 127–28; Yves Modéran, *Les Maures et l'Afrique Romaine (IVe–VIIe siècle)* (Rome: Ecole Française de Rome, 2003), pp. 675–81.

19. Berber resistance; Kusayla and the *Kahina*: Modéran, *Les Maures;* Kennedy, *Muslim Spain and Portugal,* pp. 5–7; Collins, *Visigothic Spain,* pp. 127–30.

20. On Musa ibn Nusayr and Tariq ibn Ziyad: Taha, *Muslim Conquest,* pp. 72–75; Joseph Reinaud [Haroun Khan Sherwani], *Muslim Colonies in France, Northern Italy, and Switzerland* (Lahore, Pakistan: Sh. Muhammad Ashraf, 1954), pp. 27–45; Kennedy, *Muslim Spain and Portugal,* pp. 2–7; Jayyusi, ed., *Legacy of Muslim Spain,* vol. 1, p. 4; Taha, *Muslim Conquest,* pp. 72–76.

Chapter Five

1. A critique of Henri Pirenne: Richard Hodges and David Whitehouse, *Mohammed, Charlemagne and the Origins of Europe* (Ithaca, NY: Cornell University Press, 1983), pp. 6–10.

2. The collapsing West and the Goths: Richard Fletcher, *The Barbarian Conversion: From Paganism to Christianity* (New York: Henry Holt, 1998), pp. 68–72; Peter Heather, *The Fall of the Roman Empire: A New History of Rome and the Barbarians* (New York: Oxford University Press, 2006), pp. 148–73. "Went on night and day": *Ammianus Marcellinus: The Later Roman Empire (A.D. 354–378)* (London: Penguin, 1986), p. 417. "Some fell without knowing who struck them": *Ammianus Marcellinus,* p. 436; J. F. C. Fuller, *Decisive Battles of the Western World and Their Influence Upon History* (London: Eyre & Spottiswoode, 1954), pp. 114–16; Patrick J. Geary, *Before France and Germany: The Creation and Transformation of the Merovingian World* (New York: Oxford University Press, 1988), pp. 23–27, 47–70.

3. The sack of Rome: St. Jerome, quoted in Heather, *Fall of the Roman Empire,* p. 191; Hodges and Whitehouse, *Mohammed, Charlemagne,* pp. 4–20; E. A. Thompson, *Romans and Barbarians: The Decline of the Western Empire* (Madison: University of Wisconsin Press, 1982), pp. 25–62; Heather, pp. 177–85; Finley Hooper, *Roman Realities* (Detroit: Wayne State University Press, 1979), pp. 538–39.

4. Final days of the Western Roman Empire: Geary, *Before France and Germany,* pp. 67–77; Heather, *Fall of the Roman Empire,* p. 483. On Roman Spain: Jane S. Gerber, *The Jews of Spain: A History of the Sephardic Experience* (New York: Free Press, 1992), pp. 4–5. On Vandals, Suevis, and Goths: Edward Gibbon, *The History of the Decline and Fall of the Roman Empire.* 8 vols. (London: The Folio Society, 1983; orig. eds., 1776–88), ch. 37; Jean Descola, *Histoire d'Espagne, dès origines à nos jours* (Paris: Fayard, 1959, rev. 1979), pp. 74–76.

5. On Euric and Alaric II: Descola, *Histoire d'Espagne,* p. 75; Charles Oman, *The Dark Ages, 476–918,* 7th ed. (London: Rivington, 1962, pp. 56–60, 129–35; Patrick Geary, *The Myth of Nations: The Medieval Origins of Europe* (Princeton, NJ: Princeton University Press, 2002), pp. 88–130.

6. Beginnings of Visigothic Spain: "They will not come to you at dawn": Godfrey Goodwin, *Islamic Spain* (San Francisco: Chronicle Books, 1990), p. 1; Oman, *Dark Ages,* pp. 221–27; Hugh Kennedy, *Muslim Spain and Portugal: A Political History of al-Andalus* (London, Longman, 1996), pp. 1–5.

7. The Visigoth economy: Pierre Bonnassie, *From Slavery to Feudalism in South-Western Europe* (Cambridge: Cambridge University Press, 1991), pp. 52–55; Robin Black-

burn, *The Making of New World Slavery: From the Baroque to the Modern, 1492–1800* (London: Verso, 1998), pp. 36–38.

8. "In only eight instances did a son succeed a father": Oman, *Dark Ages*, p. 129.

9. Visigothic Arianism: Oman, *Dark Ages*, pp. 2–227; Fletcher, *Barbarian Conversion*, pp. 72–75. "The whole world groaned . . . to find itself Arian": Geary, *Myth of Nations*, pp. 88–89; Abdulwahid Dhannun Taha, *Muslim Conquest and Settlement of North Africa and Spain* (London: Routledge, 1989), pp. 37–40.

10. Reccared's conversion: "The king will tolerate no one . . . who is not Catholic" (*"Le roi ne tolère personne dans son royaume qui ne soit catholique"*): Descola, *Histoire d'Espagne*, p. 91; Oman, *Dark Ages*, p. 144; Geary, *Myth of Nations*, pp. 134–35; Desmond O'Grady, *Beyond the Empire: Rome and the Church from Constantine to Charlemagne* (New York: Crossroad Publishing, 2001), pp. 166–69; Charles E. Chapman, *A History of Spain* (New York: Free Press, 1965; orig. ed. 1918), pp. 30–32.

11. Visigothic anti-Semitism: Yitzhak Baer, *A History of the Jews in Christian Spain.* 2 vols. (Philadelphia: Jewish Publication Society of America, 1961–66), vol. 1, pp. 1–21; Solomon Katz, *The Jews in the Visigothic and Frankish Kingdoms of Spain and Gaul* (Cambridge, MA: The Medieval Academy of America, 1937), pp. 10–12; Yedida Stillman and Norman Stillman, eds., *From Iberia to Diaspora: Studies in Sephardic History and Culture* (Leiden: Brill, 1999); Taha, *Muslim Conquest,* pp. 42–43, Gerber, *Jews of Spain*, p. 13. "Forced [the Jews] by power when he should have roused them by the doctrine of faith": *St. Isidore of Seville: History of the Kings of the Goths, Vandals, and Suevi,* trans. Guido Donini and Gordon B. Ford, Jr. (Leiden: E. J. Brill, 1966), p. 28; Gerber, p. 36.

12. Anti-Semitic legislation: "We can hardly doubt . . . looked upon the Arabs as liberators": Fletcher, *Barbarian Conversion,* p. 24. "Whether baptized or not baptized" (*Lex Visigothorum*): Olivia R. Constable, ed., *Medieval Iberia: Readings from Christian, Muslim, and Jewish Sources* (Philadelphia: University of Pennsylvania Press, 1997), p. 23; Baer, *History of the Jews,* vol. 1, pp. 19–21; Fletcher, pp. 293–94; Bernard S. Bachrach, *Armies and Polities in the Early Medieval West* (London: Variorum, 1993), pp. 11–30; Oman, *Dark Ages,* pp. 232–34; Collins, *Visigothic Spain,* pp. 92–111; Blackburn, *Making of New World Slavery,* pp. 45–48; Gerber, *Jews of Spain,* pp. 11–12.

13. From Tangier to Tarifa: Gibbon, *Decline and Fall,* vol. 6, pp. 337–38. *Sortes Gothica:* Marianne Barrucand and Achim Bednorz, *Moorish Architecture in Andalusia* (Cologne: Taschen, 1999), pp. 12–13; Taha, *Muslim Conquest,* p. 86; Jayyusi, ed., *Legacy of Muslim Spain,* vol. 1, p. 7.

14. Tariq crosses the Gibraltar strait and meets Roderic: Taha, *Muslim Conquest,* pp. 86–88; Kennedy, *Muslim Spain and Portugal,* pp. 10–11; Collins, *Visigothic Spain,* pp. 36–39; Jayyusi, ed., *Legacy of Muslim Spain,* vol. 1, pp. 7–8. "I do not see how I can punish him . . .": Julian in Constable, ed., *Medieval Iberia,* p. 34.

15. The Julian legend and the invasion: Oman, *Dark Ages,* pp. 233–34; Gerber, *Jews of Spain,* pp. 18–19; Collins, *Visigothic Spain,* pp. 130–38; Jayyusi, ed., *Legacy of Muslim Spain,* vol. 1, p. 8; Fletcher, *Barbarian Conversion,* p. 13. "Purely unhistoric" : Oman, p. 233; Taha, *Muslim Conquest,* pp. 91–93.

16. Preliminary to the Battle of Guadalete: "We do not know who these invaders are": Paul Fregosi, *Jihad in the West* (Amherst, NY: Prometheus Books, 1998), p. 94; Taha, *Muslim Conquest,* pp. 90–92; Kennedy, *Muslim Spain and Portugal,* p. 11.

17. The Battle of Guadalete: Kelly DeVries, *Medieval Military Technology* (Peterborough, Ontario: Broadview Press, 1995), pp. 58–59; Taha, *Muslim Conquest,* pp. 90–91; David Nicolle, *Armies of the Muslim Conquest* (London: Osprey, 1993), p. 17. "They fought a fierce battle": Constable, ed., *Medieval Iberia,* quoting Ibn 'Abd al-Hakam,

Narrative of the Conquest of al-Andalus, p. 34; Janina Safran, *The Second Umayyad Caliphate: The Articulation of Caliphal Legitimacy in al-Andalus* (Cambridge: Harvard University Press, 2001), pp. 121–24.

18. The collapse of Visigothic Hispania: "Treaty of Tudmir" in Constable, ed., *Medieval Iberia*, pp. 37–38; Jayyusi, ed., *Legacy of Muslim Spain*, vol. 1, p. 9. Arab-Jewish collaboration: Taha, *Muslim Conquest*, pp. 96–98; Baer, *History of the Jews*, vol. 1, pp. 18, 22–24; Katz, *Jews in the Visigothic and Frankish Kingdoms*, pp. 11–12.

19. "Together with willing Christians . . .": Taha, *Muslim Conquest*, p. 92.

20. Tariq's invasion route: Kennedy, *Muslim Spain and Portugal*, p. 11; Jayyusi, ed., *Legacy of Muslim Spain*, vol. 1, p. 8; Taha, *Muslim Conquest*, pp. 87–88. "Solomon's Table": Constable, ed., *Medieval Iberia*, pp. 34–35.

21. Musa begins the second invasion: "Musa himself . . . entered the long-plundered and godlessly invaded Spain . . .": Constable, ed., *Medieval Iberia*, pp. 29–32 (quote on p. 30); Taha, *Muslim Conquest*, pp. 94–95; Kennedy, *Muslim Spain and Portugal*, pp. 11–12.

22. Musa's advance: Taha, *Muslim Conquest*, pp. 98–99; Thomas Ballantine Irving, *Falcon of Spain: A Study of Eighth-Century Spain with Special Emphasis Upon the Life of the Umayyad Ruler Abdurrahman I, 756–788* (Lahore, Pakistan: Sh. Muhammad Ashraf, 1962), pp. 18–20.

23. Conquest of Merida: Constable, ed., *Medieval Iberia*, pp. 5–11; Taha, *Muslim Conquest*, p. 94; Gerber, *Jews of Spain*, p. 39.

24. On *al-Andalus* occupation policies: "His followers will not be killed or taken prisoner . . .": "Treaty of Tudmir" in Constable, ed., *Medieval Iberia*, p. 37; Kennedy, *Muslim Spain and Portugal*, pp. 12, 17.

25. Musa and Tariq meet; Caliph al-Walid orders return: Taha, *Muslim Conquest*, pp. 100–101; Kennedy, *Muslim Spain and Portugal*, p. 12; Jayyusi, ed., *Legacy of Muslim Spain*, vol. 1, p. 9.

26. Musa and Tariq ignore caliph's orders: Jayyusi, ed., *Legacy of Muslim Spain*, vol. 1, p. 9; Taha, *Muslim Conquest*, pp. 100–102. "They placed prefects throughout all the provinces . . .": Constable, ed., *Medieval Iberia*, pp. 39–42.

27. Musa and Tariq disgraced: Lewis, *The Middle East*, p. 68. "Your climate, your water, your fruits, and your baths": al-Walid quoted in Finbarr Barry Flood, *The Great Mosque of Damascus: Studies on the Makings of an Ummayyad Visual Culture* (Leiden: Brill, 2000), p. 1. "Gold and silver, assayed by the bankers . . .": Constable, ed., *Medieval Iberia*, p. 31. "Ignominiously removed from the prince's presence": Constable, ed., p. 31; Fregosi, *Jihad in the West*, pp. 99–100; Jayyusi, ed., *Legacy of Muslim Spain*, vol. 1, p. 10.

28. On conflicting geopolitics: Taha, *Muslim Conquest*, p. 102. "Lizard and gerbil eaters": Nicolle, *Armies of the Muslim Conquest*, p. 14.

29. On Leo the Isaurian: John Julius Norwich, *Byzantium: The Early Centuries* (New York: Knopf, 2001), pp. 349–58.

30. The siege of Constantinople: Norwich, *Byzantium*, p. 358; Fuller, *Decisive Battles*, pp. 340–41; Kennedy, *Armies of the Caliphs*, pp. 47–59.

Chapter Six

1. The Franks: "One of the more backward of the Teutonic races": Charles Oman, *The Dark Ages, 476–918*, 7th ed. (London: Rivington, 1962), p. 56. "If they are overcome by superior numbers . . .": Alessandro Barbero, *Charlemagne: Father of a Continent* (Berkeley: University of California Press, 2000), p. 6; Patrick J. Geary, *Before France and Germany:*

The Creation and Transformation of the Merovingian World (New York: Oxford University Press, 1988); Richard Fletcher, *The Barbarian Conversion: From Paganism to Christianity* (New York: Henry Holt, 1998), pp. 101–3. "*Francus ego civis*": Fletcher, p. 101.

2. Clovis and Clothilde: Oman, *Dark Ages*, pp. 257–60; Friedrich Heer, *Charlemagne and His World* (London: Weidenfeld and Nicolson, 1975), pp. 9–11. "Died in his white baptismal robe": Gregory of Tours, *History of the Franks*, trans. Lewis Thorpe (London: Penguin, 1974), p. 142.

3. The Catholic Franks: Geoffrey Barraclough, *The Crucible of Europe: The Ninth and Tenth Centuries in European History* (Berkeley: University of California Press, 1976), p. 10; Fletcher, *Barbarian Conversion*, pp. 101–10; Heer, *Charlemagne*, pp. 10–11; Heinrich Fichtenau, *The Carolingian Empire*, trans. Peter Munz (Toronto: University of Toronto Press, 1978), pp. 1–8; Russell Chamberlin, *Charlemagne, Emperor of the Western World* (London: Grafton, 1986), pp. 7–9, 12–23. *Lex Salica:* Fletcher, p. 106.

4. The Salic Law: "Brave in war, faithful in peace . . .": Fichtenau, *Carolingian Empire*, p. 1.

5. Clovis's superstate: Richard Hodges and David Whitehouse, *Mohammed, Charlemagne and the Origins of Europe* (Ithaca, NY: Cornell University Press, 1983), pp. 76–78; Chamberlin, *Charlemagne*, pp. 10–12; Geary, *Before France and Germany*, pp. 77–78; Edward James, *The Franks* (Oxford: Blackwell, 1991), ch. 5.

6. The Arian threat to the papacy: Fletcher, *Barbarian Conversion*, p. 75; Geary, *Before France and Germany*, p. 67.

7. *The Book of the History of the Franks*: Chamberlin, *Charlemagne*, p. 12; Richard A. Gerberding, *The Rise of the Carolingians and the "Liber Historiae Francorum"* (Oxford: Clarendon Press, 1987), pp. 2–4. Neustria and Austrasia: Chamberlin, pp. 24–25.

8. Dark Ages Frankland: Gerberding, *Rise of the Carolingians*, pp. 149–53; Chamberlin, *Charlemagne*, pp. 24–25; James, *The Franks*, ch. 6.

9. The downward spiral: "Life crept rather than ran": E. M. Almedingen, *Charlemagne: A Study* (London: Bodley Head, 1968), p. 136; Pierre Riché, *Daily Life in the World of Charlemagne* (Philadelphia: University of Pennsylvania Press, 1978), pp. 1–12; Paul Fouracre, *The Age of Charles Martel* (Harlow, UK: Pearson Education Ltd., 2000), pp. 138–45.

10. Crumbling Italy: Hodges and Whitehouse, *Mohammed, Charlemagne*, pp. 22–45; E. A. Thompson, *Romans and Barbarians: The Decline of the Western Empire* (Madison: University of Wisconsin Press, 1982), pp. 77–80. Belisarius and the aqueducts of Rome: Chamberlin, *Charlemagne*, p. 78; Thompson, p. 280; Fichtenau, *Carolingian Empire*, p. 18.

11. "*Les rois fainéants*": Geary, *Before France and Germany*, p. 225; Einhard, *The Life of Charlemagne* (Ann Arbor: University of Michigan Press, 1960), p. 24.

12. The Merovingian kings: James, *The Franks*, pp. 162–77.

13. Merovingian decay: Ivan Gobry, *Histoire des rois de France: Pépin le Bref, père de Charlemagne* (Paris: Pygmalion, 2001), ch. 1; Geary, *Before France and Germany*, ch. 6.

14. The rise of the Pippinids: Gerberding, *Rise of the Carolingians*, pp. 5–11, 92–116; Peter Brown, *The Rise of Western Christendom: Triumph and Diversity, 200–1000 AD* (Oxford: Blackwell, 1996), pp. 263–64; Jean-Henri Roy and Jean Deviosse, *La Bataille de Poitiers: Trente journées qui ont fait la France* (Paris: Gallimard, 1966), pp. 135–37.

15. Plectrude's intervention: Fouracre, *Age of Charles Martel*, pp. 57–59; Heer, *Charlemagne*, p. 16.

16. Plectrude's defeat: Fouracre, *Age of Charles Martel*, pp. 57–59.

17. Charles Martel's victory: Fouracre, *Age of Charles Martel*, pp. 60–65; Hodges and Whitehouse, *Mohammed, Charlemagne*, pp. 22–45.

18. Charles Martel in power: "Uncommonly well educated": Fouracre, *Age of Charles Martel*, pp. 75–76; Gobry, *Histoire des rois de France*, pp. 21–30.

19. Charles the Hammer's society: Fouracre, *Age of Charles Martel*, p. 150; Almedingen, *Charlemagne*, pp. 20–26; Geary, *Before France and Germany*, pp. 205–16.

20. The social landscape and "satellite imaging": Riché, *Daily Life*, pp. 18–22; Fouracre, *Age of Charles Martel*, ch. 4.

21. Household politics in *al-Andalus*: "They do not prostrate themselves before you . . .": Olivia R. Constable, ed., *Medieval Iberia: Readings from Christian, Muslim, and Jewish Sources* (Philadelphia: University of Pennsylvania Press, 1997), p. 36; Paul Fregosi, *Jihad in the West* (Amherst, NY: Prometheus Books, 1998), pp. 99–100; Salma Khadra Jayyusi, ed., *The Legacy of Muslim Spain*. 2 vols. (Leiden: Brill, 1992), vol. 1, p. 11; Hugh Kennedy, *Muslim Spain and Portugal: A Political History of al-Andalus* (London: Longman, 1996), p. 19.

22. 'Abd al-Aziz's elimination: "In the presence of the murdered man's father": Constable, ed., *Medieval Iberia*, pp. 32–46 (quote on p. 36); Jayyusi, ed., *Legacy of Muslim Spain*, vol. 1, p. 11; Kennedy, *Muslim Spain and Portugal*, p. 17.

23. On Arab-Berber immigration: Richard Fletcher, *The Quest for El Cid* (New York: Oxford University Press, 1989), pp. 14–15; Kennedy, *Muslim Spain and Portugal*, pp. 23, 33; Roger Collins, *Arab Conquest of Spain, 710–797* (Oxford: Blackwell, 1995; orig. ed. 1989), pp. 37–39, 82–83.

24. Serial *amirs*/Arab-Jewish cooperation/Covadonga: "Quarter of the Jews": Jane S. Gerber, *The Jews of Spain: A History of the Sephardic Experience* (New York: Free Press, 1992), p. 37; Jayyusi, ed., *Legacy of Muslim Spain*, vol. 1, p. 11. "A despicable barbarian": Ibn al-Qutiyya, in Constable, ed., *Medieval Iberia*, pp. 45–47; Ahmed ibn Mohammed al-Makkari [Maqqari], *The History of the Mohammedan Dynasties in Spain*. 2 vols. (London and New York: RoutledgeCurzon, 2002), vol. 2, pp. 34–35. "The slings were prepared, swords flashed, spears were brandished . . .": Constable, ed., pp. 39–42 (quote on p. 41).

25. Al-Samh's amirate: J. F. C. Fuller, *Decisive Battles of the Western World and Their Influence Upon History* (London: Eyre & Spottiswoode, 1954), pp. 340–41.

26. *Jihad* beyond the Pyrenees: Ian Meadows, "The Arabs in Occitania," *Saudi Aramco World* (March–April, 1993), pp. 24–29; Bernard S. Bachrach, *Merovingian Military Organization, 481–751* (Minneapolis: University of Minnesota Press, 1972), p. 101. "Thus to make the Mediterranean a Moslem sea": Fuller, *Decisive Battles*, pp. 340–41.

27. Al-Samh and Odo in Aquitaine: Ernest Lavisse, *Histoire de France depuis les origines jusqu'à la Révolution* (Paris: Hachette, 1911), pp. 259–260; Meadows, "The Arabs in Occitania," pp. 24–29.

28. Hisham's tax policies: G. R. Hawting, *The First Dynasty of Islam: The Umayyad Caliphate, AD 661–750* (London: Routledge, 2000), p. 106; *The Fourth Book of the Chronicle of Fredegar and the Continuations* [*Fredegarii Chronicorum Liber Quartus cum Continuationibus*], trans. J. M. Wallace-Hadrill (London: Thomas Nelson, 1960), p. 93.

29. *Sarakenoi*: Joseph Reinaud [Haroun Khan Sherwani], *Muslim Colonies in France, Northern Italy, and Switzerland* (Lahore, Pakistan: Sh. Muhammad Ashraf, 1954), pp. 59–63; Jayyusi, ed., *Legacy of Muslim Spain*, vol. 1, p. 12; Jan Retsö, *The Arabs in Antiquity: Their History from the Assyrians to the Umayyads* (London: RoutledgeCurzon, 2005), p. 506.

Chapter Seven

1. Location of the Battle of Poitiers: Maurice Mercier and André Seguin, *Charles Martel et la Bataille de Poitiers* (Paris: Librairie Orientaliste Paul Geuthner, 1944), pp. 2–20; Jean-Henri Roy and Jean Deviosse, *La Bataille de Poitiers: Trente journées qui ont fait la*

France (Paris: Gallimard, 1966), pp. 211–13; Paul Fouracre, *The Age of Charles Martel* (Harlow, UK: Pearson Education Ltd.), p. 87. "An encounter which would change the history of the world": Edward Gibbon, *The History of the Decline and Fall of the Roman Empire.* 8 vols. (London: The Folio Society, 1983; orig. eds., 1776–88), vol. 7, p. 35.

2. Odo's victory: Fouracre, *Age of Charles Martel,* pp. 84–89; Mercier and Seguin, *Charles Martel,* p. 12; Bernard S. Bachrach, *Merovingian Military Organization: 481–751* (Minneapolis: University of Minnesota Press, 1972), p. 101.

3. Odo at Toulouse: Ivan Gobry, *Histoire des rois de France: Pépin le Bref, père de Charlemagne* (Paris: Pygmalion, 2001), pp. 40–42.

4. Odo's resistance to Charles Martel: Ian Meadows, "The Arabs in Occitania," *Saudi Aramco World* (March–April, 1993), pp. 24–29; Salma Jayyusi, ed., *The Legacy of Muslim Spain.* 2 vols. (Leiden: Brill, 1992), vol. 1, p. 13; Abdulwahid Dhannun Taha, *Muslim Conquest and Settlement of North Africa and Spain* (London: Routledge, 1989), pp. 192–93.

5. Munuza and Lampegie: Hugh Kennedy, *Muslim Spain and Portugal: A Political History of al-Andalus* (London: Longman, 1996), p. xii; Mercier and Seguin, *Charles Martel,* pp. 12–14; Roy and Deviosse, *La Bataille de Poitiers,* pp. 157–60.

6. Odo's defeat at Toulouse: J. F. C. Fuller, *Decisive Battles of the Western World and Their Influence Upon History* (London: Eyre & Spottiswoode, 1954), p. 342; Gobry, *Histoire des rois de France,* pp. 40–42.

7. History's treatment of Odo/*Continuations of Fredegar* and the *Liber Pontificalis:* Fouracre, *Age of Charles Martel,* p. 85.

8. End of Munuza: Paul Fregosi, *Jihad in the West* (Amherst, NY: Prometheus Books, 1998), pp. 114–17; Fuller, *Decisive Battles,* pp. 341–42.

9. The advance of 'Abd al-Rahman al-Ghafiqi: Joseph Reinaud [Haroun Khan Sherwani], *Muslim Colonies in France, Northern Italy, and Switzerland* (Lahore, Pakistan: Sh. Muhammad Ashraf, 1954), pp. 49–52; Roy and Deviosse, *La Bataille de Poitiers,* p. 157. "Two comets appeared around the sun": Bede, *Ecclesiastical History of the English People,* rev. ed. (London: Penguin, 1990), p. 323.

10. Battlefield maneuvers at Poitiers: Taha, *Muslim Conquest,* p. 193; Roy and Deviosse, *La Bataille de Poitiers,* pp. 223–26; Ernest Lavisse, *Histoire de France depuis les origines jusqu'à la Révolution.* 18 vols. (Paris: Hachette, 1911), vol. 2, p. 260. "Only God knows how many died and vanished": *Mozarabic Chronicle of 754,* cited in Reinaud [Sherwani], *Muslim Colonies,* p. 49.

11. Significance of "la ville sacrée" and St. Martin: Gregory of Tours, *History of the Franks,* trans. Lewis Thorpe (London: Penguin, 1974), pp. 97–99 and *passim;* Richard Fletcher, *The Barbarian Conversion: From Paganism to Christianity* (New York: Henry Holt, 1998), pp. 40–47. The Saracen advance on Poitiers: Mercier and Seguin, *Charles Martel,* pp. 16–18; Roy and Deviosse, *La Bataille de Poitiers,* pp. 218–22.

12. Battlefield description: *Poitiers, Angoulême et leurs environs* (Guides Joannes) (Paris: Hachette, 1915), p. 4; Mercier and Seguin, *Charles Martel,* pp. 17–18.

13. Topography of the vicinity: sojourn by the author and spouse in Vouneuil-sur-Vienne and visit to Moussais-la-Bataille in late summer, 2002. Roy and Deviosse, *La Bataille de Poitiers,* p. 220; Mercier and Seguin, *Charles Martel,* pp. 19–20.

14. The choreography of war: Hugh Kennedy, *The Armies of the Caliphs: Military and Society in the Early Islamic State* (London: Routledge, 2001), pp. 5–10; David Nicolle, *Armies of the Muslim Conquest* (London: Osprey, 1993), pp. 10–15; Victor Davis Hanson, *Carnage and Culture: Landmark Battles in the Rise of Western Power* (New York: Doubleday, 2001), pp. 166–69, rather tendentious; Mercier and Seguin, *Charles Martel;* William E. Watson, "The Battle of Tours-Poitiers Revisited," in *Providence: Studies in Western Civiliza-*

tion, vol. 2, no. 1 (1993), published by the Department of Western Civilization, University of Providence, Rhode Island.

15. "March nor precipitate your attack": Gibbon quoted in Fuller, *Decisive Battles*, p. 344.

16. Fredegar the Continuator: "With Christ's help . . .": quoted in Mercier and Seguin, *Charles Martel*, p. 20.

17. Battlefield lineup: "L'épisode final de cette semaine de manoeuvres et d'accrochages": Mercier and Seguin, *Charles Martel*, p. 20.

18. Battlefield descriptions: Nicolle, *Armies of the Muslim Conquest*, p. 19.

19. On the slopes of Moussais-la-Bataille: "The men of the north stood as motionless as a wall": Russell Chamberlin, *Charlemagne, Emperor of the Western World* (London: Grafton, 1986), p. 24; Mercier and Seguin, *Charles Martel*, p. 20.

20. Debacles at Toulouse and Poitiers: Curiously, Muslim sources attribute the *Balat al-Shuhada* to both Poitiers and Toulouse. Ahmed ibn Mohammed al-Makkari [Maqqari], *The History of the Mohammedan Dynasties in Spain* (London and New York: RoutledgeCurzon, 2002), vol. 2, p. 33; Meadows, "The Arabs in Occitania," pp. 24–29.

21. Accepted versions of history: Roy and Deviosse, *La Bataille de Poitiers*; Fouracre, *Charles Martel*, p. 85. "Prince Charles boldly threw up his battle line": Paul Fouracre's faithful translation of the *Continuations of the Chronicle of Fredegar* on Poitiers: "Prince Charles boldly drew up his battle line against them [Arabs] and the warrior rushed in against them. With Christ's help he overturned their tents, and hastened to battle to grind them small in slaughter." J. M. Wallace-Hadrill renders a classic effusion of Fredegar's Poitiers description: "Taking boldness as his counsellor, Prince Charles set the battle in array against them [Arabs] and came upon them like a mighty man of war. With Christ's help he overran their tents, following hard after them in the battle to grind them small in their overthrow, and when 'Abd ar-Rahman perished in the battle, he utterly destroyed their armies, scattering them like stubble before the fury of his onslaught; and in the power of Christ he utterly destroyed them" (Fouracre, *Charles Martel*, pp. 148–49).

22. Origin of word *Europenses*: Donald Bullough, *The Age of Charlemagne* (London: Elek Ltd., 1965), p. 29. "Perhaps the interpretation of the Koran would now be taught in the schools of Oxford . . .": Gibbon, *Decline and Fall*, vol. 7, p. 34. "The world's fate was played out between Franks and Arabs": Henri Martin, cited in Mohamed Torki, *L'An 732 de Kairouan à Poitiers: Considérations d'ordre historique et documents sur la bataille de Poitiers et les Sarosins dans le Haut Moyen-Age français* (Tunis: Maison Tunisienne de l'édition, 1972), pp. 29–30. ". . . Asiatics and the Africans": Lavisse, *Histoire de France*, vol. 2, p. 260. ". . . The turning point of one of the most important epochs in history": Leopold von Ranke, *History of the Reformation in Germany*, trans. Sarah Austin, ed. Robert A. Johnson (New York: E. P. Dutton, 1905; orig eds. 1839–47), vol. 1, p. 5. "No more important battle in the history of the world": Hans Delbrück, *History of the Art of War* [*Geschichte der Kriegskunst im Rahmen der politischen Geschichte*], trans. Walter J. Renfroe. 4 vols. (Omaha: University of Nebraska Press, 1990).

23. Christian civilization: Pippinid hegemony: Fouracre, *Charles Martel*, p. 85; Fuller, *Decisive Battles*, p. 348. "Frankland—the greater part of modern France . . .": Pierre Riché, *Daily Life in the World of Charlemagne* (Philadelphia: University of Pennsylvania Press, 1978), p. ix.

24. Odo's bravura farewell: Lavisse, *Histoire de France*, vol. 2, p. 259; Reinaud [Sherwani], *Muslim Colonies*, p. 52. "Belt of ice": Isidorius Pacensis, quoted in Lynn White, *Medieval Technology and Social Change* (Oxford: Oxford University Press, 1962), p. 3.

25. The *jihad* resumes: Kennedy, *Muslim Spain and Portugal*, p. 24; Jayyusi, ed., *Legacy of Muslim Spain*, vol. 1, p. 16.

26. Uqba and Yusuf's advances into Gaul: Jayyusi, ed., *Legacy of Muslim Spain*, vol. 1, p. 16; Reinaud [Sherwani], *Muslim Colonies*, pp. 60–61; Patrick J. Geary, *Before France and Germany: The Creation and Transformation of the Merovingian World* (New York: Oxford University Press, 1988), p. 205.

27. The Frankish response to the *jihad* of 739: Paul the Deacon, *History of the Lombards*, trans. William Dudley Foulke, ed. Edward Peters (Philadelphia: University of Pennsylvania Press, 2003), pp. 296–97; Neil Christie, *The Lombards* (Oxford: Blackwell, 1995), p. 108; Lavisse, *Histoire de France*, vol. 2, p. 261; Reinaud [Sherwani], *Muslim Colonies*, pp. 61–63; Geary, *Before France and Germany*, p. 205.

28. *The Golden Prairies:* Macoudi [al-Masudi], *Les prairies d'or* [*Fields of Gold*], trans. C. Barbier de Meynard and P. de Courteille. 5 vols. (Paris: Imprimerie impériale, 1861–1917), vol. 1.

29. Stirrups: Bullough, *Age of Charlemagne*, p. 36; Fouracre, *Charles Martel*, pp. 146–49; Kennedy, *Armies of the Caliphs*, pp. 172–73; White, *Medieval Technology*, pp. 1–6; Bernard S. Bachrach, *Armies and Politics in the Early Medieval West* (London: Variorum, 1993), essay 12, "Charles Martel Mounted Shock Combat, The Spirit and Feudalism." "It is impossible to be chivalrous without a horse": White, *Medieval Technology*, p. 38.

30. Charles Martel's cavalry: Bachrach, *Armies and Politics*, essay 9, "Was the March Field Part of the Frankish Constitution?" pp. 178–85; Fouracre, *Charles Martel*, pp. 147–81; Riché, *Daily Life*, pp. 74–79. "Never will I give up to you the horse you demand": Riché, p. 75.

31. Financing the Pippinid military: Bachrach, *Armies and Politics*, essay 13, "Military Organization in Aquitaine Under the Early Carolingians"; J. M. Wallace-Hadrill, *The Barbarian West, 400–1000,* 4th ed. (Oxford: Blackwell, 1996), pp. 84–86.

32. John P. McKay, Bennett D. Hill, John Buckler, eds., *A History of World Societies*, 3rd ed. (Boston: Houghton Mifflin, 1992), p. 244; Riché, *Daily Life*, pp. 74–79.

33. Seizure of Church property: Fouracre, *Charles Martel*, pp. 136, 138.

34. Seizure of Church property justified: "Because of the wars which threaten": Fouracre, *Charles Martel*, p. 139. "Of all the kings and princes of the Franks": Hincmar quoted in Fouracre, p. 124; Fouracre, p. 135.

35. Pippinid Church-State collaboration: "Such things had never been seen or heard of before": Geary, *Before France and Germany*, p. 218; Wallace-Hadrill, *Barbarian West*, p. 83; C. H. Talbot, *The Anglo-Saxon Missionaries in Germany: Being the Lives of SS. Willibrord, Boniface, Sturmi . . .* (New York: Sheed and Ward, 1954), pp. xiv–xix.

36. Formation of Greater Frankland: Fouracre, *Charles Martel*, p. 150; Geary, *Before France and Germany*, pp. 212–16.

37. Death of Charles Martel: *Carolingian Chronicles: Royal Frankish Annals and Nithard's Histories,* trans. Bernhard Walter Scholz with Barbara Rogers (Ann Arbor: University of Michigan Press, 1970), p. 37; Roy and Deviosse, *La Bataille de Poitiers*, pp. 123–24.

Chapter Eight

1. The thwarted *jihad* of 739–40: Salma Khadra Jayyusi, ed., *The Legacy of Muslim Spain*. 2 vols. (Leiden: Brill, 1992), vol. 1, p. 16; Roger Collins, *Arab Conquest of Spain, 710–797* (Oxford: Blackwell, 1995), pp. 88–93.

2. Berber immigration: Titus Burckhardt, *Moorish Culture in Spain* (Louisville, KY: Fons

Vitae, 1999; orig. German ed. 1970), pp. 20–29; Maurice Lombard, *L'Islam dans sa pre-mière grandeur, VIIIe–XIe siècle* (Paris: Flammarion, 1971), pp. 94–96; Abdulwahid Dhannun Taha, *Muslim Conquest and Settlement of North Africa and Spain* (London: Routledge, 1989), pp. 167–71.

3. Berber discontent in *al-Andalus:* Taha, *Muslim Conquest,* pp. 22, 167–71. "Those that have embraced the faith and fled their homes . . .": Qur'an, 8:74.

4. The example of Berber alienation, the *wali* of Cerdanya and Duke Odo: Hugh Kennedy, *Muslim Spain and Portugal: A Political History of al-Andalus* (London: Longman, 1996), p. 24.

5. The Islamicization of *al-Andalus:* "They too are your brothers . . .": Qur'an, 8:75; Kennedy, *Muslim Spain and Portugal,* pp. 23–26; Jayyusi, ed., *Legacy of Muslim Spain,* vol. 1, pp. 12–13; Collins, *Arab Conquest,* pp. 96–100.

6. The Berber revolt in Ifriqiya and *al-Andalus:* Ahmed ibn Mohammed al-Makkari [Maqqari], *The History of the Mohammedan Dynasties in Spain.* 2 vols. (London and New York: RoutledgeCurzon, 2002), vol. 2, pp. 40–45; Collins, *Arab Conquest,* pp. 107–8; Lombard, *L'Islam,* pp. 95–96; Joseph Reinaud [Haroun Khan Sherwani], *Muslim Colonies in France, Northern Italy, and Switzerland* (Lahore, Pakistan: Sh. Muhammad Ashraf, 1954), pp. 71–73; Jayyusi, ed., *Legacy of Muslim Spain,* vol. 1, p. 17; Taha, *Muslim Conquest,* p. 235; Charles E. Chapman, *A History of Spain* (New York: Free Press, 1965; orig. ed. 1918), pp. 41–42. "Kharijism in the Maghreb and the grave troubles engendered by its consequences": Maurice Mercier and André Seguin, *Charles Martel et la Bataille de Poitiers* (Paris: Librairie Orientaliste Paul Geuthner, 1944), p. 5.

7. The Berber tax revolt; on Kharijism: John L. Esposito, ed., *The Oxford History of Islam* (New York: Oxford University Press, 2000), p. 36; John Iliffe, *Africans: The History of a Continent* (Cambridge: Cambridge University Press, 1995), p. 44.

8. On Kharijism: "Judgment belongs to God alone": Azim A. Nanji, ed., *The Muslim Almanac: A Reference Work on the History, Faith, Culture, and Peoples of Islam* (Detroit: Gale Research, 1996), pp. 61, 166; Ignaz Goldziher, *Introduction to Islamic Theology and Law,* trans. A. and R. Hamori (Princeton, NJ: Princeton University Press, 1981; orig. ed. 1910), pp. 170–75; Reza Aslan, *No god but God: The Origins, Evolution, and Future of Islam* (New York: Random House, 2005), pp. 32–33; Iliffe, *Africans,* p. 44.

9. The defeat of the *ahl al-Sham:* Kennedy, *Muslim Spain and Portugal,* p. 24; Jayyusi, ed., *Legacy of Muslim Spain,* vol. 1, p. 12.

10. Syrians to the rescue in *al-Andalus:* Jayyusi, ed., *Legacy of Muslim Spain,* vol. 1, p. 12; Kennedy, *Muslim Spain and Portugal,* p. 25.

11. Balj's *coup d'état:* Jayyusi, ed., *Legacy of Muslim Spain,* vol. 1, p. 12; Kennedy, *Muslim Spain and Portugal,* p. 25. On the Qays/Mudari vs. Kalb/Yemeni conflict: Kennedy, p. 23; Collins, *Arab Conquest,* p. 123.

12. Profile of Caliph Hisham I: G. R. Hawting, *The First Dynasty of Islam: The Umayyad Caliphate, AD 661–750* (London: Routledge, 2000), pp. 84–90.

13. Hisham's unsatisfactory successors: Hawting, *First Dynasty of Islam,* p. 93; Abu Ja'far Muhammad ibn Jarir al-Tabari (839–923), *The History of the Prophets and Kings* [*Ta'rikh al-Rusul wa'l-Muluk*]: Vol. 26, *The Waning of the Umayyad Caliphate,* trans. Carole Hillenbrand (Albany: State University of New York Press, 1988), p. 126. "This is what I have to say, and may God forgive me and you": al-Tabari, *Waning of the Umayyad Caliphate,* p. 195.

14. Caliph Marwan and revolt in Khurasan: al-Tabari, *Waning of the Umayyad Caliphate,* p. 242; Hugh Kennedy, *The Armies of the Caliphs: Military and Society in the Early Islamic State* (London: Routledge, 2001), pp. 35, 49; Hawting, *First Dynasty of Islam,* pp. 96–111.

15. The *Hashimiyya* and Abu Muslim: Bernard Lewis, *The Middle East: A Brief History of the Last 2,000 Years* (London: Weidenfeld and Nicolson, 1995), p. 75.

16. Abu'l-'Abbas and the overthrow of the Umayyads: Hawting, *First Dynasty of Islam*, p. 118; Janina M. Safran, *The Second Umayyad Caliphate: The Articulation of Caliphal Legitimacy in al-Andalus* (Cambridge: Harvard University Press, 2001), p. 126; Sabatino Moscati, "Le massacre des Umayyads dans l'histoire et dans les fragments poétiques," *Archiv Orientální* [*Journal of the Oriental Archive*, Prague], vol. 18, no. 4 (November 1950), pp. 88–115; Lewis, *Middle East*, p. 77; Muzaffar Iqbal, *Islam and Science* (Burlington, VT: Ashgate Publishing, 2002), pp. 16–17.

17. 'Abd al-Rahman ibn Mu'awiya ibn Hisham: "How like me you are, far away and in exile": al-Makkari [Maqqari], *History of the Mohammedan Dynasties*, vol. 2, p. 77; Thomas Ballantine Irving, *Falcon of Spain: A Study of Eighth-Century Spain with Special Emphasis Upon the Life of the Umayyad Ruler Abdurrahman I, 756–788* (Lahore, Pakistan: Sh. Muhammad Ashraf, 1962); Marianne Barrucand and Achim Bednorz, *Moorish Architecture in Andalusia* (Cologne: Taschen, 1999), pp. 30–31; Maria Rosa Menocal, *The Ornament of the World: How Muslims, Jews, and Christians Created a Culture of Tolerance in Medieval Spain* (Boston: Little, Brown, 2002), p. 61.

18. 'Abd al-Rahman's escape: "I saw the whole village in confusion . . .": al-Makkari [Maqqari], *History of the Mohammedan Dynasties*, vol. 1, p. 59; Hawting, *First Dynasty of Islam*, p. 91; Jayyusi, ed., *Legacy of Muslim Spain*, vol. 1, p. 19.

19. 'Abd al-Rahman's escape: "My feet scarcely touched the ground": al-Makkari [Maqqari], *History of the Mohammedan Dynasties*, vol. 2, pp. 60, 94; Jayyusi, ed., *Legacy of Muslim Spain*, vol. 1, p. 19; Safran, *The Second Umayyad Caliphate*, p. 125; Taha, *Muslim Conquest*, p. 234; Irving, *Falcon of Spain*, pp. 45–55.

20. 'Abd al-Rahman explores his Andalusian options: Jayyusi, ed., *Legacy of Muslim Spain*, vol. 1, p. 19; Taha, *Muslim Conquest*, p. 243. "He comes from such a people that if one of them peed . . .": Safran, *The Second Umayyad Caliphate*, p. 161.

21. 'Abd al-Rahman's negotiations with *Amir* Yusuf: Jayyusi, ed., *Legacy of Muslim Spain*, vol. 1, p. 19; Safran, *The Second Umayyad Caliphate*, p. 132; Hawting, *First Dynasty* p. 54.

22. 'Abd al-Rahman triumphs: Taha, *Muslim Conquest*, p. 245; Kennedy, *Muslim Spain and Portugal*, pp. 31–33.

23. 'Abd al-Rahman recruits talent: al-Makkari [Maqqari], *History of the Mohammedan Dynasties*, vol. 2, p. 76; Irving, *Falcon of Spain*, pp. 109–15; Kennedy, *Muslim Spain and Portugal*, p. 34; Barrucand and Bednorz, *Moorish Architecture*, p. 31.

24. 'Abd al-Rahman and al-Fihri opposition: Jayyusi, ed., *Legacy of Muslim Spain*, vol. 1, p. 20; Kennedy, *Muslim Spain and Portugal*, p. 34.

25. The creation of an army of slaves: Bernard Lewis, *Race and Slavery in the Middle East* (Oxford: Oxford University Press, 1990), pp. 11–18; Ronald Segal, *Islam's Black Slaves: The Other Black Diaspora* (New York: Farrar, Straus and Giroux, 2001), pp. 6–16; Nanji, ed., *Muslim Almanac*, p. 108; William Gervase Clarence-Smith, *Islam and the Abolition of Slavery* (Oxford: Oxford University Press, 2006), pp. 1–25.

26. The elimination of the Abbasid pretender: "The battle lasted long until God did His marvelous work": Kennedy, *Muslim Spain and Portugal*, p. 35.

27. "God be praised for placing a sea between us": Caliph al-Mansur, quoted al-Makkari [Maqqari], *History of the Mohammedan Dynasties*, vol. 2, p. 81; Kennedy, *Muslim Spain and Portugal*, p. 33.

28. A regime of justice for *baladiyyun*, *Shamiyyun*, Berber, or *muwalladun*: "Do not allow your hatred of a people incite you not to act equitably": *Qur'an*, 5:8; Jayyusi, ed., *Legacy of Muslim Spain*, vol. 1, p. 20.

29. Multicultural *al-Andalus*: Norman A. Stillman, *The Jews of Arab Lands: A History and Source Book* (Philadelphia: Jewish Publication Society of America, 1979), pp. 25–26; Jane S. Gerber, *The Jews of Spain: A History of the Sephardic Experience* (New York: Free Press, 1992), ch. 2; Chapman, *History of Spain* (New York: Free Press, 1965; orig. ed. 1918), p. 43; Yitzhak Baer, *A History of the Jews in Christian Spain*. 2 vols. (Philadelphia: Jewish Publication Society of America, 1961–66), vol. I, pp. 22–24.

30. Jewish contributions to the amirate: Chapman, *History of Spain*, p. 42; Lombard, *L'Islam*, pp. 93–94; Gerber, *Jews of Spain*; Nanji, ed., *Muslim Almanac*, p. 426; Stillman, *Jews of Arab Lands*, p. 26.

31. The structure of the amirate government: On the Upper, Middle and Lower Marches: Barrucand and Bednorz, *Moorish Architecture*, p. 34; Kennedy, *Muslim Spain and Portugal*, ch. 2; Jayyusi, ed., *Legacy of Muslim Spain*, vol. I, pp. 19–20.

32. Prosperity under the Falcon: Godfrey Goodwin, *Islamic Spain* (San Francisco: Chronicle Books, 1990), pp. 9–10; Lombard, *L'Islam*, pp. 161–84.

33. The east-to-west migration of crops out of monsoon India: Jayyusi, ed., *Legacy of Muslim Spain*, vol. 2, pp. 792, 974; Goodwin, *Islamic Spain*, p. 10.

34. Agricultural and urban prosperity: Burckhardt, *Moorish Culture*, p. 31; Kennedy, *Muslim Spain and Portugal*, p. 107.

35. From Egypt a Jewish trader arrives with a "cargo of flax . . .": Olivia R. Constable, "Muslim Merchants in Andalusi International Trade," in Jayyusi, ed., *Legacy of Muslim Spain*, vol. 2, pp. 759–73.

36. Hot spots of resentment and resistance in *al-Andalus*: Kennedy, *Muslim Spain and Portugal*, pp. 33–37.

37. 'Abd al-Rahman's estimate of himself: "I came fleeing hunger, the sword, and death . . .": Safran, *The Second Umayyad Caliphate*, p. 125; Kennedy, *Muslim Spain and Portugal*, p. 38.

Chapter Nine

1. Lombard threat to papacy and the Iconoclastic Controversy: John Julius Norwich, *Byzantium: The Early Centuries* (New York: Knopf, 2001), p. 358; G. R. Hawting, *The First Dynasty of Islam: The Umayyad Caliphate, AD 661–750* (London: Routledge, 2000), p. 65; James Carroll, *Constantine's Sword: The Church and the Jews* (Boston: Houghton Mifflin, 2001), p. 238.

2. The Langobards' "German disease": Paul the Deacon, *History of the Lombards*, trans. William Dudley Foulke, ed. Edward Peters (Philadelphia: University of Pennsylvania Press, 2003), pp. 310–11; Bernhard Schimmelpfennig, *The Papacy*, trans. James Sievert (New York: Columbia University Press, 1992; orig. ed. 1984), pp. 70–71, 78–80.

3. Lombards, popes, and Merovingians: Popes Zacharias and Stephen III: *Encyclopaedia Britannica*, 11th ed. Roger Grand, *Recherches sur l'origine des Francs* (Paris: Editions A. and J. Picard, 1965), pp. 30–32; Ivan Gobry, *Histoire des rois de France: Pépin le Bref, père de Charlemagne* (Paris: Pygmalion, 2001), pp. 1–30.

4. The Northumbrian priests and St. Boniface: "In the event of your coming to power": Boniface, quoted in Richard Fletcher, *The Barbarian Conversion: From Paganism to Christianity* (New York: Henry Holt, 1998), p. 236; Paul Fouracre and Richard A. Gerberding, *Late Merovingian France: History and Hagiography, 640–720* (Manchester, UK: Manchester University Press, 1996), p. 50.

5. Carloman's retirement: "A portion of Church property": Paul Fouracre, *The Age of Charles*

Martel (Harlow, UK: Pearson Education Ltd., 2000), p. 139; *Carolingian Chronicles: Royal Frankish Annals and Nithard's Histories*, trans. Bernhard Walter Scholz with Barbara Rogers (Ann Arbor: University of Michigan Press, 1970), p. 38; Russell Chamberlin, *Charlemagne, Emperor of the Western World* (London: Grafton, 1986), pp. 44–47.

6. Pippin the Short and Pope Stephen II: "Whether it was good or not that the King of the Franks should wield no royal power": *Carolingian Chronicles*, p. 39; Friedrich Heer, *Charlemagne and His World* (London: Weidenfeld and Nicolson, 1975), p. 17. "His hair was cut short and he was shut up in a monastery": Edward James, *The Franks* (Oxford: Blackwell, 1991), p. 230.

7. Pippinid-Rhineland Franks diminished the Gallo-Latin character of Merovingian Francia: James, *The Franks*, p. 176; Pierre Riché, *Daily Life in the World of Charlemagne* (Philadelphia: University of Pennsylvania Press, 1978), p. 41.

8. Pope Stephen II visits Frankland: Riché, *Daily Life*, p. 19.

9. The pope at Ponthion: "*Mefandissimi Langobardi, mefandissimi Langobardi*": Chamberlin, *Charlemagne*, p. 43; Heer, *Charlemagne and His World*, pp. 18–19. "Benches were pushed back, bedding gear and bolsters/spread across the floor": *Beowulf: A New Verse Translation*, trans. Seamus Heaney (New York: W. W. Norton, 2000), p. 87.

10. Political horse trading at Ponthion: "And we did hand it over, to be enduringly and happily possessed, to our most blessed father, Sylvester . . .": "Die Constantinische Schenkungsurkunde," in *Select Historical Documents of the Middle Ages*, ed. and trans. Ernest F. Henderson (London: George Bell, 1910), pp. 319–29; Desmond O'Grady, *Beyond the Empire: Rome and the Church from Constantine to Charlemagne* (New York: Crossroad Publishing, 2001), p. 155; Heer, *Charlemagne*, p. 14, on *Donation of Constantine*.

11. Pippinid papal alliance: Heer, *Charlemagne*, p. 19; O'Grady, *Beyond the Empire*, pp. 155–57.

12. "The Lord King Pepin [Pippin] then held a great council at Gentilly . . .": *Carolingian Chronicles*, p. 46. Constantine V's pipe-organ gift to the Frankish court: *Carolingian Chronicles*, p. 43.

13. The much-reformed Frankish Church: "*In nomine patria et filia*": Riché, *Daily Life*, p. 193; O'Grady, *Beyond the Empire*, pp. 173–78. "Inventing or recounting to the people [of] new things . . .": Riché, p. 201.

14. Rising power of the priesthood: Richard Fletcher, *The Barbarian Conversion: From Paganism to Christianity* (New York: Henry Holt, 1998), p. 200; Riché, *Daily Life*, ch. 21.

15. The Pippinid economy: Georges Duby, *Rural Economy and Country Life in the Medieval West*, trans. Cynthia Poston (Philadelphia: University of Pennsylvania Press, 1998; orig. ed. 1962), ch. 2 and *passim*; Riché, *Daily Life*, chs. 9, 13, 14; Richard Hodges and David Whitehouse, *Mohammed, Charlemagne and the Origins of Europe* (Ithaca, NY: Cornell University Press, 1983), p. 81.

16. Pippin's legacy to Carloman and Charlemagne: Heinrich Fichtenau, *The Carolingian Empire* (Toronto: University of Toronto Press, 1978), pp. 20–23; Matthias Becher, *Charlemagne* (New Haven, CT: Yale University Press, 2003), pp. 46–49; Heer, *Charlemagne*, pp. 20–21.

Chapter Ten

1. Heinrich Fichtenau, *The Carolingian Empire*, trans. Peter Munz (Toronto: University of Toronto Press, 1978), p. 26. "His eyes very large and animated": Einhard, *The Life of Charlemagne* (Ann Arbor: University of Michigan Press, 1960), p. 50.

2. On Charlemagne's literacy: Stephen Allott, *Alcuin of York, c. A.D. 732–804: His Life and Letters* (York, UK: William Sessions Ltd., 1974), p. vii; Matthias Becher, *Charlemagne* (New Haven, CT: Yale University Press, 2003), p. 5; P. L. Butzer et al., eds., *Karl der Grosse und sein Nachwirken: 1200 Jahre Kultur und Wissenschaft in Europa.* 2 vols. (Turnhout, Belgium: Brepols, 1997), vol. I, p. 42; Friedrich Heer, *Charlemagne and His World* (London: Weidenfeld and Nicolson, 1975), p. 21. "As well as his own native tongue": Einhard, *Life of Charlemagne*, p. 53.

3. Mysteries of Charlemagne's childhood: "Folly . . . to write a word concerning Charles's birth and infancy . . .": Einhard, *Life of Charlemagne*, p. 27.

4. Incest among the Franks: Heer, *Charlemagne*, pp. 23–24; Suzanne Fonay Wemple, *Women in Frankish Society: Marriage and the Cloister, 500–900* (Philadelphia: University of Pennsylvania Press, 1981), pp. 75–76; Alessandro Barbero, *Charlemagne: Father of a Continent* (Berkeley: University of California Press, 2004), p. 139; Philip E. Bennett et al., eds. *Charlemagne in the North: Proceedings of the Twelfth International Conference of the Société Rencesvals, Edinburgh, 4–11 August 1991* (Edinburgh: Société Rencesvals British Branch, 1993), p. 45; Barton Sholod, *Charlemagne in Spain: The Cultural Legacy of Roncesvalles* (Geneva: Droz, 1966), pp. 24–34; André de Mandach, *La geste de Charlemagne et de Roland: Naissance et développement de la chanson de geste en Europe* (Geneva: Droz, 1961), p. 36.

5. Competition between Carolus and Carloman: Heer, *Charlemagne*, pp. 21–23; Becher, *Charlemagne*, p. 48.

6. Machinations of Carloman: Becher, *Charlemagne*, p. 48; Heer, *Charlemagne*, pp. 21–25. On Byzantine impotence in Italy: John Julius Norwich, *Byzantium: The Early Centuries* (New York: Knopf, 2001), ch. 17.

7. The stuff of grand opera: Becher, *Charlemagne*, p. 49; Heer, *Charlemagne*, pp. 24–30.

8. Duke Bertrand's scheme: Russell Chamberlin, *Charlemagne, Emperor of the Western World* (London: Grafton, 1986), p. 65; Heer, *Charlemagne*, p. 97; Fichtenau, *Carolingian Empire*, p. 39. "The faithless and most vile Lombard people . . .": Pope Stephen III, quoted in Becher, *Charlemagne*, p. 49.

9. Papal politics and the Lombard invasion: Heer, *Charlemagne*, pp. 96–97; Bernhard Schimmelpfennig, *The Papacy* (New York: Columbia University Press, 1992), pp. 81–82. "A pitiable cipher": Heer, p. 97.

10. Bertrada's gambit and Carloman's death: Chamberlin, *Charlemagne*, pp. 65–70; Becher, *Charlemagne*, p. 51. "God has preserved you from the wiles of your brother": Identified as "the Monk Cathwulph" in Martin Bouquet, ed., *Recueil des historiens des Gaules et de la France.* 24 vols. (Paris: various publishers, 1738–1904), vol. 5, p. 634.

11. Reversal of politics, Desiderata sent home: Becher, *Charlemagne*, p. 53; Chamberlin, *Charlemagne*, p. 70.

12. *Renovatio Romani Imperii* ("Revival of the Roman Empire"): John P. McKay, Bennett D. Hill, John Buckler, eds., *A History of World Societies*, 3rd ed. (Boston: Houghton Mifflin, 1992), p. 341.

13. Housebreaking the Saxons: "They did not consider it dishonorable to transgress . . ." Einhard, *Life of Charlemagne*, p. 30. The great defeat of Rome by the Saxons in the Teutoburg Forest: J. F. C. Fuller, *Decisive Battles of the Western World and Their Influence Upon History* (London: Eyre & Spottiswoode, 1954), p. 253; Finley Hooper, *Roman Realities* (Detroit: Wayne State University Press, 1979), p. 339.

14. Charlemagne invades Saxony: Becher, *Charlemagne*, p. 54.

15. Desiderius's concerns: Barbero, *Charlemagne*, pp. 41–42.

16. The Lombard invasion of Rome: Barbero, *Charlemagne*, pp. 34–36; Becher, *Charle-*

magne, p. 53; Heer, *Charlemagne*, p. 97; Desmond O'Grady, *Beyond the Empire: Rome and the Church from Constantine to Charlemagne* (New York: Crossroad Publishing, 2001), p. 180.

17. Papal and Lombard emissaries with Charlemagne at Thionville: "For the sake of God's service and the rights of St. Peter": *Carolingian Chronicles: Royal Frankish Annals and Nithard's Histories*, trans. Bernhard Walter Scholz with Barbara Rogers (Ann Arbor: University of Michigan Press, 1970), p. 49; Barbero, *Charlemagne*, p. 27. Charlemagne's Italian invasion force: Pierre Riché, *Daily Life in the World of Charlemagne* (Philadelphia: University of Pennsylvania Press, 1978), p. 77; Kelly DeVries, *Medieval Military Technology* (Peterborough, Ontario: Broadview Press, 1995), pp. 60–62. "Each knight is to have a buckler, lance, longsword . . .": Riché, p. 77; David Nicolle, *Age of Charlemagne* (London: Osprey, 2000), pp. 8–10; Heer, *Charlemagne*, pp. 91–97.

18. Charlemagne's invasion tactics: Einhard, *Life of Charlemagne*, p. 29; Barbero, *Charlemagne*, pp. 30–32; Riché, *Daily Life*, p. 74.

19. Advancing into Italy: "Trackless mountain ridges, the heaven-aspiring cliffs . . .": Einhard, *Life of Charlemagne*, p. 179; Becher, *Charlemagne*, pp. 54–56.

20. "Baggage trains appeared that would have been worthy of the campaigns of Darius . . .": Notker "the Stammerer," quoted in Barbero, *Charlemagne*, p. 39.

21. Pavia surrenders: Becher, *Charlemagne*, p. 56. "So long as the Colosseum stands": Riché, *Daily Life*, pp. 29–30.

22. Charlemagne's triumphal Roman entry and the politics: Heer, *Charlemagne*, pp. 98–99. On the forged *Donation of Charlemagne*: Heer, p. 99.

23. Charlemagne reaffirmed as *patricius Romanorum*: Schimmelpfennig, *The Papacy*, p. 87.

24. Charlemagne returns to Saxony: "Overwhelm in war the infidel and faithless Saxon people . . .": Becher, *Charlemagne*, p. 60.

25. The Lombard insurrection and Byzantine complicity: Becher, *Charlemagne*, p. 56; Barbero, *Charlemagne*, p. 36.

26. Barbero, *Charlemagne*, p. 44.

27. Lombard kingdom destroyed; Charlemagne, now king of the Franks and the Lombards: Becher, *Charlemagne*, pp. 56–57.

28. Saracen notables at Paderborn: Sholod, *Charlemagne in Spain*, pp. 39–40; *Carolingian Chronicles*, pp. 55–56; Heer, *Charlemagne*, p. 107; Gerard Gouiran and Robert Lafont, eds. and trans., *Le Roland Occitan* (Paris: Christian Bourgeois, 1991), p. 9.

29. The Berber-Carolingian deal at Paderborn: Heer, *Charlemagne*, p. 107.

30. More on the Berber-Frankish alliance: Heer, *Charlemagne*, p. 108; Sholod, *Charlemagne in Spain*, p. 40; Roger Collins, *Arab Conquest of Spain, 710–797* (Oxford: Blackwell, 1995; orig. ed. 1989), pp. 178–80.

31. The Carolingian invasion force: "At the head of all the forces that he could muster": Einhard, *Life of Charlemagne*, p. 33. "To Saragossa came his men from Burgundy, Austrasia, Bavaria": *Carolingian Chronicles*, p. 56.

32. Charlemagne's invasion tactics: *Carolingian Chronicles*, p. 56; Einhard, p. 34.

33. The Carolingian "shock and awe": The term *Franks* becomes a Muslim generic for all Western enemies: Edward James, *The Franks* (Oxford: Blackwell, 1991), p. 1; Heer, *Charlemagne*, p. 113.

34. Charlemagne shut out of Zaragoza: E. M. Almedingen, *Charlemagne: A Study* (London: Bodley Head, 1968), p. 116; Joseph Reinaud [Haroun Khan Sherwani], *Muslim Colonies in France, Northern Italy, and Switzerland* (Lahore, Pakistan: Sh. Muhammad Ashraf, 1954), p. 89.

35. On the oriflamme banner: Becher, *Charlemagne*, p. 139.

36. Zaragoza and Pamplona close their gates, Saxons revolt: Sholod, *Charlemagne in Spain,* pp. 41–42. "The Saxons rebelled again as usual": *Carolingian Chronicles,* p. 61.

37. Charlemagne's humiliating retreat: Reinaud [Sherwani], *Muslim Colonies,* p. 89; Sholod, *Charlemagne in Spain,* pp. 41–42; Heer, *Charlemagne,* p. 113. "Bravest of the brave": *The Song of Roland* [*La Chanson de Roland*], trans. Glyn Burgess (London: Penguin, 1990).

Chapter Eleven

1. At Orreaga (Roncesvalles): The inscription on Roland's monument explained by the author: *Carolingian Chronicles: Royal Frankish Annals and Nithard's Histories,* trans. Bernhard Walter Scholz with Barbara Rogers (Ann Arbor: University of Michigan Press, 1970), p. 56; André de Mandach, *La geste de Charlemagne et de Roland: Naissance et développement de la chanson de geste en Europe* (Geneva: Droz, 1961), p. 14.

2. The Basque ambush: "The Basques forced them down into the valley . . .": Einhard, *The Life of Charlemagne* (Ann Arbor: University of Michigan Press, 1960), p. 64; *Carolingian Chronicles,* p. 56.

3. Charlemagne's destruction of Pamplona and precipitous retreat: Friedrich Heer, *Charlemagne and His World* (London: Weidenfeld and Nicolson, 1975), p. 114. "Spanish Basques and the people of Navarre": *Carolingian Chronicles,* p. 56. "A brief moment on the return journey": Einhard, *Life of Charlemagne,* p. 64.

4. The genesis of *The Song of Roland*: Alexander Murray, *Reason and Society in the Middle Ages* (Oxford: Oxford University Press, 1978), pp. 126–27; R. Ewart Oakeshott, *The Archaeology of Weapons: Arms and Armour from Prehistory to the Age of Chivalry* (London: Lutterworth Press, 1960), p. 184; *Carolingian Chronicles,* pp. 55–56; Barton Sholod, *Charlemagne in Spain: The Cultural Legacy of Roncesvalles* (Geneva: Droz, 1966), pp. 21–34; Mandach, *La geste de Charlemagne,* pp. 13–14.

5. *The Song of Roland* [*La Chanson de Roland*], trans. Glyn Burgess (London: Penguin, 1990). *The Song of Roland* begins thus: "*Carles il reis, nostre empere magnes . . .*": *Song of Roland* [*SOR*] (laisse 5). "Bravest of the brave": *SOR,* 195; "Then they ride with great zeal": *SOR,* 855; Salma Khadra Jayyusi, ed., *The Legacy of Muslim Spain.* 2 vols. (Leiden: Brill, 1992), vol. 1, pp. 20–21.

6. Turoldus transforms Roland into a Frank: The new "eye literature" and the old "ear literature": Sholod, *Charlemagne in Spain,* pp. 9, 25. "Never has any man on earth seen more": *Song of Roland,* 1040.

7. Roland's pride, Oliver's prudence: *Rollant est proz e Oliver est sage*: *Song of Roland,* 1095. The Basques are banished: Einhard, *Life of Charlemagne,* pp. 33–34; Murray, *Reason and Society,* pp. 125–27.

8. The slaughter of the brave: "Blessed martyrs/And take your place in paradise on high": *Song of Roland* [*SOR*], 1135. "We should have fought this battle and won it"—"*La prudence est plus importante que la bravoure*": *SOR,* 1730.

9. Roland and the twelve peers slaughtered; Charlemagne returns to the scene: "Had he been a Christian, he would have been a worthy baron": *Song of Roland* [*SOR*], 895. "There is no road or path there": *SOR,* 2400. "God performed a great miracle for Charlemagne,/For the sun remained where it was": *SOR,* 2460. "Striking powerfully": *SOR,* 2463. "Anyone who serves you well receives a poor reward": *SOR,* 2585.

10. The clash between Occident and Orient: Baligant "summons his men from forty kingdoms": *Song of Roland* [*SOR*], 2623. "Below Alexandria there is a seaport": *SOR,*

2627. "And on my behalf inform Marsile/That I have come with help against rhe Franks": *SOR*, 2680.

11. "Vast are the armies and handsome the divisions": *Song of Roland* [SOR], 3295. The tribes of the *Dar al-Harb* on the march: *SOR*, 3220—30.

12. There's an industry of interpretation of the "splendid folly" thesis: Robert Francis Cook, *The Sense of the Song of Roland* (Ithaca, NY: Cornell University Press, 1987), p. xii; Murray, *Reason and Society,* p. 126 ("Swansong for the reckless *fortitudo* of its defeated hero"); Karen Pratt, ed., *Roland and Charlemagne in Europe: Essays on the Reception and Transformation of a Legend* (London: King's College Center for Late Antique and Medieval Studies, 1996); Philip E. Bennett et al., eds., *Charlemagne in the North: Proceedings of the Twelfth International Conference of the Société Rencesvals, Edinburgh, 4—11 August 1991* (Edinburgh: Société Rencesvals British Branch, 1993); Donald Bullough, *The Age of Charlemagne* (London: Elek Ltd., 1965), p. 76; Norman Daniel, *Heroes and Saracens: An Interpretation of the Chansons de Geste* (Edinburgh: Edinburgh University Press, 1984), pp. 2, 3, 36—38, 73; Heer, *Charlemagne and His World,* p. 114.

13. The Franks became Europe's archetypal sword-bearers: Anthony Marx, *Faith in Nation: Exclusionary Origins of Nationalism* (Oxford: Oxford University Press, 2003), including Marx's fecund argument that "the roots of modern nationalism and its centrality to politics go back a half millennium, if not further," on p. ix; Matthias Becher, *Charlemagne* (New Haven, CT: Yale University Press, 2003), ch. 7.

14. "Let whoever can win glory before death": *Beowulf: A New Verse Translation,* trans. Seamus Heaney (New York: W. W. Norton, 2000), p. 97. The epic struggle of Christianity and Islam: Cook, *Sense of the Song of Roland,* pp. 86—87; Sholod, *Charlemagne in Spain,* pp. 15—21.

15. Another Saxon campaign: "'God,' said the king, 'how wearisome my life is'": *Song of Roland,* 4000; Bullough, *Age of Charlemagne,* p. 25. "No war ever undertaken by the Frank nation was carried out with such persistence and bitterness": Einhard, *Life of Charlemagne,* p. 30; Richard Fletcher, *The Barbarian Conversion: From Paganism to Christianity* (New York: Henry Holt, 1998), p. 214; Becher, *Charlemagne,* p. 62; Alessandro Barbero, *Charlemagne: Father of a Continent* (Berkeley: University of California Press, 2004), ch. 5; Geoffrey Barraclough, *The Crucible of Europe: The Ninth and Tenth Centuries in European History* (Berkeley: University of California Press, 1976), pp. 34—41; Heinrich Fichtenau, *The Carolingian Empire,* trans. Peter Munz (Toronto: University of Toronto Press, 1978), p. 128.

16. The show assembly in Saxony: Bullough, *Age of Charlemagne,* pp. 59—69; Becher, *Charlemagne,* p. 127; Barbero, *Charlemagne,* p. 59. The Saxon massacre at Verden: Fletcher, *Barbarian Conversion,* pp. 214—15; Bullough, p. 60; Becher, p. 67; Barbero, p. 47; Fichtenau, *Carolingian Empire,* p. 128.

17. Einhard on the necessity to "wreak vengeance and exact righteous satisfaction": Einhard, *Life of Charlemagne,* p. 31. Saxon ethnic cleansing: "Took ten thousand of those that lived on the banks of the Elbe": Einhard, p. 232; Bullough, *Age of Charlemagne,* p. 61; Fletcher, *Barbarian Conversion,* p. 215. Devil worshippers who "transgress and violate all law, human and divine": Einhard, p. 30.

18. Charlemagne's Saxon Capitulary: Fletcher, *Barbarian Conversion,* p. 215; Pierre Riché, *Daily Life in the World of Charlemagne* (Philadelphia: University of Pennsylvania Press, 1978), p. 181; Becher, *Charlemagne,* p. 67. "They promised to renounce the worship of devils": Einhard, *Life of Charlemagne,* p. 31. The surrender and baptism of Widukind: Bullough, *Age of Charlemagne,* p. 61.

19. The Saxon Capitulary, punishments: "Stands as a blueprint for the comprehensive

and ruthless Christianization of a conquered society": Fletcher, *Barbarian Conversion*, p. 215.

Chapter Twelve

1. Tensions at the edges of *al-Andalus*: "And snatched the towns located near the Franks' frontier from the Muslims": Macoudi [al-Masudi], *Les prairies d'or* [*Fields of Gold*], trans. C. Barbier de Meynard and P. de Courteille. 5 vols. (Paris: Imprimerie impériale, 1861–1917), vol. 1, p. 364.

2. Muslim unease along the frontiers: "Whilst the Muslims of al-Andalus were thus revolting . . . the people of Galicia were gathering strength": Ahmed ibn Mohammed al-Makkari [Maqqari], *The History of the Mohammedan Dynasties in Spain*. 2 vols. (London and New York: RoutledgeCurzon, 2002), vol. 2, p. 285.

3. Christian out-migration: Hugh Kennedy, *Muslim Spain and Portugal: A Political History of al-Andalus* (London: Longman, 1996), p. 49; Charles E. Chapman, *A History of Spain* (New York: Free Press, 1965; orig. ed. 1918), p. 55; Daniel Power and Naomi Standen, eds., *Frontiers in Question: Eurasian Borderlands, 700–1700* (New York: St. Martin's Press, 1999), ch. 2.

4. The Falcon's family, cadre, and slaves: Da'ja: Ibn Hazm, *The Ring of the Dove*, trans. A. J. Arberry (London: Luzac & Co., 1953), p. 22; Kennedy, *Muslim Spain and Portugal*, p. 38; Maurice Lombard, *L'Islam dans sa première grandeur, VIIIe–XIe siècle* (Paris: Flammarion, 1971), pp. 161–62.

5. Ongoing sectionalism in *al-Andalus*: al-Makkari [Maqqari], *History of the Mohammedan Dynasties*, vol. 1, p. 82; Kennedy, *Muslim Spain and Portugal*, p. 36; Marianne Barrucand and Achim Bednorz, *Moorish Architecture in Andalusia* (Cologne: Taschen, 1999), p. 34.

6. Baghdad, the model for Cordoba: *Madinat al-Salam* described: André Clot, *Harun al-Rashid and the World of The Thousand and One Nights* (New York: New Amsterdam Books, 1990), p. 20; Alexander Murray, *Reason and Society in the Middle Ages* (Oxford: Oxford University Press, 1978), p. 40.

7. Public works in *al-Andalus* and the Friday Mosque: Barrucand and Bednorz, *Moorish Architecture*, p. 31. "The Ka'bah of the West": Godfrey Goodwin, *Islamic Spain* (San Francisco: Chronicle Books, 1990), p. 40.

8. Purchase of the church and monastery for a mosque: Janina Safran, *The Second Umayyad Caliphate: The Articulation of Caliphal Legitimacy in al-Andalus* (Cambridge: Harvard University Press, 2001), p. 174; Salma Khadra Jayyusi, ed., *The Legacy of Muslim Spain*. 2 vols. (Leiden: Brill, 1992), vol. 1, p. 21.

9. Basic plan of the Great Mosque: Titus Burckhardt, *Moorish Culture in Spain* (Louisville, KY: Fons Vitae, 1999), p. 23; Barrucand and Bednorz, *Moorish Architecture*, p. 44; Goodwin, *Islamic Spain*, p. 50. On the mosque's ornamental calligraphy: Safran, *The Second Umayyad Caliphate*, pp. 62–63.

10. The Great Mosque's interior: Goodwin, *Islamic Spain*, pp. 44–45, 49; Barrucand and Bednorz, *Moorish Architecture*, p. 12.

11. A vehicle for literacy: Safran, *The Second Umayyad Caliphate*, p. 63. "We have revealed the Qur'an in the Arabic tongue": *Qur'an*, 12:2.

12. "Veneration of text and language thus went hand in hand in Islam": F. E. Peters, *The Monotheists: Jews, Christians, and Muslims in Conflict and Competition*. 2 vols. (Princeton, NJ: Princeton University Press, 2003), vol. 2, p. 209. "Run[ning] like a scarlet thread through all its word formations": Burckhardt, *Moorish Culture*, pp. 83.

13. Muslim literacy: "The day will surely come when those who disbelieve will wish that they believed that they were Muslims": *Qur'an,* 15:3. "From the beginning, then, Islam was a religion of the book and of learning, a society that esteemed knowledge and education above almost every other human activity": Jonathan Berkey, *The Transmission of Knowledge in Medieval Cairo* (Princeton, NJ: Princeton University Press, 1992), p. 296.

14. Arabic literacy rates: Berkey, *Transmission of Knowledge,* pp. 8–9. "Alas! All talented Christians know only the language and the literature of the Arabs": Peter Brown, *The Rise of Western Christendom: Triumph and Diversity, 200–1000 AD* (Oxford: Blackwell, 1996), p. 194.

15. "Eleven of whom were sons": al-Makkari [Maqqari], *History of the Mohammedan Dynasties,* vol. 1, p. 94.

16. The Falcon's balancing act of autocracy and laissez-faire: Barrucand and Bednorz, *Moorish Architecture,* p. 34; Kennedy, *Muslim Spain and Portugal,* ch. 2.

17. Jews, *muwalladun,* and Christians would ascend to high office: Maria Rosa Menocal, *The Ornament of the World: How Muslims, Jews, and Christians Created a Culture of Tolerance in Medieval Spain* (Boston: Little, Brown, 2002), p. 79. "When we grant them security; and surround them with every comfort and luxury . . .": al-Makkari [Maqqari], *History of the Mohammedan Dynasties,* vol. 2, p. 84.

18. Tolerance and taxes: Barrucand and Bednorz, *Moorish Architecture,* p. 35; Kennedy, *Muslim Spain and Portugal,* p. 40. The Malikite school of jurisprudence: Kennedy, pp. 40–41; Reza Aslan, *No god but God: The Origins, Evolution, and Future of Islam* (New York: Random House, 2005), pp. 165–66; John L. Esposito, ed., *The Oxford History of Islam* (New York: Oxford University Press, 2000), pp. 90–95.

19. The Falcon's heirs: "With sycophants, fools, and cowards": al-Makkari [Maqqari], *History of the Mohammedan Dynasties,* vol. 2, p. 95.

20. 'Abd al-Rahman's boast: "I came fleeing hunger, the sword, and death . . .": Safran, *The Second Umayyad Caliphate,* p. 125. "It is said that when 'Abd al-Rahman took over the reins of government . . .": al-Kindi, quoted in Barrucand and Bednorz, *Moorish Architecture,* p. 51.

Chapter Thirteen

1. Frankish continental military and political hegemony: Alessandro Barbero, *Charlemagne: Father of a Continent* (Berkeley: University of Callifornia Press, 2004), p. 65; Richard Fletcher, *The Barbarian Conversion: From Paganism to Christianity* (New York: Henry Holt, 1998), p. 222. "Was so puffed up with empty ambition . . .": Einhard, *The Life of Charlemagne* (Ann Arbor: University of Michigan Press, 1960), p. 68.

2. On the significance of Avar cavalry stirrups: Heinrich Fichtenau, *The Carolingian Empire,* trans. Peter Munz (Toronto: University of Toronto Press, 1978), p. 80; Peter Brown, *The Rise of Western Christendom: Triumph and Diversity, 200–1000 AD* (Oxford: Blackwell, 1996), p. 10.

3. Charlemagne's Avar campaign, first phase: "Irrational and unlettered people": Pierre Riché, *Daily Life in the World of Charlemagne* (Philadelphia: University of Pennsylvania Press, 1978), p. 5; Fichtenau, *Carolingian Empire,* p. 79; Donald Bullough, *The Age of Charlemagne* (London: Elek Ltd., 1965), p. 68; Barbero, *Charlemagne,* p. 69.

4. Islam bulwarked at the Pyrenees; Hisham's response: Hugh Kennedy, *Muslim Spain and Portugal: A Political History of al-Andalus* (London: Longman, 1996), p. 40; al-Masudi [Macoudi], *Les prairies d'or [Fields of Gold],* trans. C. Barbier de Meynard and P. de

Courteille. 5 vols. (Paris: Imprimerie impériale, 1861–1917), vol. 1, pp. 66–73; Friedrich Heer, *Charlemagne and His World* (London: Weidenfeld and Nicolson, 1975), p. 115.

5. Adoptionism (*Hispanicus error*): Bullough, *Age of Charlemagne*, pp. 112–15. "Unbelievers are those who say, God is one of three": Qur'an, 5:73.

6. The new Christian order of power and caste: Jean-Henri Roy and Jean Deviosse, *La Bataille de Poitiers: Trente journées qui ont fait la France* (Paris: Gallimard, 1966), p. 10; Georges Duby, *Rural Economy and Country Life in the Medieval West*, trans. Cynthia Poston (Philadelphia: University of Pennsylvania Press, 1998; orig. ed. 1962), Bk. 1, ch. 2, Bk. 3, ch. 3. "The species of '*potentes*' emerges": Brown, *Rise of Western Christendom*, p. 103; Paul Fouracre, *The Age of Charles Martel* (Harlow, UK: Pearson Education Ltd., 2000), pp. 146–47; Susan Reynolds, *Kingdoms and Communities in Western Europe 900–1300*, pp. 17–18. "Feudalism"—whatever it was or became: Fouracre, p. 150; F.-L. Ganshof, *Charlemagne: Sa personalité, son héritage* (Brussels: Société Royale d'Archéologie de Bruxelles, 1966).

7. Carolingian society: "comprised . . . three groups: those who fought, those who prayed, and those who labored": Riché, *Daily Life*, p. 133; Barbero, *Charlemagne*, p. 324; Riché, p. 117.

8. On the differences in Christian and Muslim enslavement: Robin Blackburn, *The Making of New World Slavery: From the Baroque to the Modern, 1492–1800* (London: Verso, 1998), pp. 8–43; William Gervase Clarence-Smith, *Islam and the Abolition of Slavery* (Oxford: Oxford University Press, 2006), pp. 4–6; Bernard Lewis, *Race and Slavery in the Middle East* (Oxford: Oxford University Press, 1990), ch. 1; Ronald Segal, *Islam's Black Slaves: The Other Black Diaspora* (New York: Farrar, Straus and Giroux, 2001), chs. 1 and 2.

9. Hardening Carolingian social stratification: "Do justice fairly, correctly and equitably . . .": Riché, *Daily Life*, p. 261; Fichtenau, *Carolingian Empire*, p. 144; Barbero, *Charlemagne*, p. 320; Riché, p. 128.

10. An agrarian society dominated by warriors and prince-bishops: Barbero, *Charlemagne*, p. 148; Duby, *Rural Economy*, Bk. 3, ch. 3; Duby, *The Early Growth of the European Economy: Warriors and Peasants from the Seventh to the Twelfth Century* (Ithaca, NY: Cornell University Press, 1974), pp. 31–34.

11. Property-holding and clerical celibacy: Riché, *Daily Life*, ch. 11; Duby, *Rural Economy*, Bk. 3, ch. 1.

12. Carolingian monogamy: "Whether she be a drunkard, irritable, immoral": Bishop Hincmar, quoted in Susanne Fonay Wemple, *Women in Frankish Society: Marriage and the Cloister, 500 to 900* (Philadelphia: University of Pennsylvania Press, 1981), p. 88.

13. Capitularies and royal emissaries (*missi dominici*): Fichtenau, *Carolingian Empire*, p. 108; Matthias Becher, *Charlemagne* (New Haven, CT: Yale University Press, 2003), p. 112. "By Christmas informs us of everything . . .": Bullough, *Age of Charlemagne*, pp. 99–100, 115–16.

14. Alcuin and Charlemagne and the intellectual awakening: Steven Allott, *Alcuin of York c. A.D. 732 to 804* (York, UK: William Sessions Ltd, 1974), pp. vii–viii; Fichtenau, *Carolingian Empire*, ch. 4 and p. 95; Luitpold Wallach, *Alcuin and Charlemagne* (Ithaca, NY: Cornell University Press, 1959); Bullough, *Age of Charlemagne*, pp. 101–2.

15. "A dozen churchmen as wise and well taught . . . as were Jerome and Augustine!": Notker of St. Gall [*De Carolo Magno*], in Einhard and Notker the Stammerer, *Two Lives of Charlemagne*, trans. Lewis Thorpe (New York: Penguin, 1969), p. 102.

16. The Palace School: "We are concerned to restore with diligent zeal the workshops

of knowledge . . .": Fichtenau, *Carolingian Empire*, p. 87; Bullough, *Age of Charlemagne*, pp. 100–102; P. L. Butzer et al., eds., *Karl der Grosse und sein Nachwirken: 1200 Jahre Kultur und Wissenschaft in Europa*. 2 vols. (Turnhout, Belgium: Brepols, 1997), pp. 42–47.

17. "By the King of Heaven, I take no account of your noble birth . . .": Fichtenau, *Carolingian Empire*, p. 32.

18. The Carolingian Renaissance: "How few care about such things!": Alexander Murray, *Reason and Society in the Middle Ages* (Oxford: Oxford University Press, 1978), p. 132. The *trivium* and the *quadrivium*, "probably never given": Fichtenau, *Carolingian Empire*, p. 91. "Every monastery and every abbey have its school": Fletcher, *Barbarian Conversion*, p. 194.

19. "In this way, the most glorious Charlemagne saw the study of letters was flourishing throughout the length and breadth of his kingdom": Notker, *De Carolo Magno*, p. 102.

20. Charlemagne at Aachen: "It was for this reason that he built his palace at Aachen": Einhard, *Life of Charlemagne*, p. 77.

21. Family worries and revolt: Becher, *Charlemagne*, pp. 123–25; Einhard, *Life of Charlemagne*, p. 76.

22. The symbolism of the Aachen palatine complex: Riché, *Daily Life*, p. 43; Fletcher, *Barbarian Conversion*, p. 51; Bullough, *Age of Charlemagne*, p. 167; Barbero, *Charlemagne*, p. 88.

23. The *chrysotriklinos* at Aachen: "Gave to God what was God's": Fichtenau, *Carolingian Empire*, p. 69. The king's prerogative to appoint bishops, Fichtenau, pp. 30, 66. On the *Libri Carolini*: Bullough, *Age of Charlemagne*, pp. 111–12; Barbero, *Charlemagne*, pp. 84–85.

24. Church and State tensions: "Although you take precedence over all mankind in dignity . . .": Pope Gelasius quoted in James Muldoon, *Empire and Order: The Concept of Empire, 800–1800* (New York: St. Martin's Press, 1999), p. 65; Murray, *Reason and Society*, p. 152; Wallach, *Alcuin and Charlemagne*, pp. 2–12.

25. Death of Pope Adrian I: "Pope Adrian I," in *The Catholic Encyclopedia*. 15 vols. (New Advent Web site, 1997; orig. ed.: Washington, DC: The Catholic University of America Press, 1913), vol. 1.

26. Charlemagne's arbitration of papal crisis and imperial elevation: Friedrich Gontard, *The Chair of Peter: A History of the Papacy* (New York: Holt, Rinehart and Winston, 1964; orig. German ed. 1959), p. 181; Bernhard Schimmelpfennig, *The Papacy* (New York: Columbia University Press, 1992), p. 91. "Pope Leo placed upon his head a crown . . .": Muldoon, *Empire and Order*, p. 21; Bullough, *Age of Charlemagne*, p. 174. See Geoffrey Barraclough's interesting minority interpretation, *The Crucible of Europe: The Ninth and Tenth Centuries in European History* (Berkeley: University of California Press, 1976), pp. 48–53.

27. "He would not have entered the church if he had known beforehand the pope's intentions": Einhard, *Life of Charlemagne*, p. 57. Carolingian political theory: Fichtenau, *Carolingian Empire*, p. 74; Muldoon, *Empire and Order*, ch. 3; Wallach, *Alcuin and Charlemagne*, pp. 10–22. "You are more noble in your wisdom": Alcuin, quoted in Becher, *Charlemagne*, p. 94; Wallach, 12–22.

28. On the Carolingian imperial vision: Muldoon, *Empire and Order*; Bullough, *Age of Charlemagne*, ch. 7 and pp. 201–7; Barbero, *Charlemagne*, ch. 5; Fichtenau, *Carolingian Empire*, ch. 3; Robert Morrissey, *L'empereur à la barbe fleurie: Charlemagne dans la mythologie et l'histoire de France* (Paris: Gallimard, 1997), pp. 9–28; Janet Coleman, *A History of Political Thought: From the Middle Ages to the Renaissance* (Oxford: Blackwell, 2000), pp. 11–26; Geoffrey Barraclough, *The Crucible of Europe: The Ninth and Tenth Centuries in European History* (Berkeley: University of California Press, 1976).

Chapter Fourteen

1. The chess game: Marilyn Yalom, *Birth of the Chess Queen: A History* (New York: HarperCollins, 2004), pp. 43–48.

2. Modernity in Cordoba: Muzaffar Iqbal, *Islam and Science* (Burlington, VT: Ashgate Publishing, 2002), p. xix.

3. Migration of knowledge ("Hindu numbers"): Alexander Murray, *Reason and Society in the Middle Ages* (Oxford: Oxford University Press, 1978), p. 167. *Bayt al-Hikma* ("House of Wisdom"): John L. Esposito, ed., *The Oxford History of Islam* (New York: Oxford University Press, 2000), p. 272.

4. The Viking plague: Hugh Kennedy, *Muslim Spain and Portugal: A Political History of al-Andalus* (London: Longman, 1996), pp. 47–48; J. M. Wallace-Hadrill, *The Barbarian West, 400–1000,* 4th ed. (Oxford: Blackwell, 1996), pp. 151–55; Gwyn Jones, *A History of the Vikings* (Oxford: Oxford University Press, 1973); James Reston, Jr., *The Last Apocalypse: Europe at the Year 1000 A.D.* (New York: Doubleday, 1998), pp. 79–81.

5. Hisham's *jihad*: "Make yourselves worthy then of such blessings": Joseph Reinaud [Haroun Khan Sherwani], *Muslim Colonies in France, Northern Italy, and Switzerland* (Lahore, Pakistan: Sh. Muhammad Ashraf, 1954), pp. 92–93, 95.

6. The creation of the Spanish March: Reinaud [Sherwani], *Muslim Colonies,* pp. 95–98; Salma Khadra Jayyusi, ed., *The Legacy of Muslim Spain.* 2 vols. (Leiden: Brill, 1992), vol. I, p. 22.

7. Pelayo's descendants commence the *Reconquista*: Ahmed ibn Mohammed al-Makkari [Maqqari], *The History of the Mohammedan Dynasties in Spain* (London and New York: RoutledgeCurzon, 2002), vol. 2, p. 34; Jayyusi, ed., *Legacy of Muslim Spain,* vol. I, pp. 11, 16; Kennedy, *Muslim Spain and Portugal,* p. 21; Daniel Power and Naomi Standen, eds., *Frontiers in Question: Eurasian Borderlands, 700–1700* (New York: St. Martin's Press, 1999), ch. 2.

8. Al-Hakam I's amirate and Frankish advances: Jayyusi, ed., *Legacy of Muslim Spain,* vol. I, pp. 22–23. "A King am I, subdued": Jayyusi, ed., vol. I, p. 401.

9. Cordoba uprisings (*al-Rabad*): al-Makkari [Maqqari], *History of the Mohammedan Dynasties,* vol. 2, p. 102; Jayyusi, ed., *Legacy of Muslim Spain,* vol. I, p. 115; Kennedy, *Muslim Spain and Portugal,* p. 43.

10. Al-Hakam's legacy: Kennedy, *Muslim Spain and Portugal,* p. 39; Jayyusi, ed., *Legacy of Muslim Spain,* vol. I, pp. 24–27; al-Makkari [Maqqari], *History of the Mohammedan Dynasties,* vol. 2, pp. 102–6.

11. Charlemagne's death: Einhard, *The Life of Charlemagne* (Ann Arbor: University of Michigan Press, 1960), pp. 59–60; Richard Fletcher, *The Barbarian Conversion: From Paganism to Christianity* (New York: Henry Holt, 1998), p. 67; Matthias Becher, *Charlemagne* (New Haven, CT: Yale University Press, 2003), pp. 123–26. The daughters were their father's comfort at the end: Becher, p. 123.

12. Charlemagne's legacy: Becher, *Charlemagne,* p. 127; Donald Bullough, *The Age of Charlemagne* (London: Elek Ltd., 1965), pp. 201–7; Heinrich Fichtenau, *The Carolingian Empire,* trans. Peter Munz (Toronto: University of Toronto Press, 1978), ch. 7.

13. The Viking infestation: "They came from the sea. Heathens!": Reston, *Last Apocalypse,* p. 79; Jayyusi, ed., *Legacy of Muslim Spain,* vol. I, p. 27.

14. *Campus stellae* ("Field of the star"): Charles E. Chapman, *A History of Spain* (New York: Free Press, 1965; orig. ed. 1918), p. 55. On 'Abd al-Rahman II's regime: Jayyusi, ed., *Legacy of Muslim Spain,* vol. I, pp. 24–27; Kennedy, *Muslim Spain and Portugal,* pp. 44–48; al-Makkari [Maqqari], *History of the Mohammedan Dynasties,* vol. 2, pp. 113–24.

15. The Battle of Clavijo: Rafael Altamira, *A History of Spain* (New York: Van Nostrand, 1949), p. 103; Americo Castro, *The Spaniards: An Introduction to Their History* (Berkeley: University of California Press, 1971), p. 387.

16. Christian assimilation and conversion: Kennedy, *Muslim Spain and Portugal*, p. 67; Jayyusi, ed., *Legacy of Muslim Spain*, vol. 1, p. 157. "A 'new religion' was in the strict sense of the term unthinkable . . .": Fletcher, *Barbarian Conversion*, p. 17.

17. The "Mozarab martyrs"; Alvarus and Eulogius: "They have forgotten their own language": Maria Rosa Menocal, *The Ornament of the World: How Muslims, Jews, and Christians Created a Culture of Tolerance in Medieval Spain* (Boston: Little, Brown, 2002), p. 66.

18. The "Mozarab martyrs"; Alvarus and Eulogius: Fletcher, *Barbarian Conversion*, p. 46; Peter Brown, *The Rise of Western Christendom: Triumph and Diversity, 200—1000 AD* (Oxford: Blackwell, 1996), p. 194; Paul Alvarus, "Life of Eulogius," trans. C. M. Sage, in Olivia R. Constable, ed., *Medieval Iberia: Readings from Christian, Muslim, and Jewish Sources* (Philadelphia: University of Pennsylvania Press, 1997), pp. 51—55; Richard Fletcher, *The Cross and the Crescent: Christianity and Islam from Muhammad to the Reformation* (New York: Viking, 2003), p. 48; Norman Daniel, *The Arabs and Medieval Europe* (London: Longman Group Ltd., 1975), ch. 2.

19. Amiral low point under 'Abd Allah: Jayyusi, ed., *Legacy of Muslim Spain*, vol. 1, pp. 31—35; al-Makkari [Maqqari], *History of the Mohammedan Dynasties*, vol. 2, pp. 131—32; Kennedy, *Muslim Spain and Portugal*, pp. 73—81.

20. 'Abd al-Rahman on stage: "His generosity, and his love of justice . . .": al-Makkari [Maqqari], *History of the Mohammedan Dynasties*, p. 147.

21. "They are the filthiest race that God ever created": Philip Riley, Frank Gerome, Robert Lembright, Henry A. Myers, and Chong-Kun Yoon, eds., *The Global Experience: Readings in World History to 1550* (New York: Prentice Hall, 2001), vol. 1, p. 336.

22. 'Abd al-Rahman III polices his realm: Kennedy, *Muslim Spain and Portugal*, ch.4; Jayyusi, ed., *Legacy of Muslim Spain*, vol. 2, pp. 35—38; Chapman, *History of Spain*, pp. 55—58.

23. Bobastro (Malaga): "Reducing its fortifications, pulling down its walls and raising everything standing . . .": Ibn Hayyan, *Muqtabis*, trans. P. M. Cobb in Constable, ed., *Medieval Iberia*, p. 70; Kennedy, *Muslim Spain and Portugal*, pp. 88—89.

24. 'Abd al-Rahman proclaims the caliphate: "Allah has favored us. He has shown His preference for us . . .": Janina Safran, *The Second Umayyad Caliphate: The Articulation of Caliphal Legitimacy in al-Andalus* (Cambridge: Harvard University Press, 2001), p. 21; Kennedy, *Muslim Spain and Portugal*, p. 90.

25. 'Abd al-Rahman III's building program; enlargement of the Friday Mosque: Manuel Nieto Cumplido, *La Mezquita-Catedral de Cordoba* (Barcelona: Editorial Escudo de Oro, n.d.). *Madinat al-Zahra*: Safran, *The Second Umayyad Caliphate*, p. 58.

26. "Their naked swords, both broad and long . . .": Robert Hillenbrand, "The Ornament of the World," in Jayyusi, ed., *Legacy of Muslim Spain*, vol. 1, pp. 112—35.

27. Homage at *Madinat al-Zahra*: Jayyusi, ed., *Legacy of Muslim Spain*, vol. 1, p. 38; Chapman, *History of Spain*, p. 57.

28. Cordoba as a world capital: Menocal, *Ornament of the World*, p. 33. Benedictine abbey of St. Gall: John P. McKay, Bennett D. Hill, John Buckler, eds., *A History of World Societies*, 3rd ed. (Boston: Houghton Mifflin, 1992), p. 289. The importance of paper: Azim A. Nanji, ed., *The Muslim Almanac: A Reference Work on the History, Faith, Culture, and Peoples of Islam* (Detroit: Gale Research, 1996), p. 190.

29. "The brilliant ornament of the world": Menocal, *Ornament of the World*, p. 32; Jane S. Gerber, *The Jews of Spain: A History of the Sephardic Experience* (New York: Free Press, 1992), p. 28.

30. The business of *al-Andalus*: Kennedy, *Muslim Spain and Portugal*, pp. 86, xxi.
31. Sephardic partnership: Hasdai's negotiations with the count of Barcelona—quotes from Ibn Hayyan, *Muqtabis*, in Constable, ed., *Medieval Iberia*, pp. 67-72. "To engage in trade wherever they wished . . .": Ibn Hayyan, *Muqtabis*, p. 71.
32. Gerbert of Aurillac's mathematics: Murray, *Reason and Society*, pp. 158-59.
33. Pope Sylvester II's influence: Murray, *Reason and Society*, p. 158; Bernard F. Reilly, *The Contest of Christian and Muslim Spain, 1031-1157* (Oxford: Blackwell, 1995), p. 255.
34. On Mozarabic demographics and culture: Reilly, *Contest of Christian and Muslim Spain*, p. 18; Menocal, *Ornament of the World*, p. 71; Kennedy, *Muslim Spain and Portugal*, p. 67.
35. The two Golden Ages (Muslim and Sefarad): Thomas F. Glick, "Science in Medieval Spain: The Jewish Contribution in the Context of Convivencia," in Vivian B. Mann et al., eds., *Convivencia: Jews, Muslims, and Christians in Medieval Spain* (New York: George Braziller/Jewish Museum of New York, 1992), pp. 83-111. Gerber, *Jews of Spain*, p. 47; Reilly, *Contest of Christian and Muslim Spain*, p. 15; Abraham ibn Daud, *The Book of Tradition (1161)*, in Constable, ed., *Medieval Iberia*, pp. 73-74; Norman A. Stillman, *The Jews of Arab Lands: A History and Source Book* (Philadelphia: Jewish Publication Society of America, 1979), pp. xv-xvi, 54.
36. The impact of *De Materia Medica*: Gerber, *Jews of Spain*, p. 49; Jayyusi, ed., *Legacy of Muslim Spain*, vol. 1, p. 124; Glick, "Science in Medieval Spain," p. 84; Menocal, *Ornament of the World*, p. 89; Esposito, ed., *Oxford History of Islam*, p. 211.
37. The splendid finale of Hasdai ibn Shaprut and 'Abd al-Rahman III: "As to the sums which entered the royal coffers": al-Makkari [Maqqari], *History of the Mohammedan Dynasties*, p. 146; Kennedy, *Muslim Spain and Portugal*, p. 93.

Chapter Fifteen

1. General tightening-up of Andalusia's borders: Macoudi [al-Masudi], *Les prairies d'or* [*Fields of Gold*], trans. C. Barbier de Meynard and P. de Courteille. 5 vols. (Paris: Imprimerie impériale, 1861-1917), vol. 1, pp. 66-67.
2. The Carolingian center failed to hold: Edward Gibbon, *The History of the Decline and Fall of the Roman Empire*. 8 vols. (London: The Folio Society, 1983; orig. eds., 1776-88), vol. 5, p. 189; Heinrich Fichtenau, *The Carolingian Empire*, trans. Peter Munz (Toronto: University of Toronto Press, 1978), p. 187; J. M. Wallace-Hadrill, *The Barbarian West, 400-1000*, 4th ed. (Oxford: Blackwell, 1996), ch. 7; Simon MacLean, *Kingship and Politics in the Late Ninth Century: Charles the Fat and the End of the Carolingian Empire* (Cambridge: Cambridge University Press, 2007). James Muldoon, *Empire and Order: The Concept of Empire, 800-1800* (New York: St. Martin's Press, 1999).
3. A mostly secure *al-Andalus*: Daniel Power and Naomi Standen, eds., *Frontiers in Question: Eurasian Borderlands, 700-1700* (New York: St. Martin's Press, 1999), p. 38; Bernard F. Reilly, *The Contest of Christian and Muslim Spain, 1031-1157* (Oxford: Blackwell, 1995), pp. 9, 17-18.
4. Umayyad succession crisis: "If you don't like the commission, I will send another to execute it": Ahmed ibn Mohammed al-Makkari [Maqqari], *The History of the Mohammedan Dynasties in Spain*. 2 vols. (London and New York: RoutledgeCurzon, 2002), vol. 2, p. 178; James Reston, Jr., *The Last Apocalypse: Europe at the Year 1000 A.D.* (New York: Doubleday, 1998), pp. 122-26; Hugh Kennedy, *Muslim Spain and Portugal: A Political History of al-Andalus* (London: Longman, 1996), ch. 5.
5. The rise of Muhammad ibn Abi Amir: Salma Khadra Jayyusi, ed. *The Legacy of Muslim*

Spain. 2 vols. (Leiden: Brill, 1992), vol. 1, p. 41; Kennedy, *Muslim Spain and Portugal,* ch. 5; Reston, *Last Apocalypse,* pp. 122–26. "With unusual pomp and magnificence": al-Makkari [Maqqari], *History of the Mohammedan Dynasties,* vol. 2, p. 182.

6. "Meanwhile [Abi Amir] filled the functions of his offices . . .": and "All this he accomplished with the help of [General] Ghalib": al-Makkari [Maqqari], *History of the Mohammedan Dynasties,* vol. 2, p. 182.

7. The bloodletting near Medinaceli: Mahmoud Makki, "The Political History of al-Andalus," in Jayyusi, ed., *Legacy of Muslim Spain,* vol. 1, p. 42.

8. Al-Mansur's new order: Peter C. Scales, *The Fall of the Caliphate of Cordoba: Berbers and Andalusis in Conflict* (Leiden: E. J. Brill, 1994), p. 39. "After the usual one for the Caliph Hisham": al-Makkari [Maqqari], *History of the Mohammedan Dynasties,* vol. 2, p. 187.

9. Al-Mansur's military and political triumphs: Jayyusi, ed., *Legacy of Muslim Spain,* vol. 2, p. 43; Kennedy, *Muslim Spain and Portugal,* ch. 5; Evariste Lévi-Provençal, *La civilisation Arabe en Espagne: Vue générale* (Paris: G. P. Maisonneuve, 1948), pp. 18–24.

10. Unchanged borders and Christian out-migration: Power and Standen, eds., *Frontiers in Question,* ch. 2.

11. Sanchuelo overreaches: Scales, *Fall of the Caliphate,* p. 40; David Wasserstein, *The Rise and Fall of the Party-Kings: Politics and Society in Islamic Spain, 1002–1086* (Princeton, NJ: Princeton University Press, 1985), p. 6; Kennedy, *Muslim Spain and Portugal,* ch. 5.

12. Sanchuelo neuters the caliph: "After searching, therefore, high ranks as well as low": al-Makkari [Maqqari], *History of the Mohammedan Dynasties,* vol. 2, p. 223; Scales, *Fall of the Caliphate,* p. 43.

13. The Umayyad Caliphate ends like silent film footage: Scales, *Fall of the Caliphate,* p. 52; Kennedy, *Muslim Spain and Portugal,* ch. 6; Wasserstein, *Rise and Fall of the Party-Kings,* pp. 79–80; Janina Safran, *The Second Umayyad Caliphate: The Articulation of Caliphal Legitimacy in al-Andalus* (Cambridge: Harvard University Press, 2001), pp. 102–5.

14. Sanchuelo's destruction: al-Makkari [Maqqari], *History of the Mohammedan Dynasties,* vol. 2, p. 226; Kennedy, *Muslim Spain and Portugal,* p. 126.

15. The competition between Caliphs Muhammad and Sulayman: al-Makkari [Maqqari], *History of the Mohammedan Dynasties,* vol. 2, p. 227; Scales, *Fall of the Caliphate,* p. 73; Makki, "Political History of al-Andalus," in Jayyusi, ed., *Legacy of Muslim Spain,* vol. 1, p. 48; Kennedy, *Muslim Spain and Portugal,* p. 127.

16. Cordoba sacked by the Berbers: "A general massacre ensued": al-Makkari [Maqqari], *History of the Mohammedan Dynasties,* vol. 2, p. 229; Scales, *Fall of the Caliphate,* p. 79.

17. The thread of legitimacy broken: al-Makkari [Maqqari], *History of the Mohammedan Dynasties,* vol. 2, p. 225; Makki, "Political History of al-Andalus," in Jayyusi, ed., *Legacy of Muslim Spain,* 1, p. 48; Scales, *Fall of the Caliphate,* p. 4.

18. The dismemberment of a caliphate: Scales, *Fall of the Caliphate,* pp. 91, 100, 180; Kennedy, *Muslim Spain and Portugal,* pp. 138, 142; Mikel de Epalza, "Mozarabs: An Emblematic Christian Minority in Islamic al-Andalus," in Jayyusi, ed., *Legacy of Muslim Spain,* vol. 1, pp. 149–70; Reilly, *Contest of Christian and Muslim Spain,* p. 6.

19. The age of the *taifas*: Reilly, *Contest of Christian and Muslim Spain,* pp. 2–3; Wasserstein, *Rise and Fall of the Party-Kings;* Scales, *Fall of the Caliphate,* pp. 205–13; Makki, "Political History of al-Andalus," in Jayyusi, ed., *Legacy of Muslim Spain,* vol. 1, pp. 46–52.

20. A Golden Age paladin: Samuel ibn Naghrela, *The Battle of Alfuente* (1038), trans. R. P. Scheindlin, in Olivia R. Constable, ed., *Medieval Iberia: Readings from Christian, Muslim, and Jewish Sources* (Philadelphia: University of Pennsylvania Press, 1997), pp. 84–90;

Jane S. Gerber, *The Jews of Spain: A History of the Sephardic Experience* (New York: Free Press, 1992), p. 53. *Al-qal'a al-hamra* ("red citadel", in Marianne Barrucand and Achim Bednorz, *Moorish Architecture in Andalusia* (Cologne: Taschen, 1999), p. 183.

21. The "Nagid" as politician and poet: "[T]hey felt resentment over my high rank": Naghrela, in Constable, ed., *Medieval Iberia*, p. 84; *Selected Poems of Shmuel HaNagid,* trans. Peter Cole (Princeton, NJ: Princeton University Press, 1996). "I am the David of my age": Maria Rosa Menocal, *The Ornament of the World: How Muslims, Jews, and Christians Created a Culture of Tolerance in Medieval Spain* (Boston: Little, Brown, 2002), p. 102. "This cursed man was a superior man": Chris Lowney, *A Vanished World: Medieval Spain's Golden Age of Enlightenment* (New York: Free Press, 2005), p. 97.

22. "Friend, lead me through the vineyards, give me wine": Gerber, *Jews of Spain*, p. 67.

23. "For the first time in a thousand years . . .": Menocal, *Ornament of the World*, p. 110; Gerber, *Jews of Spain*, pp. 65–66; Luce Lopez Baralt, "The Legacy of Islam in Spanish Literature," in Jayyusi, ed., *Legacy of Muslim Spain*, vol. 1, pp. 505–52.

24. Sefarad's spectacular personalities: Gerber, *Jews of Spain*, ch. 3; Menocal, *Ornament of the World*, pp. 101–11; 'Abd Allah ibn Buluggin (*Tibyan*), Abu Ishaq of Elvira (*Qasida*), and Abraham ibn Daud (*The Book of Tradition, 1161*), in Constable, ed., *Medieval Iberia*, pp. 91–102; Eliyahu Ashtor, *The Jews of Moslem Spain*, vol. 2/3 (Philadelphia: Jewish Publication Society, 1992), pp. 113–18.

25. On Ibn Hazm: Ibn Hazm, *Al-Fasl al-milal* ("On the Inconsistencies of the Four Gospels"), in Constable, ed., *Medieval Iberia*, pp. 81–83. *The Ring of the Dove*: Menocal, *Ornament of the World*, p. 117; Lois A. Giffen, "Ibn Hazm and the *Tawq al-Hamama*," in Jayyusi, ed., *Legacy of Muslim Spain*, pp. 420–41; Ibn Hazm, *The Ring of the Dove*, trans. A. J. Arberry (London: Luzac & Co., 1953).

26. Ill will between Ibn Hazm and the Nagid: "Stay away from these impure, evil-smelling, unclean people": Gerber, *Jews of Spain*, p. 55; Ashtor, *Jews of Moslem Spain*, pp. 52–55, 182.

27. Sancho the Great's superkingdom: Charles E. Chapman, *A History of Spain* (New York: Free Press, 1965; orig. ed. 1918), p. 71; Bernard F. Reilly, *The Kingdom of Leon-Castilla Under King Alfonso VI, 1065–1109* (Princeton, NJ: Princeton University Press, 1988), pp. 7–14; Reilly, *Contest of Christian and Muslim Spain*, p. 35.

28. The Rise of King Ferdinand I: Makki, "The Political History of al-Andalus," in Jayyusi, ed., *Legacy of Muslim Spain*, pp. 3–87, p. 57; Chapman, *History of Spain*, p. 71.

29. The Cluniac movement in Spain: Dominique Iogna-Pratt, *Order and Exclusion: Cluny and Christendom Face Heresy, Judaism, and Islam (1000–1150)*, trans G. R. Edwards (Ithaca, NY: Cornell University Press, 2003; orig. French ed. 1998), ch. 9, esp. pp. 275–76; Chapman, *History of Spain* pp. 65–66; Christopher Tyerman, *God's War: A New History of the Crusades* (Cambridge, MA: Belknap Press, 2006), p. 660; Reilly, *Contest of Christian and Muslim Spain*, pp. 66–67.

30. The siege and occupation of Barbastro (Huesca): Roger Boase, "Arab Influences on European Love-Poetry," in Jayyusi, ed., *Legacy of Muslim Spain*, vol. 1, pp. 457–82; Menocal, *Ornament of the World*, pp. 118–26; Tyerman, *God's War*, p. 660.

31. Norman acculturation in Barbastro: al-Makkari [Maqqari], *History of the Mohammedan Dynasties*, vol. 2, p. 167; Menocal, *Ornament of the World*, pp. 120–21; Boase, "Arab Influences on European Love-Poetry," in Jayyusi, ed., *Legacy of Muslim Spain*, vol. 1, pp. 462, 465; Kennedy, *Muslim Spain and Portugal*, p. 151.

32. King Sancho's murder: Richard Fletcher, *The Quest for El Cid* (New York: Oxford University Press, 1989), pp. 116–19; Reilly, *Kingdom of Leon-Castilla*, p. 87.

33. Sevillian and Castilian competition for Cordoba: Makki, "The Political History of

al-Andalus," in Jayyusi, ed., *Legacy of Muslim Spain*, vol. 1, p. 55; Reilly, *Kingdom of Leon-Castilla*, p. 81.

34. Profiles of al-Mu'tamid and Alfonso: Salma Khadra Jayyusi, "Andalusi Poetry: The Golden Period," in Jayyusi, ed., *Legacy of Muslim Spain*, vol. 1, pp. 317–66; Fletcher, *Quest for El Cid*, pp. 117–18; Reilly, *Kingdom of Leon-Castilla*, p. 92. *Qasr al-Mubarak* ("the Blessed Palace"): Juan Carlos Hernandez Nunez and Alfredo J. Morales, *The Royal Palace of Seville* (London: Scala Publishers, 1999), pp. 8–12.

35. Alfonso VI before Sevilla and the fall of Toledo: "This is the last land in Spain, and I have trod it!": Chapman, *History of Spain*, p. 72; Reilly, *Contest of Christian and Muslim Spain*, pp. 84–85; al-Makkari [Maqqari], *History of the Mohammedan Dynasties*, vol. 2, p. 255.

36. The fall of Toledo: Reilly, *Kingdom of Leon-Castilla*, p. 170; Reilly, *Contest of Christian and Muslim Spain*, pp. 85–86. "King of the Two Religions" (also "Emperor," the title Alfonso VI bestowed upon himself to preempt papal claims of supremacy in Spain): Tyerman, *God's War*, p. 660; Stephen O'Shea, *Sea of Faith: Islam and Christianity in the Medieval Mediterranean World* (New York: Walker, 2006), pp. 144–45; John Iliffe, *Africans: The History of a Continent* (Cambridge: Cambridge University Press, 1995), p. 46.

37. "The tyrant took the city of Toledo from the Muslims": al-Makkari [Maqqari], *History of the Mohammedan Dynasties*, vol. 2, p. 255. "A tabernacle of celestial virtue": Richard Fletcher, *The Barbarian Conversion: From Paganism to Christianity* (New York: Henry Holt, 1998), p. 322; Reilly, *Kingdom of Leon-Castilla*, pp. 182–83.

38. Origin and conquest of Yusuf ibn Tashufin and the Almoravids: Basil Davidson, *Africa in History: Themes and Outlines* (New York: Collier Books, 1991), p. 94; Iliffe, *Africans*, p. 46; Kennedy, *Muslim Spain and Portugal*, pp. 154–61; Makki, "The Political History of al-Andalus," in Jayyusi, ed., *Legacy of Muslim Spain*, vol. 1, pp. 60–61.

39. Yusuf ibn Tashufin, the *Murabit*: "Righteousness, the correction of injustices, and the abolition of unlawful taxes": Kennedy, *Muslim Spain and Portugal*, p. 158. Almoravid (*al-Murabitun*) ideology succinctly discussed in Majid Fakhry, *Averroes (Ibn Rushd): His Life, Works and Influence* (Oxford: Oneworld, 2001), pp. xi–xii; John L. Esposito, ed., *The Oxford History of Islam* (New York: Oxford University Press, 2000), pp. 49–51.

40. Al-Mu'tamid's famous observation: "Would rather be a camel-driver in Africa than a swineherd in Castilla": quoted in Chapman, *History of Spain*, p. 69.

41. Yusuf ibn Tashufin disembarks: Paul Fregosi, *Jihad in the West* (Amherst, NY: Prometheus Books, 1998), p. 158; Reilly, *Kingdom of Leon-Castilla*, pp. 182–86.

42. Yusuf's three alternatives to Alfonso: al-Makkari [Maqqari], *History of the Mohammedan Dynasties*, vol. 2, p. 283.

43. "Never did I charge into battle/with the hope of returning safe": Jayyusi, "Andalusi Poetry: The Golden Period," in Jayyusi, ed., *Legacy of Muslim Spain*, vol. 1, p. 359; Ambrosio Huici Miranda, *Las Grandes Batallas de la Reconquista durante las Invasiones Africanas (Almoravides, Almohades, y Benimerines)* (Madrid: CSIC, Instituto de Estudios Africanos, 1956), pp. 40–82; Reilly, *Kingdom of Leon-Castilla*, pp. 188–89.

44. Almoravid occupation of *al-Andalus*: Makki, "The Political History of al-Andalus," in Jayyusi, ed., *Legacy of Muslim Spain*, vol. 1, p. 61; Kennedy, *Muslim Spain and Portugal*, ch. 7.

45. Arrival of the Almohads: Davidson, *Africa in History*, pp. 185–87; Kennedy, *Muslim Spain and Portugal*, ch. 9; Makki, "The Political History of al-Andalus," in Jayyusi, ed., *Legacy of Muslim Spain*, vol. 1, pp. 70–75. Ibn Tumart and Almohad (*al-Muwahhidun*) ideology: Esposito, ed., *Oxford History of Islam*, pp. 50–52; Makki, pp. 68–70.

Chapter Sixteen

1. On the *Bayt al-Hikma* and precedence to the European university: Tayeb el-Hibri, *Reinterpreting Islamic Historiography: Harun al-Rashid and the Narrative of the Abbasid Caliphate* (Cambridge: Cambridge University Press, 1999), pp. 95–96; Muzaffar Iqbal, *Islam and Science* (Burlington, VT: Ashgate Publishing, 2002), p. 43; John L. Esposito, ed., *The Oxford History of Islam* (New York: Oxford University Press, 2000), p. 271.

2. Culture and science in Baghdad and Cordoba compared: El-Hibri, *Reinterpreting Islamic Historiography,* pp. 96–98, 220; Alexander Murray, *Reason and Society in the Middle Ages* (Oxford: Oxford University Press, 1978), pp. 40–42; Mahmoud Makki, "The Political History of al-Andalus," in Salma Khadra Jayyusi, ed., *The Legacy of Muslim Spain.* 2 vols. (Leiden: Brill, 1992), vol. 1, p. 25.

3. On al-Kindi: Azim A. Nanji, ed., *The Muslim Almanac: A Reference Work on the History, Faith, Culture, and Peoples of Islam* (Detroit: Gale Research, 1996), p. 189; Esposito, ed., *Oxford History of Islam,* p. 273.

4. "The work of God and the word of God": Iqbal, *Islam and Science,* p. xix.

5. *The Book of Compulsion and Comparison:* Esposito, ed., *Oxford History of Islam,* p. 157.

6. The philosophy and science of "occupied" Toledo streaming into Christian Europe: Iqbal, *Islam and Science,* pp. 178–86; Jane S. Gerber, *The Jews of Spain: A History of the Sephardic Experience* (New York: Free Press, 1992), p. 17; Etienne Gilson, *La philosophie au Moyen-Age: Dès origines patristiques à la fin du XIVe siècle* (Paris: Editions Payot, 1986), pp. 345–60.

7. Avicenna's *magnum opus:* Nanji, ed., *Muslim Almanac,* p. 194.

8. On the Toledo conveyor belt: Maria Rosa Menocal, *The Ornament of the World: How Muslims, Jews, and Christians Created a Culture of Tolerance in Medieval Spain* (Boston: Little, Brown, 2002), pp. 196–97; Gerber, *Jews of Spain,* p. 99; Bernard F. Reilly, *The Contest of Christian and Muslim Spain, 1031–1157* (Oxford: Blackwell, 1995), pp. 254–55; Gilson, *La philosophie au Moyen-Age,* p. 377; Iqbal, *Islam and Science,* pp. 187–92; Norman Kretzmann, Anthony Kenny, and Jan Pinborg, eds., *The Cambridge History of Later Medieval Philosophy* (Cambridge: Cambridge University Press, 1982), pp. 48–49. On translated Muslim and Christian scripture: Dominique Iogna-Prat, *Order and Exclusion: Cluny and Christendom Face Heresy, Judaism, and Islam (1000–1150),* trans. G. R. Edwards. (Ithaca, NY: Cornell University Press, 2003; orig. French ed. 1998), p. 338.

9. Profile of Ibn Rushd: Roger Arnaldez, *Averroes: A Rationalist in Islam,* trans. D. Streight (Notre Dame, IN: University of Notre Dame Press, 2000; orig. French ed. 1998); Majid Fakhry, *Averroes (Ibn Rushd): His Life, Works and Influence* (Oxford: Oneworld, 2001), pp. 1–4; Esposito, ed., *Oxford History of Islam,* pp. 286–89.

10. Ibn Rushd's *Commentaries* and the Toledo translation industry: Fakhry, *Averroes,* ch. 10; Arnaldez, *Averroes,* p. 31; Charles Burnett, "The Translating Activity in Medieval Spain," in Salma Khadra Jayyusi, ed., *The Legacy of Muslim Spain.* 2 vols. (Leiden: Brill, 1992), vol. 2, pp. 1036–58.

11. On Aristotle in *al-Andalus* and beyond the Pyrenees: Murray, *Reason and Society,* pp. 287–89; Fakhry, *Averroes,* ch. 10; Iqbal, *Islam and Science,* ch. 6; Miguel Cruz Hernandez, "Islamic Thought in the Iberian Peninsula," in Jayyusi, ed., *Legacy of Muslim Spain,* vol. 2, pp. 777–803; Gilson, *La philosophie au Moyen-Age,* pp. 345–60.

12. Ibn Rushd, *Incoherence of the Incoherence (Tahafut al-tahafut)* and repudiation of Neoplatonism: Fakhry, *Averroes,* pp. 16–23; Abu Hamid Muhammad al-Ghazali, *The Incoherence of the Philosophers (Tahafut al-falasifa),* trans. and annotated Michael E. Marmura

(Provo, UT: Brigham Young University Press, 2000), pp. xv–xxvii; Arnaldez, *Averroes*, pp. 77, 98; Esposito, ed., *Oxford History of Islam*, p. 289.

13. Ibn Rushd's master and the Almohad Creed: "The Almohad Creed," trans. M. Fletcher, in Olivia R. Constable, ed., *Medieval Iberia: Readings from Christian, Muslim, and Jewish Sources* (Philadelphia: University of Pennsylvania Press, 1997), pp. 190–97; Dominique Urvoy, "The *Ulama* of al-Andalus," in Jayyusi, ed., *Legacy of Muslim Spain*, vol. 2, pp. 849–77. "I found in him [caliph] a profuseness of learning . . .": Averroes, quoted in Fakhry, *Averroes*, pp. 1–2.

14. Ibn Rushd's exile: Arnaldez, *Averroes*, p. 15; Fakhry, *Averroes*, p. 2; Urvoy, in Jayyusi, ed., *Legacy of Muslim Spain*, vol. 2, pp. 870–71; Hugh Kennedy, *Muslim Spain and Portugal: A Political History of al-Andalus* (London: Longman, 1996), p. 246.

15. Almohad massacre of Jews in the Maghreb: Gerber, *Jews of Spain*, p. 81; Charles E. Chapman, *A History of Spain* (New York: Free Press, 1965; orig. ed. 1918), p. 85.

16. Ibn Rushd and Maimonides in Almeria: Sherwin B. Nuland, *Maimonides* (New York: Schocken Books, 2005), p. 35; Fakhry, *Averroes*, p. 132.

17. Ibn Rushd's great influence in the Christian West: "Rationalism was born in Spain in the mind of an Arabian philosopher as a conscious reaction against the theologism of the Arabian divines"—Etienne Gilson in *Reason and Revelation in the Middle Ages*, quoted in Fakhry, *Averroes*, pp. xv–xvi, and see pp. 165–69; Arnaldez, *Averroes*, ch. 3; Murray, *Reason and Society*, p. 261; Kretzmann, Kenny, and Pinborg, eds., *Cambridge History of Later Medieval Philosophy*, pp. 48–49, 74–78; Esposito, ed., *Oxford History of Islam*, pp. 280–89.

18. Averroism and Scholasticism in thirteenth-century Europe: Murray, *Reason and Society*, p. 261; Friedrich Gontard, *The Chair of Peter: A History of the Papacy* (New York: Holt, Rinehart and Winston, 1964; orig. German ed. 1959), pp. 292–96; Kretzmann, Kenny, and Pinborg, eds., *Cambridge History of Later Medieval Philosophy*, chs. 4, 5, 6, and see note 17, above.

19. "Utter the formula and live": quoted in Nuland, *Maimonides*, pp. 44–45. "Epistle on Martyrdom": Gerber, *Jews of Spain*, p. 82; Mark R. Cohen, *Under Crescent and Cross: The Jews in the Middle Ages* (Princeton, NJ: Princeton University Press, 1994), pp. xvi–xvii; Bernard Lewis, *The Jews of Islam* (Princeton, NJ: Princeton University Press, 1984), p. 84.

20. "No nation has ever done more harm . . .": Nuland, *Maimonides*, p. 85.

21. "Be assured, my brethren, that our opponents . . . will vanish": Nuland, *Maimonides*, p. 85.

22. Joel L. Kraemer, ed., *Perspectives on Maimonides: Philosophical and Historical Studies* (Oxford, UK, and Portland, OR: Littman Library of Jewish Civilization, 1996), pp. 8–13; Nuland, *Maimonides*, pp. 47–60.

23. *Guide for the Perplexed*: Kraemer, ed., *Perspectives on Maimonides*, p. 14; Gerber, *Jews of Spain*, p. 87.

24. God played by the rules of logic: Nuland, *Maimonides*, pp. 139–40.

25. Maimonides's medical writings: Gerber, *Jews of Spain*, p. 83; Gilson, *La philosophie au Moyen-Age*, pp. 360–61.

26. The stature of Averroës and Maimonides in Christendom: Gerber, *Jews of Spain*, p. 83; Arnaldez, *Averroes*, p. 120; Gilson, *La philosophie au Moyen-Age*, pp. 360–61; William Turner, "Teaching of Moses Maimonides," in *The Catholic Encyclopedia*. 15 vols. (New Advent Web site, 1997; orig. ed.: Washington, DC: The Catholic University of America Press, 1913), vol. 9: "Through the 'Guide of the Perplexed' [*sic*] and the

philosophical introductions to sections of his commentaries on the Mishna, Maimonides exerted a very important influence upon the Scholastic philosophers, especially on Albert the Great, St. Thomas, and Duns Scotus."

27. The Third Crusade: Christopher Tyerman, *God's War: A New History of the Crusades* (Cambridge, MA: Belknap Press, 2006), pp. 488–94.

28. The First Crusade: Steven Runciman, *The First Crusade* (Cambridge: Cambridge University Press, 1980; orig. ed. 1951), pp. 59–66; Tyerman, *God's War,* pp. 64–65, 480–81; Gontard, *Chair of Peter,* pp. 258–59.

29. Battle of las Navas de Tolosa: Ambrosio Huici Miranda, *Las Grandes Batallas de la Reconquista durante las Invasiones Africanas (Almoravides, Almohades, y Benimerines)* (Madrid: CSIC, Instituto de Estudios Africanos, 1956), pp. 241–66; Tyerman, *God's War,* p. 669; Roger Collins and Anthony Goodman, eds., *Medieval Spain: Culture, Conflict and Coexistence* (Basingstoke, UK: Palgrave Macmillan, 2002), pp. 24–27; Ahmed ibn Mohammed al-Makkari [Maqqari], *The History of the Mohammedan Dynasties in Spain.* 2 vols. (London and New York: RoutledgeCurzon, 2002), vol. 2, pp. 323–24.

30. The Fourth Lateran Council: James Carroll, *Constantine's Sword: The Church and the Jews* (Boston: Houghton Mifflin, 2001), pp. 282–83; Tyerman, *God's War,* pp. 481, 563–601; Collins and Goodman, eds., *Medieval Spain,* pp. 46–62; Yitzhak Baer, *A History of the Jews in Christian Spain.* 2 vols. (Philadelphia: Jewish Publication Society of America, 1961–66), vol. 1; Gontard, *Chair of Peter,* pp. 257–59.

Glossary

Note: Except for certain Arabic names beginning with "A" and "U," diacritical marks have been omitted.

Adoptionism: Heretical Christological conceptions nurtured in *al-Andalus*.

ahl al-Sham: "The people of Syria," denoting elite Syrian military units.

Akhbar majmu'a: Anonymous chronicle of the Muslim conquest of *al-Andalus*.

al-Andalus: Arabic for the Gothic term *landa-hlauts*.

al-Ard al-Kabirah: Arabic phrase referring to the "Great Land," or land beyond the Pyrenees.

alif, baa, taa: The first three letters of the Arabic alphabet.

Al-Lat: One of the three principal pre-Islamic goddesses of Mecca.

Almohads: Berber monotheists who overthrew the Almoravids and conquered North Africa and much of Iberia in the twelfth century.

Almoravids: Berber movement (fundamentalist) led by Yusuf ibn Tashufin; conquered North Africa and *al-Andalus* in the early twelfth century.

al-Rabad: The turbulent Cordovan neighborhood on the Guadalquivir River's left bank.

Amazighen: "Free men"; Berber self-description.

amir al-mu'minin: Commander of the Faithful.

ansars: The Believers of Mecca who protected Muhammad until his emigration to Yathrib.

ashraf: Arabic plural of *sharif,* meaning "exalted" or "eminent"; refers to members of the Arab Muslim elite.

Ashura: The tenth day of the Muslim month of Muharram, commemorated by fasting and self-punishment.

Austrasia: Northeastern (and principally Germanic) portion of the Merovingian and Carolingian kingdoms, comprising much of today's Benelux countries. The western and Latin portion of these kingdoms was Neustria.

Avars: Eurasian nomads who entered Eastern Europe in the sixth century.

Avesta: Sacred texts of Zoroastrianism, authoritatively redacted under Shapur II (309–79 CE).

Aws: One of the tribes at Yathrib, hostile to the Khazraj.

Axial Age: Designation conceived by German philosopher Karl Jaspers to denote the long period (800–200 BCE) during which the world's major religions emerged.

baladiyyun: The original Arab settlers of *al-Andalus;* those who preceded the Syrians.

Balat al-Shuhada: "Path of the Martyrs"; Arabic name for the defeat in the Battle of Poitiers in 732.

barakah: Arabic term meaning a blessed state bestowed by God.

basileus: Greek title of the emperor of the Eastern Roman Empire, in common use after the reign of Justinian I.

Bayt al-Hikma: Putative institute of learning in Abbasid Baghdad.

Bobastro: Mountain headquarters of 'Umar ibn Hafsun, rebel chieftain, in the Malaga region.

brunia: Carolingian military apparel.

cataphracts: Iranian heavy cavalry.

Chalcedonian decree: Decree issued by the Council of Chalcedon in 451, reaffirming the primacy of the Nicene Creed.

chansons de geste: Numerous poems, sung and written down between the eleventh and the fourteenth centuries, celebrating legendary and/or historical figures. The *Song of Roland* was the principal source and model for the form.

chrysotriklinos: The golden throne room in Constantinople's Great Palace.

convivencia: Spanish term for the long period of cultural and civic collaboration among Muslims, Jews, and Christians in *al-Andalus.*

Corpus Juris Civilis: Body of foundational civil law enacted under Emperor Justinian from 529 to 534.

Ctesiphon: Capital of the Parthian and Sassanian Empires.

Dar al-Harb: "House of War"—territories outside Muslim rule.

dar al-imara: Governor's palace.

Dar al-Islam: "House of Peace"—territories under Islamic law.

dawla: Arabic term applied to a regime or dynasty.

***dhimma* (or *ahl al-dhimma*):** The regime governing the status of the People of the Book (Jews, Christians, and, ambiguously, Zoroastrians).

dhimmis: Protected people living under the system of the *dhimma*.

diwan: The treasury established by Caliph 'Umar; a term gradually applied to the bureaucracy of government.

Ducatus Romanum: Duchy of Rome and the polity occupied by the See of Peter.

ereb: Semitic root of "Europe," meaning "sunset."

Euskara: Basque language.

fatwa: An opinion rendered by a distinguished scholar (*mufti*) to guide the faithful in a matter unclear or unsettled under *Sharia*.

fitna: Civil war involving caliphal succession.

foederati: German tribes allied by treaty with the Roman Republic and Empire.

fuqaha: Men learned in Islamic law.

Gemara: Rabbinical commentaries and analyses of the Mishnah.

ghanima: Arabic for spoils of war or booty.

Guadalquivir: Longest river in *al-Andalus*, flowing from Cordoba to Sevilla.

***hadith* (pl. *ahadith*):** Traditions recounting the words and deeds of Muhammad; the source of Muslim scripture.

Hajib: Arabic for chamberlain, vizier (*vizir*), prime minister.

hajj: Pilgrimage to Mecca, required of all Muslims (who can afford it) at least once in a lifetime. One of the Five Pillars of Islam.

hanifs: Pre-Islamic monotheists in Arabia.

haram: A place of sanctuary.

Hashimiyya: Early Shi'ite movement centered on Khurasan, eastern part of the Umayyad Empire.

Hephthalites: A nomadic Asian people (also called "White Huns") of indefinite ethnicity who occupied part of the Sassanian Empire for much of the fourth century and part of the fifth.

Hijaz: Arabian region on the Red Sea littoral.

hijra: The emigration of Muhammad and his followers to Medina (Yathrib) in September 622; also *hegira.*

Himyarite kingdom: Dominant kingdom in Yemen until conquered by the Aksumite kingdom of Ethiopia. The last Himyarite king, Dhu Nuwas, was a Jewish convert who persecuted Christians.

homoousian: From the Greek, meaning "common or same substance." A fundamental Christological concept enunciated by the Nicene Creed (325 CE and 381 CE) that affirmed the identity of Jesus and God the Father as two persons in one.

Hsiung-nu: Eurasian nomadic tribes known collectively as Huns.

Hudaybiyya: Muhammad's treaty with the Quraysh of Mecca, March 628.

Ifriqiya: The old Roman province of Africa, comprising Libya, Tunisia, Algeria, and Morocco.

imam: Prayer leader for Sunni Muslims; Shi'a term for Muhammad's male descendants through Fatima and Ali.

isnad: The chain of transmission by which *hadiths* (*ahadith*) are authenticated.

jahiliyyah, al-: Arabic term referring to the time of ignorance before Islam.

jihad: "Struggle" or "exertion." Greater *jihad* speaks of internal struggle for righteousness; lesser *jihad* is the defense of the Muslim community.

jinns: Fiery Arabian desert spirits capable of assuming animal and human form in order to influence good and evil.

jizya: Head tax paid by non-Muslims living as protected people under Muslim rule.

jongleurs: Medieval minstrels, singers, storytellers.

junds: Arabic for "army" or "soldiers"; specifically applied to Syrian military units.

Ka'bah: The holiest place in Islam and the direction toward which all of the world's Muslims pray. A large, cube-shaped structure in the city of Mecca shelters the Black Stone that Muslims believe God gave to Ibrahim (Abraham) and his son Ismail (Ishmael).

kafirs: Infidels, non-Believers.

kahins: Soothsayers, or pre-Islamic holy men, who were custodians of shrines.

karr wa farr: "Attack and withdraw," standard Arab military strategy.

kaviani: The gold, silver, and bejeweled battle standard of Iran's Sassanian Empire.

khagan: Chief of the Avars, Eurasian nomads.

kharaj: Islamic tax on land; not authorized by the Qur'an.

Kharijism: Militant Muslim minority sect asserting that community leadership belongs only to the religiously pure, regardless of family pedigree. Kharijites broke with Caliph Ali, assassinated him, and embraced social egalitarianism and doctrinal purity.

Khazraj: Dominant tribe in Yathrib (later Medina); hostile to the Aws.

Khurasan (Khorasan): Large area in Iran's east and northeast; the eastern part of the Sassanian Empire.

Lakhmid Kingdom: Arab kingdom of the Banu Lakhm, subordinate to the Sassanian Empire.

La Mezquita: The Great Mosque of Cordoba, begun by 'Abd al-Rahman I.

Lex Salica: The Salic Law, codified under Clovis I in the early sixth century and governing the Salian Franks.

Lex Visigothorum: A set of laws promulgated by the Sixth Council of Toledo in 638 CE.

limes: A Roman border defense system.

limpieza de sangre: Spanish and Portuguese concept pertaining to "cleanliness of blood"—i.e., devoid of Jewish and Muslim ancestry.

Lombards (Langobardi): The last of the Germanic invaders, entering northern Italy in the sixth century.

Madinat al-Nabi: "City of the Prophet" (Medina).

Madinat al-Zahra: The great palace complex erected by 'Abd al-Rahman III on the outskirts of Cordoba.

Madinat-al Salam: "City of Peace" (Abbasid Baghdad).

madrasas: Islamic schools established after the tenth century.

Maghreb: Arabic for "place of sunset"—the African region north of the Sahara and west of the Nile.

magister militum: Latin for "master of the soldiers"; the senior military commander in a war theater.

Magyars: Dominant ethnic group of disputed origins in Hungary.

Marchfield: The king's annual summons—typically between March and May—for the magnates of the realm to assemble and prepare for a military campaign.

Mashriq: Arabic for "place of sunrise"—the vast area in the East between the Mediterranean and the Persian Gulf.

mawali **(sing.** *mawla***):** Non-Arab Muslims.

mihrab: Niche in a mosque wall (*qibla*) indicating the direction of the Ka'bah in Mecca.

minbar: Pulpit in a mosque.

Mishnah: Written recordings of the oral law of Judaism.

missi dominici: Carolingian envoys of the king.

mobad: Zoroastrian high priest.

Monophysites: Christology asserting that Jesus had only one nature, as Jesus's divinity obliterated his humanity. Monophysitism was finally condemned at the Council of Chalcedon in 451.

Mozarabs: Iberian Christians living under Muslim rule and increasingly Arabized.

Muluk: *Ta'ifa* ruler (king).

Murabitun, al-: Arabic name for the Almoravids of North Africa.

Mu'tazilism: The variant Islamic school of theological emphasis and interpretation holding that reason, aided by the philosophers of classical antiquity, is compatible with divine truth as revealed in the Qur'an.

muwallad: Arabic for non-Arab convert or new Muslim, especially one in *al-Andalus*.

Nadir: One of three Jewish tribes in Medina.

Nafza: Berber tribe.

Najd: Plateau region in central Arabia.

Nestorians: Christian theology based on the preachings of Nestorius (?386–451?), patriarch of Constantinople, and holding that Jesus possessed two separate persons—human and divine. Nestorianism was condemned by the Council of Ephesus in 431 CE.

Neustria: "New Lands"—western portion of the kingdom of the Franks, originating in 511 CE with Paris and Soissons as principal cities.

noria: Waterwheel for lifting water from one level to another.

Orreaga: Basque name for Roncesvalles (Roncevaux), site of Roland's demise.

paria: Protection money paid by *ta'ifas* (kings) to powerful Christian rulers.

Parthians: Subjects of the empire founded by the Arsacid dynasty, successors to the Achaemenids and predecessors of the Sassanians.

patricius Romanorum: "Patrician (or protector) of the Romans," a distinction bestowed by the Eastern Roman emperors on Western leaders.

precarium: Free use of property without legal title to it.

qadi: Muslim judge.

qa'id: Arabic name for a chief or leader.

qanat: An ancient irrigation system still used in parts of the Middle East.

qasr: Arab palace or castle.

Qaynuqa: One of three Jewish tribes in Medina.

Qays: Arab tribe chronically hostile to Yemeni Arabs.

qibla: Arabic word for the direction Muslims face when praying. Also, the mosque wall into which the niche (*mihrab*) is built.

quadrivium: Carolingian curriculum consisting of arithmetic, music, geometry, and astronomy.

Quraysh: The Banu Quraysh, the dominant tribe in Mecca.

Qurayza: One of three Jewish tribes in Medina.

Ramadan: The ninth month of the Muslim calendar and the holiest month of the year.

rashidun: A term in Sunni and Shi'a Islam applied especially to the first four caliphs—the "rightly guided" caliphs.

razzias: Term derived from Arabic, meaning "raid."

Regnum: Latin term for the equivalent of the State.

ribat: Muslim religious retreat or militant cell.

Riddah wars: Wars of Apostasy conducted by Caliph Abu Bakr to consolidate Islam in Arabia in the aftermath of the Prophet's death.

rois fainéants: "Do-nothing kings"—Merovingian kings of Frankland.

Rusafa: Palace complex of 'Abd al-Rahman I, based on his ancestral palace complex in Syria.

sacerdotium: Latin term for the ecclesiastical realm.

Sanhaja: Major Berber tribal confederation in the Maghreb, along with the Zanata and the Masmuda.

Santiago matamoros!: "St. James the Moorslayer!"—Christian battle cry of the *Reconquista*.

saqaliba (sing. *siqlabi*): Enslaved Slavs; later applied to all white slaves and mercenaries.

Sarakenoi: Greek word for the Arabs ("people who live in tents") and origin of the word *Saracen.*

Sefarad: Jewish Iberia.

Sephardim: Iberian Jews.

Septimania: Southwestern region of Gaul under Visigoth and Muslim rule.

Serapeum: A temple dedicated to the Egyptian god Serapis; the largest and most magnificent Serapeum was erected by Ptolemy III (246–22 BCE) in Alexandria.

shahanshah: Persian title meaning "king of kings"; first used by Darius the Great (521–486 BCE).

shahada: The Muslim declaration, "There is no god but God, and Muhammad is His Messenger." One of the Five Pillars of Islam.

Shahnameh: The national epic of Iran (*The Book of Kings*), written by the Persian poet Ferdowsi in the tenth century.

Sharia: Islamic system of law based on the Qur'an.

shiatu Ali: "The party of Ali"—Shi'ites of the minority Muslim sect who maintain that leadership of the community resides solely with descendants of Muhammad through Ali and Fatima.

shura: Arabic term for consultation and the method of choosing leaders.

shurta: Police force.

sortes Gothica: Imperial lands allotted to Gothic allies; rendered into German as *landa-hlauts* and into Arabic as *al-Andalus.*

spangen: Pippinid military headgear.

Sunni: Majority Muslim sect adhering to the belief that leadership of the community belongs to the most qualified person, regardless of descent from the Prophet.

suras: Chapters of the Qur'an.

Ta'if: A prominent city in midsouthwestern Arabia, approximately 180 miles from Mecca.

ta'ifa: Muslim "petty" or "party" kings and their kingdoms, which emerged with the collapse of the Umayyad Caliphate of *al-Andalus.*

Thrace: Ancient region bordered by the Black, Aegean, and Marmara Seas and extending over parts of southern Bulgaria, northeastern Greece, and the European corner of Turkey.

trivium: Carolingian curriculum consisting of grammar, logic, and rhetoric.

ulamas: Muslim religious scholars.

ummah: The community of Believers, extending to the entire world of Islamic belief and practice.

vassi: A politically and militarily dependent social category in the Early Middle Ages.

vizir: A high-ranking official; vizier.

Völkerwanderung: German scholarly term describing "the wandering of the peoples."

wali: Arabic for "master" or "governor."

Yathrib: Arabian peninsula city renamed Medina after Muhammad's emigration from Mecca in September 622.

Yom Kippur: The Jewish Day of Atonement, falling on the tenth day of Tishri, the seventh Hebrew month.

zakat: Obligation to pay 2.5 percent of one's wealth to assist the less fortunate and to encourage conversion. One of the Five Pillars of Islam.

Zoroastrianism: Religion founded on the teachings of the prophet Zoroaster. The dominant religion of the Achaemenid, Parthian, and Sassanian Empires.

Genealogies

The Descendents of Pippin and Alpaida

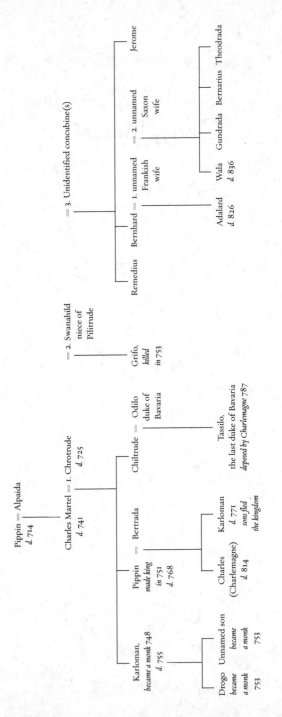

Note. Charles Martel also had a half-brother, Count Childebrand. He was either the son of Pippin, mother unidentified, or the son of Alpaida, father unidentified.

Zirid Rulers of *Ta'ifa* Granada (ca. 1026–1090)

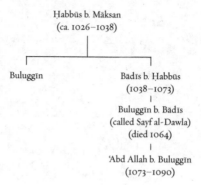

Ḥabbūs b. Māksan
(ca. 1026–1038)

Buluggīn

Bādīs b. Ḥabbūs
(1038–1073)

Buluggīn b. Bādīs
(called Sayf al-Dawla)
(died 1064)

'Abd Allah b. Buluggīn
(1073–1090)

Almoravid Rulers in *al-Andalus* (ca. 1086–1145)

Yūsuf b. Tāshūfin, (ca. 1086–1106)

'Alī b. Yūsuf (1106–1143)

Tāshūfin b. 'Alī (1143–1145)

Almohad Rulers in *al-Andalus* (ca. 1121–1223)

(Ibn Tūmart)

'Abd al-Mu'min (1130–1163)

Abū Ya'qūb Yūsuf I (1163–1184)

Abū Yūsuf Ya'qūb al-Manṣūr (1184–1199)

Muḥammad al-Naṣir (1199–1213)

Abū Ya'qūb Yūsuf II (1213–1223)

For a complete list of *ta'ifa* kingdoms and their rulers, see David Wasserstein, *The Rise and Fall of the Party-Kings* (Princeton, NJ: Princeton University Press, 1985), pp. 82–98. The Zirid genealogy is provided because the family is relevant to several texts in this collection.

Umayyad Amirs and Caliphs in Cordoba (756–1031)

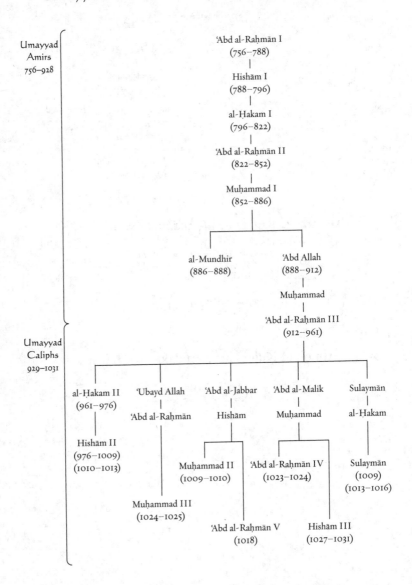

Umayyad
Amirs
756–928

'Abd al-Raḥmān I
(756–788)

Hishām I
(788–796)

al-Ḥakam I
(796–822)

'Abd al-Raḥmān II
(822–852)

Muḥammad I
(852–886)

al-Mundhir
(886–888)

'Abd Allāh
(888–912)

Muḥammad

'Abd al-Raḥmān III
(912–961)

Umayyad
Caliphs
929–1031

al-Ḥakam II
(961–976)

Hishām II
(976–1009)
(1010–1013)

'Ubayd Allāh

'Abd al-Raḥmān

'Abd al-Jabbar

Hishām

Muḥammad II
(1009–1010)

Muḥammad III
(1024–1025)

'Abd al-Raḥmān V
(1018)

'Abd al-Malik

Muḥammad

'Abd al-Raḥmān IV
(1023–1024)

Hishām III
(1027–1031)

Sulaymān

al-Ḥakam

Sulaymān
(1009)
(1013–1016)

Rulers of Asturias-León, Then Portugal, León, and Castile
(eighth–thirteenth centuries)

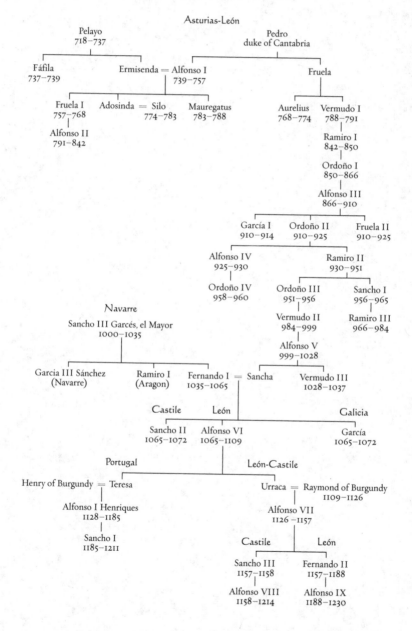

Bibliography

Primary

Abelard, Peter. *Abelard and Heloise: The Story of His Misfortunes and The Personal Letters*. Trans. with notes by Betty Radice. London: Folio Society, 1977.

al-Ghazali, Abu Hamid Muhammad. *The Incoherence of the Philosophers* [*Tahafut al-falasifa*]. Trans. and annotated Michael E. Marmura. Provo, UT: Brigham Young University Press, 2000.

al-Tabari, Abu Ja'far Muhammad ibn Jarir. *The History of the Prophets and Kings*. 39 vols. Albany: State University of New York Press, 1988. (Vol. 6, *Muhammad at Mecca*. Trans. and annotated W. Montgomery Watt and M. V. McDonald. Vol. 13, *The Conquest of Iraq, Southwestern Persia, and Egypt*. Trans. Gautier H. A. Juynboll. Vol. 18, *Between Civil Wars: The Caliphate of Mu'awiyah*. Trans. Michael G. Morony. Vol. 19, *The Caliphate of Yazid ibn Mu'awiyah*. Trans. I. K. A. Howard. Vol. 26, *The Waning of the Umayyad Caliphate*. Trans. Carole Hillenbrand. Vol. 39, *Biographies of the Prophet's Companions and Their Successors*. Trans. Ella Landau-Tasseron.)

Ammianus Marcellinus: The Later Roman Empire (A.D. 354–378). Trans. Walter Hamilton; introduction Andrew Wallace-Hadrill. London: Penguin, 1986.

Aquinas, St. Thomas. *On Faith: Summa Theologiae 2-2, qq. 1–16 of St. Thomas Aquinas (Readings in the Summa Theologiae)*. Trans. Mark D. Jordan. Notre Dame, IN: University of Notre Dame Press, 1990.

Averroes on Plato's Republic. Trans. Ralph Lerner. Ithaca, NY: Cornell University Press, 1974.

Averroes' Tahafut al-tahafut (*The Incoherence of the Incoherence*). Trans. Simon van den Bergh. London: Luzac & Co., 1954.

Bede [Venerable]. *Ecclesiastical History of the English People*, rev. ed. London: Penguin, 1990.

Beowulf: A New Verse Translation. Trans. Seamus Heaney. New York: W. W. Norton, 2000.

Carolingian Chronicles: Royal Frankish Annals and Nithard's Histories. Trans. Bernhard Walter Scholz with Barbara Rogers. Ann Arbor: University of Michigan Press, 1970.

Constable, Olivia R., ed. *Medieval Iberia: Readings from Christian, Muslim, and Jewish Sources*. Philadelphia: University of Pennsylvania Press, 1997.

"The Donation of Constantine," in *Select Historical Documents of the Middle Ages*. Trans. E. F. Henderson. London: George Bell, 1910.

Einhard. *The Life of Charlemagne*. Foreword by Sidney Painter. Ann Arbor: University of Michigan Press, 1960.

Einhard and Notker the Stammerer. *Two Lives of Charlemagne*. Trans. Lewis Thorpe. New York: Penguin, 1969.

Ferdowsi, Abolqasem. *Shahnameh: The Persian Book of Kings.* Trans. Dick Davis; foreword by Azar Nafisi. New York: Viking Penguin, 2006.

Fredegar the Continuator. *The Fourth Book of the Chronicle of Fredegar, with its Continuations* [*Fredegarii Chronicorum Liber Quartus cum Continuationibus*]. Trans. J. M. Wallace-Hadrill. London: Thomas Nelson, 1960.

Gregory of Tours. *History of the Franks.* Trans. Lewis Thorpe. London: Penguin, 1974.

The Holy Qur'an. Trans. and commentary Maulana Muhammad Ali. Lahore, Pakistan: Ahmadiyya Anjuman Isha'at-e-Islam Lahore, 1995 (orig. ed. 1917).

Huici Miranda, Ambrosio. *Las Grandes Batallas de la Reconquista durante las Invasiones Africanas (Almoravides, Almohades, y Benimerines).* Madrid: CSIC, Instituto de Estudios Africanos, 1956.

Ibn Hazm. *The Ring of the Dove.* Trans. A. J. Arberry. London: Luzac & Co., 1953.

Ibn Ishaq. *The Life of Muhammad: Apostle of Allah.* Ed. Michael Edwards. London: The Folio Society, 1964.

Ibn Khaldun. *The Muqaddimah: An Introduction to History.* Trans. Franz Rosenthal. Princeton, NJ: Bollingen Series, Princeton University Press, 1969.

Isidore of Seville. *History of the Kings of the Goths, Vandals, and Suevi.* Trans. Guido Donini and Gordon B. Ford, Jr. Leiden: E. J. Brill, 1966.

The Koran. Trans. with notes by N. J. Dawood. London: Penguin, 1999 (orig. ed. 1956).

Liber Pontificalis (The Book of the Popes). Ed. L. R. Loomis. New York: Columbia University Press, 1916.

Macoudi [al-Masudi]. *Les prairies d'or* [*Fields of Gold*]. Trans. C. Barbier de Meynard and P. de Courteille. 5 vols. Paris: Imprimerie impériale, 1861–1917.

Maimonides, Moses. *Crisis and Leadership: Epistles of Maimonides.* Trans. Abraham Halkin. Philadelphia: Jewish Publication Society of America, 1985.

———. *The Guide for the Perplexed.* Trans. Shlomo Pines. Chicago: University of Chicago Press, 1963.

McNeill, W. H., and Marilyn Robinson Waldman, eds. *The Islamic World.* New York: Oxford University Press, 1973.

Paul the Deacon. *History of the Lombards.* Trans. William Dudley Foulke; ed. Edward Peters. Philadelphia: University of Pennsylvania Press, 2003.

Procopius, *The Secret History.* Trans. G. A. Williamson. London: Penguin, 1966.

Riley, Philip, Frank Gerome, Robert Lembright, Henry A. Myers, and Chong-Kun Yoon, eds. *The Global Experience: Readings in World History to 1550.* Vol. 1. New York: Prentice Hall, 2001.

Reference Volumes

Barrucand, Marianne, and Achim Bednorz. *Moorish Architecture in Andalusia.* Cologne: Taschen, 1999.

Bennett, Philip E., et al., eds. *Charlemagne in the North: Proceedings of the Twelfth International Conference of the Société Rencesvals, Edinburgh, 4–11 August 1991.* Edinburgh: Société Rencesvals British Branch, 1993.

Burckhardt, Titus. *Moorish Culture in Spain.* Louisville, KY: Fons Vitae, 1999 (orig. German ed. 1970).

The Catholic Encyclopedia. 15 vols. New Advent Web site, 1997 (orig. ed. Washington, DC: The Catholic University of America Press, 1913).

Esposito, John L., ed. *The Oxford History of Islam.* New York: Oxford University Press, 2000.

——. *What Everyone Needs to Know about Islam.* New York: Oxford University Press, 2002.

Ferreiro, Alberto. *The Visigoths in Gaul and Spain, A.D. 418–711: A Bibliography.* Leiden and New York: E. J. Brill, 1989.

Goodwin, Godfrey. *Islamic Spain.* San Francisco: Chronicle Books, 1990.

Hernandez Nunez, Juan Carlos, and Alfredo J. Morales. *The Royal Palace of Seville.* London: Scala Publishers, 1999.

Kretzmann, Norman, Anthony Kenny, and Jan Pinborg, eds. *The Cambridge History of Later Medieval Philosophy.* Cambridge: Cambridge University Press, 1982.

Lopez Alvarez, Ana Maria, Ricardo Izquierdo Benito, and Santiago Palomero Plaza. *A Guide to Jewish Toledo.* Toledo, Spain: Codex Ediciones, 1990.

Mango, Cyril, ed. *The Oxford History of Byzantium.* New York: Oxford University Press, 2002.

Nanji, Azim A., ed. *The Muslim Almanac: A Reference Work on the History, Faith, Culture, and Peoples of Islam.* Detroit: Gale Research, 1996.

Nicolle, David. *Armies of the Muslim Conquest.* London: Osprey, 1993.

——, ed. *Historical Atlas of the Islamic World.* Ludlow, Shropshire, UK: Thalamus Publishing, 2003.

Nieto Cumplido, Manuel. *La Mezquita-Catedral de Cordoba.* Barcelona: Editorial Escudo de Oro, n.d.

Ruthven, Malise, with Azim Nanji. *Historical Atlas of Islam.* Cambridge: Harvard University Press, 2004.

Secondary

Abitbol, Michel. *Le passé d'une discorde: Juifs et Arabes du VIIe siècle à nos jours.* Paris: Perrin, 1999.

Ahmad, Aziz. *A History of Islamic Sicily.* Edinburgh: Edinburgh University Press, 1975.

al-Makkari [Maqqari], Ahmed ibn Mohammed. *The History of the Mohammedan Dynasties in Spain.* 2 vols. London and New York: Routledge Curzon, 2002.

Allott, Stephen. *Alcuin of York c. A.D. 732 to 804: His Life and Letters.* York, UK: William Sessions Ltd., 1974.

Almedingen, E. M. *Charlemagne: A Study.* London: Bodley Head, 1968.

Altamira, Rafael. *A History of Spain.* New York: Van Nostrand, 1949.

Armstrong, Karen. *The Battle for God: Fundamentalism in Judaism, Christianity and Islam.* New York: Knopf, 2000.

——. *The Great Transformation: The Beginning of Our Religious Traditions.* New York: Knopf, 2006.

——. *Muhammad: A Biography of the Prophet.* San Francisco: HarperCollins, 1992.

Arnaldez, Roger. *Averroes: A Rationalist in Islam.* Trans. D. Streight. Notre Dame, IN: University of Notre Dame Press, 2000 (orig. French ed. 1998).

Ashtor, Eliyahu. *The Jews of Moslem Spain.* Vol. 2/3. Trans. Aaron Klein and Jenny Machlowitz Klein. Introduction by David J. Wasserstein. Philadelphia: Jewish Publication Society, 1992.

Aslan, Reza. *No god but God: The Origins, Evolution, and Future of Islam.* New York: Random House, 2005.

Bachrach, Bernard S. *Armies and Politics in the Early Medieval West.* London: Variorum, 1993.

——. *Merovingian Military Organization: 481–751.* Minneapolis: University of Minnesota Press, 1972.

Baer, Yitzhak. *A History of the Jews in Christian Spain.* 2 vols. Philadelphia: Jewish Publication Society of America, 1961–66.

Barbero, Alessandro. *Charlemagne: Father of a Continent.* Berkeley: University of California Press, 2004.

Barraclough, Geoffrey. *The Crucible of Europe: The Ninth and Tenth Centuries in European History.* Berkeley: University of California Press, 1976.

Becher, Matthias. *Charlemagne.* New Haven, CT: Yale University Press, 2003.

Beinart, Haim. *The Expulsion of the Jews from Spain.* Oxford, UK, and Portland, OR: Littman Library of Jewish Civilization, 2002.

Berkey, Jonathan P. *The Formation of Islam: Religion and Society in the Near East, 600–1800.* New York: Cambridge University Press, 2003.

———. *The Transmission of Knowledge in Medieval Cairo.* Princeton, NJ: Princeton University Press, 1992.

Blackburn, Robin. *The Making of New World Slavery: From the Baroque to the Modern, 1492–1800.* London: Verso, 1998.

Blair, Peter Hunter. *The World of Bede.* Cambridge: Cambridge University Press, 1970.

Bonnassie, Pierre. *From Slavery to Feudalism in South-Western Europe.* Cambridge: Cambridge University Press, 1991.

Boyce, Mary. *Zoroastrians: Their Religious Beliefs and Practices.* London: Routledge, 2001 (orig. ed. 1979).

Brown, Peter. *The Rise of Western Christendom: Triumph and Diversity, 200–1000 AD.* Oxford: Blackwell, 1996.

Bulliet, Richard. *Conversion to Islam in the Medieval Period: An Essay in Quantitative History.* Cambridge: Harvard University Press, 1979.

Bullough, Donald. *The Age of Charlemagne.* London: Elek Ltd., 1965.

Burl, Aubrey. *God's Heretics: The Albigensian Crusade.* Thrupp, UK: Sutton, 2002.

Butler, Alfred. *The Arab Invasion of Egypt and the Last Thirty Years of Roman Dominion.* Brooklyn, NY: A & B Publishing, 1992 (orig. ed. 1902).

Butzer, P. L., et al., eds. *Karl der Grosse und sein Nachwirken: 1200 Jahre Kultur und Wissenschaft in Europa.* 2 vols. Turnhout, Belgium: Brepols, 1997.

Cahill, Thomas. *How the Irish Saved Civilization: The Untold Story of Ireland's Heroic Role from the Fall of Rome to the Rise of Medieval Europe.* New York: Doubleday, 1995.

Carroll, James. *Constantine's Sword: The Church and the Jews.* Boston: Houghton Mifflin, 2001.

Castro, Americo. *The Spaniards: An Introduction to Their History.* Berkeley: University of California Press, 1971.

———. *The Structure of Spanish History.* Princeton, NJ: Princeton University Press, 1954.

Chamberlin, Russell. *Charlemagne, Emperor of the Western World.* London: Grafton, 1986.

Chapman, Charles E. *A History of Spain.* New York: Free Press, 1965 (orig. ed. 1918).

Clanchy, M. T. *Abelard: A Medieval Life.* Oxford: Blackwell, 1997.

Clarence-Smith, W. G. *Islam and the Abolition of Slavery.* Oxford: Oxford University Press, 2006.

Clot, André. *Harun al-Rashid and the World of The Thousand and One Nights.* New York: New Amsterdam Books, 1990.

Cohen, Mark R. *Under Crescent and Cross: The Jews in the Middle Ages.* Princeton, NJ: Princeton University Press, 1994.

Collins, Roger. *Arab Conquest of Spain, 710–797.* Oxford: Blackwell, 1995 (orig. ed. 1989).

———. *Visigothic Spain, 409–711.* Oxford: Blackwell, 2004.

———, and Anthony Goodman, eds. *Medieval Spain: Culture, Conflict and Coexistence.* Basingstoke, UK: Palgrave Macmillan, 2002.

Cook, Robert Francis. *The Sense of the Song of Roland.* Ithaca, NY: Cornell University Press, 1987.

Crichton, Michael. *Eaters of the Dead: The Manuscript of Ibn Fadlan Relating His Experiences with the Northmen in A.D. 922.* New York: Knopf, 1976.

Daniel, Norman. *The Arabs and Medieval Europe.* London: Longman Group Ltd., 1975.

———. *Heroes and Saracens: An Interpretation of the Chansons de Geste.* Edinburgh: Edinburgh University Press, 1984.

———. *Islam and the West: The Making of an Image.* Oxford: Oneworld, 1993 (orig. ed. 1960).

Davidson, Basil. *Africa in History: Themes and Outlines,* rev. ed. New York: Collier Books, 1991.

Descola, Jean. *Histoire d'Espagne, dès origines à nos jours.* Paris: Fayard, 1979 (orig. ed. 1959).

Deviosse, Jean. *Charles Martel.* Paris: Librairie Jules Tallandier, 1978.

DeVries, Kelly. *Medieval Military Technology.* Peterborough, Ontario: Broadview Press, 1995.

Dixon, 'Abd al-Ameer 'Abd. *The Umayyad Caliphate, 65–86/684–705: A Political Study.* London: Luzac & Co., 1971.

Donner, Fred McGraw. *The Early Islamic Conquests.* Princeton, NJ: Princeton University Press, 1981.

Duby, Georges. *The Early Growth of the European Economy: Warriors and Peasants from the Seventh to the Twelfth Century.* Ithaca, NY: Cornell University Press, 1974.

———. *Rural Economy and Country Life in the Medieval West.* Trans. Cynthia Poston. Philadelphia: University of Pennsylvania Press, 1998 (orig. ed. 1962).

El-Hamel, Chouki. "Race, Slavery and Islam in the Maghribi Mediterranean Thought: The Question of the Haratin in Morocco." *Journal of North African Studies,* vol. 7 (autumn 2002), pp. 29–52.

El-Hibri, Tayeb. *Reinterpreting Islamic Historiography: Harun al-Rashid and the Narrative of the Abbasid Caliphate.* Cambridge Studies in Islamic Civilization. Cambridge: Cambridge University Press, 1999.

Fakhry, Majid. *Averroes (Ibn Rushd): His Life, Works and Influence.* Oxford: Oneworld, 2001.

Fichtenau, Heinrich. *The Carolingian Empire.* Trans. Peter Munz. Toronto: University of Toronto Press, 1978.

Fletcher, Richard. *The Barbarian Conversion: From Paganism to Christianity.* New York: Henry Holt, 1998.

———. *The Cross and the Crescent: Christianity and Islam from Muhammad to the Reformation.* New York: Viking, 2003.

———. *The Quest for El Cid.* New York: Oxford University Press, 1989.

Flood, Finbarr Barry. *The Great Mosque of Damascus: Studies on the Makings of an Umayyad Visual Culture.* Leiden: E. J. Brill, 2000.

Foltz, Richard. *Spirituality in the Land of the Noble: How Iran Shaped the World's Religions.* Oxford: Oneworld, 2004.

Fouracre, Paul. *The Age of Charles Martel.* Harlow, UK: Pearson Education Ltd., 2000.

Fouracre, Paul, and Richard A. Gerberding. *Late Merovingian France: History and Hagiography, 640–720.* Manchester, UK: Manchester University Press, 1996.

Fregosi, Paul. *Jihad in the West.* Amherst, NY: Prometheus Books, 1998.

Frye, Richard N. *The Golden Age of Persia: The Arabs in the East.* London: Weidenfeld and Nicolson, 1975.

Fuller, J. F. C. *Decisive Battles of the Western World and Their Influence Upon History.* London: Eyre & Spottiswoode, 1954.

Ganshof, F.-L. *Charlemagne: Sa personnalité, son héritage.* Brussels: Société Royale d'Archéologie de Bruxelles, 1966.

Geary, Patrick J. *Before France and Germany: The Creation and Transformation of the Merovingian World.* New York: Oxford University Press, 1988.

——. *The Myth of Nations: The Medieval Origins of Europe.* Princeton, NJ: Princeton University Press, 2002.

George, Anita. *Annals of the Queens of Spain.* New York: Baker & Scribner, 1850.

Gerber, Jane S. *The Jews of Spain: A History of the Sephardic Experience.* New York: Free Press, 1992.

Gerberding, Richard A. *The Rise of the Carolingians and the "Liber Historiae Francorum."* Oxford: Clarendon Press, 1987.

Ghazoul, Ferial J. *The Arabian Nights: A Structural Analysis.* Cairo: National Commission for UNESCO, 1980.

Gibbon, Edward. *History of the Decline and Fall of the Roman Empire.* 8 vols. London: The Folio Society, 1983 (orig. eds. 1776–88).

Gilman, Stephen. *The Spain of Fernando de Rojas: The Intellectual and Social Landscape of La Celestina.* Princeton, NJ: Princeton University Press, 1972.

Gilson, Etienne. *La philosophie au Moyen-Age: Dès origines patristiques à la fin du XIVe siècle.* Paris: Payot, 1986.

Gobry, Ivan. *Histoire des rois de France: Pépin le Bref, père de Charlemagne.* Paris: Pygmalion, 2001.

Godman, Peter, and Roger Collins, eds. *Charlemagne's Heir: New Perspectives on the Reign of Louis the Pious, 814 to 840.* Oxford: Clarendon Press, 1990.

Goldziher, Ignaz. *Introduction to Islamic Theology and Law.* Trans. A. & R. Hamori. Princeton, NJ: Princeton University Press, 1981 (orig. ed. 1910).

Gontard, Friedrich. *The Chair of Peter: A History of the Papacy.* New York: Holt, Rinehart and Winston, 1964 (orig. German ed. 1959).

Gouiran, Gerard, and Robert Lafont, eds. and trans. *Le Roland Occitan.* Paris: Christian Bourgeois, 1991.

Grand, Roger. *Recherches sur l'origine des Francs.* Paris: Editions A. and J. Picard, 1965.

Guichard, Pierre. *L'Espagne et la Sicile Musulmanes aux XIe et XIIe siècle.* Lyon: Presses Universitaires de Lyon, 1990.

Hanson, Victor Davis. *Carnage and Culture: Landmark Battles in the Rise of Western Power.* New York: Doubleday, 2001.

Harvey, L. P. *Islamic Spain, 1250 to 1500.* Chicago: University of Chicago Press, 1990.

Hawting, G. R. *The First Dynasty of Islam: The Umayyad Caliphate, AD 661–750.* London: Routledge, 2000 (orig. ed. 1986).

Heather, Peter. *The Fall of the Roman Empire: A New History of Rome and the Barbarians.* New York: Oxford, 2006.

Heer, Friedrich. *Charlemagne and His World.* London: Weidenfeld and Nicolson, 1975.

Hodges, Richard, and David Whitehouse. *Mohammed, Charlemagne and the Origins of Europe.* Ithaca, NY: Cornell University Press, 1983.

Holland, Tom. *Rubicon: The Last Years of the Roman Republic.* New York: Doubleday, 2003.

Hooper, Finley. *Roman Realities.* Detroit: Wayne State University Press, 1979.

Huntington, Samuel P. *The Clash of Civilizations and the Remaking of World Order.* New York: Touchstone Books, 1998.

Ibn Warraq, ed. *The Quest for the Historical Muhammad.* Amherst, NY: Prometheus Books, 2000.

Iliffe, John. *Africans: The History of a Continent.* Cambridge: Cambridge University Press, 1995.

Iogna-Prat, Dominique. *Order and Exclusion: Cluny and Christendom Face Heresy, Judaism, and Islam (1000–1150).* Trans. G. R. Edwards. Ithaca, NY: Cornell University Press, 2003 (orig. French ed. 1998).

Iqbal, Muzaffar. *Islam and Science.* Burlington, VT: Ashgate Publishing, 2002.

Irving, Thomas Ballantine. *Falcon of Spain: A Study of Eighth-Century Spain with Special Emphasis*

Upon the Life of the Umayyad Ruler Abdurrahman I, 756–788. Lahore, Pakistan: Sh. Muhammad Ashraf, 1962.

James, Edward. *The Franks.* Oxford: Blackwell, 1991.

Jayyusi, Salma Khadra, ed. *The Legacy of Muslim Spain.* 2 vols. Leiden: Brill, 1992.

Jones, Gwyn. *A History of the Vikings.* Oxford: Oxford University Press, 1973.

Kaegi, Walter E. *Byzantium and the Early Islamic Conquests.* Cambridge: Cambridge University Press, 1992.

———. *Heraclius: Emperor of Byzantium.* Cambridge: Cambridge University Press, 2003.

Kantorowicz, Ernst. *Frederick the Second, 1194–1250.* London: Constable & Co., 1931.

Katz, Solomon. *The Jews in the Visigothic and Frankish Kingdoms of Spain and Gaul.* Cambridge, MA: The Medieval Academy of America, 1937.

Keddie, Nikki. *Women in the Middle East: Past and Present.* Princeton, NJ: Princeton University Press, 2006.

Kennedy, Hugh. *The Armies of the Caliphs: Military and Society in the Early Islamic State.* London: Routledge, 2001.

———. *Muslim Spain and Portugal: A Political History of al-Andalus.* London: Longman, 1996.

Kepel, Gilles. *Jihad: The Trail of Political Islam.* Cambridge, MA: Belknap Press, 2000.

Kleinclausz, Arthur. *Charlemagne.* 2 vols. Paris: Librairie Jules Tallandier, 1977.

Kraemer, Joel L., ed. *Perspectives on Maimonides: Philosophical and Historical Studies.* Oxford, UK, and Portland, OR: Littman Library of Jewish Civilization, 1996 (orig. ed. 1991).

Lavisse, Ernest. *Histoire de France depuis les origines jusqu'à la Révolution.* 18 vols. Paris: Hachette, 1911.

Leroy, Béatrice. *Les Juifs du bassin de l'Ebre au Moyen-Age.* Biarritz, France: J. & D. Editions, 1997.

Lévi-Provençal, Evariste. *La civilisation Arabe en Espagne: Vue générale.* Paris: G. P. Maisonneuve, 1948.

Lewis, Bernard. *Islam and the West.* Oxford: Oxford University Press, 1993.

———. *The Jews of Islam.* Princeton, NJ: Princeton University Press, 1984.

———. *The Middle East: A Brief History of the Last 2,000 Years.* New York: Simon & Schuster, 1995.

———. *The Muslim Discovery of Europe.* New York: W. W. Norton, 2001 (orig. ed. 1982).

———. *Race and Slavery in the Middle East.* Oxford: Oxford University Press, 1990.

———, ed. *Islam from Muhammad to the Capture of Constantinople.* Oxford: Oxford University Press, 1987.

Lewis, Bernard, and P. M. Holt, eds. *Historians of the Middle East.* Oxford: Oxford University Press, 1962.

Lings, Martin. *Muhammad: His Life Based on the Earliest Sources.* Rochester, VT: Inner Traditions International, 1983.

Lombard, Maurice. *L'Islam dans sa première grandeur, VIIIe–XIe siècle.* Paris: Flammarion, 1971.

Lowney, Chris. *A Vanished World: Medieval Spain's Golden Age of Enlightenment.* New York: Free Press, 2005.

MacLean, Simon. *Kingship and Politics in the Late Ninth Century: Charles the Fat and the End of the Carolingian Empire.* Cambridge Studies in Medieval Life and Thought. Cambridge: Cambridge University Press, 2007.

Makiya, Kanan. *The Rock: A Tale of Seventh-Century Jerusalem.* New York: Pantheon, 2001.

Mandach, André de. *La geste de Charlemagne et de Roland: Naissance et développement de la chanson de geste en Europe,* Geneva: Droz, 1961.

Mann, Vivian B., Thomas F. Glick, Jerrilynn D. Dodds, eds. *Convivencia: Jews, Muslims, and Christians in Medieval Spain.* New York: George Braziller/Jewish Museum of New York, 1992.

Markale, Jean. *Charlemagne et Roland: Les grandes légendes de l'histoire de France.* Paris: Pygmalion, 2000.

Marx, Anthony. *Faith in Nation: Exclusionary Origins of Nationalism.* Oxford: Oxford University Press, 2003.

McKay, John P., Bennett D. Hill, and John Buckler, eds. *A History of World Societies,* 3rd ed. Boston: Houghton Mifflin, 1992.

Meadows, Ian. "The Arabs in Occitania." *Saudi Aramco World* (March–April 1993), pp. 24–29.

Menocal, Maria Rosa. *The Ornament of the World: How Muslims, Jews, and Christians Created a Culture of Tolerance in Medieval Spain.* Boston: Little, Brown, 2002.

Mercier, Maurice, and André Seguin. *Charles Martel et la Bataille de Poitiers.* Paris: Librairie Orientaliste Paul Geuthner, 1944.

Modéran, Yves. *Les Maures et l'Afrique Romaine (IVe–VIIe siècle).* Rome: Ecole Française de Rome, 2003.

Morrissey, Robert. *L'empereur à la barbe fleurie: Charlemagne dans la mythologie et l'histoire de France.* Paris: Gallimard, 1997.

Moscati, Sabatino. "Le massacre des Umayyades dans l'histoire et dans les fragments poétiques," *Archiv Orientální (Journal of the Oriental Archive,* Prague), vol. 18, no. 4 (November 1950), pp. 88–115.

Muldoon, James. *Empire and Order: The Concept of Empire, 800–1800.* New York: St. Martin's Press, 1999.

Murray, Alexander. *Reason and Society in the Middle Ages.* Oxford: Oxford University Press, 1978.

Narbaitz, Pierre. *Orria ou la Bataille de Roncevaux.* Bayonne, France: Zabal, 1978.

Newark, Tim. *Celtic Warriors, 400 BC–1600 AD.* Poole, UK: Blandford Press, 1986.

Nicolle, David. *Age of Charlemagne.* London: Osprey, 2000.

Nirenberg, David. *Communities of Violence: Persecution of Minorities in the Middle Ages.* Princeton, NJ: Princeton University Press, 1996.

Norwich, John Julius. *Byzantium: The Early Centuries.* New York: Knopf, 2001.

Nuland, Sherwin B. *Maimonides.* New York: Schocken Books, 2005.

Nykl, A. R. *Hispano-Arabic Poetry and Its Relations with the Old Provençal Troubadours.* New York: Hispanic Society of America, 1946.

Oakeshott, R. Ewart. *The Archaeology of Weapons: Arms and Armour from Prehistory to the Age of Chivalry.* London: Lutterworth Press, 1960.

O'Grady, Desmond. *Beyond the Empire: Rome and the Church from Constantine to Charlemagne.* New York: Crossroad Publishing, 2001.

Olmstead, A. T. *History of the Persian Empire: A Historical Pageant of the Greatness of Ancient Persia.* Chicago: University of Chicago Press, 1948.

Oman, Charles. *The Dark Ages, 476–918,* 7th ed. London: Rivington, 1962.

O'Shea, Stephen. *Sea of Faith: Islam and Christianity in the Medieval Mediterranean World.* New York: Walker, 2006.

Pennell, C. R. *Morocco: From Empire to Independence.* Oxford: Oneworld, 2003.

Peters, F. E. *Judaism, Christianity, and Islam: The Classical Texts and their Interpretation.* 3 vols. Princeton, NJ: Princeton University Press, 1990.

———. *The Monotheists: Jews, Christians, and Muslims in Conflict and Competition.* 2 vols. Princeton, NJ: Princeton University Press, 2003.

Pieper, Josef. *Scholasticism: Personalities and Problems of Medieval Philosophy.* New York: Pantheon, 1960.

Poitiers, Angoulême et leurs environs. Guides Joannes. Paris: Hachette, 1915.

Power, Daniel, and Naomi Standen, eds. *Frontiers in Question: Eurasian Borderlands, 700–1700.* New York: St. Martin's Press, 1999.

Pratt, Karen, ed. *Roland and Charlemagne in Europe: Essays on the Reception and Transformation of a Legend.* London: King's College Center for Late Antique and Medieval Studies, 1996.

Ranke, Leopold von. *History of the Reformation in Germany.* 6 vols. in one. Trans. Sarah Austin, ed. Robert A. Johnson. New York: Dutton, 1905 (orig. eds. 1839–47).

Reilly, Bernard F. *The Contest of Christian and Muslim Spain, 1031–1157.* Oxford: Blackwell, 1995.

———. *The Kingdom of Leon-Castilla Under Alfonso VI, 1065–1109.* Princeton, NJ: Princeton University Press, 1988.

———. *The Kingdom of Leon-Castilla Under Queen Urraca, 1109–1126.* Princeton, NJ: Princeton University Press, 1982.

———. *The Medieval Spains.* Cambridge: Cambridge University Press, 2004.

Reinaud, Joseph [Haroun Khan Sherwani]. *Muslim Colonies in France, Northern Italy, and Switzerland.* Lahore, Pakistan: Sh. Muhammad Ashraf, 1954.

Reston, James, Jr. *The Last Apocalypse: Europe at the Year 1000 A.D.* New York: Doubleday, 1998.

———. *Warriors of God: Richard the Lionheart and Saladin in the Third Crusade.* New York: Doubleday, 2001.

Retsö, Jan. *The Arabs in Antiquity: Their History from the Assyrians to the Umayyads.* London: RoutledgeCurzon, 2005.

Reynolds, Susan. *Kingdoms and Communities in Western Europe 900–1300,* 2nd ed. Oxford: Clarendon Press, 1997.

Riche, Pierre. *Daily Life in the World of Charlemagne.* Philadelphia: University of Pennsylvania Press, 1978 (orig. French ed. 1973).

Rihawi, Abdulqader. *Damascus: Its History, Development, and Artistic Heritage.* Damascus: self-published, 1977.

Robinson, Chase F. *Islamic Historiography.* Cambridge: Cambridge University Press, 2003.

Rodinson, Maxime. *Muhammad.* Trans. Anne Carter. New York: New Press, 2002 (orig. ed. 1968).

Roy, Jean-Henri, and Jean Deviosse. *La Bataille de Poitiers: Trente journées qui ont fait la France.* Paris: Gallimard, 1966.

Runciman, Steven. *Byzantine Civilization.* London: Methuen, 1975 (orig. ed. 1933).

———. *The First Crusade.* Cambridge: Cambridge University Press, 1980 (orig. ed. 1951).

Safran, Janina. *The Second Umayyad Caliphate: The Articulation of Caliphal Legitimacy in al-Andalus.* Cambridge: Harvard University Press, 2001.

Scales, Peter C. *The Fall of the Caliphate of Cordoba: Berbers and Andalusis in Conflict.* Leiden: E. J. Brill, 1994.

Schimmelpfennig, Bernhard. *The Papacy.* Trans. James Sievert. New York: Columbia University Press, 1992 (orig. ed. 1984).

Segal, Ronald. *Islam's Black Slaves: The Other Black Diaspora.* New York: Farrar, Straus and Giroux, 2001.

Sholod, Barton. *Charlemagne in Spain: The Cultural Legacy of Roncesvalles.* Geneva: Droz, 1966.

Stillman, Norman. *The Jews of Arab Lands: A History and Source Book.* Philadelphia: Jewish Publication Society of America, 1979.

Sykes, Percy. *A History of Persia.* 2 vols. London: RoutledgeCurzon, 2003 (orig. ed. 1915).

Taha, Abdulwahid Dhannun. *Muslim Conquest and Settlement of North Africa and Spain.* London: Routledge, 1989.

Talbot, C. H. *The Anglo-Saxon Missionaries in Germany: Being the Lives of SS. Willibrord, Boniface, Sturmi. . . .* New York: Sheed and Ward, 1954.

Thompson, E. A. *Romans and Barbarians: The Decline of the Western Empire.* Madison: University of Wisconsin Press, 1982.

Torki, Mohamed. *L'an 732 de Kairouan à Poitiers: Considérations d'ordre historique et documents sur la bataille de Poitiers et les Sarosins dans le Haut Moyen-Age français.* Tunis: Maison Tunisienne de l'édition, 1972.

Treadgold, Warren. *Byzantium and Its Army, 284–1081.* Palo Alto, CA: Stanford University Press, 1995.

Tyerman, Christopher. *God's War: A New History of the Crusades.* Cambridge, MA: Belknap Press, 2006.

Wallace-Hadrill, J. M. *The Barbarian West,* 4th ed. Oxford: Blackwell, 1996.

Wallach, Luitpold. *Alcuin and Charlemagne.* Ithaca, NY: Cornell University Press, 1959.

Wasserstein, David. *The Rise and Fall of the Party-Kings: Politics and Society in Islamic Spain, 1002–1086.* Princeton, NJ: Princeton University Press, 1985.

Wemple, Suzanne Fonay. *Women in Frankish Society: Marriage and the Cloister, 500 to 900.* Philadelphia: University of Pennsylvania Press, 1981.

Wheatcroft, Andrew. *Infidels: A History of the Conflict between Christendom and Islam.* New York: Random House, 2004.

Wheaton, Henry. *History of the Northmen or Danes and Normans, from the Earliest Times to the Conquest of England by William of Normandy.* London: John Murray, 1831.

White, Lynn. *Medieval Technology and Social Change.* Oxford: Oxford University Press, 1962.

Wiesehöfer, Josef. *Ancient Persia.* London: I. B. Tauris, 2006 (orig. ed. 1995).

Yalom, Marilyn. *Birth of the Chess Queen: A History.* New York: HarperCollins, 2004.

Credits

Page 3: Cameraphoto Arte, Venice / Art Resource, NY

Page 29: Corbis

Page 57: Wayne McClean

Page 85: Werner Forman / Art Resource, NY

Page 105: David Levering Lewis

Page 137: Painting by François-Louis Dejuiinne (1786–1844), Châteaux de Versailles et Trianon, Versailles. Phototograph: Réunion de Musées Nationaux / Art Resource, NY

Page 160: Ann Ronan Picture Library, London (1892). Photograph: HIP / Art Resource, NY

Page 184: G. Eric and Edith Matson Photograph Collection / Library of Congress

Page 209: Scala / Art Resource, NY

Page 224: Werner Forma / Art Resource, NY

Page 251: David Levering Lewis

Page 268: Walter B. Denny, Islamic Art Slides Archive

Page 282: Réunion des Musées Nationaux / Art Resource, NY

Page 304: Vanni / Art Resource, NY

Page 333: Scala / Art Resource, NY

Page 367: Courtesy of the Vatican Museums

Pages 434–37: Genealogical tables, from *Medieval Iberia: Readings from Christian, Muslim, and Jewish Sources.* Olivia R. Constable, ed. University of Pennsylvania Press, 1997. Reprinted by permission of the University of Pennsylvania Press.

Index

abacus, 306, 329
Aban ibn Mu'awiya, 194
Abbad, Banu, 352
'Abbad *al-Mu'tadid* "The Supporter," 352
'Abbas, al-, 194
Abbasid Empire, 220, 253, 330, 334
    capital of, 194–95
    decline of, 324
    and destruction of Rusafa, 196, 197
    and destruction of Umayyad
      Caliphate, 194
    economy of, 272
    Persian cultural influences in, 195
    science and philosophy in, 306
'Abd al-Aziz, 128, 129–30, 132, 153–54,
    157, 191, 202
'Abd Allah, King of Granada, 364
'Abd Allah (father of Prophet Muham-
    mad), 31
'Abd Allah (son of Abd al-Rahman), 208,
    271, 280, 319
'Abd Allah ibn Ali, 194
'Abd Allah ibn Muhammad, 319
'Abdallah ibn Ubayy, 41, 43, 46, 51
'Abd al-Malik (army commander), 308
'Abd al-Malik al-Muzaffar ibn al-Mansur,
    341–42
'Abd al-Malik ibn Marwan, 98, 100, 103,
    118, 132

'Abd al-Malik ibn Qatan al-Fihri, 175,
    187–88, 190
'Abd al-Malik ibn Umar ibn Marwan, 271
'Abd al-Muttalib, 31, 38
'Abd al-Rahman I "The Falcon," 195–99,
    219, 222, 232, 244, 246, 247, 298,
    307, 334, 377–79
    assessment of, 277–81
    at Battle of Carmona, 201
    becomes *amir*, 197–99
    Charlemagne contrasted with, 225–26
    civil ideology of, 202–3
    death of, 277
    Fihri clan defeated by, 201–2
    in flight from Abbasids, 196–97
    Frankish invasion and, 248–50, 252,
      268–69
    Great Mosque and, 271–75
    legacy of, 271–75
    in move to *al-Andalus,* 197–98
    non-Muslims and, 202–3, 278–79
    reign of, 202, 204–6, 270–72
    slave army of, 200–201
    sons of, 208
    succession to, 280
'Abd al-Rahman II, 312, 325, 368
    invasion of Castile and, 315
    reign of, 314–15
    Vikings and, 313–14

'Abd al-Rahman III, 206, 278, 343, 347, 352, 366
    caliphate declared by, 324–27
    death of, 331, 332
    gold dinar struck by, 324–25
    military campaigns of, 321–24
    palace city of, 325–26
    reign of, 319–20
'Abd al-Rahman V, 350
'Abd al-Rahman al-Sanchol (Sanchuelo), 341–44
'Abd al-Rahman ibn 'Abd Allah al-Ghafiqi, 158, 164–65, 173, 177, 307
'Abd al-Rahman ibn Marwan al-Jalliq, 319
'Abd al-Rahman ibn Mu'awiya ibn Hisham, 195
'Abd Shams clan, 27, 35, 36–37, 88, 91
Abelard, Peter, 374
Abi Sufyan, see Mu'awiya I
Abraha, Ethiopian viceroy, 25
Abraham (prophet), 28, 41, 56, 57, 100
Abraham bar Hiyya, 370
Abraham ibn Daud, 349
Abu Ali ibn Sina (Avicenna), 369, 371, 372
Abu Bakr, 39, 40, 41, 49, 50, 52, 53, 73, 88, 96, 98
Abu Hamid al-Ghazali, 372
Abu Ishaq, 349–51
Abu Ja'far Abdallah ibn Muhammad al-Mansur, 194–95, 198, 272
Abu'l-'Abbas (elephant), 297
Abu'l-'Abbas al-Saffah I, Abbasid Caliph, 194
Abu Lahab, 38
Abu Musa Ash'ari, 92
Abu Muslim, 193–94
Abu Sufyan ibn Harb, 42, 45, 46–47, 50, 91
Abu Talib, 30, 31, 35, 37, 38
Abu Ubayda ibn al-Jarrah, 72–73, 76, 77, 79, 83
Abu Ya'qub Yusuf, 372
Abu Yusuf Ya'qub al-Mansur, 366, 373
Abyssinia, 25
Adalghis, Prince of Lombardy, 238, 241
Adelchi (Manzoni), 229n, 235

Adoptionism, 285
Adrian I, Pope, 235–36, 239–40, 241, 242, 248, 263–66, 282–83, 285, 292, 300, 353
Adrianople, Battle of, 9, 10, 107–8, 109
Aegean Islands, 94
"affair of the necklace," 48, 54, 89
Afghanistan, 12, 76
Agincourt, Battle of, 260
Ahmed ibn Mohammed al-Makkari, 269–70, 320, 332, 338, 345, 359–60, 378
Aidan of Lindisfarne, Saint, 292
A'isha (wife of Mohammad), 41, 48, 49, 54, 86, 88, 89, 150
Aistulf, King of the Lombards, 212, 214, 215, 216, 219, 228, 230, 235
Ajnadain, Battle of, 76
Akhbar majmu'a, 196
Akhila, Duke, 119, 122, 124
'Ala ibn al-Mughith al-Yahsubi, al-, 200–201
Alamanni, 107, 138, 140, 182, 213, 214
al-Andalus, 132, 134, 136, 157, 232, 272, 307
    'Abd al-Rahman I and, see 'Abd al-Rahman "The Falcon"
    Adoptionism and, 285
    Almohad reign in, 370–71, 373–74, 375, 377
    Almoravid dynasty in, 360–66, 371, 373, 375, 377
    al-Rabad conspiracy and, 310–11
    Amirid dictatorship in, see Amirid dictatorship
    Arabic language and, 187, 277
    Balj's usurpation in, 189–91
    Barcelona treaty and, 328
    Basque nationalism and, 269
    Berber settlements in, 185–86
    Berber unrest in, 185–88, 207, 245
    caliphate formalized in, 324–25
    Carolingian order contrasted with, 286, 289
    Catholic Church in, 316–17
    Charlemagne's invasion of, see al-Andalus, Frankish invasion of
    Christian fanaticism and, 316–18, 330

Christian out-migration from, 270, 319, 330

Christian reconquest of, *see Reconquista*

civil pluralism in, 186–87

Cluniac movement in, 353

convivencia ethos in, 202–3, 349

Cordoba as showplace of, 304–5

currency of, 335

decline of Umayyad Caliphate in, 335–36, 342, 343, 346

economy of, 279–80, 335

end of Muslim rule in, 378–79

Frankland contrasted with, 334–35

Jews of, 202–4, 206, 278–79, 317, 327–28, 330–31, 349, 350–51, 370, 373

and *jihad* of 739–40, 175–77

legal system of, 280

literacy in, 277

literate culture of, 369–70

mathematics in, 329

medicine in, 330–31

non-Arab Muslims in, 311–12

non-Muslims in, 202–3, 206, 269–70, 277, 278–79

Norsemen and, 307, 313–14

papal crusades and, 353–54, 377–78

political organization of, 204–6

rebellions and uprisings in, 220, 269–70, 271, 307–8, 310–11, 319

in reign of 'Abd al-Rahman II, 314–15

in reign of 'Abd al-Rahman III, 326–27

in reign of Hakam I, 310–12

in reign of Hakam II, 335–36

science and philosophy in, 306

siege of Barbastro and, 353–55

trade and commerce in, 205–7

see also Hispania, Islamic invasion of; Spain

al-Andalus, Frankish invasion of, 243–50, 253, 255, 270, 284, 334

assessment of, 253–54

decision for, 245, 246

onset of, 246–47

Pamplona encounter in, 247–48, 252–53, 254

plan of, 246

Saracen delegation in, 243–45

Saracen partners' betrayal in, 248–49

Saxon rebellion and, 249, 253

Zaragoza encounter in, 248–49, 334

see also Roland; Roncesvalles; *Song of Roland*

Al-Anfal ("The Spoils") (*sura*), 186

Alans tribe, 106, 109, 110

al-Aqsa Mosque, 78, 133, 273

Alarcos, Battle of, 316, 366, 378

Alaric I, King of the Visigoths, 108–10, 140

Alaric II, King of the Visigoths, 110, 141

Albert the Great (Albertus Magnus), 376

Alboin, King of the Lombards, 146, 211, 235

Alcuin of York, 292–95, 299, 300, 301–2, 306, 312

Alexander II, Pope, 353, 354–55

Alexander III "The Great," King of Macedonia, 5, 70, 82, 102

Alexandria, 144, 375

Library of, 83

lighthouse of, 82

Serapeum of, 82–83

siege of, 80–83, 84

Al-Fasl fi al-milal ("On the Inconsistencies of the Four Gospels") (Ibn Hazm), 349

Alfonso I "The Catholic," King of Asturias, 309

Alfonso II "The Chaste," King of Asturias, 247, 270, 309

Alfonso V, King of Leon and Asturias, 346

Alfonso VI "The Brave," King of Leon and Castile, 355, 358–60, 361, 364–65

Alfonso VIII, King of Castile, 366, 369–70, 378

Alfuente, Battle of, 347, 348

algebra, 368

Algeria, 102, 360

Alhambra, 347

Ali ibn Abi Talib, 39, 40, 49, 52, 86, 93, 95, 96, 97, 188, 194, 324, 342
  in Battle of Siffin, 90–92
  death of, 92
  reign of, 88–90
  in rivalry for caliphate, 86–87
al-Khandaq ("The Ditch"), Battle of, 332
Allah, 33, 35
Al-Lat (goddess), 32–33, 37, 38–39
Almagest (Ptolemy), 370
Almeria, 348, 351, 365, 375
Almohad Creed (*'Aqida*), 373
Almohads ("Unitarians"), 366
  reign of, 370–71, 373–74, 375, 377
Almoravid dynasty, 360–66, 371, 373, 375, 377
Alpaide, 149
al-Qadisiyya, Battle of, 74, 76, 84
Al-Qanun (The Canon) (Avicenna), 369
Alvarus, Paul, 317–19
Amarid dictatorship, 339–46
  Berbers in, 337, 338, 340, 343, 344
  Christian kingdoms and, 339–40, 341, 343
  death of al-Mansur and, 340–41
  military campaigns of, 338, 339–40, 341, 343
  reign of Muhammad II and, 343–45
  replacement caliphs in, 345–46
  revolution in, 343–45
  rise of al-Mansur and, 336–37
  succession in, 341–42
Ambasa ibn Suhaym al-Kalbi, 159, 166
Amblève, Battle of, 150
Aminah bint Wahb, 31
Ammianus Marcellinus, 9–10, 106, 107–8
'Amr ibn al-As, 72, 79–80, 82–83, 86, 90, 91–92, 102
'Amr the One-Eyed, 72, 79, 90
Anastasius I, Eastern Roman Emperor, 60, 135, 141, 299–300
Anatolia, 66, 68, 91, 94, 134
Andalusus (Andalusia), 259, 314, 326, 327, 333, 371
Angra Mainyu, 18
Anselm (Frankish officer), 247, 253

Antioch, 144
  siege of, 60–61
Anti-Semitism, 115–17, 242
  see also Jews; Judaism
Apollinaris Sidonius, 139
Apollonius, Archbishop of Clermont, 111
Apologia for the Martyrs (Eulogius), 330
Apostolic Church, 14
'Aqida (Almohad Creed), 373
Aquitainia (Aquitaine), 140, 150, 153, 160, 162–63, 164, 183, 192, 213, 222, 228, 270, 283, 285, 289
  Muslim invasions of, 156, 157–58, 165–66, 175–76, 185
Arab Conquest, 70–103, 209–10, 309
  al-Qadisiyya in, 74, 76, 84
  Arab out-migrations in, 84
  in Asia, 83, 94–95
  Battle of Jabiya-Yarmuk in, 72–73
  Battle of Nihawand in, 75–76
  Berber setbacks in, 101–3
  Caesarea conquered in, 79–80
  Christianity and, 98–100
  conquest of Egypt in, 72, 73, 79–83
  conquest of Persia in, 73–76
  conquest of Syria in, 71–73
  cultural interplay in, 80–81
  into Europe, 156–57, 159
  fall of Ctesiphon in, 74–75
  fall of Jerusalem in, 76–79
  garrison settlements in, 75
  human-tidal-wave theory of, 71
  Jewish collaborators in, 76, 78, 98–100, 203
  and *jihad* of 739–40, 175–77
  non-Muslims and, 98–101
  in North Africa, 83, 101–3
  after Poitiers, 175–78
  in reign of Mu'awiya, 94
  role of stirrups in, 178
  siege of Alexandria in, 80–83
Arabic language, 275–76, 349
Arabs, 4, 38
  pre-Islamic, 23–24
Aragon, 315, 340, 351
Ardabast, Count, 191, 205
Arianism, 114–15, 143, 157, 166, 211

Aristotle, xxiv, 287
  in Islamic philosophy, 368–74, 376
Arles, Count of, 328
Armengol IV, Count of Urgel, 354
Armenia, 5, 7, 9, 20, 58, 66, 67, 68, 107,
  193
Armstrong, Karen, 34
Arnulf, Archbishop of Metz, 147
Artabanus, King of Parthia, 7
Asah, Banu, 36
A'sha, al- (poet), 61
Ash'arite school, 372
Aslan, Reza, 44, 54
astronomy, 369–70
Asturias, 204, 308, 309, 315, 321, 335
Aswad, al- (visionary), 53
Attila, King of the Huns, 10, 216
Aude (sister of Count Oliver), 256, 258,
  260
Augustine, Saint, 108, 112, 115, 225
Augustus Caesar, 131, 233
Aula Regia (Royal Hall), 295–96
Austrasia, 144, 147–50, 161–63, 172, 183,
  184–85, 213, 214, 222
Austria, 289
Avars, 17, 63, 66, 146, 209, 264, 299, 307,
  308, 377
  Charlemagne's campaigns against,
  283–84
Averröes (Ibn Rushd), 370–75, 376, 377,
  379
Avicebron (Solomon ibn Gabirol), 349,
  369
Avicenna (Abu Ali ibn Sina), 369, 371,
  372
Aw tribe, 40, 52
Axial Age, 11
Axum, kingdom of, 24–25, 39, 51
Ayyub ibn Habib al-Lakhmi, 155
Ayyubid dynasty, 375, 376
Azerbaijan, 5

Babylonian Captivity, 60
Babylonian Talmud, 21
Badis ibn Habbus, 347
Badr, Battle of, 42, 43, 44, 72
Badr (servant), 196–97

Baghdad, 271, 331, 367
  grandeur of, 271–72
  as seat of Islamic scholarship, 367–69
Bahira (monk), 30
Balat al-Shuhada ("Path of the Martyrs"),
  269, 334
Baligant of Babylon, 259
Balj ibn Bishr al-Qushayri, 189–90, 197,
  204–5
Banu Qasi, 204
barbarians, 9–10, 15–16, 17, 63, 68, 138,
  145–47
  see also specific tribes
Barbastro, siege of, 353–55
Barcelona, 298, 310, 312, 328–29, 334, 340
Basilica of St. Sophia, 14
Basilica of San Vitale, 16
Basques, 113, 122, 153, 187, 247, 249,
  252–53, 257, 261, 319
  nationalism of, 269
Bavaria, 182, 213, 229–30, 289
Bayeux tapestry, 254
Bayt al-Hikma (House of Wisdom), 306,
  331, 367–68, 371
Bede, Venerable, 165, 292, 293, 294
Bedouins, 17, 24, 39, 45, 50, 58, 71–72, 73,
  87, 90, 91, 92, 93, 95, 189, 193
Belisarius (Byzantine general), 15–16, 146
Bell, Richard, 52
Benedictines, 151, 288, 353
Benevento, Duke of, 241
Berbers, 92, 95, 101–4, 153, 155–56, 157,
  162, 165, 171, 175, 192, 199, 203,
  204, 278, 307, 319, 327
  in Amarid dictatorship, 337, 338, 340,
  343, 344
  in conversion to Islam, 101–2
  Hispania settlements of, 185–86
  in invasion of Hispania, 119–24, 127
  Kharijism of, 188–89
  in *Reconquista*, 358–65
Bernard, Saint, 376
Bernhard, Duke, 237, 246, 247, 248, 249
Bertrada, Queen of the Franks, 215,
  216–17, 229, 235, 297
  Charlemagne's relationship with,
  231–32, 233

Bible, 294, 350
Bidayat al-Mujtahid wa Nihayat al-Muqtasid (The Distinguished Jurist's Primer) (Ibn Rushd), 374
Bilal (slave), 36
Blessed Palace (Qasr al-Mubarak), 357
Bobastru (castle), 321–24
Bohemians, 287
Bolshevik revolution, 18
Boniface, Saint, 151, 180–81, 183, 216, 221, 232, 233, 263, 264, 265, 288, 290
    papacy-Frank alliance and, 212–15
Boniface IV, Pope, 59
Book of a Thousand Nights and One Night, The, 20
Book of Compulsion and Comparison, The (Kitab al-Jabr w'al-Muqabala) (al-Khwarazmi), 368
Book of the History of the Franks (Liber Historiae Francorum), 144, 147, 151
Book of Tradition, The (Daud), 349
Bordeaux, Count of, 246, 264
Borrel, Count of Barcelona, 326
Bourges, Count of, 246
Britain, 233, 294
Brunner, Heinrich, 178
Buddha, 28
Buddhism, 76
Bulgaria, 58, 209
Burgundy, 139–40, 162, 163, 175, 176, 183, 184–85, 213, 283, 321
Byzantine Empire, 146, 212, 228, 241, 301, 312
    Iconoclastic Controversy and, 210–11, 219, 220, 312

Caesar, Julius, 6, 81, 110, 128, 237
Caesarea, Arab conquest of, 79–80
calendars:
    Islamic, 53–54, 295
    liturgical, 294–95
calligraphy, 275, 276
Camel, Battle of the, 89, 97
Cambrai, Battle of, 150
Campania, 241
Cangas de Onís, 309
Canon, The (Al-Qanun) (Avicenna), 369

Can Rolant, 255
Cantar de Mio Cid (Song of the Cid), 327, 347
Capitulare de Villis, 291
Capitulary of Paderborn, 266
Cappadocia, 20, 66
Carcassone, 284
Carloman (brother of Charlemagne), 216, 245
    Charlemagne's rivalry with, 227–29
    death of, 231
    inheritance of, 222–23
Carloman (son of Charlemagne), 264
Carloman (son of Charles Martel), 180, 213–14, 235
Carmona, Battle of, 201
Carnage and Culture: Landmark Battles in the Rise of Western Power (Hanson), 173
Carolingian miniscule (script), 225
Carolingian order, 286–95
    Charlemagne's capitularies in, 289–91
    class in, 286–87
    economic order of, 288–89
    feudalism in, 286–87
    great families of, 286
    illiteracy in, 291
    learning and education in, 292–95
    monetary system of, 291
    Muslim Iberia and, 286, 289
    reforms and innovations in, 289–90
    and restoration of Roman Empire, 289
    social order of, 287–88, 290
    women in, 290–91
Carolingian Renaissance, 292, 294, 306
Carolus, see Charlemagne, King of the Franks
Carrhae, Battle of, 6–7
Carthage, 5, 75, 102, 117
Castile, 315, 335, 340, 343, 351
    see also Leon-Castile
Catalunya (Catalonia), 309, 321, 340, 351
Cathedral of La Seo, 131
Cathedral of St. John, 133
Catholic church, Catholicism, 112, 144, 227
    in al-Andalus, 316–17
    of Franks, 137–40, 142, 161, 172–82, 183, 212, 220–21
    of Hispania, 116

monogamy and, 256
and Saxon pacification, 266–67
of Visigoths, 112, 113–16
see also Christianity; papacy
Catholic Encyclopedia, 240
Celts, 108, 142
Cervantes, Miguel de, 316
Chalcedon, Council of, 62
Chalcedonian decree, 14
Chanson de Roland, see Song of Roland
Charlemagne, King of the Franks, 110–11,
    216, 261, 275, 277, 308, 315
    'Abd al-Rahman I contrasted with,
        225–26
    Adoptionism and, 285
    Alcuin's first meeting with, 292–95
    assessment of, 312–13
    Bertrada's relationship with, 231–33
    Campania rebellion and, 241
    Carloman's legacy and, 235–36
    Carloman's rivalry with, 227–29
    Carolingian order of, *see* Carolingian
        order
    Catholicism of, 243
    coronation of, 300–301
    death of, 312
    description of, 224–25
    domestic troubles of, 296–97
    dominions of, 283
    enforced religious conversions by,
        242–43
    Hungary invaded by, 283–84
    incest taboo and, 226–27, 256
    inheritance of, 222–23
    Italia territory annexed by, 243
    learning and education and, 292–95
    literacy of, 225–26
    Lombardy invaded by, 236–41
    longsword of, 289
    motto of, 233
    palace complex of, 295–98, 312, 325
    papal relations of, 232, 234–36,
        239–42, 282–83, 298–300
    political ambition of, 232–33, 239
    reforms and innovations of, 289–91
    and relationship of church and state,
        301–3

royal capital of, 284
Saxon campaigns of, 233–34, 240–42,
    253, 254, 262–67
show assembly of (782), 263–64
in *Song of Roland,* 258
Spanish campaign of, *see al-Andalus,*
    Frankish invasion of
succession to, 313–14
Charles III "The Simple," King of
    France, 320
Charles Martel et la Bataille de Poitiers (Mercier
    and Seguin), 168
Charles Martel "The Hammer," 145,
    148–53, 161–62, 163, 164, 176, 177,
    182, 185, 200, 205, 211, 212, 215,
    229, 233, 269, 286, 334
    assessment of, 183
    Battle of Poitiers and, 167–70, 172,
        173–74, 178–79
    church properties exploited by,
        179–81, 183, 213
    death of, 183, 184
    legitimacy of, 148–49
    literacy of, 151–52
Charles the Younger (son of Charle-
    magne), 313
"Charter of Modern Thought," 295
Chartres Cathedral, 275
chess, 305
Childebrand, Duke, 176
Childeric III, King of the Franks, 212, 215
Chilperic II, King of Neustria, 162
Chilperic III, King of Neustria, 184–85,
    198, 212
China, 70–71, 192, 272, 306
Christianity, 10, 12, 13, 25, 41, 46, 87, 276,
    277
    Adoptionism and, 285
    in Arab Conquest, 98–100
    barbarians and, 138
    of Basques, 247
    fall of Antioch and, 60
    fall of Jerusalem and, 61–62, 76–77
    Franks and, 137–40
    Lombard rejection of, 211–12
    of Pamplona, 247–48
    Roman legalization of, 10–11

Christianity (*continued*)
  Saint James as spiritual symbol of, 315–16
  slavery and, 112
  see also Catholic church, Catholicism; papacy
Chronicle of Alfonso III, 124, 132, 156
Chronicle of Fredegar, 145, 159
Church of Los Santos, 123
Church of the Resurrection, 61, 66, 69, 77, 78
Cid, El (Rodrigo Diaz), 343, 355, 365, 378
Cistercians, 353, 377
City of God, The (Augustine), 108, 225
Clavijo, Battle of, 316, 319, 321
Cleopatra, Queen of Egypt, 5–6
Clermont, Count of, 246
Clothaire IV, King of the Franks, 150, 151–52
Clothilde, Princess, 139–40
Clovis, King of the Franks, 111, 138, 144, 145, 147, 151, 152, 166, 184, 212, 218, 222, 228, 233, 242, 296
  Catholic conversion of, 139–40
  reign of, 142–43
  Visigoths defeated by, 140–41
Cluniac movement, 353, 377
Code Napoléon, 14
Commentaries (Ibn Rushd), 371
Commentaries (Maimonides), 376
Commercial Revolution, 286
Companions of the Prophet, 36–37, 39, 40–41, 52, 66, 86, 128
Constable, Olivia, 206–7
Constance, Queen of Castile, 359
Constans, Emperor of Rome, 62
Constantine I "The Great," Emperor of Rome, 10, 61, 106, 113, 138, 140, 141, 218, 219
Constantine II (antipope), 230
Constantine IV, Eastern Roman Emperor, 94
Constantine V, Eastern Roman Emperor, 211, 220, 241
Constantine VI, Eastern Roman Emperor, 274, 312

Constantine VII, Eastern Roman Emperor, 331
Constantinople, 209, 272
  in Fourth Crusade, 377
  Mu'awiya's siege of, 94
  Persian siege of, 63, 66
Constantius I, Emperor of Rome, 141
Constantius, Flavius (Constantius II), Emperor of Rome, 109
Constitution of Medina, 44, 99
Continuations of Fredegar, 164, 183
convivencia (coexistence) ethos, xxiv, 202–3, 330, 349
copts (monophysites), 11, 12, 13, 14–15, 33, 61, 62, 77, 78, 80, 81–82
Cordoba, 271–73, 306, 335, 344, 345
  al-Rabad suburb of, 310–11, 338
  Friday Mosque of, *see* Great Mosque of Cordoba
  Maymun family of, 373
  palace complex of, 304
  in reign of 'Abd al-Rahman III, 326–27
  science and philosophy in, 367
  Sevilla's subjugation of, 355–56
  as showplace of *al-Andalus,* 304–5
  ta'ifas of, 346–47
Cordoba, Archbishop of, 277
Coria, Battle of, 358
Corpus Juris Civilis, 14
Cosmas (chronicler), 13
Council of Chalcedon, 62
Council of Ephesus, 62
Council of Estinnes, 180
Council of Nicaea, 11, 62, 114, 141, 285
  Second, 299–300
Council of Orléans, 141
Council of Reims, 376
Council of the Lateran, Fourth, 252, 378–79
Council of Toledo:
  Third, 114, 115
  Sixth, 116
  Seventh, 114
  Sixteenth, 116
  Seventeenth, 116, 117
Covadonga, Battle of, 156, 309, 316

Crassus, Marcus Licinius, 6–7, 60
crop rotation, 288
crusades, 252, 378
    First, 262, 353, 375
    Second, 375
    Third, 377
    Fourth, 377
Ctesiphon, 25, 26, 272
    Arab conquest of, 74–75
Cyprus, 88, 91
Cyrus, Patriarch, 81
Cyrus II "The Great," King of Persia, 5,
    58, 69

Da'ja (wife of 'Abd al-Rahman), 270
Dakhil, al- "the Immigrant," *see* 'Abd al-
    Rahman ibn Mu'awiya ibn Hisham
Damascus, 95, 194–95
Danes, 283, 306–7
Dar al-Harb (House of War), 76, 101, 127,
    259, 269
Dar al-Islam, 88, 93, 160, 175, 189, 247, 275,
    324, 331, 334
Darius I "The Great," King of Persia, 12, 58
Dark Ages, xxii, 111, 145, 151, 254, 261, 281
    literacy in, 225
    onset of, 10
    warfare in, 168–69
Dauphine, 175–77
David, King, 265, 347
de Bois, Pierre, 374
De Carolo Magno (Notker), 293
decimal system, 99
De Intellectu (al-Kindi), 370
Delbrück, Hans, 173
De Materia Medica (Dioscorides), 331
    Hasdai's translation of, 369
Desiderata (daughter of Desiderius), 229,
    231–32, 234
Desiderius, King of the Lombards, 228,
    229–31, 235–38, 240, 241, 283
Deviosse, Jean, 168, 173–74
Dhu Nuwas, King, 24
Diaz, Rodrigo, *see* Cid, El
Diet of Paderborn, 243–44, 245, 253
Diocletian, Emperor of Rome, 8–9, 10, 131
Dioscorides, 331

*Distinguished Jurist's Primer, The (Bidayat al-
    Mujtahid wa Nihayat al-Muqtasid)* (Ibn
    Rushd), 374
Dome of the Rock, 78, 100, 133
Domesday Book, 291
Donation of Charlemagne, 239–40
Donation of Constantine, 218, 219, 236, 239,
    299
Don Quixote (Cervantes), 316
Drogon, Duke of Champagne, 148
Duchy of Rome (*Ducatus Romanum*), 210,
    212
Duero borderlands, 341
Dunash ben Labrat, 349
Dungal of Ireland, 293
Duns Scotus, John, 374
Durendal (sword of Roland), 258

Early Annals of Metz, 150
Eastern Roman Empire, 11, 13, 14, 16–17,
    51, 101, 143, 144, 209, 210
    Iranian Empire's rivalry with, 21–23,
    57–69
Eastphalia, 242
Ecclesiastical History of the English Nation
    (Bede), 294
Edict of Milan, 10
Edward, Prince of Wales "The Black
    Prince," 160
Eggihard (Frankish officer), 247, 253
Egica, King of the Visigoths, 116–17, 126
Egilona, Princess of the Visigoths, 153–54
Egypt, 4, 5–6, 11, 12, 58, 59, 62, 68, 87,
    101, 110, 197, 375
    Arab conquest of, 72–73, 79–83, 86
Einhard (Frankish scholar), 224–25, 226,
    232, 233, 237, 239, 246, 247, 250,
    253, 254, 256, 257, 263, 265, 266,
    283, 296, 297, 298, 301
Eleanor of Aquitaine, 163, 232
Elements (Euclid), 370
Elipandus, Archbishop of Toledo, 285
England, 291, 307
Enlightenment, 286, 331
Ephesus, Council of, 62
Epistle on Martyrdom (Maimonides), 375
Ermesinda (daughter of Pelayo), 309

Estinnes, Council of, 180

Ethiopia, 25, 29, 39, 51, 73

Euclid, xxiv, 370

Eudo, see Odo, Duke of Aquitania

Eulogius, Archbishop of Toledo, 318–19, 330, 353

Euric, King of the Visigoths, 110–11, 141

Europe, xxi, xxiii
    Battle of Poitiers and fate of, 172–74, 334
    Catholicization of, 220–21
    church-state relationship and, 302–3
    Lex Salica and, 142
    Muslim learning and, 368–70
    pre-civilized, 137–38
    Song of Roland as foundational document of, 254–55, 261–62

European Union, 173

Exarchate of Ravenna, 210, 212, 214

Fastrada, Queen of the Franks, 297, 312

Fatima (daughter of Muhammad), 32, 39, 40, 52, 88, 93, 96, 97, 324

Felix, Archbishop of Urgel, 285

Ferdinand I "the Great," King of Castile and Leon, 352–53, 355

Ferdinand III, King of Castile, 379

feudalism, 161, 178, 286–87

Fields of Gold, the (al-Masudi), 177, 334

Fihri clan, 175, 187–88, 200, 201–2, 271

First Crusade, 262, 353, 375

Five Pillars of Islam, 44–45, 53, 54, 103

Fletcher, Richard, 116

Florinda (daughter of Count Julian), 119–20

Forum Judicum, 279

Fourth Crusade, 377

Fourth Lateran Council, 252, 378–79

France, 137–38, 174, 184, 243, 307, 314, 320, 328, 377, 378
    nationalism of, 261, 262
    Song of Roland as national epic of, 254

Francis I, King of France, 261

Frankland (Francia), 144–45, 147, 149, 152, 174, 183, 185, 200, 206, 207, 212, 216, 220, 221, 228, 243, 308, 309, 327, 334

agriculture in, 288–89

al-Andalus contrasted with, 334–35

al-Andalus invaded by, *see al-Andalus,* Frankish invasion of

church property exploited in, 178–82, 183

collapse of, 312–14, 320, 335

continental hegemony of, 282–83

Danish incursions into, 306–7

economy of, 222, 279–80, 288–89

imperial papacy and, 181–82

Jews in, 287–88

learning and education in, 292–95

liturgical calendar of, 294–95

money in, 288, 291

Norsemen and, 320

partition of, 313–14

reforms and innovations in, 289–90

social order of, 287–89, 290

see also Carolingian order; Charlemagne

Franks, 137–40, 146, 153, 161, 179, 188, 208, 247, 262, 282
    backwardness of, 139
    Catholicism of, 137–40, 142, 161, 172–82, 183, 212, 220–21
    Clovis's reign and, 142–43
    and *jihad* of 739–40, 177
    Lex Salica and, 141–42
    papacy and, 212, 214–15
    Poitiers and identity of, 174
    in reign of Pippin III, 214–15
    Roland and warrior caste of, 260–61
    stirrups adopted by, 178
    Visigoth defeat of, 140–42
    weapons of, 237

Fredegar the Continuator, 167, 170, 172, 182

Frederick I "Barbarossa," Holy Roman Emperor, 377

French Revolution, 18

Frisians, 176, 249, 264

Frisians, Duke of, 149–50

Fritigern (Goth chieftain), 106–8

Friuli, Duke of, 241

Fuller, J.F.C., 156

Furabi, al-, 371

Gabriel (Angel), 35, 36, 38, 44, 45, 52, 57, 78, 262
Gaiseric, King of the Vandals, 117
Galen, xxiv
Galicia, 204, 315, 335, 340, 351, 353
Ganelon, Count, 255–56, 258
Ganshof, F.-L., 286
Garcia Fernandez, Count of Castile, 326, 338, 340
Garcia of Galicia, 355
Garcia Sanchez II, King of Navarra, 340
Gascony, 246
Gascony, Duke of, 246
Gaul, 142, 145, 152, 156–57, 159, 216, 222, 228, 265
Gelasius I, Pope, 299–300, 302
Gemara, 21
General Admonition of 789, 290, 299
Georgia, 20
Gerard of Cremona, 370
Gerberga, Queen (wife of Carloman), 228, 232–33, 235, 238
Gerbert of Aurillac, *see* Sylvester II, Pope
Germania, 213
Germany, 174, 233, 265, 313, 314
Ghalib ibn 'Abd al-Rahman, 337, 338
Ghana, 360
Ghassan, Banu, 26
Ghassanid kingdom, 26, 60–61, 72
Gibbon, Edward, xxiii, 7, 25, 69, 160, 169, 172–73, 294, 315–16, 326
Gibraltar, 120
Gilson, Etienne, 374
Gisela (sister of Charlemagne), 227
Godefroid, King of the Danes, 283
Godescalc Lectionary, 290
Gondeshapur (Academy), 367–68
Goths, 106–10, 211
    see also Visigoths
Granada, 346, 347–48, 350, 357, 361, 365
Gratian, Emperor of Rome, 107
Great Britain, xxi, xxii, 160
Greater Gaul (*Francia Magna*), 161
Great Mosque of Cordoba, 272–75, 277, 280, 284–85, 295–96, 297, 298, 304, 306, 325, 336, 341, 345, 356, 373, 379

Great Mosque of Damascus, 95, 100, 133, 194, 273
Great Palace of Constantinople, 298
Great Wall of China, 153
Greece, 12, 156
Green Palace (Qasr al Khadra), 95, 128
Gregory, Bishop of Tours, 139, 140, 143, 166
Gregory II, Pope, 211
Gregory III, Pope, 182, 210–11, 212
Gregory VII (Hildebrand), Pope, 354
Gregory IX, Pope, 374
Grifo (son of Charles Martel), 213
Grimoald I, Duke of Benevento, 147–48, 149
Guadalete, Battle of, 122, 130, 155, 164, 278, 309, 336
Guide for the Perplexed (Maimonides), 376
Guizot, François, 173

Hadith of Gabriel, 54
Hadrian, Emperor of Rome, 109, 274
Hafsa (daughter of 'Umar), 49, 90
Hagar, 41
Hagia Sophia, 141
Hakam, al- (historian), 119–20, 124, 127, 154
Hakam I, al-, Amir of Cordoba, 305, 309–12, 345
Hakam II, al-, Caliph of Cordoba, 206, 331–32, 335, 339
Halto (son of Duke Odo), 174
Hannibal, 69
Hanson, Victor Davis, 173
Harold Bluetooth (Harald Blatand), King of the Danes, 283
Harun al-Rashid, 277, 297, 305, 306, 331
Hasan ibn Ali, al-, 92–93, 96
Hasdai ibn Ishaq, 327–28
Hasdai ibn Shaprut, 278, 330–32, 347, 348–49, 369
Hashimite clan, 31, 35, 38, 52
Hashimiyya sect, 193–94
Hassan ibn al-Nu'man, 103
Hebrew language, 275, 348–49
Helena, Roman empress, 61
Helvetia (Switzerland), 243, 326

Hemingway, Ernest, 251
Henry IV, Holy Roman Emperor, 354
Hepthalites (White Huns), 15, 18, 19
Heraclius, Eastern Roman Emperor, 7, 59,
    61–63, 66–70, 72, 73, 76, 77, 80,
    82, 84, 94, 113, 115, 136, 320
Herman of Carinthia, 370
Herod I Agrippa, King of Judea, 315
Herod I "the Great," King of Judea, 80
Herodotus, 83
Hesse, 212, 263
Hilary, Saint, 166
Hildebrand (Pope Gregory VII), 353
Hildegard of Swabia, 234, 264, 297
Himiltrude (wife of Charlemagne), 228,
    229–30, 232
Himyarite kingdom, 24–25
Hincmar, Archbishop of Reims, 181, 291
Hind bint Utbah, 45, 50–51, 90, 91
Hindus, 192
Hisham I, Caliph of Cordoba, 101, 175,
    188, 189, 193, 195, 196, 199, 208,
    271, 277, 280, 284–85, 304–5, 334
    death of, 309–10
    in jihad against Asturia, 307–9
    reign of, 191–92
    Septimania incursion of, 284–85
Hisham II, Caliph of Cordoba, 336–39,
    342, 343, 345
Hisham III, Caliph of Cordoba, 345
Hisham ibn 'Abd al-Malik, 159, 165
Hisham ibn 'Urwa ibn al-Fihri, 202
Hispania, Islamic invasion of, 105–36,
    143, 153
    Battle of Covadonga in, 156
    Battle of Sidonia and, 123–25
    Catholicism in, 112, 113–16
    Christianity and, 153–54
    coins minted in, 132
    consolidation of, 132
    decline of the West and, 105–9
    factional conflict and, 154–55
    fall of Merida and, 129–30
    fall of Toledo and, 126–27
    Jews in, 126, 127, 128, 130, 155
    loot and plunder in, 127, 128, 130
    second invasion of, 127–28
        spoils of war and, 133–34
        Sulayman's withdrawal order and, 134
        Tarif's expedition to, 118–19
        Tariq's invasion of, 119–23
        Visigoth rule in, 110–17
        see also al-Andalus; Spain
Hispanicus error, 285
Historia Francorum (History of the Franks)
    (Gregory), 139, 140, 141, 166
History of the Decline and Fall of the Roman
    Empire, The (Gibbon), 169
History of the Lombards (Paul the Deacon),
    164, 174
History of the Prophets and Kings, The, 193
Holy Roman Empire, 239, 301, 325, 377
Honorius, Emperor of the West, 108, 109
House of War (Dar al-Harb), 76, 101, 127,
    259, 269
House of Wisdom (Bayt al-Hikma), 306,
    331, 367–68, 371
Hroswitha of Gandersheim, 326–27, 356
Hruodland, see Roland
Hudaybiyya, Treaty of, 49–50
Huddid clan, 346
Hunald, Duke of Aquitaine, 174, 228,
    245–46
Hungary, 284, 289, 308
Huns (Hsiung-nu), 66, 106, 321
Husayn ibn Ali, al-, 92, 96–97, 194
Husayn ibn Sa'ad ibn Ubada, al-, 244–46,
    248–49

Ibn 'Abd al-Hakam, 119–20, 124, 127, 154
Ibn Hayyan, 327–28, 348, 354
Ibn Hazm, 270–71, 349–51, 369
Ibn Idhari, 171–72
Ibn Ishaq, 33–34, 38–39, 44
Ibn Khaldun, 120
Ibn Rushd (Averröes), 370–75, 376, 377,
    379
Ibn Tumart, 365–66
Ibrahim (son of Muhammad), 49
Iconoclastic Controversy, 210–11, 219,
    220, 312
Ifriqiya (Tunisia), 102, 118, 187
    Fatimid dynasty of, 324
Iliad (Homer), 257

imperium Christianum (Christian Empire), 233

incest, practice of, 226–27, 256, 290

Incoherence of the Philosophers, The (Tahafut al-Falasifa) (al-Ghazali), 372

India, 12, 28, 71, 206, 272

Indiculus Luminosus (The Unmistakable Sign) (Alvarus), 317

Innocent III, Pope, 252, 300, 377–78

Iranian Empire, 84, 93, 143, 193, 379
   Arab conquest of, 71, 73–76, 86
   cultural reforms in, 20–21
   Eastern Roman Empire vs., 21–23, 57–69
   emergence of Zoroastrianism in, 11–13
   golden age of, 18–20
   implosion of, 68
   Islamicization of, 76
   Jews of, 12, 20–21
   Mazdak revolution in, 18–20
   Parthians of, 6–7, 12, 24
   Roman Empire's conflicts with, 4–11, 13, 14–16, 21–23
   Sassanian regime of, 7–8, 11, 12, 18–20, 21, 24, 28, 51
   war machine of, 20, 22, 60–61

Iraq, 4, 5, 11, 26, 68, 75, 92, 101

Ireland, 307

Irene, Empress of Byzantium, 312

Irminsul (Saxon totem), 234, 240, 242

Isaac (Mozarab Christian), 317

Isaac (son of Abraham), 41, 56

Ishmael, 41

Isidore of Miletus, 14

Isidore of Seville, Saint, 111, 114–15, 181, 287, 293, 299, 359

Islam, 21, 27, 38, 48, 126, 262
   Almohad form of, 365–66
   Arabic language and, 275–76, 277
   Buddhist clash with, 76
   calligraphy and, 275, 276
   Five Pillars of, 44–45, 53, 54, 103
   Judaism and, 41–44
   literacy and, 275–77
   lunar calendar of, 53–54
   Mecca and development of, 27–28
   proselytizing and, 99–100
   slavery and, 112, 287
   and treatment of enemies, 55
   Wars of Apostasy and, 53
   women and, 35, 54, 55
   see also Qur'an

Isma'il ibn Naghrela, *see* Samuel ibn Naghrela

Italy (Italia), 210, 289, 292, 307
   Charlemagne's annexation of, 243

Jabiya-Yarmuk, Battle of, 72–73, 76, 84, 94

Ja'far ibn 'Uthman ibn al-Mushafi, 336–37

Jalula, Battle of, 76

James, Saint, 131, 315–16, 340, 370

Jerome, Saint, 108, 114

Jerusalem, 61, 67, 84, 87, 133, 144, 377
   Arabian siege and conquest of, 76–79
   Dome of the Rock in, 78, 100, 133

Jesus of Nazareth, 28, 36, 56, 61, 77

Jews, 28, 30, 31, 38, 40, 59, 87, 252, 271, 277, 305, 375
   of al-Andalus, 202–4, 206, 273, 278–79, 317, 327–28, 330–31, 349, 350–51, 370, 373
   Arab conquest and, 76, 78, 98–100, 203
   Arab cultural symbiosis with, 349
   convivencia ethos and, 202–3, 330, 349
   Fourth Lateran Council and, 378–79
   of Frankland, 287–88
   institutionalized "otherness" of, 378–79
   and invasion of Hispania, 126, 127, 128, 130, 155
   in Iranian Empire, 12, 20–21
   of Mecca, 33, 37–38
   of Medina, 42, 43, 45–48
   in *Reconquista*, 359, 366
   in Roman-Iranian conflict, 60–62, 65
   of Yemen, 24–25
   see also Judaism

"jihad," 70

John of Biclarum, 111

John the Baptist, Saint, 96

Jordan, 4, 24, 26, 70, 155

Joseph ibn Naghrela, 351
Joshua, 264
Joyeuse (longsword), 289
Judaism, 12, 276
    Islamic aspects of, 41–42
    Muhammad's perception of, 41, 46
    see also Jews
Julian, Count, 119, 120, 125, 128, 129
Julian "the Apostate," Emperor of Rome,
    8, 10
Justin II, Eastern Roman Emperor, 17, 18,
    24, 60, 113
Justinian I, Eastern Roman Emperor, 14,
    15, 17, 20, 23, 69, 81, 84, 106, 113,
    117, 135, 146, 245

Ka'bah, 26, 27, 32–33, 35–36, 37, 97, 272
    consecration of, 49–51
    pilgrimages to, 33, 35–36
Kalb tribe, 32, 191
Kalilah and Dimnah, 20
Karbala, Battle of, 96–97
Karlamagnus Saga, 227, 254–55, 262
Karl der Grosse, see Charlemagne
Kavadh I, King of Persia, 18–19
Kavadh-Siroes, Prince of Persia, 68
Khadija bint Khuwaylid, 31–32, 34–35, 38,
    54, 58, 88, 90
Khalid ibn al-Walid, 45, 51, 53, 72, 73,
    76–77, 83
Khalid ibn Sa'id al-As, 36
Khalid ibn Sinan, 53
Khalid Yazid ibn Mu'awiya, 306
Khalifah, al-, xxi
Kharijism, 92–93, 193
    emergence of, 188–89
Khaybar oasis, siege of, 49–50
Khazraj tribe, 40, 41, 43, 51–52
Khosrow I, Persian Emperor, 15, 18,
    19–20, 367
Khosrow II, Persian Emperor, 23, 25, 30,
    57–58, 60, 61–63, 67–68, 73, 113
Khurasan, 193, 269
Khwarazmi, al-, 99, 368, 370
Kitab al-Jabr w'al-Muqabala (Book of Compulsion
    and Comparison) (al-Khwarazmi),
    368

Kusayla (Berber chieftain), 102, 118, 189

Lakhmid kingdom, 26, 72
Lampegie (daughter of Duke Odo),
    162–63, 164
Languedoc, 284, 308
Lantfrid, Duke of Alamannia, 182
Laon, Count of, 229
Las Navas de Tolosa, Battle of, 252, 378
Latin language, 275–76, 314
Lavisse, Ernest, 173
Leander, Bishop of Seville, 114
Legacy of Muslim Spain (Constable), 206–7
Leo III, Pope, 300–301, 302
Leo III "the Isaurian," Eastern Roman
    Emperor, 135–36, 210–11
Leon, kingdom of, 315, 332, 335, 337,
    351–52
Leon-Castile, 321, 340, 352, 353
Leovigild, King of the Visigoths, 113–14,
    126, 129
Letter to Yemen (Maimonides), 375–76
Lex Salica (Salic Law), 141–42
Lex Visigothorum, 116, 202
Liber Historiae Francorum (Book of the History of
    the Franks), 144, 147, 151
Library of Alexandria, 83
Libri Carolini, 299
Libya, 73, 83, 102, 103
Life of Charlemagne (Vita Caroli Magni) (Ein-
    hard), 224–25, 226, 233, 256, 257,
    265, 297, 301
Limoges, Count of, 246, 264
Lindisfarne Monastery, 306, 313
Lives of the Holy Fathers of Merida, 129
Lombards, Lombardy, 17, 63, 138, 143–44,
    146, 181, 214, 215, 233, 243, 292
    Carloman's alliance with, 228–29
    Charlemagne's invasion of, 226–41
    jihad of 739–40 and, 177
    papacy and, 210–12, 216, 218, 228,
        230–31, 235–36, 298–300
    Pippin's campaign against, 218–19
    as threat to papacy, 210–12, 216,
        218–19, 228–31
longsword (spata), 237
Lothair, King of Italy, 313, 314

Louis I "the Pious," Holy Roman
  Emperor, 264, 308, 309–10,
  312–13, 314, 328
Louis-Philippe, King of the French, 173
Luitgard, Queen of the Franks, 312
Luitprand, King of the Lombards, 177, 211,
  235
Lupicinus, Roman commander, 107
Luther, Martin, 19

Maastricht, Bishop of, 149
Macedonia, 9, 156
Madinat al-Zahra, 325–26, 339, 343, 345, 352
Maghreb, 83, 94, 95, 101, 102, 133, 172,
  187, 192, 269, 278, 324
  emergence of Kharijism in, 188–89
Magnus Aurelius Cassidorus, 293
Magyars, 320–21
Mahdi, al-, xxi
Maimonides (Musa ibn Maymun), 370,
  373–76, 379
  on Islam-Judaism relationship, 375–76
  philosophy of, 375–76
Mainz, Bishop of, 265, 266
Makhzum clan, 35
Malaga, 347
Malik ibn Anas, 311
Manat (goddess), 32–33, 37
Mani (prophet), 18, 28, 40, 46, 56
Manichaeism, 10
Mansur, al-, Abbasid Caliph, 200–201,
  271
Manzoni, Alessandro, 229n, 235
March Hispanica (Spanish March), 285,
  309, 314, 315, 328, 334, 340
Marcile, Saracen King, 255–57, 258, 259
Marcus Aurelius, 7, 106, 109
Mariya (concubine of Muhammad), 49
Marj Rahit, Battle of, 97, 155, 198
marriage, institution of, 256
Martin, Henri, 173
Martin, Saint, 166, 167
Marwan I, Ubayyad Caliph, 97–98
Marwan II, Umayyad Caliph, 97–98
Marwan ibn Muhammad, 193
Maslama, Arab commander, 134–35, 136
Maslama of Banu Hanifa, 53

Masmudas tribe, 366
Masudi, al-, 88, 177–78, 269, 334
mathematics, 306, 329, 368
Mauretania, 117
Maurice, Eastern Roman Emperor, 22, 30,
  57–58, 63, 73, 210
Maurontus of Provence, 175–76, 177
Maximian, Emperor of Rome, 8
Mazda, Ahura, 66
Mazdak i Bamdad, 18–19, 36
Mazdakism, 19, 21
Mecca, 29
  in development of Islam, 27–28
  Ethiopian invasion of, 25
  Ka'bal pilgrims and, 26–27
  Muhamad-Quraysh conflict in, 37–39,
    50–51
  Quraysh domination of, 26–27, 33
medicine, 369, 376
Medina:
  Muhammad's move to, 40–41
  Muhammad vs. Jews of, 43, 45–48,
    265
Medinaceli, Battle of, 338
Menocal, Maria, 349
Mercier, Maurice, 168
Merovech, King of the Franks, 142, 246
Merovingian line, 212–13
Mesopotamia, 5, 9
Metaphysics (Aristotle), 374
Milvian Bridge, Battle of, 138
minstrels (*jongleurs*), 261
Mishnah, 21
Mishneh Torah (Maimonides), 376
missi dominici, 291, 295
Mithradates II, King of Parthia, 5
Mithraism, 10
Mohammed and Charlemagne (Pirenne), 105
Monk of St. Gall (Notker "the Stam-
  merer"), 238, 293, 294, 295
monogamy, 256, 290
monophysites (copts), 11, 12, 13, 14–15, 33,
  61, 62, 77, 81
monotheism, 10, 11, 38
  of Muhammad, 32–33
Monothelitism, 81
"moor," 247

Morocco, 102, 136, 188, 311, 336, 358–59, 365, 375

Moses (prophet), 28, 40, 46, 56

Mozarabic Chronicle of 754, 127–28, 133–34, 166, 171

Mozarab Martyrs, 316, 317–18, 330, 353

Mu'awiya I, Caliph, 76, 89, 90–92, 101, 102, 134, 135, 192, 195, 276, 277, 281, 342

reign of, 93–94, 95, 96

Mu'awiya II, Caliph, 97

Mudari (Arab tribe), 191

Mughira, al-, 336

Mughith al-Rumi, 120, 125–26, 128, 131, 199, 279, 308

Muhammad, Prophet, 16, 25, 28, 29–36, 55, 73, 87, 100, 136, 165, 186, 265, 324, 364

and affair of the necklace, 48, 54, 89

annunciation of, 34–35

bloodlines of, 31

business acumen of, 31–32

caravan commission of, 30–31

death of, 51

description of, 30

divine revelations of, 33–36, 46, 49, 57, 60, 63–66, 71

first disciples of, 36–37

Jews vs., 35, 37–39, 43–50

Judaism as perceived by, 41, 46

Khabar oasis siege and, 49–50

marriages and concubines of, 31–32, 47, 49

martyrology of, 39–40

Mecca's surrender to, 50–51

monotheism of, 32–33

in move to Medina, 40–41

special destiny of, 30–31

successors of, 51–54

women's rights and, 89–90

Muhammad I, Emir of Cordoba, 317, 325, 368

Muhammad II al-Mahdi, Caliph of Cordoba, 343–45, 346

Muhammad III, Caliph of Cordoba, 345

Muhammad III *al-Nasr*, Almohad Caliph, 378

Muhammad al-Mahdi (Abbasid Caliph), 244

Muhammad al-Tartushi, 365

Muhammad ibn Abbad al-Mu'tamid, 356–57, 358, 360–61, 364, 365

Muhammad ibn Abi Amir (al-Mansur), 336–41, 344

death of, 340–41

emergence of, 336–37

Muhammad ibn Abi Bakr, 88, 90

Mundhir, al-, 319

Munuza, *see* 'Uthman ibn Abi Nessa

Muqtadir, al-, Amir of Zaragoza, 354, 355

Murabit (Berbers), 359

Musa ibn Maymun, *see* Maimonides

Musa ibn Nusayr, 103, 104, 118, 127–32, 133, 134, 136, 141, 148, 153, 155, 156, 172, 189, 202, 210

Mu'ta, Battle of, 70, 72, 73

Mutawakkil, al-, 361, 365

Mu'tazilism, 371–72

Nadir tribe, 40, 41, 42, 46

Naghrela family, 346–47

Narbonne, 176, 219–20, 284, 308, 309

Narbonne, Count of, 246

Narrative of the Conquest of al-Andalus (al-Hakam), 124, 127, 153, 154

Narses (Byzantine general), 15

Nasrid family, 347

nationalism, 261

Navarra, 204, 308, 309, 321, 325–26, 340, 351

neoplatonism, 368, 376

Nepos, Julius, Emperor of the West, 110

Nestorians, 11, 12, 13, 14–15, 20, 28, 33

Neustria, 144, 147–50, 152, 162, 166, 172, 183, 184–85, 213, 222

Nicaea, Council of, 11, 62, 114, 141, 285

Nicaea, Second Council of, 299–300

Nicene Creed, 11, 62, 379

Nihawand, Battle of, 75–76

Nineveh, Battle of, 66–67, 68, 69

Nobles, Battle of the, 189–90

Noble Sanctuary, 78

Normandy, 320

Norsemen (Vikings), 153, 307, 313–14, 320

Notker "the Stammerer" (Monk of St. Gall), 238, 293, 294, 295
Nuland, Sherwin, 375

Oath of Loyalty of 793, 289
Octagon Chapel, 298
Odo, Duke of Aquitania, 145, 150, 157–59, 176, 186, 228
    at Poitiers, 165–69, 171, 174, 175
    at Toulouse, 161–64
Odoacer, King of Italy, 10, 141
Odo of Metz, 297
Oliphant (ivory horn), 257
Oliver, Count, 256–58, 260
Olympic Games, 11
Oman, 92
Oman, Charles, 111, 112–13, 138–39
On Grammar (Alcuin), 293
"On the Inconsistencies of the Four Gospels" (*Al-Fasl fi al-milal*) (Ibn Hazm), 349
Origen, 80
Orlando Furioso (Ariosto), 262
Orléans, Council of, 141
Ornament of the World, The (Menocal), 349
Orthodox Catholic Church, 67
Ostrogoths, 146, 211
Otto I, Holy Roman Emperor, 301, 321, 330
Otto III, Holy Roman Emperor, 329

Pacensis, Isidore, 171, 172, 174
Pact of 'Umar, 99
Pakistan (Sind), 133, 134, 192
Palace of the Gilded Gate, 272
Palace School, 293, 295, 306, 307
Palestine, 4, 6, 24, 29, 60, 68, 155
    Arab conquest of, 73, 86
"Palm" ('Abd al-Rahman), 225
Pamplona, 247–48, 252–53, 254
papacy, 137–38, 143, 145–46, 296
    Carloman-Lombard alliance and, 228
    Charlemagne's relationship with, 232, 234–36, 239–42, 282–83, 298–300
    and coronation of Charlemagne, 300–301

Donation of Constantine and, 218–19
    and expulsion of Iberian Muslims, 377–78
    Iconoclastic Controversy and, 210–11, 219, 220, 312
    imperial, 181–82
    Lombards and, 210–12, 216, 218, 228, 230–31, 235–36, 298–300
    Pippin I's alliance with, 214–17
    Queen Bertrada's scheme and, 229–32
    Saxon pacification and, 263, 265
    threats to, 209–12
Papal States, 240, 242
paper, 306, 326
Parthians, 6–7, 12, 24
"Path of the Martyrs" (*Balat al-Shuhada*), 269, 334
Paul, Saint, 60, 80, 112, 115, 287
Paul I, Pope, 228, 230
Paul the Deacon, 164
Paulinus of Aquileia, 293
Paulus, Saint, 157
Pavia, siege of, 238, 240, 243, 245, 249
Pedro II of Aragon, 378
Pelayo, Prince of Cangas de Onís, 155–56
Pelayo (Visigoth leader), 270, 309, 316
Pena de Cervera, Battle of, 340
Persepolis, 272
"Persian Book of Kings" (*Shahnameh*), 58, 76
Peter, Saint, 60, 145
Peter of Pisa, 293, 294
Peter the Venerable, 370
Pfalzkapelle (Palace Chapel), 298
Philip (antipope), 230
Philip II, King of France (Philip Augustus), 377
philosophy, 368–69, 371, 372
Phocas, Eastern Roman Emperor, 33, 58–59
Phoenicians, 117
Physics (Aristotle), 370, 374
Pilate, Pontius, 79
Pillars of Hercules, 117, 118
Pippin, King of the Lombards, 264, 284, 292, 297
Pippin (son of Carloman), 228

Pippin I, King of Aquitaine, 313, 314
Pippin I "the Short," King of the Franks,
        213, 227, 228, 233, 235, 236, 240,
        242, 296, 300
    death of, 219, 222
    Lombardy campaigns of, 218–19
    Papal alliance of, 214–18
    partition of kingdom of, 222–23
Pippin of Heristal (Pippin II), King of
        the Franks, 148, 149, 174, 179, 181,
        229
Pippin of Landen, 147–48
Pippin the Hunchback, 228, 229, 264, 297
Pirenne, Henri, 105–6
Placidia, Galla, 108
Planisphaerium (Ptolemy), 370
Plato, xxiv, 369, 372
Plato of Tivoli, 370
Plectrude, Countess, 148–50, 151, 217, 229
poetry, 348–49, 369
Poitiers, Battle of (732), xxiii, 110, 158n,
        160–75, 177, 184, 209, 220, 243,
        286, 314
    Arab invasion of Aquitaine and,
        164–66
    Arab organization in, 169
    assessment of, 174–75
    Battle of Toulouse and, 161–64
    Charles Martel at, 167–70, 172,
        173–74, 178–79
    climax of, 170–72
    date of, 160–61
    European identity and, 172
    fate of Europe and, 172–74, 334
    landscape of, 167–68
    Porte-de-Piles fight in, 169–70
    and role of stirrups, 178
    site of, 167–68, 170–72, 247, 269
    Song of Roland and, 261
Poitiers, Battle of (1356), 160
Poitiers, Count of, 264
Pompey, 6, 58
Portugal, 128, 129, 352, 365
precarial tenure, 180–81
Priestess (Queen of the Aurès), 102–3,
        118, 189
Procopius, 14, 16, 179

Provence, 183
Ptolemy (astronomer), 370
Ptolemy I, King of Egypt, 82

Qadir, al- (Abbasid Caliph), 358–60, 371
qadis, 373–74
Qasr al Khadra (Green Palace), 95, 128
Qasr al-Mubarak (Blessed Palace), 357
Qaynuqa tribe, 40, 41, 42, 43, 49
Qays/Mudari tribe, 191
Quadripartitum (Ptolemy), 370
quadrivium (curriculum), 293–94, 295
Qur'an, 34, 72, 95, 99, 100, 103, 186, 189,
        207, 242–43, 275, 307, 310, 327,
        347–48, 350, 364, 368
    Al-Anfal ("the Spoils") sura of, 186
    compilation of, 53–55
    eighth sura of, 187
    language of, 276
    Latin translation of, 370
    in Mu'tazilite philosophy, 371
    second sura of, 78
    slavery and, 112, 200, 287
    stipulations of, 54–55
    tenth sura of, 84
    Trinity dismissed by, 285
    women and gender in, 89, 291
Quraysh clan, 26–27, 35, 37–39, 42,
        46–47, 49, 50–51, 52, 87, 88 90, 91,
        265, 342

Racemundo, Bishop of Elvira, 278–79,
        330
Ra'ha (mother of 'Abd al-Rahman I),
        195–96
Rahman (deity), 53
Raimundo, Archbishop, 369–70
Ramadan, 43, 55
Ramiro I, King of Castile, 315, 316
Ramiro II, King of Leon, 332
Ramiro of Aragon, 352
Raphael, 377
rashidun Caliphate, 85–92
    Ali's reign in, 88–92
    Battle of Siffin and, 90–92
    civil wars in, 88, 89–91
    death of 'Uthman and, 87–88

nepotism in, 86
and status of women, 89–90
'Umar's reign in, 85–87
rationalism, 374
Ravenna, 210, 212, 214, 219, 235, 241
Rayhana (concubine of Muhammad), 47
Reason and Revelation in the Middle Ages (Gilson), 374
Reccared, King of the Visigoths, 113, 115, 157
Reconquista, 110, 117, 347, 373
    Almoravid Islam and, 364–66
    Battle of Zallaqa and, 364–65
    Berbers and, 358–65
    after death of Sancho III, 351–52
    and fall of Toledo, 357–60
    Jews and, 359, 366
    Pelayo-Alfonso alliance and, 309
    religious fanaticism and, 252
    St. James as symbol of, 315–16
Reims, Council of, 376
Remigius of Reims, Saint, 140–41, 143, 218
Renaissance, 368–69, 376–77
repoblacíon (line of control), 335
Rhetoric and the Virtues (Alcuin), 300
Rhineland, 243
Richard I "the Lion Hearted," King of England, 377
Riché, Pierre, 174
Ring of the Dove, The or *The Dove's Necklace* (*Tawq al-Hamama*) (Ibn Hazm), 270–71, 350
Robert of Ketton, 370
Robinson, Maxine, 34
Roderic, King of the Visigoths, 119, 122, 123–25
Rodrigo, Archbishop of Toledo, 378
Roland, xxiii, 245, 247, 250, 288, 289, 302, 315, 347
    as archetypal superhero, 260
    monument to, 252
    "splendid fellow" thesis and, 260
    see also Song of Roland
Rollo the Norwegian, 320
Roman Empire, 3, 12, 24, 142, 144, 302, 379

barbarian invasions of, 9–10, 15–16, 17, 63, 68, 138, 145–47
Christianity legalized in, 10–11
Eastern, *see* Eastern Roman Empire
and fall of Adrianopolis, 109
Iranian Empire's conflicts with, 4–11, 13, 14–16, 21–23
Spartacus rebellion in, 6, 19
Roman Republic, 6, 19
Romizanes (Shahrbaraz), 60–62, 66–70, 81, 94
Romulus Augustulus, Emperor of Rome, 10, 14, 141, 302
Roncesvalles, 252, 254, 255, 256, 258–59, 261, 269, 270, 315
Roncevaux, Battle of, xxiii
Rotrud (daughter of Charlemagne), 312
Roy, Jean-Henri, 168, 173–74
Royal Collegiate Church of St. Mary (Iglesia de la Real Colegiata de Santa Maria), 252
Royal Frankish Annals, 183, 217, 220, 227–28, 233, 246, 249, 254, 256, 257, 297, 301
Royal Hall (*Aula Regia*), 295–96
Rumaykiyya, al-, 357
Ruolandsliet, 254–55
Ruqayya (daughter of Muhammad), 32, 40
Rusafa (residence complex), 196–97
Rusafa (villa), 205–6, 270, 280, 345
Russia, 307

Sacred Books and Early Literature of the East, 122
Sa'd ibn Abi Waqqas, 72, 73–76, 79, 83
Safwan ibn Mu'attal, 48
St. Denis, Chaplain of, 215
St. Gall abbey, 326
St. Peter's Basilica, 146, 239
St. Riquier monastery, 294
St. Sophia, 135, 136
Saladin (Salah al-Din), 376
Salamis, Battle of, 68
Salic Law (*Lex Salica*), 141–42
Sallust, 5
Samh ibn Malik al-Khawlani, al-, 156–58, 161, 174

Samuel ibn Naghrela, 347–50
Sancho, Prince of Leon, 355, 357
Sancho I "the Fat," King of Leon, 325–26
Sancho II, King of Navarra, 338
Sancho III "the Greater," King of
    Navarra, 351, 353
Sancho VII "the Strong," King of
    Navarra, 252, 378
Sancho Garcia, Prince of Castile, 340,
    344–45
Sancho Ramirez I, King of Aragon, 365
Sanchuelo ('Abd al-Rahman al-Sanchol),
    341–44
Sanctius (Mozarab Christian), 317
Santiago de Compostela, 340
Santiago Matamoros (St. James the
    Moorslayer), 315–16
San Vitale, 298
Sara (Visigoth Princess), 154
"Saracens," 159, 247
Sarah (mother of Isaac), 41
Sarakenoi, 24
Sassanians, 7–8, 11, 12, 18–20, 21, 24, 28,
    51
Saxon Capitulary, 266–67, 290, 377
Saxons, 219–20, 245, 283, 289, 299, 377
    Charlemagne's campaigns against,
        233–34, 240–42, 253, 254, 262–67
    final pacification of, 262–67
    Irminsul totem of, 234, 240, 242
Scholasticism, 371, 374, 376
School of Athens, The (Raphael), 377
science, 369–70
Second Crusade, 375
Second Temple, 61, 77–78
See of Peter, see papacy
Seguin, André, 168
Seneca, 109
Septimania, 157, 161, 176, 211, 219–20,
    270, 284, 285, 308–9
Serapeum of Alexandria, 82–83
Sergius, 67
Sevilla, 352, 361, 365
    Great Mosque of, 366
Shahin, Field Marshal, 60, 63, 66
Shahnameh ("Persian Book of Kings"), 58,
    76

Shahraplakan, Field Marshal, 66–67
Shahrbaraz (Romizanes), 60–62, 66–70,
    81, 94
Shapur I, King of Persia, 7–8, 12, 20
Shapur II "the Great," King of Persia, 9,
    13, 107, 367
Shapur III, King of Persia, 15
Shaqya ibn 'Abd al-Wahid, 271
Shi'ites, Shi'ism, 93, 97, 189, 192, 193, 271,
    375
    Fatimid dynasty of, 324
Shirin, Queen of Persia, 58
Shurta (police force), 271, 344
Sidonia, Battle of, 123–25, 161
Siete Partidas, Las, 14
Siffin, Battle of, 90–92
Siger of Brabant, 374
Sijilmasa, 324, 360
Sind (Pakistan), 133, 134, 192
Sisibut, King of the Visigoths, 113, 115–16
slaves, slavery, 222, 271
    Christianity and, 112
    Islam and, 112, 287
    Qur'an and, 112, 200, 287
    in Visigoth economy, 112
Soissons, Battle of, 150, 162
Solomon, King, 127
Solomon ibn Gabirol (Avicebron), 349,
    369
Solomon's Table, 127, 130, 133
Song of Roland, xxiii, 250, 354, 378
    beginning of, 255
    earliest written version of, 262
    ethos of heroic individual and, 260
    final line of, 262
    Frankish vengeance in, 258–59
    Ganelon's betrayal in, 255–56
    impact of, 260
    Islam and, 262
    Marsile's assaults in, 256–57
    as national epic, 254–55
    Oliphant sounded in, 257–58
    psychic power of, 261–62
    Roland as portrayed in, 255–57, 258
Song of the Cid (Cantar de Mío Cid), 327, 347
Sophronius, Patriarch, 77–78
Spain, xxii, 6, 370, 375, 377

see also al-Andalus; Hispania, Islamic
invasion of
Spanish March (*Marca Hispanica*), 285, 309,
314, 315, 328, 334, 340
Spartacus, 6, 19
spata (longsword), 237
Spoleto, Duke of, 241
Stephen II, Pope, 212, 215, 219, 222, 236,
240, 300
Pippin's meeting with, 216–18, 283
Stephen III, Pope, 230–31, 232, 235
stirrups, 178, 283–84
Strabo, 5
Strategikon (Maurice), 22, 73
Sturmi, Saint, 262–63, 266
Suanehilde, Princess of Bavaria, 182
Subh the Navarrese, 336
Sudan, xxi–xxii
Suetonius, 224, 293
Suevi, 109, 110
Sulayman (admiral), 135–36
Sulayman (son of 'Abd al-Rahman), 196,
208, 271, 280
Sulayman *al-Musta'in*, 344–45, 346
Sulayman ibn 'Abd al-Malik, 101, 131, 133,
134, 154, 156, 210
Sulayman ibn az-A'rabi, 207, 244–46,
248–49, 253
Summa de Veritate Catholicae (*Treatise on the
Truth of the Catholic Faith*) (Aquinas),
374–75
Sun Also Rises, The (Hemingway), 251
Sunnis, xxi–xxii, 93, 94, 189, 276, 280, 324
Susa, Battle of, 237–38
Switzerland (Helvetia), 243, 326
Sylvester, Patriarch of Jerusalem, 69
Sylvester II, Pope, 218, 328–29, 369
Synod of Clermont, 377
Syria, 4, 5–6, 11, 20, 24, 26, 29, 30,
59–60, 68, 79, 93, 134, 193, 199
Arab conquest of, 71, 72, 73, 86

Tabari, al- (historian), 74, 79, 80, 88, 103
Tacitus, Emperor of Rome, 112
Tahafut al-Falasifa (*The Incoherence of the
Philosophers*) (al-Ghazali), 372
ta'ifas (party, or petty, kings), 346–47

Taim, Banu, 52
Talas, Battle of, 306
Talha, 89
Talmud, 21, 279
T'ang Empire, 83
Tangier, 117–18
Tarif ibn Talib al-Mu'afire, 118–19, 120,
128, 131–32, 134, 136, 155
Tariq (Berber leader), 185
Tariq ibn Ziyad, 117, 118, 125, 126, 127, 141,
148, 153, 161, 164, 186, 210, 358
background of, 103–4
at Battle of Sidonia, 123–24
and invasion of Hispania, 119–22
Tassilo III, Duke of Bavaria, 229, 231,
234, 283–84
Tawq al-Hamama (*The Ring of the Dove*) (Ibn
Hazm), 270–71, 350
Tell Kushaf, Battle of, 194, 196
Templars, 377, 378
Temple Mount, 77–78, 92
Temple of Jupiter, 96, 133
Temple of Solomon, 61, 100, 115
Tertry, Battle of, 148
thagr (line of control), 335
Theodemir, Duke of Murcia, 130
Theodesian Code, 236
Theodora, Eastern Roman Empress,
14–15, 16, 17, 30
Theodore (brother of Heraclius), 72
Theodosius I, Emperor of Rome, 10–11,
15, 83, 141
Theodulf, Bishop of Orléans, 293
Thermopylae, Battle of, 68, 135
Theudoald IV, King of Austrasia and
Neustria, 148, 163, 174
Thierry IV, King of the Franks, 151–52,
212
Third Crusade, 377
Thomas Aquinas, Saint, 371, 374–75,
376
Thrace, 9, 106–7, 134
Thucydides, 83
Thuringia, 212–13, 263
Titus, Emperor of Rome, 61, 78
Tolbiac, Battle of, 140
Toledan Tables (al-Zarqiyal), 369

Toledo, 346, 352, 356
    Arab capture of, 126–27
    as center of learning, 369–70
    Christian capture of, 357–60
Toledo Council:
    Third, 114, 115
    Sixth, 116
    Seventh, 114
    Sixteenth, 116
    Seventeenth, 116, 117
Torah, 279
Toto of Nepi, Duke of Tuscany, 230
Toulouse, Battle of, 145, 157–59, 172
    Battle of Poitiers and, 161–64
Toulouse, Count of, 246, 264
Trajan, Emperor of Rome, 109, 274
Transcaucasia, 193
Treatise on Intellect (al-Kindi), 368
Treatise on the Truth of the Catholic Faith
        (Summa de Veritate Catholicae)
        (Aquinas), 374–75
Trench, Battle of the, 46–47, 48
trivium (curriculum), 293, 295
True Cross, 61, 69, 77
Tudmir, Treaty of, 191, 204–5
Tunisia, see Ifriqiya
Turkestan, 134
Turkey, 4, 5, 6, 60
Turoldus, 254–59, 261, 262, 334
Turpin, Archbishop, 257
Tuscans, 230
Tuscany, Duke of, 241

Ucles, Battle of, 365
Uhud, Battle of, 45–46, 91
Ulfilas, Bishop, 114
'Umar I ('Umar ibn al-Khattab), Caliph,
        39, 40, 49, 53–54, 71, 72, 73, 75, 76,
        77, 78, 80, 83, 96, 98, 169
    reign of, 85–87, 88
'Umar II, Caliph, 101, 136, 194, 199
'Umar ibn Hafsun, 319, 321–24
Umayya clan, 27, 35–36, 39, 87, 90, 91, 279
Umayyad Caliphate, 93–98, 187, 196, 281
    al-Andalus Caliphate and, 197–99
    Arabic as official language of, 133
    Berber revolt and, 188–89, 192

civil wars in, 96–98, 193–94
    Damascus made capital of, 95–96
    demise of, 192–95, 215
    Hashimite uprising in, 96–97
    Hisham's reign in, 159, 191–92
    Mu'aniya's reign in, 93–94
    nepotism in, 96
    non-Muslims in, 98–101
    in siege of Constantinople, 134–36
    Sunni-Sh'ia split in, 93–94
    tax revolts in, 188
Umm Hani, 31
Umm Kulthum, 32
university, 367–68
Unmistakable Sign, The (Indiculus Luminosus)
        (Alvarus), 317
Uqba ibn al-Hajjas al-Saluli, 175–76, 177,
        183, 185, 187–88, 307
Uqba ibn Nafi, 94, 101–3, 172, 175, 189,
        358
Urban II, Pope, 262, 377
Urraca, Queen of Castile and Leon, 355
'Uthman ibn Abi Nessa (Munuza),
        162–63, 164, 183
'Uthman ibn Affan, 37, 39, 40–41, 54, 86,
        90, 93, 96, 100, 342
    death of, 87–88
Uzbekistan, 94–95, 193
Uzzah, al-, 32–33, 37, 38–39

Vahan, General, 72–73
Valencia, Battle of, 316
Valens, Eastern Roman Emperor, 9, 106,
        107–8
Valerian, Publius Licinius, Emperor of
        Rome, 8
Valerus Majorian, Emperor of Rome,
        110
Vandals, 16, 109–10, 117
Vatican, 212, 242, 377
Verden, Battle of, 264–65, 266
Verdun, Treaty of, 243, 314, 320
Vergil, 293
Vikings (Norsemen), 153, 307, 313–14,
        320
Visigoths, 110, 118, 139, 142, 143, 153, 157,
        186, 202, 270, 274, 277, 278, 346

anti-Semitism of, 115–17
Catholicism of, 112, 113–16
Frankish defeat of, 140–41
hierarchal order of, 112–13
Hispania ruled by, 110–17
oligarchal rule of, 113–14
slave economy of, 112
Vita Caroli Magni (Life of Charlemagne) (Einhard), 224–25, 226, 233, 256, 257, 265, 297, 301
Vouillé, Battle of, 110–11, 141

Walid I, al-, 95, 99–100, 131, 133, 134, 194, 273
Walid II, al-, Caliph, 192–93
Walid ibn Mu'awiya, al-, 199
Wamba, King of the Visigoths, 122
Waraqah ibn Nawfal, 34, 38
Wars of Apostasy, 53
Wends, 264, 287
Westphalia, 242, 243, 263, 265
White, Lynn, 178
Widukind (Saxon chieftain), 234, 242, 245, 264, 266, 283
Wilfrid "the Hairy," Count of Barcelona, 328
William, Count of Toulouse, 308
William I "the Pious," Duke of Aquitaine, 353
William VIII, Duke of Aquitaine, 355
William IX, Duke of Aquitaine, 355
William of Montreuil, 353
Willibrord (priest), 151, 181, 183, 234
Willihad (abbot), 262–63
Witiza, Visigoth King, 117, 119, 121
World War II, 173
"Writing," 44
Wurzburg, Bishop of, 215
Wynfrith, *see* Boniface, Saint

Xerxes I, King of Persia, 135

Yahya al-Ma'mun, 355–56
Yahya ibn Ismail al-Qidir "the Capable," 356
Yahya ibn Yahya al-Laythi, 311
Ya'qub ibn Ishaq al-Kindi, 281, 368, 370, 371
Yazdegird III, King of Persia, 73–74, 75, 76, 88
Yazid I, Umayyad Caliph, 96–97, 102
Yazid II, Umayyad Caliph, 101
Yazid III, Umayyad Caliph, 193
Yazid ibn Abi Sufyan, 76
Year of the Elephant, 25
Yemen, 4, 24–26, 29, 40, 42, 51, 53, 155, 375
Yusuf As, 24–25
Yusuf ibn 'Abd al-Rahman, al-Fihri, 175–76, 177, 197–99, 200, 201, 271
Yusuf ibn Tashufin, 360–65

Zacharias, Patriarch, 61
Zacharias, Pope, 211–12, 214
Zaida (daughter of al-Mu'tamid), 365
Zakat (Third Pillar of Islam), 288
Zallaqa, Battle of, 364–65
Zanata Berbers, 360
Zaragoza, 248–49, 334, 346
Zarathustra, 12, 36, 56, 66
Zarqiyal, al-, 369
Zayd ibn Harithah, 32, 70, 72, 88n
Zayd ibn Thabit, 37, 41, 52, 86–87
Zaynab (daughter of Muhammad), 32, 40
Zirids (Berber tribe), 346, 347, 365
Zoroaster, 28
Zoroastrianism, 11–12, 20, 21, 28, 40, 79, 87, 99
Zubayr ibn al-Awwam, 51, 89, 97

About the Author

D AVID LEVERING LEWIS was born into a family of academics in Little Rock, Arkansas. He grew up in Wilberforce, Ohio, and Atlanta, Georgia. He graduated Phi Beta Kappa from Fisk University at age nineteen and received a master's in U.S. history from Columbia University the following year. He was awarded a PhD in modern French history from the London School of Economics and Political Science and has taught at a number of American universities, including the University of California at San Diego; Rutgers, the State University of New Jersey; Harvard University; and the University of Ghana. Lewis teaches at New York University, where he is the Julius Silver University Professor and a professor of history. He is author and editor of nine books of history and biography. In 2002, he was awarded the Columbia University Teachers College Medal for Distinguished Service to Education. His research and writing have garnered fellowships from the Woodrow Wilson International Center for Scholars, Guggenheim Foundation, Center for Advanced Study in the Behavioral Sciences, and the National Humanities Center. He is a recipient of the John D. and Catherine T. MacArthur Foundation genius award.

David Levering Lewis describes himself as a student of comparative history, a characterization borne out by a range of subjects that includes a history of anti-Semitism in France (*Prisoners of Honor: The Dreyfus Affair*) and an exploration of late-nineteenth-century conflict between British imperialism and Islamic fundamentalism (*The Race to Fashoda: European Colonialism and African Resistance in the Scramble for Africa*). A two-time winner of the Pulitzer Prize for his two-volume biography of W. E. B. Du Bois, he gained further distinction when he was recognized by the history field with two of its most prestigious awards, the Bancroft Prize and the Francis Parkman Prize. He also received the Harvard University Horace Mann Bond, the Phi Beta Kappa Ralph Waldo Emerson, the Anisfield-Wolf, and the English Speaking Union book awards. Lewis served as president of the Society of American Historians and is a member of the Academy of Arts and Sciences and the American Philosophical Society.

The author is father of two daughters and two sons, and currently resides with his wife in Europe where, during the spring of 2008, he is a fellow of the American Academy in Berlin.